Photoshop® CS Bible, Professional Edition

Deke McClelland

WILEY

Wiley Publishing, Inc.

Photoshop® CS Bible, Professional Edition

Published by
Wiley Publishing, Inc.
10475 Crosspoint Boulevard
Indianapolis, IN 46256
www.wiley.com

Copyright © 2004 by Wiley Publishing, Inc., Indianapolis, Indiana

Published simultaneously in Canada

ISBN: 0-7645-4179-X

Manufactured in the United States of America

10 9 8 7 6 5 4 3 2 1

1K/QY/QU/QU/IN

For general information on our other products and services or to obtain technical support, please contact our Customer Care Department within the U.S. at (800) 762-2974, outside the U.S. at (317) 572-3993 or fax (317) 572-4002.

Wiley also publishes its books in a variety of electronic formats. Some content that appears in print may not be available in electronic books.

Library of Congress Controle Number: 2004103999

WILEY

About the Author

Born near Verona in 1511, **Deke McClelland** was once the most popular portrait painter in all of Florence. His career came to a grinding halt a few centuries later with the advent of photography. Broken, penniless, and deeply resentful, Deke dedicated his energies to the development of a pathogen so insidious that it would one day contaminate each and every photograph on the planet. Code named the Pernicious Instrument of eXtreme EviL (or "pixel" for short), Deke smuggled his terrible creation into The New World and set it free. When his invention turned out to help rather than hurt photography, he went quite mad. He now inflicts his revenge by writing educational books and hosting training videos.

His most sinister books are the award-winning *Photoshop CS Bible* and *Photoshop CS Bible, Professional Edition* (*www.amazon.com/deke*), now in their eleventh year with more copies in print than any other guides on computer graphics. Other subversive titles include *Photoshop CS For Dummies*, *Photoshop Elements For Dummies* (both Wiley Publishing, Inc.), and *Real World Illustrator* (Peachpit Press).

Deke further shocks and appalls as host of the interactive "Video Workshop" that ships with Photoshop as well as the fiendishly exhaustive *Total Training for Adobe Photoshop CS* (*www.totaltraining.com*), the predecessor of which was named Training Product of the Year by MacNet 2.0. His other DVD- and CD-based video series include *Digital Photography with Photoshop Elements* and *Total Training for Adobe Illustrator CS* (both Total Training).

In 1989, Deke won the Benjamin Franklin Award for Best Computer Book. Since then, he has received similarly diabolical honors from the Society for Technical Communication (once in 1994 and twice in 1999), Photo>Electronic Imaging (1999), the American Society of Business Press Editors (1995 and 2000), the Western Publications Association (1999), and the Computer Press Association (1990, 1992, 1994, 1995, 1997, and twice in 2000). In 1999, Book Bytes named Deke its Author of the Year. In 2002, the National Association of Photoshop Professionals voted Deke into the Photoshop Hall of Fame.

During his fall from grace, Deke has also managed to become an Adobe Certified Expert, a member of the PhotoshopWorld Instructor Dream Team, a featured speaker on the 2003 Photoshop Fling cruise of the Eastern Caribbean, and a contributing editor for *Macworld* and *Photoshop User* magazines. Few now believe there is any hope for him.

Credits

Revisions by
Galen Fott

Acquisitions Editor
Tom Heine

Project Editor
Amy Thomas Buscaglia

Copy Editor
Beth Taylor

Editorial Manager
Robyn Siesky

Vice President & Executive Group Publisher
Richard Swadley

Vice President and Executive Publisher
Robert Ipsen

Executive Editorial Director
Mary Bednarek

Project Coordinator
Maridee Ennis

Graphics and Production Specialists
Beth Brooks
Joyce Haughey
Kristin McMullan
Lynsey Osborn

Original Artwork
©2002, Deke McClelland

Stock Photography
PhotoSpin, Corbis

Quality Control Technicians
John Greenough
Susan Moritz
Angel Perez
Charles Spencer

Proofreading
TECHBOOKS Production Services

Indexing
Sharon Hilgenberg

Preface

Welcome, gentle reader, to the *Photoshop CS Bible, Professional Edition*. Of course, this book is a "bible" only in the dictionary sense of "a book considered authoritative in its field," not in any religious sense. (This didn't stop me from trying to arrange a deal with the Gideons to distribute a copy of this book in every hotel room in America, but they didn't return my calls.) I don't want to make any assumptions about the religious persuasion of you, the prospective buyer, standing there in the bookstore. Because as it happens, the hard reality is that I know almost nothing about you, except that there's a strong possibility you have some sort of interest in Adobe Photoshop. Nevertheless, and futile though it may be, I want you—whoever you are—to feel that this book was written especially, specifically and solely for *you*.

Every time you turn a page, I want you to think, "Gosh, I feel like he is talking directly to me," because I am. I want you to smell my curiously strong Altoid-scented breath as you ripple through the pages. I want you to see my gnarled hand pointing a nail-bitten finger to direct you to all the most important Photoshop tips and tricks nestled within these pages. If you were a contestant on one of those lurid TV dating shows, today's episode would end with you and this book flying off to an all expenses-paid weekend in sunny Acapulco—that's how much this book was made for you.

Don't believe me? Check out these you-oriented stats: The *Photoshop Bible* is the longest continuously published title on Adobe Photoshop, so you know it's steadfast and tenacious. With more than a million copies in print worldwide, the *Photoshop Bible* is the bestselling reference guide on Photoshop, so you know you're getting an established, dependable standard. The *Photoshop Bible* ranks among the most award-winning and widely recommended books in the design industry, so you know it's a title you can trust.

But while the *Bible*'s pedigree clearly suggests a family and cultural heritage that's compatible with your own, that's hardly a reason to fall in love. Which is why I handcrafted this particular edition, the *Professional Edition*, with your specific needs in mind:

✦ **Your time is valuable.** The *Professional Edition* is streamlined, around 400 pages shorter than the softcover edition.

✦ **You're a visual thinker.** The *Professional Edition* places emphasis on carefully rendered illustrations and informational graphics. Loaded with more than 1,000 separate illustrations grouped into around 550 figures — more than most books twice its size — the *Professional Edition* never tells what it can show (see Figure 1).

✦ **You already know your way around Photoshop.** The *Professional Edition* skips the basic, boring stuff (preferences, file formats) in favor of pages upon pages of exciting and inspirational high-end techniques.

✦ **You have work to do.** The *Professional Edition* explains Photoshop's most practical and powerful capabilities in everyday English. After all, just because a command is complicated doesn't mean the discussion has to be.

✦ **You're not cheap, but you don't say no to value.** Unlike the softbound standard edition, the *Professional Edition* is printed entirely in full-color on glossy paper stock. And yet it costs less per page than other full-color titles.

✦ **You appreciate craftsmanship and quality.** Every photograph and illustration in the *Professional Edition* is printed at 300 pixels per inch or higher. (Go ahead, count 'em!) Even the most casual screen shots are meticulously diagrammed so you're never left wondering how an option works or where it's located.

✦ **You want brand new information.** If you've purchased previous editions of the *Bible* in softcover, you may not recognize this one. More than half the content is unique to the *Professional Edition*.

Figure 1: Unlike most books, the *Professional Edition* mates for life. So don't go buying it if you're just going to turn around and break its heart. (But feel free to break its spine if you wish.)

Needless to say, this edition has been combed over, fine-toothed-style, to weed out the old info, pour in the new, and make sure everything is totally up to date with Photoshop CS. But the guiding principles I established in the previous century with the first edition of the *Photoshop Bible* remain very much intact. As always, I make it my mission to address every topic head on — no cop-outs, no apologies. When I don't know how something works (which happens more often than I care to admit), I do the research and figure it out, sometimes discussing features directly with the programmers, sometimes taking advantage of other sources. My job is to find out the answers, make sure those answers make sense, and pass them along to you as clearly as I can.

I also provide background, opinions, and occasional attempts at chummy, even crummy humor. Like the one at the beginning of this preface. A dry listing of features followed by ponderous discussions of how they work doesn't mean squat unless I explain why the feature is there, where it fits into your workflow, and — on occasion — whether or not it's the best solution. I am alternately cranky, excited, and just plain giddy as I explain Photoshop, and I make no effort to contain my criticisms or enthusiasm. This book is me walking you through the program as subjectively as I would explain it to a friend.

Which Testament Should You Choose?

The appearance of the words *Professional Edition* in the title of this book may lead you to suspect that there is at least one other edition. And so there is. The *Photoshop CS Bible* (which I'll call the "standard edition") is a softbound publication that was published a few months prior to the *Professional Edition* and remains available throughout the life of Photoshop CS and beyond — indeed, as long as anyone is willing to purchase it. Weighing in at more than 1,000 pages, the standard edition is a great deal longer than the *Professional Edition* and covers territory that I leave unexplored in this book. Not only that, it costs $20 less. All of which may leave you wondering: "Why two books? Why does the shorter one cost more? And which one is right for me?" Here are the answers:

Why two Photoshop CS Bibles?

Over the past decade, the number one request from readers has been, "More color!" Little did you know, you were preaching to the converted. I'd been petitioning my publisher for increased color since the 2nd edition of the book — after all, there have been certain topics that I simply cannot cover in adequate detail without color. I won't go into the gory details, but I will tell you that with the *Photoshop 7 Bible, Professional Edition*, I finally got my way. (All right, so I pitched a fit. What self-respecting prima donna wouldn't?) But there was one caveat — I got full-color if *and only if* I cut the page count. So I had to be merciless in cutting content, but I was equally merciful in adding new material unique to this book. Things ultimately seemed to turn out well; therefore, you hold in your hands the *Photoshop CS Bible, Professional Edition,* still in glorious living color.

Why does the *Professional Edition* cost more?

If you're familiar with the financial demands of the print world, you know that color printing on glossy paper costs more than twice as much as black-and-white printing on uncoated stock. What you may not know is that printing is the driving factor in the high cost of creating a book. Editorial, art, and production all take a back seat. And where does that leave us authors? Locked in the trunk.

Yes, it's sad but true, the typical author is lured into the trunk of a sub-compact car with promises of "free candy," then forced to write his book in the dark on fast food napkins and the backs of oil change receipts. He's fed treacle and candle wax, with uncooked bread dough on Fridays only if all deadlines are met. Also, most authors are paid only in tips. So when you buy this book, please leave a small gratuity (something in the 15-20 percent range is standard) in the space where the book was on the shelf. I'll be by to pick it up later today.

Okay, that last paragraph was a lie. (You actually need to mail the gratuity directly to me.) But the paragraph before it was mostly true. The book costs more because it costs more to produce.

Which *Photoshop CS Bible* is right for you?

As I mentioned earlier, I wrote this book for *you*. Unless you're not who I think you are, in which case, the best *Bible* for you depends largely on your skill level.

The standard edition of the *Photoshop CS Bible* is an invaluable, cradle-to-grave resource guide with emphasis on text description over graphics. The *Professional Edition* is likewise a resource guide, but with emphasis on creative techniques, graphics and imagery, and the new capabilities of Photoshop CS. The *Professional Edition* assumes more knowledge on the part of the reader, but in return, it delivers more interesting, more exciting information.

If you're looking for specifics, topics that receive either exclusive or dramatically expanded coverage in the *Professional Edition* include Levels, Curves, the Camera Raw format, the Lens Blur filter, hue and saturation adjustments, the Channel Mixer, layer styles, history, the Render filters, actions, batch renaming and processing, arbitrary and displacement maps, the Custom filter, digital photography, red-eye reduction, Web graphics, the sRGB color space, and ImageReady. As I alluded earlier, half the pages in this book appear nowhere inside the standard edition.

That means there's a lot of stuff covered in the standard *Photoshop CS Bible* that isn't covered in this edition. The standard edition alone provides the popular shortcuts table as well as coverage of navigation, preferences, tool presets, workspaces, resampling and resolution, file formats, color channels and models, the eyedropper tool, gradients, the common selection tools, paths, text, Color Settings, and CMYK printing. My goal was to create two independent books with as little overlap as possible. I'm not advising that you get both books, but some readers will, and I want them to be absolutely satisfied.

My advice is that, if you've never read a previous edition of the *Photoshop Bible* or if you're relatively new to Photoshop, you may prefer the standard softbound *Photoshop CS Bible*. On the other hand, if you own one of the previous editions or you're reasonably adept at Photoshop, get the *Professional Edition* instead. Of the two *Bibles*, the *Professional Edition* is far and away the deluxe model, blessed with high production values, real-world techniques, detailed screen graphics, full-color photography, and scads of information that most working professionals I've come in contact with are not aware of.

Conventions

After boasting about how different this book is, here's a section that has remained pretty much the same since the old days. Fortunately, that's a good thing — even while my content improves, my conventions remain unchanged. After all, no sense messing with a good thing. For those of you who are new to the *Bible*, the following sections explain how things work.

Vocabulary

Although I try to conform to the rules of conversational English, I can't explain Photoshop in graphic and gruesome detail without occasionally reverting to the specialized language of the trade. Hence, the occasional technobabble. To help you keep up, I've italicized vocabulary words (as in *antialiasing*) with which you may not be familiar, or which I use in an unusual context. An italicized term is followed by a definition.

If you come across a strange word that is *not* italicized (that bit of italics was for emphasis), look it up in the index to find the first reference to the word in the book.

Commands and options

To distinguish the literal names of commands, dialog boxes, buttons, and so on, I capitalize the first letter in each word (for example, *click the Cancel button*). The only exceptions are option names, which can be six or seven words long and filled with prepositions (*to* and *of*) and articles (*a* and *the*). Traditionally, such words are not capitalized and this book follows that time-honored rule.

When discussing menus and commands, I use an arrow symbol to indicate hierarchy. For example, *File ⇨ Browse* indicates the Browse command from the File menu. If you have to display a submenu to reach a command, I list the command used to display the submenu between the menu name and the final command. *Image ⇨ Adjustments ⇨ Levels* means to choose the Adjustments command from the Image menu and then choose the Levels command from the Adjustments submenu.

The whole platform thing

This is a cross-platform book, meaning that it's written for both Windows and Macintosh users. Photoshop is practically identical on the two platforms, so it makes little difference. The only exceptions are the keyboard shortcuts, which can be quite different. The Ctrl key on the PC usually translates to the Command key (⌘) on the Mac. Alt usually translates to Option. And because Apple's mice do not include right mouse buttons, right-clicking on the PC often translates to Control-clicking on the Mac. Throughout the course of this book, I try to make things as unambiguous as possible by mentioning the Windows keystroke first with the Macintosh equivalent in parentheses.

Version numbers and letters

A new piece of software comes out every 15 minutes. That's not a real statistic, mind you, but I bet I'm not far off. I've had the pleasure of watching Photoshop grow from Versions 1 through 7, and now Photoshop has advanced past numbers altogether and arrived at Version CS. (I like to think of it as Photoshop, the Version Formerly Known as 8.) But by the time you read this, the version may have changed. Though I must say I can only wildly guess at what the next upgrade will be called. Photoshop CS.1? Photoshop 9 (Sorry About That Letter Thing)? Photoshop CS, p.s.? Photoshop CSI: San Jose? Photoshop: The Next Generation?

Just know that when I write *Photoshop CS*, I mean any version of Photoshop that comes before the next *major* revision of the software, whatever the heck it'll be called. Similarly, when I write *Photoshop 7*, I mean Versions 7.0 and 7.0.1; *Photoshop 6* means Versions 6.0 and 6.0.1; and so on.

Icons

Like just about every computer or self-help book available these days, this one includes alluring margin icons that call your attention to important information. The difference is, my icons are really pretty (see Figure 2). I designed these icons — inside Photoshop, naturally — to take advantage of the newly colored pages and to show off a little bit of what Photoshop can do. I'm proud to say these icons remain unique to this title.

Figure 2: The five utterly unique and original margin icons that appear inside this book. Here we see the icons magnified to 300 percent their normal size. The reduced icons feature white text for optimum readability.

On the whole, the icons are self-explanatory, but I'll explain them anyway:

 The green Photoshop CS icon explains an option, command, or other feature that is brand-spanking new to this latest version of Photoshop. If you're already familiar with previous versions of the program, you might just want to plow through the book looking for Photoshop CS icons and see what new stuff is out there.

 This book is bursting with tips and techniques. If I were to highlight every one of them, whole pages would be covered in blue light bulbs. Fortunately, I use a bit more discretion than that and reserve the Tip icon only for those tips and tricks that you're least likely to know. Figures can also serve as useful visual signposts; if you see something you like, you can bet the neighboring text has something to say on the topic.

The amber Note icon highlights a tidbit of non-essential but fascinating information. I might tell you how an option came into existence, why a feature is implemented the way it is, some details regarding the underlying math, or how things might be improved in the future.

The red Caution icon warns you that a step you're about to take may produce disastrous, inconvenient, or unpleasant results. Thankfully, I use this icon on very rare occasions, but when you see it, give it your full attention.

The purple Cross-Reference icon tells you to look elsewhere for more information on a specific topic. For example, I might mention that the icon graphics themselves rely heavily on Photoshop's custom shapes and layer effects. For more information on these key topics, read Chapter 7, "Shapes and Styles."

How to Bug Me

Even in its 15th edition, scanned by the eyes of hundreds of thousands of readers and scrutinized intensely for months at a time by myself, my crackerjack reviser Galen Fott, and my intrepid editor Amy Thomas Buscaglia, I'll bet someone, somewhere will still manage to locate errors and oversights. If you notice those kinds of things and you have a few spare moments, please let me know what you think. I always appreciate readers' comments.

If you want to share your insights, comments, or corrections, please e-mail me at *pcspro@ dekemc.com*. Don't fret if you don't hear from me for a few days, or months, or ever. I read every letter and try to implement nearly every constructive idea anyone bothers to send me. But because I receive hundreds of reader letters a week, I can respond to only a small percentage of them.

Please, don't write to ask me why your copy of Photoshop is misbehaving on your specific computer. Despite my yammering presence on the "Video Workshop" CD included with the standalone version of Photoshop CS, please keep this mind: I was not involved in developing Photoshop, I am not employed by Adobe, and I am not trained in product support. Adobe can answer your technical support questions way better than I can, so I leave it to the experts.

And please don't write to ask me if there's an accompanying CD or a Web site where you can access the images I use in this book; sorry, but there isn't. I do not make the images in this book available for two reasons. First, many are commercial stock images; understandably, their photographers would frown on me giving away their artwork for free. Second, the techniques discussed in this book are designed to work on *your* images. There's no need to slog through a tutorial before you can apply what you've learned to your own work. Instead, you can set right in making practical use of these techniques immediately.

So there it is — everything you need to know to go forward. I don't think I left anything out. But if I did, it's a big book, so there's plenty of time to bring you up to speed later. And remember, this book is for *you*, so don't hesitate to interrupt if things don't make sense or to ask questions about related topics. Needless to say, the book won't answer you, and if someone sees you talking to a book, they'd be more than justified in having you locked up. But that'll just give you that much more time to learn Photoshop.

Contents at a Glance

Contents

Painting and Brushes

Photoshop Paints Like a Pro

Once upon a time, there used to be gobs of digital painting programs. And when I say gobs, I mean bucket loads. And when I say bucket loads, I mean squillions. They had names like Lumina and Studio/32 and Deluxe Paint and Color MacCheese and — well, I really haven't the time to list them all. Suffice it to say, in the last dozen or so years, there have been more than 100 of them. At one time, there were more painting applications in circulation than word processors, spreadsheet programs, and database managers combined.

Their astonishing abundance is made all the more amazing by the fact that virtually every one of them is now stone, cold dead. The one notable exception is Corel's powerful Painter (*www.corel.com*), which enjoys a loyal but tiny following. There's also Paint Shop Pro from Jasc Software (*www.jasc.com*). But although it has the word Paint in its title, it's more of a general-purpose image editor, in many ways a lesser, not to mention less expensive, version of Photoshop.

What killed them all? Photoshop. If painting programs used to roam software shelves like bison roamed the plains, then Photoshop was the drunken cowboy perched on a train car and filling the colorful software boxes with so much virtual lead. Okay, that metaphor might be a bit extreme, but it makes my point: This one program made mincemeat of everything around it.

This fact is ironic because Photoshop never was a painting program. Traditionally, Adobe has concentrated its efforts on making Photoshop a terrific image editor. Oh, sure, Version 7 greatly expanded Photoshop's range of painting options, making it one of the most powerful painting applications in history. But the fact that artists had already abandoned other painting programs in favor of Photoshop largely seems to be an indication that folks preferred image editing to painting. So if Photoshop was a drunken cowboy, it was unintentional. Adobe was shooting at something much larger, and the painting programs just got in the way.

So why did Adobe beef up Photoshop's painting tools by integrating capabilities from an unsuccessful category of software? The answer is good timing. Although the painting programs of yore provided a wealth of amazing tools and color selection options, the hardware of the time was only barely able to keep up with them. Memory was expensive, hard drives were small, and 24-bit video was rare. As a result, painting programs tended to be slow and capable of producing only low-resolution artwork. Software has long been judged on whether it will save you time or make you money, and those old painting programs could do neither. They were, therefore, clever playthings and nothing more.

Photoshop has long since proven itself a capable, practical application, with a loyal following among professional designers. Meanwhile, the hardware has grown several times more powerful. Memory is cheap, hard drives are spacious and fast, and a modern video card can render anything Photoshop can send it in a matter of nanoseconds. So now seems a perfect time to rediscover the lost art of painting, as you and I will do throughout the following pages.

Meet the Paint and Edit Tools

Photoshop provides two basic varieties of brush tools. There are paint tools, which allow you to apply colors to an image. Then there are edit tools, which modify existing colors in an image. Either way, you operate the tool by dragging the cursor inside the image, much as you might drag a real brush across a real sheet of paper.

This might lead you to think that the paint and edit tools require artistic talent. In truth, each tool provides options for almost any level of proficiency or experience. Photoshop offers get-by measures for novices who want to make quick edits and put the tool down before they make a mess of things. It also provides a wealth of features so complex and powerful that only the most capable artist will want to approach them. But no matter who you are, you'll find the tools more flexible, less messy, and more forgiving than their traditional counterparts.

In all, Photoshop CS provides two paint tools — the brush and the pencil. You also get six edit tools — blur, sharpen, smudge, dodge, burn, and sponge. (The new color replacement tool could also be considered an edit tool, but I deal with it separately in Chapter 11.) Figure 1-1 shows all the tools along with the keyboard shortcuts for selecting them.

 When two or more tools share a slot in the toolbox, click and hold on the tool icon to display a flyout menu of all the tools, as illustrated in Figure 1-1. Or you can just press Shift plus the keyboard shortcut listed in the menu to switch from one tool to the next. For example, repeatedly pressing Shift+B cycles between the brush and pencil tools.

You can vary the performance of the active tool by using the controls in the Options bar along the top of your screen. If you don't see the Options bar, choose Window ➪ Options or double-click a tool icon in the toolbox.

The paint tools

The paint tools apply strokes of color. In most cases, you'll be painting with the foreground color, though you can also create multicolored brushstrokes using the Color Dynamics options in the Brushes palette, as we'll see later. Here's how the paint tools work:

+ **Brush:** This tool paints a line of any thickness that you specify. You can make the line sharp or blurry, but it's always slightly soft — that is to say, the edges of the brushstroke blend to some extent with the background. Known as *antialiasing*, this softness produces halftone dots when printing, ensuring smooth transitions between a brushstroke and its surroundings.

  Normally, the brush tool applies a continuous stream of color and stops applying paint whenever you stop dragging. However, if you activate the airbrush function by clicking the airbrush icon in the Options bar, the color continues to build up as long as you press the mouse button, even when you hold the cursor still. In Figure 1-2, the first line was painted with a 65-pixel soft brush and the airbrush option off. To make the second line, I turned on the airbrush setting and reduced the Flow value (also in the Options bar) to 50 percent. The result is a buildup of color at the corners and at the end of the stroke.

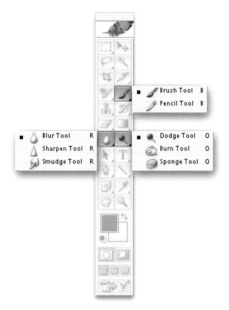

Figure 1-1: Here we see the two paint tools and six edit tools, all available from flyout menus.

 To invoke the airbrush function from the keyboard, press Shift+Alt+P (or Shift-Option-P on the Mac). Pressing Shift+Alt+P again turns the function off. For those of you who are wondering where this keystroke comes from, it's P for paint, baby, paint.

✦ **Pencil:** Like the brush tool, the pencil paints a line of any thickness in the foreground color. However, whereas brush tool lines are always soft, pencil lines are always hard-edged, with no interaction between the pencil line and background colors. Figure 1-2 shows a 45-pixel pencil line printed at 300 ppi. At such high resolutions, pencil lines appear sharp. At low resolutions, pencil lines have jagged edges.

When you select the pencil tool, a unique check box, Auto Erase, appears in the Options bar. When selected, this option instructs Photoshop to paint with the background color, in effect erasing whenever you begin painting on an area already colored with the foreground color. A throwback to old black-and-white painting programs, such as MacPaint, this option is useful when editing screen shots, custom icons, and the occasional Web graphic.

 As when painting in real life, one of the necessities of painting in Photoshop is switching out the color of your brush. The Color palette is handy, but it's not immediate enough. You need something that can keep up with the speed of your creative ideas. The solution is the eyedropper. You can select the tool directly by pressing the I key. Or access the tool temporarily by pressing the Alt key (Option on the Mac). Alt-clicking to sample a color from your image is so useful that those of you who do a lot of painting with the brush tool may find yourselves Alt-clicking almost as often as you drag.

Figure 1-2: Three lines painted with the brush and pencil tools.
To create the second stroke, I turned on the airbrush setting.
I created the color buildup at the bottom of the line by slowing
my stroke and, at the very end, holding the cursor in place for
a moment.

The edit tools

The edit tools don't apply color; rather, they influence existing colors in an image. Figure 1-3 shows the effect of dragging with each of the edit tools except the sponge. Future sections cover the tools in more detail, but here's a brief introduction:

✦ **Blur:** The first of the two focus tools, the blur tool blurs an image by lessening the amount of color contrast between neighboring pixels.

✦ **Sharpen:** The second focus tool selectively sharpens by increasing the contrast between neighboring pixels.

Generally speaking, neither the blur nor sharpen tool is as useful as its command counterparts in the Filters menu. Each provides little control and requires scrubbing at the image. The sharpen tool is especially ineffective, tending toward too much sharpening or no sharpening at all. I might use it to dab at the occasional edge, but that's about it.

✦ **Smudge:** The smudge tool smears colors in an image. The effect is rather like dragging your finger across wet paint. Although simple, this tool can be effective for smoothing out colors and textures. See "Painting with the smudge tool" later in this chapter for more information.

Blur   Sharpen   Smudge   Dodge   Burn

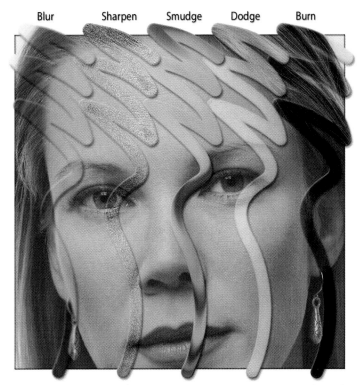

Figure 1-3: The effects of dragging with five of Photoshop's edit tools. The boundaries of each line are highlighted so you can clearly see the distinctions between line and background.

✦ **Dodge:** The first of three toning tools, the dodge tool lets you lighten a portion of an image by dragging across it. Named after a traditional darkroom technique, the dodge tool is supposed to look like a little paddle. (Yeah, I think it looks like a lollipop, too.) Before computers, a technician would wave such a paddle (or anything, really) over photographic paper to prevent light from hitting the paper and thereby leave areas less exposed. Thank golly, we no longer have to wave little paddles in our modern age.

✦ **Burn:** The burn tool is the dodge tool's opposite, darkening an area as you drag over it. Returning once again to the dark room, the technician would create a mask by, say, cutting a hole in a piece of paper or cupping his hand. Doing this would protect areas of photographic paper that had already been exposed and darken the area inside the hole. Photoshop's metaphor for this is a hand in the shape of an O, kind of a lazy man's mask. I can't testify how well that would work — never tried it myself — but I imagine the burn tool is a lot easier and more effective than the old hand trick.

If you're like most folks, you have difficulty remembering which tool lightens and which one darkens. But think of them in terms of toast, and suddenly, everything falls into place. For example, that little hand icon looks like it could be holding a piece of toast. And when you *burn* toast, it gets *darker*. Hand, toast, burn, darker. That other tool, the little paddle, is not so deft at holding toast. The toast would fall off, in which case, a small person standing below the paddle would have to *dodge* the toast. Suddenly, your load as the bearer of toast gets *lighter*. Paddle, falling toast, dodge, lighter. With these two strained but handy metaphors in mind, you'll never have problems again.

✦ **Sponge:** The final toning tool, the sponge tool, robs an image of saturation when working inside a color image or contrast when working in grayscale. Or you can set the tool so that it boosts saturation or adds contrast. For more information, stay tuned for the upcoming section "Mopping up with the sponge tool."

To access the sharpen tool temporarily when the blur tool is selected, press and hold Alt (Win) or Option (Mac) while using the tool. The sharpen tool remains available only as long as you press Alt or Option. Likewise, you can press Alt (Win) or Option (Mac) to access the blur tool when the sharpen tool is selected, to access the burn tool when the dodge tool is selected, or to access the dodge tool when the burn tool is selected. This can be a real time-saver. Say, for example, that you want to burn the image using the settings configured for the dodge tool. Rather than switching to the burn tool and changing its settings, you could select the dodge tool and Alt-drag (or Option-drag).

You can replace the blur tool with the sharpen tool in the toolbox by Alt-clicking (Option-clicking on the Mac) on the tool's icon. Alt-click (or Option-click) again to select the smudge tool and yet again to cycle back to the blur tool. Likewise, you can Alt-click (Option-click on the Mac) the dodge tool icon to cycle between the dodge, burn, and sponge tools.

The keyboard shortcut for the blur tool is R; the shortcut for the dodge tool is O (the letter shared by "dodge" and "toning tools"). These keys also toggle between the tools. When the blur tool is selected, press Shift+R to switch to the sharpen tool. Repeated pressings of Shift+R take you to the smudge tool and back to the blur tool. When the dodge tool is selected, press Shift+O to toggle to the burn tool; press Shift+O again to get the sponge.

Basic Techniques

I know several people who claim that they can't paint, and yet they create beautiful work in Photoshop. Even though they don't have sufficient hand-eye coordination to write their names on screen, they have unique and powerful artistic sensibilities, and they know many tricks that enable them to make judicious use of the paint and edit tools. I can't help you in the sensibilities department, but I can show you a few tricks to boost your ability and inclination to use the paint and edit tools.

Painting a straight line

Photoshop provides a line tool that lets you draw straight lines. It's a surprisingly flexible tool, permitting you to draw vector-based layers or pixel-based lines, and you can even add arrowheads. If you'd like to learn about it, I explain the line tool and others like it in Chapter 7.

The main reason that I use the line tool is to fashion arrows. If I don't want arrows, I usually take advantage of Photoshop's other means for creating straight lines: the Shift key. By Shift-clicking with any of the tools introduced in this chapter, you can paint or edit in straight lines.

Try this: Using the brush tool, click at one point in the image and then press Shift and click at another point. Photoshop connects the start and end points with a straight stroke of paint. You can use this same technique with the pencil, or to blur, smudge, dodge, or otherwise edit pixels in a straight line.

To create free-form polygons, continue to Shift-click with the tool. Figure 1-4 features a photograph and a tracing I made by Shift-clicking with the brush tool. Note that I experimented with different brush sizes, as explained later in the "Brush Size and Shape" section. I also used a variety of colors sampled from the image by Alt-clicking (Option-clicking on the Mac).

Most importantly, I painted the image on a separate layer to protect my original image from harm. (I discuss layers in Chapter 5.) But as a matter of principal, I only Shift-clicked with the brush tool; I never dragged.

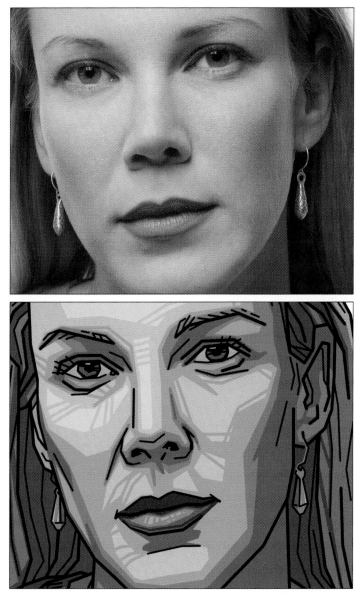

Figure 1-4: Starting from an image by photographer Barbara Penoyar (top), I created a stylized tracing (bottom) by clicking and Shift-clicking with the brush tool on a separate layer.

The Shift key makes the blur tool and even the sharpen tool halfway useful as well. Suppose that I wanted to edit the perimeter of the knife shown in Figure 1-5. The arrows in the figure illustrate the path my Shift-clicks should follow. Figure 1-6 shows the effect of Shift-clicking with the blur tool; Figure 1-7 demonstrates the effect of Shift-clicking with the sharpen tool.

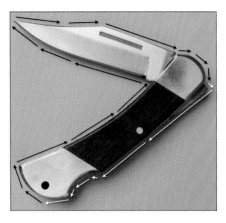

Figure 1-5: It takes one click and 21 Shift-clicks to soften or sharpen the edges around this knife using the blur or sharpen tool.

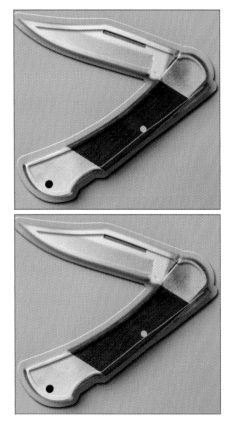

Figure 1-6: These are the results of blurring the knife's perimeter with the Strength value in the Options bar set to 50 percent (top) and 100 percent (bottom).

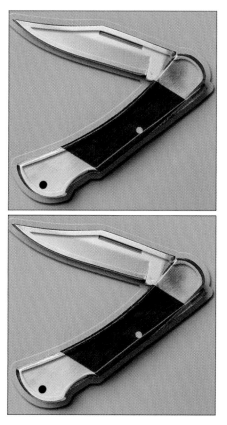

Figure 1-7: The results of sharpening the knife with the Strength value set to 35 percent (top) and 70 percent (bottom). Anything higher produced an oversharpening effect, making it too easy to cut yourself.

Painting a perpendicular line

To create a perpendicular line — that is, a line that is either vertical or horizontal — press Shift while dragging with a paint or edit tool. Releasing Shift returns the line to freeform, as illustrated in Figure 1-8. Press Shift in mid-drag to snap the line back into perpendicular alignment.

One way to exploit the Shift key's penchant for snapping to the perpendicular is to draw "ribbed" structures. To create the central outlines around the skeleton that appear at the top of Figure 1-9, I dragged from right to left with the brush tool. I painted each rib by periodically pressing and releasing Shift as I dragged. In each case, pressing Shift snapped the line to the horizontal axis, the location of which was established by the beginning of the drag.

After establishing the basic skeletal form, I added some free-form details with the brush and pencil tools, as shown in the middle image in Figure 1-9. Having painted the skeleton on a separate layer, I set it against a rock surface from the PhotoSpin image library and applied a Bevel and Emboss layer effect. (See Chapter 7 for complete information on layer effects.) Nobody's going to mistake my painting for a bona fide fossil, but it's not too shabby for a cartoon.

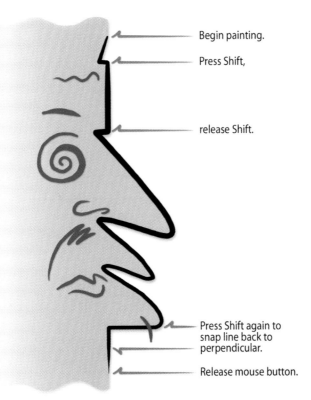

Begin painting.

Press Shift,

release Shift.

Press Shift again to snap line back to perpendicular.

Release mouse button.

Figure 1-8: Pressing Shift after you start to drag with a paint or edit tool results in a perpendicular line for as long as the key is pressed.

It's no accident Figure 1-9 features a swordfish instead of your everyday round-nosed carp. To snap to the horizontal axis, I had to establish the direction of my drag as being more or less horizontal from the get go. If I had instead dragged in a fish-faced convex arc, Photoshop would have interpreted my drag as vertical and snapped to the vertical axis.

Painting with the smudge tool

Many first-time Photoshop artists misuse the smudge tool to soften color transitions, which is the purpose of the blur tool. The smudge tool is designed to smear colors by shoving them into each other. The process bears more resemblance to finger painting than to any traditional photographic-editing technique.

In Photoshop, the performance of the smudge tool depends in part on the settings of the Strength and Finger Painting controls in the Options bar. Here's what you need to know about these options:

✦ **Strength:** The smudge tool works by repeatedly stamping the image hundreds of times throughout the length of a brushstroke. The effect is that the color appears to get "pushed" across the length of the stroke. The Strength value determines the intensity of each stamping, so higher values push colors the farthest. A Strength setting of 100 percent equates to infinity, meaning the smudge tool pushes a color from the beginning of your drag until you release your mouse button. Figure 1-10 shows a few examples.

✦ **Finger Painting:** Back in the old days, the folks at Adobe called this effect *dipping*, which I think more accurately expressed how it works. When you select this option, the smudge tool begins by applying a smidgen of foreground color, which it eventually blends in with the colors in the image. It's as if you dipped your finger in a color and then dragged it through an oil painting. Use the Strength setting to specify the amount of foreground color applied. If you turn on Finger Painting and set the Strength to 100 percent, the smudge tool behaves like the brush tool. Figure 1-11 shows examples of finger painting with the smudge tool when the foreground color is set to white.

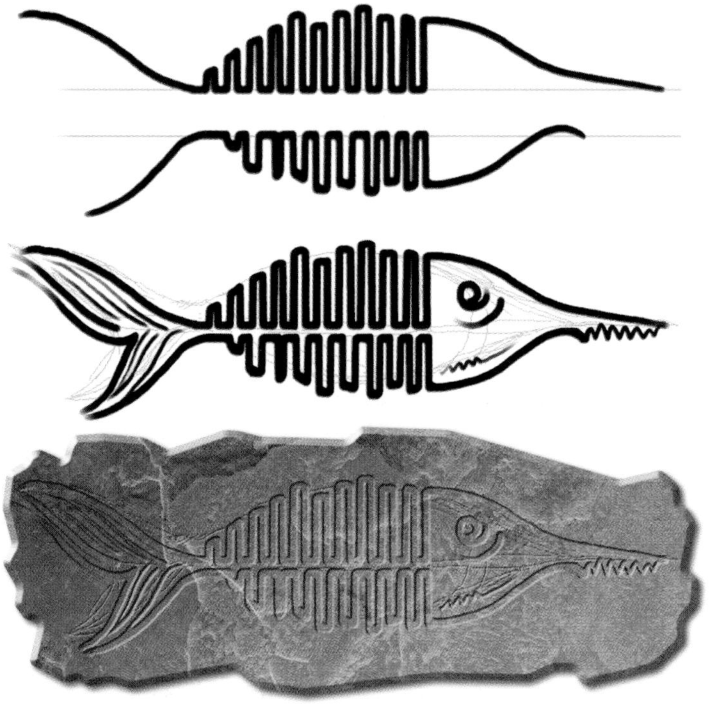

Figure 1-9: To create the basic structure for our bony pal, I periodically pressed and released Shift while dragging with the brush tool (top). Then I embellished the fish using the brush and pencil (middle). Finally, I applied a Bevel and Emboss layer effect and set the fossil against a rock surface from the PhotoSpin image library (bottom).

You can reverse the Finger Painting setting by pressing the Alt key (Option on the Mac) and dragging. If the option is off, Alt-dragging dips the tool into the foreground color. If Finger Painting is turned on, Alt-dragging smudges normally.

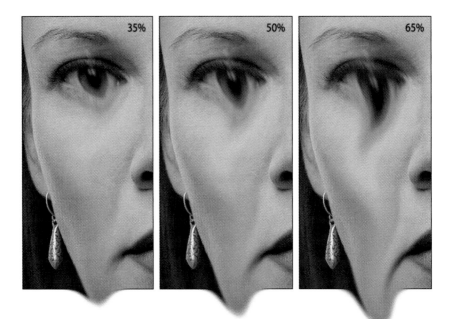

Figure 1-10: Three identical drags with the smudge tool subject to different Strength settings. In each case, I began the brushstroke at the eye and dragged downward.

The Use All Layers option instructs the smudge tool to grab colors in all visible layers and smudge them into the current layer. Whether the option is on or off, only the current layer is affected; the background and other layers remain intact.

For example, suppose the mask around the woman's eye on the left side of Figure 1-12 is on a different layer than the rest of the face. If I use the smudge tool on this mask layer with Use All Layers turned off, Photoshop ignores the face layer when smudging the mask. As a result, details such as the eye and skin remain unsmudged, as in the middle example in the figure. If I turn Use All Layers on, Photoshop lifts colors from the face layer and mixes them with the mask layer, as shown in the right-hand example.

In the case of Figure 1-12, the mask appears to smudge better when the Use All Layers check box is turned off. But this isn't always the case. In fact, turning the check box on is a great way to smudge without harming a single pixel in your image. Just make a new, empty layer in the Layers palette. Then select the smudge tool and turn Use All Layers on. Now smudge to your heart's content. Even though the active layer is empty, Photoshop is able to draw colors from other layers. Meanwhile, the colors in the underlying layers remain unharmed.

Mopping up with the sponge tool

The sponge tool is actually a pretty simple tool, hardly worth expending valuable space in a book as tiny as this one. But I'm a compulsive explainer, so here's the deal—when the sponge tool is active, you can select either Desaturate or Saturate from the Mode pop-up menu in the Options bar. Here's what they do:

✦ **Desaturate:** When set to Desaturate, the tool reduces the saturation of the colors over which you drag. When you're editing a grayscale image, the tool reduces contrast.

✦ **Saturate:** If you select Saturate, the sponge tool increases the saturation of the colors over which you drag or increases contrast in a grayscale image.

You can switch between the Desaturate and Saturate modes from the keyboard. Press Shift+Alt+D (Shift-Option-D on the Mac) to select the Desaturate option. Press Shift+Alt+S (Shift-Option-S on the Mac) for Saturate. No matter which mode you choose, higher Flow settings produce more dramatic results.

To see the sponge tool in action, take a look at Figure 1-13. Starting with the delicately featured woman from Figure 1-4, I added a virtual face-paint mask around the woman's eyes, a technique that relied heavily on the burn and sponge tools. The following steps explain how I did it.

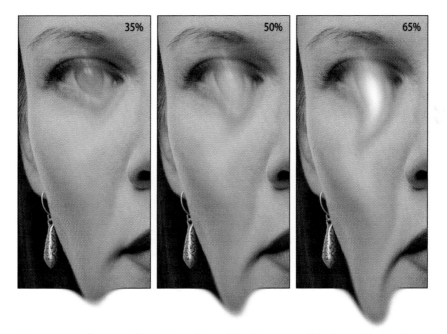

Figure 1-11: The same three drags pictured in Figure 1-10, this time with the Finger Painting option turned on and the foreground color set to white.

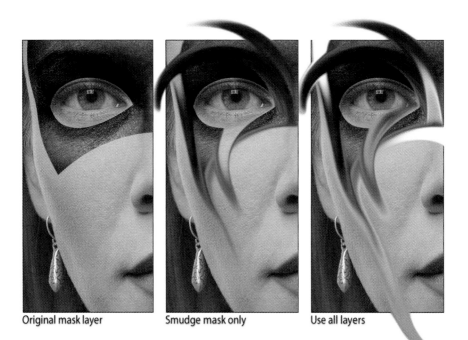

Original mask layer   Smudge mask only   Use all layers

Figure 1-12: The original image (left) features a mask on an independent layer in front of the rest of the face. I first smudged the mask with Use All Layers turned off (middle) and then with the option turned on (right). In both cases, the Strength setting was set to 80 percent; the brushstrokes were identical.

STEPS: Sponging In and Away Color Saturation

1. **Draw the mask.** To make the mask, I drew the mask outline using the pen tool set to the Paths mode. (Note that I explain the pen tool at length in the "How to Draw and Edit Paths" section in Chapter 8 of the standard *Photoshop CS Bible*.)

2. **Convert the path to a selection outline.** After drawing the mask outline and eyeholes, I converted the path to a selection outline by Ctrl-clicking on it in the Paths palette. If you're intimidated by the pen tool and Paths palette, you could create a similar selection using the lasso tool, though it wouldn't look as smooth.

3. **Jump the selection to a layer.** I next pressed Ctrl+J (⌘-J on the Mac) to copy the selection to an independent layer. This protected the image so that any edits I applied to the mask would not harm the face.

4. **Burn the mask.** Thus far, mask and face were the same colors. To set the mask apart, I darkened it with the burn tool. This involved multiple drags with the Strength set to 50 percent, focusing primarily on the outer edges. The result is the first image in Figure 1-13. (Note that no other tools or commands were used to darken the mask — that's 100 percent burn tool. See what I meant by my earlier toast analogy? That burn tool makes some tasty looking toast.)

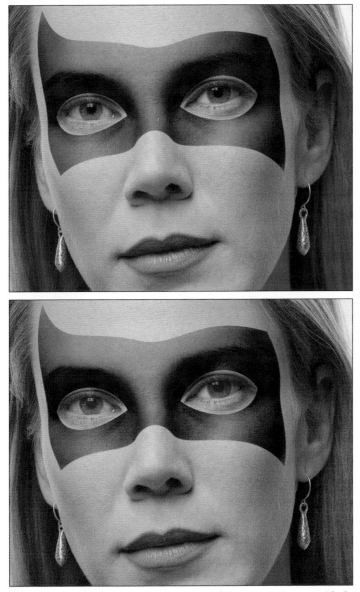

Figure 1-13: After selecting an area around the woman's eyes with the pen tool, I painted inside the selection with the burn tool, applying additional strokes under the eyebrows and around the edges of the mask to deepen the shadows (top). Next, I painted inside the mask with the sponge tool to alternatively dim colors and saturate them. Then I deselected the image and painted inside the irises, lips, and hair to make these areas more vivid (bottom).

5. **Sponge away saturation.** The mask had a nice tone to it. But to get more of a Mardi Gras effect, I wanted to introduce some difference in saturation values. I began by painting around the eyes inside the mask. Because the Mode option in the Options bar was set to Desaturate, this sucked away the color around the eyes, leaving mostly gray.

6. **Sponge in saturation.** Still armed with the sponge tool, I changed the Mode setting to Saturate and painted along the forehead of the mask and bridge of the nose. This drew out some vivid oranges. Then I switched to the face layer and painted the eyes, lips, and hair to increase their saturation as well.

7. **Dodge the eyes.** Want to make a person look better? Use the dodge tool on her eyes. Just a click or two on each eye brightens the irises and gives the person an almost hypnotic stare. A little bit of extra dodging makes her look downright freaky, like some kind of radioactive X-Men character. Which is a good thing, needless to say.

The finished image appears at the bottom of Figure 1-13. Note that although the woman now appears more brightly colored, she does not look more made up. That's because the sponge doesn't add color to an image; it merely enhances the colors that are already there. This makes the tool a bit unpredictable at times as well. For my part, I was surprised to see the hair turn a fiery orange and the tips of the earrings go purple. You never know what you'll find when you raise saturation values.

I find it very helpful to turn on the airbrush setting in the Options bar when using the sponge tool (as well as the other toning tools, dodge and burn). This way, you can gradually build up effects on the fly. When you find a section of an image that needs more sponging than most, hold your cursor in place, watch Photoshop airbrush in the effect, and then move the cursor when you've had enough.

Undoing the damage that you've done

If you make a mistake in the course of painting an image, stop and choose Edit ➪ Undo or press Ctrl+Z (⌘-Z on the Mac). If this doesn't work, press Ctrl+Alt+Z (⌘-Option-Z on the Mac) to step back through a sequence of paint strokes.

You can also undo a brushstroke by selecting a previous state in the History palette. As explained in Chapter 3, the History palette lists brushstrokes and other changes according to the tool you used to create them.

If you like the basic look of a brushstroke but you'd like to fade it back a bit, choose Edit ➪ Fade or press Ctrl+Shift+F (⌘-Shift-F on the Mac). The Fade command lets you reduce the Opacity or change the blend mode of the brushstroke you just finished painting. (If you have since clicked with another tool, the command may appear dimmed, indicating that you've lost your chance.) The Fade command is applicable to all paint and edit tools, as well as other operations inside Photoshop, so you'll be seeing a lot of it throughout this book.

Better yet, when using the brush tool or an edit tool that offers the Use All Layers option, create a new layer by pressing Ctrl+Shift+N (⌘-Shift-N on the Mac) before you paint a single line. Then you can refine your lines and erase them without harming the original appearance of your image.

Brush Size and Shape

Now that you've gotten a feeling for the basics of using the paint and edit tools, let's take a broader look at how you modify the performance of the tools. For example, every tool behaves differently according to the size and shape of your cursor, known as the *brush tip*. Different styles of brush tips are known as *brush shapes*, or just plain *brushes* (not to be confused with the brush tool, which folks sometimes call "the brush" as well). But although there's a lot of nomenclature at work here, the concept behind the brush shape is very simple. A big, round brush paints in broad strokes. A small, elliptical brush is useful for performing hairline adjustments. And if that's not enough — which it clearly isn't — you've a world of options in between and many more besides.

Selecting a brush shape

Provided that a paint or edit tool is active, there are a handful of ways to modify the brush shape:

✦ **Right-click:** Right-click anywhere inside the image window (Control-click on the Mac) to display a small palette of preset brush shapes, complete with a menu of additional options, as pictured in Figure 1-14. Scroll through the list of brush shapes, click on the one you want to use, and then press Enter or Return to hide the palette. You can also press Esc to hide the palette and leave the brush shape unchanged.

The presets palette previews how the brush looks both when you click and when you drag. If your computer includes a pressure-sensitive drawing tablet, then the strokes will appear to taper, as in the figure; otherwise, they will appear uniform. To dispense with the stroke previews, choose Large Thumbnail from the palette menu. To restore the stroke previews, choose Stroke Thumbnail.

✦ **The Brushes palette:** Choose Window ➪ Brushes or press F5 to display the Brushes palette, which appears on the left side of Figure 1-15. Click the words Brush Presets in the top-left corner of the palette to see a list of predefined brush shapes. You also get a large preview of the active brush shape at the bottom of the palette. Bear in mind, the brush shape will only appear tapered if you turn on the Shape Dynamics check box along the left side of the palette.

The primary advantage of the Brushes palette is that you can define your own brush shapes and adjust various exciting dynamics, as I discuss in the next section. If all you want to do is select a predefined brush, right-clicking (or Control-clicking) is generally simpler.

By default, the Brushes palette is wider than Photoshop's other palettes, which means it doesn't stack well on the right side of your screen. You have two ways of working around this: One is to get in the habit of pressing F5 to show and hide the palette at a moment's notice. The other is to turn off the Expanded View command in the Brushes palette menu, which lets you shrink the preset brush list to Photoshop's standard palette width, as in the right example in Figure 1-15.

✦ **Master diameter:** With the preset palette or Brushes palette on screen, you can change the size of the brush by adjusting the Master Diameter value. Measured in pixels, this value represents the thickest stroke the brush can paint. (It can get thinner based on the Shape Dynamic settings, as I explain later in this chapter.) This means you're never locked into a preset brush diameter, even when painting with custom (non-round) brushes.

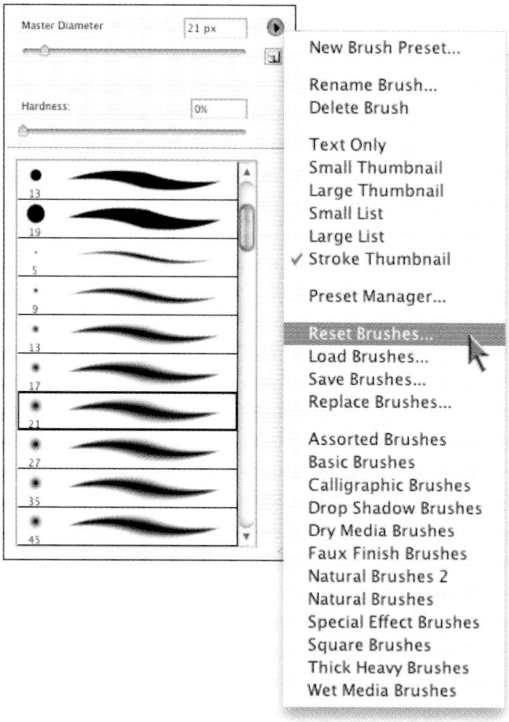

Figure 1-14: The presets palette lets you select from a list of predefined brush shapes and load other ones from disk.

Changing the brush diameter is so useful you can do it from the keyboard. Press the left bracket key, which looks like [, to make the brush smaller. Press the right bracket key, or], to make the brush bigger. (Both keys are to the right of the P key on most keyboards.) Keep an eye on the brush icon in the Options bar to see how much smaller or larger the brush diameter gets.

✦ **Preset shortcuts:** You can cycle between presets even when no palette is visible. Press the comma key to toggle to the previous brush shape in the list. Press the period key to select the next brush shape. You also can press Shift+comma to select the first brush shape in the list (1-pixel wide) and Shift+period to select the last brush.

By default, your cursor outline reflects the active brush shape. If your cursor instead looks like a crosshair or tool icon, press Ctrl+K (⌘-K on the Mac) to bring up the Preferences dialog box and press Ctrl+3 (⌘-3 on the Mac) for the Display & Cursors panel. Then select Brush Size from the Painting Cursors radio buttons. Now you can create a brush as big as 2,500 pixels in diameter and have your cursor grow accordingly.

When you use a very small brush, four dots appear around the cursor perimeter, making the cursor easier to locate. If you need a little more help, press the Caps Lock key to access the more obvious crosshair cursor.

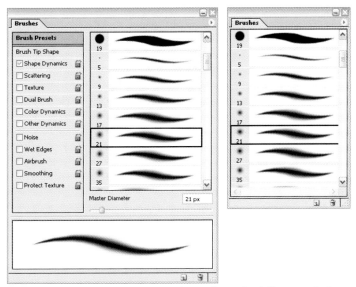

Figure 1-15: Two views of the Brushes palette, the fully expanded view (left) and the reduced view (right). The advantage of the latter is that it stacks well with Photoshop's other palettes.

Making your own brush shape

To create a custom brush shape, click the item named Brush Tip Shape inside the Brushes palette, which displays the options shown in Figure 1-16. Photoshop displays thumbnails for the predefined brushes in the top-right quadrant of the palette. Select a brush to serve as a starting point for your custom creation and then tweak away:

✦ **Diameter:** This option determines the width of the brush. If the brush shape is elliptical instead of circular, the Diameter value determines the longest dimension. You can enter any value from 1 to 2,500 pixels.

A small word of warning: Brush shapes with diameters of 15 pixels or higher are too large to display accurately in the Options bar; the stroke preview at the bottom of the Brushes palette is accurate no higher than 50 pixels. So regard the previews with a grain of salt.

✦ **Flip X** and **Flip Y:** New in Photoshop CS is the ability to flip a brush shape on either the X (horizontal) or Y (vertical) axis. Select the Flip X check box to flip the brush shape into a mirror image of itself. Select the Flip Y check box to flip the brush shape upside-down. These options are most obvious when you're using an asymmetrical brush shape.

✦ **Angle:** This option pivots a brush shape on its axes. Unless the brush is elliptical, though, you won't see a difference. So it's best to first adjust the Roundness value and then adjust the Angle.

✦ **Roundness:** Enter a Roundness value of less than 100 percent to create an elliptical brush shape. The value modifies the height of the brush as a percentage of the Diameter value, so a Roundness of 50 percent results in a short, fat brush.

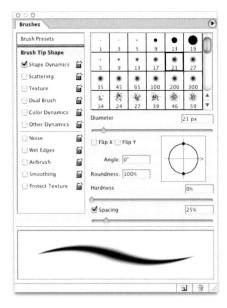

Figure 1-16: To change the size, shape, and hardness of a brush, click the item named Brush Tip Shape in the Brushes palette.

You can adjust the angle of the brush dynamically by dragging the gray arrow inside the box to the right of the Angle and Roundness options. Drag the handles on either side of the black circle to make the brush shape elliptical, as demonstrated in Figure 1-17. Drag the arrow tip to angle the brush. Or try this trick: Click anywhere in the white box to move the arrow to that point.

The Angle and Roundness settings take advantage of a terrific overall interface improvement in Photoshop CS, known as *scrubbing*. Hover your cursor over the words Angle or Roundness in the Brushes palette. You'll see a pointy finger skewered by a double-headed arrow. This means that by clicking and dragging — that's the "scrubbing" part — you can change the value with ease. Adding the Shift key makes scrubbing jump in increments of 10 percent. Holding down the Alt key (Option on the Mac) slows down the rate of change relative to your scrubbing. Happily, when painting in Photoshop, this is the only type of brush scrubbing you'll ever have to do. Though like me, you might want to keep an open jar of turpentine by your computer, just for the fragrance.

✦ **Hardness:** Except when using the pencil tool, brushes are always antialiased. You can further soften the edges of a brush by dragging the Hardness slider bar away from 100 percent. The softest setting, 0 percent, gradually tapers the brush from a single solid color pixel at its center to a ring of transparent pixels around the brush's perimeter. Figure 1-18 shows that low Hardness percentages expand the size of a 200-pixel brush beyond the Diameter value (as demonstrated by the examples in the bottom row). Even a 100-percent hard brush shape expands slightly because it is antialiased. The Hardness setting is ignored when you use the pencil tool.

Like Diameter, Hardness is one of those settings that you need regular access to. So the ever-helpful Photoshop lets you change the Hardness from the keyboard. Press Shift+[(Shift+left bracket) to make the brush softer; press Shift+] (Shift+right bracket) to make the brush harder. Both shortcuts work in 25 percent increments. For example, you have to press Shift+] four times to go from 0 percent Hardness to 100 percent.

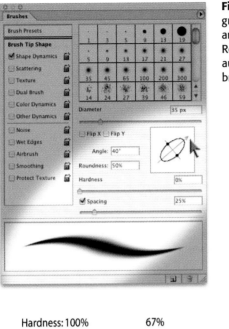

Figure 1-17: Drag the black handles and gray arrow to change the roundness and angle of the brush, respectively. The Roundness and Angle values update automatically, as does the preview of the brushstroke at the bottom of the palette.

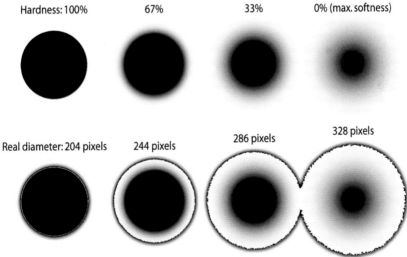

Hardness: 100%   67%   33%   0% (max. softness)

Real diameter: 204 pixels   244 pixels   286 pixels   328 pixels

Figure 1-18: A 200-pixel brush shown as it appears when set to each of four Hardness percentages. In the bottom row, I placed the brushes on a separate layer and applied a black fringe so that you can see the effective diameter of each Hardness value.

✦ **Spacing:** In real life, a brush lays down a continuous coat of paint. But that's not how it works on the computer. Photoshop actually blasts out a stream of colored spots. The Spacing option controls how frequently the spots are emitted, measured as a percentage of the brush shape. For example, suppose the Diameter of a brush is 40 pixels and the Spacing is set to 25 percent (the default setting for all predefined brushes). For every 10 pixels (25 percent of 40) you drag with the brush tool, Photoshop lays down a 40-pixel wide spot of color. A Spacing of 1 percent provides the most coverage but also slows down the performance of the tool. If you deselect the Spacing check box, the effect of the tool is wholly dependent on the speed at which you drag; this can be useful for creating splotchy or oscillating lines. Figure 1-19 shows examples.

 In my experience, ridges generally begin to appear at the default Spacing value of 25 percent, especially when painting with a mouse. If you notice lumps in your brushstrokes, lower the Spacing to 15 percent, which (as illustrated in the second example in Figure 1-19) ensures a good mix of speed and smoothness. When using a soft-edged brush, lower spacing values result in a denser, fatter stroke and higher values result in a lighter, thinner stroke. High spacing values are great for creating dotted lines.

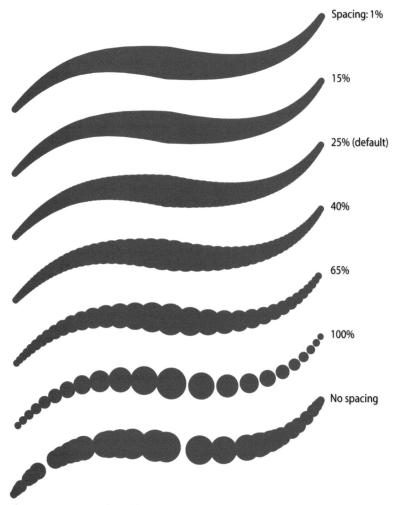

Figure 1-19: Examples of lines drawn with the brush tool subject to different Spacing values. Values greater than 100 percent are useful for creating dotted line effects. The final line was created by turning off the Spacing option.

After you edit a brush, you can save the brush for later use by clicking the tiny page icon at the bottom of the palette. Photoshop suggests a name, which you can then change. To save a brush without being asked to name it, Alt-click the page icon (or Option-click on the Mac). Photoshop stores the brush with your program preferences so that it's preserved between editing sessions.

Note that if you delete your preferences file — which goes by the name Adobe Photoshop CS Prefs on your computer's hard drive — you lose your custom brushes. To ensure that your custom brushes are saved in case you delete the preferences file or for use on another machine, choose Save Brushes from the palette menu.

To delete a brush from the list, switch back to the Brushes Presets view and drag the brush to the trash icon at the bottom of the palette.

Defining a custom brush

Photoshop allows you to not only modify the size and roundness of a brush but to define a custom brush as well. Start by making a new image and doodling the desired shape of your brush tip. For now, any squiggle will do. Then use the rectangular marquee tool to select the doodle. You don't have to be particularly careful; just select the general area around the doodle, as I've done in Figure 1-20. Photoshop is smart enough to distinguish the confines of the brush from its background.

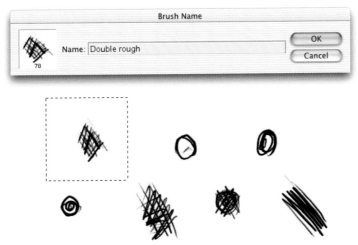

Figure 1-20: After selecting a doodle against a white background, choose Edit ⇨ Define Brush Preset and enter a name to turn the doodle into a custom brush.

Next, choose the Define Brush Preset command from the Edit menu. Photoshop invites you to give your brush a name; if you're not feeling inspired, just press Enter or Return and accept the default name, Sampled Brush 1.

After you define a custom brush, you can tweak it just like any other brush inside the Brush Tip Shape panel of the Brushes palette. You can adjust the Diameter, Angle, and Roundness (height versus width) of your new brush. As shown in Figure 1-21, the only option that appears dimmed is Hardness; you have to accept the sharpness of the brush as it was originally defined. A custom brush will even grow and shrink according to stylus pressure.

To restore a custom brush to its original size, click the Use Sample Size button in the Brush Tip Shape panel of the Brushes palette.

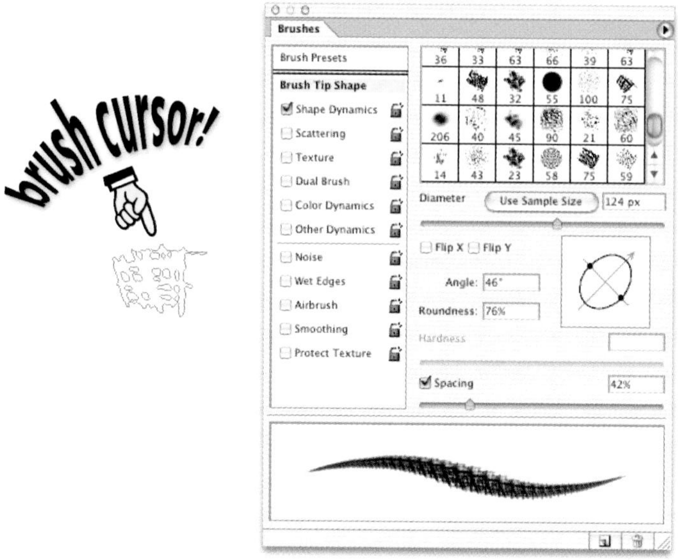

Figure 1-21: Photoshop lets you modify the size, shape, and angle of a custom brush, all of which are accurately reflected by the brush cursor.

Brush Dynamics

Photoshop has long permitted you to vary the size, opacity, and color of paint according to input from a pressure-sensitive drawing tablet. Available from companies such as Wacom (*www.wacom.com*), pressure-sensitive drawing tablets respond to how hard you press on the stylus, as well as the angle of the stylus and other attributes.

I happen to be an old fan of drawing tablets. I believe I have roughly a dozen sitting around in one form or other. So it's hardly surprising that I consider them every bit as essential as mice and keyboards. Alas, despite my opinion, I realize that you may not own a tablet. Fortunately, Photoshop permits mouse users to enjoy much of the same flexibility as their stylus-wielding colleagues. Whether you use a stylus, a mouse, or even a finger on a notebook trackpad, you can introduce an element of spontaneity into your painting.

Photoshop calls these imaginative options *brush dynamics*, and they open up a lot of opportunities for faking pressure sensitivity if you aren't using a stylus. For example, you can make a brush shape twirl as you paint. You can add noise to the edges of a stroke. You can spray shapes, add texture, combine brushes, or even paint in rainbows. And most of the settings work every bit as well with, say, the sponge as they do with the brush tool. If you're a creative type, prepare to get lost inside Photoshop and lose track of reality for a few hours, maybe even days.

Brush dynamic basics

To access Photoshop's brush dynamics when a paint or edit tool is active, bring up the Brushes palette (press F5 if it's hidden), and click the item labeled Shape Dynamics on the left side of the palette. This simultaneously activates and displays the first of six panels — including Scattering, Texture, and so on — devoted to brush dynamics. Photoshop also provides a series of check boxes (starting with Noise and ending with Protect Texture) that apply minor effects without displaying additional panels of options.

Note that all check boxes and options are available when using the brush tool, but they come and go for the other paint and edit tools. For example, the Wet Edges check box is unavailable when using the pencil tool, Color Dynamics is dimmed when using the dodge and burn tools, and so on. Even so, the sheer amount of options available for even the most limited of the edit tools verges on fantastic. Also, each tool observes an independent set of defaults. So activating, say, Shape Dynamics, Texture, and Smoothing for the brush tool does not turn them on for other tools. However, these options will again be turned on the next time you return to the brush tool.

If you want to save a group of brush dynamics for use with a variety of tools, then click the page icon along the bottom of the Brushes palette. Brush dynamics are considered to be part of a saved brush shape, and transfer from one tool to another. To save a group of brush dynamics for use with a single tool, visit the Tool Presets palette (Window ⇨ Tool Presets) and choose New Tool Preset from the palette menu. Doing so is equivalent to designing your own custom tool that you can select from the Options bar.

So there's your general overview; now let's plunge headlong into the specifics. To give you a sense of what's going on, we start with a detailed look at the options in the Shape Dynamics panel, which are arguably the most interesting, useful, and representative of all the brush dynamics. Then we take a more cursory look at the other options, which often follow in the same vein. After that, I encourage you to explore the options on your own. And as you do, don't forget to keep one eye on the big stroke preview at the bottom of the palette. It really is useful, especially when trying out settings that you haven't used before or combining options to achieve specific effects.

So have fun. And when I say "have fun," I mean, have a blast, go nuts. By which I mean, wowsers, this stuff rocks. Goodness, how I envy you, so young and naive, embarking upon brush dynamics for the very first time. You're about to be amazed, astonished, and then once again amazed. Or perhaps, after this build up, horribly disappointed. I guess it all depends on how much of a thrill you get from drawing wiggly, splattery, rough, colorful brushstrokes. Me, I love it. But you, who knows? Okay, I'll shut up now.

Shape dynamics

Inside the Brushes palette, click the Shape Dynamics option — the name, not the check box — to display the panel of options illustrated in Figure 1-22. Look carefully and you'll see that the panel is divided into three sections, which start with the words Size Jitter, Angle Jitter, and Roundness Jitter. These options permit you to vary the diameter, angle, and roundness of the brush over the course of a single stroke. But the repetition of the word "Jitter" may be misleading. It implies (to me, at least) that each group of options is related to jittering — Photoshop's word for random brush shape fluctuations — when in fact, jittering is a minor element of shape dynamics.

If I had designed this panel, it would look more like the one in Figure 1-23, with clear headlines for each section followed by the single most important option, the Control pop-up menu. Meanwhile, I'd put the least important option, Jitter, at the end. Because I believe this is the most logical way to present these options, I will explain them in this order as well.

Figure 1-22: The Shape Dynamics panel along with a quick cartoon I drew using the brush shape described in the palette and a Wacom Intuos II tablet.

The diameter settings

The first group of options controls the thickness of the brushstroke. Most important of these is the Control pop-up menu, which links the diameter of the brush to one of several variables. If you own a pressure-sensitive tablet, the most obvious setting is Pen Pressure, which is the default. This setting turns the brush into a traditional, pressure-sensitive painting tool, growing when you bear down on the stylus and shrinking when you let up.

Three settings, Pen Pressure, Pen Tilt, and Stylus Wheel, require compatible hardware. If your only pointing device is a standard mouse, selecting one of these options displays a triangular warning icon. This is Photoshop's way of telling you that, although you are welcome to select the option, it isn't really going to work. If you get the message in error — say, you get a warning for Pen Pressure even though you have a tablet installed — try clicking with the stylus on the Brushes palette. If that doesn't work, open the control panel or utility that manages the tablet to make sure the tablet is properly installed.

Figure 1-23: My suggestion for a redesign of this panel that would help it to make more sense. (It seems to make more sense to my cartoon, anyway.)

In addition to Pen Pressure, the Control pop-up menu lets you select between the following options:

✦ **Off:** Select this option to turn off your control over varying the thickness of the brush-stroke. You can still add random variations to the thickness using the Size Jitter value.

✦ **Fade:** This option works every bit as well whether you use a mouse or tablet. Select Fade to reduce the size of the brush over the course of the drag and then enter a value in the option box on the right to specify the distance over which the fading should occur. This distance is measured in steps — that is, the number of spots of color the brush plops down before reducing the size of the brush to its minimum (defined by the Minimum Diameter setting). The default value is 25, which means 25 spots of color. Exactly how long such a stroke is in, say, inches depends on the Diameter and the Spacing values in the Brush Tip Shape panel. In other words, be prepared to experiment.

The Fade option can be most useful in the creation of a specular reflection, or in layman's terms, a sparkle. Figure 1-24 shows a highly polished, gold-painted egg. To add the sparkle in the second example, I painted a series of white strokes outward from the center using the brush tool. I Shift-dragged to make each of the four horizontal and vertical strokes, using a soft brush with a diameter of 20 pixels and a Fade value of 100 steps. To make each of the diagonal strokes, I clicked in the center and Shift-clicked farther out, using a diameter of 10 pixels and a Fade value of 50 steps. To complete the effect, I clicked once in the center of the sparkle with a very large, very soft brush.

Figure 1-24: A shiny golden egg from the Corbis library (top), and that same egg with a sparkle created using the Fade setting (bottom).

✦ **Pen Tilt:** As illustrated in Figure 1-25, the tilt of a pen is its angle with respect to the tablet. Straight up and down, the pen communicates no tilt; at a severe angle, the pen communicates maximum tilt. When you set the Control option to Pen Tilt, you do two things. First, you vary the size of the brush according to pressure, just as you do when using Pen Pressure. Second, you add an element of vertical scaling so that the brush shape is oblong during a tilt. This scaling is defined by the Tilt Scale slider. All in all, it's an interesting idea, but for my money, Pen Tilt works more predictably when applied to roundness.

✦ **Stylus Wheel:** If tablet owners account for 10 percent of Photoshop users, then air-brush stylus owners account for about 1 percent of tablet users. But heck, that's still enough folks to populate a small town, so we might as well support them. For those of you who have never seen an electronic airbrush, Figure 1-26 shows what one looks like, complete with stylus wheel. Unlike the scroll wheels included with many PC mice — which are exceptionally useful for scrolling Web pages and Word documents — the wheel on an airbrush locks into position. This means you can nudge it higher or lower and leave it there. Although typically associated with properties such as Flow (which you can set from the Other Dynamics panel), the airbrush wheel is surprisingly useful for diameter as well. Move the wheel up, the brush gets thick and stays thick; move the wheel down, and you lock in a fine line, all in the middle of painting a brushstroke. Downside: A Wacom airbrush costs $100, not including the tablet. So it's a stocking stuffer. She gets earrings, he gets an airbrush. Or vice versa. Heck, send *me* the earrings — I already have an airbrush. And no, I'm not interested in a trade, just give me the earrings!

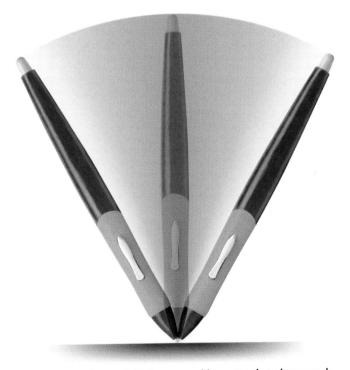

Figure 1-25: Most Wacom tablets are sensitive not only to how much pressure you apply to a stylus, but also the angle of the stylus with respect to the tablet, known as the tilt.

Accompanying the Control pop-up menu are three slider bars:

✦ **Minimum Diameter:** Use this option to determine the thinnest a brushstroke can go. Me, I say go all the way to 1 percent, baby. Why settle for more?

✦ **Tilt Scale:** I don't admit this very often, but this option puzzles me. Yes, it's only available when you set the Control option to Pen Tilt, and yes, it stretches the height of the brush to make it elliptical when you tilt the stylus. But why? You can do this just as well with the roundness options, as I explain shortly. My guess: A thoughtful engineer at Adobe wanted you to get confused by this option so you'd go out and buy this book. Really, that's my best guess. Now for those of you who did buy this book for a lucid explanation of the Tilt Scale option, sorry I couldn't help. Check out the other pages, though — they're really great.

✦ **Size Jitter:** Use this slider to add an element of pure randomness to the thickness of a brushstroke. It doesn't matter whether you use a mouse or a stylus; the brush will jitter every bit as well either way. Higher values produce a wider range of jitter. Keep an eye on the preview at the bottom of the palette to get a sense of what different settings will do.

Figure 1-26: The airbrush stylus includes a wheel that you can permanently set to increase or decrease the flow of paint, as with a traditional airbrush.

Angle and roundness

Now that you understand the diameter settings, the angle and roundness settings are pretty simple stuff. But to confirm your knowledge and ensure that we're all not just *literally* on the same page, here's how they work:

✦ **Angle Control:** As with diameter, you can link the angle of the brush to such variables as Pen Pressure, Pen Tilt, and Stylus Wheel. More pressure or tilt equals more rotation of the brush. Naturally, the changes show up best with elliptical or asymmetrical brushes. You can also link the angle to Fade, which rotates the brush over the course of a specific number of steps and then returns the brush to its normal angle (as specified in the Brush Tip Shape panel).

But this Control pop-up menu adds in two more settings, Direction and Initial Direction. The first rotates the brush according to the direction of your drag. A horizontal drag is considered the normal angle; when dragging vertically, the brush rotates 90 degrees. For maximum effect, after setting this option to Direction, go to the Brush Tip Shape panel and set the Angle value to 90 degrees (or something close) with an elliptical brush. Then raise the Spacing value to something higher than 100 percent.

Meanwhile, the Initial Direction option rotates the brush according to the very start of your drag and then locks it into position. It's a nice idea, but the angle is locked down about 2 pixels into your drag, which means Photoshop is aware of your initial direction before you are.

✦ **Angle Jitter:** This option rotates the brush randomly as you paint. As always, be sure to adjust the roundness of the brush so you can see the randomness at work.

✦ **Roundness Control:** Set this option to Fade to reduce the roundness to its minimum over the course of a specified number of steps. You can also associate the roundness with Pen Pressure, Pen Tilt, or Stylus Wheel. Of these, Pen Tilt makes by far the most sense to me, because that's what pen tilt does in real life.

✦ **Minimum Roundness:** This value determines the minimum roundness, or maximum flatness, of the brush available to the Control and Jitter settings. If the Control option is set to Off and the Roundness Jitter is 0 percent, then the Minimum Roundness slider is dimmed.

✦ **Roundness Jitter:** Use this option to introduce random variations in roundness to your brushstroke.

Two new check boxes at the bottom of the Shape Dynamics panel give you the ability to flip the jitter on its X axis, Y axis, or both at once, much like you can flip the brush tip shape. Flipping the jitter on its axis may be more control than most of us will ever need, but you can't fault Photoshop CS for offering yet another means of controlling brushstrokes.

Additional brush dynamics

For many, the Shape Dynamics settings will be enough. And certainly, they permit you to achieve an enormous range of effects. But if you're feeling ambitious, you can venture deeper, much deeper. Fortunately, the other panels of options — Scattering, Texture, and so on — follow the same logic we've seen thus far. So I'll breeze through them fairly quickly.

Figure 1-27 demonstrates several dynamic permutations as applied to the predefined custom brush Scattered Leaves. Here's how these options work:

✦ **Scattering:** Highlight the Scattering option to spread the position of the spots of color around the brushstroke. When using a custom brush, such as Scattered Leaves in Figure 1-27, the effect is like spraying a pattern of images. Raise the Scatter value to increase the spread. Select Both Axes to scatter the brush spots along the stroke as well as perpendicularly to it. Use the Control pop-up menu to link it to stylus pressure or some other variable. Finally, use the Count options to increase the population of brush spots.

✦ **Texture:** Select this option to apply a texture to a brushstroke, useful for conveying a surface such as paper or canvas. After selecting a predefined texture, set the Scale and Depth values to determine the size and degree of texture applied. Use the Mode option to define how brush and texture mix. (I discuss modes in the "Brush Modes" section near the end of this chapter, but for now, just experiment with an eye on the preview.)

If you want to vary the depth of texture throughout a stroke, turn on the Texture Each Tip check box. Then use the Control option to vary the depth according to, say, stylus pressure, or add some random Depth Jitter.

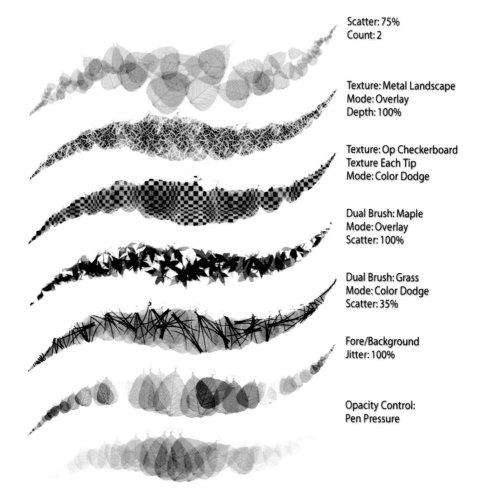

Scatter: 75%
Count: 2

Texture: Metal Landscape
Mode: Overlay
Depth: 100%

Texture: Op Checkerboard
Texture Each Tip
Mode: Color Dodge

Dual Brush: Maple
Mode: Overlay
Scatter: 100%

Dual Brush: Grass
Mode: Color Dodge
Scatter: 35%

Fore/Background
Jitter: 100%

Opacity Control:
Pen Pressure

Figure 1-27: Several brush dynamics applied to Scattered Leaves, one of Photoshop's predefined custom brushes.

✦ **Dual Brush:** The Dual Brush panel lets you mix two brushes together. Select the second brush from the list of thumbnails and use the Mode option to specify how the brushes intermix. You can also throw in settings such as Spacing, Scatter, and Count, all of which affect the second brush.

Figure 1-27 includes a couple of examples, mixing the Scattered Leaves brush with the Maple Leaves and Grass brushes, respectively. Figure 1-28 shows another example, complete with settings in the Brushes palette. Notice how by mixing a standard round brush with one of Photoshop's predefined Dry Brush options, I'm able to generate a complex brush that imparts its own texture.

✦ **Color Dynamics:** Use these options to vary the color of the stroke between the foreground and background colors depending on a fade or stylus pressure. You can also apply random changes to the hue, saturation, and brightness, or all three. The final slider bar, Purity, increases or decreases the saturation of colors throughout the brushstroke.

✦ **Other Dynamics:** The final set of brush dynamics permit you to associate the opacity, strength, flow, or exposure of the brush, depending on what tool you're using. I discuss each of these attributes in more detail in the upcoming section, "Opacity and Strength, Flow and Exposure." If you happen to own an airbrush, settings such as the Flow and Exposure are what the wheel was originally designed for.

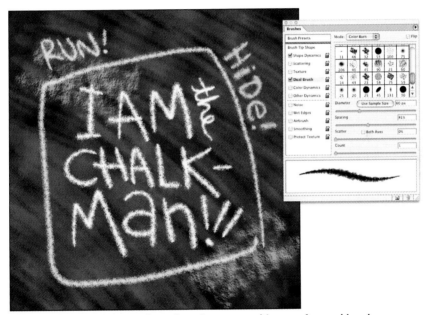

Figure 1-28: I used the Dual Brush options to combine a soft round brush and a predefined custom brush to create a fairly convincing chalk effect. I also scaled and rotated the brushes to create the light eraser stamps in the upper-left and lower-right corners.

You'll also notice that you have the ability to lock the settings you choose in the various brush dynamics panels. Click on the lock icon next to a panel name in the Brushes palette to toggle the lock option on or off. When a panel is locked, Photoshop will retain the options you've set in that panel even if you select a new brush preset that would normally contain different settings.

Noise, Wet Edges, and the rest

The list along the left side of the Brushes palette ends with five check boxes that you can use to add highlights and constraints to your brushstrokes. Not all options work with all tools, but when available, they're as effective as they are easy to use. And they work equally well with mouse or stylus.

✦ **Noise:** This option randomizes the pixels along the edge of a brushstroke. Because the option affects the edge only, softer brushes result in more noise. The middle line in Figure 1-29 shows an example.

✦ **Wet Edges:** When you select the Wet Edges check box, the brush creates a translucent line with darkened edges, much as if you were painting with watercolors. Soft brush shapes produce more naturalistic effects. The final example in Figure 1-29 shows a soft brushstroke painted in the same color as the previous brushstrokes.

Figure 1-29: Three lines painted with the brush tool. The first was painted without dynamics; the second was painted with Noise and the third with Wet Edges. The enlarged details show how the edges of the strokes compare.

✦ **Airbrush:** This check box duplicates the airbrush icon in the Options bar. When turned on, paint builds up even when you hold the cursor in place, as if spraying color from a real airbrush. The Airbrush option is not available when using the pencil tool or any of the three focus tools (blur, sharpen, and smudge).

✦ **Smoothing:** If you have difficulty drawing smooth lines and curves, turn this check box on to even out the rough spots. It slows down Photoshop's tracking time a little, but in many cases, it may be worth it. Adobe recommends this option when using a stylus, but I've found it most helpful when using optical mice, which are notoriously bad at tracking evenly on patterned surfaces, such as wood tabletops.

✦ **Protect Texture:** If you plan on painting a lot of textured lines and you want your textures to match, then select this check box. It maintains a consistent pattern from one brushstroke to the next. The effect can be subtle, but I usually advise working with the option turned on.

Opacity and Strength, Flow and Exposure

Another way to change the performance of a paint or edit tool is to adjust the Opacity and Flow values, which also go by the names Strength and Exposure, respectively, depending on the tool that you're using. When available, these controls appear in the Options bar. You can click the arrow to display a slider bar, drag the slider to raise or lower the value, and then press Enter or Return. You can also double-click the option box, type a value, and press Enter or Return. But the newest way also happens to be the best way: That scrubbing trick I mentioned earlier works in the Options bar, too.

Here's a look at how these options work:

✦ **Opacity:** The Opacity value determines the translucency of colors applied with the brush or pencil tool. At 100 percent, the applied colors appear opaque, completely covering the image behind them. (Exceptions occur when using the brush tool with Wet Edges active, which produces a translucent stroke, and when applying Mode options, discussed in the upcoming "Brush Modes" section.) At lower settings, the applied colors mix with the existing colors in the image.

You can change the opacity of brushstrokes or edits that you just applied by choosing Edit ➪ Fade or pressing Ctrl+Shift+F (⌘-Shift-F on the Mac). Then scrub the Opacity amount in the Fade dialog box. While you're in the dialog box, you can apply one of Photoshop's brush modes to further change how the modified pixels blend with the original ones.

✦ **Strength:** When using the blur or sharpen tool, the Opacity option changes to Strength. The value determines the degree to which the tool changes the focus of the image, 1 percent being the minimum and 100 percent being the maximum. Strength also appears when using the smudge tool, in which case it governs the distance the tool drags colors in the image. Another difference between Strength and Opacity: Whereas the default Opacity value for each tool when you begin using Photoshop is 100 percent, the default Strength value is 50 percent. Whether Strength is stronger than Opacity or these tools merely happen to know their own Strength is uncertain, but 50 percent is the baseline.

✦ **Flow:** The Flow option appears when using the brush tool, sponge, history brush, both stamp tools, and the eraser. Although the Flow option is always accompanied by the airbrush icon, you can use Flow and airbrush independently. The Flow value controls the opacity of each spot of color a tool delivers. So as a tool lays each spot of color onto the previous spot, the spots mix together and become more opaque. This means three things: First, a particular Flow setting will produce a more opaque line than an equivalent Opacity setting. In Figure 1-30, for example, a Flow value of 20 percent comes in slightly darker than an Opacity value of 50 percent. Second, Flow results in a progressive effect that compounds as a brushstroke overlaps itself, also demonstrated in the figure. Third, because Flow works on a spot-by-spot basis, you can increase or decrease the opacity of a line further by lowering or raising, respectively, the Spacing value in the Brush Tip Shape panel.

50% Opacity   20% Flow, 25% Spacing   20% Flow, 10% Spacing

Figure 1-30: Here we see the difference between Opacity, which controls an entire brushstroke, and Flow, which affects individual spots of paint. Where Opacity is consistent (left), Flow compounds wherever the stroke overlaps itself (middle). Tighter Spacing values also heighten the effect of Flow (right).

When using the brush, history, stamp, and eraser tools, you can combine Opacity and Flow values to achieve unique effects. You can also add in the airbrush, which compounds Flow further by adding spots of color when you slow down a brushstroke or hold the cursor still.

✦ **Exposure:** Available when using the dodge or burn tool, Exposure controls how much the tools lighten or darken the image, respectively. As with Flow, Exposure compounds when you corner or overlap a brushstroke, and includes an airbrush variation. A setting of 100 percent applies the maximum amount of lightening or darkening, which is still far short of either absolute white or black. As with Strength, the default is 50 percent.

You can change the Opacity, Strength, or Exposure setting for the active tool in 10-percent increments by pressing a number key on the keyboard or keypad. Press 1 to change the setting to 10 percent, press 2 for 20 percent, and so on, all the way up to 0 for 100 percent.

Want to change the Opacity, Strength, or Exposure setting in 1-percent increments? No problem — just press two keys in a row. Press 4 twice for 44 percent, 0 and 7 for 7 percent, and so on. This tip and the preceding one work whether or not the Options bar is visible. Get in the habit of using the number keys and you'll thank yourself later.

Changing the Flow value on the fly is trickier, but still possible. When the sponge tool is active, Flow works just like Opacity: Type a number to change the value in 10-percent increments; type two numbers to enter a specific value. But what about the brush tool and others that offer both Opacity and Flow? Typing a number changes the Opacity value *unless* the airbrush icon is active, in which case typing a number changes Flow. If the airbrush is turned off, press Shift plus a number key to change the Flow value. When the airbrush is turned on, pressing Shift plus a number key changes the Opacity value.

Brush Modes

When certain painting or editing tools are active, the Options bar provides access to Photoshop's brush modes, which control how the colors applied by the tool mix with existing colors inside an image or layer. Figure 1-31 shows which brush modes are available when you select various tools.

With the exception of the specialized modes available for the dodge, burn, and sponge tools, these brush modes are merely variations on the blend modes that are available in the Layers palette, which I examine in Chapter 6. The difference is that the blend modes in the Layers palette mix colors between layers, while the brush modes in the Options bar mix colors inside a single layer. Because of this subtle distinction, I describe the modes twice, once in the following section and again in Chapter 6. The latter discussion is more detailed, so if you don't get all the information you need here, feel free to skip ahead to Chapter 6 to find out more.

You can change brush modes from the keyboard by pressing Shift+plus (+) or Shift+minus (–). Shift+plus takes you to the next brush mode listed in the pop-up menu; Shift+minus selects the previous brush mode. It's a great way to cycle through the brush modes without losing your place in the image. Note that this doesn't work with the +/- keys on your keyboard's numeric keypad.

The 25 paint tool modes

Photoshop CS offers a total of 25 brush modes when you use the brush, pencil, or any of the other tools shown along the left side of Figure 1-31. (An additional mode, Threshold, is an alternative to Normal in certain color modes.) The brush modes are organized into six logical groups. The following figures show examples from each group, as applied to the strokes I drew by Shift-clicking with the brush tool way back in Figure 1-4.

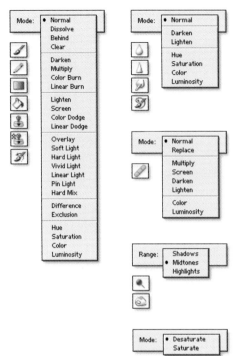

Figure 1-31: The specific Mode settings in the Options bar vary depending on which tool is active. The Mode pop-up menu changes to Range when using the dodge or burn tool.

 Just as you can cycle from one brush mode to the next from the keyboard, you can also jump directly to a specific brush mode. Just press Shift+Alt (Win) or Shift-Option (Mac) and a letter key. For example, Shift+Alt+N (Shift-Option-N on the Mac) selects the Normal mode, Shift+Alt+C (Shift-Option-C on the Mac) selects the Color mode. I list the letter key for each brush mode in parentheses along with its description:

✦ **Normal (N):** Choose this mode to paint or edit an image normally. A paint tool coats the image with the foreground color, and an edit tool manipulates the existing colors in an image according to the Opacity, Strength, Flow, and Exposure values.

Two color modes prevent Photoshop from rendering soft or translucent edges. The black-and-white and indexed modes (Image ➪ Mode ➪ Bitmap and Image ➪ Mode ➪ Indexed Color) simply don't have enough colors to go around. When painting in such a low-color image, Photoshop replaces the Normal brush mode with Threshold (L), which results in harsh, jagged edges, just like a stroke painted with the pencil tool. You can alternatively dither the soft edges by selecting the Dissolve mode, as described next.

✦ **Dissolve (I):** Dissolve scatters a random pattern of colors to simulate translucency. The pattern shows up along the edges of opaque brushstrokes or inside translucent strokes, like those in Figure 1-32. Note that this mode and the two that follow are not applicable to the edit tools. To get something resembling Dissolve with, say, the smudge tool, try applying the Noise setting in the Brushes palette.

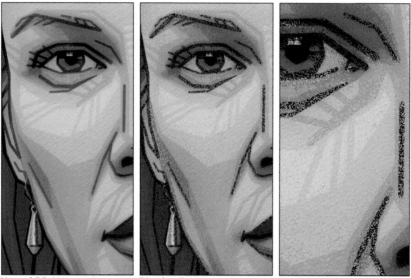

Normal (N), 50% opacity   Dissolve (I), 50% opacity   Dissolve, 200% zoom

Figure 1-32: Lines painted with the Normal (left) and Dissolve (middle) modes set to 50 percent opacity. Dissolve dithers colors to simulate translucency, as the magnified detail shows (right).

✦ **Behind (Q):** This mode is applicable exclusively to layers with transparency. When Behind is selected, the paint tools apply color behind the image on the active layer, showing through only in the transparent and translucent areas. Figure 1-33 shows how I created the Shift-click painting from Figure 1-4 by applying each coat of lighter color behind the last. Note that when working on an image without layers or on the background layer of a multi-layered image, the Behind mode is dimmed.

✦ **Clear (R):** When working on a layer other than *Background*, the Clear mode turns the brush tool, pencil, or paint bucket into an erasing tool, clearing away pixels. Given that the eraser already emulates the behavior of both the brush and pencil tools, there's not a lot of reason to use Clear with either of these tools. However, it creates a unique effect when combined with the paint bucket, thus permitting you to fill areas of colors with transparency.

✦ **Darken (K):** The first of the four darkening modes, Darken applies a new color to a pixel only if that color is darker than the pixel's present color. Otherwise, the pixel is left unchanged. The mode works on a channel-by-channel basis, so it might change a pixel in the green channel, for example, without changing the pixel in the red or blue channel.

✦ **Multiply (M):** The Multiply mode combines the foreground color with an existing color in an image to create a third color, darker than the other two. Using the multiply analogy, cyan times magenta is blue, magenta times yellow is red, yellow times cyan is green, and so on. This is the subtractive color theory at work, the same color theory practiced in CMYK printing. The effect is almost exactly like drawing with felt-tipped markers, except the colors don't bleed. The second example in Figure 1-34 shows the Multiply mode in action.

Figure 1-33: To build up the layers of color in this painting, I drew the darkest colors first and then applied progressively lighter colors using the brush tool set to the Behind mode.

✦ **Color Burn (B)** and **Linear Burn (A):** The two Burn modes are designed to simulate colored versions of the burn tool. Typically (though not always), Color Burn results in a darker, more colorful stroke than Multiply; Linear Burn is darker still and more muted, as shown in the last example in Figure 1-34. When combined with low Opacity values, the two modes can be interesting, but I wouldn't go so far as to call them particularly helpful.

✦ **Lighten (G):** Leading the lightening modes is the appropriately named Lighten, which ensures that Photoshop applies a new color to a pixel only if the color is lighter than the pixel's present color. See the first image in Figure 1-35 for an example.

✦ **Screen (S):** The inverse of the Multiply mode, Screen combines the foreground color with each colored pixel you paint to create a third color, lighter than the other two. Red on green is yellow, green on blue is cyan, blue on red is magenta. In other words, Screen obeys the rules of the additive color theory, like that used to project colors on an RGB monitor.

✦ **Color Dodge (D)** and **Linear Dodge (W):** Intended to emulate the dodge tool, these modes radically lighten an image. Color Dodge produces the more colorful effect; Linear Dodge works out to be the lightest (see the last image in Figure 1-35 for an example). As with the Burn modes, you're likely to have the most luck with the two Dodge modes at low Opacity values.

✦ **Overlay (O):** The seven modes starting with Overlay are cousins, each multiplying the dark pixels in an image and screening the light pixels. Of the seven, Overlay is the kindest and arguably the most useful. It enhances contrast and boosts the saturation of colors, rather like a colored version of the sponge tool set to Saturate. The first image in Figure 1-36 shows the Overlay mode in action.

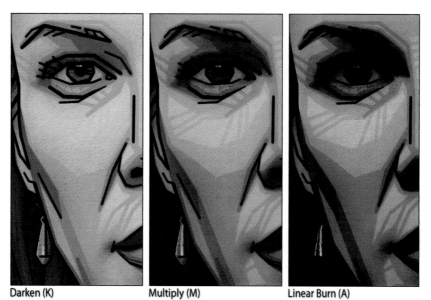

Darken (K) Multiply (M) Linear Burn (A)

Figure 1-34: Examples of three of the four darkening modes applied to grayscale versions of my Shift-click painting. In all cases, the Opacity setting is 100 percent.

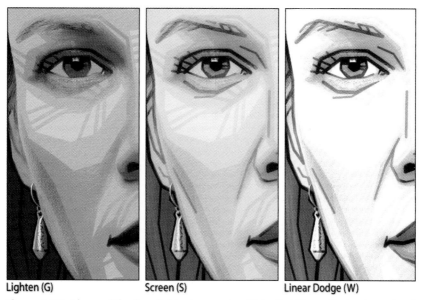

Lighten (G) Screen (S) Linear Dodge (W)

Figure 1-35: Three of the four lightening modes. Note that Linear Dodge has a tendency to send a large portion of the colors to white. The same is true of Color Dodge as well.

✦ **Soft Light (F)** and **Hard Light (H):** The Soft Light mode applies a subtle glazing of color to an image. Even black or white applied at 100 percent Opacity does no more than darken or lighten the image, but it does slightly diminish contrast. Meanwhile, Hard Light produces a much stronger effect, even stronger than Overlay. Of the modes we've seen so far, only Normal is more opaque.

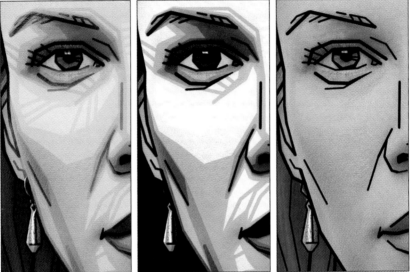

Overlay (O)   Linear Light (J)   Pin Light (Z)

Figure 1-36: The medium Overlay and extreme Linear Light modes each mix brushstrokes to darken the darkest colors in an image and lighten the lightest colors. Pin Light preserves only high frequency colors, turning less vividly colored brushstrokes invisible.

✦ **Vivid Light (V)** and **Linear Light (J):** Vivid Light works like a more colorful variation on the Hard Light mode, much like a Color Burn and Color Dodge effect combined. Linear Light produces an even higher contrast effect, as shown in the second image in Figure 1-36. Try one of these modes when you want to simultaneously burn the darkest colors in an image and dodge the lightest ones.

✦ **Pin Light (Z):** This peculiar mode drops out all but the so-called "high frequency" colors, which are the lightest, darkest, and most saturated color values, as illustrated in the last example in Figure 1-36. It is almost never useful for brushing, though it can come in very handy when applied to layers, as I discuss in Chapter 6.

✦ **Hard Mix (L):** This new mode paints using the Vivid Light brush mode and then applies a threshold operation to each color channel. The result is a stark, high-contrast mix consisting of only eight primary colors: red, green, blue, cyan, magenta, yellow, white, and black. The first example of Figure 1-37 illustrates. Note that Hard Mix produces completely different results in CMYK mode.

✦ **Difference (E):** When a paint tool is set to the Difference mode, as in the second example of Figure 1-37, Photoshop subtracts the brightness value of the foreground color from the brightness value of the pixels in the image. If the result is a negative number,

Photoshop simply makes it positive. The result of this complex-sounding operation is an inversion effect. Painting with black has no effect on an image; painting with white inverts it completely.

Because the Difference mode inverts an image, it results in an outline around the brushstroke. You can make this outline thicker by using a softer brush shape (which you get by pressing Shift+left bracket). Note that this doesn't work when using the pencil tool.

Hard Mix (L)   Difference (E)   Exclusion (X)

Figure 1-37: The Hard Mix mode produces a posterizing effect on your brushstroke. Difference and Exclusion modes subtract color values, resulting in colorful inversion effects.

✦ **Exclusion (X):** When I first asked Mark Hamburg, lead programmer for Photoshop, for his definition of Exclusion, he kindly explained, "Exclusion applies a probabilistic, fuzzy-set-theoretic, symmetric difference to each channel." Ouch, just copying and pasting that text hurt my head. In any case, I'm not sure, but I think what he meant was that Exclusion inverts an image in much the same way as Difference, except colors in the middle of the spectrum mix to form lighter colors, as in the case of the final image in Figure 1-37.

✦ **Hue (U):** Understanding this and the next few modes requires knowledge of the HSL color theory. H is for hue, the value that explains the colors in an image; S is for saturation, which represents the intensity of the colors; and L is for luminosity, which explains the lightness and darkness of colors. If you choose the Hue brush mode, therefore, Photoshop applies the hue from the foreground color without changing any saturation or luminosity values in the existing image, as in the first image in Figure 1-38.

Note that all of the HSL brush modes—Hue, Saturation, Color, or Luminosity—are exclusively applicable to color, and are therefore unavailable when painting in grayscale images.

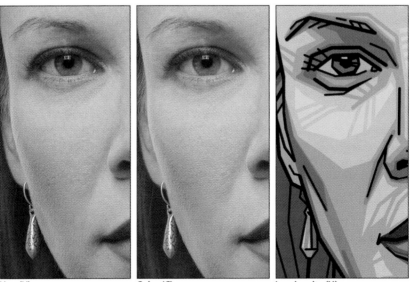

Hue (U)   Color (C)   Luminosity (Y)

Figure 1-38: The Hue mode mixes the hue values from the brushstrokes with the saturation and luminosity values of the underlying image. Color is only slightly different, preserving the saturation values from the brushstrokes as well. Luminosity is Color's opposite, brushing in lights and darks but leaving the colors unchanged.

+ **Saturation (T):** If you choose this mode, Photoshop changes the intensity of the colors in an image without changing the colors themselves or the lightness and darkness of individual pixels.

+ **Color (C):** This mode combines Hue and Saturation to change the colors in an image and the intensity of those colors without changing the lightness and darkness of individual pixels.

   In concert with the brush tool, the Color mode is most often used to colorize grayscale photographs. Here's how it works: Open a grayscale image and then choose Image ⇨ Mode ⇨ RGB Color to convert the image to the RGB mode. Then select the brush tool — with or without the airbrush turned on — and set the Mode pop-up menu to Color. From that point on, you have only to select the colors you want to use and start painting.

+ **Luminosity (Y):** The opposite of the Color mode, Luminosity changes the lightness and darkness of pixels but leaves the hue and saturation values unaffected. The final example in Figure 1-38 shows how I was able to use the Luminosity mode to trace lines and shadows without altering the color values in the original image.

The three dodge and burn modes

That takes care of the brush modes available to the paint tools, the smudge tool, and the two focus tools. I explained the Desaturate and Saturate modes available to the sponge tool in the section "Mopping up with the sponge tool." That leaves the three brush modes available to the dodge and burn tools.

You access these modes from the Range pop-up menu in the Options bar. As with other brush modes, you can select the dodge and burn modes from the keyboard. Just press Shift+Alt (Win) or Shift-Option (Mac) and the letter in parentheses as follows:

✦ **Midtones (M):** Selected by default, the Midtones mode applies the dodge or burn tool equally to all but the very lightest or darkest pixels in an image. Midtones enables you to adjust the brightness of colors without blowing out highlights or filling in shadows.

✦ **Shadows (S):** When you select this mode, the dodge or burn tool affects dark pixels in an image more dramatically than light pixels. As illustrated in Figure 1-39, medium values are likewise affected, so the Shadows option modifies a wider range of colors than Midtones.

✦ **Highlights (H):** This option lets you lighten or darken the midtones and lightest colors in an image.

Selecting Shadows when using the dodge tool or Highlights when using the burn tool has an equalizing effect on an image. For example, the first brushstroke in Figure 1-39 shows the Shadows option combined with the dodge tool. As a result, Photoshop paints an almost consistent brightness value across the course of the light-to-dark gradient. The same is true for the last brushstroke, which combines Highlights with the burn tool.

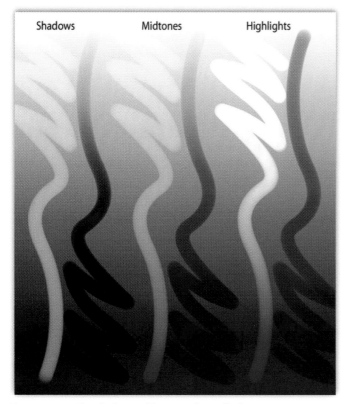

Figure 1-39: The dodge and burn tools applied at 100-percent Exposure settings subject to each of the three applicable brush modes.

✦   ✦   ✦

Cloning, Healing, and Patterns

The Gentle Art of Retouching

Painting in Photoshop is all very well and good. In fact, it's all *extremely* well and good. But it represents just the tip of an immense image-manipulation iceberg. And having melted that tip away, we come to the next strata in the pixel-based glacier, the retouchers — specifically, the clone stamp, pattern stamp, healing brush, and patch tool, all pictured in Figure 2-1. As a group, these remarkable tools permit you to cover up blemishes, smooth over imperfections, repair damaged images, and apply repeating patterns to match film grain or background elements. In short, they permit you to perform the sort of miracles that simply weren't possible in the days before computer imaging, and all without the slightest fear of damaging your artwork.

Very briefly, here's how each tool works:

✦ **Clone stamp:** The clone stamp tool replicates pixels from one area in an image to another. This one feature makes the clone stamp ideally suited to removing dust, repairing minor defects, and eliminating distracting background elements, as you'll begin to see in the very next section.

✦ **Pattern stamp:** The pattern stamp tool paints with a repeating image tile selected from Photoshop's library of predefined patterns. You can also define your own pattern using Edit ➪ Define Pattern or Filter ➪ Pattern Maker. For more information, see the section "Applying Repeating Patterns" in the latter half of this chapter.

✦ **Healing brush:** The healing brush is an expanded version of the clone stamp tool that merges texture detail from one portion of an image with color and brightness values from another. This permits you more flexibility when retouching imperfections, particularly when repairing tricky defects, such as scratches and wrinkles. Like the stamp tool, the healing brush alternatively lets you retouch with a pattern.

✦ **Patch tool:** A variation on the healing brush, the patch tool again merges the texture from one area of an image with colors and brightness values from another. The difference is that rather than brushing in changes, the patch tool repairs entire selections at a time.

Obviously, these are but the skimpiest of introductions, every bit as stingy with information as a 19th-century headmaster might have been with his Christmas gruel. But fear not, my hungry one. This chapter doles out so many courses of meaty facts, tasty techniques, and sweet, buttery insights that you'll need a whole box of toothpicks to dislodge the excess tips from your teeth.

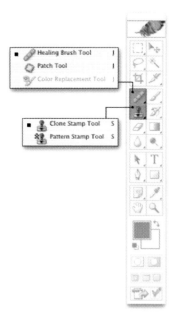

Figure 2-1: Armed with these powerful tools, you can retouch an image using another portion of that same image, another open image, or a repeating pattern.

Cloning and Healing

One of the most venerable, most practical tools in all of Photoshop is the clone stamp, which duplicates portions of an image. After selecting the tool — which you can do by pressing the S key — press the Alt key (or Option on the Mac) and click in the image window to specify the portion of the image you want to clone. This is termed the *source point*. Then paint with the tool to copy colors from that source point to another part of the image.

Closely related to the clone stamp tool is the healing brush, which clones multiple attributes of an image at a time. Press J to select the tool. Then, as with the clone stamp, Alt-click in the image (or Option-click on the Mac) to set the source of the clone. Note that the clone stamp and healing brush share a common source point, so setting the source for one tool sets it for both. Drag with the healing brush to mix the texture from the source point with the high-lights, shadows, and colors of pixels that neighbor the brushstroke.

The clone stamp tool

Let's start things off with a brief examination of the simpler of the two tools, the clone stamp. Although easy to use, it can be a little tricky at first. If you just start in dragging, Photoshop warns you that you must first define a source point. And it doesn't warn you politely. No "Sorry 'bout that," or "Ahem, pardon me, but. . . ." Just an abrupt, "Holy cow, you sorry excuse for a user! Don't you even know you have to Alt- or Option- click to define a source point to be used to repair the image? Honestly, go buy the *Photoshop Bible!*" or words to that effect. Although I do sort of like that last part, Photoshop's actual message is curt but accurate. You have to set a source point before you can proceed.

How cloning works

Here's how it works: To clone part of an image, Alt-click (Option-click on the Mac) in the image window to specify a point of reference in the portion of the image you want to clone. Then release the Alt or Option key and click or drag with the tool in some other region of the image to paint a cloned spot or line. In Figure 2-2, for example, I pressed Alt (or Option) and clicked to the right of my sporty wife's head, as demonstrated by the appearance of the target cursor. I then painted the line shown on the right. The stamp brush cursor shows the end of my drag; the clone source crosshair shows the corresponding point in the original image.

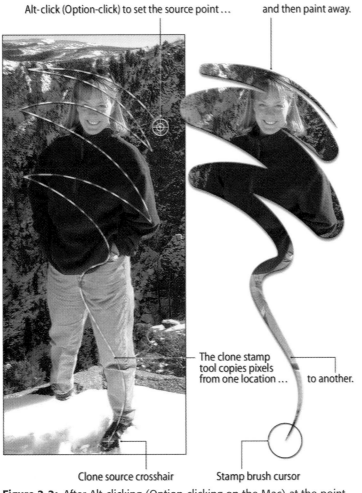

Alt-click (Option-click) to set the source point … and then paint away.

The clone stamp tool copies pixels from one location … to another.

Clone source crosshair   Stamp brush cursor

Figure 2-2: After Alt-clicking (Option-clicking on the Mac) at the point indicated by the target cursor, I dragged with the clone stamp tool to paint with the image. I painted inside a white area to make the brushstroke easier to see.

It's worth noting that the clone stamp clones the image as it existed before you began using the tool for as long as you hold down the mouse button. Even when you drag over an area that contains a clone, the tool references the original appearance of the image. This means there may be a visual disconnect between what the clone stamp tool seems to be sourcing and what it paints, as illustrated in Figure 2-3. This is actually a good thing, however, because it avoids repetition of detail, a dead giveaway of poor retouching.

Clone source crosshair   Stamp brush cursor

Throughout a drag, the clone tool copies from the original image.

Figure 2-3: During the course of a single drag, the clone stamp tool continues to clone from the image as it appeared before you began painting. This prevents you from creating more than one clone during a single drag.

Photoshop lets you clone not only within the image you're working on but from a separate image window as well. This technique makes it possible to merge two different images, as demonstrated in Figure 2-4. To achieve this effect, Alt-click (Option-click) in one image, bring a second image to the foreground, and then drag with the clone stamp tool to copy from the first image. You can also clone between layers. Just Alt-click (Option-click) one layer and then switch to a different layer and drag.

Figure 2-4: Here I used the clone stamp tool to merge my wife with a NASA photo. I employed the Multiply brush mode to achieve the shadowy edge. I also added some extra length to the snow-covered ground by cloning and recloning areas with the clone stamp tool. If you've ever seen *The Honeymooners*, you have to wonder, is this what Ralph Kramden had in mind?

Cloning options

When the clone stamp is active, the Options bar gives you access to the standard Brush, Mode, and Opacity settings that you get when using the brush tool. These permit you to mix the cloned image with the original to get different effects, as I explained in Chapter 1. You also get the Flow value and airbrush icon, which permit you to build up brushstrokes where they overlap and at points where you mouse down without moving the cursor.

You'll also find the Use All Layers check box, which lets you clone from multiple layers at a time, very useful for cloning from the composite image onto a new layer. For more information on this option, read the "Painting with the smudge tool" section of Chapter 1.

The only option associated with the clone stamp tool that's a complete departure from what we've seen so far is the Aligned check box, which locks down the relative source of a clone from one Alt- or Option-click to the next. To understand how this option works, think of the locations where you Alt-click (Option-click on the Mac) and begin dragging with the clone stamp tool as opposite ends of an imaginary straight line, as illustrated in Figure 2-5. When Aligned is turned on, the length and angle of this imaginary line remains fixed until the next time you Alt-click. As you drag, Photoshop moves the line, cloning pixels from one end of the line and laying them down at the other. The upshot is that regardless of how many times you start and stop dragging with the clone stamp tool, all brushstrokes match up as seamlessly as pieces in a puzzle.

Figure 2-5: Here I've set the clone stamp tool's blend mode to Hard Light to mix the moon image with the texture on right. I've also turned on the Aligned check box to instruct Photoshop to clone the image continuously, no matter how many times I paint a new brushstroke.

If you want to clone from a single portion of an image repeatedly, deselect the Aligned check box. Figure 2-6 shows how, with Aligned turned off, Photoshop clones from the same point every time you paint a new line with the clone stamp tool. As a result, each of the brush-strokes features some fragment of my wife's face or hair but none line up with each other. In these examples, it may appear as if having Aligned selected is the superior setting. But as you'll see in later sections, turning the option on and off both serve specific purposes.

Figure 2-6: If you turn off the Aligned check box, Photoshop clones each new line from the point at which you Alt- or Option-click.

The healing brush

I was first introduced to the healing brush in June 2001 at an Adobe-sponsored event called the Design Invitational. This was ten months before Photoshop 7 hit the shelves, and at the time, Adobe's plan was to introduce the healing brush as the central feature in the next bold upgrade to the software, the never released Photoshop 6.5. And to be honest, I was profoundly impressed. Finally, after 11 years cloning with the stamp tool, Adobe planned to release an upgrade that did more than simply duplicate pixels.

Naturally, the fellow who demoed the tool made it look like magic. The difference is that this time, magic isn't far from the truth. To get a feel for the tool, open a picture of a person's face that needs some work. For my part, I opened the picture shown in Figure 2-7. That's me, by the way, in case you were wondering what I look like. If you weren't, my apologies — after all, you've done nothing to deserve such a gruesome image — but the picture well illustrates the healing brush because it suffers myriad irregularities, not the least of which is a field of divots emblazoned across my forehead. I can only guess that these scars were the result of a bombardment of very tiny meteorites to my infant head. As suggested in Figure 2-8, my forehead and the surface of the moon bear too close a resemblance to be written off as pure chance. If you squint, you can make out the face of "The Man in Deke's Forehead" over my left eyebrow.

Isn't there enough pain in the world without this?

Figure 2-7: I am told that this is a really good picture of me. As I'm sure you can understand, that depresses me to no end. Fortunately, I can make myself appear a bit more human using the healing brush.

If you can locate an image this hideous, God bless you. If not, try to hunt down something, say, half as bad. Select the healing brush by pressing the J key, which you can remember because it's the only letter missing from the words *heal, patch, mend, fix, knit, remedy, salvage, cobble, requite,* and the antonym *wizen.* Then press Alt (or Option) and click in the image to identify the texture that you want to match. Paint over a spot, scratch, pimple, wrinkle, or scar to miraculously heal that portion of the image. And it's fast, too. It took me about five minutes to retouch every defect on my forehead. As shown in Figure 2-9, the result is a virtual skin graft of newborn flesh but without the cost or controversy.

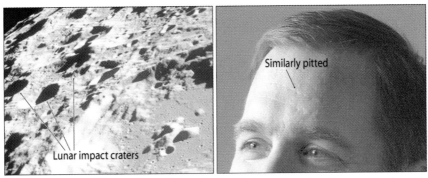

Figure 2-8: No, I didn't accidentally switch the labels on these two images. Hard as it is to believe, my forehead is indeed more dented than the lunar surface. You should see me when I sweat — my head illuminates the night sky.

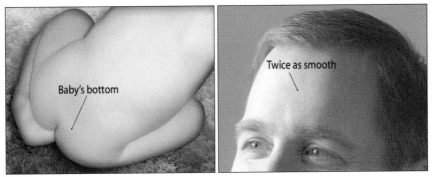

Figure 2-9: Thanks to the healing brush, my once blemished brow is now the envy of men, women, and infants alike. You won't see any more kiddo keisters kicking sand in my face.

How healing works

In dabbling with the healing brush, you'll quickly discover two things. When it works, it works incredibly well, better than any other retouching technique available inside Photoshop. But when it doesn't work, it *really* doesn't work, introducing colors and shades that appear clearly at odds with their surroundings. My experience is that, even when used carelessly, the tool produces desirable results slightly more often than it doesn't, so you may be content to paint and hope for the best. However, if you take a little time to learn what it is the healing brush is doing, you'll figure out how best to use it and when to use the clone stamp tool instead.

Naturally, I advocate the latter route, so with your approval, I'll take a moment and peel away some of the magic. The healing brush blends the pixels from the source point with the original pixels of your brushstroke. In that respect, it works a little bit like the clone stamp combined with a brush mode. But rather than blending two pixels at a time — cloned and underlying original, as a brush mode does — the healing brush blends cloned pixels with those just outside the brushstroke. The idea is that the pixels that you're painting over are messed up, but the pixels just beyond the brushstroke are in good shape and should be emulated.

Figure 2-10 illustrates what I mean. Here you see what happens when I use the healing brush to clone a photo of my son onto the slightly embossed background shown on right. Notice also that the left edge of the background is shadowed while the right edge is lit. I applied a slight bevel to the brushstroke to make it easier to see. As the healing brush clones my son, it blends the colors from the photograph and embossed background in roughly equal amounts. Photoshop dodges the brushstroke to match the light edges of the background and burns the brushstroke to match the dark edges. And it does all this according to the colors, highlights, and shadows that it encounters in tracing the very outer perimeter of the brushstroke, indicated by the dashed line on the right side of Figure 2-10.

Despite all this coloring and shading, bear in mind that the healing brush transfers the texture in its entirety from source point to brushstroke. In Figure 2-11, I Alt-clicked (Option-clicked) in the top image and dragged five times in the bottom image. In each case, the healing brush entirely replaced the pattern texture with my son's ear and eyes. At the same time, each brushstroke gets progressively darker to match the shade of the gradient in the background.

What can you deduce from this?

+ **First, the healing brush replaces the texture as you paint just as surely as if you were using the clone stamp tool.** If you want to mix textures, you'll need to employ a brush mode, as I explain in the next section.

+ **Second, the manner in which the color and shading are mixed is directly linked to the size and hardness of your brush.** Bear in mind Photoshop is looking at the outside edge of the brushstroke. As illustrated back in Figure 1-18 (see Chapter 1), the outer edge of the brush grows as the Hardness value shrinks. So soft brushes cause the healing brush to factor in more surrounding colors and shading.

The upshot is that if a brushstroke seems the wrong color, or it's too dark or light, undo it. Then modify the brush size or hardness, usually by making it smaller or harder. And try again.

Healing options

In contrast to its astonishing editing powers, there's little you can do to customize the behavior of the healing brush. It permits you neither to use custom brushes nor to apply any of the settings inside the Brushes palette. To modify a brush, you have to click the Brush icon in the Options bar. This gives you access to a few brush tip settings along with a single dynamic that lets you link brush size to pen pressure or stylus wheel.

You have no control over Opacity or Flow. (It's a shocking omission, frankly, but you can work around this problem using Edit ⇨ Fade, as I'll discuss later.) Meanwhile, the brush modes are limited to just eight. In each case, the mode merges cloned and original pixels, and then performs the additional healing blending. By way of example, Figure 2-12 shows five of the eight modes when painted over a horizontal gradient. Thanks to the dodging and burning applied by the healing brush, dark modes such as Multiply and light modes such as Screen can be substantially compromised. In fact, truth be told, most of the brush modes have little effect.

As with clone stamp, press Alt (Option) and click to set the source point …

and then paint.

The healing brush copies the texture from an area …

and blends it with colors and shades around the edges of the brushstroke.

Clone source crosshair

Stamp brush cursor

Figure 2-10: Here I used the healing brush to clone my son (left) onto an embossed background (right). The dashed line on left shows the path of the source point throughout the brushstroke. The dashed line that surrounds the brushstroke on right indicates the outer edge of the brushstroke that serves as the source for the additional coloring and shading that the healing brush performs.

The exception is Replace. Unique to the healing brush, the Replace mode clones pixels without any blending, just as if you were painting with the clone stamp tool set to Normal. The question is, why in the world would you want to do this, particularly when the healing brush set to Replace offers far fewer options than the highly customizable clone stamp tool? The answer is to test effects. Thanks to its blending routine, the healing brush sometimes takes several seconds to apply. But when set to Replace, it takes no time at all. You can test a brushstroke, make sure that it's cloning the right area, undo it, switch back to Normal, and paint the real thing. Replace is so useful that it's worth remembering its shortcut, Shift+Alt+Z (Shift-Option-Z on the Mac). Press Shift+Alt+N (Shift-Option-N) to return to Normal.

Source image

Healing brushstrokes

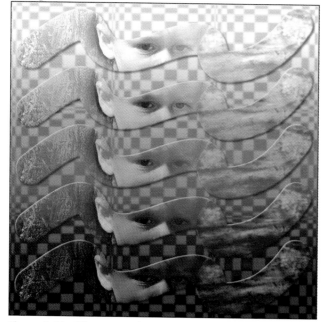

Figure 2-11: When set to the Normal brush mode, the healing brush clones the texture from the source image (above) in its entirety. The only thing that changes is the color and shade (bottom five strokes).

Other options include the Source buttons, which determine whether the healing brush clones pixels (Sampled) or paints with a predefined texture (Pattern). I explore the Pattern setting in the section "Applying Repeating Patterns" later in this chapter. You also have the Aligned check box, which aligns multiple brushstrokes to a fixed source point, as described previously in the "Cloning options" section. The Aligned check boxes for the healing brush and clone stamp tools are linked, so selecting one selects the other as well.

Source image

Healing brush modes

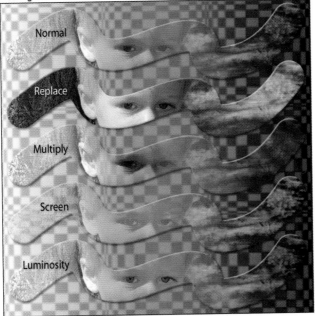

Figure 2-12: Examples of the healing brush combined with five brush modes across a light-to-dark gradient. Due to Photoshop's healing algorithms, many portions of the Multiply brushstroke are lighter than those of the Screen stroke.

Finally, new to Photoshop CS is the healing brush's Use All Layers setting in the Options bar. Much like the similarly-named option available to the clone stamp and smudge tools, turning on Use All Layers factors in information from every visible layer during the healing process. As I've mentioned previously, this feature can be a great asset because it allows you to create a new layer and perform all of your pixel manipulation on it while still retaining your original pixels on the layers below.

The patch tool

If you prefer to heal a selected area all at once, choose the patch tool from the healing brush flyout menu in the toolbox. You can also press Shift+J.

You can use the patch tool in one of two ways:

✦ **Define destination, drag onto source:** Assuming the Source option is selected in the Options bar, as by default, use the patch tool to draw an outline around the portion of the image you want to heal. This creates a selection outline. In Figure 2-13, for example, I selected my eyes. Next, drag inside the selection outline to move it to a new location. The middle image in Figure 2-13 finds me dragging the selection over my forehead. The spot at which you release the mouse button determines the source for the clone. When I dropped the selection on my forehead, Photoshop healed the forehead onto my eyes, as the final image in the figure shows.

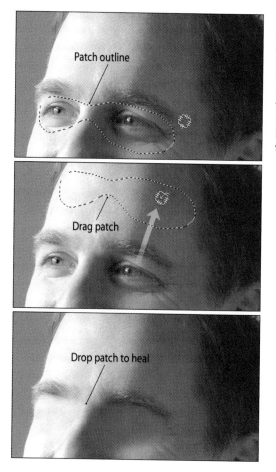

Figure 2-13: Armed with the patch tool, draw a selection outline around the portion of the image you want to heal (top), drag the selection over the clone source (middle), and release to watch the original selection heal away (bottom). You'll have to tell me if this looks good; I can't see a thing now.

✦ **Define source, drag onto destination:** If dragging the thing you want to heal onto the thing you want to clone seems backwards to you, flip it. Select the Destination radio button in the Options bar. Then use the patch tool to select the portion of the image that you want to clone. Drag the selection over the area you want to heal and release your mouse button.

Insofar as selecting is concerned, the patch tool behaves just like the standard lasso tool. You can add to a selection by Shift-dragging or delete by Alt-dragging (Option-dragging on the Mac). You can even soften a patch using Select ⇨ Feather or modify it in the quick mask mode, thus giving the patch tool more room along the edge of the selection to sample colors and shades. And there's nothing that says you have to draw a selection with the patch tool. Feel free to define the selection any way you want and then use the patch tool to move it over the source or destination area.

The patch tool lacks Opacity and brush mode controls, and you can't use it between layers or between different images. All work has to be done on a single layer, which ultimately limits its potential. On the plus side, you can patch a selection with a predefined pattern by clicking the Use Pattern button in the Options bar.

Photoshop CS introduces a few minor but interesting additions to the patch tool. Most importantly, the patch tool now gives you a preview of unaltered source pixels in your selected area while you're still dragging it around. This preview gives you a better idea of how the size and shape of the area from which you're pulling texture will fit when it combines with your original destination. Photoshop CS has also added a Transparent check box in the Options bar. When this option is selected, the patch tool pulls the texture from wherever you drag but none of the color information at all.

Retouching Photographs

Having seen how the clone stamp tool and healing brush work, the following sections examine a few sample uses for the tools. For example, say that you're confronted by the worst image in the world, shown in Figure 2-14. It's not the subject of the photo that's a problem—that's my son, after all, whom I consider to be beautiful even when shot from a distance of a few inches. Rather the problems with this image are ones of technique. The autofocus locked down a couple of seconds before the shutter release fired, giving my son ample time to rush the camera as he is wont to do. The image was shot to film and then scanned from a 35mm negative, which introduced a wealth of dust particles, hairs, and other fibers.

So the question becomes, what's a person to do when confronted with such an abomination? Naturally, one answer is to reshoot the photo using manual focus if necessary. You might also want to take a moment to clean the glass on your scanner. And come to think of it, I probably would've done well to avoid rubbing the negative in dirt, an extra step I performed to make the image as filthy as possible for purposes of this example.

But let's say none of that is an option. Let's say, my son's all grown up, I lost the original negative, and anyway my scanner blew up and burst into flames. In a nutshell, this is the only picture I have to work with. What am I to do?

After taking a moment to allow that mad feeling of panic to pass, I investigate my tools. And as luck would have it, Photoshop actually offers an automatic function for images such as this. It's called Dust & Scratches, and it's located under the Filter menu in the Noise submenu. This filter averages the colors of neighboring pixels with the intent of smearing away imperfections. Unfortunately, as it does so it smears away photographic detail as well. However, in the case of this image, there's not much detail to work with in the first place, so it's not that big of a deal. And so it comes to pass that I apply Dust & Scratches using the settings indicated in the left example of Figure 2-15. In the matter of a few seconds, the filter gets rid of every single scratch and piece of dust in the photo. But in doing so, it gums up a few details more than I would have liked, most notably reducing the size of the pupil and reflected light in my son's eye.

Original dusty, scratchy 35mm negative

Figure 2-14: A very bad photograph, made worse by a bad scanning process. How does one improve such a wretched image inside Photoshop?

So being a good father, I undo the automatic fix and set about correcting the photo manually with the healing brush and a bit of clone stamp tool. The healing brush fares well in flat areas of flesh, like the cheeks, nose, and forehead. But it introduces incongruous colors around the lips, eyes, and other edges, which is where I use the clone stamp tool instead. A half hour later, I finally arrive at the image shown on the right side of Figure 2-15. Mind you, I'm kicking myself a little bit because, although the right-hand image is an improvement, it's not what I would call vastly superior. So in purely practical terms, the result hardly justifies the effort. Then again, it's a daddy's job to toil away on pointless exercises that his kids will never appreciate, so I feel a warm glow for that.

As a final step, I apply Filter ➪ Sharpen ➪ Unsharp Mask (another feature discussed in Chapter 8), which firms up some of the detail to produce the image shown in Figure 2-16.

The lesson to draw from all this is that, although Dust & Scratches may suffice for purging fibers and defects from a low-quality photo like this one, it's hardly a professional-level tool. In fact, and I'm going to be painfully blunt here, Dust & Scratches is, generally speaking, a worthless wad of goober-covered tooth decay. In almost all cases, the better alternative is to roll up your sleeves, get real with your image, and fix its flaws manually — not to mention lovingly — with the healing brush and clone stamp tools. You'll be glad that you did.

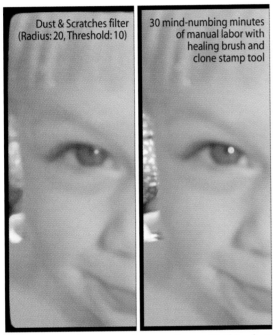

Figure 2-15: I have one of two options with this photo — apply Dust & Scratches, which takes just a few seconds but results in some pretty blobby detail (left), or fix the image manually, which takes forever but produces better results (right).

Restoring an old photograph

Dust, hairs, gloops, and other blemishes are introduced during the scanning process. But what about more severe problems that trace back to the original image? Figure 2-17 is a prime example. This photograph was shot sometime before 1910. It's a wonderful photo, but 90 years is a long time for something as fragile and transient as a scrap of paper. It's torn, faded, stained, creased, and flaking. The normally simple act of extracting it from its photo album took every bit as long as scanning it.

But despite the photo's rough condition, I was able to restore it in Photoshop, as evidenced by Figure 2-18. After about an hour and a few hundred brushstrokes, I had the image well in hand. If an hour sounds like a long time to fix a few rips and scrapes, bear in mind that photographic restoration is a labor-intensive activity that relies heavily on your talents and your mastery of Photoshop. The job of the clone stamp and healing brush tools is to make your edits believable, but they do little to automate the process. Retouching calls for a human touch, and that's where you come in.

Filter ⇨ Sharpen ⇨ Unsharp Mask
(Amount: 500, Radius: 12, Threshold: 20)

Figure 2-16: The final touch is to sharpen the image using the Unsharp Mask filter. The result is by no means perfect — Photoshop can't produce detail out of thin air — but it's adorable, and that's good enough for me.

The main trick in all this is to Alt-click (Option-click on the Mac) in an area that looks like it'd do a good job of covering up a blemish and then drag over the blemish. Repeat about 250 times, and you're done. So rather than document every single brushstroke — which would be tedious and, I fear, about as enlightening as a day at the box factory — I'll share some advice that specifically addresses the art of photo restoration:

- ✦ **Toss the bad channels:** Most images in this kind of condition are black-and-white. Scan them in color and then peruse the color channels to see which grayscale version of the image looks best. In my case, the original image had lots of yellow stains around the tears. So when I viewed the individual color channels, as illustrated in Figure 2-19, I was hardly surprised to see dark blotches in the blue channel. (Blue is the opposite of yellow, so where yellow is prominent, the blue channel was dark.) The red channel turned out to be in the best shape, so I switched to the red channel and disposed of the other two by choosing Image ⇨ Mode ⇨ Grayscale. The simple act of trashing the green and blue channels went a long way toward getting rid of the splotches.

- ✦ **View actual pixels:** When possible, work at 100 percent view size or larger. It's difficult to judge scratches and other defects accurately at smaller zoom ratios, but if you must, stick with the "smooth views" 50 percent and 25 percent.

- ✦ **Keep an eye on the source:** Keep the original photo next to you as you work. What looks like a scratch on screen may actually be a photographic element, and what looks like an element may be a scratch. Only by referring to the original image can you be sure.

Figure 2-17: This photo has seen better days. Then again,
I hope to look as good when I'm 90 years old.

✦ **Wait to crop:** Don't crop until you're finished retouching the image. You'd be surprised how useful that extra garbage around the perimeter is when it comes to covering up really big tears.

✦ **Vary the brush hardness:** Use hard brush shapes against sharp edges. But when working in general areas such as the shadow, the ground, and the wall, mix it up between soft and hard brushes using the shortcuts Shift+[and Shift+]. Staying random is the best way to avoid harsh transitions, repeating patterns, and other digital giveaways.

Figure 2-18: The same image after about an hour of work with the clone stamp tool and healing brush.

+ **Short is beautiful:** Paint in short strokes. This helps keep things random, but it also means you don't have to redraw a big long brushstroke if you make a mistake.

+ **Turn Aligned off:** Another way to stay random is to change the source of your clone frequently. That means Alt-clicking (Option-clicking) after every second or third brushstroke. And keep the Aligned check box turned off. An aligned clone is not a random one.

+ **Try out brush modes:** Feel free to experiment with the brush modes and, when using the clone stamp tool, the Opacity setting. For example, magnified in Figure 2-20, the girl has a scratch on the left eye (her right). I corrected this by cloning the right eye with the healing brush, but while the detail looked great, the healing brush over-burned the effect, as in the middle image. To fix this, I set the brush mode for the healing brush to Screen. Then I cloned a bit of the shadowed flesh onto the eye to get the finished effect.

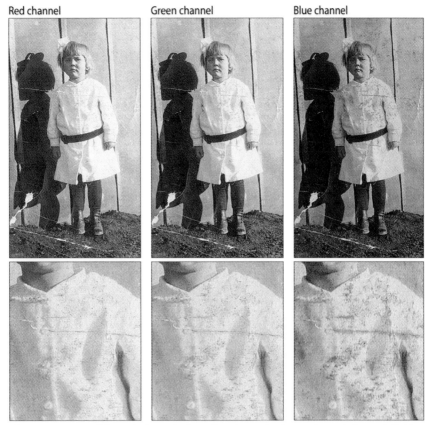

Figure 2-19: A quick peek through the color channels shows the red channel (left) to be my best choice. The blotches are most evident in the girl's blouse, enlarged in the bottom row.

✦ **Fade the clone:** You also can try applying Edit ➪ Fade to change the opacity and brush mode of the pixels you just cloned. This little trick can be extremely useful when using the healing brush, because it means you can introduce an Opacity value into the proceedings where none existed previously. Curious? After applying a healing brushstroke, choose Edit ➪ Fade or press Ctrl+Shift+F (⌘-Shift-F on the Mac). You get an Opacity value and no Mode option, exactly the opposite of what you see in the Options bar when using the tool.

✦ **Grain is good:** Don't attempt to smooth out the general appearance of grain in the image. Grain is integral to an old photo, and hiding it usually makes the image look faked. If your image gets too smooth, or if your cloning results in irregular patterns, select the problem area and apply Filter ➪ Noise ➪ Add Noise. Enter very small Amount values (2 to 6 percent). Monochromatic noise tends to work best. If necessary, press Ctrl+F (⌘-F on the Mac) to reapply the filter one or more times.

Left eye scratched

Figure 2-20: The left eye in the original image was scratched (top). I used the healing brush to copy the right eye onto the left (middle), but in trying to match the shadows on the left half of the face, Photoshop took the eye too dark. So I set the brush mode to Screen and healed a little flesh over the eye to even things out (bottom).

Heal right eye onto left

Heal flesh onto left eye, Screen mode

With Photoshop's history brush at your side, there's really no way to permanently harm an image. You can even let four or five little mistakes go and then correct them *en masse* with the history brush. Just click to the left of the state in the History palette that directly precedes your first screw-up and then drag with the history brush. To paint back to the original scanned image, click in front of the very top item in the History palette. Using the history brush is easy, satisfying, and incredibly freeing. For more information, check out "Stepping Back through Time" in Chapter 3.

Eliminating distracting background elements

The stamp and healing tools also come in handy for eliminating background action that competes with the central elements in an image. For example, Figure 2-21 shows a nifty news photo from the Reuters image library. Although the image is well-photographed and historic and all that good stuff, that rear workman doesn't contribute anything to the scene; in fact, he draws your attention away from the foreground drama. I mean, hail to the worker and everything, but the image would be better off without him. The following steps explain how I eradicated the offending workman from the scene.

Remember as you read these steps that cloning away an image element is something of an inexact science. It requires considerable patience and a dash of trial and error. So regard the following steps as an example of how to approach the process of editing your image rather than as a specific procedure that works for all images. You will undoubtedly need to adapt the process to suit the specific needs of your image.

Hey there, you with the bolts in your head

Michael Probst, Reuters

Figure 2-21: You have to love that old Soviet state-endorsed art. So bold, so angular, so politically intolerant. But you also have to lose that rear workman.

On the other hand, any approach that eliminates an element as big as the workman can also correct the most egregious of photographic flaws, including mold, holes, and fire damage. You can even restore photos that have been ripped into pieces, a particular problem for pictures of ex-boyfriends, current boyfriends, and potential boyfriends of the future. These steps qualify as major reconstructive surgery.

STEPS: Eliminating Distracting Elements from an Image

1. **My first step was to clone the area around the neck of the statue with a soft brush shape.** Abandoning the controlled clicks I recommended in the last section, I permitted myself to drag with the clone stamp tool — which generally fares better than the healing brush for this kind of work — because I needed to cover relatively large portions of the image. The apartment building (or whatever that structure is) behind the floating head is magnificently out of focus, just the thing for hiding any incongruous transitions I might create with the clone stamp tool. So I warmed up to the image by retouching this area first. Figure 2-22 shows my progress.

I covered the workman's body by cloning pixels from both his left and right sides. I also added a vertical bar where the workman's right arm used to be to maintain the rhythm of the building. Remember, variety is the key to using the clone stamp tool: If you consistently clone from one portion of the image, you create an obvious repetition the viewer can't help but notice.

Clone away rear workman's torso

Figure 2-22: Cloning over the background worker's upper torso was fairly easy. Because the background building is so regular and out of focus, it provided me with a wealth of material from which to clone.

2. **The next step was to eliminate the workman's head.** This was a little tricky because it involved rubbing up against the focused perimeter of Lenin's neck. I had to clone some of the more intricate areas using a hard-edged brush. I also ended up duplicating some of the neck edges to maintain continuity. In addition, I touched up the left side of the neck (your left, not Lenin's) and removed a few of the white spots from his face. You see my progress in Figure 2-23.

3. **Now for the hard part: eliminating the worker's legs and lower torso.** See that metal fragment that the foreground worker is holding? What a pain. Its edges were so irregular that there was no way I could restore it if I messed up while trying to eradicate the background worker's limbs. So I lassoed around the fragment to select it and chose Select ⇨ Inverse to protect it. I also chose Select ⇨ Feather and gave the selection a Radius value of 1 to soften its edges slightly. This prevented me from messing up the metal no matter what edits I made to the background worker's remaining body parts.

Clone into oblivion rear workman's head

Figure 2-23: I eliminated the workman's head and touched up details around the perimeter of Lenin's neck.

4. **From here on, it was just more cloning.** Unfortunately, I barely had anything from which to clone. See the little bit of black edging between the two "legs" of the metal fragment? That's it. This was all I had to draw the strip of edging to the right of the fragment that eventually appears in Figure 2-24. To pull off this feat, I made sure that the Aligned check box was turned off in the Options bar. Then, I Alt-clicked (or Option-clicked) on the tiny bit of edging and click-click-clicked my way down the street.

5. **Unfortunately, the strip I laid down in Step 4 appeared noticeably blobular—it looked for all the world like I clicked a bunch of times.** Darn. To fix this problem, I clicked and Shift-clicked with the smudge tool set to about 30 percent pressure. This smeared the blobs into a continuous strip but, again, the effect was noticeable. It looked as if I had smeared the strip. So I went back and cloned some more, this time with the Opacity value set to 50 percent.

6. **To polish the image off, I chose Select ⇨ Deselect and ran the sharpen tool along the edges of the metal fragment.** This helped to hide my retouching around it and further distinguished the fragment from the unfocused background. I also cropped away 120 or so pixels from the right side of the image to correct the balance.

The completed, cropped image

Figure 2-24: After about 45 minutes of monkeying around with the clone stamp tool — a practice declared illegal during Stalin's reign — the rear workman is gone, leaving us with an unfettered view of the dubious V. I. Lenin himself.

What I hope I demonstrated in these steps is this: Cloning with the stamp tool requires you to alternate between patching and whittling away. There are no rights and wrongs, no hard and fast rules. Anything you can find to clone is fair game. As long as you avoid mucking up the foreground image, you can't go wrong (so I guess there is *one* hard and fast rule). If you're careful and diligent, no one but you will notice your alterations.

Any time you edit the contents of a photograph, you tread on sensitive ground. Although some have convincingly argued that electronically retouching an image is, theoretically, no different than cropping a photograph — a technique available and in use since the first daguerreotype — photographers have certain rights under copyright law that cannot be ignored. A photographer may have a reason for including an element you want to eliminate. So, before you edit any photograph, be sure to get permission either from the original photographer or from the copyright holder, as I did for this photo.

Applying Repeating Patterns

The clone stamp tool shares a slot with the pattern stamp tool, which you can get by pressing Shift+S. Unlike the clone stamp tool, the pattern stamp tool doesn't require you to Alt-click to set a source. Instead, it paints with a repeating pattern that you select from the Pattern pop-up palette in the Options bar, as shown in Figure 2-25. You can use the pattern stamp to create frames, paint wallpaper-type patterns, or retouch patches of grass, dirt, sky, and so on.

Even better for retouching is the healing brush with the Source option set to Pattern, as shown in the bottom half of Figure 2-25. Select the pattern that you want to use from the Pattern pop-up palette. Then paint to merge the texture of the pattern with the colors and shades around the edge of the brushstroke. Again, no Alt-clicking is needed.

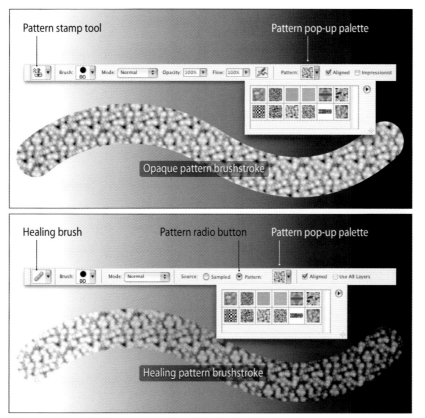

Figure 2-25: Both the stamp tool and the healing brush offer variations for painting with repeating patterns.

You can likewise apply a pattern with the patch tool. To do so, draw a selection with the tool or start with a selection defined earlier. Then select a pattern from the Pattern pop-up palette in the Options bar and click the Use Pattern button. In many ways, the effect is similar to filling a selection with a pattern using the paint bucket or Edit ➪ Fill. The difference is that the patch tool mixes the texture of the pattern with the colors and shades of the pixels around the outside edge of the selection.

Retouching with a pattern

Figure 2-26 begins our look at how and why you might apply a repeating pattern with the healing brush. The figure starts out with my face, free of meteorite craters but rife with a handful of jolly wrinkles. I rather like my wrinkles — they convey a false sense of wisdom — but in the name of higher learning, I will demonstrate how I removed them.

I first had to establish the neutral noise pattern, shown magnified to 700 percent on the right side of Figure 2-26. Combined with the healing brush, this neutral noise pattern allowed me to smooth over imperfections while matching the grain of my image. Given the repeated success I've had with it, I'm guessing it'll work for your images as well.

My semi-wrinkly face (certain to be wrinklier in future installments)   Enlarged view of neutral noise created by applying Add Noise at 6% to solid gray

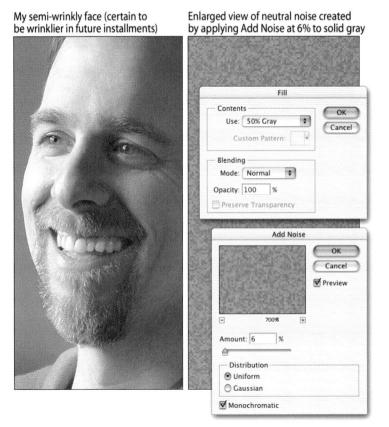

Figure 2-26: The starting point for my face (left) flanked by a 64 by 64-pixel neutral noise pattern magnified to 700 percent view size (right). I created this pattern by filling the image with medium gray and then applying the Add Noise filter with an Amount value of 6 percent and Monochromatic turned on.

I created a new image measuring 64 by 64 pixels. (The exact size isn't important, but 64 by 64 pixels is big enough to hide repetition and small enough to require little processing on the part of Photoshop.) Then I chose Edit ➪ Fill and set the Use option to 50% Gray. After clicking OK, I chose Filter ➪ Noise ➪ Add Noise, entered an Amount value of 6 percent, and selected the Monochromatic check box. This is about the right amount of noise to match the grain in a high-quality photograph.

To turn the gray noise into a pattern, I chose Edit ➪ Define Pattern. Photoshop asked me to name the pattern, and I called it Neutral Noise 6%.

I was now ready to paint with the pattern using the healing brush. For the sake of demonstration, the first image in Figure 2-27 shows what would have happened if I had applied the Neutral Noise 6% pattern using the pattern stamp tool. This way, you can see every one of the 42 brushstrokes I used to retouch the image. The second image shows what happened when I painted these exact same brushstrokes using the healing brush instead. Photoshop applied the noise to the image and fused together the wrinkles to match the surrounding skin. It may sound too good to be true, but it works like a dream.

Lines painted with pattern stamp tool set to the Neutral Noise 6% pattern

Same lines painted with healing brush, again with the Neutral Noise 6% pattern

Figure 2-27: Here you see what would happen if I used the pattern stamp tool to paint a series of Neutral Noise 6% strokes over the most prominent wrinkles in my semi-craggy semi-young face (left). But I didn't do that. Instead, I used the healing brush to paint those exact same brushstrokes (right), eliminating my wrinkles like a big hypodermic needle full of Botox.

At this point, I was having such a grand time that I just kept on painting. Pretty soon, I had painted away everything but my eyes, nose, and mouth, as the first image in Figure 2-28 shows. Some might mistake this for overkill, as it pretty much gooed away my world. But creative experiment is never overkill, and every road wandered is worth seeing to the end. So I switched to the burn tool and painted a series of shadows and dark lines. Then I used the dodge tool to lighten my eyes. I also used Filter ➪ Liquify (discussed in Chapter 9) to extend my eyeteeth into fangs. Finally, I chose Image ➪ Adjustments ➪ Hue/Saturation (discussed in Chapter 11) and colorized my flesh violet and my eyes yellow. For those of you who are thinking, "That Deke, he's a demon!" you'll be relieved to know this is just an effect. When I become possessed in real life, my skin turns more of an olive tone.

Of course, there is such
a thing as too much healing.   Or is there?

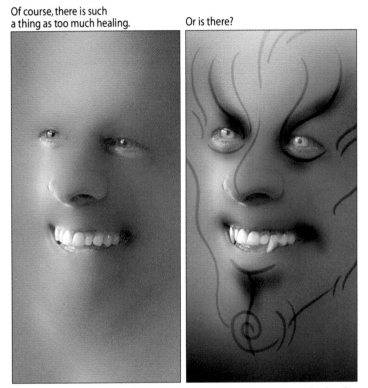

Figure 2-28: With the help of the Neutral Noise 6% pattern, the healing
brush becomes a truly effective blur tool (left). Add a few strokes of the
burn tool, dab the dodge tool on the eyes, and stretch the fangs, and
you have yourself a serviceable netherworld villain (right).

Pattern painting options

The pattern painting tools offer the usual group of settings in the Options bar that we saw
when using the clone stamp tool and healing brush. For example, there's the Aligned check
box. When turned off, Photoshop begins and ends patterns in different brushstrokes at different locations. This means that the patterns clash when they overlap. In Figure 2-29, I painted
a series of strokes using the Optical Checkerboard pattern (one of Photoshop's defaults) and
the pattern stamp tool. In the first image, the Aligned option was turned off.

If you select the Aligned check box, Photoshop aligns all patterns you apply with the stamp
tool, regardless of how many times you start and stop dragging. As in the bottom example in
Figure 2-29, all elements in the pattern remain exactly aligned throughout all the brushstrokes.

An option that's utterly unique to the pattern stamp tool is the Impressionist check box. A
very old and, I would argue, archaic feature, Impressionist adds an element of color jitter to
the brushstroke. If you select the Impressionist check box, the pattern stamp tool paints a
series of spots, randomly colored according to the colors inside the active pattern. If this
sounds peculiar at best and useless at worst, then our minds are as one. Besides, the Color
Dynamics options inside the Brushes palette (discussed in Chapter 1) render Impressionist
largely redundant.

Figure 2-29: If you turn off the Aligned check box, Photoshop starts each pattern with the beginning of the brushstroke (top), so that overlapping brushstrokes clash. Select the Aligned check box to align the patterns in all brushstrokes to match up perfectly (bottom).

Creating patterns and textures

Now that you know how to apply patterns, the question becomes, where do you find patterns? And for that matter, how do you go about making your own? The answers, it turns out, are numerous. Artists and designers generally think of Photoshop as an image editor, but it lives a secret life as a frustrated pattern laboratory. Since Version 1, Photoshop has shipped with highly specialized varieties of pattern libraries, and new patterning features are added with just about every upgrade.

The simplest way to access a pattern is from the Options bar. The Pattern option makes itself available when using the healing brush, patch tool, pattern stamp tool, or paint bucket. Click the down-pointing arrowhead to display a pop-up palette of pattern thumbnails, numbering 12 by default, some of which appear in Figure 2-30. You can also access these patterns from the Texture panel of the Brushes palette. To fill a selection with a pattern, choose Edit ⇨ Fill or press Shift+Backspace (Shift-Delete on the Mac) and select the Pattern options from the Use pop-up menu. You can even coat a layer with a pattern by choosing either the Pattern Overlay or Pattern command from, respectively, the layer style or fill layer icons at the bottom of the Layers palette (see Chapter 7).

Default dozen patterns

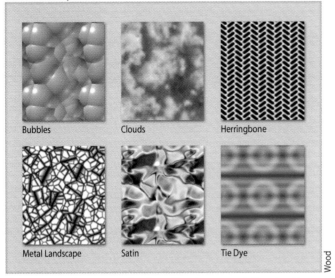

Bubbles   Clouds   Herringbone

Metal Landscape   Satin   Tie Dye

Wood

Figure 2-30: Seven samples from the dozen predefined patterns that Photoshop loads by default the first time you launch the program (and thereafter until you make changes). The seventh sample, Wood, appears in the background.

To restore the default dozen patterns at any time in the future, click the right-pointing arrowhead in the Pattern palette and choose Reset Patterns. To clean out all patterns but the default dozen, click OK. To add the default dozen to your existing patterns (which may result in duplicates), click Append.

Here are some other ways to access Photoshop's predefined patterns, as well as create your own:

✦ **Add a preset library:** In all, Photoshop CS installs a total of nine pattern libraries that you can load at will. With the Pattern pop-up palette visible, click the right-pointing arrowhead to display the palette menu. There, at the bottom of the menu are nine options, each of which loads a different library. The library called Patterns comprises the default dozen plus 12 more, so if you choose this option (which I recommend you do), click OK rather than Append to avoid repetition. Most of the other libraries include unique sets of patterns, the exception being the mostly redundant Patterns 2, which calls up patterns that you can find elsewhere. Figure 2-31 shows a few examples.

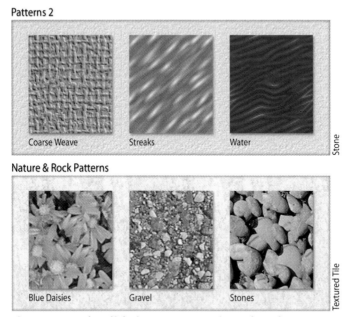

Figure 2-31: A handful of preset patterns from Photoshop's other pattern libraries. To open any one of these patterns, choose its library name from the bottom of the Pattern palette menu.

✦ **Define a pattern tile:** You can save any rectangular area as a tile that will repeat over and over inside a pattern. Just select the area with the rectangular marquee tool — no other tool will do. Then choose Edit ➪ Define Pattern. Photoshop asks you to name the pattern and then makes it available to all the Pattern pop-up palettes until you delete the pattern or replace the active library with another one. Obviously, not every rectangular selection repeats well, which is why it's so important to know how to design seamless tiles that blend to form continuous patterns. I explain how to do this shortly.

✦ **Load a displacement map:** Discussed at length in Chapter 10, a *displacement map* is a special kind of pattern that refracts colors inside an image as if you're looking through textured glass. Consider Figure 2-32. In the top row, you see each of three patterns. In the bottom row, you see the demon face from Figure 2-28 as it looks when viewed through each of the patterns expressed as a displacement map. To get one of these effects, choose Filter ➪ Distort ➪ Displace and enter the percentage values shown in the figure. Also make sure that the Displacement Map option is set to Tile. Then click OK and open one of the pattern files, Cees, Random Strokes, or Schnable Effect. You'll find these patterns as well as nine others inside a folder called Displacement Maps that's inside the Plug-Ins folder, which is inside the same folder as the Photoshop application. Naturally, every one of these images doubles as a repeating pattern. Just open it inside Photoshop and choose Edit ➪ Define Pattern.

Plug-ins\Displacement maps

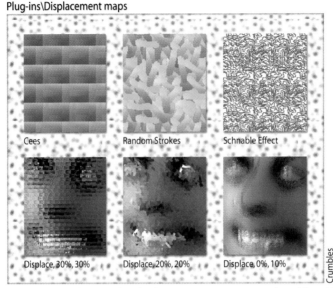

Figure 2-32: Three of the displacement map patterns that ship with Photoshop as they appear when viewed as repeating patterns (top row) and when applied to the demon image using the Displace filter (bottom).

✦ **The Texturizer:** To emboss an image with a pattern file stored on disk, choose Filter ➪ Texture ➪ Texturizer. You'll see the Texturizer filter open up inside Photoshop CS's new Filter Gallery, but more on that in Chapter 9. For now, just select Load Texture from the arrow to the right of the Texture pop-up menu on the right side of the Filter Gallery. You can open one of the pattern files stored in the previously mentioned Displacement Maps folder, or you can open one from the Adobe ImageReady Only folder inside the Patterns folder, which in turn is inside the Presets folder. For a demonstration of the Texturizer filter, see Figure 9-6 in Chapter 9.

✦ **Designing patterns with filters:** That's it for Photoshop's predefined patterns, but it's just the beginning of Photoshop's patterning capabilities. You can also create your own patterns, just as you'd expect from an accommodating program like Photoshop. And as luck would have it, you can do so without painting a single line. In fact, you can create a nearly infinite variety of background textures by applying several filters to a blank document.

Figure 2-33 presents four examples. Note that none of these textures repeats seamlessly like the pattern tiles we've looked at so far — they're each intended to fill an entire background with very little effort. To create the texture shown in the top row of the figure, I started with a blank image. Then I chose Filter ➪ Noise ➪ Add Noise, entered a value of 100 percent, and selected the Monochromatic check box. After clicking OK, I pressed Ctrl+F (⌘-F on the Mac) twice, each time repeating the filter, so that I had applied Add Noise three times in a row. Next, I chose Filter ➪ Noise ➪ Median and entered a value of 2 pixels, which averaged the noise into clumps. Finally, I chose Filter ➪ Stylize ➪ Emboss and entered 45 degrees in the Angle option box, 2 pixels for the Height value, and 100 percent for the Amount. The result is a bumpy surface that looks a bit like stucco.

Noise, Median, & Emboss

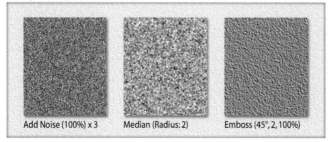

Add Noise (100%) x 3   Median (Radius: 2)   Emboss (45°, 2, 100%)

Noise, Crystallize, GBlur, Noise, & Emboss

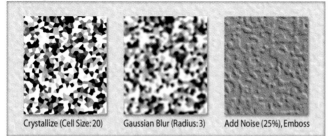

Crystallize (Cell Size: 20)   Gaussian Blur (Radius: 3)   Add Noise (25%), Emboss

Clouds, Difference Clouds, Emboss

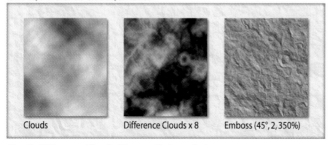

Clouds   Difference Clouds x 8   Emboss (45°, 2, 350%)

Clouds, Difference Clouds, Chrome, Emboss, Fade

Chrome (4, 10)   Emboss (45°, 2, 350%)   Edit ⇆ Fade, Pin Light

Figure 2-33: A series of four different background textures created using commands under the Filter menu, including Add Noise, Median, Crystallize, Gaussian Blur, Clouds, Difference Clouds, Chrome, and a heaping helping of Emboss.

To get the second row of effects in Figure 2-33, I started at the point labeled "Add Noise (100%) x 3" in the first row and applied Filter ⇨ Pixelate ⇨ Crystallize with a Cell Size of 20 pixels. Then I blurred the cells using Filter ⇨ Blur ⇨ Gaussian Blur and a Radius of 3 pixels. And finally, I again applied the Add Noise filter, this time at 25 percent, and the Emboss filter, using the same settings as before.

To create the third row of textures, I started with a blank image, pressed the D key to make the foreground and background colors black and white, and chose Filter ⇨ Render ⇨ Clouds. Then I applied Filter ⇨ Render ⇨ Difference Clouds and repeated the filter by pressing Ctrl+F (⌘-F) seven times in a row. In the last image, I once again applied the Emboss filter with an Amount value of 350 percent.

In the fourth row, I took up from the second effect in the third row, the one labeled "Difference Clouds x 8." Then I applied Filter ⇨ Sketch ⇨ Chrome with a Detail value of 4 and a Smoothness setting of 10. Next, I applied Emboss using the same Amount value of 350 percent as before. And finally, deciding I had gone a bit too far, I chose Edit ⇨ Fade Emboss and selected Pin Light from the Mode pop-up menu. This blended the Chrome and Emboss effects into a frothy, plastery soup.

Obviously, I could go on like this for days. To learn more about filters so that you can make up your own textures, read Chapters 8 and 9. Chapter 8 covers Add Noise, Median, Gaussian Blur, and the Fade command; Chapter 9 talks about Emboss, Crystallize, Clouds, Difference Clouds, and Chrome.

✦ **The Pattern Maker:** This command generates repeating tiles at the click of a button. More often than not, it still results in some harsh edges, but if you tough it out, you can get some interesting results. I explain how to use this command in the next section, "Using the Pattern Maker."

✦ **Marquee and clone:** Not happy with any of these solutions? Interested in creating the best seamlessly repeating pattern ever made? Well, it's a fair amount of work, but you can use the rectangular marquee and pattern stamp tools to transform an image into a custom pattern. Because this technique is more complicated as well as more rewarding than the others, I explain it in detail in the section "Building your own seamless pattern."

Using the Pattern Maker

Located under the Filter menu, the Pattern Maker is a repeating tile generator. It permits you to fill an entire image or layer with a repeating pattern — or even one massive texture — or save a pattern to Photoshop's presets for later use.

Unlike other patterning tools on the market, it does not blur the edges of an image or create reflections to ensure seamless transitions. Rather, it chops an image into random clumps, pieces those clumps together in random formation, and does its best to make a sort of chopped salad of the image so it resembles the sorts of random repetitions you see in the natural world. In most cases, the results are only marginally successful and they often exhibit unacceptably defined edges. But every so often, you get something you can actually use. If that sounds like faint praise, then bear in mind that the upside is that the Pattern Maker requires very little effort to use. It works like a free slot machine, so even though the odds are against you, you can take as many chances as you like. Just keep pulling the crank and sooner or later, you'll come up with a winner.

Generating a pattern

Start with an image that contains some basic texture like gravel or grass or something else that you'd want to repeat over a large image area. If you don't have such an image, you're in luck—Photoshop has already given you some. Inside the folder that contains the Photoshop CS application, open the Presets folder, and then open the Textures folder. Inside you should find close to 30 images with names like Leafy Bush and Snake Skin. These are photographic textures provided specifically for use with the Pattern Maker filter. For my part, I opened the image called Yellow Green Chalk.

To give myself room to work, I expanded the canvas size by choosing Image ➪ Canvas Size, turning on the Relative check box, and entering 200 for both the Width and Height options. This way, I'll have space to see my tile repeated a few times and see how it holds up as a pattern.

Next, choose Filter ➪ Pattern Maker. This displays the commodious dialog box pictured in Figure 2-34. From here, creating a texture is the three-step process described in the figure. First, outline the portion of the image upon which you want to base the pattern. (If you prefer, you can select the area before entering the Pattern Maker dialog box. Or copy an image and select the Use Clipboard as Sample check box to base the pattern on that.) Second, click the Generate button to fill the image area with a random repeating pattern. If that looks beautiful, you're in luck. But more likely, it won't look very good and you'll want to click Generate Again. And again. And again. Imagine yourself to be a crazy woodpecker, and there's a yummy bug under the Generate Again button. You'll have more fun with it that way.

That's really the gist of it. Some might argue that there's more to using the Pattern Maker than clicking the Generate button like a couch potato searching for a good TV show, but of course they'd be wrong. Still, at the risk of overcomplicating the topic, here are a few things you might want to know:

✦ **Tweaking the settings:** If the filter consistently falls short of spawning a satisfactory effect, you can modify the Tile Generation options—Width, Height, Offset, and so on, all of which I discuss in the following section—then click Generate Again to see what kind of difference your new settings make. You may want to click Generate Again two or three times before giving up on a setting and moving on.

✦ **History is now full:** The Pattern Maker saves your last 20 tiles to a temporary *history buffer* so that you can go back and compare them. After you generate your 20th tile, Photoshop warns you that the history buffer is full. After that point, an old tile drops off into the pit of pattern despair every time you generate a new one.

✦ **Managing your tiles:** Fortunately, you can manage the tiles in the history buffer, so you don't lose your best tiles. You do this using the Tile History options in the lower-right corner of the dialog box, magnified in Figure 2-35. So when you get the "History is now full" error message, go down to the Tile History options and browse through the tiles you've created so far by clicking the arrowhead icons. You can also click inside the tile number—15 of 20, for example—and enter a different tile number. When you come across a bad pattern, click the trash can icon to delete it.

✦ **Saving a tile:** After you arrive at a tile that you deem satisfactory, don't just click the OK button. Instead, click the little disk icon in the Tile History area, labeled *Save pattern* in Figure 2-35. This saves the pattern to Photoshop's presets for later use. In fact, you may want to save several patterns. They take up very little room, so you might as well.

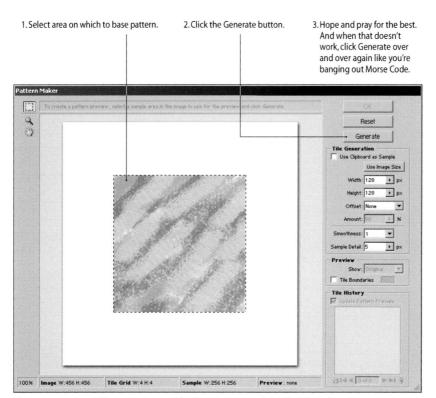

1. Select area on which to base pattern.   2. Click the Generate button.   3. Hope and pray for the best. And when that doesn't work, click Generate over and over again like you're banging out Morse Code.

Figure 2-34: Crafting a pattern with the Pattern Maker filter is a three-step process, provided of course that you regard repeatedly clicking the Generate button as a single step.

When you're finished and you've saved the pattern or patterns you want to use, click Cancel. Yes, you read that right, click Cancel. Clicking OK fills the entire image or active layer with the pattern, even if you have a selection active, which is almost never what you want. (The one exception occurs when using the Pattern Maker's exclusive Offset option, as explained in the next section.) With the pattern saved to the presets, you can apply it with more precision using the pattern stamp tool, history brush, Fill command, or other function. So clicking Cancel opens up a wider world of options.

Tile Generation options

The options in the Tile Generation section of the dialog box allow you to change the size of the repeating tile and adjust other parameters that affect how the Pattern Maker calculates patterns. To make a modified setting take effect, you must click the Generate Again button. In order, here's how the options work:

- ✦ **Use Clipboard as Sample:** When selected, this check box generates the pattern from an image you copied to the Clipboard rather than the selected area in the image window.

- ✦ **Use Image Size:** Nothing says that you have to generate a repeating tile pattern. You can fill the image with one enormous texture. To do so, click the Use Image Size button to load the size of the foreground image into the Width and Height option boxes. Then click Generate Again. It takes several seconds to generate a very large tile, so be patient.

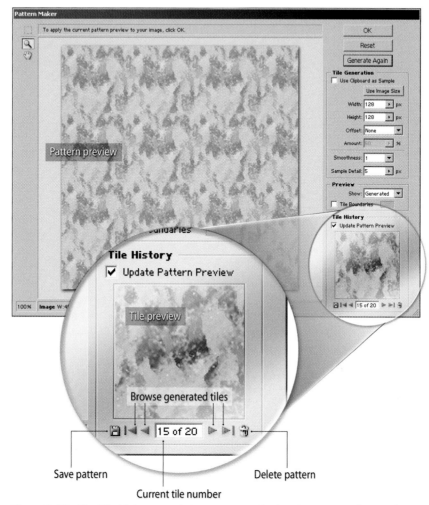

Figure 2-35: The Tile History area lets you peruse the last 20 patterns that you've created. Any time you see a pattern you like, be sure to click the disk icon to save the pattern with Photoshop's presets.

✦ **Width** and **Height:** By default, the Pattern Maker creates 128 by 128-pixel tiles, a common standard for background patterns inside your computer's operating system and on the Web. However, you can enter any values you like. And they can be different — rectangular tiles are completely acceptable.

✦ **Offset** and **Amount:** Use the Offset option to offset rows or columns of tiles in the final pattern. The Horizontal setting offsets the rows; Vertical offsets the columns. Then use the Amount value to determine the amount of offset, measured as a percentage of the tile dimensions. Figure 2-36 shows the results of applying different Offset options to a single tile. The bottom examples show the same settings, but with tile boundaries visible. To see these boundaries, turn on the Tile Boundaries check box in the Preview area of the dialog box.

Note that the Offset values only work when you apply the pattern directly from the Pattern Maker by clicking the OK button. The Offset data is not saved with a pattern and cannot be accessed from other pattern functions inside Photoshop.

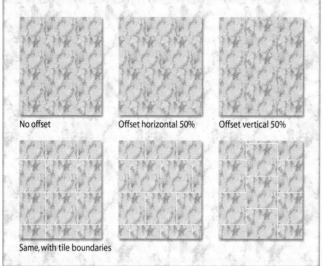

Figure 2-36: Examples of each of the three possible Offset settings, with tile boundaries hidden (top) and visible (bottom).

✦ **Smoothness:** If you keep seeing sharp edges inside your pattern, no matter how many times you regenerate it, try raising the Smoothness value. The value can only vary from 1 to 3, but higher values generally result in smoother transitions.

✦ **Sample Detail:** I mentioned earlier that the Pattern Maker works by chopping up an image and reassembling its parts. The size of those chopped up bits is determined by the Sample Detail value. Very small details result in faster pattern generation, with the potential for more cut lines and harsh transitions. A higher Sample Detail value creates a chunkier pattern, with better detail and more natural transitions, but it takes longer to generate as well. I recommend trying this value at its minimum and maximum settings, 3 and 21, to see if it makes much of a difference. If so, endure the delays and play with the value to get the desired results. If not, crank it down to 5 and focus on the other settings instead.

Bear in mind that, as you work on a pattern, you can zoom in and out of the preview area in the central portion of the dialog box to get a better idea of how the pattern will look. The Pattern Maker provides specific tools for this purpose, but it's generally easiest to rely on the keyboard shortcuts Ctrl+plus and minus (⌘-plus and minus on the Mac).

Building your own seamless pattern

Now don't get me wrong, the Pattern Maker is all very well and good for what it is — that is, a filter that slices your image into a bunch of bacon strips and throws them all over the floor in a big pile. That works for random patterns, but it doesn't work well for regular, smooth transitions between recognizable elements. For example, let's say I want to make a pattern based on the Toltec statue shown at the top of Figure 2-37. If I applied the Pattern Maker to it, I'd get something like the image shown on the bottom. If I want to simulate petrified Toltec bacon strips, then that's exactly the kind of effect I want. But I don't. So what do I do?

The following steps describe how to change a scanned image into a seamless, repeating pattern the old-fashioned way — by hand. To illustrate how this process works, Figures 2-38 through 2-41 show various stages in the creation of my Toltec pattern. You need only two tools to carry out these steps: the rectangular marquee tool and the clone stamp tool. And a bit of manual dexterity doesn't hurt.

Original image

A little ditty Pattern Maker came up with

Figure 2-37: This Toltec statue from ancient Mexico seems a perfect starting point for a repeating pattern (top). But surely I can design something better than what the Pattern Maker comes up with (bottom).

STEPS: Building a Repeating Pattern from an Image

1. **Open the image that you want to convert into a pattern.** I started with the Toltec statue from Figure 2-37. The top one, not the bacon.

2. **Select the rectangular marquee tool.** In the Options bar, select Fixed Size from the Style pop-up menu and enter specific values in the Width and Height option boxes. This way, you can easily reselect a portion of the pattern in the steps that follow, as well as use the fixed-size marquee to define the pattern when you finish. To create the patterns shown in the figures, I set the marquee to 450 by 450 pixels.

3. **Select the portion of the image that you want to feature in the pattern.** Because you've specified an exact marquee size, Photoshop selects a fixed area whenever you click. You can drag to move the marquee around in the window.

4. **Press Ctrl+C (⌘-C on the Mac).** This copies the selection to the Clipboard.

5. **Press Ctrl+N (⌘-N on the Mac) to make a new image and triple the Width and Height values.** In my case, Photoshop suggested a new image size of 450 by 450 pixels, which matches the size of the selection I copied to the Clipboard. By tripling these values, I arrived at a new image size of 1350 by 1350 pixels.

6. **Press Ctrl+V (⌘-V on the Mac).** Photoshop pastes the copied selection smack dab in the center of the window, which is exactly where you want it. This image will serve as the central tile of your repeating pattern.

7. **Ctrl-click (⌘-click on the Mac) the item labeled Layer 1 in the Layers palette.** Photoshop pasted the image on a new layer. But to duplicate the image and convert it into a pattern, you need to select it, and the easiest way to do that is to Ctrl-click (or ⌘-click) the layer name to select the pasted pixels.

8. **Press Ctrl+E (⌘-E on the Mac).** This merges the layer with the background, thereby flattening it. Or you can choose Layer ➪ Flatten Image. Either way, the selection outline remains intact.

9. **Choose Edit ➪ Define Pattern.** This establishes the selected image as a pattern tile. Give the pattern a name when Photoshop prompts you.

10. **Press Ctrl+D (⌘-D on the Mac) to deselect the image.** You neither need nor want the selection outline any more. You'll need to be able to fill and clone freely without a selection outline getting in the way.

11. **Press Shift+Backspace (Shift-Delete on the Mac) or choose Edit ➪ Fill.** Then select Pattern from the Use pop-up menu, select your new pattern from the Custom Pattern palette, and press Enter or Return. This fills the window with a 3 by 3-tile grid, as shown in Figure 2-38.

12. **Drag the title bar of the new image window to position it so you can see the portion of the image you copied in the original image window.** You want to be able to see both images at once, because you'll be cloning from one into the other. After you have your windows arranged, click the title bar of the new image, the one in Figure 2-38, to make it the active window.

13. **Select the clone stamp tool.** Press the S key, or press Shift+S if the pattern stamp tool is active.

14. **Turn off the Aligned check box in the Options bar.** Ironic as it may sound, it's easier to get the alignment between the clone-from and clone-to points established with Aligned turned off.

Figure 2-38: To build the repeating pattern shown in Figure 2-41, I started by creating a grid of nine image tiles. As you can see, the seams between the tiles are harsh and unacceptable.

15. **Specify the image you want to clone by pressing Alt (Option on the Mac) and clicking in the original image window.** No need to switch out of the new window. Alt-click (or Option-click) an easily identifiable pixel that belongs to the portion of the image you copied. The exact pixel you click is very important. In my case, I clicked the corner of the Toltec statue's mouth.

16. **Now click with the stamp tool on the matching pixel in the central tile of the new window.** If you clicked the correct pixel, the tile should not change one iota. If it shifts at all, press Ctrl+Z (⌘-Z on the Mac) and try again. Because Aligned is turned off, you can keep undoing and clicking over and over again without resetting the clone-from point in the original image.

17. **Turn on the Aligned check box.** After you click in the image without seeing any shift, select the Aligned option to lock in the alignment between the clone-from and clone-to points.

18. **Use the clone stamp tool to fill in portions of the central tile.** For example, in Figure 2-39, I extended the Toltec statue's face outward both to the left and to the right. I also extended his headdress upward into the upper Toltec's neck.

19. **Select a portion of the modified image.** After you establish one continuous transition between two tiles in any direction — up, down, left, or right — click with the rectangular marquee tool to select an area that includes the transition. In my case, I decided my best transitions were between the central and top tiles. Therefore, I selected a region that includes half the central tile and half the tile above it.

Figure 2-39: I used the clone stamp tool to copy pixels from the original image into the central tile, extending the statue's headdress and jaw line.

20. **Repeat Steps 9 through 11.** That is, choose Edit ⇨ Define Pattern, press Ctrl+D (or ⌘-D), choose Edit ⇨ Fill, select the pattern you just defined, and press Enter or Return. This fills the image with your new transition. Don't worry if the tiles shift around a bit — that's to be expected.

21. **If you started by creating a vertical transition, use the clone stamp tool to create a horizontal transition.** Likewise, if you started horizontally, now go vertically. You'll need to turn off the Aligned check box again to establish the proper alignment between clone-from and clone-to points. In my case, I shifted the clone-to point several times — alternatively building on the central statue, the one to the left of it, and the one directly above. Each time you get the clone-to point properly positioned, turn the Aligned check box back on to lock in the alignment. Then clone away.

As long as you get the clone-from and clone-to points properly aligned, you can't make a mistake. If you change your mind, realign the clone points and try again. In my case, I cloned the left side of the headdress into the cheek of the head to the left. I also cloned the bottom-left edge of the headdress from the statue above, ultimately achieving the effect shown in Figure 2-40.

22. **After you build up one set of both horizontal and vertical transitions, click with the rectangular marquee tool to select the transitions.** Figure 2-40 shows where I positioned my 450 by 450-pixel selection boundary. This includes parts of each of four neighboring heads, mostly focusing on the horizontal transition. Don't worry if the image doesn't appear centered inside the selection. What counts is that the image flows seamlessly inside the selection outline.

23. **Repeat Steps 9 through 11 again.** If the tiles blend together seamlessly, as in Figure 2-41, you're finished. If not, clone some more with the clone stamp tool and try again.

Figure 2-40: After completing a smooth transition between the upper-central tile and the tiles above and to the left of it, I selected a portion of the image and chose Edit ⇨ Define Pattern.

Figure 2-41: This south-of-the-border montage is the result of applying the finished Toltec pattern with the Fill command. The result is a transitionless tapestry of Toltec totems.

✦ ✦ ✦

Undo and History

Stepping Back through Time

The release of Photoshop 5 in 1998 gave us the History palette, and this remarkable tool remains the best implementation of multiple undos in any major application. Moving beyond simple backstepping, the History palette takes the whole reversion metaphor into *Slaughterhouse Five* territory. If you've never read the novel (or you've somehow forgotten), Kurt Vonnegut, Jr. suggests that humans live from one moment to the next like a person strapped to a boxcar, unable to change the speed or direction of the train as it hurtles through time. In most programs that offer multiple undos, you can make the train stop and back up, but you're still strapped to it. The History palette is the first tool that lets you get off the train and transport to any point on the track — instantaneously. In short, we now have a digital version of time travel.

Here are just a few of the marvelous and unique capabilities of the History palette:

+ **Undo-independent stepping:** Step backward by pressing Ctrl+Alt+Z (⌘-Option-Z on the Mac); step forward by pressing Ctrl+Shift+Z (⌘-Shift-Z). Every program with multiple undos does this, but Photoshop's default keyboard equivalents are different. Why? Because you can backstep independently of the Undo command, so that even backstepping is undoable.

+ **Before and after:** Revert to a point in history to see a *before* view of your image and then fly forward to see the *after* view. From then on, Ctrl+Z (⌘-Z on the Mac) becomes a super-undo, toggling between the before and after views. The opportunities for comparing states and changing your mind are truly colossal.

+ **Dynamic time travel:** If before and after aren't enough, how about animated history? You can drag a control to slide dynamically forward and backward through operations. It's as if you recorded the operations to videotape, and now you're rewinding and fast-forwarding through them.

+ **Sweeping away the mistakes:** Select a point in the history of your image and paint back to it using the history brush. You can let the mistakes pile up and then brush them away. This brush isn't a paintbrush; it's a hand broom. Want even more variety? Use the art history brush to paint back to the image using various artistic styles.

✦ **Take a picture, it'll last longer:** You can save any point in the History palette as a snapshot. That way, even several hundred operations after that point in history is long gone, you can revisit the snapshot.

✦ **This is your life, Image A:** Each and every image has its own history. So after performing a few hundred operations on Image A, you can still go back to Image B and backstep through operations you performed hours ago. The caveat is that the history remains available only as long as an image is open. Close the image, and its history goes away.

✦ **Undo the Revert command:** The History palette tracks the Revert command. So if you don't like the image that was last saved to disk, you can undo the reversion and get back to where you were. Also notice that when you choose File ➪ Revert, Photoshop does not ask you to confirm the reversion. There's no reason for a warning because Revert is fully undoable.

The only thing you can't do through the History palette is travel forward into the future — say, to about three days from now when you've finished your grueling project, submitted it to your client, and received your big fat paycheck. But believe it or not, that's actually good news. The day Adobe can figure out how to do your work for you, your clients will hire Photoshop and stop hiring you.

So I ask you — Photoshop, *Slaughterhouse Five*, just a coincidence? Well, yes, I suppose it is. But the fact remains, you have the option of getting off the boxcar. How you make use of your freedom CS up to you.

The History Palette

Choose Window ➪ History to view the History palette, annotated with the palette menu in full view in Figure 3-1. The History palette records each *significant* operation and adds it to a list. Things that don't inherently make a change in your image — like adjusting settings, changing preferences, or selecting a new foreground color — don't get added to the list. The oldest operations appear at the top of the list with the most recent operations at the bottom.

Each item in the list is called a *state*. That's not my word, it's Adobe's, and some folks have voiced the opinion that the term is too stiff and formal. But I think that it is dead on. Each item in the palette represents a stepping stone in the progression of the image, a condition at a moment in time — in other words, a state.

Photoshop automatically names each item according to the tool, command, or operation used to arrive at the state. The icon next to the name helps to identify the state further. But the best way to find out what a state is like is to click it. Photoshop instantaneously undoes all operations performed after that state and returns you to the state so that you can inspect it in detail. To redo all the operations you just did in one fell swoop, press Ctrl+Z (⌘-Z on the Mac) or choose Edit ➪ Undo State Change.

That one action — clicking on a state — is the gist of what you need to know to travel forward and backward through time in Photoshop. If that's all you ever learn, you'll find yourself working with greater speed, freedom, and security than is possible in virtually any other graphics application. But this represents only the first in a long list of the History palette's capabilities. Here's the rest of what you might want to know:

✦ **Changing the number of undos:** By default, Photoshop records the last 20 operations in the History palette. When you perform the 21st operation, the first state is shoved off the list. To change this behavior, choose Edit ➪ Preferences ➪ General or press

Ctrl+K (⌘-K on the Mac), which opens the Preferences dialog box, and then enter your preferred number of undoable operations in the History States option box. If your computer is equipped with 128MB or less of RAM, you might want to lower the value to 5 or 10 to maintain greater efficiency. On the other hand, if you become a time-traveling freak (like me) and have plenty of RAM—say, 1GB or more—turn it up, baby. Should you be so inclined, the History palette can hold up to 1,000 states. That's probably more than you want to use—after all, some states take up an awful lot of memory—but when working on a single image, 100 states may on rare occasions be comfortable.

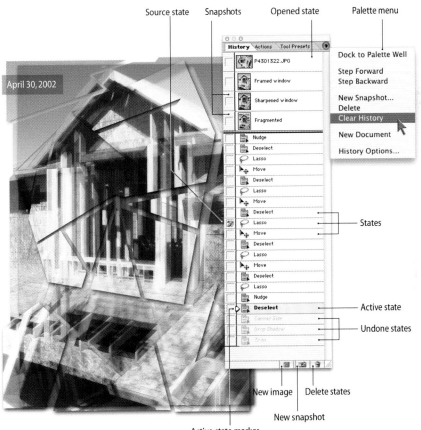

Figure 3-1: The History palette records each significant event as an independent state. To return to a state, just click on it.

✦ **Undone states:** When you revert to a state by clicking on it, every subsequent state turns gray to show that it's been undone. You can redo a grayed state simply by clicking on it. But if you perform a new operation, all grayed states disappear. You have one opportunity to bring them back by pressing Ctrl+Z (⌘-Z); if you perform another new operation, the once-grayed states are gone for good. For an exception to this behavior, see the very next paragraph.

✦ **Working with nonsequential states:** If you don't like the idea of losing your undone states — every state is sacred, after all — choose the History Options command in the palette menu and select the Allow Non-Linear History check box (see Figure 3-2). Undone states no longer drop off the list when you perform a new operation. They remain available on the off chance that you might want to revisit them. It's like having multiple possible time trails.

Here it is. Here's the option I'm talking about.

Figure 3-2: Choose History Options from the History palette menu and select Allow Non-Linear History to permit Photoshop to keep states that you have undone.

The Allow Non-Linear History check box does not permit you to undo a single state without affecting the subsequent states. For example, say that you painted with the airbrush, smeared with the smudge tool, and then cloned with the clone stamp. You can revert back to the airbrush state and then apply other operations without losing the option of restoring the smudge and clone. But you can't undo the smudge and leave the clone intact. Operations can only occur in the sequence they were applied.

✦ **Stepping through states:** As I mentioned earlier, you can press Ctrl+Alt+Z (⌘-Option-Z) to undo the active step or Ctrl+Shift+Z (⌘-Shift-Z) to redo the next step in the list. Backstepping goes up the list of states in the History palette; forward stepping goes down. So bear in mind that if the Allow Non-Linear History check box is active, back-stepping may take you to a state that was previously inactive.

✦ **Flying through states:** Drag the right-pointing active state marker (labeled in Figure 3-1) up and down the list to rewind and fast-forward, respectively, through time. If the screen image doesn't appear to change as you fly by certain states, it most likely means those states involve small brushstrokes or changes to selection outlines. Otherwise, the changes are quite apparent.

✦ **Taking a snapshot:** Every once in a while, a state comes along that's so great, you don't want it to fall by the wayside 20 operations from now. To set a state aside, choose New Snapshot from the palette menu or click the little page icon at the bottom of the History palette. To rename a snapshot after you create it, just double-click on its name at the top of the History palette and enter a new one. Or you can name a snapshot as you create it by pressing the Alt key (or Option on the Mac), clicking the little page icon, and entering a name in the dialog box.

Photoshop lets you store as many snapshots as your computer's RAM permits. Also worth noting, the program automatically creates a snapshot of the image as it appears when it's first opened. If you don't like this opening snapshot, you can change this behavior by turning off Automatically Create First Snapshot inside the History Options dialog box.

✦ **Creating a snapshot upon saving the image:** Select the Automatically Create New Snapshot When Saving check box in the History Options dialog box to create a new snapshot every time you save your image. This option is useful if you find yourself venturing down uncertain roads from one save to the next and want the ability to back-step not only to the last saved state (which you can do by choosing File ➪ Revert), but the one before that and the one before that.

✦ **Saving the state permanently:** The problem with snapshots is that they last only as long as the current session. If you quit Photoshop or if the program crashes, you lose the entire history list, snapshots included. To save a state so you can refer to it several days from now, choose the New Document command or click the leftmost icon at the bottom of the History palette. You can also drag and drop a state onto the icon. Either way, Photoshop duplicates the state to a new image window. Then you can save the state to the format of your choice.

✦ **Setting the source:** Click to the left of a state to identify it as the *source state*. The history brush icon appears where you click. The source state affects the performance of the history brush, art history brush, Fill command, and eraser, if you select Erase to History. The keystroke Ctrl+Alt+Backspace (⌘-Option-Delete on the Mac) fills a selection with the source state.

✦ **Trashing states:** If your machine is equipped with little RAM or you're working on a particularly large image, Photoshop may slow down as the states accumulate. If it gets too slow, you may want to purge the History palette. To delete any state as well as those before it, drag the state to the trash icon at the bottom of the palette. Your image updates accordingly. If the Allow Non-Linear History check box is on, clicking the trash can deletes just the active state.

To clear all states from the History palette, choose the Clear History command from the palette menu. This doesn't immediately empty the RAM, just in case you change your mind and decide you want to undo. After you perform another operation, only then does Photoshop purge the memory for real. If you want the memory emptied right away — and you're *positive* that you have no desire whatsoever to undo — press the Alt key (Option on the Mac) and choose the Clear History command. And if you're really hankering to purge, choose Edit ➪ Purge ➪ Histories — this gets rid of *all* states for *all* open documents.

Version CS makes a historical contribution to Photoshop's time traveling abilities, though it does so without actually involving the History palette. New in Photoshop CS, layer comps can take certain properties of layers and freeze them in time, in essence allowing you to revert back to a previous state. Although layer comps aren't anywhere near as omniscient as the History palette, they do have the bonus of being saved permanently within the document, so you can still view them weeks, months, or years later. We'll take a close look at layer comps in Chapter 5. But getting back to history, the new History Log preference in the General panel of the Preferences dialog box lets you keep written track of the edits you've made to an image. You can't revisit or undo any of those edits, but the log is a handy way of recording an image's history. We'll explore this feature in more detail in Chapter 13.

Painting Away the Past

The History palette represents the regimental way to revert images inside Photoshop. You can retreat, march forward, proceed in linear or nonlinear formation, capture states, and retire them. Every state plays backward in the same way it played forward. It's precise, predictable, and positively by the book.

But what if you want to get free-form? What if you want to brush away the present and paint in the past? In that case, a palette isn't going to do you any good. What you need is a pliable, emancipated, free-wheeling *tool*.

As luck would have it, Photoshop offers three candidates — the eraser, the history brush, and the art history brush. The eraser works like, well, an eraser, washing away pixels to reveal underlying pixels or exposed canvas. The eraser is a pretty straightforward tool; I cover it in depth in the standard edition of the *Photoshop CS Bible,* so we're going to skip over it here. That leaves us with the history brush, which takes you back to a kinder, simpler state, and the art history brush, which does the same but also enables you to paint using special artistic effects. Although the functions of these two tools overlap slightly, they both have very specific purposes, as becomes clear in the following sections.

As you work with these tools, remember that you can use the Edit ⇨ Fade command to blend the altered pixels with the originals, just as you can when applying any other painting or editing tool. You can adjust both the opacity and blend mode of the newly applied pixels.

The history brush

To use the history brush tool, press Y to select it and then drag in your image to selectively revert to the source state targeted in the History palette. You also can vary the translucency of your strokes using the Opacity setting in the Options bar and take advantage of brush modes. By choosing a different brush mode from the Mode pop-up menu in the Options bar, you can mix pixels from the changed and saved images to achieve interesting, and sometimes surprising, effects. We'll see the history brush in glorious, time-warping action in the upcoming section "Retouching with the History Brush," but first let's take a look at the history brush's right-brained cousin.

The art history brush

The art history brush lets you create impressionistic effects with the aid of the History palette. To get a sense for how it works, open any old file. Me, I opened the simple still life featured in Figure 3-3. Press D to get the default foreground and background colors, select the standard brush tool, and paint willy-nilly all over your image. That's right, make a total mess of it, as I did in the first example in Figure 3-4. You think it's ruined? Ah ha, but it is not. The image is now ready for you to turn into an impressionistic masterpiece.

Select the art history brush, which shares a flyout menu and keyboard shortcut (Y) with the history brush. Bring up the History palette and make sure the first snapshot is identified as the source state (assuming that you haven't made any unauthorized changes to the image since you opened it). Now paint inside your black image. Each stroke reveals a bit of your original photograph in painterly detail, as illustrated in the second image in Figure 3-4.

Hoping to punch home the effect a little more? Well, you're in luck, because I have just the recipe. First, choose Filter ⇨ Distort ⇨ Displace, enter 10 percent for both of the Scale values, select the Tile radio button, click OK, and load the Random Strokes pattern (discussed in the section "Creating patterns and textures" in Chapter 2). Photoshop adds a little bit of extra brushwork, as in the first example of Figure 3-5. Next, choose Filter ⇨ Texture ⇨ Texturizer, select the Canvas texture, and fiddle with the Scaling and Relief options to get the desired effect. Regardless of your settings, you'll get a painted canvas look, as shown on the right side of Figure 3-5. If that's not art, then my name's not Dekebrandt McVinci.

Figure 3-3: A simple still life that I shot a few years back using what was then a state-of-the-art digital camera but is now considered so low-res, it makes the digital angels cry.

Like the history brush, the art history brush paints from the source state specified in the History palette. But it does so by painting tens or even hundreds of tiny brushstrokes at a time, swirling and gyrating according to settings you select in the Options bar. Many of these settings you've seen several times before. As shown in Figure 3-6, you have the standard Brush controls, a reduced Mode option, and the tried and true Opacity value. But starting with the Style option, the art history brush goes its own way:

✦ **Style:** The art history brush paints with randomly generated worms and corkscrews of color. You can decide the basic shapes of the creepy crawlies by selecting an option from the Style pop-up menu, displayed in Figure 3-6. Combine these options with different brush sizes to vary the detail conveyed by the impressionistic image. Tight styles and small brushes give you better detail; Loose styles and big brushes produce less detail.

✦ **Area:** This value defines the area covered by a single spot of corkscrews. Larger values generally mean more corkscrews are laid down at a time; reduce the value for a more sparse look. You can get some very interesting effects by raising the Area value to its maximum, 500 pixels, and mousing down inside the image without moving the cursor. Watch those worms writhe.

Scribble a bunch of black with the brush tool   Restore original image using art history brush

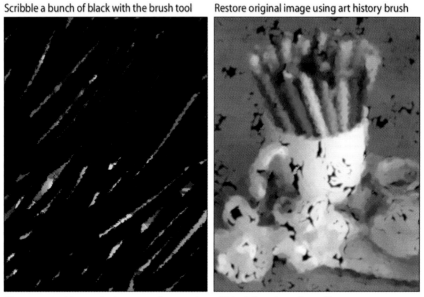

Figure 3-4: After painting a random series of black brushstrokes all over my image (left), I selected the art history brush and painted in a rough translation of the original (right).

Displace (10%, 10%, Random Strokes)   Texturizer (Canvas, 140%, 5, Top Left)

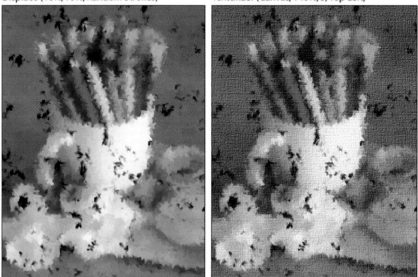

Figure 3-5: My art wasn't artsy enough, so I applied the Displace filter (left) and then added some canvas texture with the Texturizer filter (right). It took me just two minutes to create and is suitable for hanging in a dentist's waiting room, the true measure of any work of art.

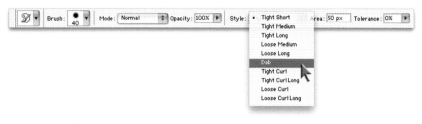

Figure 3-6: Choose an option from the Style menu to change the type of strokes applied by the art history brush.

✦ **Tolerance:** This value limits where the art history brush can paint. A value of 0 lets the brush paint anywhere; higher values let the brush paint only in areas where the current state and source state differ dramatically in color. High Tolerance values are especially useful for achieving the black velvet look that's always in vogue because it's perpetually on the verge of experiencing a major revival. Figure 3-7 shows a couple of examples painted against black using different Style settings, namely Dab and Tight Long, combined with high Area and Tolerance values. For effect, I applied the Texturizer filter set to Bricks to the second image.

If impressionism interests you, I encourage you to experiment. I mean, in keeping with my black velvet painting motif, the art history brush could do a fantastic job of painting the fringe on Elvis' jumpsuit. But otherwise, feel free to give this brush the slip. I happen to think it's pretty nifty (and surprisingly well implemented), but it definitely falls under the heading of Whimsical Creative Tools to Play with When You're Not under Deadline.

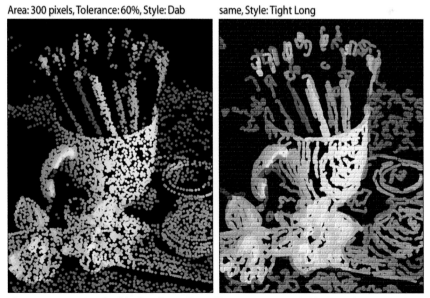

Figure 3-7: To get the black velvet effect, fill your image with black and raise the Area and Tolerance values in the Options bar. I set the brush size to 10 pixels and clicked maybe a dozen times inside each image with the art history brush.

Source state limitations

Photoshop displays the cancel cursor if you try to paint with the history brush or art history brush using a source state that's a different width or height than the current image. One pixel difference, and the source state is a moot point. This same restriction applies to filling your image with a history state by choosing Edit ➪ Fill and picking History from the Use menu, or just pressing Ctrl+Alt+Backspace (⌘-Option-Delete on the Mac).

You may also see the cancel cursor if the layer is locked, or if the source state lacks an equivalent layer. To find out exactly what the problem is, click the image with the cancel cursor to display an explanatory alert message. If the problem relates to the source state, move the source state icon in the History palette to a point after you modified the width or the height of the image. The crop tool and the Image Size, Canvas Size, Rotate Canvas, and Crop commands can mix up the history brush. If you applied one of these operations in the very last state, you either have to backstep before that operation or find some alternative to the history brush.

It's not a big deal, though. After some practice, you'll learn to anticipate this problem. Or better yet, make sure that you resize or crop your image first, before you start making other changes. Get the dimensions ironed out and then start laying down your time trails.

Retouching with the History Brush

Now that we've seen how Photoshop's particular slant on history works, let's put the past through its paces. The remainder of this chapter outlines a couple of fundamentally divergent but eminently practical history-based techniques. First, I show you how to use the History palette and its pal, the history brush, to expedite the process of retouching an old photo. Next, I turn palette and brush to the task of creating highly-customized special effects. Throughout, I take advantage of several commands that I discuss in greater depth in later chapters. But don't worry—you won't have to do a lot of time-traveling through the pages of this book to keep up. There's plenty of information in the upcoming discussions to help you make sense of it all.

Sharpening and smoothing

Let's start with the task of editing a vintage photograph. The problem with old photos is that they're usually soft and grainy, such as the first example in Figure 3-8. This means you have to find some way to both sharpen the detail and smooth away the grain—two contradictory operations. The solution is to perform both operations up front and worry about which specific areas need sharpening and smoothing later. Photoshop's history brush lets you do precisely that. You can create one sharpened version of an image, another smooth version, and then brush the two into the original as needed. As the second example in Figure 3-8 demonstrates, the resulting image looks several times better than the original and yet demands relatively little time and talent to pull off.

To start, sharpen the focus of the image by choosing Filter ➪ Sharpen ➪ Unsharp Mask. Because the sharpened state represents one extreme in this process, you want to apply the filter liberally. I recommend an Amount value of about 400 percent with a Radius of anywhere from 2.0 to 4.0 pixels, depending on the resolution of the image. Leave the Threshold set to 0; otherwise, you end up with harsh transitions between sharpened and soft areas, which look pretty ratty.

Old grainy photograph   Sharpened and smoothed using history

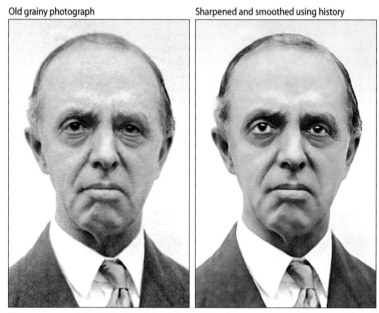

Figure 3-8: With the help of the history brush, you can transform a soft and grainy old photo (left) into a sharp and smooth vintage image (right).

In Figure 3-9, I wanted to give my image some extra color. So I shifted the image to purple by choosing Image ⇨ Adjustments ⇨ Hue/Saturation, turning on the Colorize check box, and setting the Hue value to 320. Note that this is an entirely optional step — one that happens to work well for this image though by no means for all. But it demonstrates how you can apply as many operations as you like to define the sharpened state of the image.

As it does with all operations, Photoshop automatically adds Unsharp Mask and Hue/Saturation as states in the History palette. Together, the operations result in one possible state that you can keep or undo according to your whim. However, for the purposes of this technique, it's an important state that you'll need to come back to several times over the course of editing the image. To keep the state from cycling off the History palette, you can save it as a snapshot by clicking on the little camera icon at the bottom of the palette, highlighted in Figure 3-9. (In my case, I pressed Alt or Option and clicked the icon to display the New Snapshot dialog box and give it a name.) The snapshot remains available as long as the image is open.

Now click the state prior to Unsharp Mask in the History palette. (If Unsharp Mask was the first operation you applied after opening the image, you can click the default snapshot at the top of the palette.) This reverts the image back to its pre-Unsharp Mask appearance. The undone states turn gray, but because you saved the sharpened version of the image as a snapshot earlier, it remains available at the top of the palette.

To create a smooth version of the image, choose Filter ⇨ Noise ⇨ Median. Median smoothes out film grain by averaging the colors of neighboring pixels. Raise the Radius value until the grain disappears — probably somewhere in the 4- to 8-pixel range. This will gum up the detail, but because the idea is to provide a smooth extreme, that's to be expected. Click OK to apply the filter.

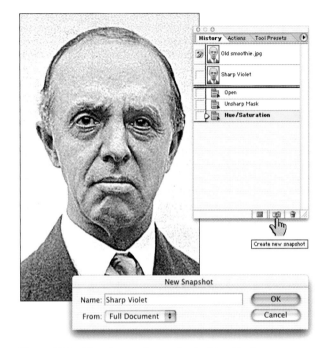

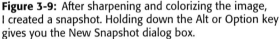

Figure 3-9: After sharpening and colorizing the image,
I created a snapshot. Holding down the Alt or Option key
gives you the New Snapshot dialog box.

If the result is a little too smooth for your taste, apply Filter ➪ Sharpen ➪ Unsharp Mask with a
relatively modest Amount setting, say 100 percent. The new operations become the final state
in the History palette. You'll want to come back to this state, so save it as a snapshot by again
clicking the camera icon at the bottom of the palette, as in Figure 3-10. Then undo the new
operations by clicking the state preceding Median.

Painting with the snapshots

You now have your original image on screen with two snapshots ready and waiting in memory:
one that's too sharp and another that's too smooth. You are ready to paint the snapshots into
the original with the history brush.

Select the history brush by pressing the Y key. Then click to the left of the sharp snapshot in
the History palette, the one I called Sharp Violet. The brush icon appears in front of the snapshot, indicating that it's the source state for the history brush and other history operations.
Trace around the important details in the image to apply the sharpened snapshot. If you're
retouching a face, for example, you should paint around the eyes, mouth, and other features
to improve their clarity and focus, as in Figure 3-11. To enhance the effect, select a brush mode
such as Hard Light or Overlay from the Options bar. Don't worry if the effect is too garish or
overdone; you can always temper it by painting from the Median snapshot or some other
state later on.

Figure 3-10: After reverting to the original image, I applied the Median filter with a Radius of 8 pixels to smooth away the film grain. I followed that up with Unsharp Mask set to an Amount of 100 percent and a Radius of 3.0. Then I saved this latest state as yet another snapshot.

After painting in all the sharpened areas, it's time to smooth away the film grain with the Median snapshot. Click in front of the Median snapshot in the History palette to make it the source state. I like to take the edge off the sharpened details by covering the entire image with a translucent coat of Median. The easiest way to do this is to press Shift+Backspace (Win) or Shift-Delete (Mac) to bring up the Fill dialog box and then set the Use pop-up menu to History and the Opacity value to 50 percent. After applying the Fill command, paint with the history brush set to 50 percent or lower to smooth out the film grain and other imperfections in the image. The result of my efforts appears in Figure 3-12.

From here on, it's just a matter of painting back and forth between the Unsharp Mask snapshot and the Median snapshot. You'll definitely want to vary the brush size as you work. You might also want to experiment with the Opacity value and brush mode setting in the Options bar. The most effective brush modes tend to be Hard Light, Screen, Multiply, and Normal. In Figure 3-13, I wasn't happy with the eyes, so I painted from the sharpened snapshot using the Screen mode. In Figure 3-14, I followed up by painting with the Median snapshot set to Multiply.

Figure 3-11: Click in front of the sharpened snapshot to make it the source state for the history brush. Then paint around the important details in the image to sharpen them. In my case, I painted around the eyes, nose, mouth, and the perimeter of the head with the brush mode set to Normal.

Figure 3-12: After switching the source state to the Median snapshot, I applied the Fill command set to History at 50 percent. Then I used the history brush, likewise set to lower Opacity values, to paint away the grain.

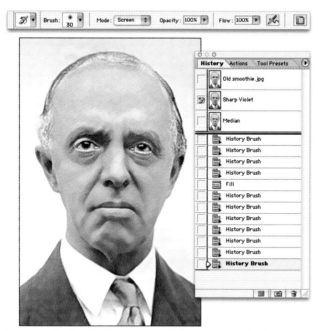

Figure 3-13: To eliminate some of the murkiness in the eyes and hair, I painted from the sharpened snapshot using the Screen mode.

Figure 3-14: To blend the sharpened eyes and hair with the other elements, I painted over them using the Median snapshot set to Multiply.

Creative History Effects

As is the case with any program that offers multiple undos, the History palette ensures that you can edit an image without worrying about making an irreversible mistake. But it also means that you can experiment with alternative futures and blend these futures with the present, just as I do in the following example.

I started with the photograph of the B-2 Bomber shown in Figure 3-15. The bomber looks pretty nifty hovering in the air like that, but it was a little static for my taste. I reckoned it'd look better as a spaceship, buzzing by at a million miles an hour propelled by a gush of flames.

To create the raw materials for my motion trails, I applied a series of filters. First I used Filter ⇨ Noise ⇨ Add Noise with an Amount value of 50 percent to give the image some grit. Then I applied two passes of Filter ⇨ Blur ⇨ Motion Blur, each set to a Distance value of 250 pixels and Angle of 5 degrees, the approximate angle of the bomber. To accentuate the stripes of color, I chose Filter ⇨ Sharpen ⇨ Unsharp Mask and entered an Amount value of 300 percent and a Radius of 12.0 pixels. Finally, I used Filter ⇨ Distort ⇨ Ripple and set the Size option to Large to give the stripes a bit of wave. The result appears in Figure 3-16.

Figure 3-15: This B-2 Bomber photo is pretty cool now, but I'm going to make it look like a spaceship from *Earth vs. the Flying Saucers,* only more modern.

The effects are interesting, but they obliterate the bomber. Luckily, the History palette recorded the original state of my image so I could return to it at my leisure. But before doing so, I chose the History Options command from the History palette menu and selected the Allow Non-Linear History check box. This told Photoshop to save the filtered states even if I decide to undo them.

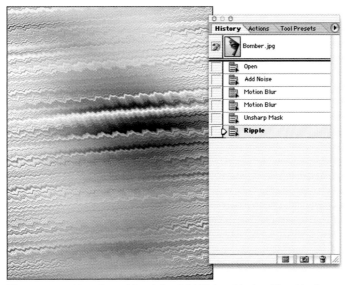

Figure 3-16: Here I combined the Add Noise, Motion Blur, Unsharp Mask, and Ripple filters to dissolve the bomber into a series of wavy motion lines.

Confident that I wouldn't lose my effects, I reverted the image to its original state by clicking the Open item at the top of the History palette. Then I took up the history brush, resolved to paint the filtered effects into the bomber on my own terms. For starters, I selected the second Motion Blur state and painted to the left of the bomber to create a unidirectional motion trail, as in Figure 3-17.

Figure 3-17: After turning on the Allow Non-Linear History check box, I restored the Open state, set the second Motion Blur state as the source, and brushed in a unidirectional motion blur.

I can't emphasize enough how handy it is that the history brush permits you to apply one state to another using different brush modes. I selected the Ripple state as the source for the history brush and painted it in using the Overlay mode. Then I set the source state to the original Open state and brushed it in using Multiply. The net result is a rushing effect that enhances the bomber without annihilating it, as pictured in Figure 3-18.

But for my purposes, a fast bomber wasn't enough. To give it that intergalactic touch, it had to be emitting fire. To make the fire, I set the foreground and background colors to red and yellow, and applied Filter ⇨ Render ⇨ Clouds. I followed that up with Filter ⇨ Render ⇨ Difference Clouds four times in a row to round out the billowy flames, which appear in Figure 3-19.

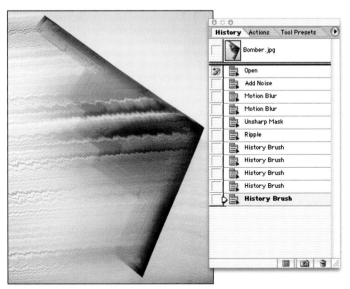

Figure 3-18: To introduce the Ripple state as heat trails, I set it as the source and painted it in with the history brush set to the Overlay mode. To burn in some of the original edges, I also brushed in the Open state using the Multiply mode.

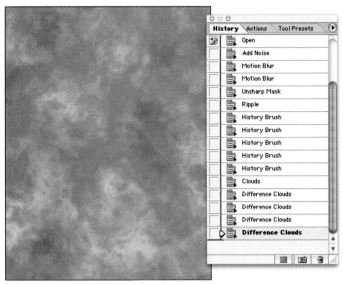

Figure 3-19: To make the fire, I set the foreground color to red, the background color to yellow, and applied the Clouds filter. Then I applied Difference Clouds four times to achieve a roiling effect.

Even more than the previous filters, Clouds and Difference Clouds drowned out the spaceship. So I clicked the History Brush state immediately preceding Clouds to revert to that point. Then I selected the final Difference Clouds state as the source for the history brush and painted in the fire using a combination of Opacity settings and brush modes. Figure 3-20 shows the completed spaceship in glorious flight.

The timeline of the History palette lets you plan a network of possible futures. It's like standing at a fork in the road with the option of going all directions at once. In my case, the road forked in two directions, the Motion Blur experiment in one direction and the Clouds effects in the other. In my experience, no other program lets you paint with time in such a dynamic and satisfying manner.

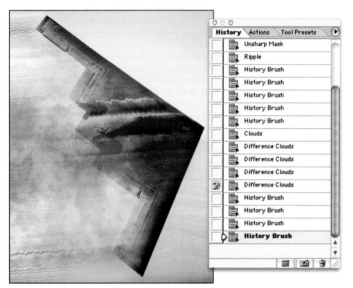

Figure 3-20: After reverting to the state prior to Clouds, I tagged the final Difference Clouds state as the source and brushed in the raging fire.

✦   ✦   ✦

Masks and Extractions

Making Selections Using Masks

If you are or aspire to be a professional Photoshop user, then it's quite likely you've played with the basic selection tools, namely the marquee tools, the lassos, and the magic wand. On occasion, you may even resort to the pen tools, which let you draw precise curves and convert them to selections or clipping paths. You may, in fact, be so confident and content with these tools that you venture to wonder what more a skilled Photoshop craftsman could possibly need.

Well, as it so happens, plenty. Every one of the tools I just mentioned is only moderately suited to the task of making selections in images. The lasso tools let you create free-form selections, but none of the tools — not even the magnetic lasso — can account for differences in focus levels. The magic wand selects areas of color, but it usually results in ragged edges and leaves important colors behind. The pen tool is extremely precise, but it results in mechanical outlines that may appear incongruous with the natural imagery they contain.

That's why you need masks. Blessed with all the benefits of the other selection tools, masks let you create free-form selections, select areas of color, and generate amazingly precise selections. However, masks also address all the deficiencies associated with those selection tools. They can account for different levels of focus, they give you absolute control over the look of the edges, and they create selections every bit as natural as the image itself.

In fact, a mask *is* the image itself. Masks use pixels to select pixels. Masks are your way to make Photoshop see what you see using the data inherent in the photograph. Masks enable you to devote every one of Photoshop's powerful capabilities to the task of creating a selection outline. Masks are, without a doubt, the most accurate selection mechanism available in Photoshop.

If you're not entirely clear about what I mean by the term *mask*, I'll tell you: A mask is a selection outline expressed as a grayscale image.

+ Selected areas appear white.

+ Deselected areas appear black.

+ Partially selected parts of the image appear in gray. Feathered edges are also expressed in shades of gray, from light gray near the selected area to dark gray near the deselected area.

Figure 4-1 shows a selection outline and its equivalent mask. The left example shows an elliptical selection outline that I feathered by choosing Select ⇨ Feather. To the right is the same selection expressed as a mask. The selected area is white and is said to be *unmasked*; the deselected area is black, or *masked*. Note that while you can't see the feathering effect in the selection outline — marching ants can't accurately express softened edges — in the equivalent mask it's completely visible.

Marching ants-style selection outline

Mask viewed by itself

Figure 4-1: A feathered selection outline (left) and its equivalent mask (right).

When you look at the mask at the right of Figure 4-1, you may wonder where the heck the image went. One of the wonderful things about masks is that you can view them independently of an image, as in Figure 4-1, or with an image, as in Figure 4-2. In the second figure, the mask is expressed as a color overlay. By default, the color of the overlay is a translucent red, like a sheet of rubylith film used in printing. Areas covered with the rubylith are masked (deselected); areas that appear normal — without any red tint — are unmasked (selected). When you return to the standard marching ants mode, any changes you make to your image affect only the unmasked areas.

Now that you know roughly what masks are (the definition becomes progressively clearer throughout this chapter), the question remains: What good are they? Because a mask is essentially an independent grayscale image, you can edit the mask using paint and edit tools, filters, color correction options, and almost every other Photoshop function. You can even use the selection tools, including the marquee, lasso, and others. With all these features at your disposal, you can't help but create a more accurate selection outline in a shorter amount of time.

Working in Quick Mask Mode

As I mentioned at the outset of this chapter, I'm guessing that you've experimented with Photoshop's selection tools, using the lasso, magic wand, or what have you to create a *selection mask*. Although selection masks give you an idea of what masks are all about, in truth, they only scrape the surface. The rest of this chapter revolves around using masks to define complex selection outlines.

Mask & image viewed together

Figure 4-2: Here is the mask from Figure 4-1, shown as it appears when viewed along with the image.

The most straightforward environment for creating a mask is the *quick mask mode*. In the quick mask mode, a selection is expressed as a rubylith overlay. All deselected areas appear coated with red, and selected areas appear without red coating. You can then edit the mask as desired and exit quick mask mode to return to the standard selection outline. The quick mask mode is — as its name implies — expeditious and convenient, with none of the trappings or permanence of more conventional masks. It's kind of like a fast food restaurant — you use it when you aren't overly concerned about quality and you want to get in and out in a hurry.

How the quick mask mode works

Typically, you'll at least want to rough out a selection with the standard selection tools before entering the quick mask mode. That's what I've done in the left example of Figure 4-3; in this case I used the pen tool to create an outline to select the sculpted head, leaving holes in my selection for the eyes. Then I inverted the selection by choosing Select ➪ Inverse (that's Ctrl+Shift+I under Windows or ⌘-Shift-I on the Mac) so that the eyes and wild painted hair were selected, and the face was not. After your selection mask is roughed in, you can then concentrate on refining and modifying your selection inside the quick mask, rather than having to create the selection from scratch. (Naturally, this is only a rule of thumb. I violate the rule several times throughout this chapter, but only because the quick mask mode and I are such tight friends.)

To enter the quick mask mode, click the quick mask mode icon in the toolbox, as I've done in the right example of Figure 4-3. Or press Q. You can see the red overlay over the head, masking it off. The head receives the mask because it is not selected. The hair and the eyes look the same because those areas are selected and, therefore, not masked.

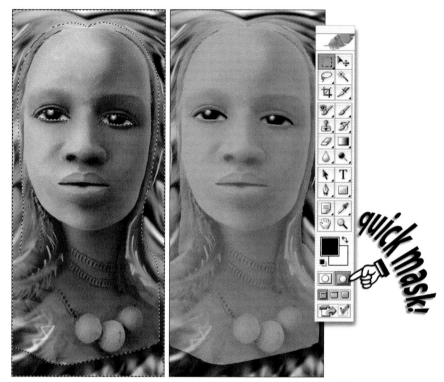

Figure 4-3: You can see the marching ants-style selection in the left image, indicating that the painted hair and eyes are selected. Clicking the quick mask mode icon (right) instructs Photoshop to express the selection temporarily as a rubylith overlay.

Notice that the selection outline disappears when you enter the quick mask mode. This happens because the outline temporarily ceases to exist. Any operations you apply affect the mask itself and leave the underlying image untouched. When you click the marching ants mode icon (to the left of the quick mask mode icon) or press Q, Photoshop converts the mask back into a selection outline and again enables you to edit the image.

If you click the quick mask mode icon and nothing changes on screen, your computer isn't broken; you simply didn't select anything before you entered quick mask mode. When nothing is selected, Photoshop makes the whole image open for editing. In other words, everything's selected. (Only a smattering of commands under the Edit, Layer, and Select menus require something to be selected before they work.) If everything is selected, the mask is white; therefore, the quick mask overlay is transparent and you don't see any difference on screen. This is another reason why it's better to select something before you enter the quick mask mode — you get an immediate sense you're accomplishing something.

In quick mask mode, you can edit the mask in the following ways:

✦ **Subtracting from a selection:** Paint with black to add red coating and, thus, deselect areas of the image. You can selectively protect portions of your image by merely painting over them.

✦ **Adding to a selection:** Paint with white to remove red coating and, thus, add to the selection outline, as demonstrated in the left half of Figure 4-4. Assuming the background color is set to white, you can use the eraser tool to whittle away at the masked area. Or you can swap the foreground and background colors so that you can paint in white with the brush tool.

Figure 4-4: I painted in white using a soft-edged brush to enlarge the selected area (left). After switching out of quick mask mode, I was then able to use the brush and smudge tools to draw hair from the top of the forehead (right).

✦ **Adding feathered selections:** If you paint with a shade of gray, you add feathered selections. You also can feather an outline by painting with black or white combined with a soft brush shape, as shown in the left image in Figure 4-4. Here, I'm painting in white with a soft-edged brush, adding a nice feathered edge to the top of the selection. Then after re-entering the world of the marching ants, a little painting and smudging creates the image on the right side of the figure.

✦ **Cloning selection outlines:** If you have a selection outline that you want to repeat in several locations throughout the image, the quick mask is your friend. Select the transparent area with one of the standard selection tools, press and hold Ctrl+Alt (⌘-Option on the Mac), and drag it to a new location in the image, as shown in Figure 4-5. Although I use the rectangular marquee tool in the figure, the magic wand tool also works well for this purpose. To select an antialiased selection outline with the wand tool, set the Tolerance value to about 10 and be sure the Anti-aliased check box is active. Then click inside the selection. It's that easy.

Figure 4-5: To clone the eye sockets selection, I marquee-dragged around it. Then I pressed Ctrl+Alt (⌘-Option on the Mac) and dragged it first to the top, and then to the bottom (left). This enabled me to switch out of quick mask mode and paint details into the new eye sockets (right).

✦ **Transforming selection outlines:** You can scale or rotate a selection independently of the image, just as you can with the Transform Selection command. Enter the quick mask mode, select the mask using one of the standard selection tools, and choose Edit ⇨ Free Transform or press Ctrl+T (⌘-T on the Mac). See Chapter 5 for more information on Free Transform and related commands.

These are only a few of the unique effects you can achieve by editing a selection in the quick mask mode. Others involve tools and capabilities I haven't yet discussed, such as filters and color corrections. Nonetheless, you'll get a sense of how a few of these more advanced techniques work later in this chapter.

After you finish editing your selection outlines, click the marching ants mode icon (to the left of the quick mask mode icon) or press Q again to return to the marching ants mode. Your selection outlines again appear flanked by marching ants, and all tools and commands return to their normal image-editing functions. Figure 4-6 shows the results of switching to the marching ants mode and pressing Ctrl+J (⌘-J on the Mac) to float the selection to a new layer. I then filled the background layer with white and threw in a drop shadow for good measure.

As demonstrated in the left example of Figure 4-6, the quick mask mode offers a splendid environment for feathering one selection outline, while leaving another hard-edged or antialiased. Granted, because most selection tools offer built-in feathering options, you can accomplish this task without resorting to the quick mask mode. But the quick mask mode enables you to change feathering selectively after drawing selection outlines, something you can't accomplish with Select ⇨ Feather. The quick mask mode also enables you to see exactly what you're doing. Kind of makes those marching ants look piddly and insignificant, huh?

Figure 4-6: The results of creating new layers from the selected areas in the right examples of Figures 4-4 (left) and 4-5 (right). This allows us to see the quick mask selections independently of other portions of the image.

Changing the red coating

By default, the protected region of an image appears in translucent red in the quick mask mode, but if your image contains a lot of red, the mask can be difficult to see. Luckily, you can change it to any color and any degree of opacity that you like. To do so, double-click the quick mask icon in the toolbox (or double-click the *Quick Mask* channel in the Channels palette) to display the dialog box shown in Figure 4-7.

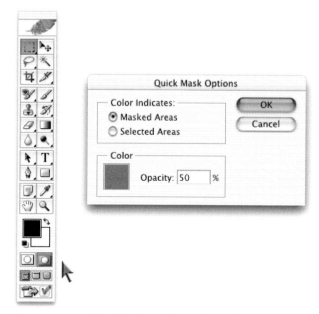

Figure 4-7: Double-click the quick mask mode icon in the toolbox to access the Quick Mask Options dialog box. You then can change the color and opacity of the protected or selected areas when viewed in the quick mask mode.

✦ **Color Indicates:** Choose Selected Areas to reverse the color coating so that the translucent red coating covers selected areas, and deselected areas appear normally. Choose Masked Areas (the default setting) to cover deselected areas in color.

You can reverse the color coating without ever entering the Quick Mask Options dialog box. Simply Alt-click (Win) or Option-click (Mac) the quick mask icon in the toolbox to toggle between coating the masked or selected portions of the image. The icon itself changes to reflect your choice.

✦ **Color:** Click the Color icon to display the Color Picker dialog box and select a different color coating. You can lift a color with the eyedropper after the Color Picker dialog box comes up; just keep in mind that you probably want to use a color that isn't in the image so that you can better see the mask.

✦ **Opacity:** Enter a value to change the opacity of the translucent color that coats the image. A value of 100 percent naturally makes the coating absolutely opaque.

Change the color coating to achieve the most acceptable balance between being able to view and edit your selection and being able to view your image. For example, the default red coating shows up poorly in print, so I raised the Opacity value to 65 percent before shooting the screens featured in Figures 4-3 through 4-5.

Gradations as masks

If you think that the Feather command is a hot tool for creating softened selection outlines, wait until you get a load of gradations in the quick mask mode. There's no better way to create fading effects than by selecting an image with the gradient tool.

Fading an image

Just to make this more difficult for me to explain, I'm going to show you how to create a gradient mask by using an image of an actual mask, shown in Figure 4-8. This mask is no doubt some primitive sacred relic from a bygone civilization, but that won't stop me from turning it into a towering monolith like you might find on Easter Island. Here we go:

Figure 4-8: In this section, I'll use a linear gradient in the quick mask mode to make the mask (left) rise from the middle of the field (right).

Switch to the quick mask mode by pressing Q. Then use the gradient tool (which you can get by pressing the G key) to draw a linear gradation from black to white. The white portion of the gradation represents the area you want to select. I wanted to select the top portion of the mask, so I drew the gradation from just below the lower lip to the bottom of the nose, as shown in the first example in Figure 4-9. Because the gradient line is a little hard to see, I've added an arrow to show the direction of the drag.

Banding can be a problem when you use a gradation as a mask. To eliminate the banding effect, therefore, apply Filter ⇨ Noise ⇨ Add Noise at a low setting one or more times. To create the right example in Figure 4-9, I applied the Add Noise filter using an Amount value of 10 percent and the Uniform distribution setting.

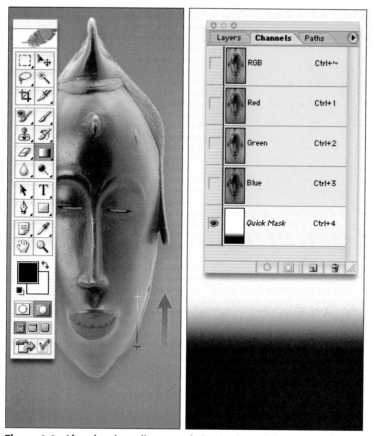

Figure 4-9: After drawing a linear gradation in the quick mask mode over the bottom of the image (left), I hid the image and applied the Add Noise filter with an Amount of 10 (right).

In the right example in Figure 4-9, I hid the image so that only the gradient mask is visible. As the figure shows, the Channels palette lists the *Quick Mask* item in italics. This is because Photoshop regards the quick mask as a temporary channel. You can hide the image and view the gradient mask in black and white by clicking the eyeball in front of the color composite view, in this case RGB. Or just press the tilde key (~) to hide the image. Press tilde again to view gradient mask and image together.

To apply the gradation as a selection, I returned to the marching ants mode by again pressing Q. I then Ctrl-dragged (⌘-dragged on the Mac) the selected portion of the mask and dropped it into the open field, as seen in the left half of Figure 4-10. Not content with this level of desecration, I pressed Ctrl+T (⌘-T) to enter the free transform mode. Then I scaled and distorted the image by Ctrl-dragging (⌘-dragging) the corner handles (see Chapter 5). I also used the dodge and burn tools to enhance the highlights and shadows. The end result appears on the right side of Figure 4-10.

Figure 4-10: The result of selecting the top portion of the mask using a gradient mask and then Ctrl-dragging (⌘-dragging on the Mac) and dropping the selection into the field (left). Throw in a little more tweaking, and you've got your own personal Easter Island (right), minus the eggs and bunnies, of course.

Applying special effects gradually

You also can use gradations in the quick mask mode to fade the outcomes of filters and other automated special effects. For example, I wanted to apply a filter around the edges of the image that appears in Figure 4-11. I began by deselecting everything in the image by pressing Ctrl+D (⌘-D on the Mac) and switching to the quick mask mode. Then I selected the gradient tool, selected the linear gradient style icon in the Options bar, and selected the Foreground to Transparent gradient from the Gradient drop-down palette. I also selected the Transparency check box in the Options bar.

I pressed D to make the foreground color black. Then I dragged with the gradient tool from each of the four corners of the image inward to create a series of short gradations that trace around the focal point of the image, as shown in Figure 4-12. (As you can see, I've hidden the image so that you see the mask in black and white.) Because I've selected the Foreground to Transparent option, Photoshop adds each gradation to the previous gradation.

Figure 4-11: This time around, my intention is to surround the foreground image with a gradual filtering effect.

To jumble the pixels in the mask, I applied Filter ⇨ Noise ⇨ Add Noise with an Amount value of 10 percent. You see the effect in Figure 4-12.

The only problem is that I want to select the outside of the image, not the inside. So I need the edges to appear white and the inside to appear black, the opposite of what you see in Figure 4-12. No problem. All I do is press Ctrl+I (⌘-I on the Mac) to invert the image. Inverting inside the quick mask mode produces the same effect as applying Select ⇨ Inverse to a selection.

Finally, I switched back to the marching ants mode by again pressing Q. Then I applied Filter ⇨ Render ⇨ Clouds to get the atmospheric effect you see in Figure 4-13.

Notice the corners in the mask in Figure 4-12? These corners are soft and rounded, but you can achieve all kinds of corner effects with the gradient tool. For harsher corners, select the Foreground to Background gradient and select Lighten from the Mode pop-up menu in the Options bar. For some *really* unusual corner treatments, try out the Difference and Exclusion brush modes. Wild stuff.

Creating gradient arrows

The following steps explain how to add cool fading arrows to any image, similar to the one shown back in Figure 4-9. Photoshop not only makes it easy to use gradients for fading effects, it's also a breeze to create dramatic drop shadows for image elements, as demonstrated in Figures 4-14 and 4-15. The steps involve a gradient layer mask, the Free Transform command, the line tool, and a little old-fashioned layer opacity.

Figure 4-12: Inside the quick mask mode, I dragged from each of the four corners with the gradient tool (as indicated by the green arrows) and applied the Add Noise filter set to 10 percent.

Figure 4-13: After switching back to the marching ants mode, I chose Filter ⇨ Render ⇨ Clouds to create the smoky effect shown here. Now that's what I call CD burning.

STEPS: Creating Fading Arrows with Drop Shadows

1. **Draw an arrow with the line tool, creating a shape layer.** First, select the line tool and make sure the Shape Layers button is selected in the Options bar. Click on the Geometry Options and give your line an arrowhead at the end. No doubt a bit of trial and error will be necessary to get the right settings. (To create the arrow in the top example of Figure 4-14, I used a Weight of 25, both a Width and Length of 400 percent, and a Concavity setting of 25 percent.) Set the foreground color to white and then drag to draw your arrow in the desired direction.

For the straight dope on using the shape tools, check out Chapter 7.

Figure 4-14: Use the line tool with appropriate arrowhead settings to draw an arrow (top). To create the perspective distortion effect, select the points on the left side of the arrow and rotate them using Free Transform. Add a drop shadow layer style for extra dimension (bottom).

2. **Use rotation to add a perspective effect to the arrow.** I pressed A and then Shift+A to switch to the white arrow tool. Then I selected the three points on the left side of the arrow. Next I chose Edit ➪ Free Transform Points and moved the origin point from the center to the upper-right corner by adjusting the reference point location in the Options bar. Then I dragged outside the arrow to rotate the selected points.

3. **Apply a drop shadow.** I clicked the layer style icon at the bottom of the Layers palette and selected Drop Shadow. I accepted the default settings, but you can tweak as you wish. The bottom image in Figure 4-14 shows the result.

4. **Create a layer mask.** Choose Layer ➪ Add Layer Mask ➪ Reveal All. Or just click the Add a Mask icon at the bottom of the Layers palette (as I explain in Chapter 5).

5. **Draw a gradient mask.** Select the gradient tool and make sure the Black to White gradient is selected in the Options bar. Then draw a gradient on the arrow, starting at the end of the arrow and extending to around the middle, as shown in the top example of Figure 4-15.

6. **Lower the overall opacity of the arrow.** Now I've got a nice fade to transparency within the arrow, but it seems that the top of the arrow is obscuring too much of the image. No problem; I just reduce the Opacity of the arrow layer in the Layers palette to 70 percent. The bottom image in Figure 4-15 shows the result. Isn't it neat how you can combine the sharp edges of the vector shape tools with the soft edges of the layer mask? Well, *I* think so.

Figure 4-15: Drag from the end of the arrow upward to create a gradient layer mask that makes the arrow seem to fade into view (top). Then lower the layer's Opacity value. The result makes it much easier to keep your eye on the ball (bottom).

Generating Masks Automatically

In addition to the quick mask mode and selection masking, Photoshop offers several tools that automate the masking process — or at least, automate *some* parts of the process. You still need to provide some input to tell the program exactly what you're trying to mask. Three of these tools — the magic eraser, background eraser, and Extract command — employ basic masking theory, but they do it in such a way as to hide the unpleasant details from you, the user. And rather than selecting pixels, they delete them. I give these three tools an in-depth workout in the standard edition of the *Photoshop CS Bible*. But this full-color version of the *Bible* is the perfect place to demonstrate Photoshop's other automatic masker, the Color Range command. Color Range generates selection outlines based on the colors inside the image. And if that sounds like the magic wand, then prepare yourself for something much, much better.

Using the Color Range command

Located under the Select menu, the Color Range command enables you to generate selections based on color ranges. Use the familiar eyedropper cursor to specify colors that should be considered for selection and colors that you want to rule out. In truth, the Color Range command is a lot like the magic wand tool, except that it enables you to select colors with more precision and to change the tolerance of the selection on the fly.

When you choose Select ➪ Color Range, Photoshop displays the Color Range dialog box shown in Figure 4-16. Like the magic wand with the Contiguous option turned off, Color Range selects areas of related color all across the image, whether or not the colors are immediate neighbors. Click in the image window to select and deselect colors, as you do with the wand. But rather than adjusting a Tolerance value before you use the tool, you adjust a Fuzziness option any old time you like. Photoshop dynamically updates the selection according to the new value. Think of Color Range as the magic wand on steroids.

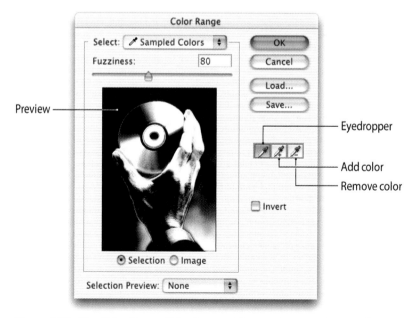

Figure 4-16: The Color Range dialog box enables you to generate a mask by dragging with the eyedropper tool and adjusting the Fuzziness option.

So why didn't the folks at Adobe merely enhance the functionality of the magic wand instead of adding this strange command? Well, the Color Range dialog box offers a preview of the mask—something a tool can't do—which is pretty essential for gauging the accuracy of your selection. And the magic wand gets points for convenience, if nothing else. If Adobe were to combine the two functions, you would lose functionality.

When you move your cursor outside the Color Range dialog box, it changes to an eyedropper. Click to specify the color on which you want to base the selection—I call this the base color— as if you were using the magic wand. Or click inside the preview, labeled in Figure 4-16. In either case, the preview updates to show the resulting mask.

You can also do the following:

✦ **Add colors to the selection:** To add base colors to the selection, select the add color tool inside the Color Range dialog box and click inside the image window or preview. You can access the tool while the standard eyedropper is selected by Shift-clicking (just as you Shift-click with the magic wand to add colors to a selection). You can even Shift-drag with the eyedropper to add multiple colors in a single pass, something you can't do with the magic wand.

✦ **Remove colors from the selection:** To remove base colors from the selection, click with the remove color tool or Alt-click (Option-click on the Mac) with the eyedropper. You can also drag or Alt-drag (Option-drag on the Mac) to remove many colors at a time.

If adding or removing a color sends your selection careening in the wrong direction, press Ctrl+Z (⌘-Z on the Mac). Yes, the Undo command works inside the Color Range dialog box as well as out of it.

✦ **Adjust the Fuzziness value:** This option resembles the magic wand's Tolerance value because it determines the range of colors to be selected beyond the ones on which you click. Raise the Fuzziness value to expand the selected area; lower the value to contract the selection. A value of 0 selects the clicked color only. Unlike changes to Tolerance, however, changing the Fuzziness value adjusts the selection on the fly; no repeat click-ing is required, as it is with the wand tool.

Fuzziness and Tolerance also differ in the kind of selection outlines they generate. Tolerance entirely selects all colors within the specified range and adds antialiased edges. If the selection were a mask, most of it would be white with a few gray pixels around the perimeter. By contrast, Fuzziness entirely selects only the colors on which you click and Shift-click, and it partially selects the other colors in the range. That's why most of the mask is expressed in shades of gray. The light grays in the mask repre-sent the most similar colors; the dark grays represent the least similar pixels that still fall within the Fuzziness range. The result is a tapering, gradual selection, much more likely to produce natural results.

✦ **Reverse the selection:** Select the Invert check box to reverse the selection, changing black to white and white to black. As when using the magic wand, it may be easier to isolate the area you don't want to select than the area you do want to select. When you encounter such a situation, select Invert.

✦ **Toggle the preview area:** Use the two radio buttons below the preview area to control the preview's contents. If you select the first option, Selection, you see the mask that will be generated when you press Enter or Return. If you select Image, the preview shows the image.

Press and hold Ctrl (Win) or ⌘ (Mac) to toggle between the two previews. My advice is to leave the option set to Selection and press Ctrl or ⌘ when you want to view the image.

✦ **Control the contents of the image window:** The Selection Preview pop-up menu at the bottom of the dialog box enables you to change what you see in the image window. Leave the option set to None—the default setting—to view the image normally in the image window. Select Grayscale to see the mask on its own. Select Quick Mask to see the mask and image together. Select Black Matte or White Matte to see what the selection would look like against a black or white background.

Although they may sound weird, the Matte options enable you to get an accurate picture of how the selected image will mesh with a different background. Figure 4-17 shows an original image at the top left with the grayscale mask on the right. The mask calls for the shadows in the disc, fingers, and wrist to be selected, with the highlights deselected. The two Matte views help you see how this particular selection looks against two backgrounds as different as night and day. Use the Fuzziness option in combination with Black Matte or White Matte to come up with a softness setting that will ensure a smooth transition.

Selection Preview:

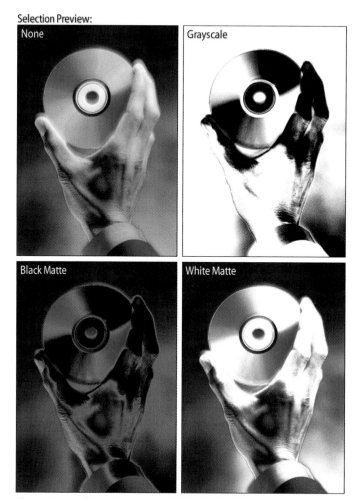

Figure 4-17: The options in the Selection Preview pop-up menu change the way the Color Range command previews the selection in the image window.

✦ **Select by predefined colors:** Choose an option from the Select pop-up menu at the top of the dialog box to specify the means of selecting a base color. If you choose any option besides Sampled Colors, the Fuzziness option and eyedropper tools become dimmed to show they are no longer operable. Instead, Photoshop selects colors based on their relationship to a predefined color. For example, if you select Red, the program entirely selects red and partially selects other colors based on the amount of red they contain. Colors composed exclusively of blue and green are not selected.

The most useful option in this pop-up menu is Out of Gamut, which selects all the colors in an RGB or Lab image that fall outside the CMYK color space. You can use this option to select and modify the out-of-gamut colors before converting an image to CMYK.

✦ **Load and save settings:** Click the Save button to save the current settings to disk. Click Load to open a saved settings file. To use a settings file on a PC, it must end in the extension *.axt*.

After you define the mask to your satisfaction, click OK or press Enter or Return to generate the selection outline. Although the Color Range command is more flexible than the magic wand, you can no more expect it to generate perfect selections than any other automated tool. After Photoshop draws the selection outline, therefore, you'll probably want to switch to quick mask mode and paint and edit the mask to taste.

If you learn nothing else about the Color Range dialog box, at least learn to use the Fuzziness option and the eyedropper tools. Basically, you can approach these options in two ways. If you want to create a diffused selection with gradual edges, set the Fuzziness option to a high value — 60 or more — and click and Shift-click two or three times with the eyedropper. To create a more precise selection, enter a Fuzziness of 40 or lower and Shift-drag and Alt-drag (Option-drag on the Mac) with the eyedropper until you get the exact colors you want.

Figure 4-18 shows some sample results. To create the left images, I clicked once with the eyedropper tool in the disc and set the Fuzziness value to 40. To create the right images, I raised the Fuzziness value to 180; then I clicked, Shift-clicked, and Alt-clicked with the eyedropper to lift exactly the colors I wanted. The top examples show the effects of filling the selections with white. In the two bottom examples, I copied the selections and pasted them against an identical cloud background. In all four cases, the higher Fuzziness value yields more generalized and softer results; the lower value produces a more exact but harsher selection.

A few helpful Color Range hints

You can limit the portion of an image that Select ➪ Color Range affects by selecting part of the image before choosing the command. When a selection exists, the Color Range command masks only those pixels that fall inside it. Even the preview area reflects your selection.

You also can add or subtract from an existing selection using the Color Range command. Press Shift when choosing Select ➪ Color Range to add to a selection. Press Alt (Win) or Option (Mac) when choosing Color Range to subtract from a selection.

If you get hopelessly lost when creating your selection and you can't figure out what to select and what to deselect, click with the eyedropper tool to start over. This clears all the colors from the selection except the one you click. Or you can press Alt (Option on the Mac) to change the Cancel button to a Reset button, which returns the settings inside the dialog box to those in force when you first chose Select ➪ Color Range.

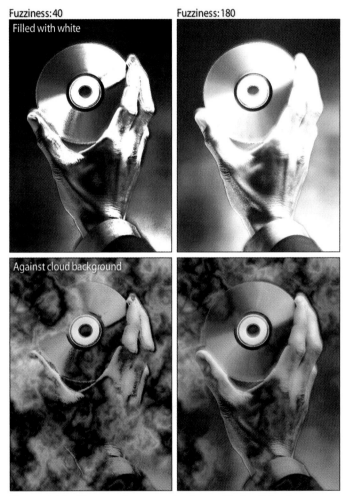

Fuzziness: 40   Fuzziness: 180
Filled with white

Against cloud background

Figure 4-18: After creating two selections with the Color Range command — one with a low Fuzziness value (left) and one with a high one (right) — I alternately filled the selections with white (top) and pasted them against a different background (bottom).

Creating an Independent Mask Channel

The problem with masks generated via the quick mask mode and Color Range command is that they're here one day and gone the next. Photoshop is no more prepared to remember them than it is a lasso or wand selection.

Most of the time, that's okay. You'll only use the selection once, so there's no reason to sweat it. But what if the selection takes you a long time to create? What if, after a quarter hour of Shift-clicking here and Alt-dragging there, adding a few strokes in the quick mask mode, and getting the selection outline exactly right, your boss calls a sudden meeting or the dinner bell rings? You can't just drop everything; you're in the middle of a selection. But nor can you convey your predicament to non-Photoshop users because they'll have no idea what you're talking about and no sympathy for your plight. Sure, you could just leave your computer running...but what if there's a sudden power outage? What if someone else needs to use the computer? Other people have important stuff to do too, you know. Be considerate.

The simplest solution is to back up your selection, save your file, and move on to the next phase of your life. In fact, anytime that you spend 15 minutes or more on a selection, you should save it. After all, you never know when all heck is going to break loose, and 15 minutes is just too big a chunk of your life to waste. (The average person racks up a mere 2.5 million quarter hours, so use them wisely!) You wouldn't let 15 minutes of image-editing go by without saving, and the rules don't change just because you're working on a selection.

Saving a selection outline to a mask channel

The following steps describe how to back up a selection to an independent mask channel, which is any channel above and beyond those required to represent a grayscale or color image. Mask channels are saved along with the image itself, making them a safe and sturdy solution.

STEPS: Transferring a Selection to an Independent Channel

1. **Convert the selection to a mask channel.** One way to do this is to choose Select ➪ Save Selection or right-click (Control-click on the Mac) in the image window and choose Save Selection from the pop-up menu, which saves the selection as a mask. The dialog box shown in Figure 4-19 appears, asking you where you want to put the mask. In most cases, you'll want to save the mask to a separate channel inside the current image. To do so, make sure that the name of the current image appears in the Document pop-up menu. Then select New from the Channel pop-up menu, enter any name for the channel that you like, and press Enter or Return.

   If you have an old channel you want to replace, select the channel's name from the Channel pop-up menu. The radio buttons at the bottom of the dialog box become available, permitting you to add the mask to the channel, subtract it, or intersect it. These radio buttons work like the equivalent options that appear when you make a path into a selection outline (as discussed in the previous chapter), but they blend the masks together, instead. The result is the same as if you were adding, subtracting, or intersecting selection outlines, except it's expressed as a mask.

   Alternatively, you can save the mask to a new multichannel document all its own. To do this, choose New from the Document pop-up menu and press Enter or Return.

    Man, what a lot of options! If you only want to save the selection to a new channel and be done with it, you needn't bother with the Save Selection command or dialog box. Just click the make channel icon at the bottom of the Channels palette (labeled in Figure 4-19). Photoshop automatically creates a new channel, converts the selection to a mask, and places the mask in the channel.

   Regardless of which of these many methods you choose, your selection outline remains intact.

2. **View the mask in the Channels palette.** To do so, click the appropriate channel name in the Channels palette — automatically named *Alpha 1* unless you assigned a name of your own. In Figure 4-19, I replaced the contents of a channel called Existing Mask, so this is where my mask now resides.

   This step isn't the least bit mandatory. It just lets you see your mask and generally familiarize yourself with how masks look. Remember, white represents selection, black is deselected, and gray is partial selection.

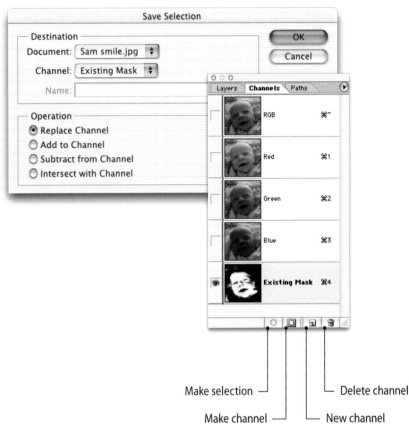

Make selection — └ Delete channel

Make channel — └ New channel

Figure 4-19: The Save Selection dialog box enables you to convert your selection outline to a mask and save it to a new or existing channel.

If you didn't name your mask in Step 1 and you want to name it now, double-click the Alpha 1 name in the Channels palette and enter a new name.

3. **Return to the standard image-editing mode by clicking the first channel name in the Channels palette.** Better yet, press Ctrl+1 (⌘-1 on the Mac) if you're editing a grayscale image or Ctrl+tilde (⌘-tilde on the Mac) if the image is in color.

4. **Save the image to disk to store the selection permanently as part of the file.** A handful of formats — PICT, Pixar, PNG, TIFF, Targa, PDF, and native Photoshop — accommodate RGB images with an extra mask channel. But only TIFF, PDF, and the native Photoshop format can handle more than four channels, all saving up to 56 channels in all. I generally use the TIFF format with LZW compression when saving images with masks. Because TIFF supports layers, you aren't restricted to the Photoshop format for multilayered images with masks.

Both the native Photoshop format and TIFF can compress masks so that they take up substantially less room on disk. The Photoshop format does this automatically, and you can save a TIFF image using LZW compression without fear. In both cases, this run-line compression is entirely safe. It does not change a single pixel in the image; it merely writes the code in a more efficient manner.

If you performed the steps in the "Creating gradient arrows" section earlier in this chapter, you know that you can also save a quick mask to its own channel for later use. But in case you missed those steps, or you're saving them for a special occasion, here's how it works. When you enter the quick mask mode, the Channels palette displays an item called *Quick Mask*. The italic letters show the channel is temporary and will not be saved with the image. (To clone it to a permanent channel, drag the *Quick Mask* item onto the page icon at the bottom of the Channels palette.) Now save the image to the TIFF or Photoshop format, and you're backed up.

Converting a mask to a selection

To retrieve your selection later, choose Select ➪ Load Selection. A dialog box nearly identical to the one shown in Figure 4-19 appears except for the addition of an Invert check box. Select the document and channel that contain the mask you want to use. You can add it to a current selection, subtract it, or intersect it. Select the Invert option if you want to reverse the selected and deselected portions of the mask.

Want to avoid the Load Selection command? Ctrl-click (Win) or ⌘-click (Mac) the channel name in the Channels palette that contains the mask you want to use. For example, if I Ctrl-clicked the Existing Mask item in Figure 4-19, Photoshop would load the equivalent selection outline into the image window.

But wait, there's more:

✦ You can press Ctrl+Alt (⌘-Option on the Mac) plus the channel number to convert the channel to a selection. For example, Ctrl+Alt+4 would convert the Existing Mask channel shown in Figure 4-19.

✦ You can also select the channel and click the far-left mask selection icon at the bottom of the Channels palette. But for my money, this takes too much effort.

✦ To add a mask to the current selection outline, Ctrl+Shift-click (⌘-Shift-click on the Mac) the channel name in the Channels palette.

✦ Ctrl+Alt-click (⌘-Option-click on the Mac) a channel name to subtract the mask from the selection.

✦ And Ctrl+Shift+Alt-click (⌘-Shift-Option-click on the Mac) to find the intersection.

You can convert color channels to selections as well as mask channels. For example, if you want to select the black pixels in a piece of scanned line art in grayscale mode, Ctrl-click (Win) or ⌘-click (Mac) the first item in the Channels palette. This selects the white pixels; press Ctrl+Shift+I (⌘-Shift-I on the Mac) or choose Select ➪ Inverse to reverse the selection to the black pixels.

Viewing mask and image

Photoshop lets you view any mask channel along with an image, just as you can view mask and image together in the quick mask mode. To do this, click in the first column of the Channels palette to toggle the display of the eyeball icon. An eyeball in front of a channel name indicates you can see that channel. If you are currently viewing the full-color image, for example, click in front of the mask channel name to view the mask as a translucent color coating, again as in the quick mask mode. Or if the contents of the mask channel appear by themselves on screen, click in front of the composite name (RGB, CMYK, or LAB) to display the image as well.

When the mask is active, you can likewise toggle the display of the image by pressing the tilde (~) key. Few folks know about this shortcut, but it's a good one to assign to memory. It works whether the Channels palette is open or not, and it permits you to focus on the mask without moving your mouse all over the screen.

Using a mask channel is different from using the quick mask mode in that you can edit either the image or the mask channel when viewing the two together. You can even edit two or more masks at once. To specify which channel you want to edit, click the channel name in the palette. To edit two channels at once, click one and Shift-click another. All active channel names appear highlighted.

You can change the color and opacity of each mask independently of other mask channels and the quick mask mode. Double-click the mask channel thumbnail or choose the Channel Options command from the Channels palette menu. (This command is dimmed when editing a standard color channel, such as Red, Green, Blue, Cyan, Magenta, Yellow, or Black.) A dialog box similar to the one shown back in Figure 4-7 appears, but this one contains a Name option box so you can change the name of the mask channel. You can then edit the color overlay as described in the "Changing the red coating" section earlier in this chapter.

If you ever need to edit a selection outline inside the mask channel using paint and edit tools, click the quick mask mode icon in the toolbox. It may sound a little like a play within a play, but you can access the quick mask mode even when working within a mask channel. Make sure the mask channel color is different from the quick mask color, so you can tell what's happening.

Building a Mask from an Image

So far, everything I've discussed in this chapter has been pretty straightforward. Now, seeing as how this is the *Professional Edition* and everything, it's time to see how the professionals do things. This final section explains every step required to create a mask for a complex image. Here's how to select the image you never thought you could select, complete with wispy little details such as leaves, stray pieces of string, very small rocks, and hair.

Take a gander at Figure 4-20 and see what I mean. This little cutie presents us with three big challenges: the stray bits of hair roaming about her head and shoulders, the veritable rainbow of colors in her dress, and the wide range of brightness levels in the background. Can you imagine selecting any one of them with the magnetic lasso or magic wand? No way. As demonstrated in Figure 4-20, these tools lack sufficient accuracy to do any good. The dress and background share too many colors for the background eraser to work. Meanwhile, you'd be fit for an asylum by the time you finished selecting the hairs with the pen tools, and the edges aren't definite enough for Select ⇨ Color Range to latch onto.

So, what's the solution? Manual masking. Although masking styles vary as widely as artistic styles, a few tried-and-true formulas can work for just about everyone. First, you peruse the channels in an image to find the channel that lends itself best to a mask. You're looking for high degrees of contrast, especially around the edges. Next, you copy the channel and boost the level of contrast using Image ⇨ Adjustments ⇨ Levels. (Some folks prefer Image ⇨ Adjustments ⇨ Curves, but the Levels command is more straightforward.) Then you paint or edit the mask until you get it just the way you want it.

Figure 4-20: She may look like a sweetheart, but this kid's elaborate details and indistinct transitions are too much for Photoshop's selection and extraction tools. This is a job for manual masking.

The only way to get a feel for masking is to try it out for yourself. The following steps explain exactly how I masked this girl and pasted her against a different background. The final result is so realistic, you'd think she was born there.

STEPS: Masking a Monstrously Complicated Image

1. **Browse the color channels.** Press Ctrl+1 (⌘-1 on the Mac) to see the red channel, Ctrl+2 (⌘-2) for green, and Ctrl+3 (⌘-3) for blue. Note that this assumes you're working inside an RGB image. You can also peruse CMYK and Lab images. If you're editing a grayscale image, you have only one channel, and that's Black, Jack.

   Figure 4-21 shows the three channels in my RGB image. Of the three, the green channel offers the most contrast between the hair, the dress, and the background. Hey, it ain't much, but it's better than nothing.

2. **Clone the channel.** Drag the channel onto the little page icon at the bottom of the Channels palette to create a duplicate of the channel. Naturally, I clone the green channel. Now you can work on the channel without harming the image itself.

3. **Choose Filter ⇨ Other ⇨ High Pass.** The next thing you want to do is to force Photoshop to bring out the edges in the image so you don't have to hunt for them manually. And when you think edges, think filters. All of Photoshop's edge-detection prowess is packed into the Filter menu. Several edge-detection filters are available to you — Unsharp Mask, Find Edges, and many others that I discuss in Chapters 8 and 9. But the best filter for finding edges inside a mask is Filter ⇨ Other ⇨ High Pass.

   High Pass selectively turns an image gray. High Pass may sound strange, but it's quite useful. The filter turns the non-edges completely gray while leaving the edges mostly intact, thus dividing edges and non-edges into different brightness camps, based on the Radius value in the High Pass dialog box. Unlike in most filters, a low Radius value produces a more pronounced effect than a high one, in effect locating more edges.

   Figure 4-22 shows the cloned green channel on left with the result of the High Pass filter on right. I used a Radius of 10, which is a nice, moderate value. The lower you go, the more edges you find and the more work you make for yourself. A Radius of 3 is accurate, but it'll take you an hour to fill in the mask. Granted, 10 is less accurate, but if you value your time, it's more sensible.

4. **Choose Image ⇨ Adjustments ⇨ Levels or press Ctrl+L (⌘-L on the Mac).** After adding all that gray to the image, follow it up by increasing the contrast. And the best command for enhancing contrast is Levels. Although I discuss this command in depth in Chapter 12, here's the short version: Inside the Levels dialog box, raise the first Input Levels value to make the dark colors darker, and lower the third Input Levels value to make the light colors lighter. (For now you can ignore the middle value.)

   Figure 4-23 shows the result of raising the first Input Levels value to 110 and lowering the third value to 155. As you can see in the left-hand image, this gives me some excellent contrast between the black hairs and white background.

   To demonstrate the importance of the High Pass command in these steps, I've shown what would happen if I had skipped Step 3 in the right-hand image in Figure 4-23. I applied the same Levels values as in the left image, and yet the image is overly dark and quite lacking in edges. Look at that wishy-washy hair. It's simply unacceptable.

Red Green Blue

Figure 4-21: Of the three color channels, the green channel offers the best contrast between hair, dress, and background. Take my word for it.

Clone the Green channel High Pass filter, Radius: 10 pixels

Figure 4-22: After cloning the green channel (left), I applied the High Pass filter with a Radius value of 10 to highlight the edges in the image (right).

Levels after High Pass   Levels only

Input Levels: 110   1.00   155

Figure 4-23: Here are the results of applying the Levels command to the mask after the High Pass step (left) and without High Pass (right). As you can see, High Pass has a very positive effect on the edge detail.

5. **Identify the edges.** By way of High Pass and Levels, Photoshop has presented you with a complex coloring book. From here on, it's a matter of coloring inside the lines. But you have to make sure your lines are coherent. In my case, the hair edges showed up as black lines against white, but the dress showed up as white lines against black. To keep things consistent, I selected the general region of the dress using the lasso tool and then chose Image ➪ Adjustments ➪ Invert (Ctrl+I under Windows, ⌘-I on the Mac) to swap the blacks and whites. As shown in the first example in Figure 4-24, the image looks the worse for this change, but the outlines are easier to follow.

6. **Use the lasso tool to remove the big stuff you don't need.** To simplify things, get rid of the stuff you know you don't need. All you care about is the area where the girl meets her background — mostly around the hair and dress. Everything else goes to white or black.

In the second example in Figure 4-24, I selected a general area inside the girl by Alt-clicking with the lasso tool (or Option-clicking on the Mac). Then I filled it with black by pressing Alt+Backspace (Option-Delete on the Mac).

In Figure 4-25, I selected the area outside the girl and filled it with white by pressing Ctrl+Backspace (⌘-Delete on the Mac). Notice that I was able to accomplish a lot with the lasso tool, but not everything is as it should be. The areas inside the hair and around the right sleeve, in particular, will require some careful attention with the brush tool.

Incidentally, be sure to press Ctrl+D (⌘-D on the Mac) to eliminate the selection before continuing to the next step.

Invert dress region   Select along edges & fill black

Figure 4-24: To ensure a consistent line between foreground and background, I selected the area around the dress with the lasso tool and inverted it (left). Then I selected the area inside the girl and filled it with black (right).

Select outside areas & fill white

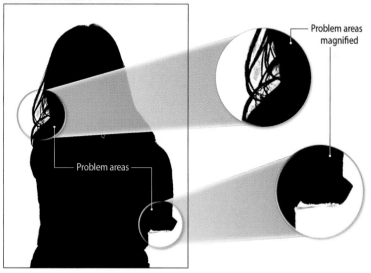

Figure 4-25: By selecting the area outside the girl and filling it with white, I was able to clearly distinguish between foreground and background. But that still left a few messy edges, identified by the circles.

7. **Paint inside the lines with the brush tool.** This tends to be the most time-consuming part. Now you have to paint inside the lines to make the edge pixels black or white. For this image, I used the brush tool with a hard brush size of about 5 to 10 pixels. I used the X key to switch between painting with black and white. The first image in Figure 4-26 shows the fruits of my labors. As you can see, I made a few judgment calls and decided — sometimes arbitrarily — where the hair got so thick that background imagery wouldn't show through. You may even disagree with some of my brushstrokes. But you know what? It doesn't matter. Despite whatever flaws I may have introduced, my mask is more than accurate enough to select the girl, as I will soon demonstrate.

8. **Invert the mask.** You may or may not need to perform this step. Based on the condition of the edges after I chose the High Pass command, my girl ended up black against a white background. But I want to select the girl, so she needs to be white. Therefore, I pressed Ctrl+I (⌘-I on the Mac) to swap the blacks and whites. If your foreground image ends up white after Step 7, then skip this step.

9. **Switch to the color composite view.** Press Ctrl+tilde (⌘-tilde on the Mac). Or if you're working in a grayscale image, press Ctrl+1 (⌘-1). By the way, now is a good time to save the image if you haven't already done so. Remember, TIFF is a terrific format for this purpose.

10. **Ctrl-click (Win) or ⌘-click (Mac) the mask channel to convert it to a selection.** This mask is ready to go prime time.

Clean up edges   Invert for final mask

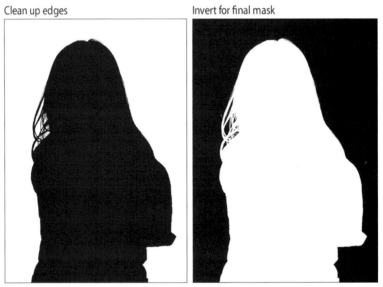

Figure 4-26: I fixed the problem areas by hand using the brush tool (left). Then I inverted the entire mask so the area inside the girl was white and the area outside was black (right).

11. **Ctrl-drag (Win) or ⌘-drag (Mac) the selection and drop it into a different image.**
Figure 4-27 shows the result of dropping the girl into a background of giant orange squash not unlike the one she holds in her arms. Thanks to my mask, she looks as natural in her new environment as she did in her previous one. In fact, an uninitiated viewer might have difficulty believing this isn't how she was originally photographed. But if you take a peek at Figure 4-20, you can confirm that Figure 4-27 is indeed an artificial composite. I painted in a few extra hairs to sell the composition, but that's because I'm an obsessive fussbudget. In most cases, you won't need to bother.

Figure 4-27: I guess all this time I've actually been working on a Halloween mask. Anyway, thanks to the wonders of masking, our girl has found a new life in a more sincere pumpkin patch.

Figure 4-27 looks great, in part because I performed a little extra finessing by brushing in color from the new background. I set the brush tool to the Color mode. Then I Alt-clicked (Option-clicked on the Mac) in the Background layer to lift colors from the new background and dragged to paint them into the hair. After a minute or two of this color painting, I arrived at the final composition. Now if that isn't compositing perfection, well gee whiz, I don't know what is.

✦　　　✦　　　✦

Working with Layers

Layers, Layers Everywhere

I'd like to begin my discussion of layers with a little look at Photoshop's history, peeling back the years like an onion's layers (if you'll pardon the strained simile). In 1994, when layers debuted in Version 3 of Photoshop, they were little more than their name implies — sheets of pixels that you could edit and transform independently of each other. But since then, layers have become increasingly sophisticated and complicated. Photoshop 4 forced you to embrace the feature by creating a new layer every time you imported an image; but it also rewarded you with floating *adjustment layers* that let you correct colors without permanently affecting a single pixel (see Chapter 11). Photoshop 5 witnessed the birth of layer effects, which included editable drop shadows, glows, and edge bevels (see Chapter 7). Photoshop 6 permitted you to bundle and color-code layers into logical clusters (this chapter), turn layers into floating holes (Chapter 6), and even add vector-based lines and shapes (Chapter 7). Photoshop 7 gave you the ability to adjust the fill opacity from the Layers palette but otherwise maintained the status quo.

Photoshop CS improves the way you work with layers by introducing layer comps, which we'll examine at the end of this chapter. It's a fairly helpful new feature, but I believe there's still room for improvement. For example, one day I hope to see Photoshop integrate parametric effects, in which filters such as Unsharp Mask and Motion Blur are fully editable, interactive, and interchangeable, on the order of Adobe's motion graphics powerhouse, After Effects. But in the meantime, Photoshop's layers still provide us with a rewarding amount of freedom and flexibility.

For those of you who are wondering what I'm talking about, permit me to back up for a moment. The first and foremost benefit of layers is that they add versatility. Because each layer in a composition is altogether independent of other layers, you can change your mind at a moment's notice. Consider the top example in Figure 5-1. Here we see a mock-up for a promotional piece I created for a video series called *Total Training for Adobe Photoshop*, in which I would not actually appear as a lovable robot named roboDeke. I created the top image one morning, utilizing the Layers palette to its fullest extent. Really, just about every element you see in the image is on a separate layer: the background, the motorcycle toy, the chains, each individual bunch of text, and even roboDeke himself. Satisfied with my work, I set it aside and took the rest of the day off.

The next morning, I checked out my multilayered masterpiece with fresh eyes, only to find that I felt it needed some improvement. Luckily, I had worked so extensively in layers that I was able to give my work an extensive overhaul, resulting in the true masterpiece you see at the bottom of Figure 5-1. I made innumerable changes, as reflected in the Layers palette shown in the figure: roboDeke has hair, antennae, and a much more substantial goatee, he's been shrunk and repositioned, the finger and arrow are gone from the image, many of the text elements have been restyled, the background is blurred, and so on. (In fact, there are more than 20 differences between the two images. Can you circle them all?)

Figure 5-1: Thanks to the flexibility of layers, you can arrange a bunch of elements one way one moment (top) and quite differently the next (bottom). Layers let you modify a composition without sacrificing quality.

Layers make it harder to make mistakes, they make it easier to make changes, and they expand your range of options. More than anything else, they permit you to restructure a composition and examine how it was put together after you assemble it. Layers can be very challenging to use or relatively simple. But whatever you do, don't shy away. If a layer might help, there's no reason not to add one. Layers are a big fact of life inside Photoshop, and it's important to know how to create, modify, organize, and exploit them to their full potential. And that's what this chapter is all about.

Sending a Selection to a Layer

To its credit, Photoshop lets you establish a new layer in roughly a million ways. If you want to add a selected portion of one image to another image, the easiest method is to Ctrl-drag (Win) or ⌘-drag (Mac) the selection and drop it into its new home, as demonstrated in Figure 5-2. Photoshop makes you a new layer, lickety-split.

Be sure to Ctrl-drag (⌘-drag on the Mac) or use the move tool. If you merely drag the selection with the marquee, lasso, or wand, you drop an empty selection outline into the new image window. Also, be aware that pressing Ctrl (Win) or ⌘ (Mac) delivers the move tool. But if the pen, arrow, or shape tool is active, you get the arrow tool instead, which won't work for you. Press V to get the good old move tool and then try dragging again.

When you drop the selection, your selection outline disappears. Not to worry, though. Now that the image resides on an independent layer, the selection outline is no longer needed. You can move the layer using the move tool, as you would move a selection. You can even paint inside what was once the selection by selecting the first of the Lock buttons in the Layers palette. I explain both the move tool and the Lock buttons in greater detail throughout this chapter.

If you want to clone a selection to a new layer inside the same image window — useful when performing complex filter routines and color corrections — choose Layer ➪ New ➪ Layer Via Copy. Or press Ctrl+J (⌘-J on the Mac), as in Jump.

Other ways to make a layer

Those are only two of the million ways to create a new layer in Photoshop. Here are the other 999,998 (or so):

✦ Copy a selection (Ctrl+C or ⌘-C) and paste it into another image (Ctrl+V or ⌘-V). Photoshop pastes the selection as a new layer.

✦ If you want to relegate a selection exclusively to a new layer, choose Layer ➪ New ➪ Layer Via Cut or press Ctrl+Shift+J (⌘-Shift-J on the Mac). Rather than cloning the selection, Layer Via Cut removes the selection from the background image and places it on its own layer.

✦ To convert a floating selection — one which you've moved or cloned — to a new layer, press Ctrl+Shift+J (⌘-Shift-J on the Mac). The Shift key is very important. If you press Ctrl+J (⌘-J) without Shift, Photoshop clones the selection and leaves an imprint of the image on the layer below.

✦ To create an empty layer — as when you want to paint a few brushstrokes without harming the original image — choose Layer ➪ New ➪ Layer or press Ctrl+Shift+N (⌘-Shift-N on the Mac). Or click the new layer icon at the bottom of the Layers palette (labeled in Figure 5-3).

✦ When you create a new layer, Photoshop positions it in front of the active layer. To create a new layer behind the active layer, Ctrl-click (⌘-click on the Mac) the new layer icon.

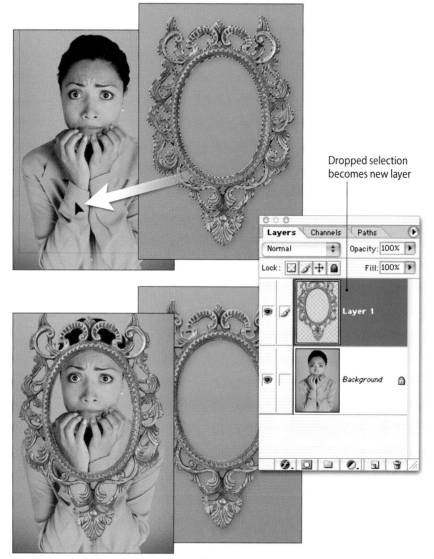

Figure 5-2: Ctrl-drag (Win) or ⌘-drag (Mac) a selected portion of an image and drop it into a different image window to introduce the selection as a new layer. As you can see in the Layers palette, the frame becomes a new layer in front of the frightened woman.

Incidentally, you can also create a new layer by choosing New Layer from the Layers palette menu. But as you can see in Figure 5-3, nearly all the palette commands are duplicated in the Layer menu. The only unique palette commands are Dock to Palette Well, which sends the Layers palette tab to the Options bar, and Palette Options, which lets you change the size of the thumbnails in front of the layer names. Turns out, you can perform the latter technique more easily by right-clicking (Control-clicking on the Mac) in the palette's empty space below the layers and choosing an option.

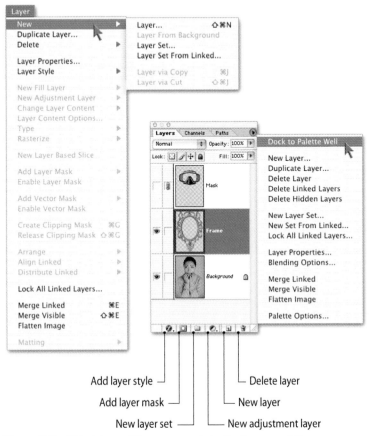

Add layer style

Add layer mask

New layer set

Delete layer

New layer

New adjustment layer

Figure 5-3: All but two of the commands in the Layers palette menu are duplicated in the Layer menu.

When you choose the Layer Via Copy or Layer Via Cut command or click the new layer icon, Photoshop automatically names the new layer for you. Unfortunately, the automatic names — Layer 1, Layer 2, and so on — are fairly meaningless and don't help to convey the contents of the layer.

If you want to specify a more meaningful name, add the Alt key (Option on the Mac). Press Ctrl+Alt+J (⌘-Option-J) to clone the selection to a layer, press Ctrl+Shift+Alt+J (⌘-Shift-Option-J) to cut the selection, or Alt-click (Option-click) the new layer icon to create a blank layer. In any case, you see the dialog box shown in Figure 5-4. Enter a name for the layer. If you like, you can also assign a color to a layer, which is helpful for identifying a layer name at a glance. Then press Enter or Return. (For now, you can ignore the other options in this dialog box.)

When creating a new layer from the keyboard, press Ctrl+Shift+Alt+N (⌘-Shift-Option-N on the Mac) to bypass the dialog box. Note that pressing Alt or Option works both ways, forcing the dialog box to display on some occasions and suppressing it on others. The only time it produces no effect is when pasting or dropping an image. Too bad — I for one would get a lot of use out of it.

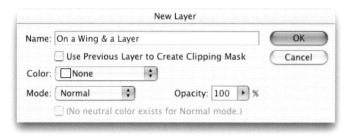

Figure 5-4: Press Alt (or Option on the Mac) when making a new layer to force the display of the New Layer dialog box, which lets you give the layer a name.

To rename a layer, just double-click on the name and type the new name directly into the Layers palette.

Duplicating a layer

To clone the active layer, you can choose Layer ➪ Duplicate Layer. But that's the sucker's way. The more convenient way is to drag the name or icon of the layer you want to clone onto the new layer icon at the bottom of the Layers palette.

To specify a name for the cloned layer or to copy the layer into another image, Alt-drag (Option-drag on the Mac) the layer onto the new layer icon. Always the thoughtful program, Photoshop displays the dialog box shown in Figure 5-5. You can name the cloned layer by entering something in the As option box. To copy the layer to some other open image, choose the image name from the Document pop-up menu. Or choose New and enter the name for an entirely different image in the Name option box, as the figure shows.

You can clone a layer by simply Ctrl-Alt-dragging (⌘-Option-dragging) it inside the image window. This way, you clone the layer and reposition it in one operation. Just be sure not to begin your drag inside a selection outline; if you do, you create a floating selection.

Layer Basics

Regardless of how you create a new layer, Photoshop lists the layer along with a little thumbnail of its contents in the Layers palette. The new layer appears highlighted to show that it's active, and the layer's name appears in bold. The little paintbrush icon in front of the layer name also indicates an active layer.

To the left of the paintbrush icon is a column of eyeballs, allowing you to hide and display layers temporarily. Click an eyeball to hide the layer. Click where the eyeball previously was to bring it back and redisplay the layer. Whether hidden or displayed, all layers remain intact and ready for action.

To view a single layer by itself, Alt-click (or Option-click) the eyeball icon before the layer name to hide all other layers. Alt-click (Option-click) in front of the layer again to bring all the layers back into view.

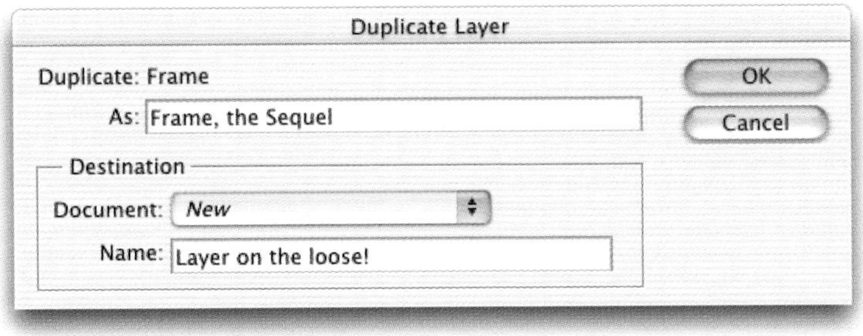

Duplicate Layer

Duplicate: Frame

As: | Frame, the Sequel |

OK

Cancel

┌─ Destination ──────────────────
Document: | New | ▲▼

Name: | Layer on the loose! |

Figure 5-5: You can duplicate the layer into an entirely different image by Alt-dragging (or Option-dragging) the layer onto the new layer icon in the Layers palette.

Switching between layers

You can select a different layer by clicking on its name in the Layers palette. This layer becomes active, enabling you to edit it. Note that only one layer may be active in Photoshop — you can't Shift-click to select and edit multiple layers, I'm sorry to say. So although you *can* link multiple layers and combine them into sets — as I explain in the section "Moving, Linking, and Aligning Layers" — you cannot select, paint, filter, or otherwise change the pixels on more than a single layer at a time.

If your image contains several layers — like the one back in Figure 5-1 — it might prove inconvenient, or even confusing, to switch from one layer to another in the Layers palette. Luckily, Photoshop offers a better way. With any tool, Ctrl+Alt-right-click (Ô-Option-Control-click on the Mac) an element in your composition to go directly to the layer containing the element. For example, Ctrl+Alt-right-clicking on the dangling hooks in Figure 5-1 would take me to the chains layer.

Why such an elaborate keyboard trick? Here's how it breaks down:

✦ Ctrl (⌘ on the Mac) gets you the move tool. If the move tool is already selected, you don't have to press Ctrl or ⌘; Alt-right-clicking or Option-Control-clicking works just fine.

✦ Right-clicking (Control-clicking on the Mac) brings up a shortcut menu. When you right-click or Control-click with the move tool — or Ctrl-right-click or ⌘-Control-click with any other tool — Photoshop displays a pop-up menu that lists the layer that the image is on and any other layers in the image, as in Figure 5-6. (If a layer is completely transparent at the spot where you right-click or Control-click, then that layer name doesn't appear in the pop-up menu.) Select the desired layer to go there.

✦ The Alt key (Option on the Mac) bypasses the pop-up menu and goes straight to the clicked layer.

Add them all together, and you get Ctrl+Alt-right-click or ⌘-Option-Control-click, depending on your platform. It's a lot to remember, but believe me, it's a great trick once you get the hang of it.

If you'd prefer Photoshop to always go directly to the layer on which you click and avoid all these messy keyboard tricks, press V to select the move tool. The first check box in the Options bar is called Auto Select Layer. Turn it on. Now whenever you click a layer with the move tool — or Ctrl-click (Ô-click on the Mac) with some other tool — Photoshop goes right to that layer.

Ctrl-right-click
(⌘-Control-click)

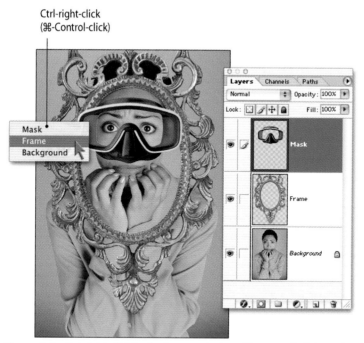

Figure 5-6: Ctrl-right-click in the image window (⌘-Control-click on the Mac) to view a pop-up menu. The menu lists all of the layers in the image that contain pixel data at the spot where you clicked.

Understanding transparency

Although the selection outline disappears when you convert a selection to a layer, no information is lost. Photoshop retains every little nuance of the original selection outline — whether it's a jagged border, a little bit of antialiasing, or a feathered edge. Anything that wasn't selected is now transparent. The data that defines the opacity and transparency of a layer is called the *transparency mask*.

To see this transparency in action, click the eyeball icon in front of the Background item in the Layers palette. This hides the background layer and enables you to view the new layer by itself. In Figure 5-7, I hid the background woman from Figure 5-6 to view the mask and frame on their own. The transparent areas are filled with a checkerboard pattern. Opaque areas look like the standard image, and translucent areas — where they exist — appear as a mix of image and checkerboard.

If the checkerboard pattern is hard to distinguish from the image, you can change the appearance of the pattern. Press Ctrl+K and then Ctrl+4 (⌘-K and then ⌘-4 on the Mac) to go to the Transparency & Gamut panel of the Preferences dialog box. Then edit the colors as you see fit.

If you apply an effect to the layer while no portion of the layer is selected, Photoshop changes the opaque and translucent portions of the image but leaves the transparent region intact. For example, if you press Ctrl+I (⌘-I on the Mac) or choose Image ➪ Adjustments ➪ Invert, Photoshop inverts the image but doesn't change a single pixel in the checkerboard area. If you click in the left column in front of the Background item to bring back the eyeball icon, you may notice a slight halo around the inverted image, but the edge pixels blend with the background image as well as they ever did. In fact, it's exactly as if you applied the effect to a selection, as demonstrated in Figure 5-8. The only difference is that this selection is independent of its background. You can do anything you want to it without running the risk of harming the underlying background.

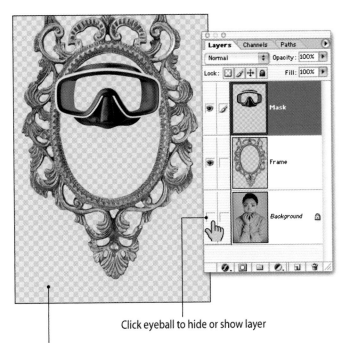

Click eyeball to hide or show layer

Checkerboard indicates transparency

Figure 5-7: When you hide the background layer, you see a checkerboard pattern that represents the transparent portions of the layer.

Only a few operations affect the transparent areas of a layer, and most of these are limited to tools. You can paint on transparent pixels to make them opaque. You can clone with the clone stamp or smear pixels with the edit tools. To send pixels back to transparency, paint with the eraser. All these operations change both the contents of the layer and the composition of the transparency mask.

You can fill all pixels also by pressing Alt+Backspace (Option-Delete on the Mac) for the foreground color and Ctrl+Backspace (⌘-Delete on the Mac) for the background color. To fill the pixels in a layer without altering the transparency mask, toss in the Shift key. Shift+Alt+Backspace (Shift-Option-Delete) fills the opaque pixels with the foreground color; Ctrl+Shift+Backspace (⌘-Shift-Delete) fills them with the background color. In both cases, the transparent pixels remain every bit as transparent as they ever were.

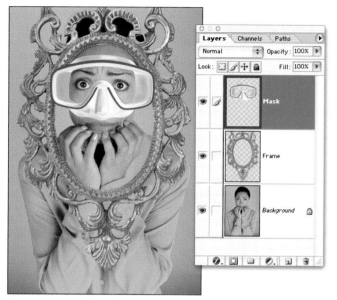

Figure 5-8: Applying the Invert command to the mask layer inverts only the mask without affecting any of the transparent pixels. The woman and the frame remain every bit as visible as ever.

When a portion of a layer (other than the background layer) is selected, pressing plain old Backspace (Delete on the Mac) eliminates the selected pixels and makes them transparent, revealing the layers below.

Transparent pixels take up next to no space in memory, but opaque and translucent pixels do. Thus, a layer containing 25 percent as many pixels as the background layer takes up roughly 25 percent as much space. Mind you, I wouldn't let this influence how you work in Photoshop, but it is something to keep in mind.

Modifying the background layer

At the bottom of the layer stack is the *background layer*, the fully opaque layer that represents the base image. The background image is as low as you go. Nothing can be slipped under the background layer, and pixels in the background layer cannot be made transparent, unless you first convert the background to a floating layer.

To make the conversion, double-click the item labeled Background in the Layers palette. A dialog box appears. Enter a name for the new layer — Photoshop suggests Layer 0 — and press Enter or Return. You can now change the order of the layer or erase down to transparency.

To skip the dialog box and accept Layer 0 as the new layer name, press Alt (or Option on the Mac) and double-click the Background item in the Layers palette.

In Figure 5-9, I converted the background woman to a layer. This particular image included a predrawn path that encircled the scared subject. I Ctrl-clicked (⌘-clicked on the Mac) on the path to convert it to a selection outline and then I pressed Ctrl+Shift+I (⌘-Shift-I) to reverse the selection. Finally, I pressed Backspace (Delete) to erase the pixels outside the woman, as the figure demonstrates. From this point on, I can reorder all of the layers or add layers behind the woman. I can also introduce a new background layer.

 Although InDesign 2.0 can easily handle layered Photoshop files complete with all transparency intact, QuarkXPress 6.0 can't. If you want to export transparency to Quark, you have to use a clipping path.

Convert background to independent layer

Ctrl-click (⌘-click) path to make selection

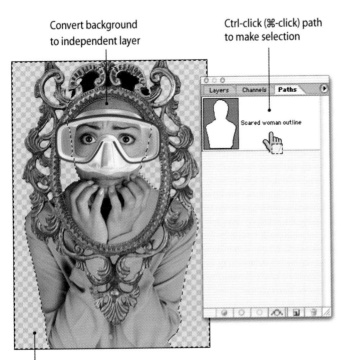

Inverse, delete selected pixels

Figure 5-9: After converting the image of the scared woman to a layer, I Ctrl-clicked (⌘-clicked on the Mac) on the path, inversed the selection, and pressed Backspace (Delete on the Mac) to reveal the transparent void below.

 To convert the active layer to a background layer when there is currently no background layer, choose Layer ➪ New ➪ Background From Layer. It doesn't matter whether the active layer is at the top of the stack, the bottom, or someplace in between — Photoshop takes the layer and makes a new background out of it.

To establish a blank background, create an empty layer by pressing Ctrl+Shift+N (⌘-Shift-N on the Mac) and then choose Layer ➪ New ➪ Background From Layer. In Figure 5-10, I did just that. Next I used the Add Noise and Emboss filters to create a paper texture pattern (as explained in Chapter 2). Then I selected the Frame layer and chose Layer ➪ Layer Style ➪ Drop Shadow to add a drop shadow that matched the contours of the frame. Finally, I switched back to the Scared Woman layer and gave our frightened friend a drop shadow as well. (I tell all there is to know about layer styles in Chapter 7.)

Create new background layer   Add drop shadows

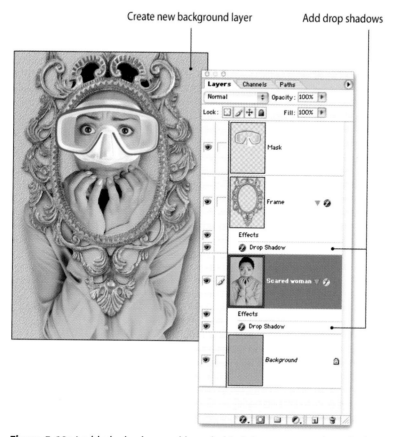

Figure 5-10: I added a background layer behind the woman and applied a paper texture and drop shadows to give me — I mean, to give my *composition* — a false sense of depth.

Photoshop permits only one background layer per image. If an image already contains a background layer, the command Layer ⇨ New ⇨ Background From Layer changes to Layer From Background, which converts the background layer to a floating layer, as when you double-click the Background item in the Layers palette.

Reordering layers

What good are layers if you can't periodically change what's on the top and what's on the bottom? You can reorder layers in two ways. First, you can drag a layer name up or down in the scrolling list to move it forward or backward in layering order. The only trick is to make sure that the black bar appears at the point where you want to move the layer before you release the mouse button, as illustrated in Figure 5-11.

The all-important black bar

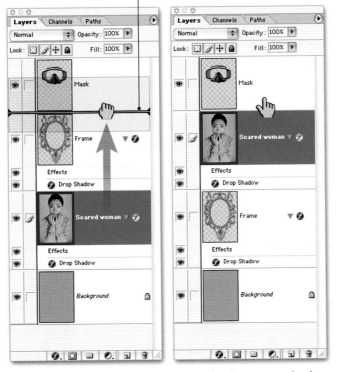

Figure 5-11: Drag a layer between two other layers to make the all-important black bar appear (left). Then release the mouse button to change the hierarchy of the layer (right).

The second way to reorder layers is to choose a command from the Layer ⇨ Arrange submenu. For example, choose Layer ⇨ Arrange ⇨ Bring Forward to move the active layer up one level; choose Layer ⇨ Arrange ⇨ Send to Back to move the layer to above the background layer.

You can move faster if you remember the following keyboard shortcuts:

✦ **Ctrl+Shift+] (Win) or ⌘-Shift-] (Mac):** Press Ctrl+Shift+right bracket (Win) or ⌘-Shift-right bracket (Mac) to move the active layer to the top of the stack.

✦ **Ctrl+Shift+[(Win) or ⌘-Shift-[(Mac):** This shortcut moves the active layer to the bottom of the stack, just above the background layer.

✦ **Ctrl+] (Win) or ⌘-] (Mac):** This nudges the layer up one level.

✦ **Ctrl+[(Win) or ⌘-[(Mac):** This nudges the layer down.

You can neither reorder the background layer nor move any other layer below the background until you first convert the background to a floating layer, as explained in the previous section.

Blending layers

Photoshop lets you blend layers like no other program in the business. In fact, Photoshop does such a great job that it takes me an entire chapter — Chapter 6 — to explain these options in detail. I offer this section by way of introduction so that you're at least aware of the basics. If you have bigger questions, Chapter 6 is waiting to tell all.

The Layers palette provides four basic ways to blend pixels between layers (see Figure 5-12). None of these techniques permanently changes as much as a pixel in any layer, so you can always return and reblend the layers at a later date.

✦ **The Opacity value:** Enter a value in the Opacity option box near the top of the Layers palette to change the opacity of the active layer or floating selection. If you reduce the Opacity value to 50 percent, for example, Photoshop makes the pixels on the active layer translucent, so the colors in the active layer mix evenly with the colors in the layers below.

If any tool other than a paint or an edit tool is active — including the selection and navigation tools — you can press a number key to change the Opacity value. Press 1 for 10 percent, 2 for 20 percent, up to 0 for 100 percent. Or you can enter a specific Opacity value by quickly pressing two number keys in a row. For example, press 3 and then 7 for 37 percent.

✦ **The Fill value:** The Fill option lets you adjust the opacity of pixel information in the layer — anything painted, drawn, or typed — without affecting the opacity of any layer effects that might be applied. For instance, if you have a text layer with the Drop Shadow layer effect applied, lowering the Fill slider to 0 fades out the text itself, leaving just the ghostly drop shadow behind. As with all other blending-related options, I explain the Fill option in excruciating detail in Chapter 6.

✦ **The blend mode pop-up menu:** Choose an option from the blend mode pop-up menu — open in Figure 5-12 — to mix every pixel in the active layer with the pixels below it, according to one of several mathematical equations. For example, when you choose Multiply, Photoshop really does multiply the brightness values of the pixels and then divides the result by 255, the maximum brightness value. Blend modes use the same math as the brush modes covered in Chapter 1. In fact, the two terms are sometimes used interchangeably. But you can accomplish a lot more with blend modes, which is why I spend so much time examining them in Chapter 6.

As with Opacity, you can select a blend mode from the keyboard when a selection or navigation tool is active. Press Shift+plus to advance incrementally down the list; press Shift+minus to inch back up. You can also press Shift+Alt (or Shift-Option on the Mac) and a letter key to select a specific mode. For example, Shift+Alt+M (Shift-Option-M) selects the Multiply mode. Shift+Alt+N (Shift-Option-N) restores the mode to Normal.

✦ **Blending Options:** Choose Layer ⇨ Layer Style ⇨ Blending Options or double-click a layer thumbnail to display the Layer Style dialog box. The General Blending area of this dialog box provides access to a Blend Mode pop-up menu and an Opacity value, but it also offers a world of unique functions. As discussed in Chapter 6, you can hide one or more color channels, specify which colors are visible in the active layer, and force other colors to show through from the layers behind it. Select an item from the left-hand list to apply a layer style, as discussed in Chapter 7.

Although far short of the whole story, that should be enough to prepare you for anything I throw at you throughout the remainder of this chapter. And did I mention that Chapter 6 has a lot more to say about blend modes? Oh, yeah, I guess I did.

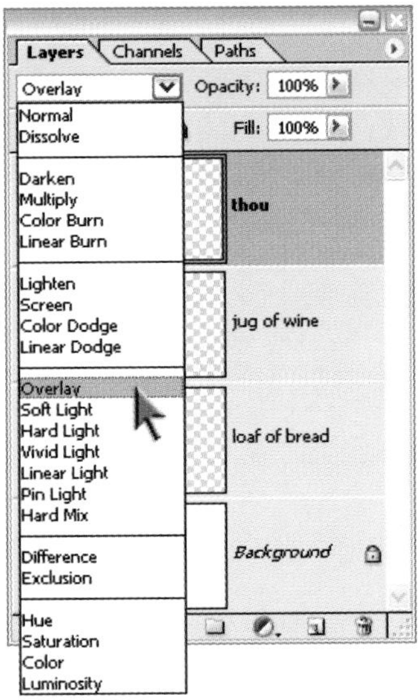

Figure 5-12: The blend mode pop-up menu and the Opacity and Fill option boxes enable you to mix layers without making any permanent changes to the pixels.

Fusing several layers

Although layers are wonderful and marvelous creatures, they have their price. Layers expand the size of an image in RAM and ultimately lead to slower performance. And only four formats — PDF, TIFF, the new PSB, and the native PSD format — permit you to save layered compositions.

In the interest of slimming the size of your image, Photoshop provides the following methods for merging layers together:

✦ **Merge Down (Ctrl+E or ⌘-E):** Choose Layer ➪ Merge Down to merge a layer with the layer immediately below it. (Both layers need to be visible.) When generating screen shots, I use this command 50 or 60 times a day. I paste the screen shot into the image window, edit the layer as desired, and then press Ctrl+E (Win) or ⌘-E (Mac) to set it down. Then I can save the screen shot to the smallest possible file on disk, essential when e-mailing the screens to my editor.

If the active layer is part of a clipping mask or is linked to other layers — two conditions I discuss later in this chapter — the Merge Down command changes to Merge Clipping Mask or Merge Linked, respectively. Again, these commands use Ctrl+E (⌘-E on the Mac) as a shortcut. Merge Down is forever changing to suit the situation.

✦ **Merge Visible (Ctrl+Shift+E or ⌘-Shift-E):** Choose the Merge Visible command to merge all visible layers into a single layer. If the layer is not visible — that is, if no eyeball icon appears in front of the layer name — Photoshop doesn't eliminate it; the layer simply remains independent.

To create a merged clone, press Alt (or Option) when applying either Layer ➪ Merge Down or Layer ➪ Merge Visible. Pressing Alt (Option) and choosing Merge Down — or pressing Ctrl+Alt+E (⌘-Option-E on the Mac) — clones the contents of the active layer into the layer below it. Pressing Alt (Option) and choosing Merge Visible — or pressing Ctrl+Shift+Alt+E (⌘-Shift-Option-E) — copies the contents of all visible layers to the active layer.

More useful, I think, is the ability to copy the merged contents of a selected area. To do so, choose Edit ➪ Copy Merged or press Ctrl+Shift+C (Ô-Shift-C on the Mac). You can then paste the selection into a layer or make it part of a different image.

◆ **Flatten Image:** This command merges all visible layers and throws away the invisible ones. The result is a single, opaque background layer. Photoshop does not give this command a keyboard shortcut because it's so dangerous. More often than not, you'll want to flatten an image incrementally using the two Merge commands.

Note that Photoshop asks whether you want to flatten an image when converting from one color mode to another. You can choose not to flatten the image (by pressing D), but this may come at the expense of some of the brighter colors in your image. Also, many blend modes that you might have assigned to layers perform differently in RGB than they do in CMYK.

Dumping layers

You can also merely throw a layer away: Drag the layer name onto the trash can icon at the bottom of the Layers palette. Or click the trash can icon to delete the active layer.

When you click the trash can icon, Photoshop displays a message asking whether you really want to toss the layer. To give this message the slip, Alt-click (or Option-click) the trash can icon.

Here's a much juicier tip for you: If the active layer is linked to one or more other layers (see the upcoming section "Linking layers"), you can delete all linked layers in one fell swoop by Ctrl-clicking the trash can icon (that's ⌘-clicking on the Mac).

Saving a flattened version of an image

As I mentioned earlier, only four file formats — PDF, TIFF, PSB, and the native Photoshop format — save images with layers. If you want to save a flattened version of your image — that is, with all layers fused into a single image — in some other file format, choose File ➪ Save As or press Ctrl+Shift+S (⌘-Shift-S on the Mac) and select the desired format from the Format pop-up menu. If you select a format that doesn't support layers — such as JPEG, GIF, or EPS — the program dims the Layers check box.

The Save As command does not affect the image in memory. All layers remain intact. And if you select the As a Copy check box with the Layers option deselected — which I recommend you do — Photoshop doesn't even change the name of the image in the title bar. It merely creates a flattened version of the image on disk. Nevertheless, be sure to save a layered version of the composition as well, just in case you want to edit it in the future.

Selecting the Contents of Layers

A few sections back, I mentioned that every layer except the background includes a *transparency mask*. This mask tells Photoshop which pixels are opaque, which are translucent, and which are transparent. Like any mask, Photoshop lets you convert the transparency mask for any layer — active or not — to a selection outline. In fact, you use the same keyboard techniques that you use to convert channels to selections (see "Converting a mask to a selection" in Chapter 4):

✦ Ctrl-click (or on the Mac, ⌘-click) an item in the Layers palette to convert the transparency mask for that layer to a selection outline.

✦ To add the transparency mask to an existing selection outline, Ctrl+Shift-click (⌘-Shift-click) the layer name. The little selection cursor includes a plus sign to show you that you're about to add.

✦ To subtract the transparency mask, Ctrl+Alt-click (⌘-Option-click) the layer name.

✦ And to find the intersection of the transparency mask and the current selection outline, Ctrl+Shift+Alt-click (⌘-Shift-Option-click) the layer name.

If you're uncertain that you'll remember all these keyboard shortcuts, you can use Select ➪ Load Selection instead. After choosing the command, select the Transparency item from the Channel pop-up menu. (You can even load a transparency mask from another open image if the image is exactly the same size as the one you're working on.) Then use the Operation radio buttons to merge the mask with an existing selection.

Selection outlines exist independently of layers, so you can use the transparency mask from one layer to select part of another layer. For example, to select the part of the background layer that exactly matches the contents of another layer, press Shift+Alt+[(Shift-Option-[on the Mac) to descend to the background layer and then Ctrl-click (or ⌘-click) the name of the layer you want to match.

The most common reason to borrow a selection from one layer and apply it to another is to create manual shadow and lighting effects. After Ctrl-clicking (or ⌘-clicking) a layer, you can use this selection to create a shadow that precisely matches the contours of the layer itself. No messing with the brush or the lasso tool — Photoshop does the tough work for you.

Now, you might think that with Photoshop's extensive range of layer styles (covered in Chapter 7), manual drop shadows and the like would be a thing of the past. After all, you have only to choose Layer ➪ Layer Style ➪ Drop Shadow and, bang, the program adds a shadow to the layer. But the old, manual methods still have their advantages. You don't have to visit a complicated dialog box to edit a manual drop shadow. You can reposition a manual shadow from the keyboard, and you can modify a manual shadow with more precision than you can an automatic one. For one such example, read the section "Adding a cast shadow to a layer" in Chapter 8.

Moving, Linking, and Aligning Layers

You can move an entire layer or the selected portion of a layer by dragging in the image window with the move tool. If you have a selection going, drag inside the marching-ants outline to move only the selection; drag outside the selection to move the entire layer.

You can temporarily access the move tool when some other tool is active by pressing Ctrl (Win) or ⌘ (Mac). To nudge a layer, press Ctrl or ⌘ with an arrow key. Press Ctrl+Shift (⌘-Shift on the Mac) to nudge in 10-pixel increments.

If part of the layer disappears beyond the edge of the window, no problem. Photoshop saves even the hidden pixels in the layer, enabling you to drag the rest of the layer into view later.

Note that this works only when moving all of a layer. If you move a selection beyond the edge of the image window using the move tool, Photoshop clips the selection at the window's edge the moment you deselect it. Also be aware: If you move your cursor outside the image window, Photoshop thinks you are trying to drag-and-drop pixels from one image to another and responds accordingly.

If you Ctrl-drag (Win) or ⌘-drag (Mac) the background image with no portion of it selected, you get an error message telling you that the layer is locked. If some portion of the layer is selected, however, you can drag that selected portion, and Photoshop will fill in the hole with the background color.

Linking layers

Photoshop lets you move multiple layers at a time. To do so, you have to establish a *link* between the layers you want to move and the active layer. Begin by selecting the first layer in the Layers palette you want to link. Then click in the second column to the left of the other layer you want to link. A chain-link icon appears in front of each linked layer, as in Figure 5-13. This icon shows that the linked layers move in unison when you Ctrl-drag (or ⌘-drag) the active layer. To break the link, click a link icon, which hides the icon.

Link icons

Link column

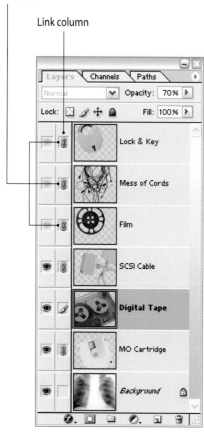

Figure 5-13: Click in the second column in the Layers palette to display or hide link icons. Here I've linked all layers except the background, so I can drag them in unison.

Dragging inside a selection outline moves the selection independently of any linked layers. Dragging outside the selection moves all linked layers at once.

To link many layers at a time, drag up and down the link column. To unlink the active layer from all others, Alt-click (on the Mac, Option-click) the paintbrush icon in the link column.

You can also link layers with the shortcut menu. As you may recall from the "Switching between layers" section earlier in this chapter, you can bring up a pop-up menu listing the layers in an image by Ctrl-right-clicking (⌘-Control-clicking) on an image element with any tool. Add Shift while selecting a layer from the pop-up menu to link or unlink the layer rather than switch to it.

But that's not all. If you're plum crazy for shortcuts, you can change the link state without visiting the pop-up menu by — drumroll please — Ctrl+Shift+Alt-right-clicking (⌘-Shift-Option-Control-clicking) an element in the image window. Okay, I love shortcuts, but even *I* have to admit that this one is gratuitous!

When you drag-and-drop linked layers into another document, all linked layers move together and the layers retain their original order. If you want to move just one layer without its linked buddies, drag the layer name from the Layers palette and drop it into another open image window.

If you hold down Shift when dropping, Photoshop centers the layers in the document. If the document is exactly the same size as the one from which you dragged the layers, Shift-dropping lands the image elements in the same position they held in the original document. And finally, if something is selected in the document, the Shift-dropped layers are centered inside that selection.

Uniting layers into sets

Linking isn't the only way to keep layers together. You can toss multiple layers into a folder called a *set*. To create a new set, click the little folder icon along the bottom of the Layers palette. Or better yet, Alt-click (Option-click) the icon to display the dialog box shown in Figure 5-14. Here you can name the set, assign a color, and set the blend mode and opacity.

![New Layer Set dialog box]
```
                    New Layer Set

   Name: Tummy contents                    (   OK   )

   Color:  ☐ Yellow  ⬍                      ( Cancel )

   Mode:  Pass Through  ⬍  Opacity: 100  ▶ %
```

Figure 5-14: Choose the New Layer Set command or Alt-click (Option-click on the Mac) the folder icon at the bottom of the Layers palette to create and name a new set.

Notice in Figure 5-14 that a unique Mode option — Pass Through — appears when working with sets. This tells Photoshop to observe the blend modes assigned to the individual layers inside the set. By contrast, if you apply a different blend mode such as Multiply to the set, Photoshop overrides the blend modes of the layers inside the set and applies Multiply to them all.

The set appears as a folder icon in the Layers palette scrolling list. To add a layer to the set, drag the layer name in the scrolling list and drop it on the folder icon. Layers that are part of a set appear indented, as in Figure 5-15. The triangle to the left of the folder icon — sometimes called the "twirly"—permits you to expand and collapse the layers inside the set, a tremendous help when working inside images with a dozen or more layers. Figure 5-16 shows the layers associated with a typically complex image. When all sets are expanded, the layers don't even begin to fit on screen. But with sets collapsed, you can assess the construction of the image at a glance.

Photoshop CS also lets you place sets inside other sets, in a process called *nesting*. Nesting layer sets can be a great way to better organize your layers, and Photoshop CS allows you to nest sets up to five levels deep, like those concentric Russian dolls. To place one set inside of another, simply drag and drop it onto the other set in the same manner you would a layer. As it does when you place a layer into a set, Photoshop applies the blend mode of the master set to every layer and nested set within it when the mode is not set to Pass Through.

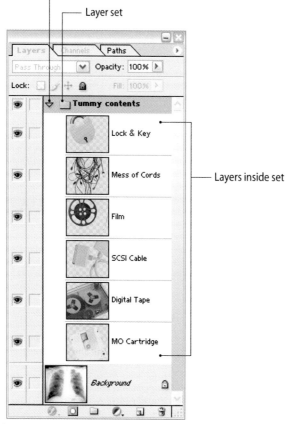

Figure 5-15: Click the "twirly" to the left of a folder icon to show or hide all layers in a set.

Figure 5-16: Sets are a terrific help when working with complex, multilayer compositions, such as this old Web page of mine. Witness the difference between all sets expanded (first palette) and all sets collapsed (second).

Here are some other ways to create and modify sets:

✦ Double-click a set name to rename it.

✦ Drag a set name up or down the palette to move it.

✦ When a set is expanded, you can drag a layer within the set, move a layer out of the set, or drop a layer into the set at a specific position.

✦ Drag a set name and drop it onto another set to empty all layers from the former into the latter.

✦ To duplicate a set, drag it onto the folder icon at the bottom of the Layers palette.

✦ Hate dragging all those layers into a set? Wish you could move more than one at a time? Well, you can't, but you can do the next best thing. Link the layers that you want to make part of a set. Then choose New Set From Linked from the Layers palette menu. All linked layers go into the new set.

✦ In case you're wondering, *Can I link layers in different sets?*, yes, you can. And if you're also wondering, *Can I link sets together?*, I'll be happy to tell you that it's possible not only to link sets, but also to link individual layers to whole sets. You have to admit, it's pretty hot stuff.

✦ As you know, Ctrl-right-clicking (⌘-Control-clicking) in the image window displays a shortcut menu of layers under the cursor. If one of the layers belongs to a set, Photoshop lists the set name along with the individual layer names in the shortcut menu. Select the set name to make it active.

✦ Ctrl-click (⌘-click) on the triangle next to a folder icon to open or close the set, displaying or hiding the layers and nested sets it contains. Alt-click (Option-click) the triangle next to a folder icon to show or hide every element contained in the set, including nested sets and layer styles.

Anytime a set name is active in the Layers palette, you can move or transform all layers in the set as a unit, much as if they were linked. To move or transform a single layer inside the set, just select that layer and go about your business as you normally would.

Locking layers

Photoshop lets you protect a layer by locking it. But unlike other programs that lock or unlock layers in their entirety, Photoshop lets you lock some attributes of a layer and leave other attributes unlocked. Figure 5-17 labels the four Lock buttons available in the Layers palette. Here's how they work:

✦ **Lock transparency:** This button protects the transparency of a layer. When selected, you can paint inside a layer without harming the transparent pixels. This option is so useful that I devote an entire section to the topic (see "Preserving transparency" later in this chapter).

✦ **Lock pixels:** Select this button to prohibit the pixels in the active layer from further editing. Paint and edit tools will no longer function, nor will filters or other pixel-level commands. However, you'll still be able to move and transform the layer as you like. Note that selecting this button dims and selects the Lock Transparency button as well. After all, if you can't edit pixels, you can't edit pixels — whether they're opaque or transparent.

✦ **Lock position:** Select this button to prevent the layer from being moved or transformed. You can, however, edit the pixels.

✦ **Lock all:** To lock everything about a layer, select this button. You can't paint, edit, filter, move, transform, delete, or otherwise change a hair on the layer's head. About all you can do is duplicate the layer, move it up and down the stack, add it to a set, and merge it with one or more other layers. This button is applicable to layers and sets alike.

Photoshop shows you which layers are locked by displaying two kinds of lock icons in the Layers palette. As labeled in Figure 5-17, the hollow lock means one attribute or other is locked; the filled lock means all attributes are locked.

Applying Transformations

Photoshop treats some kinds of edits differently than others. Edits that affect the geometry of a selection or a layer are known collectively as *transformations*. These transformations include scaling, rotating, flipping, slanting, and distorting. (Technically, moving is a transformation as well.) Transformations are a special breed of edits inside Photoshop because they can affect a selection, a layer, multiple layers, or an entire image at a time.

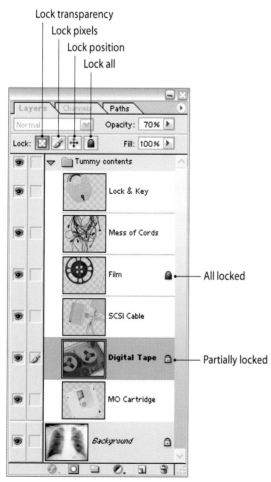

Lock transparency
Lock pixels
Lock position
Lock all

— All locked

— Partially locked

Figure 5-17: The Lock buttons at the top of the Layers palette let you protect certain layer attributes.

Transforming the entire image

Photoshop has two varieties of transformations. Transformation commands that affect the entire image — including all layers, paths, channels, and so on — are listed in the Image menu. Those that affect layers and selected portions of layers are in the Edit menu, or in the case of selection outlines, in the Select menu.

The following list explains how to apply transformations to every pixel in an image, regardless of whether the image is selected or not:

✦ **Scale:** To resize the image, use Image ➪ Image Size and enter new Width and Height values as desired. Make sure that the Resample Image check box is turned on. The default resampling method, Bicubic, used to be pretty much the only way to go. But Photoshop CS gives you two excellent new methods: Bicubic Smoother and Bicubic Sharper. When you're enlarging images, Bicubic Smoother is your best bet — it tries to reinterpret your image with the smoothest pixel transitions possible. Bicubic Sharper is recommended for preserving the sharpness of an image that you're reducing. You can also enter new Width and Height values as desired.

✦ **Rotate:** To rotate the entire image, choose a command from the Image ➪ Rotate Canvas submenu. To rotate an image scanned on its side, choose the 90° CW or 90° CCW command. (That's clockwise and counterclockwise, respectively.) Choose 180° to spin the image on its head. To enter some other specific value, choose Image ➪ Rotate Canvas ➪ Arbitrary.

You can use the Arbitrary command in combination with the measure tool to fix a crooked scanned image. Here's how: Select the measure tool from the eyedropper flyout in the toolbox (or press I and then Shift+I twice). Drag along what should be a vertical or horizontal edge in the image. Then choose Image ➪ Rotate Canvas ➪ Arbitrary. Look, the Angle value is preset to the angle you just measured. That Photoshop, it's one sharp cookie. Press Enter or Return, and the job's done.

Whenever you apply the Arbitrary command, Photoshop has to expand the canvas size to avoid clipping any of your image. This results in background-colored wedges at each of the four corners of the image. You need to either clone with the clone stamp tool to fill in the wedges or clip them away with the crop tool.

✦ **Flip:** Choose Image ➪ Rotate Canvas ➪ Flip Horizontal to flip the image so left is right and right is left. To flip the image upside down, choose Image ➪ Rotate Canvas ➪ Flip Vertical.

No command is specifically designed to slant or distort the entire image. In the unlikely event you're keen to do this, you'll have to link all layers and apply one of the commands under the Edit ➪ Transform submenu, as explained in the next section.

Transforming layers and selected pixels

To transform a selection, a layer, or a collection of linked layers, you can apply one of the commands in the Edit ➪ Transform submenu. Nearly a dozen commands are here, all of which you can explore on your own. I'm not copping out; it's just that it's unlikely you'll use any of these commands on a regular basis. They aren't bad, but one command — Free Transform — is infinitely better.

With Free Transform, you can scale, flip, rotate, slant, distort, and move a selection or layer in one continuous operation. This one command lets you get all your transformations exactly right before pressing Enter or Return to apply the final changes. I demonstrate this command on the charming image shown in Figure 5-18. Each of the elements in this image resides on an independent layer. The dog layer is active, and the fire and shadow are linked to this layer. Therefore, dog, fire, and shadow will transform together.

Get it? Okay, so here's how it works: To initiate the command, press Ctrl+T (⌘-T on the Mac) or choose Edit ➪ Free Transform. Photoshop surrounds the selection, layer, or linked layers with an eight-handle marquee. You are now in the Free Transform mode, which prevents you from doing anything except transforming the image or canceling the operation.

Figure 5-18: This dog, his fiery breath, and his shadow reside on separate layers. But because they are linked together, they will transform as one.

Here's how to work in the Free Transform mode:

✦ **Scale:** Drag one of the eight square handles to scale the image inside the marquee. To scale proportionally, Shift-drag a corner handle. To scale about the central *transformation origin* (labeled in Figure 5-19), Alt-drag (or Option-drag) a corner handle.

By default, the origin is located in the center of the layer or selection. But you can move it to any place inside the image — even outside of the transformation box — by dragging it. The origin snaps to the grid and guides as well as to the center or any corner of the layer.

✦ **Flip:** You can flip the image by dragging one handle past its opposite handle. For example, dragging the left side handle past the right side handle flips the image horizontally.

If you want to perform a simple flip, it's generally easier to choose Edit ➪ Transform ➪ Flip Horizontal or Flip Vertical. Better yet, right-click (on the Mac, Control-click) in the image window and choose one of the Flip commands from the shortcut menu. Quite surprisingly, you can choose any of the shortcut menu commands while working in the Free Transform mode.

✦ **Rotate:** To rotate the image, drag outside the marquee, as demonstrated in Figure 5-19. Shift-drag to rotate in 15-degree increments.

✦ **Skew:** Ctrl-drag (⌘-drag) a side handle (including the top or bottom handle) to slant the image. To constrain the slant, which is useful for producing perspective effects, Ctrl+Shift-drag (⌘-Shift-drag) a side handle.

✦ **Distort:** You can distort the image by Ctrl-dragging (⌘-dragging) a corner handle. You can tug the image to stretch it in any of four directions.

To tug two opposite corner handles in symmetrical directions, Ctrl+Alt-drag (⌘-Option-drag) either of the handles. I apply this technique to our ferocious dog in Figure 5-20.

✦ **Perspective:** For a one-point perspective effect, Ctrl+Shift-drag (⌘-Shift-drag) a corner handle. To move two points in unison, Ctrl+Shift+Alt-drag (⌘-Shift-Option-drag) a corner handle.

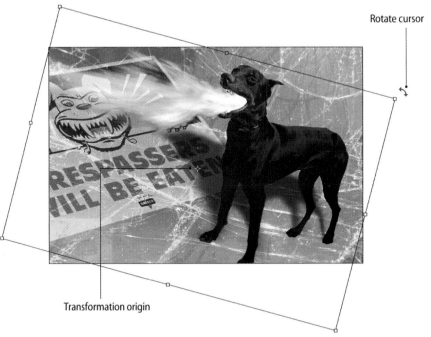

Rotate cursor

Transformation origin

Figure 5-19: After pressing Ctrl+T (⌘-T on the Mac) to initiate the Free Transform command, drag outside the marquee to rotate the layer.

✦ **Move:** Drag inside the marquee to move the image. This is useful when you're trying to align the selection or layer with a background image and you want to make sure the transformations match up properly.

✦ **Undo:** To undo the last modification without leaving the Free Transform mode altogether, press Ctrl+Z (⌘-Z on the Mac).

✦ **Zoom:** You can change the view size by choosing one of the commands in the View menu. You can also use the keyboard zoom shortcuts: Ctrl+spacebar-click, Alt+spacebar-click, Ctrl+plus, or Ctrl+minus (on the Mac, that's ⌘-spacebar-click, Option-spacebar-click, ⌘-plus, or ⌘-minus).

✦ **Apply:** Press Enter or Return to apply the final transformation and interpolate the new pixels. You can also double-click inside the marquee or click the checkmark button in the Options bar.

 If the finished effect looks jagged after you've applied the transformation, it's probably because you selected Nearest Neighbor from the Image Interpolation pop-up menu in the Preferences dialog box. To correct this problem, press Ctrl+Z (⌘-Z on the Mac) to undo the transformation and then press Ctrl+K (⌘-K). Selecting Bicubic from the Image Interpolation menu is your best all-around choice for a default. (This preference sets the default interpolation method in the Image Size dialog box, too.) Then press Ctrl+Shift+T (⌘-Shift-T) to reapply the transformation.

✦ **Cancel:** To cancel the Free Transform operation, press Escape, click the "no" symbol button in the Options bar, or press Ctrl+period (⌘-period).

Distort cursor

Figure 5-20: Press Ctrl and Alt (⌘ and Option) and drag a corner handle to move it and its opposite corner handle in symmetrical directions. The result is a free-form skew.

 To transform a clone of a layer or selected area, press Alt (Option) when choosing the Free Transform command or press Ctrl+Alt+T (⌘-Option-T).

If no part of the image is selected, you can transform multiple layers at a time by first linking them, as described in the "Linking layers" section earlier in this chapter.

 To replay the last transformation on any layer or selection, choose Edit ➪ Transform ➪ Again or press Ctrl+Shift+T (⌘-Shift-T on the Mac). This technique is great to use if you forgot to link all the layers that you wanted to transform. You can even transform a path or selection outline to match a transformed layer. It's a handy feature. In fact, throw the Alt (or Option) key in there, and the transformation can be repeated on a clone of the selected layer.

Neither Free Transform nor any of the commands in the Edit ➪ Transform submenu are available when a layer or linked layer is locked, either with the Lock Position or Lock All button. If a transformation command appears dimmed, therefore, the Lock buttons are very likely your culprits.

Numerical transformations

To track your transformations numerically, display the Info palette (F8) before you apply the Free Transform command. Even after you initiate Free Transform, you can access the Info palette by choosing Window ➪ Info. You can also track the numerical equivalents of your transformations in the Options bar. Shown in Figure 5-21, the Options bar contains a series of numerical transformation controls anytime you enter the Free Transform mode. These values not only reflect the changes you've made so far but also permit you to further transform the selection or layer numerically.

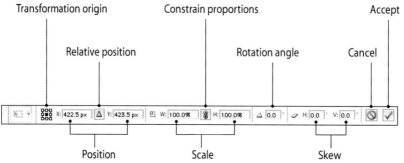

Figure 5-21: Normally, the options in the Options bar change only when you select a different tool, but choosing Free Transform adds a series of controls that permit you to transform a selection or layer numerically.

For the most part, the controls in the Options bar are straightforward. Click in the grid of nine squares to reposition the transformation origin. Use the X and Y values to change the location of the origin numerically. (This is another opportunity to utilize Photoshop CS's new scrubbing function, described in detail in Chapter 1.) Click the triangular delta symbol to measure the movement relative to the transformation origin. Use the W and H values to scale the selection or layer. Click the link button to constrain the W and H values and resize the selection or layer proportionally. The angle value rotates; the H and V values skew.

I imagine most folks use the Options bar strictly for scaling and rotating. You'd need the spatial awareness of a NASA navigation system to predict a numerical slant.

Masking and Layers

Layers offer special masking options unto themselves. You can paint inside the confines of a layer as if it were a selection mask; you can add a special mask for a single layer; or you can group multiple layers and have the bottom layer in the group serve as the mask. Quite honestly, these are the kinds of thoughtful and useful functions I've come to expect from Photoshop. Although they're fairly complicated to use — you must be on your toes once you start juggling layer masks — these functions provide new realms of opportunities.

Preserving transparency

As you may recall, I mentioned we'd be talking more about the Lock Transparency button, first mentioned in the "Locking layers" section and labeled in Figure 5-22. Well, sure enough, the time has come to do exactly that. When selected, this button prevents you from painting inside the transparent portions of the layer. And although that may sound like a small thing, it is in fact the most useful Lock option of them all.

Lock transparency

Figure 5-22: The Lock Transparency button enables you to paint inside the layer's transparency mask without harming the transparent pixels.

Suppose I want to paint inside the girl shown in Figure 5-22. (You remember her, right?) If this were a flat, nonlayered image, I'd have to draw a selection outline carefully around her. But there's no need to do this when using layers. Because the girl lies on a different layer than her background, a permanent selection outline tells Photoshop which pixels are transparent and which are opaque. This is the *transparency mask.*

The first example in Figure 5-23 shows the girl on her own with the background hidden. The transparent areas outside the mask appear in the checkerboard pattern. When the Lock Transparency button is turned off, you can paint anywhere you want inside the layer. Selecting the Lock Transparency button activates the transparency mask and places the checkerboard area off-limits.

The bottom image in Figure 5-23 shows what happens after I select Lock Transparency and use the clone stamp tool to paint in the scared woman image. I also painted in some black with the brush tool. Notice that no matter how much I painted, it never leaked out onto the background.

Although this enlightening discussion pretty well covers it, I feel compelled to share a few additional words about Lock Transparency:

✦ You can turn Lock Transparency on and off from the keyboard by pressing the standard slash character, /, right there on the same key with the question mark.

✦ The Lock Transparency option is dimmed when the background layer is active because this layer is entirely opaque. There's no transparency to lock, eh? (That's my impression of a Canadian explaining layer theory. It maybe needs a little polishing, but I think it's just aboot perfect.)

Figure 5-23: The layered girl as she appears on her own (top) and when the scared woman has been clone stamped in with the Lock Transparency button turned on (bottom).

And finally, here's a question for all you folks who think you may have Photoshop mastered. Which of the brush modes (explained in Chapter 1) is the exact opposite of Lock Transparency? The answer is Behind. To see what I mean, turn off Lock Transparency. Then select the brush tool and choose the Behind brush mode in the Options bar. Now paint. Photoshop applies the foreground color exclusively *outside* the transparency mask, thus protecting the opaque pixels. So it follows, when Lock Transparency is turned on, the Behind brush mode is dimmed.

Creating layer-specific masks

In addition to the transparency mask that accompanies every layer (except the background), you can add a mask to a layer to make certain pixels in the layer transparent. Now, you might ask, "Won't simply erasing portions of a layer make those portions transparent?" The answer, of course, is yes. And, I hasten to add, that was a keen insight on your part. But when you erase, you delete pixels permanently. By creating a layer mask, you instead make pixels temporarily transparent. You can return several months later and bring those pixels back to life again simply by adjusting the mask. So layer masks add yet another level of flexibility to a program that's already a veritable image-editing contortionist.

To create a layer mask, select the layer you want to mask and choose Layer ⇨ Add Layer Mask ⇨ Reveal All. Or more simply, click the layer mask icon at the bottom of the Layers palette, as labeled in Figure 5-24. A second thumbnail preview appears to the left of the layer name, also labeled in the figure. A second outline around the preview shows the layer mask is active.

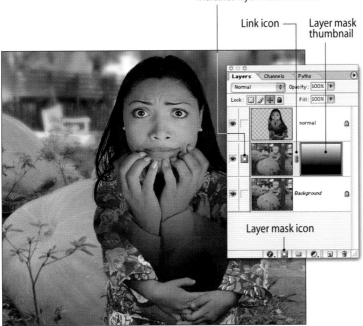

Figures labels: Indicates layer mask is active · Link icon · Layer mask thumbnail · Layer mask icon

Figure 5-24: The black area in the layer mask (which you can see in the thumbnail view in the Layers palette) translates to transparent pixels in the layer.

If the second outline is hard to see, check the icon directly to the right of the layer's eye icon. If the icon is a paintbrush, the layer, and not the mask, is active. If the icon is a square with a little dotted circle, the mask is active.

To edit the mask, simply paint in the image window. Paint with black to make pixels transparent. Because black represents deselected pixels in an image, it makes these pixels transparent in a layer. Paint with white to make pixels opaque.

Thankfully, Photoshop is smart enough to make the default foreground color in a layer mask white, and the default background color black. This ensures that painting with the brush makes pixels opaque, whereas painting with the eraser makes them transparent, just as you would expect.

In Figure 5-24, I floated the background to a new layer, applied Gaussian Blur with a Radius of 8 pixels, and drew a simple white to black gradient in the layer mask using the gradient tool. The result was a fading blur, so that the farthest away elements appear the least in focus. If I decide that I want the fade to be more abrupt, not to worry. I merely drag a shorter distance in the layer mask with the gradient tool.

Photoshop goes nuts in the layer mask department, adding lots of bells and whistles to make the function both convenient and powerful. Here's everything you need to know:

+ **Reveal Selection:** If you select some portion of your layer, Photoshop automatically converts the selection to a layer mask when you click the layer mask icon at the bottom of the palette. The area outside the selection becomes transparent. (The corresponding command is Layer ⇨ Add Layer Mask ⇨ Reveal Selection.)

+ **Hide Selection:** You can also choose to reverse the prospective mask, making the area inside the selection transparent and the area outside opaque. To do this, choose Layer ⇨ Add Layer Mask ⇨ Hide Selection. Or better yet, Alt-click (Win) or Option-click (Mac) the layer mask icon in the Layers palette.

+ **Hide everything:** To begin with a black mask that hides everything, choose Layer ⇨ Add Layer Mask ⇨ Hide All. Or press Ctrl+D (⌘-D on the Mac) to deselect everything and then Alt-click (Option-click) the layer mask icon.

+ **View the mask:** Photoshop regards a layer mask as a layer-specific channel. You can actually see it listed in italics in the Channels palette. To view the mask on its own — as a black-and-white image — Alt-click (Option-click) the layer mask thumbnail in the Layers palette. Alt-click (Option-click) again to view the image instead.

+ **Layer mask rubylith:** To view the mask as a red overlay, Shift+Alt-click (or Shift-Option-click) the layer mask icon. Or simply press the backslash key, \, which is above the Enter key (Return on the Mac).

After you have both layer and mask visible at once, you can hide the mask by pressing \, or you can hide the layer and view only the mask by pressing the tilde key (~). So many alternatives!

+ **Change the overlay color:** Double-click the layer mask thumbnail to access the Layer Mask Display Options dialog box, which enables you to change the color and opacity of the rubylith.

+ **Turn off the mask:** You can temporarily disable the mask by Shift-clicking on the mask thumbnail. A red X covers the thumbnail when it's disabled, and all masked pixels in the layer appear opaque. Click the thumbnail to put the mask back in working order.

+ **Switch between layer and mask:** As you become more familiar with layer masks, you'll switch back and forth between layer and mask quite frequently, editing the layer one minute and editing the mask the next. You can switch between layer and mask by clicking on their respective thumbnails. As I mentioned, look to the icon to the right of the eye icon to see whether the layer or the mask is active.

You can also switch between layer and mask from the keyboard. Press Ctrl+tilde (⌘-tilde on the Mac) to make the layer active. Press Ctrl+\ (⌘-\) to switch to the mask.

✦ **Link layer and mask:** A little link icon appears between the layer and mask thumbnails in the Layers palette. When the link icon is visible, you can move or transform the mask and layer as one. If you click the link icon to turn it off, the layer and mask move independently. (You can always move a selected region of the mask or layer independently of the other.)

✦ **Convert mask to selection:** As with all masks, you can convert a layer mask to a selection. To do so, Ctrl-click (on the Mac, ⌘-click) the layer mask icon. Throw in the Shift and Alt (or Option) keys if you want to add or subtract the layer mask with an existing selection outline.

✦ **Apply mask to set:** You can also apply a mask to a set of layers. Just select the set and click the layer mask icon. The mask affects all layers in the set. If a layer in the set contains its own mask, no worries; Photoshop's smart enough to figure out how to mix them together. For another method of masking multiple layers, see the section "Masking groups of layers," coming up soon.

When and if you finish using the mask — you can leave it in force as long as you like — you can choose Layer ➪ Remove Layer Mask. Or just drag the layer mask thumbnail to the trash can icon. Either way, an alert box asks whether you want to discard the mask or permanently apply it to the layer. Click the button that corresponds to your innermost desires.

Pasting inside a selection outline

One command, Edit ➪ Paste Into (Ctrl+Shift+V or ⌘-Shift-V), creates a layer mask automatically. Choose the Paste Into command to paste the contents of the Clipboard into the current selection, so that the selection acts as a mask. Because Photoshop pastes to a new layer, it converts the selection into a layer mask. But here's the interesting part: By default, Photoshop turns off the link between the layer and the mask. This way, you can Ctrl-drag (or ⌘-drag) the layer inside a fixed mask to position the pasted image.

Once upon a time in Photoshop, there was a command named Edit ➪ Paste Behind. (Or something like that. It might have been Paste in Back. My memory's a little hazy.) The command (whatever its name) pasted a copied image in back of a selection. Although the command is gone, its spirit still lives. Now you press Alt (Win) or Option (Mac) when choosing Edit ➪ Paste Into. Or just press Ctrl+Shift+Alt+V (⌘-Shift-Option-V on the Mac). Photoshop creates a new layer with an inverted layer mask, masking away the selected area.

Masking groups of layers

About now, you may be growing fatigued with the topic of layer masking. But one more option requires your immediate attention. You can group multiple layers into something called a *clipping mask*, in which the lowest layer in the group masks the others. Where the lowest layer is transparent, the other layers are hidden; where the lowest layer is opaque, the contents of the other layers are visible.

There are two ways to create a clipping mask:

✦ Alt-click (or Option-click) the horizontal line between any two layers to group them into a single unit. Your cursor changes to the mask cursor labeled in Figure 5-25 when you press Alt (Option on the Mac). To break the layers apart again, Alt-click (or Option-click) the line.

✦ Select the higher of the two layers you want to combine into a clipping mask. Then choose Layer ⇨ Create Clipping Mask or press Ctrl+G (⌘-G). To make the layers independent again, choose Layer ⇨ Release Clipping Mask or press Ctrl+Shift+G (⌘-Shift-G).

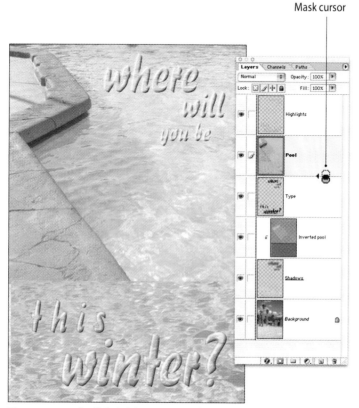

Mask cursor

Figure 5-25: Alt-click (Win) or Option-click (Mac) the horizontal line between two layers to group them.

Figures 5-25 and 5-26 demonstrate two steps in a piece of artwork I created years ago for *Macworld* magazine. I had already created some text on an independent layer using the type tool, and I wanted to fill the text with water. So I added some photographs I shot of a swimming pool to a layer above the text, as shown in Figure 5-25. Then I combined the text and pool images into a clipping mask. Because the text was beneath the water, Photoshop masked the pool images according to the transparency mask assigned to the text. The result is a water pattern that exactly fills the type, as in Figure 5-26.

If you're familiar with Illustrator, you may recognize this clipping mask metaphor as a relative to Illustrator's clipping mask. One object in the illustration acts as a mask for a collection of additional objects. In Illustrator, however, the topmost object in the group is the mask, not the bottom one. So much for consistency.

Clipping mask

Figure 5-26: After combining the pool water and type layers into a single clipping mask, Photoshop applies the type layer's transparency mask to the pool layer.

Working with Layer Comps

For years, users of Photoshop have been clamoring for a savable History palette. This is particularly true of designers who are often required to submit to their clients a bunch of variations on a particular concept. True, there have been a handful of tricks available for keeping different versions of images within one file, mostly having to do with creatively organizing layer sets and toggling visibilities. But it still hasn't been easy enough. When it comes to saving different snapshots of an image that can be quickly called up later, Photoshop has never been able to deliver the goods. Well now, with the addition of the new Layer Comps palette, Photoshop CS comes one significant step closer.

The Layer Comps palette, shown in Figure 5-27, allows you to record the status of certain aspects of your layers and save those states as *layer comps* inside the file. Then, later, with the click of a button in the Layer Comps palette, you can jump between those states, presenting your client with a "Better here...or better here?" kind of choice. And if that sounds like a savable History palette, it's really not. The drawback here is that the Layer Comps palette has a selective memory.

Figure 5-27: The new Layer Comps palette enables you to leap through time without having to save up for that vintage DeLorean.

The key to successfully working with layer comps is to be extremely conscious of what they are and aren't capable of tracking. A saved layer comp can store and recall information about the visibility, opacity, and blend modes of the layers in an image. Layer comps can also record whether or not styles are applied to each layer and the settings of those styles. And finally, layer comps can remember the position of a layer. That doesn't mean you can shuffle the order of layers up and down in the Layers palette; by remembering the "position," I mean the position of a layer's pixel info within the image window. In other words, if you drag an element to the left or right with the move tool, layer comps can track that and remember it.

What you need to keep in mind, however, is that layer comps don't even attempt to track any pixel changes to your images. This applies to painting, creating gradients, using the patch tool — any operation that alters the pixels (as well as text contents) of an image is not recorded in the Layer Comps palette. The palette will turn the other way and pretend you've done nothing at all.

That said, layer comps can be a great and useful asset, especially when you're at the stage of assembling the final pieces into a composition. To save a layer comp, bring up the Layer Comps palette by choosing Window ⇨ Layer Comps or by clicking the Layer Comps tab in the Options bar's docking well (the palette is docked there by default). Next, click the new layer comp icon (it's the one that looks like a little page) at the bottom of the palette to access the New Layer Comp dialog box. Here, you set a name for your layer comp and any comments that might help you identify the state you're saving. This dialog box is also where you specify exactly what gets tracked by this layer comp. You have three check boxes available to you:

+ **Visibility:** Turn on this option to track the visibility of layers and layer masks.

+ **Position:** This option tracks the horizontal and vertical position of a layered object. In other words, if you drag the contents of a layer around within the image window, layer comps can remember that. But it's important to emphasize changing the pixel content of the layer — say, if you marquee a section of a layer and drag it over to a corner — is not restorable through layer comps.

+ **Appearance (Layer Style):** This option saves all layer style attributes, including knock-outs and effects, as well as the Opacity value and blend mode assigned to each layer.

Click OK to confirm your settings and, presto, you've created a new layer comp. Figure 5-28 shows a multilayered image which has been saved as a layer comp; the image itself depicts a couple of my bulgy-eyed image-editing mascots. On the left, you see my Little Puppet Friend who (as performed by my *Photoshop Elements For Dummies* co-author Galen Fott) has popped up in several of my video series for Total Training. And on the right is Shenbop the frog who, despite being technically dead, was a featured player in a comic strip I drew back in the halcyon days of my youth. Ah, my youth, my youth...

Figure 5-28: The new Layer Comps palette (upper left) is sort of like a History palette that works exclusively on the Layers palette (right). Changes to some aspects of your layers can be saved and recalled with a single click.

Um, where was I? Oh yeah, layer comps. You can tell that you're looking at a saved state of this image because the little icon in the left column of the Layer Comps palette sits alongside the LPF/Shenbop item. As soon as you make any layer comp-friendly changes to your image, the icon will snap back to the topmost layer comp, known as the Last Document State. This means that trackable changes have been made to the image since your last saved layer comp. Now, you can save this new state as another layer comp, as I've done in Figure 5-29. To return to a saved state, simply click in the space to the left of the desired layer comp.

If you compare Figure 5-29 with Figure 5-28, you'll see that I made quite a few changes. Starting at the bottom of the Layers palette, I changed the Color Overlay and Pattern Overlay layer styles on the left background and right background layers, switching the orange/pink combination for a blue/green one. Using the move tool, I dragged my LPF layer to the right and my Shenbop layer to the left, turning off their Drop Shadow layer styles and adding Outer Glows instead. I also turned off the panel layer's Outer Glow, and added a Drop Shadow layer style. And finally I toggled the visibility of the two text layers on the top. To save the two different fonts into layer comps, I had to use two different text layers, since layer comps don't remember changes to the actual pixel contents of a layer. That's the kind of limitation that makes layer comps a little less than wonderful, but in a way I'm looking a gift horse in the mouth. Instead of hating layer comps for what they aren't, why not love them for what they are? Layer comps do give you the unprecedented ability to toggle the visibility of multiple layers on and off with a single click—even layers that are intermingled with other layers in the Layers palette. Heck, by stacking a sequence of images into a single layered file, layer comps can even be used to turn Photoshop into a sort of ersatz PowerPoint when making presentations.

Figure 5-29: Do you like this layout better than the one in Figure 5-28? That's the strength of layer comps; they make it easy for you — or your persnickety client — to compare changes in an image.

Working with the Layer Comps palette is pretty easy once you get used to it, but there are a few things you should know:

✦ Use the left- and right-pointing arrowheads at the bottom of the palette to cycle through your various layer comps. Click the right-pointing arrowhead to view the next saved layer comp down the list and click the left-pointing arrowhead to view the previous layer comp. To cycle through only specific comps, Ctrl-click (⌘-click on the Mac) or Shift-click to select them and then click the arrowheads.

✦ To the right of the arrowhead icons is the update layer comp icon (it's the one with two arrows that form a circle). Click this icon to assign changes to an existing selected layer comp. The layer comp icon in the left column of the palette leaps over to the layer comp you've selected, and the layer comp is updated to reflect the current state of the Layers palette.

✦ To delete a layer comp, simply select it and click the trash can icon, just as you would to delete a layer in the Layers palette. Here, you also have the added benefit of being able to select and drag multiple layer comps to the trash icon at once.

✦ You can always return the image to its most recent unsaved layer state by clicking in the left column next to the Last Document State item in the palette.

✦ To duplicate a layer comp, simply choose Duplicate Layer Comp in the Layer Comps palette menu.

✦ Choosing Layer Comp Options for a selected layer comp gives you another crack at the settings in the New Layer Comp dialog box. Who says there are no second chances in life?

Being the fragile creatures that they are, layer comps do have a tendency to break down every once in a while. Luckily, though, they're pretty good at letting you know when they're unhappy. Whenever you make a change that will throw any of your layer comps out of whack — such as merging or deleting layers — the affected comps will display a little triangle with an exclamation point. You can either undo the destructive move or click on one of the triangle icons, in which case you'll be presented with a warning explaining that you've betrayed the layer comp. Clicking the warning's Clear button basically updates the layer comp, in essence telling it to accept the changes that have been made to its little world, and to roll with those changes.

Blend Modes and Knockouts

It's High Time to Blend, Friend

When recording artist Paul Simon first asserted that there must be 50 ways to leave your lover, I couldn't help but think he was inflating the number a little. I mean, some of the methods he proposed were pretty flimsy. Is it really that simple for Gus to get on a bus? Won't he just have to come back later for a clean shirt and a change of underwear? And when he cautions Roy not to be coy, Simon seems to be more interested in rhymin' than in providing concrete, helpful suggestions. In the end, the song fails to deliver on its own premise. Between Jack, Stan, Roy, Gus, and Lee, Simon gets around to offering a scant five ways to leave your lover, just 10 percent of the number promised. What happened to Take a ride on the ferry, Larry; Tell her you're gay, Ray; and Show her the door, Thor? And how about the ladies? Might not Sue, Beth, and Anne benefit from some help in leaving their lovers as well?

Don't get me wrong, I love the song. But personally, I think Mr. Simon might have had an easier time of it if he had decided to list the many ways you can combine and compare differently colored pixels in Photoshop. Forget 50, there must be 50 thousand! Just think of the brush modes from Chapter 1: Try Linear Burn, Vern; then a touch of Pin Light, Dwight; lighten up with some Screen, Dean — and paint yourself free. Granted, it would have failed commercially, but assuming Simon again listed no more than 10 percent of the possibilities, the song could have filled seven albums.

Here we are, hundreds of pages into the book, and we've seen how you can smear and blur pixels, trace and sharpen pixels, undo your way back to the stone age, select pixels using other pixels, layer pixels in front of other pixels, and much, much more. Any time that you edit, retouch, mask, composite, or filter an image, you're actually breeding the image with itself or with another image to create a new and unique offspring. Did I say 50 thousand? I meant 50 million!

And yet, despite all that we've seen so far, we're not even close to being finished. Consider the subject of this chapter, *blend modes*, one of the most alluring experiments in Photoshop's great genetics laboratory. Alternatively known as *transfer modes* and *calculations*, blend modes permit you to mix the color of a pixel with that of every pixel in a straight line beneath it. A single blend mode can be as powerful as a mask, a filter, and a retouching tool combined. Best of all, it's

temporary. As long as one image remains layered in front of another, you can replace one calculation with another as easily as you change a letter of text in a word processor.

To appreciate the most rudimentary power of blend modes, consider Figure 6-1. The first image shows me rendered in robot form on an independent layer with the New Yankee Photoshop set in the background. Aside from the text and accompanying color bars, these are the only layers in the image. For the most part, the robot is as opaque as if I had cut it out with scissors and glued it to the wood behind it. (Admittedly, I'd have to be very skilled with scissors and glue, but you get the idea.) The soft edges of the shadow to the right of the robot mix slightly with the pixels below them. But beyond that, every pixel is a digital hermit, steadfastly avoiding interaction.

Figure 6-1: One roboDeke means good training (top), but treat yourself to multiple roboDekes subject to all kinds of blend modes (bottom), and you get the kind of educational overload that leaves you begging for mercy.

The second image in Figure 6-1 paints a different picture. Here I've created several clones of the robot and mixed them with both the background and each other using Photoshop's wide array of calculation capabilities. The robot image itself never changes; each layer contains the same 400 or so thousand pixels that, when combined, scream out, "We are roboDeke!" In all, there are ten layers: three angled robots in the background, one apiece subject to the Hard Light and Linear Light modes on the left, followed by two overlapping layers, one the result of Linear Dodge and the other a function of Multiply and an Opacity value of 50 percent. I created the final photonegative robot using three layers, one subject to Difference, another inverted and subject to Screen, and then again inverted and again subject to Difference.

Naturally, we'll get into the specifics of every one of these blend modes — including the ever-popular Difference sandwich — later in this chapter. But before we do, a few basics are in order. We'll be investigating two fundamental ways to mix images:

✦ **The Layers palette:** You can combine the active layer with underlying pixels using the Opacity and Fill values, along with the blend mode pop-up menu, all members of the Layers palette. Figure 6-2 shows these illustrious items in the context of the list of layers for Figure 6-1. To learn everything there is to know about the Opacity and Fill options, read the next section. Blend modes are covered in the section after that.

✦ **Blending options:** Right-click a thumbnail in the Layers palette (Control-click on the Mac) and choose Blending Options to display the Blending Options panel of the extensive Layer Style dialog box. Along with the Blend Mode, Opacity, and Fill Opacity options, you get an assortment of advanced blending options, including the Knockout pop-up menu and Blend If sliders. The Knockout options let you use one layer to cut a floating hole into one or more layers below it. Using the Blend If sliders, you can drop colors out of the active layer and force colors to show through from layers below. For more information about these and other options, read "Advanced Blending Options" later in this chapter.

Blend modes are not Photoshop's most straightforward feature. There may even come a time when you utter the words, "Blend modes are stupid." They demand a generous supply of experimentation and even then they'll try to fool you. I was a math major in college (with a double-major in art, for what it's worth), so I well understand the elementary arithmetic behind many of Photoshop's calculations. And yet, despite roughly a decade of experience with blend modes in Photoshop and other programs, I am frequently surprised by their outcome.

The key, therefore, is to combine a basic understanding of how blend modes and other compositing features work with your natural willingness to experiment, grow, and bond with pixels. Sometime when you don't have a deadline looming over your head, take some multilayered composition you have lying around and hit it with a few calculations. Even if the result is a disaster that you wouldn't share with your mother, let alone a client, you can consider it time well spent, Kent.

Opacity and Fill

The Opacity value permits you to mix the active layer with the layers beneath it in prescribed portions. By way of example, consider Figure 6-3. The first image shows one of my favorite postage stamps, in which patriot and statesman Paul Revere looks for all the world like Betsy Ross. Although quite thoroughly emasculated, he is shown at full opacity, 100 percent. In the second example, I have reduced his Opacity setting to 20 percent, thereby transforming him from Paul Revere in drag to the ghost of Paul Revere in drag.

Blend mode pop-up menu   Opacity/Fill slider bar

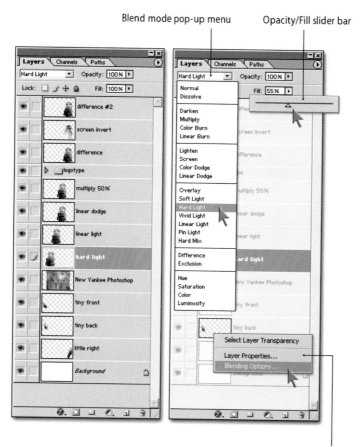

Shortcut menu

Figure 6-2: The list of layers in the "Army of roboDekes" composition, with a few essential layer blending functions labeled on right.

The result is a lot like mixing a drink. Suppose you pour one part vermouth and four parts gin into a martini glass. (Any martini enthusiast knows that's too much vermouth, but bear with me on this one.) The resulting beverage is ⅕ vermouth and ⅘ gin. If the vermouth were a layer, you could achieve the same effect by setting the Opacity to 20 percent, as I did with Paul Revere. So in the case of the right half of Figure 6-3, 20 percent of what you see is Revere and the remaining 80 percent is background.

The option directly below Opacity in the Layers palette is Fill, which controls the *fill opacity* of a layer. Where Opacity controls the translucency of everything associated with a layer, Fill adjusts the opacity of the filled areas only. Now at first blush, there won't seem to be any difference. Things change, however, if you add one or more layer effects. In Figure 6-4, I added a drop shadow and outer bevel to each of the stamp layers. (You can add a layer effect to a layer by choosing an option from the cursive *f* icon at the bottom of the Layers palette, as discussed in Chapter 7.) Now the difference between Opacity and Fill becomes apparent — Opacity affects pixels and layer effects alike; Fill affects pixels and leaves effects unchanged.

Fill is also more absolute than Opacity. You can lower the Opacity value to 1 percent, just shy of altogether transparent. But Photoshop lets you take Fill all the way down to 0 percent. Why?

Because that allows you to reduce the fill of a layer to nothing while leaving the effects intact. Figure 6-5 shows the results of lowering the Fill value to first 20 and then 0 percent.

Figure 6-3: Paul Revere at 100 percent Opacity (left) and faded into the background (right).

Figure 6-4: By adding a layer effect or two, the difference between Opacity and Fill becomes obvious. Opacity makes layer and effects translucent (left); Fill alters the layer independently of its effects (right).

When a selection or navigation tool is active, you can change the Opacity setting for a layer from the keyboard. Press a single number key to change the Opacity in 10-percent increments. That's 1 for 10 percent, 2 for 20 percent, up to 0 for 100 percent, in order along the top of your keyboard. If you have the urge to be more precise, press two keys in a row quickly to specify an exact two-digit Opacity value.

Figure 6-5: Using the Fill value, you can subordinate a layer to its effect (left) or fade the layer away entirely (right).

Hankering to change the Fill just as easily? Then press the Shift key. Shift+1 changes the Fill value to 10 percent; Shift+0 makes it 100 percent. Shift plus two numbers enters a two-digit value.

You also can change the setting by dragging the Opacity or Fill slider in the Layers palette (labeled back in Figure 6-2). Click the arrowhead to the right of the option to display the slider bar and then drag the triangle to change the value. Or press the up and down arrows to nudge the triangle along; press Shift with the arrow key to nudge the value in 10-percent increments. Press Enter or Return to confirm the slider setting or press Escape to restore the previous setting.

Incidentally, both the Opacity and Fill options are dimmed when working on the background layer or in a single-layer image. There's nothing underneath, so there's nothing to mix. Naturally, this goes double when editing a black-and-white or indexed image, or when editing a single channel or mask, because neither of these circumstances supports layers.

Blend Modes

Photoshop CS offers a total of 23 blend modes, starting with Normal and ending with Luminosity. If you've been reading the chapters sequentially, you'll notice this isn't the first time I've touched on Normal, Dissolve, Darken, and the like. In fact, given that the blend modes mimic the brush modes (discussed in Chapter 1) both in name and in function, we're covering some familiar territory. But you'll soon find that there's a big difference between laying down a color or pattern with a brush and merging the myriad colors that inhabit a single layer. This difference is the stuff of the following pages.

For you visual learners, I'll be demonstrating the effects of Normal, Luminosity, and the others using the images pictured in Figure 6-6. The default order of the images is the order pictured in the figure — that is, the Blistered Paint pattern (one of the predefined patterns included with Photoshop) on top and the tranquil background at the bottom. However, I sometimes slide the pattern layer below the gradient layer if it better suits the discussion. In any case, bear in mind how these control images look, because I'll be using two or more of them throughout future figures.

Figure 6-6: To demonstrate the effects of Photoshop's blend modes, I'll be compositing these images in more or less the order shown here (with some occasional swapping around). The tranquil background is in fact the background layer, so no blend mode can ever be applied to it. Note that the right half of the face layer is transparent, and the layer includes an automated drop shadow, fading off to the right.

You apply every one of the blend modes to a layer from the keyboard by pressing Shift+Alt (Shift-Option on the Mac) plus a letter, provided that the active tool doesn't offer its own brush mode options. (If the tool supports brush modes — as in the case of the brush tool, pencil, clone stamp, healing brush, and others — the shortcuts set the mode for the tool and not the layer.)

Some of the shortcut letters make perfect sense — Shift+Alt+N for Normal and Shift-Option-S for Screen. Others are a bit of a stretch — such as Shift+Alt+W for Linear Dodge or Shift-Option-Z for Pin Light. That's why I've come up with the following helpful pneumonic. Reading from the top of the blend mode menu to the bottom, it's "Nik mba gsd wof hvjz lex utcy," pronounced "Nick mubba gus-sid woff heev-jizz lex ootsie." Sing that to a song Big Bird might have sung (see Figure 6-7), and you'll have your blend mode shortcuts memorized in no time.

It's the most remarkable word I've ever seen!

Figure 6-7: Just sing this magical word and you'll be the smartest bird the world has ever seen. I promise.

Of course, it's always possible a few people won't be able to wrap their brains around my simple approach. Which is why I list the shortcut letter in parentheses with each blend mode description and illustrate the shortcut inside the figures. So whether predictable or not, we got your blend modes covered.

One more note: Every so often, I allude to a little something called a composite pixel. By this I mean the pixel color that results from all the mixing that's going on beneath the active layer. For example, your document may contain hordes of layers with all sorts of blend modes in effect, but as long as you're working on, say, Layer 23, Photoshop treats the image formed by Layers 1 through 22 as if it were one flattened image filled with a bunch of static composite pixels.

Cool? Keen. So without any further notes or clarifications, here they are, the 23 blend modes, in order of appearance:

✦ **Normal (N):** In combination with Opacity and Fill settings of 100 percent, this option displays every pixel in the active layer normally, regardless of the colors in the underlying layers. When you use opacity values (whether Opacity or Fill) of less than 100 percent, the color of each pixel in the active layer is averaged with the composite pixel in the layers behind it. Figure 6-8 shows examples applied to the face layer on its own.

✦ **Dissolve (I):** This option specifically affects feathered or softened edges. If the active layer is entirely opaque with hard edges, Dissolve has no effect. But when the edges of the layer fade into view, as is the case around the neck and chin in Figure 6-9, Dissolve randomizes, or *dithers*, the pixels. If you look closely, you'll see that Dissolve does not dither pixels in the drop shadow; as I discuss in Chapter 7, layer effects are governed by their own, independent blend modes. Things change, however, when you drop the Opacity value below 100 percent, in which case Dissolve dithers all pixels, as demonstrated in the second example of the figure.

✦ **Darken (K):** The first of the four darkening modes, Darken applies colors in the active layer only if they are darker than the corresponding pixels below. Keep in mind that Photoshop compares the brightness levels of pixels in a full-color image on a channel-by-channel basis. So although the blue component of a pixel in the active layer may be darker than the blue component of the underlying composite pixel, the red and green components may be lighter. In this case, Photoshop would assign the blue component but not the red or green, thereby subtracting blue and shifting the pixel toward yellow. Darken is most useful for covering up light portions of an image while letting dark areas show through.

Figure 6-8: The face layer subject to the Normal mode when combined with Opacity values of 100 percent (top) and 60 percent (bottom). The superimposed character indicates the keyboard shortcut Shift+Alt+N (Shift-Option-N on the Mac) and 6 for 60 percent opacity.

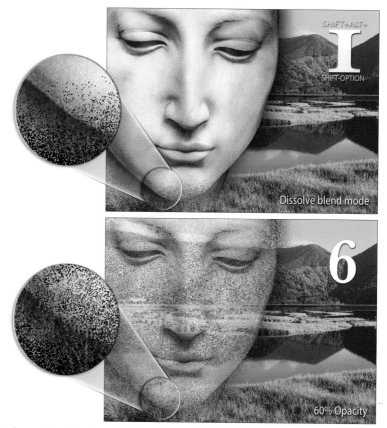

Figure 6-9: Here I applied the Dissolve mode to a layer at 100 percent (top) and 60 percent (bottom) Opacity settings. Instead of creating translucent pixels, Dissolve turns pixels on and off to simulate transparency, as shown by the magnified details.

To illustrate Darken and the other darkening modes, I first established a light background by setting the pattern layer on top of the background and lowering its Opacity to 70 percent. Then I placed the gradient layer on top of that and set it to the Screen mode, which left the white portion of the gradient visible and dropped out the black portion. The result appears in the top example of Figure 6-10. I then added the face layer and set it to the Darken mode, as shown at the bottom of the figure. The result is a face that appears smooth in the midtones and the shadows and patterned in the light areas, with relatively sharp transitions between the two.

✦ **Multiply (M):** Multiply is one of the rare blend modes that emulate a real-world scenario. Imagine that the active layer and the underlying composite are both photos on transparent slides. The Multiply mode produces the same effect as holding these slides up to the light, one slide in front of the other. Because the light has to travel through two slides, the outcome invariably combines the darkest elements from both images. So unlike Darken, Multiply universally darkens, resulting in smooth transitions, ideal for preserving contours and shadows, as in the top image in Figure 6-11.

If the Multiply mode produces too dark an effect, reduce the Opacity or Fill value. If it isn't dark enough, clone the layer by pressing Ctrl+J (Ô-J on the Mac). In the second example in Figure 6-11, I cloned the face layer and threw away its drop shadow to avoid darkening the shadow. Then I merged the two layers by pressing Ctrl+E (Ô-E). As fortune would have it, the visual effect remained the same, effectively creating a single layer with twice the darkness of the original. This technique holds true throughout Photoshop: Provided that two layers share a common blend mode, you can merge the layers and preserve the effect.

Figure 6-10: A backdrop composed of the background, pattern, and gradient layers (top) followed by an application of the face in the Darken mode (bottom). Only those pixels in the face that are darker than the pixels in the patterned backdrop remain visible.

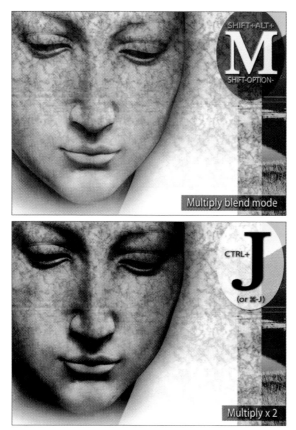

Figure 6-11: The Multiply blend mode (top) produces the same effect as holding two overlapping transparencies up to the light. To get an even darker effect, I duplicated the layer, removed its drop shadow, and merged the two face layers into one (bottom).

♦ **Color Burn (B)** and **Linear Burn (A):** If the Multiply mode darkens your images, then the two Burn modes char them. They both use colors in the active layer to reduce brightness values, resulting in radical color transformations. As demonstrated in Figure 6-12, Color Burn results in crisp, often colorful, toasted edges; Linear Burn creates a smoother, less vibrant effect. Both modes have an uncanny ability to draw colors from background layers. For example, even though I lightened the background by applying Screen to the pattern layer in Figure 6-12, we see more contrast in this figure than in the single-pass Multiply example from Figure 6-11. So for high-contrast stamping effects, these are the blend modes to use.

♦ **Lighten (G):** The next four options use the active layer to lighten those below it. If you select Lighten, for example, Photoshop applies colors in the active layer only if they are lighter than the corresponding pixels in the underlying image. As with Darken, Photoshop compares the brightness levels of all channels in a full-color image.

To set the stage for the lightening figures, I modified the background layers, restoring the pattern layer to Normal and switching the gradient layer to Multiply. As a result, Photoshop dropped out the whites in the gradient and kept the blacks, as in the first image in Figure 6-13. In the second image, I assigned the Lighten blend mode to the face. But I also modified the drop shadow—which would have otherwise remained black—by changing its color to white and its blend mode to Screen. The result is a drop glow, which I describe in the section "Inside the Layer Style dialog box" in the next chapter. (If you're having problems finding this discussion, look for the full-page Figure 7-19.)

Figure 6-12: After applying Screen to the pattern layer, I applied the Color Burn (top) and Linear Burn (bottom) blend modes to the face layer. Even though the background is lighter, many portions of the face appear darker than they did after a single application of Multiply.

Figure 6-13: Here I prepared a dark background by assigning Multiply to the gradient layer (top). Then I applied Lighten to the face layer and changed its drop shadow to white (bottom).

✦ **Screen (S):** From a creative standpoint, Screen is the opposite of Multiply. In fact, remember those transparent slides from the Multiply analogy? Well this time, place them both in separate projectors and point them at the same screen. The result is the effect you get with Screen. Rather than creating a darker image, as you do with Multiply, you create a lighter image, as demonstrated in Figure 6-14.

You can use the Screen blend mode to emulate film that has been exposed multiple times. Ever seen Thomas Eakin's pioneering *Jumping Figure*, which shows rapid-fire exposures of a naked man jumping from one location to another? Each shot is effectively screened onto the other, lightening the film with each and every exposure. The photographer was smart enough to limit the exposure time so as not to overexpose the film; likewise, you should only apply Screen when working with images that are sufficiently dark so that you avoid overlightening. Screen is equally useful for creating glows, retaining just the light colors in a gradient, and creating light noise effects such as snow and stars.

Figure 6-14: The Screen mode produces the same effect as shining two projectors at the same screen. In this case, one projector contains the background layers, and the other contains the face (top). Want a more pronounced ghosting effect? Just duplicate the Screen layer (bottom).

✦ **Color Dodge (D)** and **Linear Dodge (W):** When you apply one of the two Dodge modes, each color in the layer becomes a brightness-value multiplier. Light colors such as white produce the greatest effect, and black drops away. As a result, the Dodge modes are Photoshop's most dramatic whitening agents, the equivalent of mounting your image on a gel and projecting it from a spotlight. (This is not an exact equivalent, mind you, but it's close enough to give you an idea of what to expect.) Of the two, Color Dodge produces the sharper, rougher effect; Linear Dodge smoothes out the transitions (see Figure 6-15). Because they send so much of an image to white, the Dodge modes are most useful for simulating hot spots and other intensely bright effects.

✦ **Overlay (O), Soft Light (F),** and **Hard Light (H):** Photoshop's six Light modes darken the darkest colors and lighten the lightest colors, thereby allowing the midtones to intermix, so that foreground and background remain independently identifiable. Of the six, the first three — Overlay, Soft Light, and Hard Light — are arguably the most useful, so I'll begin with them.

Each of these three modes alternatively multiplies the blacks and screens the whites, but to different degrees. For example, where Overlay favors the background layers, Hard Light emphasizes the active layer. In fact, the two are direct opposites — Layer A set to Overlay in front of Layer B produces the same effect as Layer B set to Hard Light in front of Layer A. Meanwhile, Soft Light is a modified version of Hard Light that results in a more subtle effect than either Hard Light or Overlay.

Figure 6-15: After slightly darkening the gradient layer and fading the pattern layer, I applied Color Dodge (top) and Linear Dodge (bottom) to the face. Never subtle, both modes simultaneously bleach the image and draw out some of the dark outlines from the Blistered Paint pattern.

When experimenting with these modes, my advice is to always start with Overlay. If Overlay produces too strong an effect, reduce the Opacity or Fill value to favor the composite pixels. Figure 6-16 shows three compositions created using the background, face, and pattern layers. Throughout, the face is set to Normal, fully opaque. To add texture to the image, I set the blend mode for the pattern layer to Overlay. But as we can see in the first example, this overwhelms the image. So I pressed the 5 key to reduce the Opacity to 50 percent, resulting in the second image.

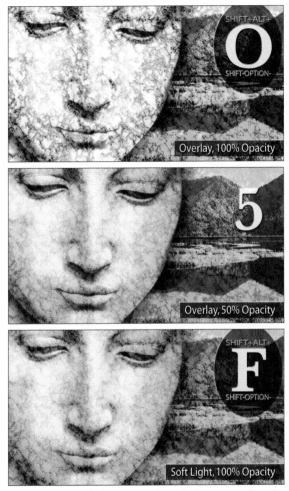

Figure 6-16: With the pattern layer in front, I applied the Overlay mode (top), experimented with reducing its Opacity setting to 50 percent (middle), and finally settled on the Soft Light mode with an Opacity of 100 percent (bottom).

Alternatively, you can switch from Overlay to Soft Light, as I did in the final example in Figure 6-16. On first glance, the second and third examples in the figure — one showing Overlay at 50 percent and the other Soft Light at full opacity — look very close to identical. But on closer inspection, you will notice that where the balance of lights and darks is roughly equivalent, their distribution is quite different. The Overlay example favors the details in the face; the Soft Light example favors the marbleized edges of the Blistered Paint pattern.

On the other hand, if the Overlay mode at 100 percent seems too subtle, you can try cloning the layer to double the Overlay effect, or switching to the Hard Light mode. Figure 6-17 demonstrates the difference. I start with the gradient layer set to Screen and the face set to Overlay. (For the present, the pattern layer is hidden.) The face is too light, so I clone the face to another layer by pressing Ctrl+J (⌘-J on the Mac) and delete its drop shadow. The final image compares this effect to sticking with a single layer and applying the Hard Light mode instead. In this particular case, Hard Light provides the best marriage of emphasis on the face and balance with the background.

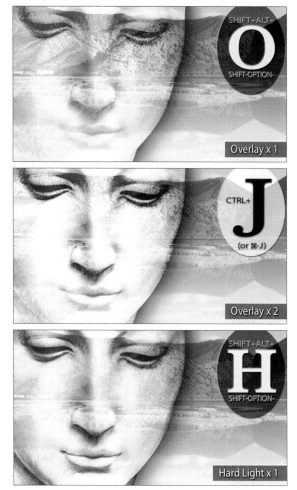

Figure 6-17: Here I have the face layer in front with the gradient set to Screen behind it. Working on the face, I first applied the Overlay mode (top) and then duplicated the face to another layer (middle). Deciding I didn't like the contrast, I deleted the cloned layer and changed the original to Hard Light (bottom).

✦ **Vivid Light (V)** and **Linear Light (J):** If Overlay and its ilk combine Multiply and Screen, then the next two Light modes combine Dodge and Burn. More specifically, Vivid Light combines Color Dodge and Color Burn, where Linear Light combines Linear Dodge and

Linear Burn. Figure 6-18 shows examples. This time, I've reduced the Opacity setting for the gradient layer to 50 percent and brought back the pattern layer, also at 50 percent Opacity, but set to Soft Light. Sandwiched in between is the face, set to Vivid Light at top and Linear Light at bottom.

Figure 6-18: The effect of setting the face to the Vivid Light (top) and Linear Light (bottom) modes. Because the effects are so hot, I sandwiched them between a Soft Light pattern layer and a Screen gradient layer, each with Opacity settings of 50 percent.

I find both of these modes useful for enhancing contrast, especially when combined with gradients. In Figure 6-19, we have the usual gang: the Blistered Paint pattern at 50 percent Soft Light and the face layer at 100 percent Normal. But this time, I've alternated the gradient layer, fully opaque, between Vivid Light in the first example and Linear Light in the second. In the final example, I cloned the face and set it to Linear Light as well. Setting both gradient and face to Linear Light invokes a heightened, haunting effect; cloning the face before applying Linear Light prevents the face and gradient from interacting.

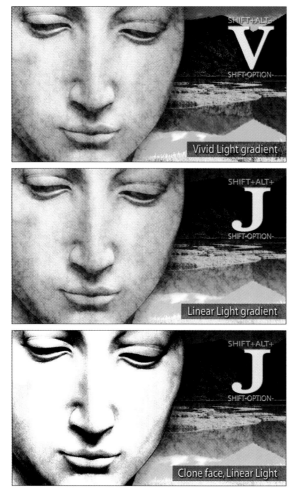

Figure 6-19: The effects of applying Vivid Light (top) and Linear Light (middle) to the gradient layer. In both cases, the Opacity value is 100 percent. I then cloned the face layer and set it to Linear Light as well (bottom).

+ **Pin Light (Z):** One of the simplest modes in all of Photoshop, Pin Light keeps the darkest blacks and the lightest whites and then makes everything else invisible. For the sake of comparison, the first example in Figure 6-20 shows the gradient layer set to Pin Light. (The face has been restored to Normal.) As you can see, only the very top and bottom of the gradient are visible; otherwise, the tranquil background lies exposed.

I find Pin Light particularly useful for modifying edge filters. In the second example in Figure 6-20, I cloned the face to a new layer and applied Filter ➪ Sharpen ➪ Unsharp Mask with an Amount of 100 percent and a Radius of 20 pixels. By applying the Pin Light mode, I retained just the lightest and darkest edges of the sharpened layer, as the final image shows. The result is a more subtle effect that still manages to exhibit thick, high-contrast outlines.

Figure 6-20: After returning the face to the Normal mode, I set the gradient layer to Pin Light (top). Then I cloned the face and sharpened the edges using the Unsharp Mask filter (middle). Finally, I applied the Pin Light mode to keep just the lightest and darkest pixels (bottom).

✦ **Hard Mix (L):** The first time you apply this new blend mode to an image you may be inclined to run screaming from your computer and hide under your bed until your screen saver kicks in. Oh, all right, it's not that bad. But the results that Hard Mix produces don't fit a standard definition of "pretty." Think functional as opposed to beautiful and you'll be on the right track. As shown in Figure 6-21, the Hard Mix blend mode combines the pixels in your layers using the Vivid Light blend mode and then performs a color threshold operation on them.

To achieve the Hard Mix effect in previous versions of Photoshop, here's what you'd have to do: Take two layers blended with Vivid Light and lower the opacity of the top one to 50 percent. Press Ctrl+Shift+E (⌘-Shift-E on the Mac) to merge the visible layers.

Then select the red channel in the Channels palette to isolate it. Choose Image ➪ Adjustments ➪ Threshold. When the Threshold dialog box comes up, click OK to accept the default settings. Repeat this process with both the green and blue channels. Finally, click the RGB channel item to view the composite image. Whew, no wonder they named it *Hard* Mix. I bet right now you're thanking your lucky stars that Adobe has simplified the process by doing it all for you in a single blend mode.

Figure 6-21: In the top image, I've set only the face layer to Hard Mix. Although it is by no means smooth or anti-aliased, Hard Mix has done a great job of completely isolating the eyes from the face. As you can see in the bottom image, applying Hard Mix to a number of layers gives you something of a catastrophe.

Or maybe not. It's also quite possible that you're wondering why on Earth you'd ever want to achieve this effect. Essentially, Hard Mix mixes two layers and pushes the colors to their absolute extreme: A hint of auburn becomes a harsh, deafening red; a sprinkle of cool aquamarine is transformed into bright, brash blue; you get the picture. All in all, Hard Mixed pixels come in only eight colors: black, white, red, green, blue, cyan, magenta, and yellow. It's sort of a live posterizing effect. You remember Posterize; it's that command under the Image ➪ Adjustments menu that you almost never use.

✦ **Difference (E)** and **Exclusion (X):** Difference inverts lower layers according to the brightness values in the active layer. White inverts the composite pixels absolutely, black inverts them not at all, and the other brightness values invert them to some degree in between. In the first example in Figure 6-22, I applied the Difference mode to the face layer, which is set against the gradient layer set to Screen. The light colors from the background show through the black pixels around the eyebrows, nose, and mouth, while the light areas in the face invert the lake and mountains.

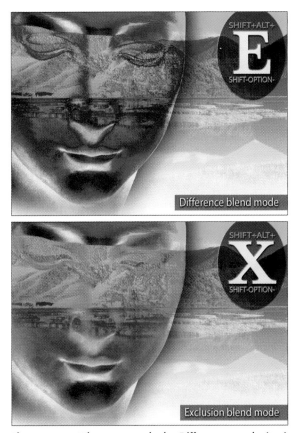

Figure 6-22: When you apply the Difference mode (top), white pixels invert the pixels beneath them; black pixels leave the background untouched. The Exclusion mode (bottom) performs a similar effect, but instead of inverting medium colors, it changes them to gray.

Exclusion works just like Difference except for one, er, difference. Illustrated in the second example in Figure 6-22, Exclusion sends midtones to gray — much as Pin Light sends midtones to transparent — creating a lower-contrast, often smoother effect.

Because these modes invert colors, they can produce interesting effects when combined with inverted layers. Figure 6-23 shows examples in which Difference is applied to the face. In the first example, I inverted the face layer by pressing Ctrl+I (⌘-I on the Mac). In the second example, I restored the face to its previous appearance and then inverted the gradient layer, so it went from white at the top to black at the bottom.

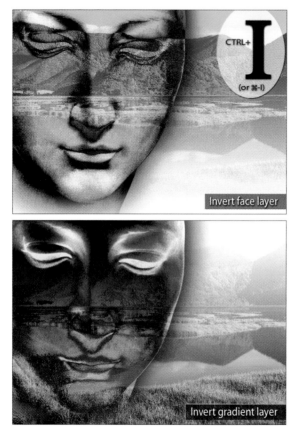

Figure 6-23: Since the Difference mode inverts colors, it only stands to reason that you can invert Difference layers and neighboring layers to achieve still more effects. Here I've alternated between inverting the face layer (top) and the gradient (bottom). In both cases, the face is set to Difference, the gradient is set to Screen.

One of my favorite uses for the Difference and Exclusion modes is to create a "Difference sandwich," in which you slide a filtered version of an image onto a layer between two originals. I explain this and related techniques in the upcoming section "Sandwiching a filtered image."

✦ **Hue (U):** Hue and the remaining three blend modes make use of the HSL color model to mix colors between the active layer and the underlying composite. When you select Hue, Photoshop retains the hue values from the active layer and mixes them with the saturation and luminosity values from the underlying image.

To demonstrate the HSL blend modes, I first created the composition shown in Figure 6-24. It includes many of the same layers as before, with the rear gradient set to 100 percent Screen, the face to 100 percent Normal, and the pattern layer hidden. In front of the face, I added a layer filled with a red-to-white gradient. Then I grouped the red gradient with the face below it, so the gradient fills the face and nothing else.

Figure 6-24: Starting where I left off in Figure 6-22, I set the face layer to Normal. Then I added a red-to-white gradient in front of the face and grouped it with the face layer, preventing the new gradient from spilling out into its background.

Now for the demonstration: I next applied the Hue blend mode to the red-to-white gradient. As far as Photoshop is concerned, the hue of the gradient is uniformly red, varying strictly in saturation as it fades to white. Hence, the Hue mode retains the red from the gradient and blends it with the saturation and luminosity values from the face layer, in effect colorizing the face red, as in Figure 6-25.

✦ **Saturation (T):** When you select this option, Photoshop retains the saturation values from the active layer and mixes them with the hue and luminosity values from the underlying image. In the case of Figure 6-25, the red-to-white gradient is most saturated at the top and least saturated at the bottom, resulting in vivid colors in the eye and dull colors below the mouth.

The Saturation mode produces such subtle effects that you'll typically want to apply it in combination with other blend modes. For example, after applying a random blend mode to a layer, you might duplicate the layer and then apply the Saturation mode to either boost or downplay the colors, much like printing a gloss or matte coating over an image.

✦ **Color (C):** This option combines the Hue and Saturation modes. As shown in the third example in Figure 6-25, Photoshop retains both the hue and saturation values from the active layer and mixes them with the luminosity values from the underlying layers. Because the saturation ingredient of the Color mode produces such a slight effect, Color frequently produces a very similar effect to Hue.

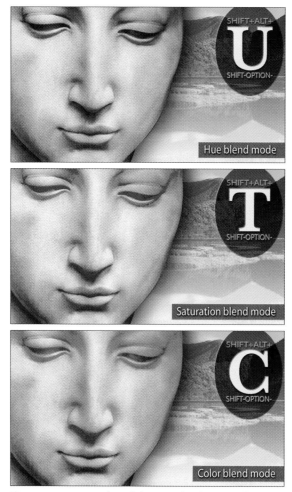

Figure 6-25: Examples of the Hue (top), Saturation (middle), and Color (bottom) blend modes, each applied to the red-to-white gradient. The gradient is constant in hue and varies in saturation, which is why the top of the face appears so vivid in the Saturation and Color examples.

✦ **Luminosity (Y):** The Luminosity blend mode retains the lightness values from the active layer and mixes them with the hue and saturation values from the composite pixels below. Just as the Color mode uses the layer to colorize its background, the Luminosity mode uses the background to colorize the layer.

Luminosity is one of my favorite modes, so forgive me if I get a little carried away with the examples. To start things off, I applied Luminosity to the red-to-white gradient layer. Because the gradient is uniform in brightness (only the saturation varies), the result is a flattening of surface detail in the face, as in the first example in Figure 6-26. The shadows of the eyes, nose, and mouth are distinguishable only by their bluish coloring. Next, I hid the red-to-white gradient layer and set the face layer to Luminosity. As you can see in the figure's middle example, this blends the rich volumetric textures of the face with the background colors. Finally, I set the rear gradient layer to Luminosity. The black-to-white gradient is composed exclusively of brightness values, so it has the effect of burning the top of the image and dodging the bottom, as the final example shows.

Figure 6-26: The results of applying the Luminosity mode to the red-to-white gradient layer (top), the face (middle), and the rear black-to-white gradient (bottom). Note that the red-to-white gradient is hidden in the final two examples.

Blend modes are amazing. They permit you to try out so many permutations that you can lose yourself in hours of experimentation. Figure 6-27 gives you a sense of the wonders you can achieve by combining a mere trio of blend modes — one each from the lighten, Light, and HSL categories — in concert. The figure begins with the face and the tranquil background, and also adds in a vertical coil postage stamp printed in 1946. The face and stamp are set to

Normal with the stamp layer lowered to an Opacity value of 70 percent. In the second image, I introduce two more layers, the by-now familiar pattern and gradient. The gradient is fully opaque and set to Normal. Topping off the stack, the pattern enjoys the Overlay blend mode and an Opacity setting of 30 percent. In the final image, I changed the gradient layer to the Screen mode and reduced the Opacity setting to 60 percent. Then I assigned Luminosity to the face and stamp.

Figure 6-27: I started with three layers, all set to Normal with the stamp at 70 percent Opacity (top). Next, I introduced the gradient and pattern layers. The gradient is opaque; the pattern is set to 30 percent Overlay (middle). I changed the gradient layer to 60 percent Screen. Then I combined the face and stamp layers into a layer set and assigned the Luminosity blend mode (bottom).

Or did I? Clearly if you look at the final image in Figure 6-27, you can see that the brightness values from the face and stamp interact with the colors from the background. But had I applied Luminosity independently to the layers, they would interact with each other as well, with some of the blend of background and stamp leaking into the face. And yet, there is no such interaction. It's as if the stamp thinks the face is opaque, while the background can see through both.

And that's exactly what's happening. How? By combining the layers that should not interact into a set and applying a blend mode to the set instead of the layers. In the case of Figure 6-27, for example, I added the face and stamp to a set. The modes for both layers were Normal, so the face would cover the stamp. The default mode for a set is Pass Through, which merely means Photoshop will ignore the set and adopt the modes assigned to the independent layers. By changing this set mode to Luminosity, I instructed Photoshop to override the blend modes assigned to the individual layers and adopt Luminosity instead. The result is two layers blending as if they were one.

Blend mode madness

Remember that scene in *Amadeus* where Mozart is telling the king about some obscure opera that he's writing — "Marriage of Franz Joseph Haydn" or something like that — and he's bragging about how many folks he plans to have singing on stage at the same time? Turns out, you can do that same thing with Photoshop. Not with melody or recitative or anything like that, but with imagery. Just as Mozart might have juggled several different melodies and harmonies at once, you can juggle layers upon layers of images, each filtered differently and mixed differently with the images below it.

Predicting the outcome of these monumental compositions takes a brain the magnitude of Mozart's. But experimenting with different settings takes no intelligence at all, which is where I come in.

The hierarchy of blend modes

The most direct method for juggling multiple images is "sandwiching." By this I mean placing a heavily filtered version of an image between two originals. This technique is based on the principal that more than half the blend modes — including Normal, Dissolve, Color Dodge and Burn, the six Light modes, and the four HSL modes — change depending on which of two images is on top.

For example, Figure 6-28 shows two layers, A and B, and what happens when I blend them with the Overlay mode. When the man is on top, as in the third example, the Overlay mode favors the sun; but when the sun is on top, Overlay favors the man. How fair is that?

Fortunately, Overlay is balanced by its opposite, Hard Light, which operates with a keener sense of justice, favoring the layer to which it's applied. For example, I could have achieved the exact effect shown in the third example in Figure 6-28 by placing the man under the sun and setting the sun to Hard Light. Flip-flop the layers and apply Hard Light to the man to get the last example.

Another obvious example of blend mode opposites is Color and Luminosity. If I were to position the man in front of the sun and apply Color, the sun would turn a kind of peachy, fleshy color. The same thing would happen if I placed the sun in front and applied Luminosity.

The moral of this minutia is that the order in which you stack your layers is as important as the blend mode you select. Even modes that have no stacking opposites — Color Dodge, Linear Light, and others — produce different effects depending on which layer is on top. For your general edification, Figure 6-29 shows a few examples.

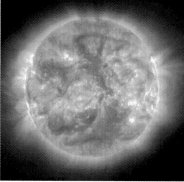

Layer A (the mighty sun)   Layer B (a cheerful countenance)

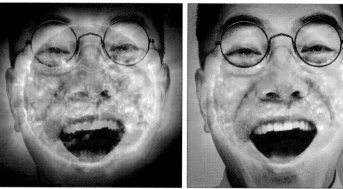

Overlay, Layer B on A (man in the sun)   same mode, Layer A on B (sun in the man)

Figure 6-28: After establishing two layers, sun and man, I placed the man on top and applied Overlay to get the third image. Then I switched the order of the layers and applied Overlay to the sun to get the last image.

An interesting upshot of Figure 6-29 is that you can see which layer each mode favors. Like Overlay, Color Dodge favors the composite pixels below the active layer. This holds true for Color Burn as well. Meanwhile, Linear Light, Pin Light, and all the other modes with Light in their names favor the active layer. Modes that do not change based on layering order — Multiply, Screen, Difference, and the like — favor neither front nor rear layer.

Sandwiching a filtered image

When you sandwich a filtered image between two originals — which, as you may recall, is what all this is leading up to — you can lessen the effect of the filter and achieve different effects than those I discuss in Chapter 9. Layers and blend modes give you the flexibility to experiment as much as you want and for as long as you please.

In Figure 6-30, I copied the happy man's face to a new layer and then applied Filter ➪ Sketch ➪ Charcoal with the foreground and background colors set to their defaults, black and white. The right-hand image lists the specific settings.

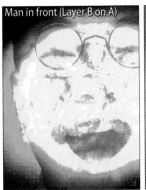

Man in front (Layer B on A)

Color Dodge   Linear Light   Pin Light

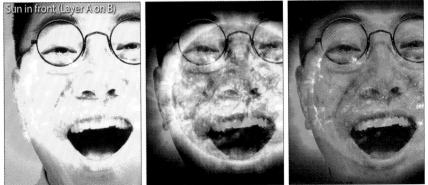

Sun in front (Layer A on B)

Color Dodge   Linear Light   Pin Light

Figure 6-29: A series of blend modes shown with the man in front (top row) and the sun in front (bottom row).

Control layer (unfiltered image)   Filter ➪ Sketch ➪ Charcoal (5, 5, 50)

Figure 6-30: The fixings for our blend mode sandwich include the original happy man layer (left) and a cloned version on an independent layer subject to the Charcoal filter (right). The original will be our bread, the Charcoal will be our meat. I mean, come on, who wouldn't want charcoaled meat? (Okay, *besides* vegetarians.)

Like most filters under the Sketch submenu, Charcoal absolutely destroys the detail in the image, replacing all brightness values with the foreground and background colors, in this case, black and white. Fortunately, because I applied Charcoal to a clone of the image, I can use a blend mode to restore some of the detail. Figure 6-31 shows two of the myriad possibilities that exist — one using the Multiply mode, which kept the blacks in the Charcoal effect and threw away the whites, and the other using Pin Light, which allowed colors from the original image to show through the gray areas of the Charcoal rendering.

Charcoal on control, Multiply   same, Pin Light

Figure 6-31: Each of two blend modes applied to the Charcoal meat in front of a slice of original image bread. This is what we image-editing professionals like to call an open-face blend mode sandwich, great when you only have time for a light snack.

But that's just the beginning. By once again cloning the background layer and moving it above the Charcoal layer, so that the filtered image resides between two originals, I can increase my opportunity for blend mode variations. In this sandwich, the original images serve as the bread and the Charcoal layer is the meat (or the eggplant, for you vegetarians). Figure 6-32 shows the effects of applying a total of four blend modes to the top slice of bread, which in turn interact with the two blend modes applied to the Charcoal meat in the previous figure. For example, in the lower-left example, I applied the Multiply mode to the filtered image and the Linear Light mode to the cloned original in front of that. The result is a brightly colored image with charcoal shadows and a bright, white background.

Creating a Difference sandwich

Check out the last example in Figure 6-32 and you'll see a purist's sandwich, Pin Light on the meat and Pin Light on the bread. That's one of the best, most reliable sandwich combinations you can create. If blend modes were condiments, Pin Light would be mustard — it works for everything.

But every purist has a favorite, and for me, the best sandwich dressing out there is Difference. By applying Difference to both the filtered layer and the cloned original on top, you do a double-invert, first inverting the filter into the original image and then reinverting the original into the composite. The result is a subtler and utterly unique culinary combination.

Multiply meat, Color Dodge bread

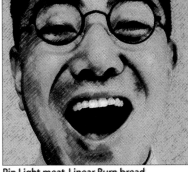
Pin Light meat, Linear Burn bread

Multiply meat, Linear Light bread

Pin Light meat, Pin Light bread

Figure 6-32: When you've got a hunger, only a full sandwich will do. Here I've thrown on several top slices of bread, each slathered with a different, delicious blend mode.

Figure 6-33 shows a small sampling of the several thousand possible variations on the Difference sandwich theme. In the top row of the figure, I've vigorously applied a series of standard filters — so vigorously, in fact, that I've pretty well ruined the image. But have no fear. By stacking it on top of the original, cloning the original on top of it, and applying the Difference mode to both layers, you can restore much of the original image detail, as the bottom row of examples shows.

A few notes about the Difference sandwich:

✦ First, the effect doesn't work nearly as well if you start reducing the Opacity values, so fully opaque is usually the best way to go.

✦ If you want to lighten or darken the effect, try adding a Levels adjustment layer to the top of the stack, as discussed in Chapter 12.

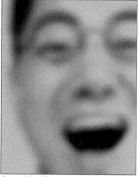

Gaussian Blur (Radius: 12)   Diffuse Glow (8, 10, 10)   Mosaic (Cell Size: 16)

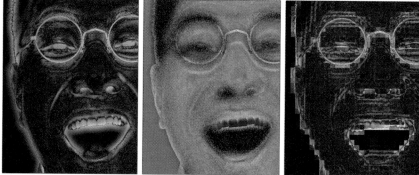

Filtered image in front of original, Difference blend mode

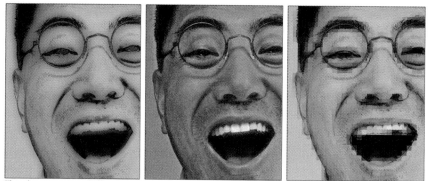

The always yummy Difference sandwich

Figure 6-33: Three different filtering effects as they appear on their own (top row), combined with the original image using the Difference mode (middle row), and when inserted into a Difference sandwich (bottom row).

✦ If you want to lower the contrast, try substituting Difference with the Exclusion mode.

✦ Finally, Difference is one of those blend modes that produces the same effect regardless of how you order the layers. This means you can filter either the middle layer or the bottom layer in the sandwich and get the same effect. But the top layer must be the original image. Using the sandwich analogy, you can put the meat between the two slices of bread, or both slices of bread on top of the meat. In either case, set the top two layers to Difference, and life will be a dream, sweetheart.

Advanced Blending Options

Opacity got you down? Blend modes just not enough? Why then, you need the Advanced Blending options, a collection of settings so absolutely terrific you'll be reaching for the phone and calling your mother to thank her for giving birth to you (as well you should anyway — mothers work so very hard).

To display the Advanced Blending options, you have three options: First, you can double-click on the layer thumbnail. Second, if you want to modify the Advanced Blending options for a specialty layer — such as type or an adjustment layer — right-click on the layer name or thumbnail (Control-click on the Mac) and choose the Blending Options command. You can also right-click inside the image window with one of the selection tools and access Blending Options that way. Third, you can press Alt (or Option) and double-click the layer name. So you decide.

In any case, you'll see the vast and stately Layer Style dialog box. This one multipaneled window holds controls for adding layer effects, changing the opacity and blend mode of a layer, and achieving some special blending tricks, which I'll be discussing here. By default, you should see the Blending Options panel, pictured in Figure 6-34. If you're working in some other area of the dialog box, click the Blending Options item at the top of the list on the left side of the dialog box.

You already know how the two General Blending options, Blend Mode and Opacity, work. The same goes for the Fill Opacity slider (though as we'll see, it takes on broader meaning inside this dialog box). These are the same options found in the Layers palette and discussed in the first half of this chapter. The next few sections explain the Advanced Blending options, spotlighted in Figure 6-34. Like so many aspects of blend modes, these options can be perplexing at first. But after you get the hang of them, they enable you to gain a degree of control over your layers unrivaled by any other image editor.

Many of the Advanced Blending options affect the performance of layer effects, such as drop shadows, glows, bevels, and so on. These effects fall into the broader category of layer styles, which I discuss at length in the second half of Chapter 7, starting with the section "The Bold and Beautiful Layer Styles."

Blending interior layer effects

I should say at the outset, the Fill Opacity value behaves exactly like the Fill option in the Layers palette. Enter a number into one option and it appears in the other as well. They are as one. The same goes for the Blend Mode setting inside the dialog box and the selected mode in the Layers palette. However, we are about to discover a few ways to modify the performance of these options that are only possible from the Advanced Blending options.

As you may recall, the Opacity value controls the translucency of all aspects of a layer, including pixels and layer effects alike. This is a fact of life, regardless of any other settings that may be in place. Meanwhile, the Blend Mode and Fill Opacity settings modify the interaction of pixels independently of most or all layer effects. This caveat, "most or all," is where things get interesting.

Click here for Blending Options

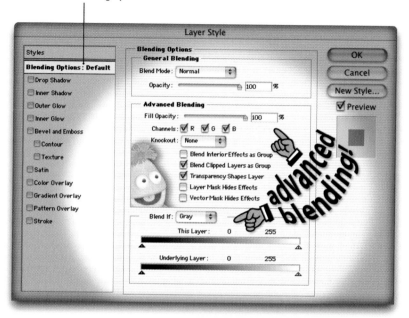

Figure 6-34: Using the Advanced Blending options, you can turn a layer into a floating hole, make specific color ranges invisible, and more.

You see, Photoshop divides layer effects into two groups that you can control independently of each other. *Interior effects* fall inside the boundaries of the filled areas of a layer and include the Inner Shadow, Inner Glow, Satin, and three Overlay effects. *Exterior effects* fall either outside or both inside and outside the boundaries of a layer. These include the effects Drop Shadow, Outer Glow, Bevel and Emboss, and Stroke.

Using blend modes and Fill Opacity, Photoshop permits you the option of modifying interior effects independently from exterior effects. The catalyst at the heart of this behavior is the check box labeled Blend Interior Effects as Group. When turned off, as by default, blend modes and Fill Opacity affect the pixels on a layer only. But if you turn the check box on, Photoshop applies the blend mode and Fill Opacity to the interior layer effects as well—only the exterior effects remain unchanged.

Figures 6-35 and 6-36 show examples. In Figure 6-35, we see a layer to which I've assigned three interior effects—Color Overlay, Pattern Overlay featuring the Wrinkles pattern (one of Photoshop's defaults), and a thick white Inner Glow—as well as three exterior effects—Drop Shadow, Stroke, and Bevel and Emboss set to a Stroke Emboss. When I lower the Fill Opacity to 20 percent, the pixels that make up the scanned stamp drop away, but the layer effects do not change. However, if I also turn on Blend Interior Effects as Group, Photoshop reduces the opacity of the three interior effects to 20 percent as well. Figure 6-36 shows the similar relationship that exists between Blend Interior Effects as Group and a couple of blend modes, Multiply and Difference. When the check box is off, the interior effects remain unchanged; when the check box is on, the interior effects are treated as just another part of the layer.

Figure 6-35: The results of taking a layer subject to three interior effects and three exterior effects (top), reducing the Fill Opacity value to 20 percent (middle), and then selecting the Blend Interior Effects as Group check box (bottom).

Note, however, that neither Fill Opacity nor blend mode affects the exterior effects under any circumstance. This is a little odd, since some exterior effects actually fall inside the boundaries of the layer. In particular, the Stroke effect is set to trace the inside of the layer, and the Stroke Emboss covers the stroke. In fact, the only effect that truly exists outside the layer is the drop shadow. However, as far as Photoshop is concerned, an exterior effect is an exterior effect, regardless of where it happens to fall.

Blending clipping masks

Just as you can control whether interior layer effects blend with filled areas of a layer, you can choose to blend the upper layers in a clipping mask along with the base layer or leave them unchanged. By default, the Blend Clipped Layers as Group check box is turned on, thus blending all layers in a clipping mask as a single unit. So the blend modes inside the group interact, and then the group as a whole interacts with other layers in the composition. To adjust the blending of the base layer in a clipping mask by its lonesome, deselect the check box. Then, only the Opacity slider will impact the other layers in the group.

Multiply, ▣ Blend Interior Effects as Group off   Difference, ▣ Blend Interior Effects off

Multiply, ☑ Blend Interior Effects as Group on   Difference, ☑ Blend Interior Effects on

Figure 6-36: Two blend modes, Multiply (left) and Difference (right), when applied to the stamp layer with Blend Interior Effects as Group turned off (top) and on (bottom). The effect is most obvious on the thick Inner Glow, which turns invisible in the Multiply image and inverts colors when set to Difference.

For those of you who are thinking, "Yes, that's all very well and good, but what the heck does that gibberish you just wrote mean?" cast your curious eyes to Figure 6-37. Here, I've pasted the happy man on a separate layer, grouped him with the stamp layer so that the man's face falls entirely inside the stamp's edges, and then set the blend mode for the stamp (which is now the base layer for the group) to Hard Light and the Fill value to 50 percent. Using the Blend Interior Effects as Group and Blend Clipped Layers as Group check boxes, I was able to achieve the following effects:

Hard Light, Fill: 50%, ▤Blend Int. Effects off ▤Blend Clipped Layers as Group off

same, ☑Blend Interior Effects as Group on ▤Blend Clipped Layers as Group off

again, ▤Blend Interior Effects as Group off ☑Blend Clipped Layers as Group on

finally, ☑Blend Interior Effects as Group on ☑Blend Clipped Layers as Group on

Figure 6-37: After adding a face to the composition and grouping it with the stamp, I set the stamp's blend mode to Hard Light and the Fill Opacity to 50 percent. Then I experimented with turning each of the Blend as Group check boxes on and off.

✦ **Both options off:** By turning off Blend Clipped Layers as Group, I was able to maintain the happy man's face at the Normal blend mode and full opacity. But because Blend Interior Effects as Group was also turned off, the Inner Glow and other effects wrap around the face, just as they do any other layers in the clipping mask. The result appears at upper left in the figure.

✦ **Interior Effects on, Clipped Layers off:** If I turn Blend Interior Effects as Group on, the interior effects — including the Inner Glow and Pattern Overlay — recede behind the clipped face, as in the upper-right image in Figure 6-37. However, exterior effects such as Stroke and Stroke Emboss remain in force.

✦ **Interior Effects off, Clipped Layers on:** Pictured in the lower-left example in Figure 6-37, this is the default condition for a new clipping mask. The face adopts the blend mode and fill opacity assigned to the stamp layer. The interior effects, on the other hand, remain as opaque as ever.

✦ **Both options on:** If you want everything to be governed by the base layer of the clipping mask — including clipped layers and interior effects — then turn both options on. The result appears in the lower-right example in Figure 6-37.

Masking and unmasking effects

The remaining check boxes — Transparency Shapes Layers, Layer Mask Hides Effects, and Vector Mask Hides Effects — permit you to manage the boundaries of interior and exterior effects alike. These options take us into some weird and rarefied territory, but don't panic. I'm going to briefly explain each one and then walk you through a real-world example.

✦ **Transparency Shapes Layer:** One of the strangest sounding features in all of Photoshop, turning off this check box deactivates the transparency mask that is normally associated with a layer, permitting layer effects and clipped layers to spill outside the boundaries of a layer to fill the entire image window. If the layer includes a layer mask, then effects and clipped layers fill the mask instead. So it serves two purposes: First, you can fill an image or clipping group with a Color Overlay or other interior effect associated with a layer. And second, you can substitute a transparency mask with a layer or vector mask. I'll be showing both of these in the following pages.

✦ **Layer Mask Hides Effects:** When turned on, this check box uses the layer mask to mask both the pixels in the layer and the layer effects. When turned off, as by default, the layer mask defines the boundary of the layer, and the effect traces around this boundary just as it traces around other transparent portions of the layer.

✦ **Vector Mask Hides Effects:** As I discuss in the next chapter, Photoshop's shape tools allow you to draw vector-based shapes, which you can fill with flat colors, gradients, patterns, or even layered images. When working inside a layer inside a shape, you can use the Vector Mask Hides Effects check box to specify whether the shape defines the outline of the layer (check box off) or clips layer effects just as it clips pixels (check box on). For complete information on defining a layer mask, read the "Editing the stuff inside the shape" section in Chapter 7.

Okay, so much for the basics. But why would you ever use these options? The short answer is, because something has gone wrong and you want to correct it. Don't like how your layer effects look? Turn one of these options on or off and see if it makes a difference. Of course, it helps to have a little experience with these options before you start randomly hitting switches, so let's work through an example.

The top image in Figure 6-38 is basically a repeat of the first image in Figure 6-37 — the stamp layer is set to Hard Light with a Fill Opacity of 50 percent. The face layer is grouped with the stamp and both the Blend Interior Effects as Group and Blend Clipped Layers as Group check boxes are turned off. Now let's say I decided to add a layer mask to the stamp layer. Nothing fancy, just a gradient from black at the bottom of the image to white near the middle, as shown in the second example in Figure 6-38. Naturally, this made the layer transparent at the bottom and opaque toward the middle, but it had an unexpected consequence. The mask shaped the boundaries of the layer, giving it a very soft edge that the layer effects didn't quite know how to accommodate. Rather than fading into view, the Inner Glow effect starts abruptly at the point where the layer becomes fully opaque, right under the guy's nose (see the final image in Figure 6-38). As it turns out, it really wasn't the inner glow's fault — it was a function of the Stroke being set to Inside — but who cares? The plain fact of the matter is that it looks absolutely awful.

One's proclivity in a situation like this is to say, "Gosh, I guess I can't combine a layer mask with Inner Glow and an inside Stroke effect. I think I'll go soak my head now." But instead you should keep your head dry and consult your Advanced Blending options. In the first image in Figure 6-39, I fixed the problem by simply turning on the Layer Mask Hides Effects check box. This way, rather than constraining the effects, the layer mask fades them out just like a good gradient mask is supposed to do.

Figure 6-38: Starting with the face masked inside the stamp (top),
I added a layer mask to the stamp layer using the gradient tool (middle).
But instead of fading the effects, the mask shoved the edges of the
Stroke and Inner Glow so far upward I worry that our once chipper
fellow may soon run out of breath (bottom).

The second example in Figure 6-39 shows what happened when I turned off the Transparency Shapes Layer check box (on by default). Suddenly, the layer effects are no longer constrained by the boundaries of the stamp layer and grow to fill the entire layer mask. Edge-dependent effects, such as Inner Glow, Drop Shadow, and Stroke disappear. Meanwhile, the Color and Pattern Overlay effects expand to fill the image.

Next, I added a vector mask to the stamp layer. To do this, I pressed the Ctrl key (⌘ on the Mac) and clicked the layer mask icon at the bottom of the Layers palette. After selecting the custom shape tool and selecting the highway sign symbol from the Shape menu in the Options bar, I pressed the plus key (+) to make sure the Add to Path Area button was active and drew my shape. Photoshop automatically traced the Drop Shadow, Inner Glow, and

Stroke effects around the shape, as in the final example in Figure 6-39. However, if for some reason this weren't to occur, I had only to visit my handy Advanced Blending options and turn off the Vector Mask Hides Effects check box.

Figure 6-39: After fading out the Inner Glow and Stroke effects by selecting the Layer Mask Hides Effects check box (top), I turned off Transparency Shapes Layer, which permitted the Pattern Overlay effect to fill most of the image (middle). Then I added a vector mask to the stamp layer and left the Vector Mask Hides Effects check box off, as by default (bottom).

Dumping whole color channels

That takes care of the most complex of the check boxes. All that remain are the Channels options. Located directly below the Fill Opacity slider in the Layer Style dialog box, the Channels check boxes let you hide the layer inside one or more color channels. For example, turning off R makes the layer invisible in the red channel, sending colors careening toward vivid red or turquoise (all red or no red), depending on the colors in the layers underneath.

I have a tendency to make bold pronouncements on the features I like and loathe inside Photoshop, and the Channels check boxes fall into the latter category. They are, for the most part, useless. There are exceptions, of course — in a CMYK image, it can prove helpful to drop a layer inside, say, the Black channel — but for general RGB image editing, they just don't cut the mustard, which is too bad because if slightly retooled, they could. For example, I would very much like to control the translucency of a layer on a channel-by-channel basis, but instead we have only on or off controls. One lives in hope for something better.

Making knockouts

Okay, enough grousing. Back to the good stuff. Like the Knockout pop-up menu.

Knockout turns the contents of the active layer into a floating hole that can bore through one or more layers behind it. It's like a layer mask, except that you can use it to mask multiple layers, and their layer effects, at a time. You can also apply layer effects to the knockout, making them extremely flexible.

Creating a knockout is arguably more abstruse than it ought to be, but it ultimately makes a kind of twisted sense. You specify how deep the hole goes using the Knockout pop-up menu. Then use the Fill Opacity or Blend Mode option to define the translucency of the hole. The Knockout pop-up menu provides the following three options:

- ✦ **None:** This setting is the same as turning the knockout function off. The layer is treated as a standard layer, not a hole.

- ✦ **Shallow:** Choose this option to cut a hole through a group of layers inside a set and expose the layer immediately below the set. In a clipping mask where Blend Clipped Layers as Group is turned off, Shallow burrows down to the layer directly below the base layer of the group. When Blend Clipped Layers as Group is turned on, the knockout layer burrows down to the base layer in the group. If the layer resides neither inside a set nor a clipping mask, it typically cuts a hole down to the background layer.

- ✦ **Deep:** The final setting bores as far down as the background layer, even if the knockout layer resides inside a set. A notable exception occurs when working inside a clipping mask. If the Blend Clipped Layers as Group check box is on, Deep burrows down to the base of the clipping mask, just like Shallow.

See, I told you it was abstruse. But in truth, making a knockout has less to do with what option you choose from the Knockout pop-up menu and more to do with Fill Opacity, layering order, and sets. Consider my revolutionary idea in motoring shown in Figure 6-40. Here we have a pair of friendly highway markers that tell you where to go. I call out, "Where's the Garden State?" and they yell back, "You're on it, you knucklehead!" Forget global positioning systems — invest in talking highway markers today.

I created my brave new vision using vector masks, as I explained a few pages back in the "Masking and unmasking effects" section. If you look closely, you may notice that I replaced the one-time stamp layer with a pattern, threw out the now unnecessary Pattern Overlay effect, and deleted the gradient layer mask (first featured in Figure 6-38). Finally, I added posts behind the signs and set the background image — a photograph of New Mexico's Ship Rock — on an independent layer, so I could reposition it if need be. Okay, so the signs cast drop shadows onto the Ship Rock image — that's not realistic. But bear in mind, it's all conceptual. The real highway markers will be much cooler.

Figure 6-40: If you're like me, the first thing you do upon arriving in a new city is rent a car and spend a few hours driving around, playing the radio too loud and trying to look at an elaborately detailed map while hurtling past one exit after another at 70 miles per hour. Wouldn't it be easier if someone would invent talking highway markers? Here's my sketch, now get on it. Remember, I get 25 percent of net.

At this point, I decided that these shouldn't be little signs, like the highway markers we see now. They should be great huge things that emerge from the ground like the ancient Moai heads of Easter Island. Otherwise, how will you be able to hear them as you speed on by? To do this, I needed the markers to fade up from the ground. For a single sign, I could use a layer mask, but for multiple signs, I needed a knockout layer.

In Figure 6-41, I started things off by creating a new layer and filling it with a slightly angled black-to-transparent gradient. Then I double-clicked on the gradient thumbnail in the Layers palette and set the Knockout option to Shallow, which is a good place to start. But nothing happened. That's because you need to follow up by telling Photoshop how transparent to make the knockout. You can do this using a blend mode — for example, setting the gradient to Screen would make the black transparent, thereby cutting a hole. But the most straight-forward method is to lower the Fill Opacity value. By reducing the value to 0 percent, I instructed Photoshop to use the filled portions of the gradient layer to burrow through all layers below. (Transparent portions of the knockout layer have no effect.) Note that you have to use the Fill value; the standard Opacity value does not work for this purpose.

So far so good, except for one tiny problem: The knockout went too far, masking all the way down to the white background layer, as illustrated in the second image in Figure 6-41. I set the Knockout to Shallow, which is the least amount of knockout I can apply, but without clipping groups or layer sets to guide it, Photoshop goes ahead and drills down to the bottom of the stack. How do I tell Photoshop to drill down to the Ship Rock layer instead? By combining the knockout and the layers I want to mask into a single set.

So I link the gradient knockout layer to the many layers that make up the signs and posts (using the link icons on the left side of the Layers palette). Then I choose New Set From Linked from the Layers palette menu. That's all there is to it. The Shallow setting tells the knockout to bore through to the layer immediately below the set, which is the Ship Rock layer. The result appears at the bottom of Figure 6-41.

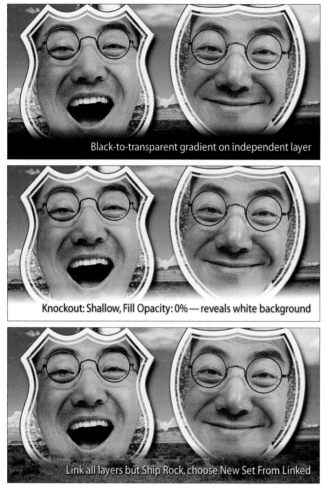

Figure 6-41: To mask through the many layers that make up the two signs, I made a new layer and filled it with a black-to-transparent gradient (top). Then I set the Knockout option to Shallow and reduced the Fill Opacity to 0 percent, which masked down to the white background (middle). To constrain the knockout, I combined all layers except the Ship Rock image into a set (bottom).

After all this work to make a so-called shallow knockout even shallower, why would you ever choose Deep? Because your image may contain a network of layer sets and clipping groups, and you want to cut all the way through to the background. For example, let's say I wanted to create a floating crop boundary. In other words, I didn't want to throw away any background details for good, nor did I want to reduce the size of my image window. I merely wanted to add an empty border around my image to indicate how the final composition should be cropped.

To make my crop boundary, I created a new layer and used the rectangular marquee tool to draw the perimeter of my final image. Then I pressed Ctrl+Shift+I to inverse the selection (⌘-Shift-I on the Mac) and filled the area outside the crop with black. (Incidentally, I didn't have to use black; any color will do. It's just important to make the knockout pixels opaque.) The first example in Figure 6-42 shows my progress thus far.

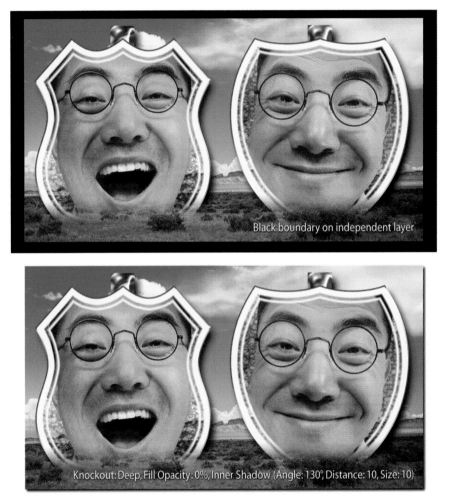

Figure 6-42: To establish a floating crop boundary, I created a new layer and filled the area outside the desired crop with black (top). Then I set the Knockout to Deep and reduced the Fill Opacity value to 0 percent. I also added an Inner Shadow effect to the knockout layer, which resulted in what appears to be a drop shadow behind the image (bottom).

To turn the blackness into knockout, I double-clicked on the layer thumbnail to bring up the Advanced Blending options, set the Fill Opacity to 0 percent, and set the Knockout to Shallow. The knockout works, but it only goes down as far as the Ship Rock layer. This is because I've gone and created the crop layer inside my new set. So I have two choices: move the crop layer in front of the set, in which case it'll burrow through everything inside and outside the set, or just set the Knockout option to Deep. The latter seemed easier, so that's what I did.

Finally, I decided I wanted my cropped image to have some depth. So I added a drop shadow. However, if I were to apply the Drop Shadow effect, the knockout would cast the shadow into the image. I want the shadow to go into the knockout, so I apply the Inner Shadow effect instead. The final image appears at the bottom of Figure 6-42.

At this point, I could move my crop boundary, add to it, change the effects, or otherwise modify it without worrying about harming a single pixel in the composition. Couldn't I do this same thing by simply filling the crop layer with white, as Photoshop artists have been doing for years? Yes, but there are two benefits to using a knockout layer instead: You have more flexibility where layer effects are concerned, and you can later turn around and composite this cropped image against a different background or frame. Simply put, no other cropping technique is this flexible.

Dropping Out and Forcing Through

Found at the bottom of the Blending Options panel of the Layer Style dialog box, the Blend If slider bars rank among Photoshop's oldest and most powerful compositing capabilities. Pictured in Figure 6-43, these options enable you to drop out pixels in the active layer and force through pixels from lower layers according to their brightness values. You can even use them in combination with the Knockout option. For example, if you set the Knockout to Deep, you force through pixels from the background layer instead of from the layer immediately below the active layer.

Here's how the Blend If options work:

✦ **Blend If:** Select a color channel from the Blend If pop-up menu to apply the effects of the slider bars according to the contents of a single color channel. If you choose Gray, as by default, Photoshop bases the changes on the grayscale composite. Each time you select a different Blend If option, the slider triangles change to the positions at which you last set them for that color channel. Regardless of how you set the sliders, Photoshop applies your changes evenly to all channels in the image; the selected channel is merely used for the calculation.

✦ **This Layer:** This slider bar lets you exclude ranges of colors according to brightness values in the active layer. You exclude dark colors by dragging the black triangle to the right; you exclude light colors by dragging the white triangle to the left. In either case, the excluded colors disappear from view.

✦ **Underlying Layer:** The second slider forces colors from the underlying layers to poke through the active layer. Any colors outside the range set by the black and white triangles will not be covered and are therefore visible regardless of the colors in the active layer.

✦ **Preview:** Don't forget to select the Preview check box on the right side of the Layer Style dialog box so you can see the effects of your modifications in the image window every time you adjust a setting.

These options are far too complicated to fully explain in a bulleted list. So I invite you to learn more by reading the following sections. You'll be glad you did.

Figure 6-43: Little Puppet Friend ranks the Blend If slider bars among Photoshop's most powerful capabilities, and I'm forced to agree.

Color range slider bars

To demonstrate the Blend If options, I've taken the sculpted face and tranquil background composition first introduced in Figure 6-6 and added an oldie but goodie element from *Photoshop Bibles* of yore, The Thinker. (For you longtime readers who might be saying, "Oh no, not The Thinker again! Retire that guy already!" notice that this time, he's facing a different direction. I used to flip him so he was facing right, but this time I kept him facing left, just as photographer Wernher Krutein shot him. No, that's okay, no need to thank me. Putting a smile of genuine satisfaction on a loyal reader's face is reward enough for me.) As shown in Figure 6-44, The Thinker includes a soft drop shadow to distinguish him from the rest of the composition. Like all layers in this composition, he rests contemplatively behind a thin veil of the Blistered Paint pattern set to the Overlay blend mode at 20-percent Opacity.

The first Blend If slider bar, This Layer, hides pixels in the active layer according to their brightness values. You can abandon dark pixels by dragging the left slider triangle and abandon light pixels by dragging the right triangle. Figure 6-45 shows examples of each.

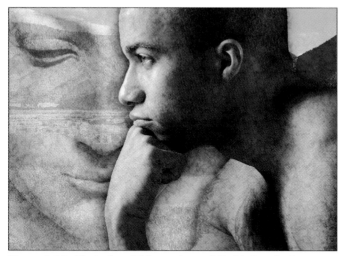

Figure 6-44: *Photoshop Bible* regular and Corbis Royalty Free stock image, The Thinker joins the composition for this very special demonstration of the Blend If slider bars.

✦ To create the first example in Figure 6-45, I first set the blend mode to Screen. Then I dragged the black slider triangle until the value immediately to the right of the words This Layer read 130, thereby hiding all dark pixels whose brightness values were 130 or lower.

✦ To create the second example, I changed the blend mode to Multiply. I reset the black slider triangle to 0 and dragged the white slider triangle to 175, which hid those pixels with brightness values of 175 or higher.

✦ The final image in the figure shows the second Thinker layered in front of the first. With the help of the This Layer slider bar, I can combine the Screen and Multiply blend modes to produce an image that is both lighter and darker than its background.

Drag the triangles along the Underlying Layer slider bar to force pixels in the underlying layers to show through, again according to their brightness values. To force dark pixels in the underlying image to show through, drag the black slider triangle; to force light pixels to show through, drag the white slider triangle.

Here's how I achieved the effects in Figure 6-46:

✦ To achieve the effect in the top example in Figure 6-46, I started off by applying the Linear Light blend mode. Then I dragged the black slider triangle until the first Underlying Layer value read 130. This forced the dark colors in the sculpted face and tranquil background with brightness values of 130 or lower to show through.

✦ In the second example, I changed the blend mode to Luminosity. Then I restored the black Underlying Layer triangle to 0 and dragged the white triangle to 175, uncovering pixels at the bright end of the spectrum.

✦ The final image shows the two effects combined, one copy of The Thinker in the Linear Light mode with Underlying Layer values of 130 and 255 and another in front of that set to Luminosity with Underlying Layer values of 0 and 175. The right eye from the sculpted face blends in with The Thinker's face like another one of his tattoos.

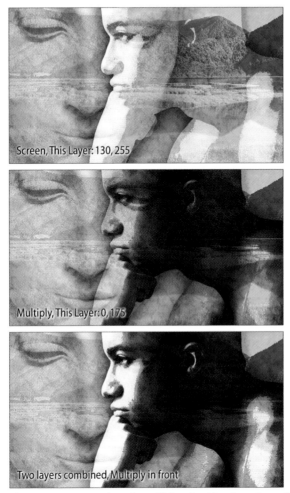

Figure 6-45: Examples of modifying the blend mode and This Layer settings inside the Layer Style dialog box. The final image shows the copy of The Thinker that I set to Multiply layered in front of the copy set to Screen to get a high-contrast effect.

Bear in mind, like every other adjustment made in the Layer Style dialog box, changes made to the Blend If slider bars are temporary. These options hide pixels; they don't delete them. As long as the layer remains intact, you can revisit the Blend If sliders and restore hidden pixels or hide new ones.

Fuzziness

The problem with hiding and forcing colors with the slider bars is that you achieve some pretty harsh color transitions. Although printed at high resolutions, both Figures 6-45 and 6-46 exhibit occasional jagged edges. Luckily, you can soften the color transitions by dropping and forcing pixels gradually over a fuzziness range, which works much like the Fuzziness value in the Color Range dialog box, leaving some pixels opaque and tapering others off into transparency.

Linear Light, Underlying Layer: 130, 255

Luminosity, Underlying Layer: 0, 175

Two layers combined, Luminosity in front

Figure 6-46: Here I changed the Underlying Layer settings to force through the darkest (top) and lightest (middle) pixels from the sculpted face and tranquil background layers. The third image shows the two effects combined.

To taper the opacity of pixels in either the active layer or the underlying image, press the Alt key (or Option on the Mac) and drag one of the triangles in the appropriate slider bar. The triangle splits into two halves, and the corresponding value above the slider bar splits into two values separated by a slash, as demonstrated in Figure 6-47.

The left triangle half represents the beginning of the fuzziness range — that is, the brightness values at which the pixels begin to fade into or away from view. The right half represents the end of the range — that is, the point at which the pixels are fully visible or invisible. Figure 6-48 shows a bit of fuzziness applied to the This Layer slider. Here are the specifics:

✦ In the top example, I set the blend mode to Screen. After splitting the black slider triangle by Alt-dragging (Option-dragging on the Mac), I set one half of the triangle to 40 and the other to 220. Colors with a brightness value of 40 or darker turn transparent, they fade into view from 41 to 219, and they become opaque from 220 on up.

✦ In the second image, I selected the Multiply blend mode and restored both halves of the black triangle to 0. Then, I Alt-dragged (or Option-dragged) the white triangle to split it. I moved the left half of the split triangle to 20 and the right half to 190. The result is an extremely gradual drop-off. Those few pixels with brightness values from 0 to 20 are opaque, the pixels become gradually translucent from 21 to 189, and pixels of 190 and brighter are transparent.

✦ Finally, I combined both effects on separate layers, with the Multiply effect on top. As shown in the bottom example in Figure 6-48, the result is a perfect blending of Multiply and Screen, with the background images showing through in the midtones.

Figure 6-47: "If only people knew to Alt-drag (Win) or Option-drag (Mac) the slider triangles to split them in half," thinks Little Puppet Friend. "Then they could specify a range over which brightness values will fade into transparency."

Using the Underlying Layer slider is a bit trickier. It typically works best when you're trying to force through very bright or dark details, such as the highlights in the sculpted face or the shadows in the mountains. It also helps to work with a foreground layer that has lots of flat areas of color for the background to show through. Here's what I did to create Figure 6-49:

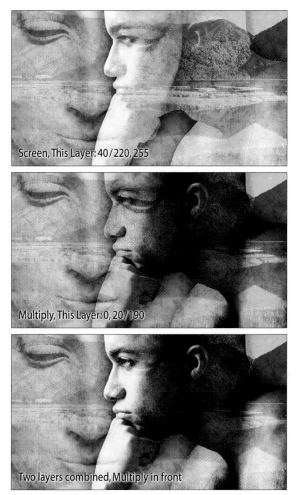

Screen, This Layer: 40/220, 255

Multiply, This Layer: 0, 20/190

Two layers combined, Multiply in front

Figure 6-48: By Alt-dragging (Win) or Option-dragging (Mac) a This Layer slider triangle, you can create gradual transitions between the opaque and transparent portions of a layer.

✦ For starters, I applied Filter ➪ Other ➪ High Pass to The Thinker layer. As shown in the first example in Figure 6-49, this created lots of gray areas that would serve as ample neutral ground for the Blend If slider bars.

✦ I next applied the radical Linear Dodge mode to this layer. I first dropped out most of the dark colors in The Thinker layer by setting the halves of the black This Layer triangle to 80 and 230. Then I split the black triangle for the Underlying Layer slider, leaving the left half at 0 and moving the right half to 190. This forced through virtually all of the darkest pixels from the rear layers, fading them out as they got lighter.

✦ Finally, I duplicated the layer, applied the Multiply mode, and reset the black triangles to 0. I experimented with the white triangles, ultimately setting the This Layer halves to 110 and 180 and the Underlying Layer halves to 90 and 200. The result is a vibrant composition that contrasts elements of the sculpted face with the outline of The Thinker.

Figure 6-49: After combining a High Pass effect with the Linear Dodge and Multiply blend modes, I used both the This Layer and Underlying Layer slider bars to drop out foreground colors and force through background colors. In the end, I was able to bring out some interesting details from the Michelangelo sculpture and mountain range.

Shapes and Styles

Adobe Gumbo

As any longtime user of Adobe products will tell you, things were sure a lot simpler in the old days. You wanted to work in a pixel-based environment, touching up photos and creating artistic images? Photoshop was the only place to be. You wanted to work with vectors, creating object-based art with razor-sharp edges? Illustrator was made just for you. You wanted to create motion graphics for video? Look no further than After Effects, my friend.

But now, things are different. Many people actually use After Effects as an image editor, completely ignoring that program's powerhouse animation capabilities and just taking advantage of its immensely flexible effects palette, arguably a better way to work with filters than anything Photoshop provides. Illustrator is giving bitmap graphics a full body hug now, signified by the fact that pixels are now one of the built-in units of measurement. And while Photoshop's paths have always been vector-based, the shape tools bring all the advantages of drawing with vectors into Photoshop, ensuring that anything you create with them will stay sharp, whether the final destination is a high-end printer or the World Wide Web.

And it doesn't stop there; Adobe InDesign has extremely capable vector drawing tools; Photoshop Elements can create animated GIFs, just like ImageReady; and After Effects outputs to the Flash format, just like LiveMotion, Adobe's dedicated Web animation tool. Sometimes it seems that all these products will eventually converge into one towering Swiss army knife of a graphics application, and when someone admires your work and asks what program you used to create it, you'll simply answer: "I did it in Adobe Amalgam 1.0."

Until that day arrives, we'll have to take things piecemeal. First up in this chapter are Photoshop's aforementioned shape tools. These permit you to draw object-oriented paths filled with anything from solid colors to gradients to photographic images. Other bitmap image-editing programs may have done it before Photoshop did, but as is so often the case, none has done it better.

Next, we turn our attention to layer styles. Although the promise of "instant drop shadows and glows" might sound at first like a cheap trick unworthy of inclusion in Photoshop's professional high-end tool set, they've actually proven to be an invaluable addition. Not only do

✦ ✦ ✦ ✦

In This Chapter

Drawing object-oriented shapes

Setting polygon, line, and custom shape options

Combining shapes into compound paths

Defining custom shapes

Filling shapes with gradients, patterns, and imagery

Creating and modifying automatic layer effects

Working inside the Layer Style dialog box

Duplicating effects

Saving effects and blending options as styles

✦ ✦ ✦ ✦

they give you painstaking control over drop shadows, glows, and bevels, but you can coat layers with gradients, patterns, and contoured wave patterns, as well as trace outlines around layers. When combined with the Advanced Blending options discussed in Chapter 6, layer styles blossom into a powerful special-effects laboratory, one of the most far-reaching and flexible Adobe has ever delivered. Furthermore, you can save the effects and reapply them to future layers.

These features may not be the reason you started to use Photoshop in the first place, and there's no question that they take time and patience to fully understand. But you'll be rewarded with greater proficiency and versatility in the long run — and you'll be that much farther down the road to mastery when the Day of the Grand Adobe Application Convergence finally arrives.

Drawing Shapes

Photoshop provides six *shape tools* that allow you to draw geometric and predefined shapes. By default, the shapes are separated off into independent *shape layers*, which are a mix of objects and pixels. The vector-based outlines of the shapes print at the maximum resolution of your printer, while the interiors may consist of solid colors, gradients, or pixel-based patterns and images.

The pros and cons of shapes

What good are object-oriented shapes inside Photoshop? Well, I'll tell you:

✦ **Shapes are editable.** Unlike pixels, you can change a shape by moving points and control handles. Likewise, you can scale, rotate, skew, or distort shapes, or even transform specific points and segments inside shapes. Nothing is ever set in stone.

✦ **Shapes help to disguise low-resolution images.** Sharply defined edges can add clarity to a printed image. The first example in Figure 7-1 shows a standard image printed at 75 pixels per inch. The second example shows that same 75-ppi image, but this time using an object-oriented shape outline. The low resolution works fine for the blurry fill, but where clarity is needed, the mathematical outline is there to serve.

✦ **You can color a shape with a layer style.** As we see later in this same chapter, layer effects such as drop shadows and beveled edges are equally applicable to shape layers as they are to standard image layers. And it's amazing what wild effects a person can achieve with a shape, a style, and no talent whatsoever. Take me, for example. To create Figure 7-1, I drew a fleur-de-lis shape and applied the Striped Cone style from the Styles palette.

✦ **Shapes result in smaller file sizes.** As a rule, an object takes up less space on disk than an image. Expressed in PostScript code, a typical path outline consumes 8 bytes per anchor point, as compared with 3 bytes for a single RGB pixel. But while a shape may contain as few as 4 points in the case of a rectangle or ellipse, an image routinely contains hundreds of thousands of pixels. For example, the illustration pictured in Figure 7-1 consumes 172K on disk when saved as a native PSD file. If I rasterized the image at an equivalent resolution — say, 600 ppi — using exclusively pixels, the file would balloon to 3.5MB, or more than 20 times the size.

✦ **You can preview clipping paths directly inside Photoshop.** Before object-oriented shapes, you were never quite sure if you traced an image properly with a clipping path until you imported it into InDesign, QuarkXPress, or some other application. Now you can preview exactly what your clipping path will look like directly inside Photoshop.

✦ **Shapes expand with an image.** When working with straight pixels, I advise against using Image ⇨ Image Size to resample an image upward on the grounds that it adds pixels without adding meaningful detail. But you can enlarge shapes as much as you want. Because a shape is mathematically defined, it remains crystal clear no matter how big or small you make it. Layer styles are likewise capable of resizing to match a new image size.

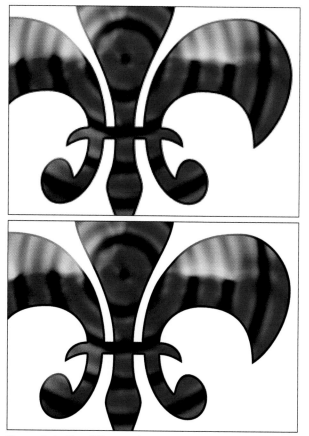

Figure 7-1: The difference between a 75-ppi graphic saved as a flat image (top) and as an object-oriented path outline (bottom). Although the blurry interiors appear identical, the shape outline becomes several times sharper when expressed as a path.

If vectors are so great, why not forsake pixels and start drawing entirely with shape layers instead? Although a shape can clip a continuous-tone photograph, it can't replace one. Although there have been all kinds of experiments using objects and fractals, pixels are still the most viable medium for representing digital photographs. Because Photoshop's primary job is photo editing, pixels are (for the foreseeable future) the program's primary commodity.

One downside to shape layers is compatibility. Photoshop has stretched the TIFF and PDF formats to accommodate any kind of layer — shape layers included — but that doesn't mean other programs have any idea what Photoshop is doing. Of all the formats, PDF is the most likely to work with other programs. Just be sure to proof the document on a laser printer before taking it to a commercial printer. After all, when you create objects in Photoshop, you're working on the bleeding edge, so be prepared for the consequences.

The shape tools

Now that I've painted my rosy picture, let's dig in and look at the tools. Or, if you're not feeling brave enough, take a break and come back later. Either way, it's up to you. As you've probably discovered by now, I like to give my readers lots of autonomy. That way, you're responsible for your own actions and you can't sue me if you go and poke your eye out with the line tool before you know how to use it.

Now as I was saying, click the rectangle tool to display a flyout menu of six shape tools, pictured in Figure 7-2. Or press U to select the rectangle tool. Then press Shift+U to switch from one shape tool to the next. Either way — remember, it's totally up to you; on my lawyer's advice, I make no recommendations — the six shape tools work as follows:

✦ **Rectangle tool:** It used to be a running gag that the hardest thing to do in Photoshop was to draw a simple rectangle. You had to draw a rectangular marquee and then fill it. Not actually hard, I guess, but what person outside the walls of a sanitarium would think to approach it that way? But the gag is dead — these days drawing a rectangle is easy. Drag to draw a rectangle from one corner to the other, Shift-drag to draw a square, Alt-drag (Option-drag on the Mac) to draw the shape outward from the center.

While drawing a rectangle or any other shape, press the spacebar to reposition the shape. Then release the spacebar and continue dragging to resize the shape as you normally do.

✦ **Rounded rectangle tool:** When you select the rounded rectangle tool, a Radius value becomes available in the Options bar. If you think of each rounded corner as a quarter of a circle, the Radius value is the radius (half the diameter) of that circle. Bigger values result in more roundness.

To lower or raise the Radius value in 1-pixel increments, press the bracket keys, [and]. Press Shift+[or] to lower or raise the value in 10-pixel increments.

✦ **Ellipse tool:** The ellipse tool draws ovals. Shift-drag for circles; Alt-drag (Option-drag) to draw the oval outward from the center.

✦ **Polygon tool:** This tool draws regular polygons, which are straight-sided shapes with radial symmetry. Examples include isosceles triangles (3 sides), squares (4 sides), pentagons (5 sides), hexagons (6 sides), heptagons (7 sides), octagons (8 sides), decagons (10 sides), dodecagons (12 sides), and a bunch of other shapes with so many sides that they're virtually indistinguishable from circles. Enter a Sides value in the Options bar to set the number of sides in the next polygon you draw.

Or better yet, press the bracket keys, [and], to decrease or increase the Sides value from the keyboard. You can also draw stars and rounded shapes with the polygon tool by clicking on the Geometry Options button, as discussed in Step 4 of the next section.

✦ **Line tool:** Some of you may be thinking, "Deke, you blithering nincompoop, how can you call these 'shape tools' when one of them draws lines?" Well, despite your name-calling, I'll tell you. The truth is, even the line tool draws shapes. Enter a Weight value into the Options bar to define the thickness of the so-called "line," and then drag in the image window. The result is an extremely long and skinny rectangle. As you see shortly, this makes editing a line exceedingly difficult, and calling this tool a "line tool" is some-what of a misnomer. Honestly, it really breaks my heart that The Squirt Gun that Shoots Jelly has to live on the Island of Misfit Toys while The Line Tool that Draws Shapes gets to roam around free as a bird.

Okay, so the line tool is weird. But you can modify the Weight value in single pixel incre-ments by pressing the [and] keys. You can also add an arrowhead to a line using the Geometry Options button, discussed in Step 4 of the next section.

✦ **Custom shape tool:** If you're familiar with Adobe Illustrator, Photoshop's shape tools may occasionally disappoint. You can't edit the roundness of an existing rectangle or add sides to a polygon while drawing it. And the kindest thing you can say about the line tool is that it's non-traditional. Fortunately, the custom shape tool makes up for the oversights and transgressions of its predecessors. Select a preset shape from the Shape option in the Options bar and then draw it in the image window. It's a symbol library of instant clip art.

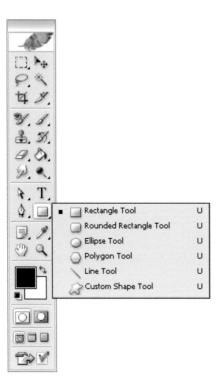

Figure 7-2: Click the rectangle tool to display the shape tools flyout menu. Or press U and Shift+U to switch between tools.

The shape drawing process

The act of drawing a shape can be as simple as dragging with a tool. How that shape manifests itself, however, depends primarily on which of the first three buttons labeled in Figure 7-3 is depressed. The first option creates a new shape layer when you draw with the shape tool. The second option creates a conventional path, available for inspection in the Paths palette. And the final option creates a pixel-based shape. In this last case, Photoshop doesn't add a new layer; it merely recolors the pixels on the active layer.

And that's just the beginning. Photoshop offers the aspiring shape artist a wealth of additional controls. Just for the record, here's the in-depth way to approach the process of drawing a shape layer.

STEPS: Creating a New Shape Layer

1. **Select the shape tool you want to use.** Remember, U is the keyboard shortcut for the shape tools.

2. **Specify the color.** Select a color for the shape from the Color palette. Alternatively, you can click either the foreground color icon in the toolbox or the Color swatch in the Options bar, and then select a color from the Color Picker. If you want to fill the shape with a gradient, pattern, or image, you can do that after you finish drawing the shape, as I explain in the upcoming section "Editing the stuff inside the shape."

3. **Specify how you want to draw the shape.** Pictured in Figure 7-3, the first three buttons in the Options bar determine what the shape tool draws. Because we're creating a shape layer, you'll want to make sure the first button is selected.

4. **Modify the geometry options.** Click the down-pointing arrowhead to the right of the tool buttons in the Options bar (labeled "Geometry options" in Figure 7-3) to see a pop-up palette of options geared to the selected shape tool. These permit you to constrain rectangles, ellipses, and custom shapes; indent the sides of a polygon to create a star; round off the corners of a polygon or star; and add arrowheads to the end of a line.

   Most of the geometry options are self-evident, but a few are tricky. When using the polygon tool, turn on the Star option to draw a star, and then use Indent Sides By to determine the angle of the spikes. Higher percentages mean sharper spikes. You can also round off the outside corners of a star or polygon or the inside corners of a star.

   When adding arrowheads to a line, the Width and Height values are measured relative to the line weight. A positive Concavity value bends the base of the arrowhead in; a negative value bends it out.

   The most unusual option is Snap to Pixels, which is associated with the two rectangle tools. Object-oriented shapes don't have any resolution, so their sides and corners can land in the middle of pixels. To prevent potential antialiasing in rectangles, select the Snap to Pixels check box to precisely align them with the pixels in the image.

5. **Modify other tool-specific settings.** Depending on the tool, you may see options to the right of the geometry options arrowhead. The polygon tool offers a Sides option; the line tool offers a Weight option. You can edit either by pressing the bracket keys, [and].

   When drawing a custom shape, click the button to the right of the word Shape to display a pop-up palette of presets, as revealed in Figure 7-3. Press [or] to cycle from one preset shape to another. You can load more shapes by choosing the Load Shapes command or by choosing one of the shape libraries — Animals, Arrows, Banners, and so forth — listed in the second half of the menu.

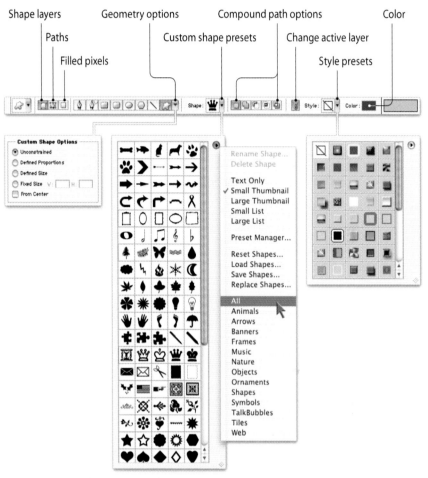

Figure 7-3: Use the options in the Options bar to specify the kind of shape you want to draw.

To load all custom shapes that ship with Photoshop, choose the All command. When Photoshop asks you if you want to replace the current shapes with the new ones, click OK.

6. **Apply style and color.** Unlike the other options discussed so far, you can assign a layer style or color to a shape either before you draw it or afterward. The key is the link icon, labeled "Change active layer" in Figure 7-3. When turned on, the style and color options affect the active shape layer. When turned off, they affect the next shape you draw.

The Style pop-up palette offers the very same presets available from the Styles palette, which I cover in the "Saving effects as styles" section at the end of this chapter. To cycle from one preset to another, press the comma (,) or period (.) key — the former selects the previous style and the latter selects the next. Shift+comma selects the first style; Shift+period selects the last style.

7. **Draw the shape.** Because you set the tool to draw a shape layer in Step 3, Photoshop automatically creates a new layer. As shown in Figure 7-4, the Layers palette shows a colored fill (labeled "Layer contents" in the figure) with a clipping path — or *vector mask*, in Photoshop parlance — to the right of it, masking the fill. If you assigned a layer style, a list of one or more effects appears under the layer name.

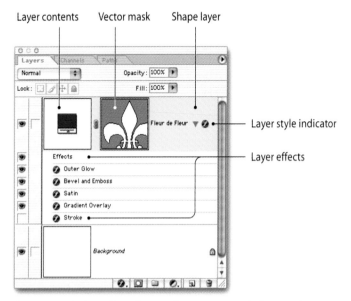

Figure 7-4: A shape layer is actually a vector mask that masks a color, gradient, pattern, or other fill directly inside Photoshop.

8. **Switch tools and draw more shapes.** By default, Photoshop creates a new shape layer for each new shape that you draw. If you prefer to keep adding paths to an active shape layer so that all shapes share the same fill, click the Add to Shape Area button in the Options bar. (It's labeled in Figure 7-5.) Then draw a new shape.

If you hit the Enter, Return, or Escape key, the current shape layer is deactivated, signifying that you no longer want to add shapes to that layer. This change is visible in the Layers palette; notice that the vector mask thumbnail no longer has a selection border around it. To reactivate the layer, simply click the thumbnail.

That's it. You now have one or more shape layers that you can use as you please. From this point on, it's a matter of editing the shape, as explained in the following sections.

Combining and editing shapes

A few years back, there was an image editor called Live Picture. Its creators heralded it as the first image editor to provide "infinite incremental undos." In fact, the program had a run-of-the-mill single-level Undo/Redo command. The infinite incremental undos were actually a result of an object metaphor that pervaded the program. After drawing an element, you had the option of changing it — less an automated backstep and more a manual adjustment.

By this twisted marketing logic, Photoshop's shape layers likewise permit infinite incremental undos. Although I'm being deliberately ironic, there is much to be said for a mask that is perpetually editable. Don't like a segment? Change it. Don't like a point? Move it. Hate the entire shape? Delete it. Here's how:

✦ **Compound path options:** As explained in Step 8 in the previous section, you can draw multiple shapes on a single layer. Because they all share a single fill, Photoshop thinks of the shapes as being bits and pieces of a single, complex path. In the language of the PostScript printer language, such a path is called a *compound path*. This leads Photoshop to wonder, what do I do when the bits and pieces overlap? Because they share a fill, they could just merge together. Or perhaps you'd rather use one shape to cut a hole in the other. Or maybe you'd like the intersection to be transparent.

You specify your preference by selecting one of the compound path buttons, labeled in Figure 7-5. On by default, the first button instructs Photoshop to create a shape on an independent layer—in effect, ensuring that there is no compound path interaction. Click the second button or press the plus key (+) to add the new shape to the others. Click the third button or press the minus key (–) to subtract the new shape from the others. The fourth button retains the intersection, and the fifth makes the intersection transparent. Feel free to experiment with these Boolean operations till you're bool in the face. (That's a little geek joke. Hope you enjoyed. Now if you'll excuse me, I'm going to go have a nice cup of chicken boolean.)

Create new shape layer

Add to shape area

Subtract from shape area

Intersect shape areas

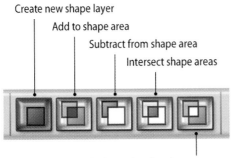

Exclude overlapping shape areas

Figure 7-5: The five compound path buttons let you control the interaction of compound paths. The last four are available only when editing or adding to an existing shape layer.

✦ **Selecting shapes:** To select and edit shapes, use the arrow tools. Press A to get the black arrow tool, which selects entire shapes at a time. Then click a shape to select it. To temporarily access the arrow tool, press the Ctrl key (⌘ on the Mac) when using a shape tool.

✦ **Moving and transforming:** Armed with the black arrow tool, drag a selected shape to move it. Select the Show Bounding Box check box in the Options bar to access the transformation controls. Or press Ctrl+T (⌘-T on the Mac) to enter the free transform mode. Then drag a handle to scale, drag outside the bounding box to rotate, and Ctrl-drag (⌘-drag) a handle to skew or distort. If you need a transformation refresher, check out the section "Applying Transformations" in Chapter 5.

✦ **Arranging and combining shapes:** After selecting a shape with the black arrow tool, you can apply any of the four available compound path buttons. (Create New Shape Layer is unavailable, because it affects new shapes only.) As you make your selection, bear in mind that the topmost shape takes precedence. So if Shape A is set to Add, Shape B is set to Intersect, and Shape B is in front, then Photoshop fills only the intersection. Meanwhile, the stacking order is entirely dependent on the order in which you draw the shapes, with more recent shapes in front. (The Layer ⇨ Arrange commands affect whole layers; they can't be used to reorder shapes.)

After you get the effect you're looking for, you can fix the relationship by selecting two or more paths and clicking the Combine button in the Options bar. Photoshop then fuses the selected paths into one.

Although it sounds impossible, you can combine a single path on a layer by itself. Select a shape with the black arrow and press the minus key (–) to fill everything *but* the shape. Press the plus key (+) to reset the layer to normal.

✦ **Selecting points and segments:** Press Shift+A to get the white arrow tool, which selects individual points and segments. Move individually selected points by dragging them; transform such points by pressing Ctrl+T (⌘-T on the Mac). To select an entire path independently of any others on a layer, Alt-click (Option-click) its outline.

✦ **Adding and deleting points:** The best tool for reshaping a shape is the pen tool, which you get by pressing the P key. First select part of the shape with one of the arrow tools. Then click a segment to insert a point that will serve as a sharp corner; drag to add a smooth point, which defines a continuous arc. Click on an existing point to delete it.

✦ **Disabling a vector mask:** Shift-click the vector mask thumbnail in the Layers palette to turn it off and make visible the entire contents of the layer. Shift-click the thumbnail again to turn the vector mask on.

✦ **Deleting a vector mask:** Click the vector mask thumbnail and then click the trash can icon at the bottom of the Layers palette to delete the shapes from the layer. You can also just drag the thumbnail to the trash can icon.

To delete an entire shape layer, just press the Backspace key (or Delete on the Mac). If the path outline is active, Photoshop will ask you if you want to delete the entire layer, just the mask, or just the paths inside the mask. Select the first option and click OK to get rid of the entire layer. And if the path outline isn't active when you press Backspace or Delete, Photoshop will just delete the layer, no questions asked.

✦ **Adding a vector mask to an existing layer:** To add a vector mask to any kind of layer — even one that contains standard image pixels — first choose Layer ⇨ Add Vector Mask ⇨ Reveal All. Then select a shape tool, press the + key to make sure Photoshop is ready to add a shape, and draw as you normally would. There you have it: an image inside a vector mask.

Better yet, instead of choosing the Reveal All command, just press the Ctrl key (⌘ on the Mac) and click the add layer mask icon at the bottom of the Layers palette. This creates a blank vector mask, ready for you to add shapes. Grab yourself a shape tool, press the + key, and start drawing.

✦ **Defining your own custom shape:** If you create a shape that you think you might want to repeat in the future, select the shape with either arrow tool and choose Edit ⇨ Define Custom Shape. Then name the shape and press Enter or Return. Photoshop adds the shape to the presets so you can draw it with the custom shape tool.

Editing the stuff inside the shape

The following are a few ways to modify the color and general appearance of shape layers. (Gosh, I've never written such a short introduction in my life. Of course, now I've gone and ruined it with this parenthetical, but what the heck.)

✦ **Changing the color:** To change the color of a shape layer, double-click the layer contents thumbnail in the Layers palette. Then select a new color from the Color Picker dialog box. Or better yet, change the foreground color and then press Alt+Backspace (Option-Delete on the Mac).

✦ **Changing the blending options:** You can change the blend mode and Opacity value for a shape layer using the standard controls in the Layers palette. Or double-click the vector mask thumbnail to display the Blending Options section of the Layer Style dialog box, covered in Chapter 6. You can also apply or modify layer effects, as I explain later in this chapter.

✦ **Changing the layer style:** Another way to apply or switch out layer effects is to apply a predefined style from the Styles palette. Just click a preset in the Styles palette and Photoshop automatically applies it to the active layer.

✦ **Fill with a gradient or repeating pattern:** Don't want to fill your shape with a solid color? Don't have to. To fill the active shape layer with a gradient, choose Layer ⇨ Change Layer Content ⇨ Gradient. Or choose Layer ⇨ Change Layer Content ⇨ Pattern to apply a repeating pattern. Figure 7-6 shows the dialog box for each. Most of the options will be familiar to the serious Photoshop user. The only unusual options are in the Pattern Fill dialog box. The Scale value lets you resize the pattern inside the shape; Link with Layer makes sure that the shape and pattern move together; and Snap to Origin snaps the pattern into alignment with the origin.

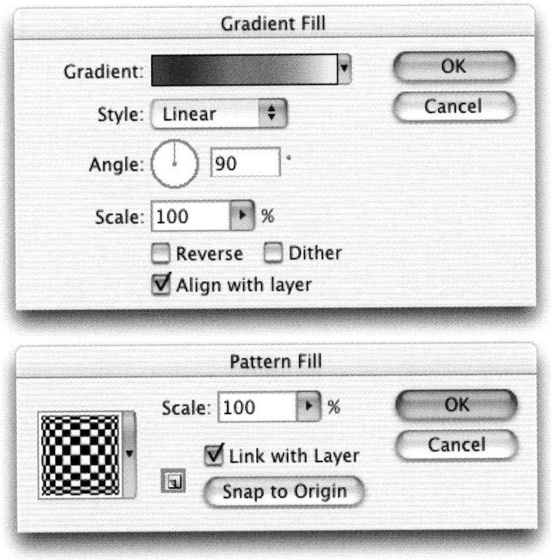

Figure 7-6: Gradients and patterns inside a shape layer are considered dynamic fills, which means you can edit them simply by double-clicking the layer contents thumbnail and editing the options above.

You can reposition a gradient or pattern inside its shape just by dragging inside the image window while the dialog box is up on screen.

After applying a gradient or pattern, you can edit it just by double-clicking the layer contents thumbnail in the Layers palette. Photoshop calls these kinds of editable contents *dynamic fills*.

✦ **Making a color adjustment shape:** Where layer content is concerned, shape layers have unlimited potential. You can even fill a shape with a color adjustment. Just choose Levels, Curves, Hue/Saturation, or any of the other color correction classics from the Layer ➪ Change Layer Content submenu. Read the "Adjustment Layers" section in Chapter 11 for more information.

✦ **Painting inside a shape layer:** Wish you could paint or edit the contents of a shape layer? Well, thanks to subtle genetic alterations to Photoshop's core subroutines, you can. Assuming the shape is filled with a solid color, gradient, or pattern (this technique is not applicable to adjustment layers), choose Layer ➪ Rasterize ➪ Fill Content. From this point on, the fill is no longer dynamic. This means you can't double-click its thumbnail to edit it. However, you can edit it like any other layer full of pixels. Paint inside it, clone from another layer with the healing brush, apply a filter, go nuts.

✦ **Filling a vector mask with an image:** Applying a vector mask to an image is a more delicate operation. Fortunately, there are several ways to do it, so you can select your favorite. I mentioned one method at the end of the previous section. Here's another: Draw a shape not as a new shape layer, but rather as a path by selecting the Paths button in the Options bar. Then select the layer that you want to mask (it must be a floating layer, not the background) and choose Layer ➪ Add Vector Mask ➪ Current Path.

Want to avoid that command? After establishing a path, Ctrl-click (on the Mac, ⌘-click) the add layer mask icon at the bottom of the Layers palette to make the path clip the active image layer.

✦ **From clipping mask to vector mask:** What if you've already gone and made a shape layer, and now you want to fill that shape with an image? Move the image to an independent layer in front of the shape layer. Then press Ctrl+G (⌘-G on the Mac) to group it with the shape layer. You now have a clipping mask with the shape masking the contents of the image above it.

✦ **Fusing image and shape layer:** If you want for any reason to fuse those two layers together, you can't just hit Ctrl+E (⌘-E on the Mac). Here's what you have to do: First, select the shape layer and choose Layer ➪ Rasterize ➪ Fill Content to convert the dynamic fill to pixels. Then you can select the image layer and press Ctrl+E (⌘-E on the Mac) to merge it with the shape layer below.

If all this isn't enough, there is one more way to push the boundaries of shape layers and wring the last vestiges of cogent reasoning out of your by-now fragile mind. How? By adding a layer mask to a shape layer. That's right, Photoshop lets you combine pixel masking and vector masking in one layer, permitting you to mix soft edges and razor sharp outlines.

In Figure 7-7, I first Ctrl-clicked (⌘-clicked) the vector mask thumbnail in the Layers palette to load the fleur-de-lis shape as a selection outline. Then I converted the selection to a layer mask by clicking the add layer mask icon at the bottom of the Layers palette. The result was a layer mask that was identical to the vector mask. Why in the world would I want to do that?

Layer mask thumbnail

Add layer mask

Figure 7-7: Add a layer mask to a shape layer to add pixel-based softening to the razor-sharp vector mask.

Why, to serve as a jumping off point, of course. In Figure 7-8, I applied Filter ➪ Blur ➪ Gaussian Blur to feather the layer mask. Then I applied Filter ➪ Pixelate ➪ Crystallize, to add mosaic edges. The result is organic, rippling edges along the inside of a sharp vector shape. The layer mask masks the layer, and then the vector mask masks that. Pretty spiffy, huh?

I explain the Gaussian Blur command in Chapter 8. For more information on Crystallize, see Chapter 9.

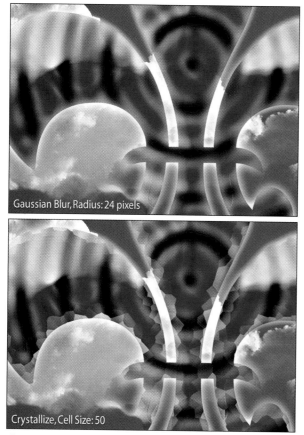

Figure 7-8: Applying the Gaussian Blur (top) and Crystallize filters to the layer mask mixes a soft pixelated effect with the hard edges provided by the vector mask (bottom).

The Bold and Beautiful Layer Styles

As I mentioned at the beginning of this chapter, a simple description of what layer styles can do for you might sound a bit cheesy. Would a serious artist really want to trust an automated, instantaneous feature to create shadows and glows, relying on canned, prefab effects to imbue her images with a sense of depth? Well, considering the amount of control and power Adobe has packed into Photoshop's layer styles, *this* serious artist says: Bring it on, baby. While creating these effects by hand used to be a slow, painstaking process with permanent results, layer styles are fast, flexible, and totally non-destructive. Shadows, glows, beveled edges, strokes, and textures: These are only a small part of what layer styles can deliver. So enough chit-chat; let's get stylin'.

First of all, a quick note on nomenclature. I tend to refer to these features — drop shadows, glows, and whatnot — as layer *effects*. But Photoshop seems to refer to them as layer *styles*. I mean, you apply them using the Layer Style dialog box, right? Technically, you use the Layer Style dialog box to add effects to a layer, which you then might save as a style to be called up later in the Styles palette. Kind of confusing, if you ask me. So, you say styles, I say effects, let's call the whole thing *awf*-ully powerful, no matter what the name.

The following are just a few of the many advantages to Photoshop's unique brand of layer effects:

✦ First, they stick to the layer. Move or transform the layer and the effect tags along with it.

✦ Second, the effect is temporary. As long as you save the image in one of the four layered formats — native Photoshop (PSD), TIFF, PDF, or PSB — you can edit the shadows, glows, bevels, overlays, and strokes long into the future.

✦ Third, layer effects are equally applicable to standard layers, shape layers, and editable text. This is unusual because both shape layers and editable text prohibit many kinds of changes.

✦ Fourth, thanks to the Contour presets, layer effects enable you to create effects that would prove otherwise exceedingly difficult or even impossible.

✦ Fifth, you can combine multiple effects on a single layer.

✦ Sixth, you can copy an effect from one layer and paste it onto another.

✦ Seventh, you can save groups of effects for later use in the Styles palette.

✦ Eighth, the effects show up as items in the Layers palette. You can expand and collapse a list of effects, as well as temporarily disable and enable effects by clicking the familiar eyeball icons.

✦ Ninth — why the heck do you need a ninth advantage? Didn't television teach us that *Eight Is Enough*? But what the heck. Ninth, layer effect strokes print as vector output, so they're guaranteed to be smooth. There, satisfied?

Now that you're champing at the bit to get your hooves on these effects, the following sections tell you how, why, and what for.

The basic varieties of layer effects

To apply a layer effect, start with an image on an independent layer. In Figure 7-9, I painted a white seven on an independent layer using the brush tool and a Wacom tablet. But you can use any kind of layer, including a shape layer or even text. Then click the add layer style icon at the bottom of the Layers palette — the one that looks like a florin (cursive *f*) — and choose any of the commands following Blending Options. Or double-click anywhere on the layer thumbnail to display the Layer Style dialog box and then select an effect from the left-hand list. Use the check box to turn an effect on or off; highlight the effect name to edit its settings.

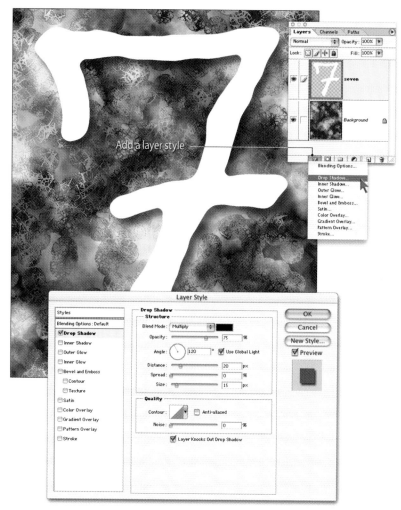

Figure 7-9: Starting with an independent layer, click the add layer style icon at the bottom of the Layers palette and choose an effect (top). Then adjust the settings inside the sprawling but highly capable Layer Style dialog box (bottom).

You can select from one of the following effects:

◆ **Drop Shadow:** The Drop Shadow command applies a common, everyday drop shadow, as seen in the first example in Figure 7-10. You specify the color, opacity, blend mode, position, size, and contour of the shadow; Photoshop makes it pretty.

◆ **Inner Shadow:** This command applies a drop shadow inside the layer, as demonstrated in the second example in Figure 7-10. The command simulates the kind of shadow you'd get if the layer were punched out of the background — that is, the background looks like it's in front, casting a shadow onto the layer. Figure 7-10 should give you an inkling of the fact that Inner Shadow is especially effective with type.

Drop shadow, Distance: 25, Size: 30   Inner shadow, Distance: 20, Size: 10

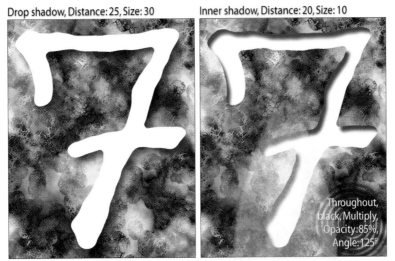

Throughout, black, Multiply, Opacity: 85%, Angle: 125°

Figure 7-10: Photoshop's two Shadow effects can make it look like the affected layer hovers above (left) or below (right) the layer behind it.

✦ **Outer Glow:** The Outer Glow command creates a traditional halo, as seen in the first example in Figure 7-11. Note that I also pressed Shift+Alt+Backspace (Shift-Option-Delete) to fill the seven with black. Throughout this and future figures, I'll be switching the fill color between black, white, and gray to best suit the layer effect.

✦ **Inner Glow:** This command applies the glow effect inside the boundaries of the layer rather than outside, as demonstrated in the second example in Figure 7-11.

Outer glow, Size: 30   Inner glow, Size: 20

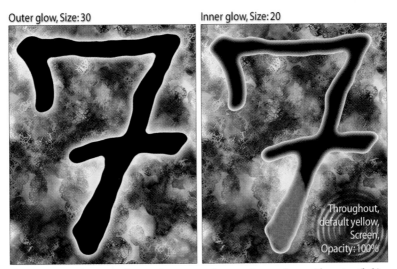

Throughout, default yellow, Screen, Opacity: 100%

Figure 7-11: The two Glow styles can make your layer glow with outer (left) or inner (right) beauty. I filled my seven with black instead of white to better show off the glows.

To create a neon strip around the perimeter of a layer, apply both the Outer Glow and Inner Glow styles. Figure 7-12 shows one such example of a neon edge (top right), as well as a few other effects you can obtain by mixing and matching shadows and glows.

Drop shadow + inner shadow

Outer glow + inner glow

Drop shadow + inner glow

Inner shadow + outer glow

Figure 7-12: Even if you never venture beyond the Shadow and Glow styles, you can invent some intriguing combinations.

✦ **Bevel and Emboss:** The Bevel and Emboss option produces one of five distinct edge effects, as defined using the Style pop-up menu. The first four appear in Figure 7-13; the fifth one is exclusively applicable to stroked layers and requires the Stroke effect to be turned on. You can add a three-dimensional beveled edge around the outside of the layer, as in the first example in the figure. The Inner Bevel effect (top right) produces a beveled edge inside the layer. The Emboss effect (bottom left) combines inner and outer bevels. And the Pillow Emboss effect (bottom right) reverses the inner bevel so the image appears to sink in and then rise back up along the edge of the layer.

Outer bevel, Depth: 200, Size: 30

Inner bevel, Depth: 200, Size: 20

Emboss, Depth: 300, Size: 25

Pillow emboss, Depth: 200, Size: 15

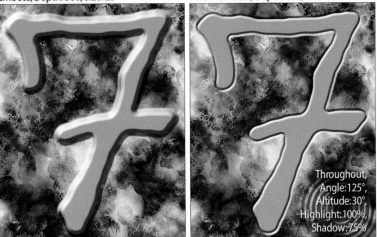

Throughout,
Angle: 125°,
Altitude: 30°,
Highlight: 100%,
Shadow: 75%

Figure 7-13: The examples above demonstrate four of the effects available when you choose Layer ⇨ Layer Style ⇨ Bevel and Emboss. I used Edit ⇨ Fill to fill my seven with 50% Gray to better show off the highlights and shadows that Bevel and Emboss creates.

✦ **Contour and Texture:** The Contour and Texture options aren't actual effects, but rather modify the Bevel and Emboss effect. The Contour settings create waves in the surface of the layer that result in rippling lighting effects. Texture stamps a pattern into the surface of the layer, which creates a texture effect. Figure 7-14 illustrates these two options.

Inner bevel, Contour: Ring, Range: 20%   same, Texture, Pattern: Molecular

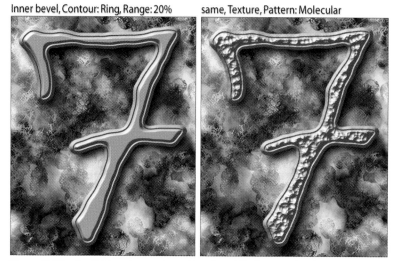

Figure 7-14: Available when using a Bevel and Emboss style, the Contour option lets you sculpt around the boundary of a layer (left). Meanwhile, the Texture option applies a lighted surface texture to the shape (right).

✦ **Satin:** This option creates waves of repeating color that follow the outline of the layer, like the blue ripples in Figure 7-15. You define the behavior of the waves using the Contour options. One of the stranger effects, Satin can be difficult to predict. But as long as you keep the Preview check box turned on, you can see the results of your experimentations as you work.

✦ **Color, Gradient, and Pattern Overlay:** These three options coat the layer with a solid color, gradient, or repeating pattern, respectively. They work almost identically to the three dynamic fills available to shape layers, as discussed in the section "Editing the stuff inside the shape" earlier in this chapter. All three can be quite useful when defining your own style presets, or when colorizing a flat layer like my white seven.

Figure 7-16 shows off the Gradient and Pattern Overlay effects. In the upper-left example, I applied a black-to-white gradient using the Multiply blend mode and an Opacity setting of 50 percent. Upper right, I filled the layer with the Optical Checkerboard pattern. The figure goes on to show the two effects combined and then heaped on top of the previous inner bevel and satin effects. I then added in a blue Color Overlay effect to produce the two permutations in Figure 7-17. Bear in mind, throughout, the color of the seven layer is actually white. Everything else is layer effects.

✦ **Stroke:** Use this option to trace a colored outline around a layer. The first example in Figure 7-18 features a dark blue stroke combined with a stroke emboss from the Bevel and Emboss effect category. The settings for the stroke emboss are a Depth of 200 percent, a Size of 20 pixels, and Gloss Contour set to Ring – Double. The Stroke effect is often preferable to Edit ➪ Stroke because you can edit the effect long after applying it. By comparison, Edit ➪ Stroke recolors pixels.

Satin, Angle: 125°, Distance: 50, Size: 30   same, with contoured inner bevel

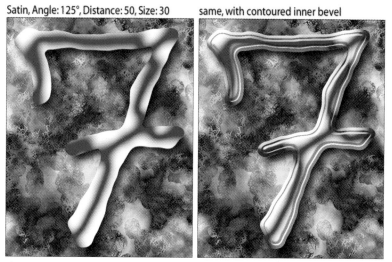

Figure 7-15: After making my seven white, I applied the Satin option (left) and then added a contoured inner bevel to produce a dramatic, reflective effect (right).

The Layer Style dialog box is a vast labyrinth of options. So it's handy to know a few additional ways to get around. To switch between effects without turning them on or off, press Ctrl (⌘ on the Mac) plus a number key. Ctrl+1 (⌘-1) highlights Drop Shadow, Ctrl+2 (⌘-2) highlights Inner Shadow, Ctrl+3 (⌘-3) highlights Outer Glow, and so on, all the way to Ctrl+0 (⌘-0) for Stroke. You cannot get to Blending Options, Contour, or Texture from the keyboard.

Inside the Layer Style dialog box

The Layer Style dialog box offers 13 panels containing more than 100 options. That may seem like a ridiculous number of settings, but in truth, every one of them serves a unique and often highly practical purpose. And thankfully, many of the options are familiar from other parts of the program. The Blend Mode pop-up menu provides access to the same modes discussed in Chapters 1 and 6. You make an effect translucent by entering a value in the Opacity option box.

Other options appear multiple times throughout the course of the dialog box. For example, all the options that appear in the Inner Shadow panel also appear in the Drop Shadow panel; the options from the Outer Glow panel appear in the Inner Glow panel; and so on. The modified dialog box in Figure 7-19 shows four representative effects panels — Inner Shadow, Inner Glow, Bevel and Emboss, and Texture — which together contain most of the options you'll encounter.

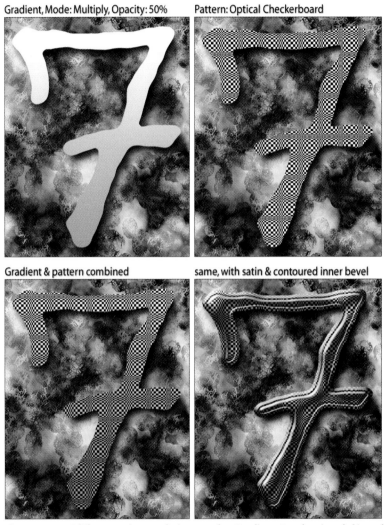

Figure 7-16: While attractive on their own, the Gradient Overlay (top left) and Pattern Overlay (top right) options can be combined to create the graduated effect shown in the bottom-left example. Add in my Satin and Inner Bevel settings from Figure 7-15, and the bottom-right image is the ravishing result.

Color, Mode: Overlay + gradient & pattern   same, with satin & contoured inner bevel

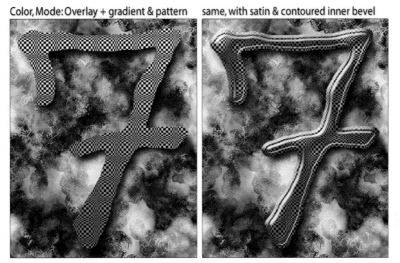

Figure 7-17: A blue Color Overlay effect as it appears when added to the final two examples from Figure 7-16. In each case, the blend mode is set to Overlay and the Opacity is 100 percent.

Stroke, 7 pixels, with stroke emboss   + inner glow, satin, color, gradient, & pattern

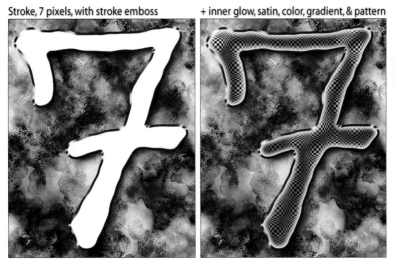

Figure 7-18: The Stroke effect is an editable alternative to the Edit ⇨ Stroke command and can be used in combination with a stroke emboss (left) as well as other layer effects (right).

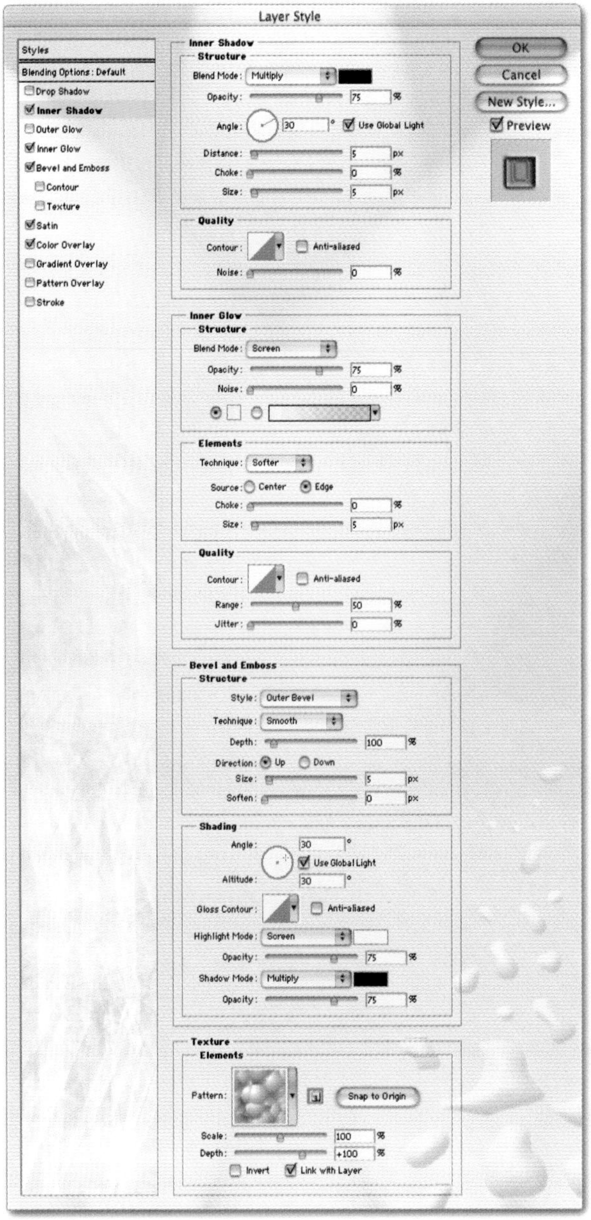

Figure 7-19: A modified snapshot of the Layer Style dialog box, featuring the Inner Shadow, Inner Glow, Bevel and Emboss, and Texture panels.

The following items explain the options in the order that they appear throughout the panels. I explain each option only once, so if an option appears multiple times — as so many do — look for its first appearance in a panel to locate the corresponding discussion in the following list. (Hey, we have to do our part to save paper. Your friendly neighborhood forest thanks you.)

✦ **Blend Mode:** This pop-up menu controls the blend mode. So much for the obvious. But did you know that you can use the Blend Mode menu to turn an effect upside-down? Select a light color and apply the Screen mode to change a drop shadow into a directional halo. Or use a dark color with Multiply to change an outer glow into a shadow that evenly traces the edge of the layer. Don't be constrained by pedestrian notions of shadows and glows. Layer effects can be anything. Figure 7-20 offers proof.

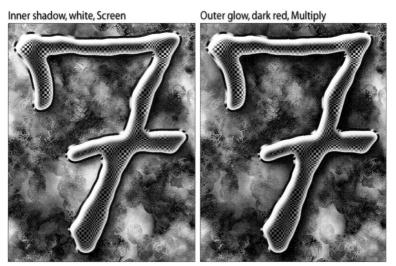

Inner shadow, white, Screen   Outer glow, dark red, Multiply

Figure 7-20: Starting with the last example in Figure 7-18, I added a white inner shadow (left) to create a soft beveling effect and then surrounded the whole thing with a dark red outer glow (right). We'll never get that seven mixed up with its background.

✦ **Color Swatch:** To change the color of the shadow, glow, or beveled edge, click the color swatch. When the Color Picker is open, click in the image window to eyedrop a color from the layered composition. When editing a glow, you can apply a gradient in place of a solid color. Click the gradient preview to create a custom gradation or select a preset from the pop-up palette.

✦ **Opacity:** Use this option to make the effect translucent. Remember, a little bit of effect goes a long way. When in doubt, reduce the Opacity value.

✦ **Angle:** Associated with shadows, bevels, the Satin effect, and gradients, this value controls the direction of the effect. In the case of shadows and bevels, the option controls the angle of the light source. With Satin, it controls the angle at which contour patterns overlap. And with a gradient, the Angle value represents the direction of the gradient.

You can avoid the numerical Angle option and simply drag an effect inside the image window. When the Drop Shadow or Inner Shadow panel is visible, drag inside the image window to move the shadow with respect to the layer. You can also drag the contour effect when working in the Satin panel. Other draggable effects include Gradient Overlay and Pattern Overlay, although dragging affects positioning, not angle.

✦ **Use Global Light:** In the real world, the sun casts all shadows in the same direction. Oh, sure, the shadows change minutely from one object to the next, but what with the sun being 90 million miles away and all, the changes are astronomically subtle. I doubt if a single-celled organism, upon admiring its shadow compared with that of its neighbor, could perceive the slightest difference. The fact that single-celled organisms lack eyes, brains, and other perceptual organs does not in any way lessen the truth of this powerful argument.

As I was saying, one sun means one lightness and one darkness. By turning on the Use Global Light check box, you tell Photoshop to cast *all* direction-dependent effects — drop shadows, inner shadows, and the five kinds of bevels — in the same direction. If you change the angle of a drop shadow applied to Layer 1, Photoshop rotates the sun in its heaven and so changes the angle of the pillow emboss applied to Layer 9, thus proving that even a computer program may subscribe to the immutable laws of nature.

Conversely, if you turn the check box off, you tell nature to take a hike. You can change an Angle value in any which way you like and none of the other layers will care.

If you have established a consistent universe, you can edit the angle of the sun by choosing Layer ➪ Layer Style ➪ Global Light. Change the Angle value and all shadows and bevels created with Use Global Light turned on will move in unison. You can also set the Altitude for bevels. "Sunrise, sunset," as the Yiddish fiddlers say. That doesn't shed any light on the topic, but when in doubt, I like to quote a great musical to class up the joint.

✦ **Distance:** The Drop Shadow, Inner Shadow, and Satin panels feature a Distance value that determines the distance between the farthest edge of the effect and the corresponding edge of the layer. Like Angle, this value is affected when you drag in the image window.

✦ **Spread/Choke:** Associated with the Drop Shadow and Outer Glow panels, the Spread option expands the point at which the effect begins outward from the perimeter of the layer. Spread changes to Choke in the Inner Shadow and Inner Glow panels, in which case it contracts the point at which the effect begins. Note that both Spread and Choke are measured as percentages of the Size value, explained next.

✦ **Size:** One of the most ubiquitous settings, the Size value determines how far an effect expands or contracts from the perimeter of the layer. In the case of shadows and glows, the portion of the Size that is not devoted to Spread or Choke is given over to blurring. For example, if you set the Spread for Drop Shadow to 0 percent and the Size to 30 pixels, as in the top-left example in Figure 7-21, Photoshop blurs the shadow across 100 percent of the 30-pixel size. If you set the Spread to 100 percent as in the bottom-right example, then 0 percent is left for blurring. The shadow expands 30 pixels out from the perimeter of the layer and has a sharp edge. This makes the effect seem larger, but in fact, only the opaque portion of the effect has grown.

Size and Depth observe a similar relationship in the Bevel and Emboss panel, with Depth taking the place of Spread or Choke. When adjusting a Satin effect, Size affects the length of the contoured wave pattern. And in Stroke, Size controls the thickness of the outline.

Drop shadow, Size: 30 pixels, Spread: 0% same, Spread: 25%

and again, Spread: 50% ditto, Spread: 100%

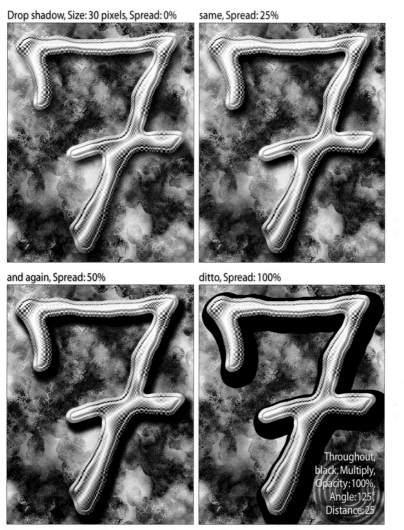

Throughout,
black, Multiply,
Opacity: 100%,
Angle: 125,
Distance: 25

Figure 7-21: The effect of raising the Spread percentage value from 0 (top left) to 100 (bottom right) on my now-familiar number seven. Note that for purposes of contrast, I changed the color of the Satin effect to white. (Feel free to insert your own Moody Blues joke here.)

✦ **Contour:** Photoshop creates most effects — namely shadows, glows, bevel, and the Satin effect — by fading a color from a specified Opacity value to transparent. The rate at which the fade occurs is determined by the Contour option. Click the down-pointing arrowhead to select from a palette of preset contours; click the contour preview to design your own. If you think of the Contour preview as a graph, the top of the graph represents opacity and the bottom represents transparency. So a straight line from top to bottom shows a consistent fade. A spike in the graph shows the color hitting opacity and then fading away again. Figure 7-22 shows a few examples applied to — hooray! — a new layer. In case you're curious, I painted this S shape with a scatter brush, and then filled it with the Molecular Pattern Overlay effect, topping it all off with an Inner Bevel garnish.

The most challenging contours are associated with Bevel and Emboss. The Gloss Contour option controls how colors fade in and out inside the beveled edge, as if the edge were reflecting other colors around it. (Figure 7-28 offers a glimpse.) The indented Contour effect — below Bevel and Emboss in the Layer Style list — wrinkles the edge of the layer so that it casts different highlights and shadows.

Outer glow, Size: 70 pixels, Contour: Linear   same, Contour: Gaussian

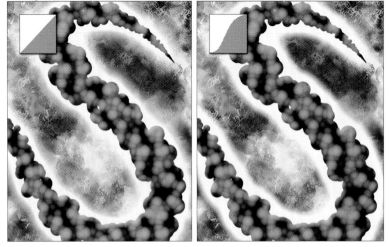

ibid, Contour: Ring   encore, Contour: Ring – Triple

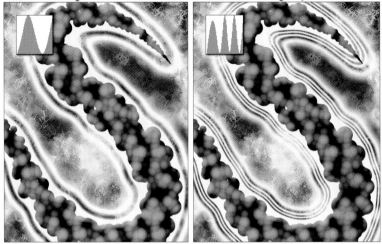

Figure 7-22: Four Contour presets combined with an Outer Glow effect. Note that the final Contour (Ring – Triple) is available only if you bring up the menu off the Contour pop-up palette and choose the Contours library. The settings used throughout include the Screen blend mode, 100-percent Opacity, 15-percent Spread, and Softer Technique.

✦ **Anti-aliased:** If a Contour setting consists of sharp corners, you can soften them by turning this check box on. Most presets have rounded corners, making antialiasing unnecessary.

✦ **Noise:** Associated strictly with shadows and glows, the Noise value randomizes the transparency of pixels. It's like using the Dissolve blend mode, except that you have control over how much randomization to apply. The Noise value does not change the color of pixels; that is the job of an option called Jitter.

✦ **Layer Knocks Out Drop Shadow:** In the real world, if an object was translucent, you could see through it to its own shadow. However, this turns out to be an unpopular law of nature with most image editors, a lawless bunch if ever there was one. So when creating a drop shadow, Photoshop gives us the Layer Knocks Out Drop Shadow check box, which when selected makes the drop shadow invisible directly behind the layer. Turn the option off for a more natural effect.

✦ **Technique:** Moving out of the Shadow panels and into Outer Glow, the first unique option is the Technique pop-up menu. Also available when creating bevel effects (see Figure 7-27), Technique controls how the contours of the effect are calculated. When a glow is set to Softer, as in all of the examples in Figure 7-22, Photoshop applies a modified Gaussian Blur to ensure optimal transitions between the glow and background elements. Your other option is Precise, which calculates the effect without the Gaussian adjustment, as in Figure 7-23. Mind you, the effect may remain blurry, but strictly as a function of the Spread and Contour settings. Precise may work better in tight corners, common around type and shape layers. Otherwise, stick with Softer.

The Bevel and Emboss panel doesn't provide the same kind of blurring functions that you get with shadow and glow effects, so the Technique option works a bit differently. The default setting, Smooth, averages and blurs pixels to achieve soft, rounded edges. The two Chisel settings remove the averaging to create saw-tooth abrasions into the sides of the layer. Chisel Hard results in thick cut marks; Chisel Soft averages the perimeter of the layer to create finer cuts. Up the Soften value (described shortly) to blur the abrasions.

✦ **Source:** When working in the Inner Glow panel, Photoshop wants to know where the glow starts. Should it glow inward from the perimeter of the layer (Edge) or outward from the middle (Center)? Figure 7-24 shows an example of each.

✦ **Range:** The two Glow panels and the Contour panel (subordinate to Bevel and Emboss) use Range values to modify the Contour settings. This value sets the midpoint of the contour with respect to the middle of the size. As seen in the first example in Figure 7-25, values less than 50 percent move the midpoint away from the source, extending the effect. Values greater than 50 percent shrink the effect, as shown in the second example.

✦ **Jitter:** Where the Noise value randomizes the transparency of pixels, Jitter randomizes the colors. This option is operable only when creating gradient glows in which the gradation contains two or more colors (not a color and transparency).

✦ **Depth:** The first unique Bevel and Emboss setting is Depth, which makes the sides of a bevel steeper or shallower. In most cases, this translates to increased contrast between highlights and shadows as you raise the Depth value. Figure 7-26 shows examples.

The Texture panel includes its own Depth setting. Here, Photoshop renders the pattern as a texture map, lighting the white areas of the pattern as high and the black areas as low. The Depth value determines the depth of the texture. The difference is you can enter a negative value, which inverts the texture. Meanwhile, you also have an additional Invert check box, which you can use to reverse the lights and darks in the pattern. So a positive Depth value with Invert turned on produces the same effect as a negative Depth value with Invert turned off.

Technique: Precise, Contour: Linear   Contour: Gaussian

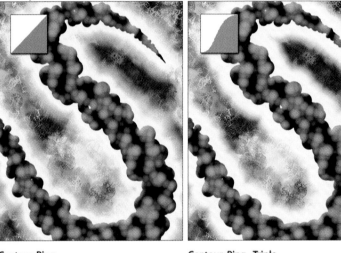

Contour: Ring   Contour: Ring–Triple

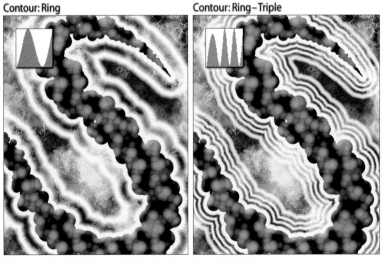

Figure 7-23: This figure is identical to Figure 7-22 in every way, save one: It's printed on a different page. Well, that, plus here the Technique option is set to Precise.

Inner glow, Contour: Ring, Source: Edge   same, Source: Center

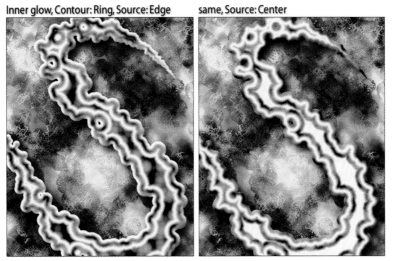

Figure 7-24: The two settings for the Source option in the Inner Glow panel. The other settings used in both examples are as follows—Blend Mode: Screen, Opacity: 100 percent, Technique: Precise, Choke: 15 percent, and Size: 40 pixels.

Outer & inner glows, Range: 20%   same, Range: 80%

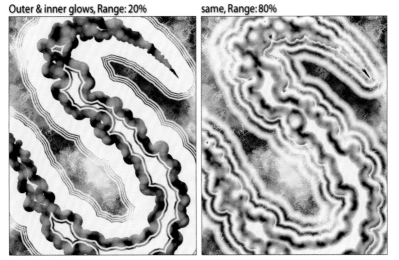

Figure 7-25: The Range setting at 20 percent (left) and 80 percent (right). The outer glow in both examples uses the Contour preset Ring – Triple; the inner glow uses the Ring preset with the Source set to Center.

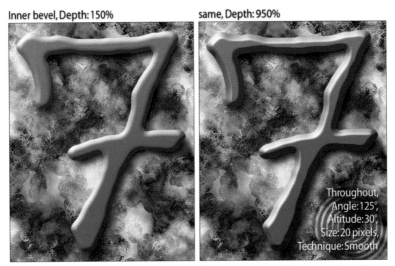

Inner bevel, Depth: 150%   same, Depth: 950%

Throughout,
Angle: 125°,
Altitude: 30°,
Size: 20 pixels,
Technique: Smooth

Figure 7-26: The return of the seven with an inner bevel Depth setting of 150 percent (left) and 950 percent (right). The color of the seven has again been changed to gray, with the Drop Shadow, Color Overlay, and Gradient Overlay effects in attendance.

✦ **Direction:** When working in the Bevel and Emboss panel, you see two radio buttons: Up and Down. If the Angle value indicates the direction of the sun, then Up positions the highlight along the edge near the sun and the shadow along the opposite edge. Down reverses things, so the shadow is near the light source. Presumably, this means the layer sinks into its background rather than protrudes out from it. But, in practice, the layer usually appears merely as though it's lit differently.

✦ **Soften:** This value sets the amount of blur applied to the beveled highlights and shadows. Small changes make a big difference when the Technique option is set to one of the Chisel options. Figure 7-27 provides a hard look at this squishy option.

✦ **Altitude:** The Bevel and Emboss panel includes two lighting controls, Angle and Altitude. The Angle value is just that: the angle of the sun with respect to the layer. The Altitude, demonstrated in Figure 7-28, is measured on a half circle drawn across the sky. A maximum value of 90 degrees puts the sun directly overhead (noon); 0 degrees puts it on the horizon (sunrise). Values in the medium range — 30 to 60 degrees — generally produce the best results. If you find the effect to be too sharp, you can temper it with the Soften setting, as shown in Figure 7-29.

✦ **Scale:** The Texture and Pattern Overlay panels include Scale values, which scale the pattern tiles inside the layer. Values greater than 100 percent swell the pattern; values lower than 100 percent shrink it.

✦ **Link/Align with Layer:** When turned on, this check box centers a gradient inside a layer. If you want to draw a gradient across many layers, turn the option off to center the gradient inside the canvas. When editing a pattern, this option links the pattern to the layer so the two move together.

✦ **Position:** The final Layer Style option appears in the Stroke panel. The Position pop-up menu defines how the width of the stroke aligns with the perimeter of the layer. Photoshop can draw the stroke outside the edge of the layer, inside the edge, or center the stroke exactly on the edge. It's up to you.

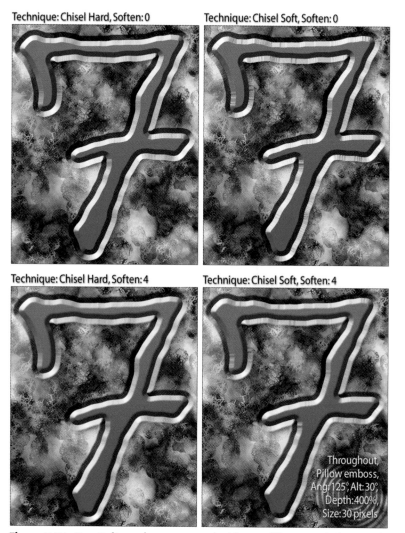

Figure 7-27: Two Soften values compared with two different Technique settings in the Pillow Emboss effect. Note that higher Soften values (bottom two examples) smooth out the otherwise jagged Technique settings without altogether getting rid of the sculpted edges.

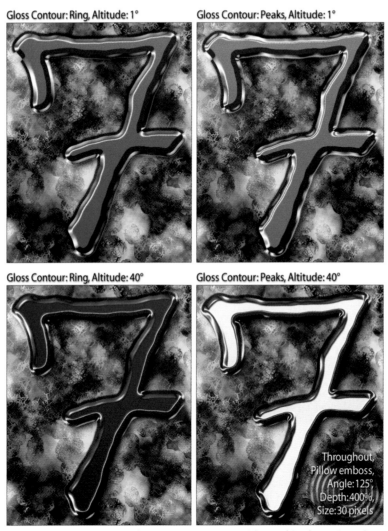

Gloss Contour: Ring, Altitude: 1°   Gloss Contour: Peaks, Altitude: 1°

Gloss Contour: Ring, Altitude: 40°   Gloss Contour: Peaks, Altitude: 40°

Throughout,
Pillow emboss,
Angle: 125°,
Depth: 400%,
Size: 30 pixels

Figure 7-28: A couple of Gloss Contour presets with an Altitude setting of 1 degree (top) and 40 degrees (bottom). Note that the higher setting brings out major differences between the two Gloss Contour presets.

Gloss Contour: Ring, Altitude: 1°, Soften: 4   Gloss Contour: Peaks, Altitude: 40°, Soften: 2

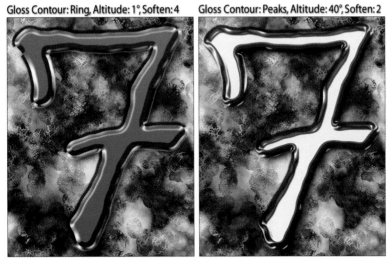

Figure 7-29: The first and last examples from Figure 7-28 with a touch of the Soften option.

Modifying and Saving Effects

After you apply a layer effect, Photoshop stamps the layer with a florin symbol (*f*), as shown in Figure 7-30. A triangular toggle switch lets you collapse the effects to permit more room for layers inside the palette. From that point on, you can edit an effect by double-clicking its name in the Layers palette. Or double-click the florin symbol to display the Blending Options panel of the Layer Style dialog box.

Disabling effects

To temporarily disable all effects applied to a layer, choose Layer ➪ Layer Style ➪ Hide All Effects. Or better yet, just click the eyeball in front of the word "Effects" in the Layers palette. Click the eyeball spot again to show the effects. You can likewise hide and show individual effects — without permanently disabling them — by clicking eyeballs. Photoshop even goes so far as to save hidden effects. This makes it easy to bring an effect back to life later without re-entering settings.

To permanently delete an effect, drag it and drop it onto the trash icon at the bottom of the Layers palette. To delete all effects, drag the word "Effects" to the trash.

Duplicating effects

After you apply an effect to a layer, the effect becomes an element that you can copy and apply to other layers. Select the layer with the effects you want to duplicate and choose Layer ➪ Layer Style ➪ Copy Layer Style. Or right-click (on the Mac, Control-click) the layer name in the Layers palette and choose Copy Layer Style from the shortcut menu. Then select another layer, right-click (Control-click) it, and choose Paste Layer Style. To paste a copied effect onto multiple layers at a time, link them together (as explained in the section "Linking layers" in Chapter 5) and choose the Paste Layer Style to Linked command.

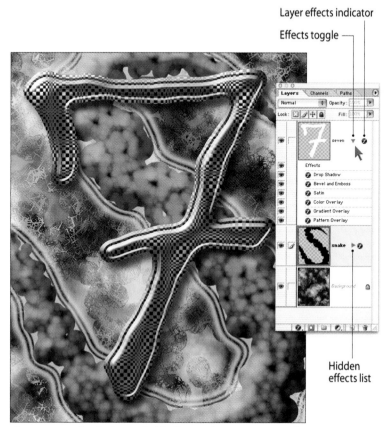

Layer effects indicator

Effects toggle

Hidden
effects list

Figure 7-30: The florin symbol indicates that one or more layer effects have been applied to the layer. Use the triangular effects toggle to hide and show the list of effects.

The Copy and Paste Layer Style commands bypass the Clipboard. This means you can copy an image and then copy an effect without displacing the image.

Paste Layer Style duplicates all effects associated with one layer onto another. But what if you want to duplicate a single effect only? Just drag the effect name from one layer and drop it below another in the Layers palette. Be sure you see a bar below the layer name when dropping the effect — otherwise, it won't take.

Scattering effects to the four winds

When you apply an effect, Photoshop is actually doing all the manual layer work for you in the background. This means if Photoshop doesn't seem to be generating the precise effect you want, you can take over and edit the layers to your satisfaction. Choose Layer ⇨ Layer Style ⇨ Create Layers to resolve the automated effect into a series of layers and clipping masks. In some cases, a warning appears telling you that one or more attributes of an effect cannot be represented with layers. Go ahead and give it a try; you can always undo. If you like what you see, inspect it and edit at will.

After choosing Create Layers, you're on your own. From that point on, you lose the ability to edit the effects from the Layer Style dialog box (unless, of course, you decide to go back in time via the History palette).

Effects and blending options

If you like layer effects as much as I do — and as you've probably gathered, I really, *really* like layer effects — there's no doubt you'll eventually find yourself experiencing a curious phenomenon. After you've gone and heaped on a bunch of different effects, particularly Color, Gradient, and Pattern Overlays, your layer may no longer respond to blend modes. For example, Figure 7-31 shows two very familiar layers together: the seven and the S. I applied the Overlay blend mode to the seven layer (much as I would apply hot sauce to a seven-layer burrito). Then I applied the Soft Light blend mode to the S layer and reduced the Fill Opacity value to 50 percent.

Two layers, two blend modes, one Fill value . . . and yet nothing happens. As the first image in Figure 7-31 shows, the seven and S still look like they did in Figure 7-30. It's as if both layers are still set to Normal with 100 percent Opacity. What gives? Well, both layers contain opaque interior effects, the Pattern Overlay being the primary culprit. But there's an easy workaround: I just double-clicked on each layer and turned on the Blend Interior Effects as Group check box in the Blending Options panel. The remaining images in Figure 7-31 show what happens when I turn on this check box for just the seven layer, just the S layer, and both layers. This one setting supplies me with the interaction between layers that I was looking for. And by the way, you can save this and other Advanced Blending options along with a layer style, as I explain in the next section.

Saving effects as styles

Okay, here comes that confusing nomenclature thing I was talking about earlier. Photoshop lets you use the Layer Style dialog box to create and save layer effects and blending options for later use as layer styles, which then show up as items in the Styles palette. Whew. In layman's terms, if you like them fancy shadows and purty glows and such what you has done made, you kin tuck 'em away to use agin after a spell. Now then, there are three ways to create a style:

✦ **Click the New Style icon.** When working in the Layer Style dialog box, click the New Style icon to display the options shown at the bottom of Figure 7-32. Name your style and then use the check boxes to decide which settings in the Layer Style dialog box are preserved. The first check box saves the effects covered in this chapter, the second saves the blending options discussed in the previous chapter.

✦ **Click in the Styles palette.** Choose Window ➪ Styles to view the Styles palette. Then move your cursor inside the palette and click with the paint bucket, as shown at the top of Figure 7-32. Photoshop shows you the New Style dialog box. Set the options as described previously.

✦ **Drag and drop a layer.** Start with both the Layers and Styles palettes open. Now drag any layer, active or not, and drop it in the Styles palette. Again, Photoshop shows you the New Style dialog box.

After you press Enter or Return, Photoshop saves the style as a new preset. As with any preset, you can apply it to future images during future Photoshop sessions. Just click a style to apply it to the active layer or drag the style and drop it on any layer name (active or not) in the Layers palette. And don't forget, Photoshop ships with scads of preset styles that you can explore at your leisure. Load a set of styles from the Styles palette menu, apply one to your favorite layer, and take a look at how it's put together in the Layer Style dialog box. It's a great way to get a feel for the amazing variety of effects that are possible in Photoshop.

Blend Interior Effects as Group turned off.   Blend Interior Effects on for the seven, …

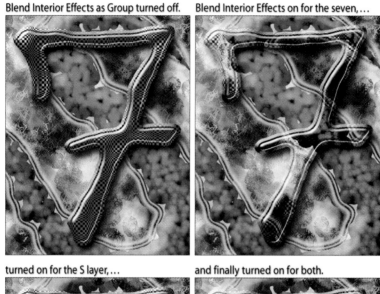

turned on for the S layer, …   and finally turned on for both.

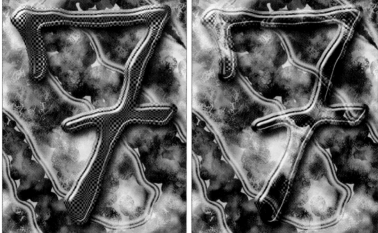

Figure 7-31: Here I applied the Overlay and Soft Light blend modes to the seven and S layers, respectively, with the Blend Interior Effects as Group option turned off (upper left). Then I alternately turned the option on for the seven layer only (upper right), the S layer only (lower left), and finally for both layers (lower right).

Figure 7-32: Click in the Styles palette (top) to display the New Style dialog box (bottom), which lets you name the style and define exactly which attributes from the layer get saved.

A style may include blending options, layer effects, or both. Applying a new style to a layer replaces all blending options and/or effects associated with that style. If you would rather add the blending options and effects from a style to the existing blending options and effects associated with a layer, Shift-click an item in the Styles palette.

Sadly, there is no way to update a style. And even if you could, the style and layer are not linked, so updating the style would have no effect on the layer. Photoshop lets you create new styles, rename existing styles, and delete old ones — but that's about it. Sorry to end on a downer, there.

✦   ✦   ✦

Corrective Filtering

Filter Basics

In Photoshop, filters enable you to apply automated effects to an image. Although named after photographers' filters, which typically correct lighting fluctuations and perspective, Photoshop's filters can accomplish a great deal more. You can slightly increase the focus of an image, introduce random pixels, add depth to an image, or completely rip it apart and reassemble it into a murky pile of goo. A variety of special effects are made available via filters.

At this point, a little bell should be ringing in your head, telling you to beware of standardized special effects. Why? Because everyone who has Photoshop — or its cocky young offspring Photoshop Elements — has access to the same filters that you do. If you rely on filters to edit your images for you, your audience will quickly recognize your work as poor or at least unremarkable art.

Imagine this scenario: You're wasting away in front of your TV, flipping aimlessly through the channels. Just as your brain is about to shrivel and implode, you stumble across a really cool commercial for an SUV where it keeps on rolling along implacably as the background behind it changes something like 17 times. Really eye-catching, unusual stuff, and I would say it was a terrific commercial if only I could remember precisely which SUV it was selling. Ah, well.

The commercial ends, and you're so busy basking in the glow that you neglect for a split second to whack the channel-changer. Before you know it, you're midway through an advertisement for a monster truck rally. Like the SUV commercial, this ad is riddled with special effects — spinning letters, a reverberating voice-over slowed down to an octave below the narrator's normal pitch, and lots of big machines filled with little men filled with single brain cells working overtime. Watching this obnoxious commercial is like being beaten over the head with a sledgehammer, and then run over several times by a steamroller for good measure.

You see, in and of themselves, special effects aren't bad. It's all in how you use them. The SUV commercial manages to entice your eye and draw you into its constantly morphing world, making the vehicle look very hip and cool. The monster truck rally's effects are more of the hard-sell, hit-you-over-the-head variety. Not only are these effects devoid of substance, but, more importantly, they're devoid of creativity.

This chapter and the two that follow, therefore, are about the creative application of special effects. Rather than trying to show an image subject to every single filter — a service already performed quite adequately by the manual included with your software — these chapters explain exactly how the most important filters work and offer some concrete ways to use them.

You also learn how to apply several filters in tandem and how to use filters to edit images and selection outlines. My goal is not so much to teach you what filters are available — you can find that out by tugging on the Filter menu — but how and when to use filters.

A first look at filters

You access Photoshop's special effects filters by choosing commands from the Filter menu. These commands fall into two general camps — *corrective* and *destructive*.

Corrective filters

Corrective filters are workaday tools that you use to modify scanned or otherwise captured images and prepare an image for printing or screen display. In many cases, the effects are subtle enough that the viewer won't even notice that you applied a corrective filter. As demonstrated in Figure 8-1, these filters include those that change the focus of an image, enhance color transitions, and average the colors of neighboring pixels. Find these filters in the Filter ➪ Blur, Noise, Sharpen, and Other submenus.

Many corrective filters have direct opposites. Blur is the opposite of Sharpen, Add Noise is the opposite of Median, and so on. This is not to say that one filter entirely removes the effect of the other; only reversion functions such as the History palette provide that capability. Instead, two opposite filters produce contrasting effects.

Corrective filters are the subject of this chapter. Although they number fewer than their destructive counterparts, I spend more time on them because they represent the functions you're most likely to use on a day-to-day basis.

Destructive filters

The destructive filters produce effects so dramatic that they can, if used improperly, completely overwhelm your artwork, making the filter more important than the image itself. For the most part, destructive filters reside in the Filter ➪ Distort, Pixelate, Render, and Stylize submenus. A few examples of overwhelmed images appear in Figure 8-2.

Destructive filters can produce way-cool effects, and many people gravitate toward them when first experimenting with Photoshop. But the filters invariably destroy the original clarity and composition of the image. Granted, every Photoshop function is destructive to a certain extent, but destructive filters change your image so extensively that you can't easily disguise the changes later by applying other filters or editing techniques.

Destructive filters are the subject of Chapters 9 and 10. Rather than explaining every one of these filters in detail, I try to provide a general overview.

Effects filters

Photoshop also provides a subset of 47 destructive filters called the *effects* filters. These filters originally sire from the Gallery Effects collection, developed by Silicon Beach, which got gobbled up by Aldus (of PageMaker fame), and finally acquired by Adobe Systems. Not knowing what exactly to do with this grab bag of plug-ins, Adobe integrated them into Photoshop.

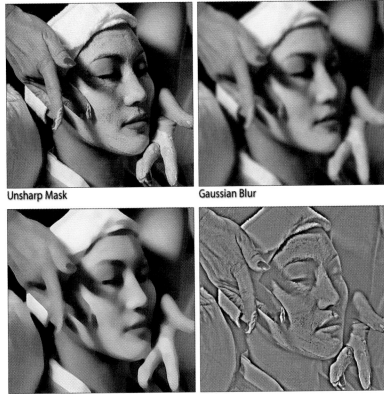

Unsharp Mask Gaussian Blur

Median High Pass

Figure 8-1: A woman getting a facial subject to four corrective filters, including one each from the Sharpen, Blur, Other, and Noise submenus (reading clockwise from upper left).

Although the effects filters themselves haven't really changed that much since Gallery Effects 1.5 came out in 1993, Photoshop CS introduces an easy and fun method of applying and editing the filters: the Filter Gallery. In previous versions, the effects filters were like every other filter; they had to be applied individually, and there was no quick way of viewing how different effects would interact with each other. All of that has changed with the introduction of the Filter Gallery, which lets you access all of the effects filters from within one convenient dialog box. Even more impressive, the Filter Gallery lets you stack as many of these filters as you want on top of one another, and even reorder them to achieve different effects. It's a cool addition to the program, and one we'll be exploring in more detail in the next chapter.

In addition to the Filter Gallery dialog box, most of the effects filters also reside in the Filter ⇨ Artistic, Brush Strokes, Sketch, and Texture submenus (see Figure 8-3 for some examples). A few have trickled out into other submenus, including Filter ⇨ Distort ⇨ Diffuse Glow, Glass, and Ocean Ripple; and Filter ⇨ Stylize ⇨ Glowing Edges.

Shear   Color Halftone

Lighting Effects   Emboss

Figure 8-2: The effects of applying four destructive filters, one each from the Distort, Pixelate, Stylize, and Render submenus (clockwise from upper left). Note that Lighting Effects is applicable to color images only.

Fading a filter

In many cases, you apply filters to a selection or image at full intensity — meaning that you marquee an area using a selection tool if desired, choose a filter command, enter whatever settings you deem appropriate if a dialog box appears, and sit back and watch the fireworks.

What's so full intensity about that? Sounds normal, right? Well, the fact is, you can reduce the intensity of the last filter applied by choosing Edit ➪ Fade or pressing Ctrl+Shift+F (⌘-Shift-F on the Mac). This command permits you to mix the filtered image with the original, unfiltered one.

As shown in Figure 8-4, the Fade dialog box provides you with the basic tools of image mixing — an Opacity value and a blend mode pop-up menu. To demonstrate the wonders of Edit ➪ Fade, I've applied two particularly destructive filters from the Filter Gallery to the woman getting a facial — Stylize ➪ Glowing Edges and Sketch ➪ Bas Relief. The right-hand images show the effects of pressing Ctrl+Shift+F and applying two blend modes, Screen and Vivid Light, with the Opacity value set to 100 and 65 percent, respectively.

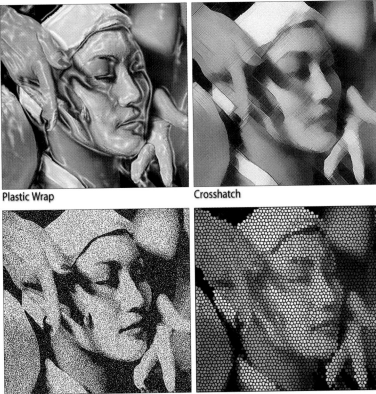

Plastic Wrap Crosshatch

Reticulation Stained Glass

Figure 8-3: The *effects* filters come from Gallery Effects, a little toy surprise that Adobe accidentally acquired when it purchased Aldus Corporation. Here we see the impact of one filter each from the Filter ⇨ Artistic, Brush Strokes, Texture, and Sketch submenus (clockwise from upper left).

Creating layered effects

The drawback of the Fade command is that it's only available immediately after you apply a filter (or other applicable edit). If you so much as modify a selection outline after applying the filter, the Fade command dims, only to return when you apply the next filter.

Therefore, you may find it more helpful to copy a selection to a separate layer (by pressing Ctrl+J on the PC or ⌘-J on the Mac) before applying a filter. This way, you can perform other operations, and even apply many filters in a row, before mixing the filtered image with the underlying original.

Filtering inside a border

And here's another reason to layer before you filter: If your image has a border around it — like the ones shown in Figure 8-5 — you don't want Photoshop to factor the border into the filtering operation. To avoid this, select the image inside the border and press Ctrl+J (⌘-J on the Mac) to layer it prior to applying the filter. The reason is that most filters take neighboring pixels into consideration even if they are not selected. By contrast, when a selection floats, it has no neighboring pixels, and therefore the filter utilizes the selected pixels only.

Figure 8-4: Press Ctrl+Shift+F (⌘-Shift-F on the Mac) to mix the filtered image with the unfiltered original. I don't know about you, but I'd take a Glowing Edges facial over a Bas Relief one any day.

Figure 8-5 shows the results of applying two filters discussed in this chapter — Unsharp Mask and Motion Blur — when the image is anchored in place and when it's layered. In all cases, the 2-pixel border was not selected. In the left examples, the Unsharp Mask filter leaves a high-contrast residue around the edge of the image, while Motion Blur duplicates the left and right edges of the border. Both problems vanish when the filters are applied to layered images, as seen on the right.

Even if the area outside the selection is not a border per se — perhaps it's just a comparatively dark or light area that serves as a visual frame — layering comes in handy. You should always layer the selection unless you specifically want edge pixels to be calculated by the filter.

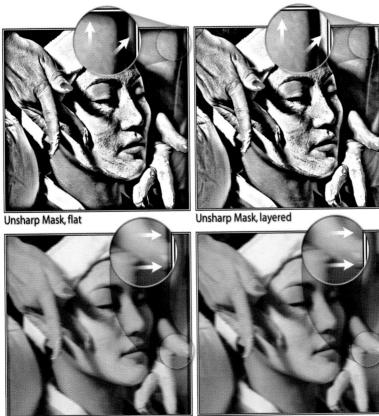

Unsharp Mask, flat

Unsharp Mask, layered

Motion Blur, flat

Motion Blur, layered

Figure 8-5: The results of applying two sample filters to images surrounded by borders. In each case, only the image was selected; the border was not. Layering the right examples prevented the borders from affecting the performance of the filters.

Undoing a sequence of filters

Okay, here's one last reason to layer before you filter. Copying an image to a layer protects the underlying image. If you just want to experiment a little, pressing Ctrl+J (⌘-J) is often more convenient than restoring a state in the History palette. After applying four or five effects to a layer, you can undo all that automated abuse by Alt-clicking (Option-clicking) the trash icon at the bottom of the Layers palette, which deletes the selected layer with no fuss. The underlying original remains unharmed.

Heightening Focus and Contrast

If you've ever tried to improve a digital or scanned snapshot in Photoshop, you've no doubt had your way with many of the commands in the Filter ➪ Sharpen submenu. By increasing the contrast between neighboring pixels, the sharpening filters enable you to compensate for image elements that were photographed or scanned slightly out of focus.

The Sharpen, Sharpen More, and Sharpen Edges commands are easy to use and immediate in their effect. However, you can achieve better results and widen your range of sharpening options if you learn how to use the Unsharp Mask command, which I discuss at length in the following pages.

Using the Unsharp Mask filter

The first thing you need to know about the Unsharp Mask filter is that it has a weird name. The filter has nothing to do with unsharpening—whatever that is—nor is it tied into Photoshop's masking capabilities. Unsharp Mask is named after a traditional film compositing technique (which is itself oddly named) that highlights the edges in an image by combining a blurred film negative with the original film positive.

That's all very well and good, but the fact is most Photoshop artists have never touched a stat camera (an expensive piece of machinery, roughly twice the size of a washing machine, used by image editors of the late Jurassic, pre-Photoshop epoch). Even folks like me who used to operate stat cameras professionally never had the time to delve into the world of unsharp masking. In addition—and much to the filter's credit—Unsharp Mask goes beyond traditional camera techniques.

To understand Unsharp Mask—or Photoshop's other sharpening filters, for that matter—you first need to understand some basic terminology. When you apply one of the sharpening filters, Photoshop increases the contrast between neighboring pixels. The effect is similar to what you see when you adjust a camera to bring a scene into sharper focus.

Two of Photoshop's sharpening filters, Sharpen and Sharpen More, affect whatever area of your image is selected. The Sharpen Edges filter, however, performs its sharpening operations only on the *edges* in the image—those areas that feature the highest amount of contrast.

Unsharp Mask gives you both sharpening options. It can sharpen only the edges in an image or it can sharpen any portion of an image according to your exact specifications, whether it finds an edge or not. It fulfills the exact same purposes as the Sharpen, Sharpen Edges, and Sharpen More commands, but it's much more versatile. Simply put, the Unsharp Mask tool is the only sharpening filter you'll ever need.

When you choose Filter ⇨ Sharpen ⇨ Unsharp Mask, Photoshop displays the Unsharp Mask dialog box, shown in Figure 8-6, which offers the following options:

✦ **Amount:** Enter a value between 1 and 500 percent to specify the degree to which you want to sharpen the selected image. Higher values produce more pronounced effects.

✦ **Radius:** This option determines the thickness of the sharpened edge. Low values produce crisp edges. High values produce thicker edges with more contrast throughout the image.

✦ **Threshold:** Enter a value between 0 and 255 to control how Photoshop recognizes edges in an image. The value indicates the numerical difference between the brightness values of two neighboring pixels that must occur if Photoshop is to sharpen those pixels. A low value sharpens lots of pixels; a high value excludes most pixels from the running.

The preview options offered by the Unsharp Mask dialog box are absolutely essential visual aids that you're likely to find tremendously useful throughout your Photoshop career. Just the same, you'll be better prepared to experiment with the Amount, Radius, and Threshold options and less surprised by the results if you read the following sections, which explain these options in detail and demonstrate the effects of each.

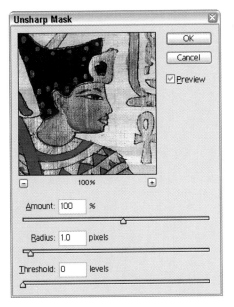

Figure 8-6: Despite any conclusions you may draw from its bizarre name, the Unsharp Mask filter sharpens images according to your specifications in this dialog box.

Specifying the amount of sharpening

If Amount were the only Unsharp Mask option, no one would have any problems understanding this filter. If you want to sharpen an image ever so slightly, enter a low percentage value. Values between 25 and 50 percent are ideal for producing subtle effects. If you want to sharpen an image beyond the point of good taste, enter a value somewhere in the 300 to 500 percent range. And if you're looking for moderate sharpening, try out some value between 50 and 300 percent. Figure 8-7 shows the results of applying different Amount values. For purposes of demonstration, the Radius and Threshold values are fixed at 2.0 pixels and 0 level, respectively.

If you're not sure how much you want to sharpen an image, try out a small value in the 25 to 50 percent range. Then reapply that setting repeatedly by pressing Ctrl+F (⌘-F on the Mac). As you can see in Figure 8-8, repeatedly applying the filter at a low setting produces a very nearly identical result to applying the filter once at a higher setting. For example, you can achieve the effect shown in the middle image in the figure by applying the Unsharp Mask filter three times at 50 percent or once at 238 percent. (The math is a bit complicated — 1.5 cubed minus 1 = 2.375, or roughly 238 percent — but don't worry about that. The point is, you can work incrementally.)

The benefit of using small values is that they enable you to experiment with sharpening incrementally. As the figure demonstrates, you can add sharpening bit by bit to increase the focus of an image. You can't, however, reduce sharpening incrementally if you apply too high a value; you must press Ctrl+Z (⌘-Z on the Mac) and start again.

Original image (PhotoSpin)

Amount: 25%

Amount: 50%

Amount: 75%

Amount: 100%

Amount: 150%

Throughout, Radius: 2.0 pixels, Threshold: 0 level

Amount: 200%

Amount: 350%

Amount: 500%

Figure 8-7: The results of sharpening an image with the Unsharp Mask filter using eight different Amount values. The Radius and Threshold values used for all images were 2.0 and 0, respectively.

Just for fun, Figure 8-9 shows the results of applying the Unsharp Mask filter to each of the color channels in an RGB image independently, as well as in pairs. (To switch between channels, press Ctrl or ⌘ plus a number key, 1 through 3.) In each case, I maxed out the Amount value to 500 percent and set the Radius and Threshold to 4.0 and 0, respectively. You can see how the filter creates a crisp halo of color, especially around the outside edge of the woman's face. Sharpening the red channel creates a red halo on the face and brings out blue-green details in the facial cream; sharpening the red and green channels together creates a yellow halo on the face and bluish details in the cream; and so on. Applying the filter to one or both of the red and green channels produced the most noticeable effects because these channels contain the lion's share of the image detail. The blue channel contained the least detail — as is typical — so sharpening this channel produced the least dramatic results.

Note that Photoshop applies filters to images one channel at a time, so when you apply the Unsharp Mask command to a full-color image, it actually applies the command in a separate pass to each of the color channels. Therefore, the command always results in the color halos shown in Figure 8-9; it's just that the halos get mixed together, minimizing the effect. To avoid any haloing whatsoever, convert the image to the Lab mode (Image ⇨ Mode ⇨ Lab Color) and apply Unsharp Mask to only the Lightness channel in the Channels palette. (Do not filter the a and b channels.) This sharpens the brightness values in the image and leaves the colors untouched.

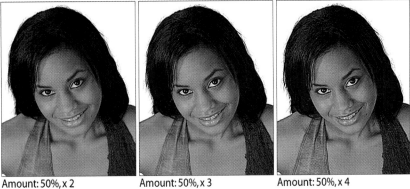

Amount: 50%, x 2   Amount: 50%, x 3   Amount: 50%, x 4

Throughout, Radius: 2.0 pixels, Threshold: 0 level

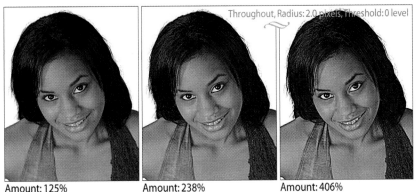

Amount: 125%   Amount: 238%   Amount: 406%

Figure 8-8: Repeatedly applying the Unsharp Mask filter at 50 percent (top row) is nearly equivalent on a pixel-by-pixel basis to applying the filter once at higher settings (bottom row).

Setting the thickness of the edges

The Unsharp Mask filter works by identifying edges and increasing the contrast around those edges. The Radius value tells Photoshop how thick you want your edges. Large values produce thicker edges than small values.

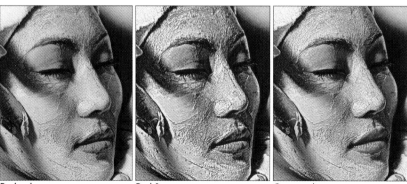

Red only   Red & green   Green only

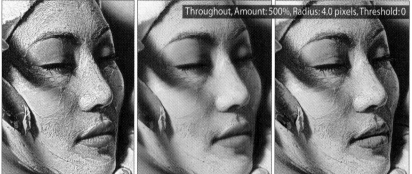

Throughout, Amount: 500%, Radius: 4.0 pixels, Threshold: 0

Green & blue   Blue only   Blue & red

Figure 8-9: The results of applying Unsharp Mask to a single color channel or a pair of color channels are relatively predictable once you get the hang of it. For example, if you apply the filter to the red channel only, the edges appear red where light, and turquoise (the inverse of red) where dark.

The ideal Radius value depends on the resolution of your image and the quality of its edges:

✦ When creating screen images — such as Web graphics — use a very low Radius value, such as 0.5. This results in terrific hairline edges that look so crisp, you'll think you washed your bifocals.

✦ If a low Radius value brings out weird little imperfections — such as grain, scan lines, or JPEG compression artifacts — raise the value to 1.0 or higher. If that doesn't help, don't fret. I include two different sure-fire image-fixing techniques later in this chapter, one designed to sharpen grainy old photos, and another that accommodates compressed images.

✦ When printing an image at a moderate resolution — anywhere from 120 to 180 ppi — use a Radius value of 1.0. The edges will look a little thick on screen, but they'll print fine.

✦ For high-resolution images — around 300 ppi — try a Radius of 2.0. Because Photoshop is printing more pixels per inch, the edges have to be thicker to remain nice and visible.

If you're looking for a simple formula, I recommend 0.1 of Radius for every 15 ppi of final image resolution. That means 75 ppi warrants a Radius of 0.5, 120 ppi warrants 0.8, 180 ppi warrants 1.2, and so on. If you have a calculator, just divide the intended resolution by 150 to get the ideal Radius value.

You can of course enter higher Radius values, as high as 250, in fact. Higher values produce heightened contrast effects, almost as if the image had been photocopied too many times, generally useful for producing special effects.

But don't take my word for it; you be the judge. Figure 8-10 demonstrates the results of specific Radius values combined with Amount and Threshold values of 200 percent and 0 level, respectively.

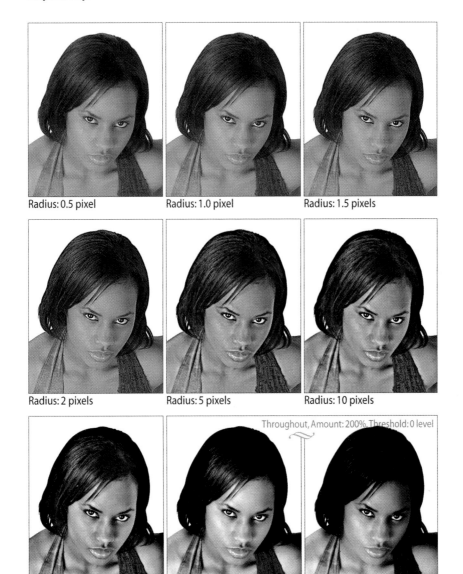

Radius: 0.5 pixel   Radius: 1.0 pixel   Radius: 1.5 pixels

Radius: 2 pixels   Radius: 5 pixels   Radius: 10 pixels

Throughout, Amount: 200%, Threshold: 0 level

Radius: 20 pixels   Radius: 50 pixels   Radius: 250 pixels

Figure 8-10: The results of applying nine different Radius values, ranging from precise edges to very gooey.

Figure 8-11 shows the results of combining different Amount and Radius values. You can see that a large Amount value helps to offset the softening of a high Radius value. For example, when the Amount value is set to 75 percent, as in the first row, the Radius value appears to smooth out the sharpening effect when raised from 0.5 pixel to 2.0 pixels and higher. But when the Amount is raised to 300 percent, as in the last row, the higher Radius values genuinely enhance contrast.

Amount: 75%, Radius: 0.5   Amount: 75%, Radius: 2.0   Amount: 75%, Radius: 10.0

Amount: 150%, Radius: 0.5   Amount: 150%, Radius: 2.0   Amount: 150%, Radius: 10.0

Amount: 300%, Radius: 0.5   Amount: 300%, Radius: 2.0   Amount: 300%, Radius: 10.0

Figure 8-11: The effects of combining different Amount and Radius settings. The Threshold value for each image was 0 level, the default setting.

Recognizing edges

By default, the Unsharp Mask filter sharpens every pixel in a selection. However, you can instruct the filter to sharpen only the edges in an image by raising the Threshold value from 0 to some other number. The Threshold value represents the difference between two neighboring pixels — as measured in brightness levels — that must occur for Photoshop to recognize them as an edge.

Suppose that the brightness values of neighboring pixels are 10 and 20. If you set the Threshold value to 5, Photoshop reads both pixels, notes that the difference between their brightness values is more than 5, and treats them as an edge. If you set the Threshold value to 20, however, Photoshop passes them by. A low Threshold value, therefore, causes the Unsharp Mask filter to affect a high number of pixels and vice versa.

In the top row of images in Figure 8-12, the high Threshold values result in tiny slivers of sharpness that outline only the most substantial edges in the woman's face. As I lower the Threshold value incrementally in the second and third rows, the sharpening effect takes over more and more of the face, ultimately sharpening all details uniformly in the lower-right example.

Sharpening grainy photographs

Having completed my neutral discussion of Unsharp Mask, king of the Sharpen filters, I hasten to interject a little bit of commentary, along with a helpful solution to a common sharpening problem.

First, the commentary: While Amount and Radius are the kinds of superior options that will serve you well throughout the foreseeable future, I urge young and old to observe Threshold with the utmost scorn and rancor. The idea is fine — we can all agree that you need some way to draw a dividing line between those pixels that you want to sharpen and those that you want to leave unchanged. But the Threshold setting is nothing more than a glorified on/off switch that results in harsh transitions between sharpened and unsharpened pixels.

Consider the picture of Frederick Douglass in Figure 8-13. Like so many vintage photographs, this particular image of the famed abolitionist is a little softer than we're used to seeing these days. But if I apply a heaping helping of Unsharp Mask — as in the second example in the figure — I bring out as much film grain as image detail. The official Photoshop solution is to raise the Threshold value, but the option's intrinsic harshness results in a pockmarked effect, as shown on the right. Photoshop has simply replaced one kind of grain with another.

These abrupt transitions are quite out of keeping with Photoshop's normal approach. Paintbrushes have antialiased edges, selections can be feathered, the Color Range command offers Fuzziness — in short, everything mimics the softness found in real life. Yet right here, inside what is indisputably Photoshop's most essential filter, we find no mechanism for softness whatsoever.

While we continue to wait for Photoshop to give us a better Threshold — one with a Fuzziness slider or similar control — you can create a better Threshold using a very simple masking technique. Using a few filters that I explore at greater length throughout this chapter and the next, you can devise a selection outline that traces the essential edges in the image — complete with fuzzy transitions — and leaves the non-edges unmolested. So get out your favorite old vintage photograph and follow along with these steps.

Threshold: 80 levels

Threshold: 50 levels

Threshold: 30 levels

Threshold: 20 levels

Threshold: 15 levels

Threshold: 10 levels

Threshold: 5 levels

Throughout, Amount: 500%, Radius: 4.0 pixels

Threshold: 2 levels

Threshold: 0 level

Figure 8-12: The results of applying nine different Threshold values. To best show off the differences between each image, I set the Amount and Radius values to 500 percent and 4.0 pixels, respectively.

Soft vintage image Sharpened, Threshold: 0 Sharpened, Threshold: 20

Figure 8-13: The original photograph is a bit soft (left), a condition I can remedy with Unsharp Mask. Leaving the Threshold value set to 0 brings out the film grain (middle), but raising the value results in equally unattractive artifacts (right).

STEPS: Creating and Using an Edge Mask

1. **Duplicate one of the color channels.** Bring up the Channels palette and drag one of the color channels onto the little page icon. Mr. Douglass is colorized from a gray-scale image, so it really doesn't matter which channel I duplicate — they're all roughly the same.

2. **Choose Filter ➪ Stylize ➪ Find Edges.** As I explain in Chapter 9, the Find Edges filter automatically traces the edges of your image with thick, gooey outlines that are ideal for creating edge masks.

3. **Press Ctrl+I (⌘-I on the Mac).** Or choose Image ➪ Adjustments ➪ Invert. Find Edges produces black lines against a white background, but in order to select your edges, you need white lines against a black background. The Invert command reverses the lights and darks in the mask, as in the first example in Figure 8-14.

4. **Choose Filter ➪ Other ➪ Maximum.** The next step is to thicken up the edges. The Maximum filter expands the white areas in the image, serving much the same function in a mask as Select ➪ Modify ➪ Expand serves when editing a selection outline. Enter a Radius value and press Enter or Return. In my case, a Radius of 4 pixels worked nicely, but for best results you should experiment with different values based on the resolution of your image.

5. **Choose Filter ➪ Noise ➪ Median.** You need fat, gooey edges, and the current ones are a bit tenuous. To firm up the edges, choose the Median filter, enter the same Radius value you did for the Maximum filter, in my case 4, and press Enter or Return.

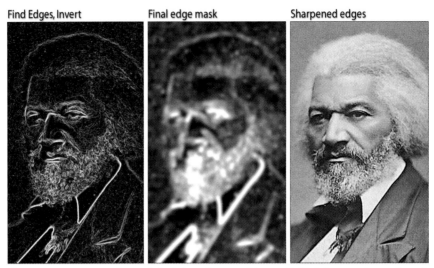

Figure 8-14: I copy a channel, find the edges, and invert (left). I then apply a string of filters to expand and soften the edges (middle). After converting the mask to a selection outline, I reapply Unsharp Mask with winning results (right).

6. **Choose Filter ⇨ Blur ⇨ Gaussian Blur.** Unfortunately, the Maximum filter results in a bunch of little squares that don't do much for our cause. You can merge the squares into a seamless line by choosing the Gaussian Blur command and entering 4, the same radius you entered for Maximum. Then press Enter or Return.

The completed mask is pictured in the second example of Figure 8-14. Though hardly an impressive sight to the uninitiated eye, you're looking at the perfect edge mask — soft, natural, and extremely accurate.

7. **Return to the standard composite view.** Press Ctrl+tilde (Win) or ⌘-tilde (Mac) in a color image. In a grayscale image, press Ctrl+1 (Win) or ⌘-1 (Mac).

8. **Convert the mask to a selection outline.** Ctrl-click (Win) or ⌘-click (Mac) the mask name in the Channels palette. Photoshop selects the most essential edges in the image without selecting the grain.

9. **Choose Filter ⇨ Sharpen ⇨ Unsharp Mask.** In the last example in Figure 8-14, I applied the highest permitted Amount value, 500 percent, and a Radius of 2.0.

10. **Whatever values you use, make sure the Threshold is set to 0.** And always leave it at 0 from this day forward.

In case Figures 8-13 and 8-14 are a little too subtle, I include enlarged views of the great abolitionist's face in Figure 8-15. The top image shows the result of using the Threshold value; the bottom image was created using the edge mask. Which one appears sharper and less grainy to you?

Sharpened, Threshold: 20 (speckled)

Sharpened with edge mask (smooth)

Figure 8-15: Enlarged views of the last examples from Figures 8-13 (top) and 8-14 (bottom). A good edge mask beats the Threshold value every time.

Using the High Pass filter

The High Pass filter falls more or less in the same camp as the sharpening filters but is not located under the Filter ➪ Sharpen submenu. This frequently overlooked gem enables you to isolate high-contrast image areas from their low-contrast counterparts.

When you choose Filter ➪ Other ➪ High Pass, Photoshop offers a single option: the familiar Radius value, which can vary from 0.1 to 250.0. High Radius values distinguish areas of high and low contrast only slightly. Low values change all high-contrast areas to dark gray and low-contrast areas to a slightly lighter gray. A value of 0.1 changes all pixels in an image to a single gray value and is therefore useless.

Converting an image into a line drawing

The High Pass filter is especially useful as a precursor to Image ➪ Adjustments ➪ Threshold, which converts all pixels in an image to black and white. As illustrated in Figure 8-16, the Threshold command produces entirely different effects on an image depending on the setting you apply with the High Pass filter. In fact, applying the High Pass filter with a low Radius value and then issuing the Threshold command converts your image into a line drawing.

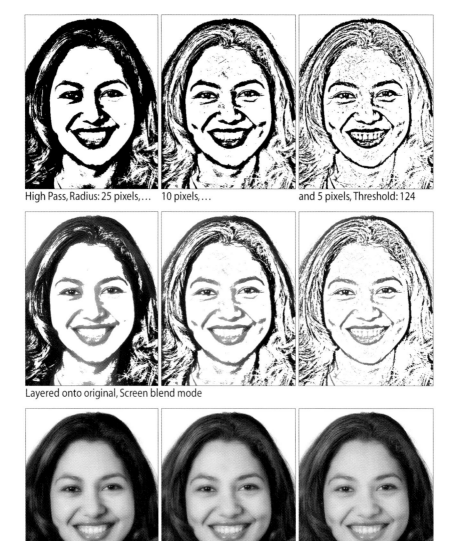

High Pass, Radius: 25 pixels, ...   10 pixels, ...   and 5 pixels, Threshold: 124

Layered onto original, Screen blend mode

Gaussian Blur (Radius: 8 pixels), Overlay blend mode, Opacity: 50%

Figure 8-16: After sending three copies of the image to a separate layer and applying different High Pass values, I chose Image ⇨ Adjustments ⇨ Threshold (top row). I then applied the Screen blend mode to drop out the black pixels, resulting in colored line drawings (middle). Finally, I chose Filter ⇨ Blur ⇨ Gaussian Blur, changed the blend mode to Overlay, and reduced the Opacity to 50 percent (bottom).

In the first row of Figure 8-16, I start with three applications of the High Pass filter, with Radius settings of 25, 10, and 5 pixels, respectively. I then applied the Threshold command with a Threshold Levels value of 124, meaning that all colors darker than 124 — a bit darker than medium gray — become black and all values lighter than 124 become white. (For more information on brightness values, see the Levels discussion in Chapter 12.) In the second row, I layered the black-and-white drawings in front of original versions of the image and applied the Screen mode, so that colors from the image filled in the black lines.

Why else might you want to change your image to a bunch of unsightly gray values and then apply Threshold or the like? One reason is to create a mask, as discussed at length in the "Building a Mask from an Image" section back in Chapter 4. (As you may remember, there I used the Levels command instead of Threshold, but both commands are variations on a common theme.)

Or you might simply want to bolster the edges in an image, as illustrated in the final row of Figure 8-16. Here, I began by applying Filter ⇨ Blur ⇨ Gaussian Blur (the subject of the next section) with a Radius value of 8 pixels. Like the Threshold option in the Unsharp Mask dialog box, Image ⇨ Adjustments ⇨ Threshold results in harsh, jagged transitions. Gaussian Blur softens them to produce more gradual transitions. Then I applied the Overlay mode and reduced the Opacity setting to 50 percent. The result is a glowing image with thicker, more defined edges, great for smoothing away blemishes and generally toning down an otherwise severe or unkind image.

I should mention that Photoshop provides several automated edge-tracing filters — including Find Edges, Trace Contour, and the Filter Gallery's Glowing Edges, many of which I cover in the next chapter. But High Pass affords more control than any of these commands and permits you to explore a wider range of alternatives. Also worth noting, several Filter Gallery filters — most obviously Sketch ⇨ Photocopy — lift much of their code directly from High Pass. Although it may seem at first glance a strange effect, High Pass is one of the seminal filters in Photoshop.

Blurring an Image

The commands under the Filter ⇨ Blur submenu produce the opposite effects of their counterparts under the Filter ⇨ Sharpen submenu. Rather than enhancing the amount of contrast between neighboring pixels, the Blur filters diminish contrast to create softening effects.

Applying the Gaussian Blur filter

The preeminent Blur filter, Gaussian Blur, blends a specified number of pixels incrementally, following the bell-shaped Gaussian distribution curve I touched on earlier. When you choose Filter ⇨ Blur ⇨ Gaussian Blur, Photoshop produces a single Radius option box, in which you can enter any value from 0.1 to 250.0. (Beginning to sound familiar?) Radius values of 1.0 and smaller blur an image slightly; moderate values, between 1.0 and 10.0, turn an image into a rude approximation of life without glasses on; and higher values blur the image beyond recognition.

Moderate to high Radius values can be especially useful for creating that hugely amusing *Star Trek* Iridescent Female effect. I'm referring to the old *Star Trek*, of course, the one with the 10-pound tricorders and radically cool sideburns. Take yourself back, if you will, to one of the many moments when a chubby Captain Kirk meets some bewitching ambassador or scientist who has just beamed aboard his ship. He takes her hand in sincere welcome and warns her that the ship is not equipped with seat belts and has been known to come to sudden halts and send people careening in different directions even though there is no independent source of gravity. Then we see it — the close-up of the fetching actress shrouded in a kind of gleaming halo that prevents us from discerning if her lips are chapped or her mascara is clumping, all because some cockeyed cinematographer smeared Vaseline all over the camera lens. I mean, what wouldn't you give to be able to recreate this effect in Photoshop?

Figure 8-17 shows a suitably comely lass. For the sake of this example, we'll assume she has her pointy ears tucked up into her hat, and some intergalactic beautician has tweezed her eyebrows into a more humanoid shape. The following steps explain how to give her that glorious Kirk-O-Vision glow.

Gaussian Blur, Radius: 8 pixels   Normal, 65% Opacity

Darken, 100% Opacity   …plus Linear Dodge, 80% Opacity

Figure 8-17: After applying Gaussian Blur (top left), I used the Fade command to lower the Opacity to 65 percent (top right) and to apply the Darken mode with 100 percent Opacity (bottom left). Overlaying another application of Gaussian Blur with Opacity at 80 percent and Linear Dodge mode in force created the final example in the figure.

STEPS: The Captain Kirk Myopia Effect

1. **Select a portion of the image if desired.** If you only want to apply the effect to a portion of the image, feather the selection with a Radius in the neighborhood of 5 to 8 pixels.

2. **Choose Filter ➪ Blur ➪ Gaussian Blur.** Enter some unusually large value into the Radius option box — say, 8.0 — and press Enter or Return. The results are shown in the first example of Figure 8-17.

3. **Press Ctrl+Shift+F (⌘-Shift-F on the Mac) to bring up the Fade dialog box.** To achieve the effect shown in the second example of Figure 8-17, I reduced the Opacity value to 65 percent, making the blurred image slightly translucent. This way, you can see the hard edges of the original image through the filtered one.

4. **You can achieve additional effects by selecting options from the Mode pop-up menu.** For example, I created the third example in Figure 8-17 by raising the Opacity back up to 100 percent and selecting the Darken mode option, which uses the colors in the filtered image to darken the original. I built upon this effect by pressing Ctrl+F (⌘-F on the Mac) to reapply my Gaussian Blur settings, pressing Ctrl+Shift+F (⌘-Shift-F on the Mac) to bring back the Fade command, lowering the Opacity to 80 percent, and choosing the Linear Dodge mode, as seen in the last example of Figure 8-17.

You know, though, as I look at this woman, I'm beginning to have my doubts about her and Captain Kirk. I mean, she has Harry Mudd written all over her. (And if you don't get that joke, good for you. Despite your enthusiasm for Photoshop, you're not really a geek after all. Me, I wrote the gag, so I'm beyond redemption.)

Directional blurring

In addition to its everyday blurring functions, Photoshop provides two *directional blurring* filters, Motion Blur and Radial Blur. Instead of blurring pixels in feathered clusters like the Gaussian Blur filter, the Motion Blur filter blurs pixels in straight lines over a specified distance. The Radial Blur filter blurs pixels in varying degrees depending on their distance from the center of the blur. The following pages explain both of these filters in detail.

Motion blurring

The Motion Blur filter makes an image appear as if either the subject of the image or the camera itself was moving when you shot the photo. When you choose Filter ➪ Blur ➪ Motion Blur, Photoshop displays the dialog box shown in Figure 8-18. You enter the angle of movement into the Angle option box. Alternatively, you can indicate the angle by dragging the straight line inside the circle to the right of the Angle option, as shown in the figure. (Notice that the arrow cursor actually appears outside the circle. After you begin dragging on the line, you can move the cursor anywhere you want and still affect the angle.)

You then enter the distance of the movement in the Distance option box. Photoshop permits any value between 1 and 999 pixels. The filter distributes the effect of the blur over the course of the Distance value, as illustrated by the examples in Figure 8-19.

Mathematically speaking, Motion Blur is one of Photoshop's simpler filters. Rather than distributing the effect over a Gaussian curve — which one might argue would produce a more believable effect — Photoshop creates a simple linear distribution, peaking in the center and fading at either end. It's as if the program took the value you specified in the Distance option, created that many clones of the image, offset half the clones in one direction and half the clones in the other — all spaced 1 pixel apart — and then varied the opacity of each.

Figure 8-18: Drag the line inside the circle to change the angle of the blur.

Using the Wind filter

The problem with the Motion Blur filter is that it blurs pixels in two directions. If you want to distribute pixels in one absolute direction or the other, try the Wind filter, which you can use either on its own or in tandem with Motion Blur.

When you choose Filter ➪ Stylize ➪ Wind, Photoshop displays the Wind dialog box shown in Figure 8-20. You can select from three methods and two directions to distribute the selected pixels. Figure 8-21 compares the effect of the Motion Blur filter to each of the three methods offered by the Wind filter. Notice that the Wind filter does not blur pixels. Rather, it evaluates a selection in 1-pixel-tall horizontal strips and offsets the strips randomly inside the image.

To get the best results, try combining the Motion Blur and Wind filters with a blending mode. For example, as shown in Figure 8-22, I cloned the entire image to a new layer and applied the Wind command twice to the topmost layer, first selecting the Stagger option and then selecting Blast (top example). Next, I applied the Motion Blur command with a 0-degree Angle and a Distance value of 100 (second example). I then selected Lighten from the blend mode pop-up menu (third example). Finally, to keep the front of the truck from being obscured by the blurring effect, I added a layer mask and filled it with a gradient starting on the right with black and ending in white near the middle. I also did a little painting in the mask to control exactly where the motion streaks appeared in the image. (For the full monty on layer masks, turn to Chapter 5.)

The result is a perfect blend between two worlds. The motion effect at the bottom of Figure 8-22 doesn't obliterate the image detail, as the Wind filter does in Figure 8-21. And thanks to the layer mask, the motion appears to run in a single direction — to the left — something you can't accomplish using Motion Blur on its own.

Original

Motion Blur, Angle: 0°, Distance: 50 pixels

Distance: 100 pixels

Distance: 250 pixels

Distance: 500 pixels

Distance: 999 pixels

Figure 8-19: A single green rectangle followed by five different applications of the Motion Blur filter. Only the Distance value varied, as labeled. A 0-degree Angle value was used in all five examples.

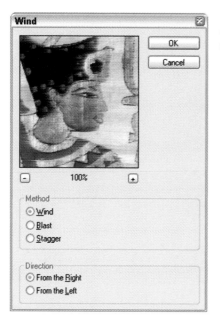

Figure 8-20: Use the Wind filter to randomly distribute a selection in 1-pixel horizontal strips in one of two directions.

Radial blurring

Choosing Filter ➪ Blur ➪ Radial Blur displays the Radial Blur dialog box shown in Figure 8-23. The dialog box offers two Blur Method options: Spin and Zoom.

If you select Spin, the image appears to be rotating about a central point. You specify that point by dragging in the grid inside the Blur Center box (as demonstrated in the figure). If you select Zoom, the image appears to rush away from you, as if you were zooming the camera while shooting the photograph. Again, you specify the central point of the Zoom by dragging in the Blur Center box. Figure 8-24 features examples of both settings.

After selecting a Blur Method option, you can enter any value between 1 and 100 in the Amount option box to specify the maximum distance over which the filter blurs pixels. Pixels farthest away from the center point move the most; pixels close to the center point barely move at all. Keep in mind that large values take more time to apply than small values. The Radial Blur filter, incidentally, qualifies as one of Photoshop's most time-consuming operations.

Select a Quality option to specify your favorite time/quality compromise. The Good and Best Quality options ensure smooth results by respectively applying bilinear and bicubic interpolation, the same interpolation options that the Image Size command uses to resample pixels when changing the size of an image. However, they also prolong the amount of time the filter spends calculating the new colors of pixels in your image.

Figure 8-21: The difference between the effects of the Motion Blur filter (top) and the Wind filter (other three). In each case, I selected From the Right from the Direction radio buttons.

Figure 8-22: Combining the Wind filter (top) with Motion Blur (second image), the Lighten blend mode (third image), and a layer mask (bottom).

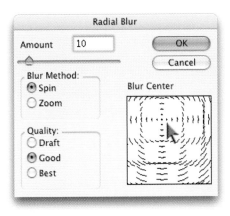

Figure 8-23: Drag inside the Blur Center grid to change the point about which the Radial Blur filter spins or zooms the image.

The Draft option renders the image using a diffusion dither, which leaves a trail of loose and randomized pixels but takes less time to complete. I used the Draft setting to create the top-right and bottom-left images in Figure 8-24; I selected the Good option to create the middle-left image and the Best option to create the middle and bottom images on the right.

Using the Lens Blur filter

A great new addition to Photoshop CS is the Lens Blur filter, designed to simulate the optical camera blurring that occurs in the real world. For years, photographers have experimented with depth-of-field to determine the relative focus of foreground and background elements in their photos. While a crisp, uniformly in-focus image can be great in many circumstances, sometimes a shallow depth-of-field (where one section is sharply in focus while others are blurred) can perfectly set the tone for an image, creating separation between foreground and background elements. Now, you can start with an entirely in-focus photo and perform the selective blurring quite realistically later in Photoshop. Not content to simply be a compound blur effect, however, the Lens Blur filter also offers you a blissfully obsessive amount of control over Iris, Highlight, and Noise settings.

Choose Filter ➪ Blur ➪ Lens Blur to bring up the large Lens Blur dialog box, shown in Figure 8-25. On the left side of the dialog box is the image preview, which scales to fit entirely inside the dialog box by default. If you want to adjust the zoom ratio, use the plus and minus signs in the lower-left corner or click the right-pointing arrowhead and choose an option from the resulting pop-up menu. As usual, you can hold down the spacebar and drag over your image to position it within the preview area. Next to the zoom options is the progress bar, which lets you know that Photoshop is still working hard during some of the slower, more complex Lens Blur calculations. The right side of the bulky Lens Blur dialog box contains the following options:

> ✦ **Preview:** When the Preview check box is turned on, the Lens Blur filter automatically updates the image preview every time you make any sort of adjustment. This is usually a good and necessary thing, but sometimes this calculation-intense filter can take a while to give you a preview, in which case you may want to turn off the Preview option. Even better is the ability to choose between Faster and More Accurate previews. (You can't blame Photoshop for trying to put a positive spin on things, but bear in mind that these radio buttons might just as easily be labeled Less Accurate and Slower.) Generally, I'm guessing you'll say "Accurate-schmaccurate!" and leave this set to Faster. Remember, these radio buttons are only for preview purposes. As soon as you click OK, Photoshop renders the best possible result it can.

Original image (Corbis)

Radial Blur, Spin, Amount: 10, Draft

Spin, Amount: 10, Good

Spin, Amount: 10, Best

Zoom, Amount: 30, Draft

Zoom, Amount: 30, Best

Figure 8-24: Five examples of the Radial Blur filter set to both Spin and Zoom, subject to different Quality settings. I specified Amount values of 10 pixels for the Spin examples and 30 for the Zooms. Each effect is centered about the bridge of the woman's nose.

Figure 8-25: The new Lens Blur filter lets you apply realistic blurring effects to your always perfectly-in-focus snapshots.

✦ **Depth Map:** Here's where the wonders of the Lens Blur filter really become apparent. The Depth map source you specify contains information that assigns an imaginary depth position in space to every individual pixel in an image. By default, the Source pop-up menu offers three options: None, which performs blurring on each pixel in an image uniformly; Transparency, which determines what gets blurred in an image based on the transparency values of the pixels; and Layer Mask, which bases blur levels on the grayscale values in an image's layer mask. Under the default settings, the black areas of the mask are treated as though they are in the foreground and the white areas are treated as though they are in the background, although you can reverse this by clicking the Invert check box or by adjusting these settings manually. If you've added alpha channels to your image, those too are available to choose as depth maps from the Source pop-up menu.

The focal distance for an image is the imaginary plane in space that your camera is focusing on. Anything closer to the camera or farther away from the camera will fall out of focus to some degree. Adjusting the setting of the Blur Focal Distance slider changes which color in your depth map will represent the in-focus plane of your image. A value of 0 brings the pure black pixels into focus, a value of 255 brings the pure white pixels into focus, and any setting in-between sets a different level of gray as in focus.

3D graphics programs like Alias' Maya can easily crank out depth maps that correspond to rendered images, and this is a great use for Photoshop's new Lens Blur filter. Figure 8-26 shows my Little Puppet Friend's first foray into the hot and happening digital world. (He changes with the times, does my LPF.) The top left image shows an austere scene, rendered as a Maya IFF file. At top right you'll see the depth map that Maya rendered, which I have inverted by pressing Ctrl+I (⌘-I on the Mac). Because I inverted Maya's depth map, objects get brighter as they recede into the distance, which is how Lens Blur operates by default. (Photoshop CS comes with an IFF plug-in, but you need to manually install it from the installer CD. Look in the Goodies folder located in the Optional Plug-Ins folder inside the File Format folder.)

To apply this depth map to my image, I loaded the appropriate alpha channel using the Source pop-up menu. While I could have just dragged the Blur Focal Distance slider to determine which part of the image I wanted to be in focus, the Lens Blur filter provides a quicker, more precise way to designate any portion of a layer as being in focus. Simply click on any pixel in the preview image and watch as the Blur Focal Distance slider snaps to attention. The Lens Blur filter takes the pixel you've chosen, looks at the corresponding grayscale level for that pixel in the depth map, and adjusts the BFD (calm down, that's Blur Focal Distance) to accommodate your desire. If Invert is selected, clicking on a portion of the image will instead set it as out of focus. That's why I inverted my depth map manually; I wanted to be able to take advantage of the click-to-set-BFD feature. In the bottom left example in Figure 8-26, I clicked on the nearest puppet head, which set the BFD to 6; in the bottom right example, I clicked on the middle puppet head, automatically setting the BFD to 111.

"Well Deke, that's all well and good for 3D images with their self-generated depth maps," you might be thinking, "but what good does this Lens Blur filter do me with my real world photos?" Yes, once again, the natural world with its icky flowers and trees and cameras and stuff can't possibly hold a candle to the magical, anything-is-possible digital world. Life as we know it is indeed tough, but if real depth maps don't exactly pop out of your camera, there's nothing to stop you from faking one. Try this: Create a layer mask and draw a black-to-white transparency gradient in your image. Then apply the Lens Blur filter with the Source set to Layer Mask. The result will be an image that gradually increases in blurriness according to your gradient. Or add an alpha channel to your layer and use the brush tool to paint in random splotches of blacks and grays to emulate the random, selective focus that's so popular right now among music video directors and people with broken camera lenses.

In Figure 8-27, I took an image of a hip young urbanite, created a new alpha channel, and quickly made a depth map using the magnetic lasso and gradient tools. Next, I chose Filter ⇨ Blur ⇨ Lens Blur, set my newly-made depth map channel as Source, and watched as the background sprung into sharp focus and our hair-dyed hero sunk into softitude. The problem, as you can see in the middle image in Figure 8-27, was that I'd reversed my values when I first created the depth map—I'd colored my desired foreground white and background black, and by default the Lens Blur filter focuses on black. While I could have exited the dialog box and performed an invert on the channel in question, this time I just used the Invert check box, which gave me a quick, easy fix.

Figure 8-26: My Little Puppet Friend pops his head up into a 3D-rendered environment, all to better help you understand Photoshop CS's new Lens Blur filter.

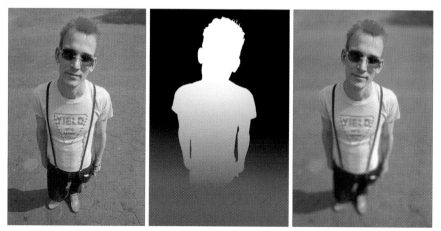

Figure 8-27: The extreme perspective of this image (left) is nice but I decided that a more shallow depth-of-field would lend our subject the "In Your Face!" feeling I was after. I created an alpha channel for use as a depth map (center). Then, I applied the Lens Blur filter, clicked the Invert check box, and blurred the other pixels at a Radius value of 33 (right).

✦ **Iris:** The characteristics of genuine lens blur in a photograph can depend a lot on the shape of the iris in the camera lens that captured the photo. Photoshop's Lens Blur filter gives you a number of options for simulating many different types of lens irises. From the Shape pop-up menu you can select anything from a triangular iris to an octagonal one. Experiment with the various Shape options in conjunction with the Blade Curvature and Rotation settings to create different types of realistic details and imperfections in your lens blur effects. As the number of sides in your iris increases, along with the Blade Curvature, your blur highlights will become more and more smooth until they are virtually circular.

The Radius setting is where you set the focal depth for your blurring effect. If you think back on the focal plane that I talked about just a couple of paragraphs ago, the *focal depth* regulates how quickly things get out of focus as they get farther away from the focal plane. You can think of it as the Photoshop counterpart to a camera's f-stop (which regulates depth-of-field in real life), though the fact that Photoshop doesn't know the focal length of the lens that captured the image prevents you from getting a direct, mathematical correlation.

✦ **Specular Highlights:** When you blur an image through one of the other blurring filters in Photoshop, colors can get averaged and bright whites can become shades of gray. Photographers are well aware of the fact that no matter how much a photo is optically blurred, whites remain bright white. The Lens Blur filter accounts for this with the Specular Highlights section of the dialog box. Decrease the Threshold amount to add areas that will be affected by the highlights and increase the Brightness level to blast the image with pools of white. In addition to being optically accurate, the Specular Highlights settings can also add a nice, otherworldly quality to an image.

✦ **Noise:** When you apply a drastic blur to sections of an image, it tends to smooth out detail and color values. But as we've seen, the name of Lens Blur's game is realism, and no matter how blurry a photograph is, it would look unnatural to lose film's inherent grain detail. Thankfully, the Noise options can help artificially pull this detail back in.

Adjust the Amount slider until the noise in the blurred section matches the original photo's noise in the in-focus section. Below the slider, select either Uniform or Gaussian to set the type of noise (for my money, Gaussian is the way to go). Finally, you can make sure the noise you generate won't affect the color in your image by clicking on the Monochromatic check box.

 Although the Lens Blur filter is unquestionably a welcome addition to Photoshop, it has some limitations that you'd do well to keep in mind. Most notable is the filter's inability to deal with transparency. This problem is due to a basic limitation of depth maps; when distance is represented by a grayscale value of a pixel, that value is absolute. When a foreground element like glass or hair has its own detail, but allows some of the background to show through, what should the pixel depth value be? It has to pick one or the other, so either a transparent object's details will be inappropriately blurred, or the background elements that are visible through the same object will be inappropriately in focus.

Also, depth maps may or may not be antialiased, and with antialiased depth maps, weird edges can occur. Antialiasing in a visible channel is a great way of fooling the eye and simulating a sharp edge, but the same intermediate gray pixels that fool the eye can create some goofy effects when used as a blur map, since each gray represents a different depth. The effect gets worse the fuzzier the map. So, when in doubt, try to make sharp-edge transitions when you have a foreground element you want to isolate against a busy background, or prepare for some manual touching up after the fact.

Softening a selection outline

Gaussian Blur and other Blur filters are equally as useful for editing masks as they are for editing image pixels. Applying Gaussian Blur to a mask has the same effect as applying Select ➪ Feather to a selection outline. But Gaussian Blur affords more control. Where the Feather command affects all portions of a selection outline uniformly, you can apply Gaussian Blur selectively to a mask, permitting you to easily mix soft and hard edges within a single selection outline.

Another advantage to blurring a mask is that you can see the results of your adjustments on screen, instead of relying on the seldom-helpful marching ants. For example, suppose that you want to create a shadow that recedes away from a subject in your composition. You've managed to accurately select the foreground image — how do you now feather the selection exclusively inward, so that it appears smaller than the object that casts it? Although you can pull off this feat using selection commands such as Contract and Feather, it's much easier to apply filters such as Minimum and Gaussian Blur inside a mask. But before I go any further, I need to back up and explain how Minimum and its pal Maximum work.

Minimum and Maximum

Filter ➪ Other ➪ Minimum expands the dark portions of an image, spreading them outward into other pixels. Its opposite, Filter ➪ Other ➪ Maximum, expands the light portions of an image. In traditional stat photography, these techniques are known, respectively, as *choking* and *spreading*.

When you are working in the quick mask mode or in an independent mask channel, applying the Minimum filter has the effect of incrementally contracting the selected area, subtracting pixels uniformly around the edges of the selection outline. The Minimum dialog box presents you with a single Radius value, which tells Photoshop how many edge pixels to delete. Just the opposite, the Maximum filter incrementally increases the size of white areas, which adds pixels uniformly around the edges of a selection.

Adding a cast shadow to a layer

The following steps describe how to use the Minimum and Gaussian Blur filters to contract and feather an existing selection outline to create a shadow that leans away from the foreground subject of a composition. Figures 8-28 through 8-30 illustrate the steps in the project. Figure 8-31 shows the final cast shadow.

STEPS: Filtering a Selection Outline in the Quick Mask Mode

1. **Select the foreground image.** My foreground image was the screwball character from the Corbis image library pictured in Figure 8-28. I had already set him up on an independent layer from the background. These steps work best if you do the same. (To learn how, see Chapter 5.) To select this scary fellow, I converted the layer's transparency mask to a selection outline by Ctrl-clicking (⌘-clicking on the Mac) on the layer's name in the Layers palette.

Figure 8-28: This maniacally gleeful human resides on an independent layer. (That way he can't harm the other pixels.) To select him, I Ctrl-clicked (or ⌘-clicked) on his layer in the Layers palette.

2. **If you're working on a layer, switch to the background image.** The quickest route is Shift+Alt+[(that's Shift-Option-[on the Mac).

3. **Press Q to enter the quick mask mode.** You can create a new mask channel if you prefer, but the quick mask mode is more convenient.

4. **Choose Filter ⇨ Other ⇨ Minimum.** Enter a Radius value to expand the transparent area into the rubylith. In Figure 8-29, I entered a Radius value of 20 pixels. This expanded the size of the black, or masked, area and made the selection smaller.

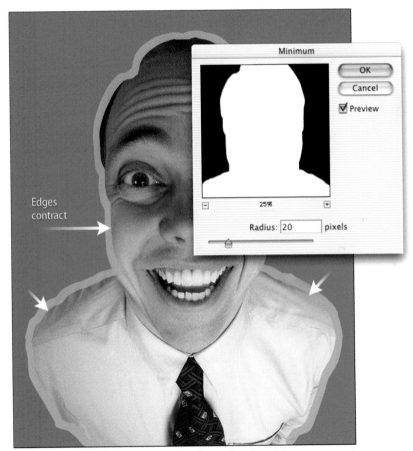

Figure 8-29: The Minimum filter decreases the size of the transparent area inside the quick mask mode, thereby choking the selection outline.

5. **Choose Filter ⇨ Blur ⇨ Gaussian Blur.** To create a soft shadow, I entered a Radius equal to the Radius I used in the Minimum dialog box, which was 20 pixels. Smaller values are likewise acceptable. The only potential problem with larger values is that they expand the shadow beyond the boundaries of the image, which in all probability is not the effect you want. When you click OK, Photoshop blurs the transparent area.

6. **Press Q to exit the quick mask mode.** Ah, back in the workaday world of marching ants.

7. **Send the selection to an independent layer.** The easiest way to do this is to press Ctrl+J (⌘-J on the Mac). You now have a shadow filled with colors from the background layer.

8. **Choose the Multiply mode.** You can choose Multiply from the pop-up menu at the top of the Layers palette, or press Shift+Alt+M (Shift-Option-M). As discussed in Chapter 6 this burns the shadow into its background, so it looks darker, as a shadow should. Because your foreground image is in the way, you may not be able to see the effect of this step, but don't worry—you will soon.

9. **Scale and distort the shadow.** Press Ctrl+T (⌘-T) to invoke the Free Transform command. Then drag the top handles in the bounding box to scale the shadow; press Ctrl (⌘) and drag a handle to distort the shadow. For the best effect, you'll need a big distortion. As demonstrated in Figure 8-30, you may have to zoom out and expand the size of the image window to give yourself lots of room to work. When you get the effect you want, press Enter or Return to apply the distortion.

Figure 8-30: Press Ctrl+T (⌘-T on the Mac) to enter the Free Transform mode. Then Ctrl-drag (⌘-drag) a corner handle to distort the shadow.

Thanks to the fact that you applied the Multiply blend mode to the shadow, it appears darker than the rest of the background. You can adjust its opacity or fill it with a different color if you like. I elected to fill my background with one of Photoshop's predefined patterns, called Molecular. As shown in Figure 8-31, this permitted me to transform the subject of my montage from an overly enthusiastic sycophant into an overly enthusiastic tour guide. As I said, you could achieve a similar effect using Select ➪ Modify ➪ Contract and Select ➪ Feather, but unless you have a special aversion to the quick mask mode, it's easier to be sure of your results when you can see exactly what you're doing using filters.

Figure 8-31: Suddenly, he's not scary anymore, he's just passionate about his work. No doubt, we could all learn a lesson from this plainly insane man.

Noise Factors

Photoshop offers four loosely associated filters in its Filter ➪ Noise submenu. One filter adds random pixels — known as *noise* — to an image. The other three, Despeckle, Dust and Scratches, and Median, average the colors of neighboring pixels in ways that theoretically remove noise from poorly scanned images. But in fact, they function nearly as well at removing essential detail as they do at removing extraneous noise. In the following sections, I show you how the Noise filters work, demonstrate a few of my favorite applications, and leave you to draw your own conclusions.

Adding noise

Noise adds grit and texture to an image. Noise makes an image look like you shot it in New York on the Lower East Side and were lucky to get the photo at all because someone was throwing sand in your face as you sped away in your chauffeur-driven, jet-black Maserati Bora, hammering away at the shutter release. In reality, of course, a guy over at Sears shot the photo for you, after which you toodled around in your minivan trying to find a store that sold day-old bread. But that's the beauty of Noise. It makes you look cool, even when you aren't.

You add noise by choosing Filter ⇨ Noise ⇨ Add Noise. Shown in Figure 8-32, the Add Noise dialog box features the following options:

✦ **Amount:** This value determines how far pixels in the image can stray from their current colors. The value represents a color range rather than a brightness range and is expressed as a percentage. You can enter a value as high as 400 percent. The percentage is based on 256 brightness values per channel if you're working with a 24-bit image and 32,768 brightness values for 16-bit images. So with a 24-bit image (8-bit channels), the default value of 12.5 percent is equivalent to 32 brightness levels, which is 12.5 percent of 256.

For example, if you enter a value of 12.5 percent for a 24-bit image, Photoshop can apply any color that is 32 shades more or less red, more or less green, *and* more or less blue than the current color. If you enter 400 percent, Photoshop theoretically can go 1024 brightness values lighter or darker. But that results in colors that are out of range; therefore, they get clipped to black or white. The result is higher contrast inside the noise pixels.

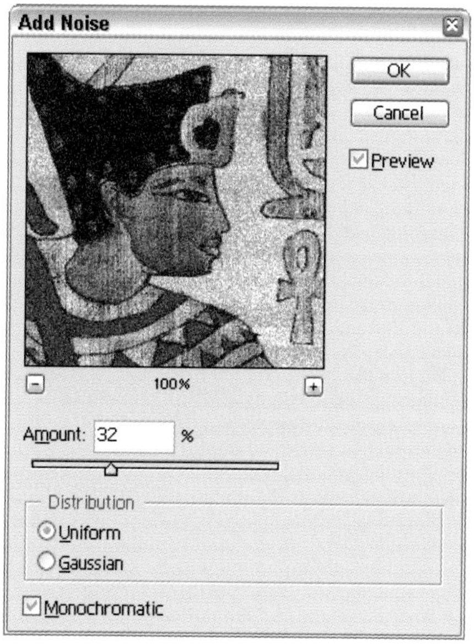

Figure 8-32: The Add Noise dialog box asks you to specify the amount and variety of noise you want to add to the selection.

✦ **Uniform:** Select this option to apply colors absolutely randomly within the specified range. Photoshop is no more likely to apply one color within the range than another, thus resulting in an even color distribution.

✦ **Gaussian:** When you select this option, you instruct Photoshop to prioritize colors along the Gaussian distribution curve. The effect is that most colors added by the filter either closely resemble the original colors or push the boundaries of the specified range. In other words, this option results in more light and dark pixels, thus producing a more pronounced effect.

✦ **Monochromatic:** When working on a color image, the Add Noise filter distributes pixels randomly throughout the different color channels. However, when you select the Monochrome check box, Photoshop distributes the noise in the same manner in all channels. The result is grayscale noise. (This option has no effect on grayscale images, because the noise can't get any more grayscale than it already is.)

Figure 8-33 compares three applications of Uniform noise to identical amounts of Gaussian noise, the latter of which produces higher contrast. The final row in the figure demonstrates the generally more visually appealing Monochromatic-type noise. In each case, the Distribution was set to Uniform.

Noise variations

Normally, the Add Noise filter adds both lighter and darker pixels to an image. If you prefer, however, you can limit the effect of the filter to strictly lighter or darker pixels. To do so, apply the Add Noise filter, and then apply the Fade command (Ctrl+Shift+F on the PC or ⌘-Shift-F on the Mac) and select the Lighten or Darken blend mode. Or you can copy the image to a new layer, apply the filter, and merge the filtered image with the underlying original.

Figure 8-34 shows sample applications of lighter and darker noise. After copying the image to a separate layer, I applied the Add Noise filter with an Amount value of 40 percent and selected Gaussian. To create the upper-left example in the figure, I selected Lighten from the blend mode pop-up menu. To create the upper-right example, I selected the Darken mode. In each case, I added a layer of strictly lighter or darker noise while at the same time retaining the clarity of the original image.

To achieve the streaked noise effects in the bottom examples of Figure 8-34, I applied Motion Blur and Unsharp Mask to the layered images. Inside the Motion Blur dialog box, I set the Angle value to –30 degrees and the Distance to 30 pixels. Then I applied Unsharp Mask with an Amount value of 200 percent and a Radius of 1. Naturally, the Threshold value was 0.

Chunky noise

My biggest frustration with the Add Noise filter is that you can't specify the size of individual specks of noise. No matter how you cut it, noise only comes in 1-pixel squares. It may occur to you that you can enlarge the noise dots in a layer by applying the Maximum or Minimum filter. But in practice, doing so simply fills in the image, because there isn't sufficient space between the noise pixels to accommodate the larger dot sizes.

Luckily, Photoshop provides several alternatives. One is the Pointillize filter, which adds variable-sized dots and then colors those dots in keeping with the original colors in the image. Though Pointillize lacks the random quality of the Add Noise filter, you can use it to add texture to an image.

Uniform, Amount: 6%   Uniform, 12%   Uniform, 25%

Gaussian, Amount: 6%   Gaussian, 12%   Gaussian, 25%

Monochromatic, Amount: 6%   Monochromatic, 12%   Monochromatic, 25%

Figure 8-33: The Gaussian option (middle row) produces more pronounced effects than the Uniform option (top) at identical Amount values. Select the Monochromatic check box to apply the noise evenly in all channels (bottom).

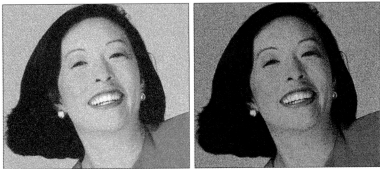

Add Noise, Amount: 40%, Lighten ... Darken

Motion Blur, –30°, 30 pixels, Lighten ... Darken

Figure 8-34: You can limit the Add Noise filter to strictly lighter (left) or darker (right) noise by applying the filter to a layered clone. To create the rainy and scraped effects (bottom examples), I applied Motion Blur and Unsharp Mask to the noise layers.

To create the top-left image in Figure 8-35, I chose Filter ➪ Pixelate ➪ Pointillize and entered 5 into the Cell Size option box. After pressing Enter or Return to apply the filter, I pressed Ctrl+Shift+F (⌘-Shift-F on the Mac) to fade the filter, changing the Opacity value to 50 percent. The effect is rather like applying chunky bits of noise. The top-right image is similar, but with the Opacity value at 100 percent and with the Pin Light blend mode applied. (For more on blend modes, see Chapter 6.)

The Filter Gallery filters provide a few noise alternatives. Sketch ➪ Halftone Pattern adds your choice of dot patterns, as shown in the two middle examples in Figure 8-35 (Size and Contrast settings were the same for both examples). But like all filters in the Sketch submenu, it replaces the colors in your image with the foreground and background colors. Texture ➪ Grain is a regular noise smorgasbord, permitting you to select from 10 different Grain Type options, each of which produces a different kind of noise. The bottom examples in Figure 8-35 show off two of the Grain options, Clumped and Speckle. The Intensity and Contrast remained the same in each; I added a Soft Light blend mode in the Speckle example.

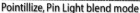

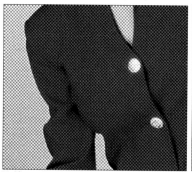
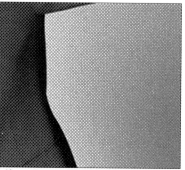

Pointillize, Cell Size: 5, 50% Opacity   Pointillize, Pin Light blend mode

Halftone Pattern, Size: 2, Contrast: 3   Halftone Pattern, Pin Light blend mode

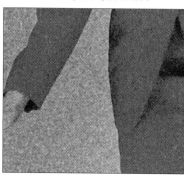
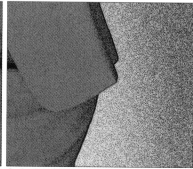

Grain, Intensity: 80, Contrast: 50, Clumped   Grain, Speckle, Soft Light blend mode

Figure 8-35: The results of applying several different Add Noise-like filters, including Pointillize, Halftone Pattern, and Grain.

Removing noise with Despeckle

Now for the noise removal filters. Strictly speaking, the Despeckle command probably belongs in the Filter ➪ Blur submenu. It blurs a selection while at the same time preserving its edges — the idea being that unwanted noise is most noticeable in the continuous regions of an image. In practice, this filter is nearly the exact opposite of the Sharpen Edges filter.

The Despeckle command searches an image for edges using the equivalent of an Unsharp Mask Threshold value of 5. It then ignores the edges in the image and blurs everything else with the force of Filter ➪ Blur ➪ Blur More, as shown in the upper-left image in Figure 8-36.

Despeckle

Median, Radius: 1 pixel

Radius: 3 pixels

Radius: 5 pixels   Radius: 8 pixels   Radius: 12 pixels

Figure 8-36: The effects of the Despeckle filter (upper left) and Median filter, the latter of which averages the colors of pixels in an image according to a Radius value.

Averaging pixels with Median

Another command in the Filter ➪ Noise submenu, Median removes noise by averaging the colors in an image, one pixel at a time. When you choose Filter ➪ Noise ➪ Median, Photoshop produces a Radius option box. For every pixel in a selection, the filter averages the colors of the neighboring pixels that fall inside the specified radius — ignoring any pixels that are so different that they might skew the average — and applies the average color to the central pixel. You can enter any value between 1 and 100. However, even at relatively low settings like 12 pixels, significant blurring occurs, as is evident in the bottom-right image in Figure 8-36. At the maximum Radius value, the face would decline into a blurry, gummy goo, with all image detail obliterated.

As with Gaussian Blur, you can achieve some very interesting and useful effects by backing off the Median filter with the Fade command. But rather than creating a *Star Trek* glow, Median clumps up details, giving an image a plastic, molded quality, as demonstrated by the examples in Figure 8-37. To create every one of these images, I applied the Median filter with a Radius of 5 pixels. For the second example, I pressed Ctrl+Shift+F (⌘-Shift-F) to display the Fade dialog box and lowered the Opacity value to 65 percent. For the bottom-left image, I raised the Opacity back up to 100 percent in the Fade dialog box and applied the Darken blend mode. And for the final example, I took the Opacity back down to 80 percent and used the Linear Dodge mode.

Another difference between Gaussian Blur and Median is that Gaussian Blur destroys edges and Median invents new ones. This means you can follow up the Median filter with Unsharp Mask to achieve even more pronounced sculptural effects.

Median, Radius: 5 pixels   Normal, 65% Opacity

Darken, 100% Opacity   …plus Linear Dodge, 80% Opacity

Figure 8-37: After applying the Median filter to our Vulcan vixen, I reversed the effect slightly using Edit ⇨ Fade Median. I varied the blend modes and Opacity values, as labeled beneath the images.

Sharpening a compressed image

The other night, I caught part of *Mission Impossible II*, and it had this scene where the bad guys are using — get this — a "digital camera." Just to make sure we didn't think they had one of those run-of-the-mill film cameras, the actors say "digital camera" about 15 times. Then without warning, things turn especially unsuspenseful as the good guys steal the camera's "memory card," take it back to their top-secret unmarked van, and look at the pictures using another "digital camera."

I mean, here are a bunch of guys who are so plugged into state-of-the-art technology that they have tiny walky-talkies in their ears and they fool each other by wearing utterly realistic masks of each other's faces. (Of course, they had those masks back in the TV show, so I'm beginning to think they're just fanciful sci-fi.) And yet where photography is concerned, the best the villains can muster is a Kodak DC290 with a 32MB CompactFlash card. That mission isn't just possible, it's probable. What's next? Pilfering an Olympus D-520 from an old lady's handbag? Scoring a bag of 16MB Memory Sticks from an unscrupulous Radio Shack clerk? A gripping scene in which the hero loses his lens cap and then remembers that he left it in the pocket of a blazer that he just that morning dropped off at the cleaners?

The fact is, digital cameras are one of the hottest and most commonplace gadgets around. And it's hardly surprising. Your typical midrange device is not only fun to use, but it also shoots three million or more pixels and lets you download the images to your computer in a matter of seconds. Yet despite the $300 to $500 entry price, even a halfway decent 3-megapixel camera captures at best half the resolution theoretically attainable with run-of-the-mill 35mm film.

To give you an idea, a 3 million-pixel photograph measures 5.5 by 7.5 inches when printed at the glossy prepress standard of 267 pixels per inch. That's not bad, but bear in mind, most midrange digital photographs receive a heaping helping of JPEG compression, and all are upsampled from the mere 8 bits of data captured by the CCD to the 24 bits that we see on screen. As a result, no pixel is altogether accurate in its representation of the real world.

Naturally, the brunt of this dilemma falls to the world's real heroes, we graphic and design professionals. Our mission, should we choose to accept it, is to take these imperfect images and render them suitable for printing. Fortunately, armed with color adjustment commands such as Levels and Hue/Saturation and our trusty corrective filters Median, Gaussian Blur, and Unsharp Mask, we have everything we need to smooth over extreme imperfections and enhance the most fragile details. In the following steps, I show how to save an irreplaceable photograph from near extinction. Hopefully, you won't encounter anything as dramatic as the image pictured in Figure 8-38, but even a reasonably sound photograph may benefit from this approach. And if you ever find yourself with an image that appears beyond repair, you'll know what to do. Now read fast — this book will self-destruct in five seconds.

Figure 8-38: Captured with a 1-megapixel Agfa ePhoto CL30, this digital photograph suffers all the woes of many low-end and midrange digital photographs — dark color, low contrast, random compression artifacts, and gummy detail.

STEPS: Fixing a Digital Photograph

1. **Fix the brightness and contrast.** Choose the command Image ➪ Adjustments ➪ Levels or press Ctrl+L (⌘-L on the Mac). Then balance the brightness and contrast of the image as I explain in Chapter 12. The most important option is the middle Input Levels value—the gamma value—which lets you lighten the midtones. I raised the gamma of my image to 1.6, a huge leap. This not only lightened the colors, but it also washed them out, making them trend more toward gray, as in Figure 8-39.

Figure 8-39: Raising the gamma value in the Levels dialog box to 1.6 corrected the brightness of the image, but it left the colors washed out.

2. **Copy the image to a new layer.** The best tool for making colors more vivid is Hue/Saturation. Unfortunately, this command has the side effect of enhancing JPEG compression artifacts, often radically. So before applying the command, duplicate the image to a new layer by pressing Ctrl+J (⌘-J).

3. **Increase the color saturation.** Choose Image ➪ Adjustments ➪ Hue/Saturation or press Ctrl+U (⌘-U). Then increase the Saturation value well beyond what seems sensible. For example, I raised the Saturation of my image to 70 percent. Don't worry that the image looks absurdly grainy (see Figure 8-40); you'll need an extreme effect when it comes time to blend this layer with the original image in Step 6.

4. **Choose the Median filter.** The next step is to reduce the undesirable grain and enhance the highly desirable edge detail. You achieve the first using the Median command. Choose Filter ➪ Noise ➪ Median and then enter a Radius value of 4 pixels or higher until the compression artifacts appear almost entirely smoothed away. (In Figure 8-41, I used a Radius value of 6.) Don't worry that the Median command makes the photograph appear doughy or indistinct; you'll recover the focus of the image shortly.

Figure 8-40: Boosting the Saturation value in the Hue/Saturation dialog box by 70 percent made the photograph much more vivid. However, it also brought out JPEG compression artifacts that interrupt the natural edges and color transitions.

Figure 8-41: I set the Radius values for the Median and Gaussian Blur filters to 6 and 2 pixels, respectively. This gums and blurs away the compression artifacts so that all we have is smooth color.

5. **Choose Filter ⇨ Blur ⇨ Gaussian Blur.** Now that you've gummed up the detail a bit and rubbed out most of the compression, use the Gaussian Blur filter with a Radius of 2.0 or thereabouts to blur the gummy detail slightly. This softens the edges that the Median filter creates. (You don't want any fake edges, after all.)

Note that the result is by no means a perfect image. The photograph should look over-saturated and gummy, as if it were molded out of brightly colored plastic. You have created an extreme correction — a radical combination of saturation, averaging, and blurring that you simply cannot reproduce in more delicate applications.

6. **Lower the layer's opacity.** Blend the exaggerated layer with the original image behind it using the Opacity value. If your image had few faults to begin with, you may want to go as low as a few percent — say, 5 percent or even lower. (Bear in mind, a low Opacity value favors the original image over the filtered layer.) Just a little dab of detail enhancement can make a perceptible difference. For more objectionable images such as mine, higher Opacity values are warranted. In Figure 8-42, I applied a value of 50 percent, which weighted the original and filtered images equally. This is about as high as you'll want to go — placing more weight on the extreme filtered layer than the original image generally results in a surreal effect. Bear in mind, what we're trying to achieve is not an image that looks radically corrected, but rather one that looks as if it didn't require correction in the first place.

Figure 8-42: I lowered the Opacity value of the filtered layer to 50 percent, evenly mixing the oversaturated filtered image with the undersaturated original.

7. **Merge the image.** Press Ctrl+E (⌘-E on the Mac) to fuse the two layers into one. The result is a base image that will better respond to standard enhancements. Now you can apply color and focus adjustments as if the image were scanned from a high-quality film source.

8. **Continue to correct the image as you normally would.** For my part, I again boosted the saturation of my colors using Hue/Saturation — albeit far more subtly than before. Then I applied the Unsharp Mask filter with an Amount value of 100 percent and a Radius of 4.0 pixels to arrive at the final image shown in Figure 8-43.

Figure 8-43: After merging the layers, I increased the Saturation of the image to 25 percent and applied the Unsharp Mask filter with an Amount value of 100 percent and a Radius of 4 pixels.

Depending on how your image looked before you started, you may or may not achieve something resembling absolute perfection. For example, my snapshot still suffers compression artifacts and wonky color aberrations. Nevertheless, the image looks far better than it looked before I started (see Figure 8-38). It also looks significantly better than it would have had I applied Hue/Saturation and Unsharp Mask directly to the original image without creating a duplicate layer and employing Median and Gaussian Blur.

Note that these steps work well for sharpening other kinds of compressed imagery as well, including old photographs that you over-compressed without creating backups and images that you've downloaded from the Internet. If applying the Unsharp Mask filter brings out the goobers, try these steps instead.

Using the Average filter

If the Median filter is a refined, dignified tea party in the British countryside, then Photoshop's new Average filter is the most reckless, wild Mardi Gras tea party you've ever seen. Whereas Median performs a pixel-by-pixel examination of your image and averages the color values smoothly based on a radius you select, the Average filter sizes up all of the color values present and then with a resounding "Booyah!" smooshes them into one gigantic, uncontrollable, uniform mass.

Choosing Filter ➪ Blur ➪ Average will, on most color images, immediately replace your image with a grayish wall of nothing. Gee, thanks, Photoshop. That gray void is what you usually end up with when you average all of the varied color values in an image. Consequently, on its own, Average isn't much more than a minor curiosity. But believe it or not, there are some uses for this filter. The trick is to use it in tandem with selections and blend modes.

When just a portion of your image is selected, the Average filter only makes calculations from and applies changes to only the selected area. Marquee over a patch of grass, and the averaged area becomes a flat, solid green. Use the magic wand to grab a handful of sky, and Average turns it into a smooth, perfect firmament. And though these averages may not be all that photographic or impressive on their own, when you begin to blend averaged sections of an image with the original underlying pixels the filter really proves its worth.

For instance, let's say you've got an image of a lovely, smiling face, marred only by slight imperfections in color. Create a selection that includes only the skin areas of the face and press Ctrl+J (⌘-J on the Mac) to copy your selection to a new layer. Choose Filter ➪ Blur ➪ Average and watch as the various color differences in your floating face layer completely disappear. The new layer is clean, yes, though not entirely believable. Lower the layer's opacity to around 70 percent and set the blend mode to Hue. Now you're applying the smooth color of the averaged layer with the texture detail of the original image. As if by magic, your image is jaundiced no more.

You can also experiment with blend modes to achieve stylized results, as shown in Figure 8-44. I began by duplicating the background layer to a layer above it. Next, I selected the different color zones of the woman's face on the new layer using Select ➪ Color Range and applied the Average filter to each individually (top right). Then I tried out a few blend modes and Opacity values on the layer until I found a combination that worked (bottom left). Finally, I manually selected different elements of the face, copied them to new layers, then selected them and applied the Average filter (bottom right), for a somewhat-above-average effect.

Her Macaulay Culkin impression is no match...

...for Photoshop's Average filter.

Vivid Light, 80% Opacity...

...plus a little manual labor home alone.

Figure 8-44: Here I used the Average filter together with the Vivid Light blend mode and a little manual labor to smooth out color transitions and create some nice stylistic effects.

✦   ✦   ✦

Pixelate, Distort, and Render

Destructive Filters

While corrective filters enable you to eliminate image flaws and apply special effects, destructive filters are all about special effects. Even though Photoshop offers nearly twice as many destructive filters as corrective counterparts, destructive filters are less frequently used and ultimately less useful.

Don't get me wrong — these filters are a superb bunch. But because of their vast quantity and limited appeal, I don't explain each and every one of them. Rather, I concentrate on the ones that I think you'll use most often, breeze over a handful of others, and let you discover on your own the ones that I totally ignore.

A million wacky effects

Did I say totally ignore? Heck, I guess I can't just go and ignore half of the commands in the Filter menu — they're not completely useless, after all. In fact, I would actually go so far as to call one or two of them somewhat useful. So here are the briefest of all possible descriptions of the filters that I don't explain elsewhere, in the order that they appear in the Filter menu:

✦ **The Artistic filters:** As a rule, the effects under the Filter ➪ Artistic submenu add a painterly quality to your image. Colored Pencil, Rough Pastels, and Watercolor are examples of filters that successfully emulate traditional mediums. Other filters — Fresco, Palette Knife, and Smudge Stick — couldn't pass for their intended mediums in a dim room filled with dry ice.

✦ **The Brush Strokes filters:** I could argue that the Brush Strokes submenu contains filters that create strokes of color. This is true of some of the filters — including Angled Strokes, Crosshatch, and Sprayed Strokes. Others — Dark Strokes and Ink Outlines — generally smear colors, while still others — Accented Edges and Sumi-e — belong in the Artistic submenu. Whatever.

✦ **Diffuse Glow:** Another of the Gallery Effects that I ignore — the present paragraph notwithstanding — Filter ➪ Distort ➪ Diffuse Glow sprays a coat of dithered, background-colored pixels onto your image. In a way, this filter reminds me of a fortune cookie that contains a nutty parable like, "The wise man eats breakfast before the bugs have time to walk in his marmalade." It's not so much a dumb fortune as no fortune at all. If I want advice, I'll get an advice cookie — in the meantime, predict my future, you stupid cookie! Likewise, Diffuse Glow is not so much a dumb distortion filter as no distortion filter at all. Nonetheless, one cannot deny that it is also dumb, which is why it occupies a special place of contempt in my heart.

✦ **Dust & Scratches:** The clever reader will notice that I omitted any but the briefest mention of Filter ⇨ Noise ⇨ Dust & Scratches in the previous chapter. Could that be because it's a shoddy piece of crud that doesn't do what it implies it does? Yes, it could. Dust & Scratches is nothing more than the Median filter with a Threshold option tacked onto it. Imagine if Unsharp Mask didn't have a Threshold option (as I wish it didn't) and then there was this other filter that used the same math as Unsharp Mask plus it tossed in a Threshold setting. And it was called Complete Image Fixer. Well, that's how much faith you can put in Dust & Scratches. It doesn't remove dust, it doesn't fix scratches, it just averages pixels. Every once in a while, I see someone defend this filter and show how it can actually be useful under special circumstances. Some of these techniques are very interesting, but everything I've seen can be accomplished just as well with Median. Personally, I think a filter that *added* dust and scratches to an image would be more useful.

✦ **Fragment:** Ooh, it's an earthquake! Another entry in our Lame Filters Parade, Filter ⇨ Pixelate ⇨ Fragment repeats an image four times in a square formation and lowers the opacity of each to create a sort of jiggly effect. You don't even have any options to control it, so in a way it makes Dust & Scratches look good. On the plus side, at least it doesn't promise to do anything, except take up space in the Filter menu.

✦ **3D Transform** and **Texture Fill:** Well, it finally happened: Adobe took the keys away from granddad. Age-old, venerable, and largely useless, these two remnants of a bygone era are conspicuous in their absence with the release of Photoshop CS. And that's fine with me; I was sick to death of their talk about the "old days," when Photoshop ran on a blackboard, and there were only two colors of chalk. But if you have an unaccountable fit of nostalgia and want these filters back, all is not lost. Adobe has merely consigned 3D Transform and Texture Fill to that old age home for has-been software: the installer CD. Just manually install these relics from your Photoshop CS CD, and sure enough they'll be back, heckling the other filters from the Filter ⇨ Render submenu like Statler and Waldorf in the balcony of the Muppet theatre.

✦ **Clouds** and **Difference Clouds:** I told you there would be some filters in this parade that I actually liked, and here they are. You can use Clouds and Difference Clouds to create a layer of haze over an image. The Clouds filter creates an abstract and random haze between the foreground and background colors. Difference Clouds works exactly like layering the image, applying the Clouds filter, and selecting the Difference blend mode in the Layers palette. Figure 9-1 demonstrates what mere words can't describe.

To strengthen the colors created by the Clouds filter, press Shift when choosing the command. This same technique works when using the Difference Clouds filter as well. In fact, I don't know of any reason *not* to press Shift while choosing one of these commands, unless you have some specific need for washed-out effects.

Also, if you want to make a repeating texture using Clouds and Difference Clouds, make sure your image size is a square with pixel dimensions that are based on a power of two — something like 128 by 128 or 256 by 256 will work well. Your cloudy image will seamlessly tile, making it perfect for creating Web page backgrounds and the like.

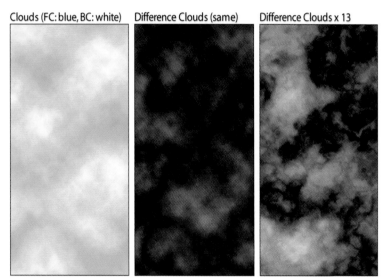

Clouds (FC: blue, BC: white)   Difference Clouds (same)   Difference Clouds x 13

Figure 9-1: The effect of applying the Clouds filter with blue and white as the foreground and background colors, respectively (left). I then applied Difference Clouds (middle) and repeated the filter a dozen additional times (right). Repeated applications of Clouds always yield variations on the same theme; repeated applications of Difference Clouds soon result in roiling, plasma-like textures.

✦ **Fibers:** Like Clouds and Difference Clouds, the new Fibers filter uses Perlin-based fractal noise to achieve a realistic randomness that, when stretched out in one direction, looks less like fluffy clouds and more like — well, fibers. The problem is, that's basically the long and short of this filter. Whereas a program like, say, Adobe's own After Effects gives you a truckload of options through which to tweak and adjust the noise it can generate, Photoshop's Fibers filter will have none of it. It can only hear the noise in its head, and it'll be danged if it's gonna change.

Sadly, there's no way to change the angle of the fibers generated by the filter (another limitation that seems somewhat obvious), but you can cheat your way around this. Here's a way to utilize the filter: Apply Fibers to a layer, duplicate it, and then rotate the top layer 90 degrees. Set the top layer to the Darken blend mode and you should wind up with a somewhat realistic interwoven pattern.

✦ **Lens Flare:** Okay, Lens Flare is a wacky filter, and you probably won't use it very often, but it's another one that I like. Found in the Render submenu, Lens Flare adds sparkles and halos to an image to suggest light bouncing off the camera lens. Even though photographers work their buns off trying to make sure that these sorts of reflections don't occur, you can add them after the fact. You can select from one of three Lens Type options, adjust the Brightness slider between 10 and 300 percent (though somewhere between 100 and 150 is bound to deliver the best results), and move the center of the reflection by dragging a point around inside the Flare Center box. In addition, you can Alt-click (on the Mac, Option-click) inside the preview to position the center point numerically. By way of example, Figure 9-2 shows the effects of the three different Lens Type settings. In each case the Brightness value was set to 140 percent.

Original digital photograph

Lens Flare, 50-300mm Zoom

Lens Flare, 35mm Prime

Lens Flare, 105mm Prime

Figure 9-2: Starting with a very dark photograph that I
shot at El Morro in Puerto Rico, I applied each of the three
Lens Type settings available in the Lens Flare dialog box.

If you want to add a flare to a grayscale image, first convert it to the RGB mode. Then apply the filter and convert the image back to grayscale. The Lens Flare filter is applicable only to RGB images.

And here's another tip (I'm known around town as a good tipper). Another thing the Alt or Option key can do for you in this and many other filter dialog boxes: If you hold down Alt or Option as you drag the slider, you can see the preview update on the fly.

Let's keep 'em coming. Here's another great tip for using Lens Flare. Before choosing the filter, create a new layer, fill it with black, and apply the Screen blend mode by pressing Shift+Alt+S (Shift-Option-S on the Mac) with a non-painting tool selected. Now apply Lens Flare. You get the same effect as you would otherwise, but the effect floats above the background image, protecting your original image from harm. You can even move the lens flare around and vary the Opacity value, giving you more control over the final effect. Frankly, I've grown more and more fond of Lens Flare over time — it's also a very flexible tool for making specular highlights.

✦ **The Sketch filters:** In Gallery Effects parlance, Sketch means "color sucker." Beware, most of these filters replace the colors in your image with the current foreground and background colors. If the foreground and background colors are black and white, the Sketch filter results in a grayscale image; otherwise, you get a mixture of two colors. (The exceptions are Chrome, which converts the image to shades of gray regardless of the foreground and background colors, and Water Paper, which retains the image's original colors.) Charcoal and Conté Crayon create artistic effects, Bas Relief and Note Paper add texture, and Photocopy and Stamp are stupid effects that you can produce better and with more flexibility using High Pass.

To retrieve some of the original colors from your image after applying a Sketch filter, press Ctrl+Shift+F (⌘-Shift-F on the Mac) to display the Fade dialog box and try out a few different Mode settings. Overlay and Luminosity are particularly good choices. In Figure 9-3, I applied the Halftone Pattern filter with the foreground and background colors set to dark green and light blue. The result is a photo that looks as if it were projected on an old-style computer monitor. To combine the texture from the filtered image with the colors from the original, I chose Edit ➪ Fade and changed the blend mode to Overlay. Shown in the third image, the result brings back the reds and yellows inside the leaf but keeps the filtered greens inside the previously gray background. If you'd prefer to forsake all color from the filtered image, set the blend mode to Luminosity, as in the last example.

✦ **Diffuse:** Located in the Stylize submenu — as are the three filters that follow — Diffuse dithers the edges of color, much like the Dissolve brush mode dithers the edges of a soft brush. The most intriguing option, Anisotropic, barely dithers at all. One academic site I found defines Anisotropic as "a diffusion process that encourages intraregion smoothing while inhibiting interregion smoothing." (Say that to your friends and watch them shun you.) In other words, Anisotropic smoothes over low-contrast areas and roughs up edges. Try this: After applying the Diffuse filter set to Anisotropic, follow up with a bit of Unsharp Mask to get an oil painting effect, as in Figure 9-4.

✦ **Solarize:** For those of you who are wondering, "Hey, Deke, out of Photoshop's generous supply of dicey filters, which one is the worst of them all," this is it. The Grand Marshal in my Lame Filters Parade, Filter ➪ Stylize ➪ Solarize is really just a color-correction effect that inverts the lightest colors in the image and leaves the darkest colors unchanged. (If you're familiar with the Curves command, the map for Solarize looks like a pyramid.) It really belongs in the Image ➪ Adjustments submenu or, better yet, swept up after the parade along with all the confetti and horse poop.

Original image

Halftone Pattern, Size: 2, Contrast: 18, Pattern Type: Line

Edit ⇨ Fade Halftone Pattern, Mode: Overlay

same, Mode: Luminosity

Figure 9-3: Starting with a stock art photo (top), I set the foreground and background colors to medium green and light turquoise, respectively, and then applied Filter ⇨ Sketch ⇨ Halftone Pattern (second). Then I used the Fade command to select the Overlay blend mode (third) and then Luminosity (bottom).

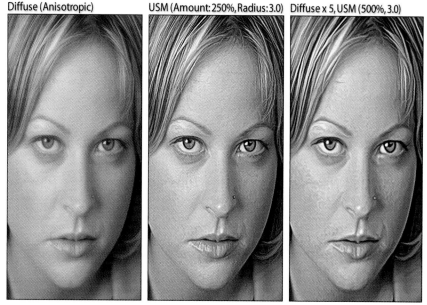

Figure 9-4: Here I applied Filter ➪ Stylize ➪ Diffuse set to Anisotropic (left). The effect is subtle, so I followed up with a heavy application of Unsharp Mask (middle). If you're looking for a more pronounced effect, apply Diffuse several times in a row, and then add Unsharp Mask (right).

✦ **Tiles:** This filter does its best to break an image up into a bunch of square, randomly spaced rectangular tiles. You specify how many tiles fit across the smaller of the image's width or height — a value of 10, for example, creates 100 tiles in a perfectly square image — and the maximum distance each tile can shift. You can fill the gaps between tiles with foreground color, background color, or an inverted or normal version of the original image. A highly intrusive and not particularly stimulating effect.

✦ **Extrude:** The more capable cousin of the Tiles filter, Extrude breaks an image into tiles and forces them toward the viewer in three-dimensional space. The Pyramid option is a lot of fun, devolving an image into a collection of spikes. When using the Blocks option, you can select a Solid Front Faces option that renders the image as a true 3D mosaic. The Mask Incomplete Blocks option simply leaves the image untouched around the perimeter of the selection where the filter can't draw complete tiles.

Actually, I kind of like Extrude. For the sheer heck of it, Figure 9-5 shows two examples of Extrude applied to what was once a statue. In the middle image, I set the Type to Blocks, the Size to 6, the Depth to 30 and Random, with the Solid Front Faces radio button selected. The example on the right shows the Pyramids option, with Size at 10 and Depth at 20. Pretty great, huh? I only wish that the filter would generate a selection outline around the masked areas of the image so that I could get rid of anything that hadn't been extruded. It's a wonderful effect, but it's not one that lends itself to many occasions.

Original digital photo   Blocks, Size: 6, Depth: 30   Pyramids, Size: 10, Depth: 20

Figure 9-5: Two examples of the fun Extrude filter, which can turn the most dignified image into one of those toys with hundreds of thin metal rods that you press your face into to create an impression. You know what I mean? What the heck are those things called, anyway?

♦ **The Texture filters:** As a group, the commands in the Filter ➭ Texture submenu are my favorite filters from the old Gallery Effects collection. Craquelure, Mosaic Tiles, and Patchwork apply interesting depth textures to an image. Texturizer provides access to several scalable textures and permits you to load your own (as long as the pattern is saved in the Photoshop format), as demonstrated in Figure 9-6. The one semi-dud Texture filter is Stained Glass, which creates polygon tiles like Photoshop's own Crystallize filter, only with black lines around the tiles. But as shown back in Figure 8-3 in Chapter 8, even it can prove interesting.

♦ **De-Interlace:** Your typical consumer video camera captures 60 *fields* per second. Each field comprises half the horizontal rows of pixels that you see on your TV set. So the first field contains the odd-numbered rows, the second field contains the even-numbered rows, the third field contains the next set of odd-numbered rows, and so on. The thing is, moving objects shift between the odd and even fields. So when you grab a still frame, every other horizontal row of pixels may appear out of alignment. The solution posed by Filter ➭ Video ➭ De-Interlace is to throw away either the odd or even rows of pixels — which is up to you — and average the remaining pixels. It's not perfect, but it's better than zigzag frames.

Figure 9-6: Filter ⇨ Texture ⇨ Texturizer lets you select from four built-in patterns — including the first three shown here — and load your own. In the last example, I loaded the *Water.psd* pattern located in the folder Photoshop CS/Presets/Patterns/Adobe ImageReady Only.

✦ **NTSC Colors:** Used throughout the United States and elsewhere, the aging NTSC broadcast standard relies on a 16-bit color space that is largely a subset of RGB (though the colors are defined differently). Many colors — including highly saturated reds, yellows, greens, and purples — fall outside NTSC's allowable range, as do absolute white and black. The results of recording such unsafe colors to analog tape vary. Some colors may bleed into each other or jitter on screen. In the case of the worst offender, bright white, the luminance information bleeds into the audio track and produces an irritating buzz. So when recording a still image from Photoshop to tape, you may want to first adjust your colors using Filter ➪ Video ➪ NTSC Colors. Unfortunately, this is a very old, very crude filter, so it tends to produce banding inside gradations. Worse, it has no effect on black or white. Better solution: Export your images for use in After Effects or some other video application.

✦ **Offset:** Ironically, we end our look at Photoshop's also-ran filters with a very useful, albeit arcane, command. Filter ➪ Other ➪ Offset shifts the pixels inside a selection, layer, or image window. It has two uses: First, you can move a layer by a prescribed number of pixels. With a layer other than background active, choose the Offset filter, enter values into the Horizontal and Vertical options, and then select Set to Transparent. You can even replay the movement by pressing Ctrl+F (⌘-F on the Mac). Second, you can wrap a repeating background around an image. Make sure you're working with a flat image or on the background layer. Then choose Offset and this time, select the Wrap Around radio button. Any pixels shifted beyond the bottom edge of the image appear at the top; pixels shifted off the right edges appear on left; and so on. I must admit, I don't use Offset all that often, but every once in a while, it comes in very handy.

Also among the filters I've omitted from this chapter are Photoshop's two custom effects filters: Filter ➪ Other ➪ Custom and Filter ➪ Distort ➪ Displace. These filters are actually quite useful, which is why I cover them in depth in the very next chapter.

Certainly, there is room for disagreement about which filters are good and which are awful. After I wrote a two-star *Macworld* review about the first Gallery Effects collection back in 1992 — I must admit, I've never been a big fan — a gentleman showed me page after page of excellent artwork he created with the filters. Another person showed me her collection of amazing Lens Flare imagery. I mean, here's a filter that basically just creates a bunch of bright spots, and yet this talented person was able to go absolutely nuts with it.

The moral is that just because I consider a filter or other piece of software to be a rotting pile of chunky, sticky putrescence doesn't mean that a creative artist can't come along and put it to remarkable use. I mean, if they can make art with elephant feces, you must be able to do something with Solarize. But that's because *you* are good, not the filter. So if you're feeling particularly creative today, give the preceding filters a try. Otherwise, skip them with a clear conscience.

A note about RAM

Memory — that is, real RAM — is a precious commodity when applying destructive filters. Photoshop's scratch disk function generally enables you to edit larger images than your computer's RAM might permit. But many of the filters in the Distort and Render submenus operate exclusively in memory. If they run out of physical RAM, they choke.

Fortunately, there is one potential workaround: When editing a color image, try applying the filter to each of the color channels independently. One color channel requires just a third to a fourth as much RAM as the full-color composite. Sadly, this technique does not help Lens Flare, Lighting Effects, or NTSC colors. These delicate flowers of the filter world are compatible only with full-color images; when editing a single channel, they appear dimmed.

However, nice as these techniques are, there is a better one. RAM is cheap, so when in doubt, buy more. As with clothes and toilet paper, you can never have enough RAM.

The Filter Gallery

As I've mentioned previously, for years, Adobe has made virtually no changes or improvements to the somewhat lackluster Gallery Effects filters. And while Photoshop CS has continued the hallowed tradition of not attempting to revamp the filters themselves, it has introduced the Filter Gallery (shown in Figure 9-7), which is a one-stop-shopping depository for all 47 Gallery Effects filters. The germ of the idea for this feature can be found, I believe, in Photoshop's spunky younger sibling, Photoshop Elements. That application features a Filters palette which makes great use of the same little generic sailboat sample image that appears in Photoshop's Filter Gallery. But as often happens, when Photoshop borrows an idea from Elements, it makes it immensely more useful. Users of previous versions of Photoshop will gasp at the ease with which you can jump from filter to filter, adjust filter settings, and even stack filters on top of one another (like layers) — all within a single dialog box. Why, it's so impressive, it might even make you reconsider your one-time dismissal of Mosaic Tiles.

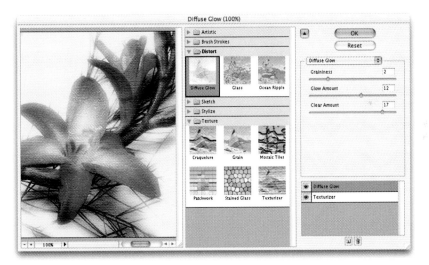

Figure 9-7: The new Filter Gallery makes it faster than ever to compromise the quality of your artwork through cheap and rampant overuse of the age-old Gallery Effects filters.

To access the Filter Gallery, either choose one of the Gallery Effects filters as you would choose any filter or choose Filter ➪ Filter Gallery. One of the complaints often lobbed at the Gallery Effects filters in the past was that image previews were limited to tiny squares within the filter dialog boxes. Thankfully, that's all changed in Photoshop CS. One of the first things you'll notice about the Filter Gallery is the gigantic image preview area on the left side of the dialog box. As with the Lens Blur filter dialog box discussed in Chapter 8, you can adjust the zoom level of the preview using the – and + icons or the pop-up menu under the right-pointing arrowhead at the bottom-left corner of the dialog box. You can also drag from the little grip in the lower-right corner of the preview area to make the preview bigger. Click on the up-pointing arrowhead to the left of the OK button to toggle the visibility of the filter area in the middle section of the dialog box and create even more room for your image preview. Also similar to the Lens Blur filter is the progress bar that appears next to the zoom controls during particularly time-consuming renders.

The middle section of the Filter Gallery dialog box is where you access the filters themselves. The filters are organized in an assortment of folders that correspond to their respective submenus inside the Filter menu. Twirl down the triangles (or simply click on a folder's name) to reveal the aforementioned sailboat thumbnails, each altered to represent the effect applying a particular filter. Click on any of the thumbnails to apply the effect to your image and bring up its settings on the right side of the dialog box. Once you've enabled an effect, you can adjust its settings as you would any other filter. From here, you can more or less go nuts — hop recklessly from folder to folder or filter to filter in the middle section or select a filter from the pop-up menu located above the settings.

The real power of the Filter Gallery, however, can be found in the bottom-right corner of the window, where the applied filters are displayed in much the same manner as layers in the Layers palette. They also work in a similar fashion, if only because the stacking order of the filters plays a large role in determining how the final affected image looks. By default, you've only got one layer of effects in the Filter Gallery, and selecting a new filter wipes away the last one you tried. But adding additional layers is as easy as clicking on the new layer icon (it's the little page) at the bottom of the dialog box and then selecting a different filter from the thumbnails. Additionally, you can stack the same filter on top of itself, again and again, with different variations on the settings to create some interesting effects. Click on the eyeball icons next to the filter layers to toggle the visibility of any of the effects. Reordering the layers of filters in the Filter Gallery is as simple as clicking one and dragging it up or down the stack. To remove any of the filters, simply highlight its layer and click the trash icon. To remove all currently applied filters, Ctrl-click (⌘-click on the Mac) the Cancel button, which changes to a Default button for as long as the Ctrl (or ⌘) key is pressed.

The only real downside to the Filter Gallery is the lack of an option to turn the thing off. As useful as it can often be, there are times when you'd like to quickly apply one of the Gallery Effects filters and be done with it. Admittedly, it was quite a bit faster to access individual Gallery Effect filters in previous versions of the program. Nevertheless, the Filter Gallery is a very positive addition to Photoshop, and we can only hope there will come a day in which we have a similar system for applying and organizing filters that we might actually want to use more than once in a blue moon.

The Pixelate Filters

The Filter ➪ Pixelate submenu features a handful of commands that rearrange your image into clumps of color:

- ✦ **Color Halftone:** This highly practical filter allows you to suggest the effect of a halftone pattern. When applied to a CMYK image, Photoshop simulates a commercially reproduced color separation. Otherwise, the filter merely affects those channels that it can. For example, when working inside an RGB image, the Channel 4 value is ignored, because there is no fourth color channel. (Alpha channels are ignored.) When working on a grayscale image or mask, the Screen Angles value for Channel 1 is the only angle that matters.

- ✦ **Crystallize:** This filter organizes an image into irregularly shaped nuggets. You specify the size of the nuggets by entering a value from 3 to 300 pixels in the Cell Size option.

✦ **Facet:** Facet fuses areas of similarly colored pixels to create a sort of hand-painted effect.

✦ **Fragment:** I already harped on this filter, so here's a quick summary: It jumbles, it bumbles, but more than anything, it dumbles.

✦ **Mezzotint:** This filter renders an image as a pattern of dots, lines, or strokes. See the upcoming "Creating a mezzotint" section for more information.

✦ **Mosaic:** The Mosaic filter blends pixels together into larger squares. You specify the height and width of the squares by entering a value in the Cell Size option box.

✦ **Pointillize:** This filter is similar to Crystallize, except it separates an image into disconnected nuggets set against the background color. As usual, you specify the size of the nuggets by changing the Cell Size value.

The Crystal Halo effect

By applying one of the Pixelate filters to a feathered selection, you can create what I call a Crystal Halo effect, named for the Crystallize filter, which tends to deliver the most successful results. The following steps explain how to create a Crystal Halo, using the worlds in Figures 9-8 and 9-9 as examples.

STEPS: Creating a Crystal Halo Effect

1. **Select the foreground element around which you want to create the halo.** In my case, I select the world.

2. **Choose Select ➪ Inverse.** Or press Ctrl+Shift+I (⌘-Shift-I on the Mac). The halo appears outside the foreground element, so you have to deselect the foreground and select the background.

3. **Press Q to switch to the quick mask mode.** Now you can edit your selection and see the results of your changes.

4. **Copy the mask.** Press Ctrl+A and Ctrl+C to select the entire mask and copy it to the Clipboard. (That's ⌘-A, ⌘-C on the Mac.) We'll need this image later to complete the effect.

5. **Choose Filter ➪ Other ➪ Minimum.** As I explained in the previous chapter, this filter enables you to increase the size of the deselected area. The size of the Radius value depends on the size of the halo you want to create. I entered 50 because I wanted a generous 50-pixel halo.

6. **Choose Filter ➪ Blur ➪ Gaussian Blur.** Then enter a Radius value equal to the amount you entered into the Minimize dialog box, in my case, 50 pixels. The result appears on the left side of Figure 9-8.

7. **Choose Filter ➪ Pixelate ➪ Crystallize.** Enter a moderate value in the Cell Size option box. I opted for the value 20 to convert the blurred edges to a series of chunky nuggets. The filter refracts the edges, almost as if you were viewing them through textured glass.

8. **Invert the mask.** Press Ctrl+I (⌘-I on the Mac) to swap the blacks and whites. This deselects the area outside the halo.

Quick mask, Minimum: 50, GBlur: 50   Crystallize: 20, Invert, Paste, Fade: Multiply

Figure 9-8: Create a heavily feathered selection outline (left) and then apply the Crystallize filter, invert the mask, and paste the original selection (right).

9. **Paste the copied selection outline.** Press Ctrl+V (⌘-V on the Mac) to paste the version of the mask you copied in Step 4.

10. **Choose Edit ⇨ Fade, and then Multiply.** To blend the original mask with the crystallized version, press Ctrl+Shift+F (⌘-Shift-F on the Mac) and choose Multiply from the Mode pop-up menu. This burns one mask into the other, leaving only the halo selected, as in the right example in Figure 9-8.

11. **Press Q to return to the marching ants mode.** Then use the selection as desired. I merely pressed Ctrl+Backspace (⌘-Delete on the Mac) to fill the selection with white, as shown in the top-left image in Figure 9-9.

Figure 9-9 shows several variations on the Crystal Halo effect. To create the upper-right image, I substituted Filter ⇨ Pixelate ⇨ Color Halftone for the Crystallize filter in Step 7. To create the lower-left image, I applied the Mosaic filter in place of Crystallize, using a Cell Size value of 14 pixels. Finally, to create the lower-right image, I applied Pointillize with a Cell Size of 5 pixels.

Creating a mezzotint

A *mezzotint* is a special halftone pattern that replaces dots with a random pattern of swirling lines and wormholes. Photoshop's Mezzotint filter is an attempt to emulate this effect. Although not entirely successful—true mezzotinting options can be properly implemented only as PostScript printing functions, not as filtering functions—they do lend themselves to some pretty interesting interpretations.

The filter itself is straightforward. You choose Filter ⇨ Pixelate ⇨ Mezzotint, select an effect from the Type submenu, and press Enter or Return. A preview box enables you to see what each of the ten Type options looks like. Figure 9-10 shows off four of the effects at 300 ppi.

When applied to grayscale artwork, the Mezzotint filter always results in a black-and-white image. When applied to a color image, the filter automatically applies the selected effect independently to each of the color channels. Although all pixels in each channel are changed to either black or white, you can see a total of eight colors — black, red, green, blue, yellow, cyan, magenta, and white — in the RGB composite view. The upper-left example of Figure 9-11 shows an image subject to the Mezzotint filter in the RGB mode.

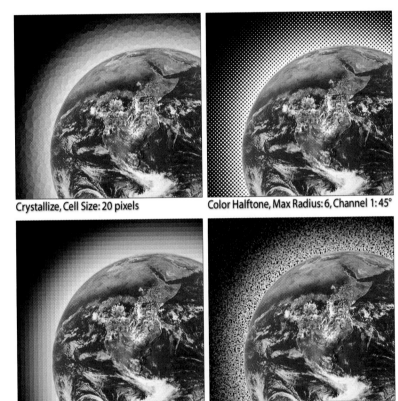

Crystallize, Cell Size: 20 pixels   Color Halftone, Max Radius: 6, Channel 1:45°

Mosaic, Cell Size: 14 pixels   Pointillize, Cell Size: 5 pixels

Figure 9-9: These images illustrate the effects of applying each of four filters to a heavily feathered selection in the quick mask mode and then filling the resulting selection outlines with white.

If the Mezzotint filter affects each channel independently, it follows that the color mode in which you work dramatically affects the performance of the filter. For example, if you apply Mezzotint in the Lab mode, you again whittle the colors down to eight, but a very different eight — black, cyan, magenta, green, red, two muddy blues, and a muddy rose — as shown in the middle-left example of Figure 9-11. If you're looking for bright happy colors, don't apply Mezzotint in the Lab mode.

In CMYK, the filter produces roughly the same eight colors that you get in RGB — white, cyan, magenta, yellow, violet-blue, red, deep green, and black. However, as shown in the bottom-left example of Figure 9-11, the distribution of the colors is much different. The image appears lighter and more colorful than its RGB counterpart. This happens because the filter has a lot of black to work with in the RGB mode but very little — just that in the black channel — in the CMYK mode.

The right column of Figure 9-11 shows the effects of the Mezzotint filter after using Edit ⇨ Fade to mix the filtered image with its original. In each case, I chose Overlay from the Mode pop-up menu and set the Opacity value to 40 percent. As you can see, fading Mezzotint permits me to achieve more subtle and functional effects.

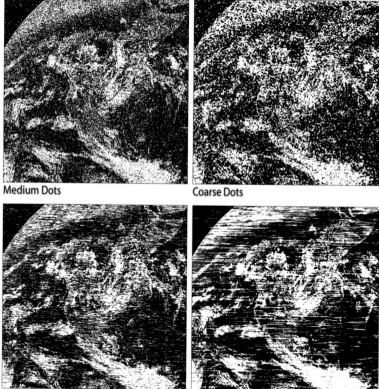

Medium Dots

Coarse Dots

Short Lines

Long Strokes

Figure 9-10: The results of applying the Mezzotint filter set to each of four representative effects. In each case, the filter changes all pixels in each channel to black or white.

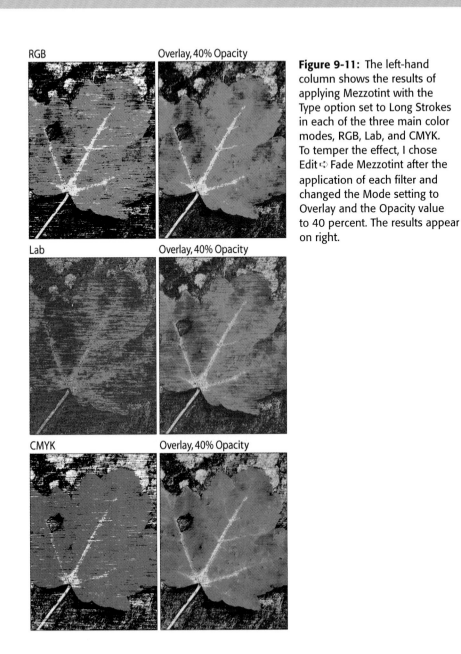

RGB

Overlay, 40% Opacity

Lab

Overlay, 40% Opacity

CMYK

Overlay, 40% Opacity

Figure 9-11: The left-hand column shows the results of applying Mezzotint with the Type option set to Long Strokes in each of the three main color modes, RGB, Lab, and CMYK. To temper the effect, I chose Edit ➪ Fade Mezzotint after the application of each filter and changed the Mode setting to Overlay and the Opacity value to 40 percent. The results appear on right.

Edge-Enhancement Filters

The Filter ➪ Stylize submenu offers access to a triad of filters that enhance the edges in an image. The most popular of these is undoubtedly Emboss, which adds dimension to an image by making it look as if it were carved in relief. The other two, Find Edges and Trace Contour, are less commonly applied but every bit as capable and deserving of your attention.

Embossing an image

The Emboss filter works by searching for high-contrast edges (just like the Sharpen Edges and High Pass filters), highlighting the edges with black or white pixels, and then coloring the low-contrast portions with medium gray. When you choose Filter ⇨ Stylize ⇨ Emboss, Photoshop displays the Emboss dialog box shown in Figure 9-12. The dialog box offers three options:

✦ **Angle:** The value in this option box determines the angle at which Photoshop lights the image in relief. For example, if you enter a value of 90 degrees, you light the relief from the bottom straight upward. The white pixels therefore appear on the bottom sides of the edges, and the black pixels appear on the top sides. Figure 9-13 shows four reliefs lit from different angles and with different Height settings.

✦ **Height:** The Emboss filter accomplishes its highlighting effect by displacing one copy of an image relative to another. Using the Height option, you specify the distance between the copies, which can vary from 1 to 100 pixels. Lower values produce crisper effects, as demonstrated in Figure 9-13. Values above 4 goop up things pretty well unless you also enter a high Amount value. Together, the Height and Amount values determine the depth of the image in relief.

The Height value is analogous to the Radius value in the Unsharp Mask dialog box. You should therefore set the value according to the resolution of your image — 1 for 150 ppi, 2 for 300 ppi, and so on.

✦ **Amount:** Enter a value between 1 and 500 percent to determine the amount of black and white assigned to pixels along the edges. Values of 50 percent and lower produce almost entirely gray images. Higher values produce sharper edges, as if the relief were carved more deeply.

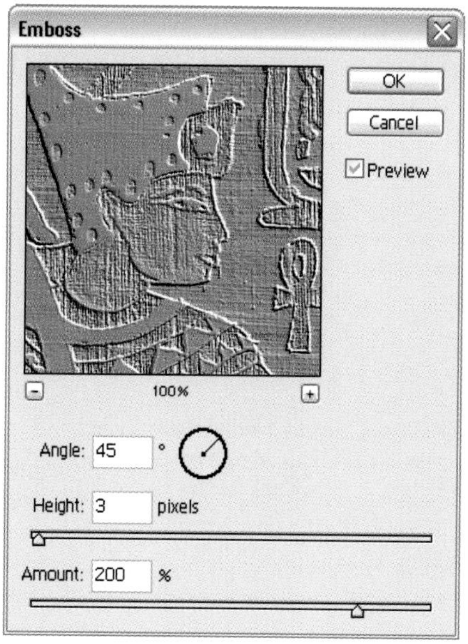

Figure 9-12: The Emboss dialog box lets you control the depth of the filtered image and the angle from which it is lit.

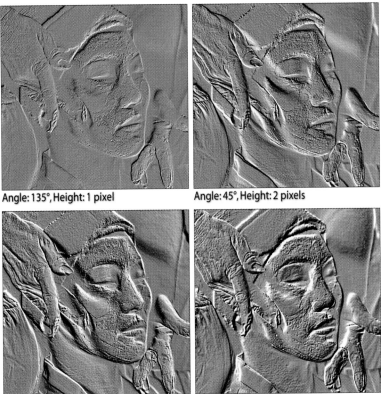

Angle: 135°, Height: 1 pixel   Angle: 45°, Height: 2 pixels

Angle: –135°, Height: 3 pixels   Angle: –45°, Height: 4 pixels

Figure 9-13: Reliefs lit with four different Height settings and from four different angles, in increments that are multiples of 45 degrees. Imagine a light source in the center of the grouping of four images.

As a stand-alone effect, Emboss is only so-so. It's one of those filters that makes you gasp with delight the first time you see it but never quite lends itself to any practical application after you become acquainted with Photoshop. But if you think of Emboss as an extension of the High Pass filter, it takes on new meaning. You can use it to edit selection outlines in the quick mask mode, just as you might use the High Pass filter. You also can use it to draw out detail in an image.

Figure 9-14 shows the result of choosing Edit ➪ Fade immediately after applying the Emboss filter. First, I applied the Emboss filter at an Angle of 135 degrees, a Height of 2 pixels, and an Amount of 500 percent. Then I pressed Ctrl+Shift+F (⌘-Shift-F on the Mac) to display the Fade dialog box. To create the top-right example, I selected Darken from the Mode pop-up menu and lowered the Opacity to 65 percent. This added shadows to the edges of the image, thus boosting the texture without unduly upsetting the original brightness values. I selected the Overlay blend mode and raised the Opacity back to 100 percent to create the bottom-left example, and then switched to Pin Light at 80 percent Opacity for the bottom-right image.

Emboss, Angle: 135°, Height: 2, 500%   Darken, 65% Opacity

Overlay, 100% Opacity   Pin Light, 80% Opacity

Figure 9-14: After applying the Emboss filter, I used my old friend the Fade command to experiment with blend modes and Opacity levels.

To create a color relief effect, first float the image to an independent layer by pressing Ctrl+J (⌘-J on the Mac). This way, you'll be free to experiment with the Opacity and blend mode settings in the Layers palette, not only right after applying the filter, but well into the future. After applying the Emboss filter, try modifying the blend mode setting to something like Overlay, Color Dodge, or Luminosity — all illustrated in Figure 9-15 — just to name a few. In each case, the blend mode retains the colors from the original image while applying the lightness and darkness of the pixels from the filtered selection. The effect looks something like an inked lithographic plate, with steel grays and vivid colors mixing together.

While this figure chiefly demonstrates various effects you can achieve by fading the Emboss filter, the final example uses a different technique to improve upon the example directly above it. Rather than let the gray choke out the colors below, I double-clicked on the thumbnail for the layer in the Layers palette to bring up the Layer Style dialog box. Then I dragged and Alt-dragged (or Option-dragged) the triangles in the Underlying Layer slider bar to the settings listed in the final example, thus permitting the blacks and whites to show through. For more information on the powerful Underlying Layer slider, read the section "Dropping Out and Forcing Through" in Chapter 6.

Normal, 30% Opacity

Emboss, Angle: 135°, Height: 2 pixels, Amount: 500%

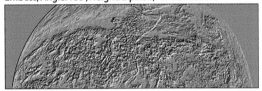

Figure 9-15: Before applying Emboss (second example), I floated the Earth to an independent layer. Then I experimented with different blend mode and Opacity combinations, as the third, fourth, and fifth examples illustrate. Of the three, Luminosity chokes out the black sky and white clouds with gray. So I modified the Underlying Layer settings in the Layer Style dialog box, permitting the blacks and whites to show through (last example).

Overlay blend mode, 85% Opacity

Color Dodge blend mode, 60% Opacity

Luminosity blend mode, 100% Opacity

Luminosity, 100%, Underlying Layer: 10/30, 95/215

Tracing around edges

Photoshop provides three filters that trace around pixels in your image and accentuate the edges. All three filters live on the Filter ⇨ Stylize submenu:

✦ **Find Edges:** This filter detects edges similarly to High Pass. Low-contrast areas become white, medium-contrast edges become gray, and high-contrast edges become black, as in the first example in Figure 9-16. Hard edges become thin lines; soft edges become fat ones. The result is a thick, organic outline that you can overlay onto an image to give it a waxy appearance. To achieve the bottom-left effect in the figure, I chose Edit ⇨ Fade Find Edges and applied the Overlay mode.

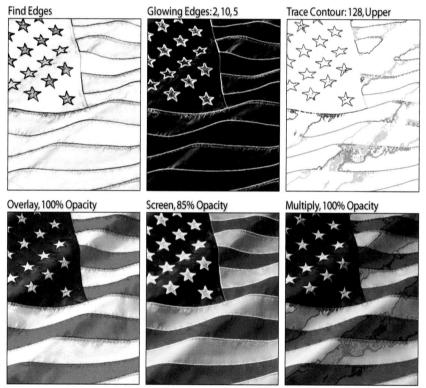

Find Edges   Glowing Edges: 2, 10, 5   Trace Contour: 128, Upper

Overlay, 100% Opacity   Screen, 85% Opacity   Multiply, 100% Opacity

Figure 9-16: The top row of images demonstrates the effect of the three edge-tracing commands available from the Filter ⇨ Stylize submenu. After applying each command, I used the Fade command to apply the blend modes and Opacity values demonstrated in the bottom row.

✦ **Glowing Edges:** This Gallery Effects filter is a variation on Find Edges, with two important differences: Glowing Edges produces an inverted effect, changing low-contrast areas to black and edges to white, as in the top-middle image in Figure 9-16. This filter also enables you to adjust the width, brightness, and smoothness of the traced edges. For example, the top-middle image in Figure 9-16 uses an Edge Width of 2, an Edge

Brightness of 10, and a Smoothness of 5. Glowing Edges is a great backup command. If you aren't satisfied with the effect produced by the Find Edges filter, choose Glowing Edges instead and adjust the options as desired. If you want black lines against a white background, press Ctrl+I (⌘-I on the Mac) to invert the effect.

✦ **Trace Contour:** Illustrated on the right side of Figure 9-16, Trace Contour is a little more involved than the others and slightly less interesting. The filter traces a series of single-pixel lines along the border between light and dark pixels. Choosing the filter displays a dialog box containing three options: Level, Upper, and Lower. The Level value indicates the lightness value above which pixels are considered to be light and below which they are dark. For example, if you enter 128 — medium gray, the default setting used in Figure 9-16 — Trace Contour draws a line at every spot where an area of color lighter than medium gray meets an area of color darker than medium gray. The Upper and Lower options tell the filter where to position the line — inside the lighter color's territory (Upper) or inside the space occupied by the darker color (Lower).

Like Mezzotint, Trace Contour applies itself to each color channel independently and renders each channel as a 1-bit image. A collection of black lines surrounds the areas of color in each channel; the RGB, Lab, or CMYK composite view shows these lines in the colors associated with the channels. When you work in RGB, a cyan line indicates a black line in the red channel (no red plus full-intensity green and blue becomes cyan). A yellow line indicates a black line in the blue channel, and so on. You get a single black line when working in the grayscale mode.

Creating a metallic coating

The edge-tracing filters are especially fun to use in combination with Edit ⇨ Fade. I became interested in playing with these filters after trying out the Chrome filter included with the first Gallery Effects collection. Now included with Photoshop as Filter ⇨ Sketch ⇨ Chrome, this filter turns an image into a melted pile of metallic goo. No matter how you apply Chrome, it completely wipes out your image and leaves a ton of jagged color transitions in its wake. It's really only useful with color images, and then only if you follow up with the Fade command and a blend mode. Even then, I've never been particularly satisfied with the results.

But all that experimenting got me thinking: How can you create a metallic coating, with gleaming highlights and crisp shadows, without depending on Chrome? Find Edges offers a way. First, copy your image to a separate layer by pressing Ctrl+J (⌘-J on the Mac). Then apply the Gaussian Blur filter. A Radius value between 1.0 and 4.0 produces the best results, depending on how gooey you want the edges to be. Next, apply the Find Edges filter. Because the edges are blurry, the resulting image is light, so I recommend you darken it using Image ⇨ Adjustments ⇨ Levels. (Raise the first Input Levels value to 100 or so, as explained in Chapter 13.) The blurry edges appear in the top-left example in Figure 9-17.

To produce the bottom-left image, I mixed the layer with the underlying original using the Overlay blend mode. The result is a shiny effect that produces a metallic finish without altogether destroying the detail in the image.

If you decide you like this effect, there's more where that came from. The second and third columns of Figure 9-17 show the results of applying Filter ⇨ Sketch ⇨ Bas Relief and (for comparison's sake) Filter ⇨ Sketch ⇨ Chrome, respectively. After applying each filter, I chose Edit ⇨ Fade and selected the Overlay mode, repeating the effect I applied to the Gaussian Blur and Find Edges layer. In this case, the Overlay mode actually makes the Chrome filter look quite respectable.

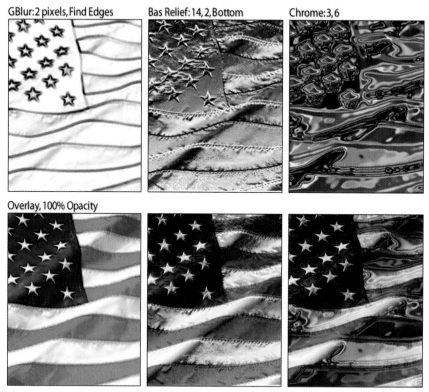

Figure 9-17: After applying Gaussian Blur and Find Edges to a layered version of the image (top left), I composited the filtered image with the original using the Overlay mode (bottom left). The second and third columns show similar effects achieved using the Bas Relief and Chrome effects filters.

Distortion Filters

For the most part, commands in the Distort submenu are related by the fact that they move colors in an image to achieve unusual stretching, swirling, and vibrating effects. They're rather like the transformation commands from the Edit menu in that they perform their magic by relocating and interpolating colors rather than by altering brightness and color values.

The distinction, of course, is that whereas the transformation commands let you scale and distort images by manipulating four control points, the Distort filters provide the equivalent of hundreds of control points, all of which you can use to affect different portions of an image. In some cases, you're projecting an image into a fun-house mirror; other times, it's a reflective pool. You can fan images, wiggle them, and change them in ways that have no correlation to real life, as illustrated in the disturbing but illuminating Figure 9-18.

A kind and decent man   What'd you have to go and do that for?

Figure 9-18: This is your image (left); this is your image on distortion filters (right). Six filters, in fact: Spherize, Twirl, Polar Coordinates, Shear, Wave, and Ripple. I also used Liquify for some of the effects toward the top of the image, including those creepy cat-like eyes.

Distortion filters are powerful tools. Although they are easy to apply, they are extremely difficult to use well. Here are some rules to keep in mind:

✦ **Practice makes practical:** Distortion filters are like complex vocabulary words. You don't want to use them without practicing a little first. Experiment with a distortion filter several times before trying to use it in a real project. You may even want to write down the steps you take so that you can remember how you created an effect. Then again, why bother writing down steps when you can use the new History Log feature to save a record for you? Chapter 13 gives the lowdown on the History Log preference.

✦ **Use caution during tight deadlines:** Distortion filters are enormous time-wasters. Unless you know exactly how you want to proceed, you may want to avoid using them when time is short. The last thing you need when you're working under the gun is to get trapped trying to pull off a weird effect.

✦ **Apply selectively:** The effects of distortion filters are too severe to inflict all at once. You can achieve marvelous, subtle effects, however, by distorting feathered and layered selections. Although I would hardly call the image in Figure 9-18 subtle, no single effect was applied to the entire image. For instance, the black edges were created with the Ripple filter. I also skipped ahead of myself a bit and used the Liquify command to create the distortion in the topmost face and in the main pair of eyes. The upcoming section "Distorting with the Liquify command" explains how to use this tool.

✦ **Combine creatively:** Don't expect a single distortion to achieve the desired effect. If one application isn't enough, apply the filter again. Experiment with combining different distortions.

Distortion filters interpolate between pixels to create their fantastic effects. This means the quality of your filtered images depends on the setting of the Interpolation option in the General Preferences dialog box. If a filter produces jagged effects, the Nearest Neighbor option is probably selected. Try selecting the Bicubic or Bilinear option instead.

Reflecting an image in a spoon

Most folks take their first venture into distortion filters by using Pinch and Spherize. Pinch maps an image on the inside of a sphere or similarly curved surface; Spherize maps it on the outside of a sphere. It's sort of like looking at your reflection on the inside and outside of a spoon.

You can apply Pinch to a scanned face to squish the features toward the center or apply Spherize to accentuate the girth of the nose. Figure 9-19 illustrates both effects. It's a laugh, and you pretty much feel as though you're onto something that no one else ever thought of before. (At least that's how I felt — but I'm easily amazed.)

You can pinch or spherize an image using either the Pinch or Spherize command. Note that a positive Amount value in the Pinch dialog box produces a similar effect to a negative value in the Spherize dialog box. There is a slight difference between the spatial curvature of the 3D calculations: Pinch pokes the image inward or outward using a rounded cone — we're talking bell-shaped, much like a Gaussian model. Spherize wraps the image on the outside or inside of a true sphere. As a result, the two filters yield subtly different results. Pinch produces a soft transition around the perimeter of a selection; Spherize produces an abrupt transition. If this doesn't quite make sense to you, just play with one, try out the same effect with the other, and see which you like better.

Another difference between the two filters is that Spherize provides additional options that enable you to wrap an image on the inside or outside of a vertical or horizontal cylinder, as shown in Figure 9-20. To try out these effects, select the Horizontal Only or Vertical Only options from the Mode pop-up menu at the bottom of the Spherize dialog box. Perhaps counterintuitively, Horizontal Only wraps an image around a vertical cylinder and vice versa. There's just no accounting for the peculiarities of calculus, you know?

Both filters can affect elliptical regions only. If a selection outline is not elliptical, Photoshop applies the filter to the largest ellipse that fits inside the selection. As a result, the filter may leave behind a noticeable elliptical boundary between the affected and unaffected portions of the selection. To avoid this effect, select the region that you want to edit with the elliptical marquee tool and then feather the selection before filtering it. This softens the effect of the filter and provides a more gradual transition (even more so than Pinch already affords).

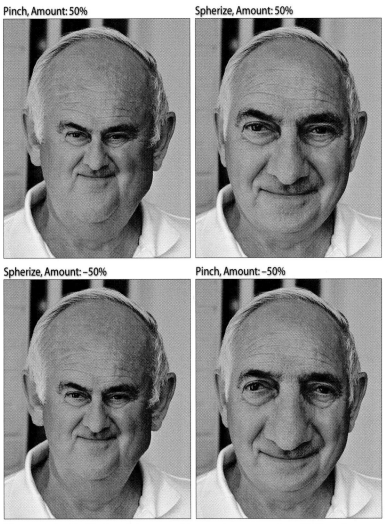

Pinch, Amount: 50%

Spherize, Amount: 50%

Spherize, Amount: –50%

Pinch, Amount: –50%

Figure 9-19: My kind and decent subject endures more humiliating abuse—
thanks to the Pinch and Spherize filters. Notice how negative values make
Pinch spherize, and Spherize pinch.

One of the more remarkable properties of the Pinch filter is that it lets you turn any image
into a conical gradation. Figure 9-21 illustrates how the process works. First, you may want
to blur the image to eliminate any harsh edges between color transitions. Then apply the
Pinch filter at full strength (100 percent). Reapply the filter several more times. Each time
you press Ctrl+F (⌘-F on the Mac), the center portion of the image recedes farther and farther into the distance, as shown in Figure 9-21. After 10 repetitions, the face in the example
all but disappeared.

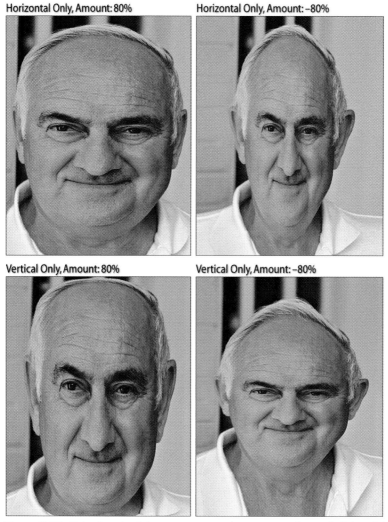

Figure 9-20: Spherize also lets you wrap your image around a vertical (top left) or horizontal (bottom left) cylinder. Or try your hand at wrapping the image around the inside of the cylinder (right examples).

Next, apply the Radial Blur filter set to Spin 10 pixels or so to mix the color boundaries a bit. The result is a type of gradation that you can't create using Photoshop's gradient tool.

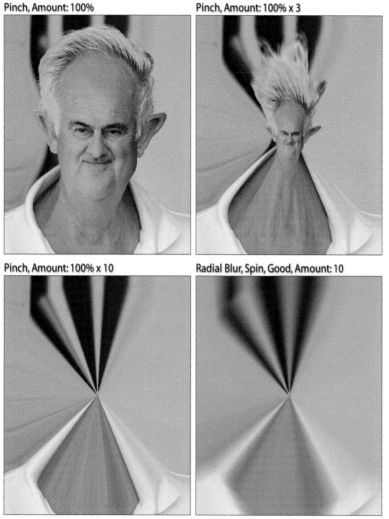

Pinch, Amount: 100%

Pinch, Amount: 100% x 3

Pinch, Amount: 100% x 10

Radial Blur, Spin, Good, Amount: 10

Figure 9-21: I pinched the image 10 times and applied the Radial Blur filter with its default settings to create a conical gradation.

Twirling spirals

The Twirl filter rotates the center of a selection while leaving the sides fixed in place. The result is a spiral of colors that looks for all the world as if you poured the image into a blender set to a very slow speed.

When you choose Filter ⇨ Distort ⇨ Twirl, you can enter a positive value from 1 to 999 degrees to spiral the image in a clockwise direction. Enter a negative value to spiral the image in a counterclockwise direction. Figure 9-22 shows 30-degree and 100-degree spirals in both positive and negative directions. As you are probably already aware, 360 degrees make a full circle, so the maximum 999-degree value equates to a spiral that circles around almost three times, as shown in the bottom-right example in Figure 9-23.

The Twirl filter produces smoother effects when you use lower Angle values. Therefore, you're better off applying a 100-degree spiral 10 times rather than applying a 999-degree spiral once, as you can see in Figure 9-23.

Twirl, Angle: 30°   Twirl, Angle: 100°

Twirl, Angle: –30°   Twirl, Angle: –100°

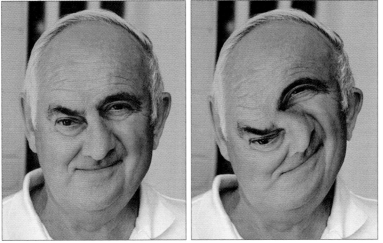

Figure 9-22: You can adjust the direction of the Twirl filter to suit whichever side of the equator you happen to be on.

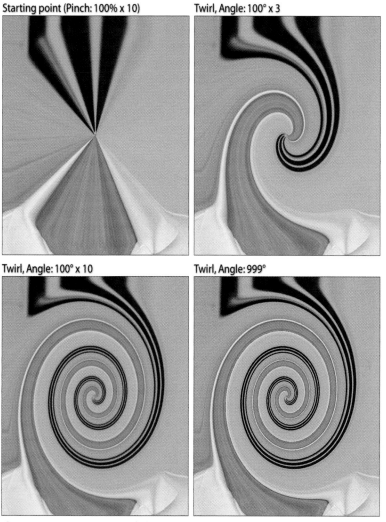

Starting point (Pinch: 100% x 10)

Twirl, Angle: 100° x 3

Twirl, Angle: 100° x 10

Twirl, Angle: 999°

Figure 9-23: Our poor Pinch-headed subject (upper left) gets subjected to the tortures of the Twirl filter (upper right). Repeatedly applying the Twirl filter at a moderate value (bottom left) produces a smoother effect than applying the filter once at a high value (bottom right).

In addition to creating ice-cream swirls like those shown in Figure 9-23, you can use the Twirl filter to create organic images virtually from scratch, as witnessed by Figures 9-24 and 9-25. To create the images shown in Figure 9-24, I started with Mr. Pinch-head (top left) and used the Spherize filter to flex the image vertically by entering 100 percent in the Amount option box and selecting Vertical Only from the Mode pop-up menu. After repeating this filter several times, I eventually achieved a stalactite-stalagmite effect, as shown in the top-right example of the figure. To increase the contrast in the image, I applied Unsharp Mask and followed that up with a little Gaussian Blur to make things creamier. I then repeatedly applied the Twirl filter to curl the straight spikes like two symmetrical hairs. The result merges the simplicity of pure math with the beauty of bitmapped imagery.

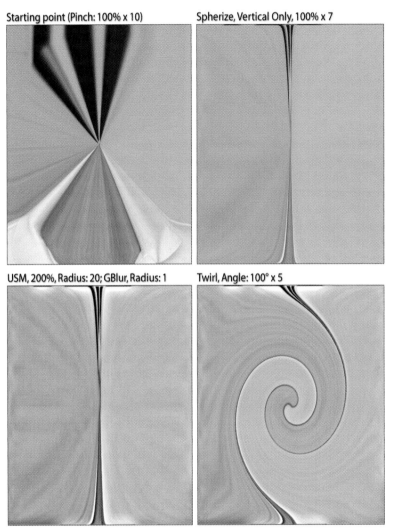

Figure 9-24: You can create surprisingly naturalistic effects using distortion filters exclusively.

Figure 9-25 illustrates a droplet technique designed years ago by a friend of mine whom I have long regarded as one of the most extraordinary digital artists out there, Mark Collen. I took the liberty of breaking down the technique into the following steps for your edification.

STEPS: Creating a Thick-Liquid Droplet

1. **Press D to restore the default foreground and background colors.**

2. **Shift-drag with the rectangular marquee tool to select a square portion of an image.**

3. **Create a linear gradation by dragging inside the selection outline with the gradient tool.** Before you drag, select the linear gradient style in the Options bar and select the

foreground to background gradient from the Gradients drop-down palette, also in the Options bar. Drag a short distance near the center of the selection from upper left to lower right, creating the gradation shown in the top-left image in Figure 9-25.

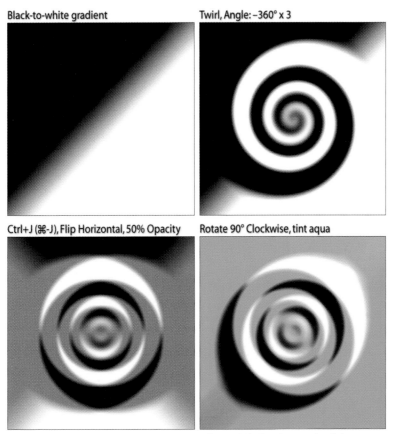

Figure 9-25: Although they appear as if they might be the result of the ZigZag filter, these images were created entirely by using the gradient tool, the Twirl filter, and a couple of transformations.

4. **Choose the Twirl filter and apply it at −360 degrees so that the spiral moves counterclockwise.** To create the top-right image in the figure, I applied the Twirl filter three times. Each repetition of the filter adds another ring of ripples.

5. **Press Ctrl+J (Win) or ⌘-J (Mac) to copy the selection to a layer.**

6. **Choose Edit ➪ Transform ➪ Flip Horizontal.**

7. **Lower the Opacity value to 50 percent.** You can do this from the keyboard by selecting the rectangular marquee tool and pressing 5. The result appears in the lower-left example in Figure 9-25.

8. **Choose Edit ➪ Transform ➪ Rotate 90° CW.** This rotates the layer a quarter turn, thus creating the last image in the figure. You can achieve other interesting effects by choosing Lighten, Darken, and others from the brush modes pop-up menu.

Now, if a few twirls and transformations can produce an effect this entertaining in black and white, just imagine what you can do in color. On second thought, don't imagine; check out Figure 9-26 instead. Starting with one of Photoshop's predefined gradients — Blue, Red, Yellow — I followed the previous Steps 1 through 4, which resulted in the top-left example. I next pressed Ctrl+J (or ⌘-J on the Mac) to clone the image to a separate layer, chose Edit ⇨ Transform ⇨ Flip Horizontal, and applied the Difference mode from the Layers palette, thus producing the top-right example.

Blue, Red, Yellow;
Twirl: –360° x 3

Ctrl+J (⌘-J), Flip Horizontal,
Difference blend mode

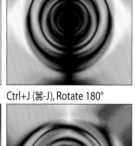

Figure 9-26: Starting with the preset Blue, Red, Yellow gradient, I followed Steps 1 through 4 (top left). In the next three examples, I made extensive use of floating copies of layers with the Difference blend mode applied. I then finished up with a little Spherize, ZigZag, Lens Flare, and Unsharp Mask to mutate the concentric rings into vividly colored puddles (bottom).

Ctrl+J (⌘-J), Rotate 90° CW

Ctrl+J (⌘-J), Rotate 180°

Spherize (100%), ZigZag (100%,10),
Lens Flare (170%), Unsharp Mask (500%, 20, 0)

From there, it was largely a matter of cloning the layer and applying more transformations. I again pressed Ctrl+J (⌘-J) and then chose Edit ➪ Transform ➪ Rotate 90° Clockwise to achieve the second effect on the left. Then I pressed Ctrl+J (⌘-J) and chose Edit ➪ Transform ➪ Rotate 180° to get the second effect on the right. Because the Difference mode remains in effect for each new layer, the bright colors from one layer invert the colors from the layers below, producing a wild array of colors that go well beyond the original blue, red, and yellow.

To produce the final effect, I applied a series of filters to the top layer only. First I chose Filter ➪ Distort ➪ Spherize and set the Amount value to 100 percent. Then I chose Filter ➪ Distort ➪ ZigZag; entered 100 percent and 10, respectively, for the Amount and Ridges values; and set the Style option to Pond Ripples. Next, I chose Filter ➪ Render ➪ Lens Flare and set the Brightness value to 170 percent with a Lens Type of 50–300m Zoom. The flare starts in the upper-right corner of the image. Finally, I applied Filter ➪ Sharpen ➪ Unsharp Mask with the settings listed in the figure. With its colorful bubbles and deeply etched concentric rings, the final image is perhaps the ultimate embodiment of groovy.

If that went a little fast for you, not to worry. More important than the specific effects is this general category of distortion drawings, which I call *synthetics*, because you create them not from digitized photographs but out of thin air. A filter such as Pinch or Twirl permits you to create wild imagery without ever drawing a brushstroke or scanning a photograph. If you can do this much with a simple three-color gradation, just think of what you can do if you throw in a few more colors. Pixels are little more than fodder for these very powerful functions.

Creating concentric pond ripples

I don't know about you, but when I think of zigzags, I think of cartoon lightning bolts, wriggling snakes, scribbles — anything that alternately changes directions along an axis, like the letter *Z*. The ZigZag filter does arrange colors into zigzag patterns, but it does so in a radial fashion, meaning that the zigzags emanate from the center of the image like spokes in a wheel. The result is a series of concentric ripples. If you want parallel zigzags, check out the Ripple and Wave filters, described in the next section. (The ZigZag filter creates ripples and the Ripple filter creates zigzags. Go figure.)

When you choose Filter ➪ Distort ➪ ZigZag, Photoshop displays a dialog box offering the following options:

✦ **Amount:** Enter an amount between negative 99 and positive 100 in whole-number increments to specify the depth of the ripples. If you enter a negative value, the ripples descend below the surface. If you enter a positive value, the ripples protrude upward.

To illustrate how the Amount value works, I first prepared the sample image pictured in Figure 9-27. Starting with our much-maligned Mr. Pinch as seen in the upper-left example (oh, you're a lean one, Mr. Pinch), I copied the image to an independent layer, rotated it 180 degrees, and applied the Overlay blend mode (upper right). I floated this layer, used Overlay again, and applied the Twirl filter repeatedly (lower left). Finally, I pasted in the flag image seen earlier, inverted it, used Difference mode on the layer, and flattened the entire image (lower right). Pretty cool, huh? Figure 9-28 shows the final image subject to the ZigZag filter with two different Amount values.

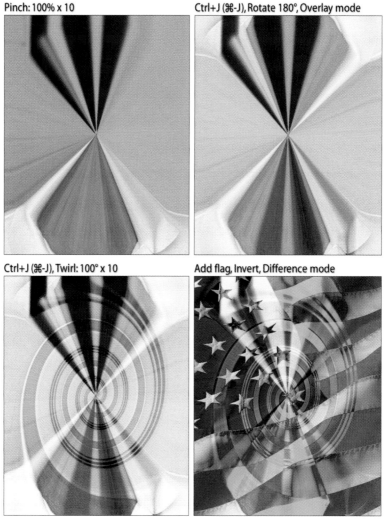

Pinch: 100% x 10

Ctrl+J (⌘-J), Rotate 180°, Overlay mode

Ctrl+J (⌘-J), Twirl: 100° x 10

Add flag, Invert, Difference mode

Figure 9-27: Mr. Pinch does his duty as a proud American, resulting in a kaleidoscopic sample image.

✦ **Ridges:** This option box controls the number of ripples in the selected area and accepts any value from 0 to 20. Figure 9-29 illustrates the difference between a Ridges value of 5 (top row) and 20 (bottom row).

✦ **Style:** The options in this pop-up menu determine how Photoshop moves pixels with respect to the center of the image or selection.

- **Around Center:** Select this option to rotate pixels in alternating directions around the center without moving them outward, as shown in the left columns of Figures 9-28 and 9-29. This is the only option that produces what I would term a zigzag effect.

- **Out From Center:** When you select this option, Photoshop moves pixels outward in rhythmic bursts according to the value in the Ridges option box. The middle columns of Figures 9-28 and 9-29 show some examples.

- **Pond Ripples:** This option is really a cross between the previous two. It moves pixels outward and rotates them around the center of the selection to create circular patterns. As demonstrated in the right columns of Figures 9-28 and 9-29, this option truly results in a pond ripple effect.

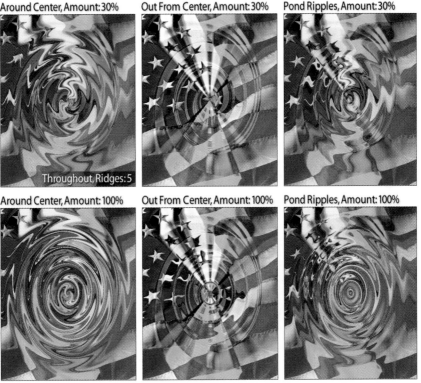

Figure 9-28: The results of applying the ZigZag filter using Amount values of 30 percent (top row) and 100 percent (bottom row) and each of the three Style settings. In all cases, the Ridges value was 5.

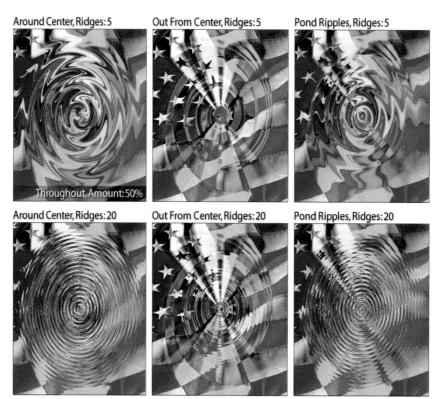

Figure 9-29: The effects of the ZigZag filter using two Ridges values and each of the three Style pop-up menu settings. In all cases, the Amount value was 50.

Creating parallel ripples and waves

Photoshop provides four means to distort an image in parallel waves, as if the image were lying on the bottom of a shimmering or undulating pool. Of the four, the ripple filters — which include Ripple, Ocean Ripple, and Glass — are only moderately sophisticated, but they're also relatively easy to apply. The fourth filter, Wave, affords you greater control, but its options are among the most complex Photoshop has to offer.

The Ripple filter

To use the Ripple filter, choose Filter ➪ Distort ➪ Ripple. Photoshop displays the Ripple dialog box, giving you the following options:

✦ **Amount:** Enter an amount between negative and positive 999 in whole-number increments to specify the width of the ripples from side to side. Negative and positive values change the direction of the ripples, but visually speaking, they produce identical effects. The ripples are measured as a ratio of the Size value and the dimensions of the selection — all of which translates to, "Experiment and see what happens." You can count on getting ragged effects from any value over 300, as illustrated in Figure 9-30.

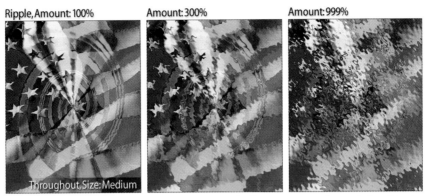

Figure 9-30: The effects of three different Ripple filter Amount values. Notice that the transitions turn jagged between 300 and 999 percent, so high values are generally discouraged.

✦ **Size:** Select one of the three options in the Size pop-up menu to change the length of the ripples. The Small option results in the shortest ripples and therefore the most ripples. Combining the Small option with a relatively high Amount value results in a textured-glass effect. The Large option results in the longest and fewest ripples. Figure 9-31 shows an example of each Size option.

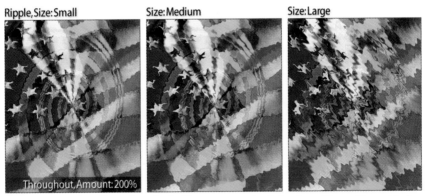

Figure 9-31: The effects the Ripple filter set to each of the three Size settings. Medium generally produces the most even effects.

You can create a blistered effect by overlaying a negative ripple onto a positive ripple. Try this: First, copy the selection. Then apply the Ripple filter with a positive Amount value — say, 300. Next, paste the copied selection and apply the Ripple filter at the exact opposite Amount value, in this case, –300. Press 5 to change the Opacity value to 50 percent. The result is a series of diametrically opposed ripples that cross each other to create teardrop blisters.

Ocean Ripple and Glass

The Ocean Ripple and Glass filters are gifts from Gallery Effects. Both filters emulate the effect of looking at an image through textured glass. These two distorters so closely resemble each other that they would be better merged into one. But where the effects filters are concerned, interface design is as fickle and transitory as the face on the cover of *Tiger Beat Magazine*.

The Ocean Ripple filter's two parameters, Ripple Size and Ripple Magnitude, are illustrated in Figure 9-32. Compare the examples horizontally to observe an increase in Ripple Size values from 3 to the maximum of 15; compare vertically to observe an increase in Ripple Magnitude from 5 to the maximum of 20. As you can see, you can vary the Ripple Size value with impunity. But raise the Ripple Magnitude value, and you're looking through sculpted glass.

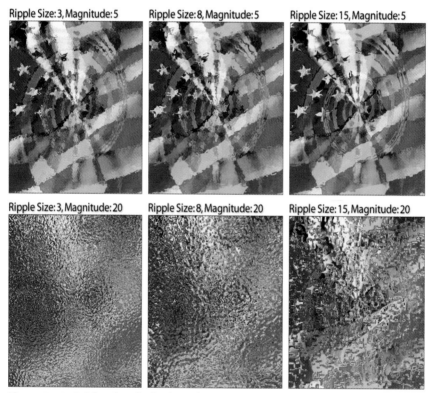

Figure 9-32: Raising the Ripple Size value spreads out the effect; raising the Ripple Magnitude adds more depth and contrast to the ripples.

The principal difference between Glass and Ocean Ripple is that while Ocean Ripple uses one preset distortion texture, Glass gives you four to choose from, plus it lets you load your own (similar to Texturizer). You can invert the texture — high becomes low, low becomes high — and also scale it to change its size relative to the layer you're distorting. Figure 9-33 uses the Tiny Lens texture throughout and demonstrates how different the effect can be depending on the Distortion and Smoothness settings. Compare the examples in the figure horizontally for proof that Distortion is perhaps the best-named parameter in all of Photoshop. Smoothness, on the other hand, is sort of like an "anti-Ripple Magnitude" setting. High Smoothness settings in Glass are analogous to low Ripple Magnitude settings in Ocean Ripple.

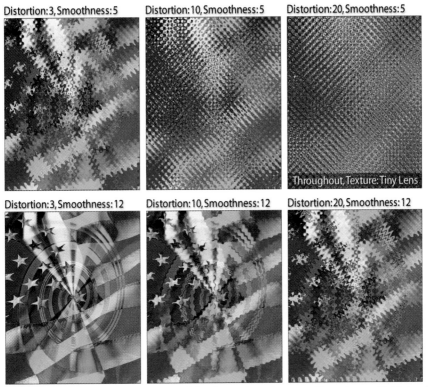

Distortion: 3, Smoothness: 5 — Distortion: 10, Smoothness: 5 — Distortion: 20, Smoothness: 5

Throughout, Texture: Tiny Lens

Distortion: 3, Smoothness: 12 — Distortion: 10, Smoothness: 12 — Distortion: 20, Smoothness: 12

Figure 9-33: For maximum privacy while showering, choose a Glass door with high Distortion and low Smoothness settings (upper right).

The Wave filter

Now that you've met the Ripple family, it's time to ride the Wave. I've come to love this filter — I use it all the time — but it's complex enough to warrant its own book. It wouldn't be a very big book and no one would buy it, but you never know what a freelancer like me will do next. Keep an eye out for *Wave Filter Bible* at your local bookstore.

In the meantime, choose Filter ➪ Distort ➪ Wave (that's the easy part) to display the Wave dialog box shown in Figure 9-34. Photoshop presents you with the following options, which make applying a distortion every bit as easy as operating an oscilloscope:

✦ **Number of Generators:** Right off the bat, the Wave dialog box boggles the brain. A friend of mine likened this option to the number of rocks you throw in the water to start it rippling. One generator means that you throw in one rock to create one set of waves. You can throw in two rocks to create two sets of waves, three rocks to create three sets of waves, and all the way up to a quarryful of 999 rocks to create, well, you get the idea. In case you don't, Figure 9-35 shows what happens when I throw a total of 16 rocks at the reflected image of a neon sign. If you enter a high value, however, be prepared to wait a few years for the preview to update. If you can't wait, press Escape, which turns off the preview until the next time you enter a value in the dialog box.

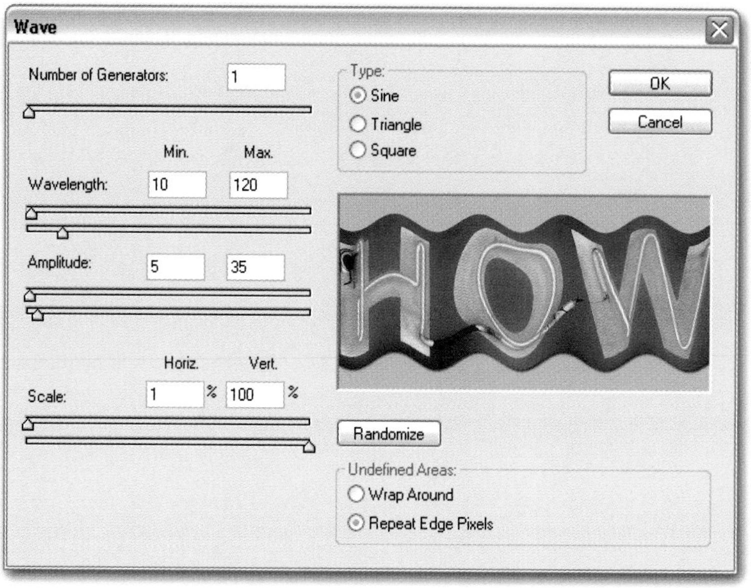

Figure 9-34: The Wave dialog box lets you wreak scientific havoc on an image. Put on your pocket protector, take out your slide rule, and give it a whirl.

✦ **Wavelength and Amplitude:** Beginning to feel like you're playing with a ham radio? The Wave filter produces random results by varying the number and length of waves (Wavelength) as well as the height of the waves (Amplitude) between minimum and maximum values, which can range from 1 to 999. (The Wavelength and Amplitude options, therefore, correspond in theory to the Size and Amount options in the Ripple dialog box.) Figure 9-36 demonstrates the difference between Wavelength and Amplitude.

✦ **Scale:** You can scale the effects of the Wave filter between 1 and 100 percent horizontally and vertically. For clarity's sake, all the effects featured in Figures 9-35 and 9-36 use only Vertical Scale, with Horizontal Scale set at the minimum of 1 percent. Increasing Horizontal Scale would make the waves go back and forth as well as up and down.

✦ **Type:** You can select from three kinds of waves. As exhibited in Figures 9-35 and 9-36, the Sine option produces standard sine waves that rise and fall smoothly in bell-shaped curves, just like real waves. The Triangle option, shown in the first and third examples of Figure 9-37, creates zigzags that rise and fall in straight lines, like the edge of a piece of fabric cut with pinking shears. The Square option, illustrated in the second and last examples of Figure 9-37, has nothing to do with waves at all, but rather organizes an image into a series of rectangular groupings, reminiscent of Cubism. You might think of this option as an extension of the Mosaic filter. All examples in Figure 9-37 utilize a Number of Generators setting of 1.

Number of Generators: 1

Number of Generators: 5

Number of Generators: 10

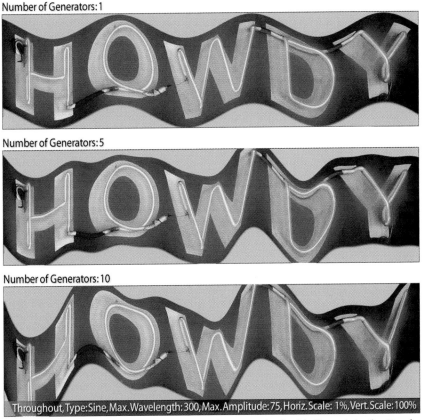

Throughout, Type: Sine, Max. Wavelength: 300, Max. Amplitude: 75, Horiz. Scale: 1%, Vert. Scale: 100%

Figure 9-35: The only difference between the examples in this figure is in the Number of Generators. Adding generators increases random action by creating more intersecting waveforms.

✦ **Randomize:** The Wave filter is random by nature. If you don't like the effect you see in the preview box, click the Randomize button to stir things up a bit. You can keep clicking the button until you get an effect you like.

✦ **Undefined Areas:** The Wave filter distorts a selection to the extent that gaps may appear around the edges. You can fill those gaps either by repeating pixels along the edge of the selection, as in the figures, or by wrapping pixels from the left side of the selection onto the right side and pixels from the top edge of the selection onto the bottom.

Max. Wavelength: 120, Max. Amplitude: 35

Max. Wavelength: 350, Max. Amplitude: 35

Max. Wavelength: 120, Max. Amplitude: 115

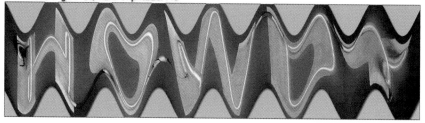

Max. Wavelength: 350, Max. Amplitude: 115

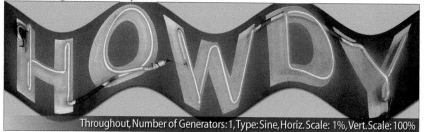

Throughout, Number of Generators: 1, Type: Sine, Horiz. Scale: 1%, Vert. Scale: 100%

Figure 9-36: With all other parameters set according to the specifications at the bottom of the figure, increasing Wavelength creates a larger horizontal distance between the peaks of waves. Increasing Amplitude creates a higher wave peak.

Type: Triangle, Max. Wavelength: 120, Max. Amplitude: 35

Type: Square, Max. Wavelength: 120, Max. Amplitude: 35

Type: Triangle, Max. Wavelength: 20, Max. Amplitude: 70

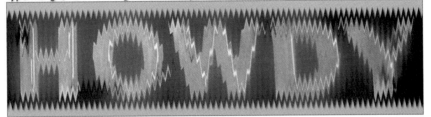

Type: Square, Max. Wavelength: 20, Max. Amplitude: 70

Throughout, Number of Generators: 1, Horiz. Scale: 1%, Vert. Scale: 100%

Figure 9-37: The effects of the unsmooth Triangle and Square types, using relatively high Wavelength and low Amplitude values (top two examples) versus relatively low Wavelength and high Amplitude values (bottom two examples).

Distorting an image along a curve

The Distort command (Edit ➪ Transform ➪ Distort), which isn't discussed elsewhere in this book, creates four corner handles around an image. You drag each corner handle to distort the selected image in that direction. Unfortunately, you can't add other points around the edges to create additional distortions, which can be frustrating if you're trying to achieve a specific effect. If you can't achieve a certain kind of distortion using Edit ➪ Free Transform, the Shear filter may be your answer.

Shear distorts an image or selection along a path. When you choose Filter ➪ Distort ➪ Shear, you get the dialog box shown in Figure 9-38. Initially, a single line that has two points at either end appears in the grid at the top of the box. When you drag the points, you slant the image in the preview. This, plus the fact that the filter is named Shear — Adobe's strange term for skewing (it appears in Illustrator as well) — leads many users to dismiss the filter as nothing more than a slanting tool. But in truth, it's more versatile than that.

You can add points to the grid line simply by clicking on it. A point springs up every time you click an empty space in the line. Drag the point to change the curvature of the line and distort the image along the new curve. To delete a point, drag it off the left or right side of the grid. To delete all added points and return the line to its original vertical orientation, click the Defaults button.

The Undefined Areas options work just as they do in the Wave dialog box (described in the preceding section). You can either fill the gaps on one side of the image with pixels shoved off the opposite side by selecting Wrap Around or repeat pixels along the edge of the selection by selecting Repeat Edge Pixels.

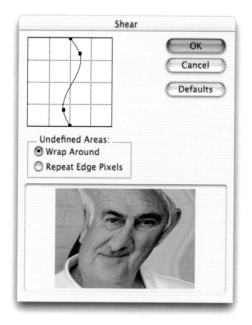

Figure 9-38: Click inside the grid line in the upper-left corner of the Shear dialog box to add points to the line. Drag these points to distort the image along the curve.

Although Shear was obviously conceived to create horizontal distortions, you may find you need to create a vertically-based distortion instead. If you can't change the filter, why not change the image? As shown in Figure 9-39, simply rotating the image on its side allowed me to give the desired slant to my subject's face.

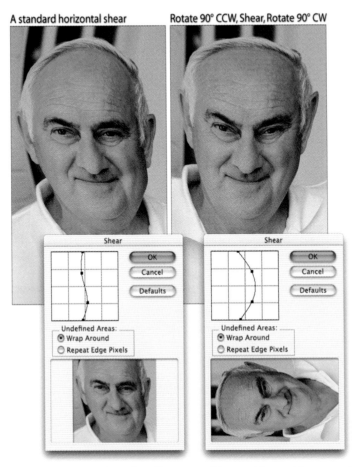

Figure 9-39: Not liking the effect I was able to achieve with a normal application of Shear (left), I chose Image ➪ Rotate Canvas ➪ 90° CCW, which allowed me to vertically distort my image with the Shear filter (right). Finally, I chose Image ➪ Rotate Canvas ➪ 90° CW to restore the image to its original upright position.

Changing to polar coordinates

The Polar Coordinates filter is another one of those gems that a lot of folks shy away from because it doesn't make much sense at first glance. When you choose Filter ➪ Distort ➪ Polar Coordinates, Photoshop presents a dialog box with two radio buttons, as shown in Figure 9-40. You can either map an image from rectangular to polar coordinates or from polar to rectangular coordinates.

All right, time for some global theory. The first image in Figure 9-41 shows a stretched detail of a world map. This map falls under the heading of a *Mercator projection*, meaning that Greenland is all stretched out of proportion, looking as big as the United States and Mexico combined.

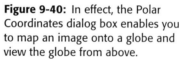

Figure 9-40: In effect, the Polar Coordinates dialog box enables you to map an image onto a globe and view the globe from above.

The reason for this has to do with the way different mapping systems handle longitude and latitude lines. On a spherical globe, lines of latitude converge at the poles. On a Mercator map, they run absolutely parallel. Because the Mercator map exaggerates the distance between longitude lines as you progress away from the equator, it likewise exaggerates the distance between lines of latitude. The result is a map that becomes enormous at each of the poles.

When you convert the map to polar coordinates (by selecting the Rectangular to Polar radio button in the Polar Coordinates dialog box), you look down on it from the extreme North or South Pole. This means that the entire length of the top edge of the Mercator map becomes a single dot in the exact center of the polar projection. The length of the bottom edge of the map wraps around the entire perimeter of the circle. The second example in Figure 9-41 shows the result. For this to be completely realistic, I would have to start with a map of just the top half of the globe, with the equator running along the bottom edge, but you get the idea. And as you can see, the Rectangular to Polar option can also wrap text around a circle. (Photoshop CS's new text on a path feature combined with the ellipse tool is probably a better way to get circular text, if that's what you're looking for. While I decided not to cover the black and white world of text in a colorful book like this one, I explain how to create text in the standard edition of the *Photoshop CS Bible*.)

If you select the Polar to Rectangular option, the Polar Coordinates filter produces the opposite effect. Imagine for a moment that the image shown in the upper-left corner of Figure 9-42 is a fan spread out into a full circle. Now imagine closing the fan, breaking the hinge at the top, and spreading out the rectangular fabric like an accordion. The center of the fan unfolds to form the top edge of the fabric, and what was once the perimeter of the circle is now the bottom edge of the fabric. This can be especially useful for examining the composition of a spiraling or concentric effect, as demonstrated in the upper-right image in Figure 9-42.

Alternatively, if you're feeling ornery, try it out on a guy's face. As the second row of images in Figure 9-42 illustrates, the Polar to Rectangular setting can melt a person's eyes down his cheeks and give you a once-in-a-lifetime opportunity to look up his nose. It's not attractive, but isn't the world filled with enough good-looking people?

Figure 9-41: The world expressed in rectangular (top) and polar (bottom) coordinates. The decorative ornament atop the first image becomes a happy inhabitant of the North Pole in the second.

But I guess my favorite use for this setting is to expand synthetic effects. The last example in Figure 9-42 shows the Polar to Rectangular option applied to the final twirl drops image from Figure 9-26. As a special bonus, notice that the right side of each of the filtered images matches up perfectly with its left side. In the rainbow pool, for example, that subtle cyan splash flows from the right edge of the image into the left edge. This means the image will transition seamlessly when repeated horizontally, perfect for building patterns.

From 10 pinches & 7 twirls …   we get a wavy pattern.

 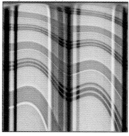

Figure 9-42: A pair of circular images (left) converted from polar to rectangular coordinates (right). The final example shows the result of applying the Polar to Rectangular option to the twirl-drops image from Figure 9-26.

A crazy guy in a circle …   turns into a manatee!

Where once there were twirl drops …

there is now a rainbow pool.

The Polar Coordinates filter is a great way to edit gradations. After drawing a linear gradation with the gradient tool, try applying Filter ➪ Distort ➪ Polar Coordinates with the Polar to Rectangular option selected. (Rectangular to Polar just turns it into a radial gradation, sometimes with undesirable results.) You get a redrawn gradation with highlights at the bottom of the selection. Press Ctrl+F (⌘-F on the Mac) to reapply the filter to achieve another effect. You can keep repeating this technique until jagged edges start to appear. Then press Ctrl+Z (⌘-Z) to return to the last smooth effect.

Distorting with the Liquify command

The final essential distortion function isn't located under the Filter ➪ Distort submenu. In fact, in many respects, it's not a filter at all. The Liquify command is more of a separate distortion utility that just happens to run inside Photoshop. It enables you to perform any number of distortions — you can warp, shift, twirl, expand, contract, and even copy pixels. It grants you multiple undos and redos before you apply the final effect. And unlike other distortion filters, which apply a uniform effect across a layer or selection, Liquify lets you modify pixels by pushing them around with a brush.

The result is a distortion filter that doubles as a powerful retouching tool. Consider the images in Figure 9-43. Raphael's original oil painting on the left shows a lad who, in his day, was no doubt regarded as the perfect gentleman. But I worry that if he were to attempt to transport from his century to ours, his ways would be misunderstood. It might be his hair style, all curly on the sides but slicked down on top. Or it could be his languid expression, as if his delicate features had become lost in a torpid sea of big, round face. Then there's his raised pinky, which speaks perhaps too loudly of a young man who very much enjoys the feel of a dainty teacup in his hand. But whatever the culprit, I sense that this boy's presence would not receive warm applause and hearty handshakes were he to step onto a modern metropolitan thoroughfare or playground. In fact, there's the very real possibility that today's spirited teens would greet him with a vigorous beating and help themselves to his lunch money.

But thanks to the Liquify command, I was able to transform Raphael's masterwork into the swaggering, first-person-shooter playing, ill-informed but fiercely opinionated high school graduate that we see on the right. Oh sure, he still wears his hair long and likes to dress like his grandmother, but like any good Catholic boy, he's got the chutzpah to pull it off. There's still a bit of stiffness in that pinky, but you know he's only doing that because it seems to irritate people.

English teachers and ex-spelling bee champions may notice my habitually strange spelling of the word "liquefy" throughout this and the following pages. Rather than referring to the "Liquefy command," which would not match your screen, or the condescending "Liquify (sic) command," which you would get sic of quickly, I merely bend like the reed and adopt Adobe's spelling. Photoshop's engineers assure me that "liquify" is an acceptable alternative spelling, and they seem to be technically right. But here's a head-scratcher: If you use the type tool to enter the word "liquify" and then choose Edit ➪ Check Spelling, Photoshop will suggest *liquefy*, *liquefied*, *liquefier*, *liquefies*, and *liquefying*, but it always wants to replace that second I with an E. In fact, even after I pointed this out in the last edition of this book, subjecting Adobe to public humiliation and scorn for their glaring inconsistency, they still haven't bothered to add "liquify" to Photoshop's dictionary. I mean, how hard would that be? Don't they read my books to find out how to use their software? Hello? Is this thing on?

Figure 9-43: Using only the Liquify command, I was able to transform Raphael's 16th-century vision of St. Sebastian from a languid, matronly aristocrat (left) into a self-assured senior who managed to snag the part of Judas in his high school's production of *Jesus Christ Superstar* (right).

Liquify basics

To enter the world of Liquify (sic) — oops, wasn't going to do that — choose the Liquify command from the Filter menu or press the keyboard shortcut Ctrl+Shift+X (⌘-Shift-X on the Mac). Photoshop displays the immense Liquify image window shown in Figure 9-44, breathtaking in its wealth of tools and options.

The miniature toolbox on the left side of the window contains tools for distorting your image. You drag or click with the tools as explained in the next section. (You can even select tools from the keyboard, as indicated by keys in parentheses.) But before you begin, here are a few basic facts:

✦ All tools respond to the Brush Size setting on the right side of the window. Press the right and left bracket keys, [and], to raise and lower the brush size from the keyboard by 2 pixels. This is a bit of a departure from Photoshop's standard painting tools, where pressing [or] routinely changes the brush size by 10 pixels or more. To change the brush size inside the Liquify window more rapidly, press and hold [or]. Or press Shift with a bracket key to change the brush size by 20 pixels. Throughout, your cursor reflects the approximate brush size.

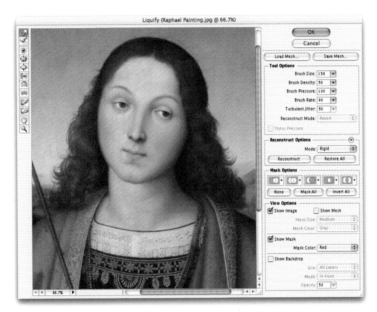

Liquify (Raphael Painting.jpg @ 66.7%)

Figure 9-44: Choose Filter ➪ Liquify to shove pixels around in your image by dragging them with a brush.

✦ The Brush Density setting determines how much feathering the edges of your cursor will have while you are creating your distortions. A smaller Brush Density setting means that effects will be more localized to the center of the brush.

✦ The Brush Pressure option controls the impact of the tools; higher values produce more pronounced effects. If you work with a pressure-sensitive tablet, select the Stylus Pressure check box to make Photoshop adjust the tool pressure based on the amount of pressure you put on the pen stylus.

✦ Available when you use the reconstruct, twirl clockwise, pucker, bloat, and turbulence tools, the Brush Rate option controls the strength of these tools when you click on a particular area but keep the cursor still. The higher the Brush Rate setting, the faster distortions will apply to the area.

You can use the standard shortcuts Ctrl+plus to zoom in and Ctrl+minus to zoom out (⌘-plus and minus on the Mac). Use the scroll bars to reposition the image, or press the spacebar to get the hand tool and drag the image inside the window. The Liquify window also provides zoom (Z) and hand (H) tools for your navigation pleasure.

✦ If you select a portion of your image prior to choosing Filter ➪ Liquify, any deselected areas are considered *frozen*, which just means that they're unaffected by the distortion tools. You can freeze and then *thaw* — make available for editing — portions of the image as explained in the upcoming section, "Freezing and thawing pixels." You can even create partially frozen or thawed areas, which further limits the impact of the distortion tools. Photoshop CS has introduced a number of new ways to control which pixels are frozen and which are thawed. In addition to a selection, you can freeze or unthaw pixels based on a combination of the transparency information in the image and even through a layer mask. Hey, did you ever notice that "thaw" and "unthaw" have the same meaning? Sort of like "flammable" and "inflammable." Things like that interest me. Sometimes I feel very lonely.

✦ By default, frozen regions are covered with a red translucent coating, just like masked areas in the quick mask mode. You can change the appearance of the overlay by selecting a new color from the Mask Color pop-up menu in the View Options section of the Liquify window. If you don't want to see the coating at all, turn off the Show Mask check box.

✦ If your image contains layers, then you will see only the current layer against a transparent checkerboard background when you enter the Liquify window. To see other layers, turn on the Show Backdrop check box in the bottom-right corner of the window. You can either view all layers, or select a specific layer from the nearby pop-up menu. The Opacity option controls how well you can see the other layers.

✦ Use the new Mode pop-up menu in the Show Backdrop settings to specify exactly how the layer you're currently distorting interacts with the other layers in the image. Regardless of what you see, Photoshop lets you edit only the active layer.

✦ Select the Show Mesh check box to display gridlines on top of the image. You can use the gridlines as a guide if you want to apply very precise distortions. You can even apply your distortions while viewing only the grid by deselecting the Show Image check box. Set the grid size and color by selecting options from the Mesh Size and Mesh Color pop-up menus.

✦ You can save a distortion for later use by clicking the Save Mesh button. To use the mesh on both the Mac and PC, the file name needs to end with the extension *.msh*. Click Load Mesh to load a distortion stored on disk. Note that Photoshop is smart enough to scale the mesh to fit the current image, so a mesh specifically designed for one image may turn out to be useful for another.

As with other Save buttons found throughout Photoshop's myriad dialog boxes, the Save Mesh button may strike you as the kind of nifty option that may prove useful every once in a while. But I strongly urge you to use it *every time you use the Liquify command.* Did you get that? Last thing you should do, right before you click the OK button, is click Save Mesh. Why? Because Photoshop does not automatically keep track of your previous Liquify settings. So if you spend 15 minutes or so working inside the Liquify window, click OK, and then decide that the distortion doesn't work exactly as well as you had hoped, you're left with two unpleasant options: Choose Liquify and try to tweak the image further, which can result in incremental damage to the detail, or undo the previous operation and start over again. But if you saved the mesh, then you always have that last distortion to come back to. And the beauty is, a mesh is purely mathematical until it's applied. So you can use one mesh as a jumping-off point for another without doing incremental damage. Pixels only get involved after you click OK. So don't forget, save your mesh, save your mesh, save your mesh.

Oh, and by the way, save your mesh.

The Liquify tools

Okay, so much for the basics. I can see that you're itching to start mucking around in your pixels. So here's how the distortion tools along the left side of the Liquify window work:

Forward warp (W): Drag to shove the pixels under your cursor around the image. At first, it may feel a lot like the smudge tool. But instead of smearing pixels, you're incrementally moving points in the mesh that distorts the image. The first example in Figure 9-45 shows a few large-scale changes made with a large brush and the default Pressure value. That's a lot of fun, of course, but it's only practical if you're trying to produce a caricature of Carrot Top, which, let's face it, would be redundant. And yet, when used properly, the forward warp tool is the Liquify command's most practical tool. To create the second image, I used the forward warp tool set to a smaller brush size. But the biggest difference was in the length of my strokes. Instead of dragging, say, 10 to 20 pixels at a time, I dragged one or two pixels. As you can see, making lots of little adjustments — in my case, somewhere in the neighborhood of 30 strokes — produces the best results.

Forward warp tool, Size: 100, Pressure: 50   same, Size: 50, Pressure: 50, short strokes

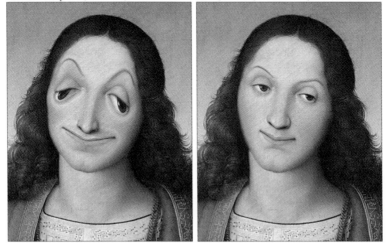

Figure 9-45: Making big strokes with the forward warp tool produces wacky results (left); short, careful drags give you more control (right). But you have to be patient. It took six strokes to make the big changes on left and about 30 to make the subtle changes on right — broadening the nose, expanding the lips, raising the chin, and lifting the eyelids and brows.

 Reconstruct (R): Rather than a distortion tool, the reconstruct tool is more of a reversion tool, in that it undoes the twisting and turning that the other Liquify tools inflict on your image. If you've gone on a destructive binge with the other tools, you can use the reconstruct tool to selectively push and pull pixels back into place. Since you're always referencing the original pixels of the image until you click OK and close the Liquify window, you maintain the ability to restore the image to its original state without any loss of quality. You specify the type of reconstruction you want to perform by choosing an option from the Reconstruct Mode pop-up menu in the Tool Options area. I'll discuss these options in more detail in the upcoming section "Reconstructing and reverting."

Twirl clockwise (C): Click or drag to spin pixels under your cursor in a clockwise direction. Unless you've got one of those Goofy watches that goes backward, which would be more like "clock-unwise." Okay, I'll stop now.

 This tool's companion, the twirl counterclockwise tool, no longer owns a slot in the Liquify toolbox. (Now it knows how the airbrush tool felt in Photoshop 7.) But you can still access the twirl counterclockwise tool by pressing the Alt key (Option key on the Mac) when you use the twirl clockwise tool. You can press and release Alt in mid-drag to switch the twirl direction on the fly. Figure 9-46 shows how I curled the lad's hair using the twirl clockwise tool.

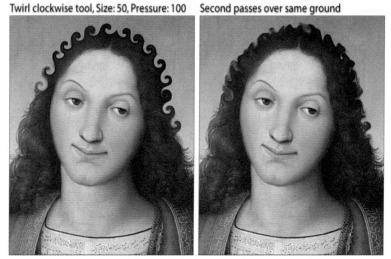

Twirl clockwise tool, Size: 50, Pressure: 100   Second passes over same ground

Figure 9-46: Here I used the twirl clockwise tool to give St. Sebastian a *faab*-ulous new hairstyle. I started by clicking and holding in 15 locations to rough in the basic curls (left). Then I clicked and dragged between those curls to fill in the effect (right).

Pucker (S): With that new keyboard shortcut (it used to be P), why not just rename this the *sucker* tool? Drag with this tool to suck pixels toward the center of the brush cursor. The effect is similar to applying the Pinch filter with a positive Amount value. If you mouse down instead of dragging, Photoshop steadily increases the extent of the distortion until you release the mouse button.

Bloat (B): When you drag or mouse down with this tool, pixels underneath the cursor move outward, like a stomach after too many trips to the buffet line. As is the case with the pucker tool, the longer you hold down the mouse button, the stronger the effect you get.

Press the Alt key (or Option on the Mac) to toggle between the pucker and bloat functions on the fly.

The pucker and bloat tools rock. In fact, I use them only slightly less frequently than the forward warp tool. They are particularly valuable for removing weight or adding bulk. For example, in the first image in Figure 9-47, I used the pucker tool exclusively to slim details in the image. I clicked and dragged around the jaw line. I also clicked and held on the nose and mouth and around the chin. The result is an increasingly feminine version of the one-time man. In the second image, I completed the operation by bloating the eyes, eyelids, and lips. Forget all that stuff about chromosomes; the difference between men and women comes down to Pucker and Bloat.

Push left tool (O): The O stands for "Oh darn it, they gave this tool a weird new name, and a perplexing new keyboard shortcut to boot." Anyway, as you drag with this tool, pixels underneath the cursor move in a direction perpendicular to your drag. For example, if you drag up, pixels get pushed to the left (hence the name). Drag straight down, and pixels move to the right. It sort of follows, then, that dragging in a clockwise circle around an object in your image makes it get bigger, and dragging counterclockwise makes it smaller. To reverse the direction of the pixels, press the Alt key (Option on the Mac).

Pucker tool, Size: 100, Pressure: 20   Press Alt (Option on Mac) to bloat eyes, lips

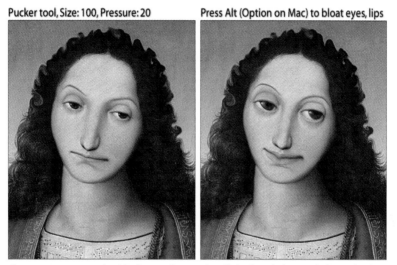

Figure 9-47: Armed with the pucker tool, I clicked and dragged along the jaw, chin, nose, and mouth (left) to reduce the masculine elements of what had become a fairly meaty guy. Then I pressed Alt (Option on the Mac) and moused down on the eyes, eyelids, and lips to fill out his feminine attributes.

At first, the push left tool may seem unwieldy, resulting in dramatic and sometimes unpredictable movements. But you can control it using two techniques. First, reduce the Brush Pressure value to 25 or lower. Figure 9-48 illustrates the difference between drags performed using Pressure settings of 50 and 20. Second, try using it in a straight line by clicking at one point and Shift-clicking at another, as you might with Photoshop's painting and editing tools. The result is a neat line, great for reducing flab along straight elements, such as arms and legs.

Mirror (M): In Photoshop 7, this was called the reflection tool, though it still had the keyboard shortcut of M. And now Adobe has renamed it the *mirror* tool, which goes with the shortcut. Maybe there's hope for a sucker tool after all. Dragging with this tool does create a reflection, albeit one you might see in a funhouse mirror. As you drag, Photoshop copies pixels from the area perpendicular to the direction you move the cursor. So if you drag up, you clone pixels to the right of the cursor into the area underneath the cursor; drag down to clone pixels from left to right, as shown in Figure 9-49. Press the Alt key (Option on the Mac) to reflect from another direction on the fly.

Turbulence (T): The turbulence tool is a variation on the forward warp tool that distorts pixels in random directions as you drag. When you select this tool, Photoshop grants you access to a fifth Tool Options value labeled Turbulent Jitter. If the Brush Size value controls how many pixels are affected at a time and Brush Pressure controls the strength of the stroke, then Turbulent Jitter specifies just how much random variation is permitted. The minimum value of 1 causes the turbulence tool to behave much like the forward warp tool; a maximum value of 100 mixes pixels in all directions.

Push left tool, Size: 400, Pressure: 50   same, Pressure: 20

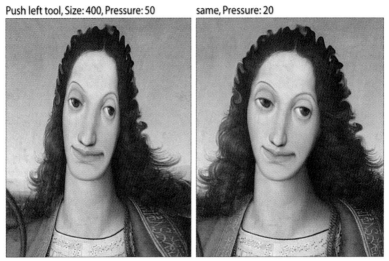

Figure 9-48: Here I dragged down on the left side of the face and up on the right to slim the face with the push left tool. The first image used a Brush Pressure value of 50, which produces extreme results. For the second image, I reperformed the edits using a Pressure value of 20. I would still characterize the effect as extreme, but it's better.

Mirror tool, Brush Size: 400, drag up on the left, down on the right

Figure 9-49: Using the mirror tool, I dragged up on the left side of the woman and down on her right side. Pixels are reflected in a clockwise direction.

Figure 9-50 illustrates a few examples. For purposes of demonstration, all four images were created using a very large Brush Size, 400, and the maximum Pressure value, 100. For each image in the top row, I held the brush in place for 15 seconds. The random variations built up from one moment to the next. Not surprisingly, a Turbulent Jitter value of 30 produced a more dramatic effect than one of 10. But things become a bit more complicated when you drag with the tool. For each image in the bottom row, I created two brushstrokes from the bottom of the image to the top, once on the right side of the face and again on the left. This time, the higher Turbulent Jitter value produces more random fluctuation, but both images result in roughly equivalent amounts of distortion, as dictated by the fixed Size and Pressure values.

Turbulence tool, Jitter: 10 …

Jitter: 30, hold 15 seconds on face

same, Jitter: 10 …

Jitter: 30, drag up both sides of face

Figure 9-50: Four variations created using the turbulence tool, twice holding the mouse in place (top row) and twice dragging with the tool on the left and right sides of the face (bottom row). Throughout, the Size and Pressure were set to 400 and 100, respectively.

After all that, what good is the tool? When combined with low Turbulent Jitter values, I find it helpful for introducing small tremors or, if you prefer, turbulence into an image. At higher values, 30 and up, things go haywire very quickly.

After you drag with any of these tools, you can undo the effect by pressing Ctrl+Z (⌘-Z on the Mac). You also have the option of multiple undos. Press Ctrl+Alt+Z (⌘-Option-Z on the Mac) to backstep through your operations. Press Ctrl+Shift+Z (⌘-Shift-Z) to redo undone distortions. To learn how to go back in time nonsequentially and explore additional reversion options, read the section "Reconstructing and reverting."

Freezing and thawing pixels

As I mentioned a few paragraphs ago, if you make a selection in your image, Photoshop automatically freezes unselected pixels when you enter the Liquify dialog box. This means that any distortions you apply don't affect them. In previous versions of Photoshop, you couldn't thaw these pixels from inside the Liquify window. But Photoshop CS lets us thaw pixels, freeze new ones, and determine frozen pixels based on transparency and layer masks in ways never before possible.

To freeze a portion of your image from the Liquify window, you have two options:

 Freeze mask (F): Press F to select the freeze mask tool and then drag over areas that you want to protect. You can adjust the brush size, density, and pressure as you can when working with the distortion tools. But in this case, the Brush Pressure setting determines how deeply frozen the pixels become. At anything less than 100 percent, the pixels become partially distorted when you drag over them with a distortion tool. If you set the pressure to 50 percent, the distortion is applied with half the pressure used in unfrozen areas. Likewise, the Brush Density setting controls how deeply pixels become frozen toward the outside of the brush. To freeze the entire image, click the Mask All button in the Mask Options settings.

 Thaw mask (D): D is for *defrost*, I guess. To thaw areas that were once frozen, again making them slaves to the distortion tools, paint over them with the thaw mask tool. The tool options affect this tool just as they do the freeze mask tool. To thaw the entire image, click the None button in the Mask Options settings.

Just as you can inverse a selection outline or invert a mask in the quick mask mode, you can click the Invert All button to quickly freeze any unfrozen pixels and thaw any frozen ones.

Among the more complex additions to the Liquify dialog box in Photoshop CS are the Mask Options settings, located below the Reconstruct Options. Above the None, Mask All, and Invert All buttons I just mentioned, you're presented with five different buttons, each giving you a different option for interacting with the current mask. And each of those buttons has three options, when relevant; you can use information from the layer's current selection, transparency, or layer mask.

+ **Replace selection** replaces the current mask, completely wiping out any freezing or thawing you've done, and replacing it with a mask drawn from the layer's current selection, transparency, or layer mask.

+ **Add to selection** keeps all thawed areas in the current mask, and also thaws other areas according to the layer's current selection, transparency, or layer mask.

+ **Subtract from selection** keeps all frozen areas in the current mask, and also freezes other areas according to the layer's current selection, transparency, or layer mask.

✦ **Intersect with selection** only allows an area to stay thawed if it is thawed both in the current mask *and* according to the layer's current selection, transparency, or layer mask.

✦ **Invert selection** takes the current mask and inverts it, but only within the thawed areas according to the layer's current selection, transparency, or layer mask.

If these many and varied options strike you as, um, overkill, you're probably right. I mean, I can see how basing a mask on a layer's selection, transparency, or layer mask might be helpful *initially*, but it's hard to imagine freezing and thawing for several minutes, and then suddenly declaring "Now, I want to intersect this mask with the layer's transparency!" But these are new features, and once I've used them enough and uncovered the inherent mysteries, I'll probably be raving about them in the next edition of this book. Stay tuned.

Reconstructing and reverting

In the Reconstruct Options section of the Liquify window, you see a Mode pop-up menu plus two buttons, Reconstruct and Restore All. You can use these options not only to revert an image to the way it looked before you applied a distortion, but also to redo a distortion so that it affects the image differently.

The following list outlines reversion possibilities:

✦ **Undo:** The Liquify window doesn't give you a History palette, but Ctrl+Alt+Z and Ctrl+Shift+Z still let you undo and redo sequences of operations. (That's ⌘-Option-Z and ⌘-Shift-Z on the Mac.)

✦ **Reset:** To return everything back to the way it was the very first time you opened the Liquify window, Alt-click (Win) or Option-click (Mac) the Cancel button, which changes to Reset. Not only do you restore your original image, you restore the Liquify window's default settings.

Believe it or not, Reset and other reversion techniques are undoable. I know, it's too cool. Just press Ctrl+Z (⌘-Z on the Mac) to get your edits back.

✦ **Restore All:** To revert the image without resetting all values to their defaults, click the Restore All button. This affects frozen and thawed areas alike.

Liquify also offers a handful of reconstruction techniques that are more controlled and more complex than the reversion options. When you select the reconstruct tool, these options become available to use with that tool in the Tool Options. Just paint where you want to reconstruct, using the other Tool Options to determine the severity of your reconstruction.

The reconstruction options are also available, quite naturally, in the Reconstruct Options section. Click Reconstruct to apply a reconstruction in the currently selected Mode. And if you want another option for applying these options, click the little arrow in the upper-right corner of the Reconstruct Options section. Here, you can choose one of the Mode options, which will take you to another dialog box. Drag the slider or type in a number to determine the amount of reconstructing you want to do in that chosen mode; the preview window will update as you drag. Once you like what you see, click OK and the reconstruction will be applied.

All the reconstruction modes calculate the change to the image based on the warp mesh (grid). To get a better feel for how each mode works, deselect the Show Image check box, turn on Show Mesh and then apply a simple distortion across a portion of the grid. Freeze part of the distorted region and then keep an eye on the grid lines at the intersections between frozen and unfrozen regions as you try out each of the modes. The modes, available in the reconstruct tool's Reconstruct Mode options and in the Mode menu of the Reconstruct Options, are:

✦ **Revert:** The Revert mode restores unfrozen portions of the image to their original appearance, without regard to the borders between the frozen and unfrozen areas. Compare this to the Restore All button, which restores frozen and unfrozen areas alike.

✦ **Rigid:** This mode extends the distortion only as needed to maintain right angles in the mesh where frozen and unfrozen areas meet. The result is unfrozen areas that look very much like they did originally but smoothly blend into the frozen areas.

✦ **Stiff:** Stiff interpolates the distortion so that the effect tapers away as you move farther from the boundary between the frozen and unfrozen areas.

✦ **Smooth, Loose:** These two modes extend the distortion applied to the frozen areas into the unfrozen areas. The Smooth setting tries to create smooth transitions between frozen and unfrozen areas. Loose shares more of the distortion from the frozen area with the unfrozen area. You'll achieve the most dramatic results when frozen and unfrozen areas have been distorted differently.

✦ **Displace, Amplitwist,** and **Affine:** The last three modes are only available with the reconstruct tool in the Reconstruct Mode menu. Using these modes, you can apply one or more distortions that are in force at a specific reference point in the image. Click to set the reference point and then drag through unfrozen areas to distort them. Use the Displace mode to move pixels to match the displacement of the reference point; select Amplitwist to match the displacement, rotation, and scaling at the reference point; and choose Affine to match all distortions at the reference point.

Although Liquify certainly gives you plenty of ways to reconstruct distortions, predicting the outcome of your drags with the reconstruct tool can be nearly impossible. So be prepared to experiment. And if you don't get the results you want, remember, you can undo a reconstruction just as easily as a distortion.

Lighting an Image

Photoshop ventures into 3D drawing territory with the Lighting Effects filter. This very complex function enables you to shine lights on an image, color the lights, position them, focus them, specify the reflectivity of the surface, and even light an image based on a texture map. The one downside is that it's applicable exclusively to RGB images. But of course, if you want to apply it to a grayscale or CMYK image, you can convert the image to RGB, apply Lighting Effects, and then convert back to the original color space.

When you choose Filter ➪ Render ➪ Lighting Effects, Photoshop displays a complex dialog box, pictured in Figure 9-51. (Okay, after Liquify, it doesn't seem *that* complex, does it?) The dialog box is split into two parts: the left half, in which you actually position light with respect to a thumbnail of the selection or active layer, and the right half, which contains a billion or so intimidating but useful options.

The easiest way to apply the filter is to choose one of the predefined lighting effects from the Style pop-up menu that heads up the right half of the dialog box, see how it looks in the preview area, and — if you like it — press Enter or Return to apply the effect.

But if you want to create your own effects, you have to work a little harder. Here are the basic steps involved in creating a custom effect.

Preview area (stage)   Hot spot (source)   Color swatches

Footprint   Focus point

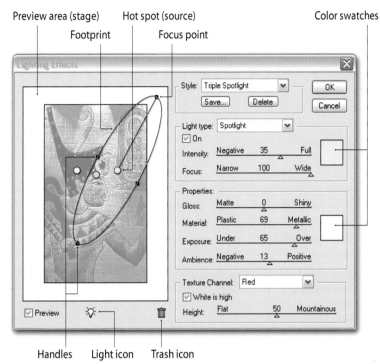

Handles   Light icon   Trash icon

Figure 9-51: The Lighting Effects dialog box lets you light an image as if it were hanging in a gallery, lying on a floor, or perhaps resting too near a hot flame.

STEPS: Creating a Custom Lighting Effect

1. **Drag from the light icon at the bottom of the dialog box into the preview area to create a new light source.** I call this area the *stage* because the image behaves as if it's painted on the floor of a stage and the lights are hanging above it.

2. **Select the kind of light you want from the Light Type pop-up menu.** It's just below the Style pop-up menu. You can select from Directional, Omni, and Spotlight:

   • Directional works like the sun, producing a generalized, unfocused light that hits a target from an angle. Because the light source is distant, the image is lit more or less evenly throughout.

   • Omni is a bare light bulb hanging in the middle of the room, shining in all directions from a center point.

   • Spotlight is a focused beam that is brightest at the source and tapers off gradually.

   Each of the three Light Type options is illustrated in Figure 9-52 as it relates to its focus point, hot spot, and footprint (discussed in the following steps).

3. **Specify the color of the light by clicking the top color swatch.** You can also muck about with the Intensity slider bar to control the brightness of the light. If Spotlight is selected, the Focus slider becomes available. Drag the slider toward Narrow to create a bright laser of light; drag toward Wide to diffuse the light and spread it over a larger area.

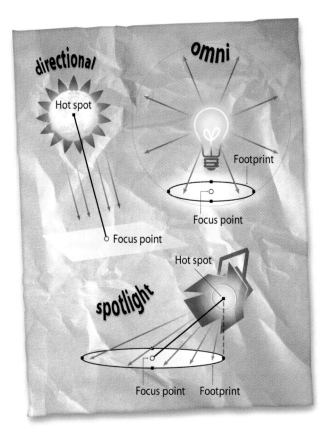

Figure 9-52: The Directional option produces a broad, distant light source (top left); Omni casts light in all directions (top right); and Spotlight shines a focused beam (bottom).

4. **Move the light source by dragging the focus point.** If you selected a color for your light, the *focus point* appears as a colored circle in the stage. When Directional or Spotlight is selected, the focus point represents the spot at which the light is pointing. When Omni is active, the focus point is the actual bulb. Please, don't burn yourself.

5. **If Directional or Spotlight is active, you can change the angle of the light by dragging the hot spot.** The *hot spot* represents the light source, and often marks the location that will receive the most light. When you use a Directional light, the hot spot appears as a black square at the end of a line joined to the focus point. The same holds true when you edit a Spotlight; however, a spotlight also includes an elliptical footprint (explained in Step 6) decorated with four handles. The hot spot is the handle that's joined to the focus point by a line.

To make the light brighter, drag the hot spot closer to the focus point. Dragging the hot spot away from the focus point dims the light by increasing the distance that it has to travel. It's like pointing a flashlight from the living room into the garage — the light grows dimmer as the source moves farther away.

6. **With Omni or Spotlight in force, you can edit the elliptical footprint of the light.** When Omni is in force, a circle surrounds the focus point. When editing a Spotlight, you see an ellipse. Either way, this shape represents the *footprint* of the light, which is the plane at which the light intersects the image. In other words, it's the approximate area of the image affected by the light. (It's the maximum area affected by a Spotlight. The Omni setting produces light in all directions. Therefore, the footprint represents the area of direct light; indirect light falls outside the footprint.)

   You can change the size of the light by dragging the handles around the footprint. Enlarging the shape is like raising the light source. When the footprint is small, the light is close to the image so it's concentrated and very bright. When the footprint is large, the light is high above the image, so it's more generalized.

   When editing the footprint of a Spotlight, Shift-drag a handle to adjust the width or height of the ellipse without affecting the angle. To change the angle without affecting the size, Ctrl-drag (or ⌘-drag) a handle.

7. **Introduce more lights as you see fit.**

   Duplicate a light in the stage by Alt-dragging (or Option-dragging) its focus point. To delete the active light, drag the focus point onto the trash can icon below the preview area.

8. **Change the Properties and Texture Channel options as you see fit.** I explain these in detail after the steps.

9. **If you want to save your settings for future use, click the Save button.** Photoshop invites you to name the setup, which then appears as an option in the Style pop-up menu. If you want to get rid of one of the presets, select it from the pop-up menu and click the Delete button.

10. **Press Enter or Return to apply your settings to the image.**

That's almost everything. The only parts I left out are the Properties and Texture Channel options. The Properties slider bars control how light reflects off the surface of your image:

✦ **Gloss:** Is the surface dull or shiny? Drag the slider toward Matte to make the surface flat and nonreflective, like dull enamel paint. Drag the slider toward Shiny to make it glossy, as if you had slapped on a coat of lacquer.

✦ **Material:** This option determines the color of the light that reflects off the image. According to the logic employed by this option, Plastic reflects back the color of the light; Metallic reflects the color of the object itself. If only I had a bright, shiny plastic thing and a bright, shiny metal thing, I could check to see whether this logic holds true in real life (like maybe that matters).

✦ **Exposure:** I'd like this option better if you could vary it between Sun Block 65 and Melanoma. Unfortunately, the more prosaic titles are Under and Over — exposed, that is. This option controls the brightness of all lights like a big dimmer switch. You can control a single selected light using the Intensity slider, but the Exposure slider offers the added control of changing all lights in the stage (preview) area and the ambient light (described next) together.

✦ **Ambience:** The last slider enables you to add *ambient light*, which is a general, diffused light that hits all surfaces evenly. First, select the color of the light by clicking the color swatch to the right. Then drag the slider to cast a subtle hue over the stage. Drag toward Positive to tint the image with the color in the swatch; drag toward Negative to tint the stage with the swatch's opposite. Keep the slider set to 0 — dead in the center — to cast no hue.

The Texture Channel options enable you to treat one channel in the image as a *texture map*, which is a grayscale surface in which white indicates peaks and black indicates valleys. (This assumes the White Is High check box is selected. If you turn that option off, everything flips, and black becomes the peak.) The texture map results in an embossed effect, much like that created with the Emboss filter but with three important advantages. First, the embossing is much more realistic, with naturalistic shadows and smooth transitions around corners. Second, you can light the surface from many angles at once. And third, the final outcome invariably appears in color.

All you have to do is choose a channel from the Texture Channel pop-up menu to serve as the embossed surface. Then adjust the Height slider to indicate more or less Flat terrain or huge Mountainous cliffs and gorges.

By way of example, Figure 9-53 shows what can only be described as a Bible-appropriate tableau followed by the same tableau subject to the Lighting Effects filter. Brian Maffitt, the artist behind this particular piece, started with the preset Triple Spotlight and then modified the positions, colors, and intensities of the spotlights to better suit the image. He left the Texture Channel option set to None, so naturally no texture was applied.

Original digital photo   Triple Spotlight (modified), no texture

Figure 9-53: To be revered in front of a stained glass window is all very well and good (left). But add a triad of spotlights, and you can become a saint (right).

Figure 9-54 shows what happens if you take this very same image and add in a bit of surface texture. The texture in question is none other than the photo's own green channel, so the etching follows the natural contours of the image. One example shows the result of a Height value of 10, the other shows a Height value of 25. In each case, Lighting Effects exaggerates the inherent edges in the photograph.

But the best texture maps are those that you create by hand. In Figure 9-55, I started by creating a new channel in the Channels palette, filling it with noise (using Filter ⇨ Noise ⇨ Add Noise with an Amount value of 100 percent and Distribution set to Gaussian), and chunking up the noise with Filter ⇨ Pixelate ⇨ Pointillize set to a Cell Size of 6. To ensure that the texture affected just the background and left the foreground characters unharmed, I had to erase away the foreground. So I used the lasso tool to select the general area surrounding the people, feathered the selection (using Select ⇨ Feather with a Radius value of 6 pixels), and filled the selection with white. Having completed the texture map, I pressed Ctrl+tilde (~) to return to the composite RGB view (that's ⌘-tilde on the Mac). Working once again from the original digital photo in Figure 9-53, I chose the Lighting Effects filter, set the Texture Channel option to Alpha 1 — the default name for the channel I just created — and entered a Height value of 30. The resulting effect, complete with smooth foreground and rough background, appears on the right side of Figure 9-55.

Texture Channel: Green, Height: 10   same, Height: 25

Figure 9-54: Sometimes, an image's best texture map is itself. Here we see the results of setting the Texture Channel option to the green channel and varying the Height values from smooth (left) to bumpy (right).

Add Noise: 100%, Pointillize: 6   Texture Channel: Alpha 1, Height: 30

Figure 9-55: After creating a special mask channel using the Add Noise and Pointillize filters (left), I applied my texture map with the Lighting Effects filter. My reward was this resplendent triumvirate, rendered in stucco (right), a welcome vision to a world in desperate need of casually dressed people bearing glad tidings.

✦   ✦   ✦

Custom Effects

Creating a Home-Grown Effect

This last-of-the-filters chapter covers two often overlooked but important entries—Custom and Displace—that permit you to create your own, custom-tailored special effects. Both require some mathematical reasoning skills, and even then, you'll probably have occasional difficulty predicting the outcomes. If math isn't your bag, if number theory clogs up your synapses to the extent that you feel like a worthless math wimp, by all means don't put yourself through the torture. Skip all the mathematical background in this chapter and read the "Applying Custom Values" and "Using Displacement Maps" sections to try out some specific, no-brainer effects.

On the other hand, if you're not scared silly of math and you want to understand how to eventually create effects of your own, read on, you hearty soul.

The Custom filter

The Custom command enables you to design your own *convolution kernel,* which is a variety of filter in which neighboring pixels get mixed together. The kernel can be a variation on sharpening, blurring, embossing, or a half-dozen other effects. You create your filter by entering numerical values into a matrix of options.

When you choose Filter ⇨ Other ⇨ Custom, Photoshop displays the dialog box shown in Figure 10-1. It sports a 5×5 matrix of option boxes followed by two additional options, Scale and Offset. The matrix options can accept values from negative to positive 999. The Scale value can range from 1 to 9,999, and the Offset value can range from negative to positive 9,999. The dialog box includes Load and Save buttons so that you can load settings from disk and save the current settings for future use.

Like most of Photoshop's filters, the Custom filter also includes a constantly updating preview box, which you'll have lots of time to appreciate if you decide to try your hand at designing your own effects. Select the Preview check box to view the effect of the kernel in the image window as well.

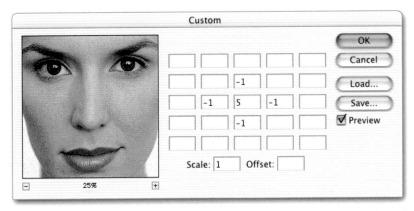

Figure 10-1: The Custom dialog box lets you design your own convolution kernel by multiplying the brightness values of pixels.

Here's how the filter works: When you press Enter or Return to apply the values in the Custom dialog box to a selection, the filter passes over every pixel in the selection, one at a time. For each pixel being evaluated — which I call the PBE, for short — the filter multiplies the PBE's current brightness value by the number in the center option box (the one that contains a 5 in Figure 10-1). To help keep things straight, I call this value the CMV, for *central matrix value.*

The filter then multiplies the brightness values of the surrounding pixels by the surrounding values in the matrix. For example, Photoshop multiplies the value in the option box just above the CMV by the brightness value of the pixel just above the PBE. It ignores any empty matrix option boxes and the pixels they represent.

Finally, the filter totals the products of the multiplied pixels, divides the sum by the value in the Scale option, and then adds the Offset value to calculate the new brightness of the PBE. It then moves on to the next pixel in the selection and performs the calculation all over again. Figure 10-2 shows a schematic drawing of the process.

Perhaps seeing all of this spelled out in an equation will help you understand the process. Then again, perhaps not — but here it comes anyway. In the following equation, NP stands for *neighboring pixel* and MV stands for the corresponding matrix value in the Custom dialog box.

New brightness value = (((PBE × CMV) + (NP1 × MV1) + (NP2 × MV2) + . . .) ÷ Scale) + Offset

Luckily, Photoshop calculates the equation without any help from you. All you have to do is punch in the values and see what happens.

Custom filter advice

Now obviously, if you go around multiplying the brightness value of a pixel too much, you end up making it white. And a filter that turns an image white is pretty darn useless. The key, then, is to filter an image and at the same time maintain the original balance of brightness values. To achieve this, just be sure that the sum of all values in the matrix is 1. For example, the default values in the matrix shown back in Figure 10-1 are 5, –1, –1, –1, and –1, which add up to 1.

If the sum is greater than 1, use the Scale value to divide the sum down to 1. Figures 10-3 and 10-4 show the results of increasing the CMV to 6, 7, and 8. This raises the sum of the values in the matrix to 2, then 3, and finally 4.

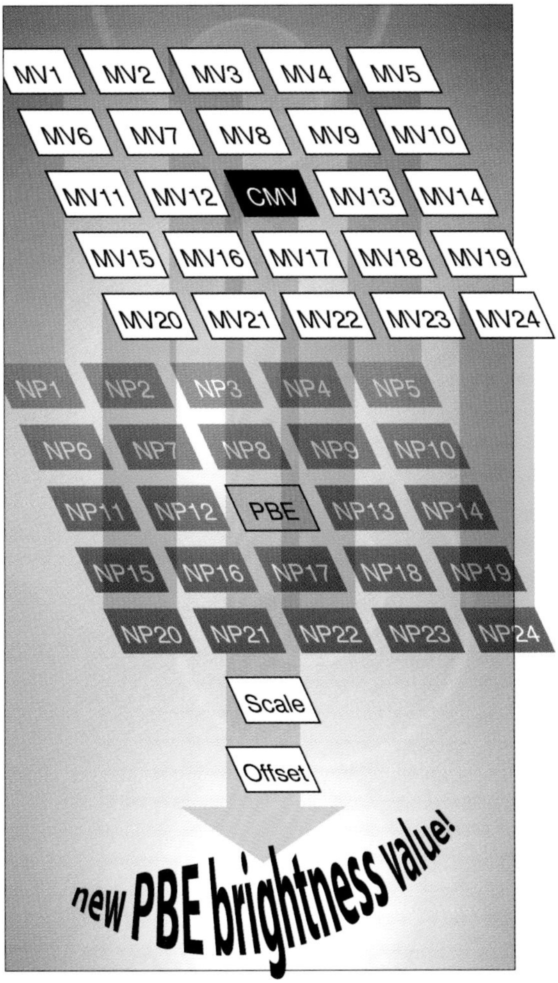

Figure 10-2: The Custom filter multiplies each matrix value by the brightness value of the corresponding pixel, adds the products together, divides the sum by the Scale value, adds the Offset value, and applies the result to the pixel being evaluated.

In Figure 10-3, I entered the sum into the Scale option to divide the sum back down to 1 — any value divided by itself is 1, after all. The result is that Photoshop maintains the original color balance of the image while at the same time filtering it slightly differently. When I did not raise the Scale value, the image became progressively lighter, as illustrated in Figure 10-4.

If the sum is less than 1, increase the CMV until the sum reaches the magic number. For example, in Figure 10-5, I lowered the values to the left of the CMV and then above and to the right of the CMV by 1 apiece to increase the sharpening effect. To ensure that the image did not darken, I also raised the CMV to compensate. When I did not raise the CMV, the image turned black.

Although a sum of 1 provides the safest and most predictable filtering effects, you can use different sums, such as 0 and 2, to try out more destructive filtering effects. If you do, be sure to raise or lower the Offset value to compensate. For some examples, see the "Non-1 variations" section later in this chapter.

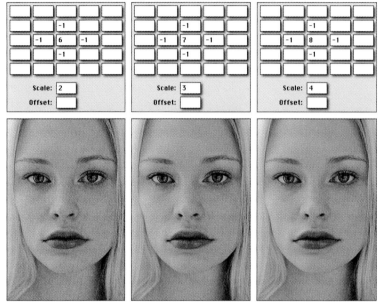

Figure 10-3: Raising the Scale value to reflect the sum of the values in the matrix maintains the color balance of the image.

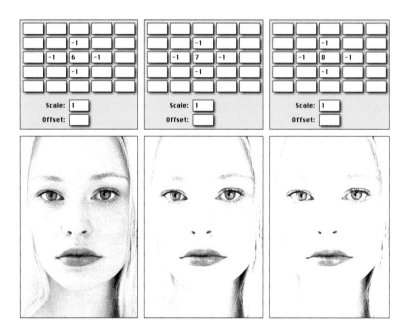

Figure 10-4: Raising the sum of the matrix values without counterbalancing it in the Scale option lightens the image.

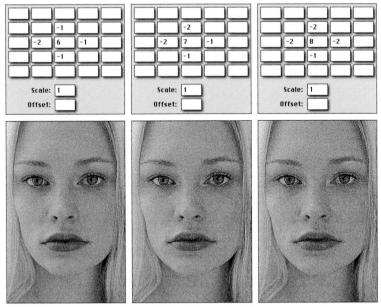

Figure 10-5: Raising the CMV to compensate for the lowered values in the matrix maintains the color balance of the image.

Applying Custom Values

The following sections show you ways to sharpen, blur, and otherwise filter an image using specific matrix, Scale, and Offset values. It is my sincere hope that by the end of the Custom filter discussions, you will not only know how to repeat my examples, but also know how to apply what you've learned to design special effects of your own.

Symmetrical effects

Values that are symmetrical both horizontally and vertically about the central matrix value produce sharpen and blur effects:

✦ **Sharpening:** A positive CMV surrounded by negative values sharpens an image, as demonstrated in the first example of Figure 10-6. Figures 10-3 through 10-5 also demonstrate varying degrees of sharpening effects.

✦ **Blurring:** A positive CMV surrounded by symmetrical positive numbers — balanced, of course, by a Scale value as explained in the preceding section — blurs an image, as demonstrated in the second example of Figure 10-6.

✦ **Blurring with edge-detection:** A negative CMV surrounded by symmetrical positive values blurs an image and adds an element of edge-detection, as illustrated in the last example of the figure. These effects are unlike anything provided by Photoshop's standard collection of filters.

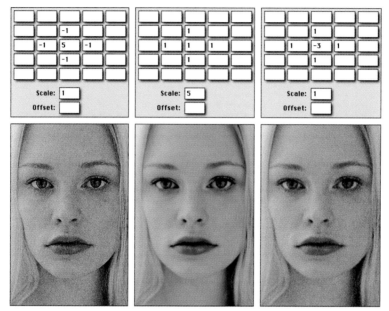

Figure 10-6: Symmetrical values can result in sharpening (left), blurring (middle), and edge-detection (right) effects.

Sharpening

The Custom command provides as many variations on the sharpening theme as the Unsharp Mask filter. In a sense, it provides even more, for whereas the Unsharp Mask filter requires you to sharpen an image inside a Gaussian radius, you get to specify exactly which pixels are taken into account when you use the Custom filter.

To create Unsharp Mask-like effects — well, more like the sharpen tool, actually — enter a large number in the CMV and small values in the surrounding option boxes, as demonstrated in the first two examples of Figure 10-7. To go beyond Unsharp Mask, you can violate the radius of the filter by entering values around the perimeter of the matrix and ignoring options closer to the CMV, as demonstrated in the last example of Figure 10-7.

You can sharpen an image using the Custom dialog box in two basic ways. First, you can enter lots of negative values into the neighboring options in the matrix and then enter a CMV just large enough to yield a sum of 1. This results in radical sharpening effects, as demonstrated in the examples in Figure 10-7.

Second, you can tone down the sharpening by raising the CMV and using the Scale value to divide the sum down to 1. Figure 10-8 shows the results of raising the CMV and Scale values to lessen the impact of sharpening effects typical of those performed in the first two examples of Figure 10-7. Figure 10-9 shows what happens when you apply slightly more adventurous values. Although the arithmetic is a little more involved, the values remain symmetrical and the sums remain 1.

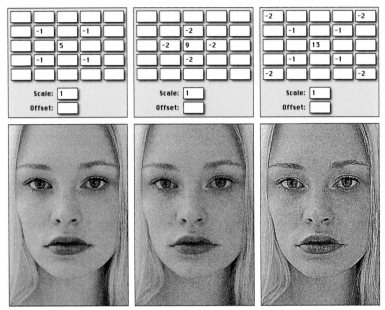

Figure 10-7: To create severe sharpening effects, enter a CMV just large enough to compensate for the negative values in the matrix (first and second examples). To heighten the sharpening effect even further, shift the negative values closer to the perimeter of the matrix (last example).

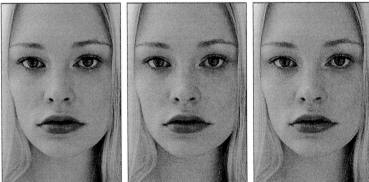

Figure 10-8: To sharpen more subtly, increase the central matrix value and then enter the sum into the Scale value.

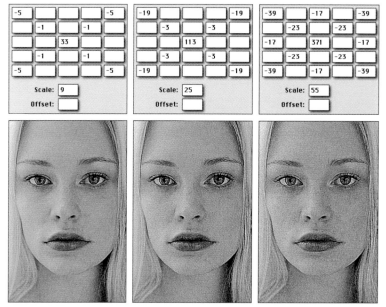

Figure 10-9: When you soften the effect of radical sharpening, you create a thicker, higher-contrast effect, much as when raising the Radius value in the Unsharp Mask dialog box.

Blurring

The philosophy behind blurring is very much the same as that behind sharpening. To produce extreme blurring effects, enter lots of values or high values into the neighboring options in the matrix, enter 1 into the CMV, and then enter the sum into the Scale option. Examples appear in Figure 10-10. To downplay the blurring, raise the CMV and the Scale value by equal amounts. In the last example of Figure 10-10, I used the same neighboring values as in the middle image, but I increased the CMV and the Scale value by 3.

Edge-detection

Many of you are probably beginning to get the idea by now, but just in case you're the kind of person who believes that friends don't let friends do math, I'll breeze through it one more time in the venue of edge-detection. If you really want to see those edges, enter 1s and 2s into the neighboring options in the matrix and then enter a CMV just *small* enough — it's a negative value, after all — to make the sum 1. The first two examples in Figure 10-11 illuminate.

To lighten the edges and bring out the blur, raise the CMV and enter the resulting sum into the Scale option box. The last example in Figure 10-11 pushes the boundaries between edge-detection and a straight blur.

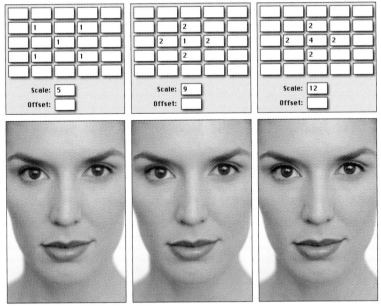

Figure 10-10: To create severe blurring effects, enter 1 for the CMV and fill the neighboring options with 1s and 2s (first two images). To blur more subtly, increase the central matrix value and the Scale value by equal amounts (last image).

Non-1 variations

Every image shown in Figures 10-6 through 10-11 is the result of manipulating matrix values and using the Scale option to produce a sum total of 1. Earlier in this chapter, I told you what can happen if you go below 1 (black images) or above 1 (white images). But I haven't shown you how you can use non-1 totals to produce interesting, if somewhat washed-out, effects.

The key is to raise the Offset value, thereby adding a specified brightness value to each pixel in the image. By doing this, you can offset the lightening or darkening caused by the matrix values to create an image that has half a chance of printing well.

Lightening overly dark effects

The first image in Figure 10-12 uses nearly the same values used to create the extreme sharpening effect in the last image of Figure 10-7. The only difference is that the CMV is 1 lower (12, down from 13), which in turn lowers the sum total from 1 to 0.

The result is a dark image with hints of brightness at points of high contrast. The image reads well on screen, but many of the details are likely to fill in during the printing process. To prevent the image from going too dark, lighten it using the Offset value. Photoshop adds the value to the brightness level of each selected pixel. A brightness value of 255 equals solid white, so you don't need to go too high. As illustrated by the last example in Figure 10-12, an Offset value of 100 is enough to raise most pixels in the image to a medium gray.

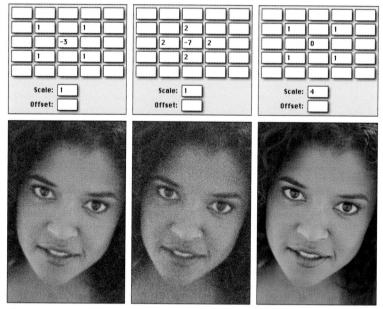

Figure 10-11: To create severe edge-detection effects, enter a negative CMV just small enough to compensate for the positive values in the matrix (first two examples). To blur the edges, increase the central matrix value and then enter the sum into the Scale value (final example).

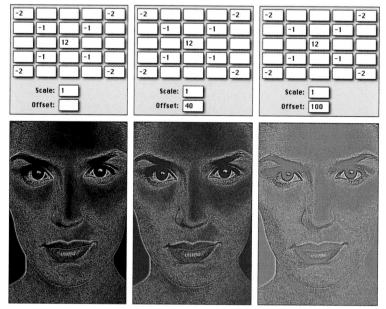

Figure 10-12: Three examples of a sharpening kernel with a sum total of 0. The only difference is that I lightened the second and third examples incrementally by entering positive values into the Offset option box.

Darkening overly light effects

You also can use the Offset value to darken filtering effects with sum totals greater than 1. The images in Figures 10-13 and 10-14 show sharpening and edge-detection effects whose matrix totals add up to 2. On their own, these filters produce effects that are too light. However, as demonstrated in the middle and right examples in the figures, you can darken the effects of the Custom filter to create high-contrast images by entering a negative value into the Offset option box.

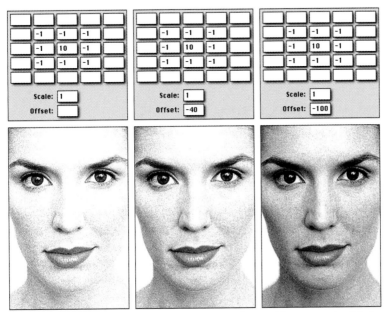

Figure 10-13: Three examples of sharpening effects with sum totals of 2. I darkened the images incrementally by entering negative values into the Offset option box.

Using extreme offsets

If a brightness value of 255 produces solid white and a brightness value of 0 is solid black, why in blue blazes does the Offset value permit any number between negative and positive 9,999, a number 40 times greater than solid white? The answer lies in the fact that the matrix options can force the Custom filter to calculate brightness values much darker than black and much lighter than white. Therefore, you can use a very high or very low Offset value to boost the brightness of an image in which all pixels are well below black or diminish the brightness when all pixels are way beyond white.

Figure 10-15 shows exaggerated versions of the sharpening, blurring, and edge-detection effects. The sum totals of the matrixes (when divided by the Scale values) are –42, 53, and 42, respectively. Without some help from the Offset value, each of these filters would turn every pixel in the image black (in the case of the sharpening effect) or white (blurring and edge-detection). But as demonstrated in the figure, using enormous Offset numbers brings out those few brightness values that remain. The images are so polarized that there's little difference between the three effects, the first image being an inverted version of the last. The second row shows the results of choosing Edit ⇨ Fade Custom immediately after applying the Custom filter and selecting the Luminosity blend mode.

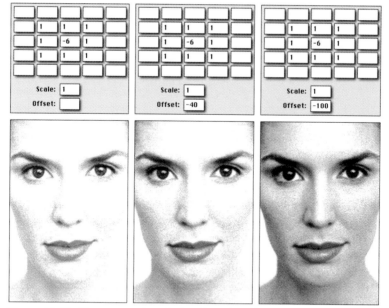

Figure 10-14: Three examples of edge-detection effects with sum totals of 2, darkened incrementally with progressively lower Offset values.

Other custom effects

By now, I hope that you understand what an absolute trip the Custom filter can be, provided that you immerse yourself in the old adventurous spirit. Quite honestly, I could keep showing you ways to use the Custom filter for another 20 or 30 pages. But then my publisher would come unglued because I'd never finish the book, and you'd miss the pleasure of discovering variations on your own.

Nonetheless, you're probably wondering what happens if you just go absolutely berserk, in a computer-geek sort of way, and start entering matrix values in unusual or even arbitrary arrangements. The answer is that as long as you maintain a sum total of 1, you achieve some pretty interesting and even usable effects. Many of these effects will be simple variations on blurring, sharpening, and edge-detection.

Directional blurs

Figure 10-16 shows examples of entering positive matrix values all in one row, all in a column, or in opposite quadrants. As you can see, as long as you maintain uniformly positive values, you get a blurring effect. However, by keeping the values lowest in the center and highest toward the edges and corners, you can create directional blurs. The first example resembles a slight horizontal motion blur, the second looks like a slight vertical motion blur, and the last example looks like it's vibrating horizontally and vertically.

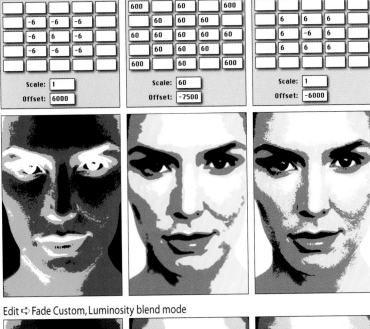

Edit ➪ Fade Custom, Luminosity blend mode

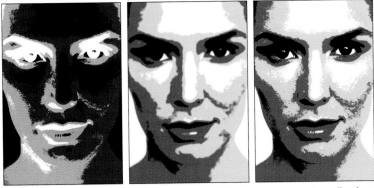

Figure 10-15: You can create high-contrast effects by exaggerating all values in the matrix and then compensating with a very high or very low Offset value (top row). When you back off the effect using Edit ➪ Fade (bottom row), these dramatic effects become interesting indeed.

Embossing

So far, we aren't going very nuts, are we? Despite their unusual formations, the matrix values in Figures 10-16 still manage to maintain symmetry. Well, now it's time to lose the symmetry, which typically results in an embossing effect.

Figure 10-17 shows three variations on embossing, all of which involve positive and negative matrix values positioned on opposite sides of the CMV. (The CMV happens to be positive merely to maintain a sum total of 1.)

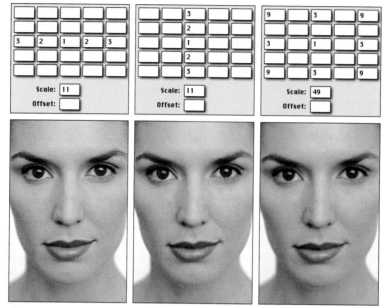

Figure 10-16: Enter positive matrix values in a horizontal formation (left) or vertical formation (middle) to create slight motion blurs. By positioning positive values in opposite corners of the matrix, you create a vibrating effect (right).

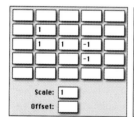
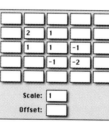
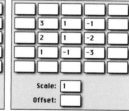

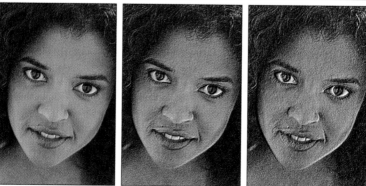

Figure 10-17: You can create embossing effects by distributing positive and negative values on opposite sides of the central matrix value.

This type of embossing has no hard and fast light source, but you might imagine that the light comes from the general direction of the positive values. Therefore, when I swapped the positive and negative values throughout the matrix (all except the CMV), I approximated an underlighting effect, as demonstrated by the images in Figure 10-18.

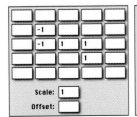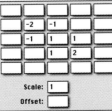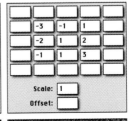

Figure 10-18: Change the location of positive and negative matrix values to change the general direction of the light source.

In truth, it's not so much a lighting difference as a difference in edge enhancement. White pixels collect on the side of an edge represented by positive values in the matrix; black pixels collect on the negative-value side. So when I swapped the locations of positive and negative values between Figures 10-17 and 10-18, I changed the distribution of white and black pixels in the filtered images.

Embossing is the loosest of the Custom filter effects. As long as you position positive and negative values on opposite sides of the CMV, you can distribute the values in almost any way you see fit. Figure 10-19 demonstrates three entirely arbitrary arrangements of values in the Custom matrix, downplayed by raising the CMV and entering the sum of the matrix values in the Scale option box. And notice that unlike Filter ➪ Stylize ➪ Emboss, which sacrifices color and changes low-contrast areas to gray, the Custom filter preserves the natural colors in the image.

Displacing Pixels in an Image

Photoshop's second custom effects filter is Filter ➪ Distort ➪ Displace, which enables you to distort and add texture to an image by moving the colors of certain pixels in a selection. You specify the direction and distance that the Displace filter moves colors by creating a second image called a *displacement map*, or *dmap* (pronounced *dee-map*) for short. The brightness values in the displacement map tell Photoshop which pixels to affect and how far to move the colors of those pixels:

◆ **Black:** The black areas of the displacement map move the colors of corresponding pixels in the selection a maximum prescribed distance to the right and/or down. Lighter values between black and medium gray move colors a shorter distance in the same direction.

◆ **White:** The white areas move the colors of corresponding pixels a maximum distance to the left and/or up. Darker values between white and medium gray move colors a shorter distance in the same direction.

◆ **Medium gray:** A 50 percent brightness value, such as medium gray, ensures that the colors of corresponding pixels remain unmoved.

Suppose that I start with the hammer pictured at the outset of Figure 10-20. Next, I create a new image window the same size as the hammer. (I do this by choosing File ⇨ New and then choosing the hammer image from the bottom of the Window menu.) This new image will serve as the displacement map. I divide the image roughly into four quadrants. As shown in the middle example of Figure 10-20, I fill the upper-left quadrant with white, the lower-right quadrant with black, and the other two quadrants with medium gray. Note that the green arrows are not actually part of the dmap. They appear in the figure merely to indicate the direction in which the quadrants will move colors in the displaced image.

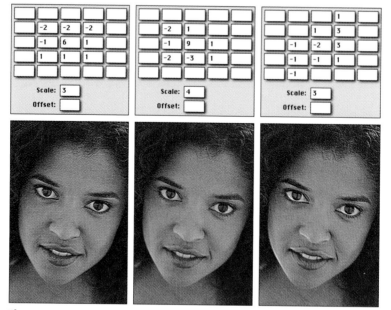

Figure 10-19: You can create whole libraries of embossing effects by experimenting with different combinations of positive and negative values. To emboss more subtly, increase the central matrix value and the Scale values by equal amounts.

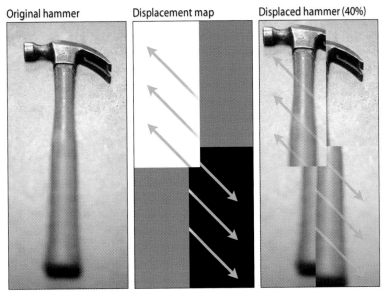

Figure 10-20: The Displace filter moves colors in an image (left) according to the brightness values in a separate image, called the displacement map (middle). The green arrows indicate the direction that the dmap moves colors in the displaced image (right).

When finished, I save the dmap image in the native Photoshop (PSD) format so that the Displace filter can access it. I then return to the hammer image, choose Filter ➪ Distort ➪ Displace, change both the Horizontal and Vertical Scale values to 40 percent each, and open the dmap from disk. The result is the image shown in the last example in Figure 10-20. In keeping with the distribution of brightness values in the dmap, the colors of the pixels in the upper-left quadrant of the carving image move up and to the left, the colors of the pixels in the lower-right quadrant move down and to the right, and the colors in the upper-right and lower-left quadrant remain intact.

A dmap must be a grayscale or color image, and you must save the dmap as a flattened image in the native Photoshop file format. The Displace command does not recognize PICT, TIFF, or any of the other non-native file formats. It's an old filter, so it has its peculiarities.

At this point, you likely have two questions: How do you use the Displace filter, and why in the world would you possibly want to? The hows of the Displace filter are covered in the following section. To discover some whys — which should in turn help you dream up some whys of your own — read the "Using Displacement Maps" section later in this chapter.

Displacement theory

Like any custom filtering effect worth its weight in table salt, you need a certain degree of mathematical — or at least, geometric — reasoning skills to predict the outcome of the Displace filter. Though I was a math major in college (well, actually, I double-majored in math and fine arts, and I must admit to paying the lion's share of attention to the latter), I was frankly befuddled by the results of my first few experiments with the Displace command. Don't be surprised if you are as well. With some time and a modicum of effort, however, you can learn to anticipate the approximate effects of this filter.

Direction of displacement

A moment ago, I mentioned that the black areas of a dmap move colors in an image to the right and/or down and the white areas move colors to the left and/or up. This may have caused you to wonder what all this "and/or" guff is about. "Is it right or is it down?" you may have puzzled, and rightly so.

The truth is that the direction of a displacement can go either way. It's up to you, as it were. Here's how it works: A dmap can contain one or more channels. If the dmap is a grayscale image with one color channel only, the Displace filter moves colors that correspond to black areas in the dmap both down *and* to the right, depending on your specifications in the Displace dialog box. The filter moves colors that correspond to white areas in the dmap both up and to the left.

Figure 10-21 shows two examples of an image displaced using a single-channel dmap, which appears on the left side of the figure. (To create this dmap, I took the middle image from Figure 10-20 and applied Filter ⇨ Blur ⇨ Gaussian Blur with a Radius value of 60 pixels.) I displaced the middle image both horizontally and vertically at 20 percent and the right image at 40 percent. Therefore, the colors in the right image travel twice the distance as those in the middle image, but all colors travel the same direction. (The upcoming section "The Displace dialog box" explains exactly how the percentage values work.)

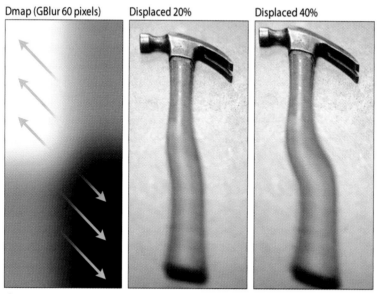

Dmap (GBlur 60 pixels)   Displaced 20%   Displaced 40%

Figure 10-21: After blurring the displacement map from the previous figure (left, with arrows added to show direction), I applied this single-channel dmap to the hammer image at 20 percent (middle) and 40 percent (right).

However, if the dmap contains more than one channel—whether it's a color image or a grayscale image with an independent mask channel—the first channel (red in the case of an RGB image) indicates horizontal displacement, and the second channel (green in RGB) indicates vertical displacement. All other channels are ignored. Therefore, the Displace filter moves colors that correspond to black areas in the first channel to the right and colors that correspond to white areas to the left. It then moves colors that correspond to the black areas in the second channel downward and colors that correspond to white areas upward.

Figure 10-22 examines an RGB image that contains a series of gradations. The first example shows the red channel, which transitions from gray to black to white to black and finally back to gray. The second example shows the green channel, which is filled with a white-to-black-to-white gradient. If the blue channel is filled with gray, the RGB dmap looks like the full-color image on right.

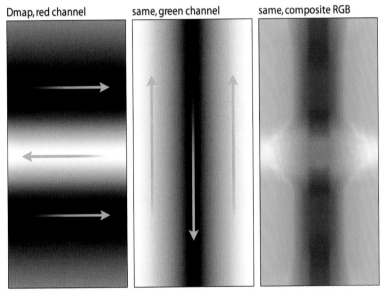

Figure 10-22: The red (left) and green (middle) channels of a full-color displacement map (right). In a dmap, red shifts colors horizontally and green shifts them vertically.

Figure 10-23 shows the effects of applying the RGB displacement map to the hammer. The first example shows a strictly horizontal displacement (again, set to 40 percent). The second example shows a vertical displacement. And the third shows both displacements calculated together.

Brightness value transitions

If you look closely at the images in Figure 10-23, you'll notice stretching effects, most noticeable along the left edge of the image. Although very common with displacement maps, this is an effect you'll most likely want to avoid.

Displaced horizontally   Displaced vertically   Displaced both

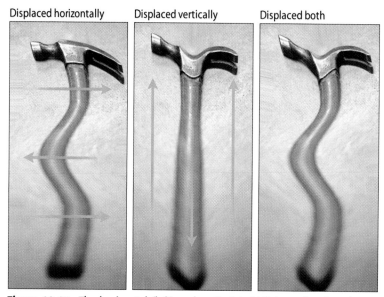

Figure 10-23: The horizontal (left) and vertical (middle) results of applying the RGB dmap from the previous figure. The final image shows horizontal and vertical displacements combined. In all cases, the Scale values are 40 percent.

The cause of the stretching is twofold: First, the left and right edges of both channels in the dmap from Figure 10-22 are laced with black and white, which displace pixels around the perimeter of the hammer image. This forces Photoshop to duplicate border pixels; hence the stretching. Second, neighboring brightness values in a gradient may be less similar than they appear. These differences are magnified when the gradient is expressed as a displacement map.

The solution to the first problem is a gray border. The solution to the second is blurring. In the first example of Figure 10-24, I pressed Ctrl+A (⌘-A on the Mac) to select the entire image and then chose Edit ⇨ Stroke. I entered a Width value of 50 pixels, changed the Color swatch to 50 percent gray, and set the Location option to Inside. After clicking OK, I got a nice thick gray border, which keeps the edge pixels stationary. Next, I chose Filter ⇨ Blur ⇨ Gaussian Blur and set the Radius to 40 pixels. By keeping the blur value slightly smaller than the stroke value, I was able to maintain some gray pixels along the perimeter of the dmap, as shown in the second example. Finally, I applied my modified dmap to the original hammer image, thus achieving a smoother effect, as shown in the third example in Figure 10-24.

Okay, you might think, the hammer in Figure 10-24 looks a little smoother than its counterpart in Figure 10-23. But if we put the two images under the virtual microscope, we find that the former is *way* smoother. In Figure 10-25, we see both hammers enlarged to 200 percent their normal size and sharpened using Unsharp Mask set to a maximum Amount of 500 percent. True, the stretch marks are conspicuously absent in the right-hand image, but that's not all. Ragged edges between highlights and shadows in the first hammer are rendered crisp and clear in the second. So a blurry dmap actually results in a sharper displaced image — further proof that truth is stranger than fiction.

Edit ⇨ Stroke, 50% Gray   Gaussian Blur, Radius: 40   Smoother displacement

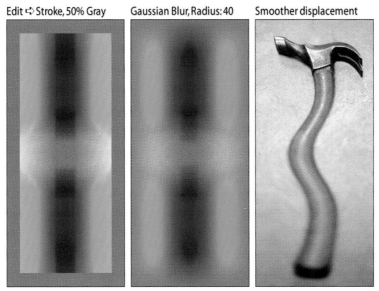

Figure 10-24: For a smoother displacement, select the entire image and stroke it with gray (left). Then blur the stroke and dmap generously (middle). The result of this dmap exhibits virtually no stretch marks (right).

Displaced image with stretched pixels   Smoother results with blurred dmap

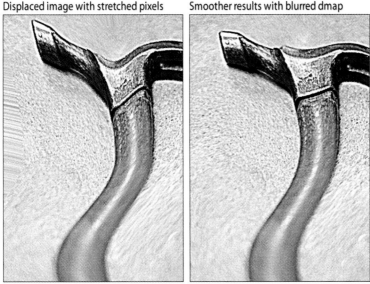

Figure 10-25: Magnified versions of the hammers from Figures 10-23 and 10-24, subject to a hefty dose of Unsharp Mask. The second hammer is several times smoother. In fact, if I were shopping for wiggly hammers, I would gladly pay a dollar more for the one on the right. (And you thought displacement maps had no practical value.)

The Displace dialog box

When you choose Filter ⇨ Distort ⇨ Displace, Photoshop displays the Displace dialog box. ("Displays the Displace" is the modern equivalent of "Begin the Beguine," don't you know.) Pictured in minimalist splendor in Figure 10-26, the Displace dialog box provides the following options:

✦ **Scale:** You can specify the degree to which the Displace filter moves colors in an image by entering percentage values in the Horizontal Scale and Vertical Scale option boxes. At 100 percent, black and white areas in the dmap each have the effect of moving colors 128 pixels. That's 1 pixel per each brightness value over or under medium gray. You can isolate the effect of a single-channel dmap vertically or horizontally — or ignore the first or second channel of a two-channel dmap — by entering 0 percent into the Horizontal or Vertical option box, respectively.

Figure 10-27 shows the effect of distorting an image exclusively horizontally (top row) and vertically (bottom row) using a variety of positive, negative, and even radical Scale values. In all cases, I used the single-channel dmap originally pictured in the first example in Figure 10-21. (Obviously, I could have just as easily applied a multichannel dmap. But this was already aptly demonstrated in Figure 10-23, and the ever-sensitive Figure 10-27 hates to steal the thunder from its predecessors.)

✦ **Displacement Map:** If the dmap contains fewer pixels than the image, you can either scale it to match the size of the selected image by selecting the Stretch To Fit radio button or repeat the dmap over and over within the image by selecting Tile. The first row of Figure 10-28 shows a single-channel dmap magnified to twice its normal size. It starts as a simple gradient stroked with gray and ends twirled to 999 degrees. The second row of images show the hammer subject to each of the dmaps above it with the Horizontal and Vertical Scale values set to 25 percent and Stretch To Fit selected. The bottom row shows the same settings, except this time I selected Tile. The Displace command is unique in permitting you to distort an image using a repeating pattern.

✦ **Undefined Areas:** These radio buttons let you tell Photoshop how to color pixels around the outskirts of the selection that are otherwise undefined. By default, the Repeat Edge Pixels radio button is selected, which repeats the colors of pixels around the perimeter of the selection. This can result in extreme stretching effects, as shown in the middle example in Figure 10-29. To repeat the image inside the undefined areas instead, as demonstrated in the final example in the figure, select the Wrap Around option.

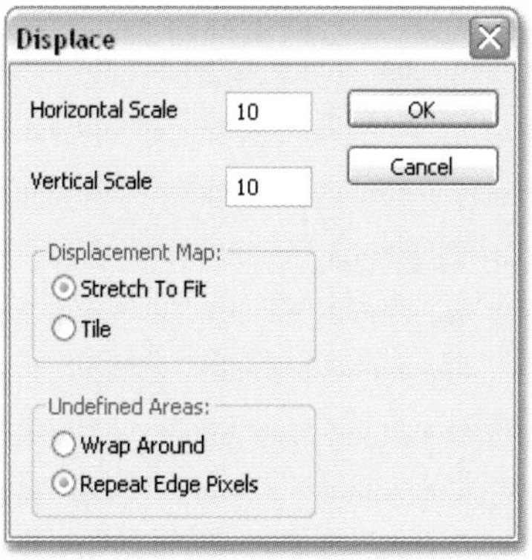

Figure 10-26: Use these options to specify the degree of distortion, how the filter matches the displacement map to the image, and how it colors the pixels around the perimeter of the selection.

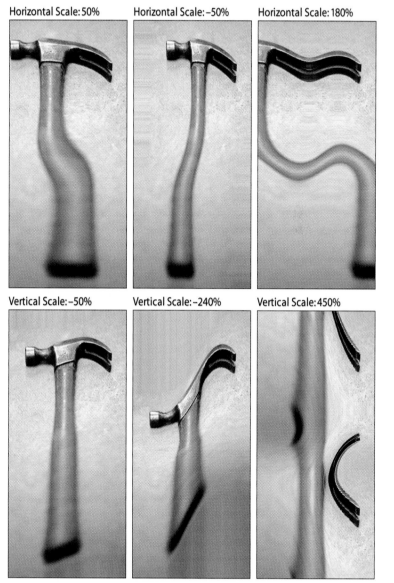

Figure 10-27: The results of applying the displacement map from Figure 10-21 to the hammer exclusively horizontally (top row) and vertically (bottom row) at each of several different percentage values. As illustrated by the right-hand examples, values over 100 percent can produce some surprising liquid image effects.

The Repeat Edge Pixels setting was active in all displacement map figures prior to Figure 10-29. But as you may recall, I frequently avoided stretching effects by coloring the edges of the dmap with medium gray and gradually lightening or darkening the brightness values toward the center.

Gradient & gray stroke   Gaussian Blur, Radius: 12   Twirl, Angle: 999°

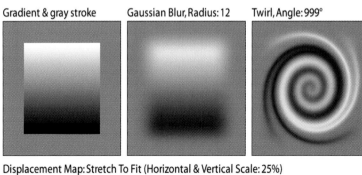

Displacement Map: Stretch To Fit (Horizontal & Vertical Scale: 25%)

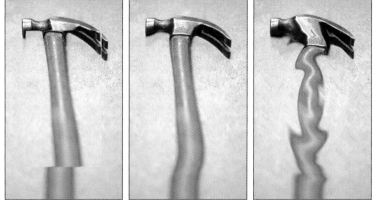

Displacement Map: Tile (same Scale values)

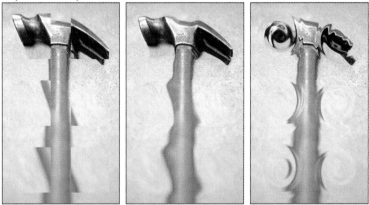

Figure 10-28: Using a sequence of tiny dmaps, each measuring only a sixth the size of the hammer (top row), I alternatively stretched the dmap to fit the hammer image (middle row) and repeated the dmap using the Tile setting (bottom row).

After you finish specifying options in the Displace dialog box, press Enter or Return to display the Open dialog box, which invites you to select the displacement map saved to disk. Only native Photoshop documents show up in the scrolling list.

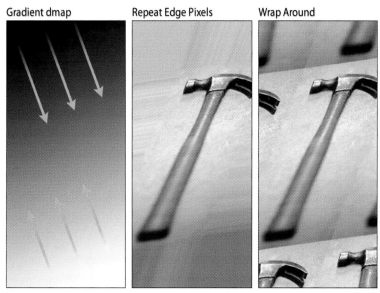

Gradient dmap · Repeat Edge Pixels · Wrap Around

Figure 10-29: After creating a straightforward, single-channel gradient dmap (left), I applied the Displace filter using two different Undefined Areas settings, Repeat Edge Pixels (middle) and Wrap Around (right).

Using Displacement Maps

So far, all the displacement maps demonstrated involve gradations of one form or another. Gradient dmaps distort the image over the contours of a fluid surface, like a reflection in a fun-house mirror. In this respect, the effects of the Displace filter closely resemble those of the Pinch and Spherize filters as well as the Free Transform command, all described in previous chapters. But the Displace filter also offers its share of unique functions, including the ability to add texture to an image.

Applying predefined dmaps

Since the Displace filter was introduced in Photoshop 2.0, the program has shipped with a collection of predefined dmap files. These reside in the Displacement Maps folder that's inside the Plug-Ins folder, inside the folder that contains the Photoshop application file. I first introduced these special files in the "Creating patterns and textures" section of Chapter 2, but now let's take a look at them in more depth.

Figure 10-30 details four of the dozen images in the Displacement Maps folder. As you can see, the files contain sometimes independent information in the red and green channels. The blue channel is left white, hence the tendency of the colors toward blue, cyan, and magenta. In the final column of Figure 10-30, I've filled the blue channels with 50 percent gray. This merely helps the colors to print better; because the Displace filter ignores the blue channel, it has no effect on the performance of the displacement map.

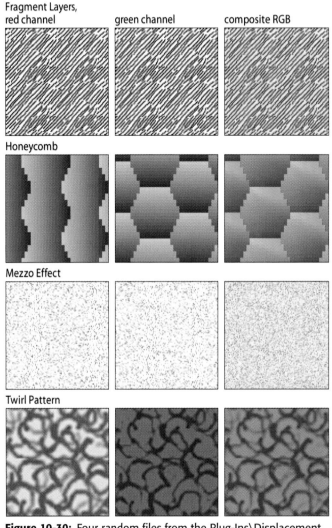

Figure 10-30: Four random files from the Plug-Ins\Displacement Maps folder. Note that the red (left column) and green (middle column) channels often differ, thus conveying unique horizontal and vertical displacement information. The final column shows the full-color dmap, with the blue channel set to 50 percent gray.

Figure 10-31 shows a sample image subjected to each of the four dmaps from Figure 10-30. The second and third columns in Figure 10-31 show the image displaced exclusively horizontally or vertically by the amounts described in the labels (either 10 or 20 percent). Figure 10-32 shows the image displaced using a host of arbitrary Horizontal and Vertical Scale values applied in tandem. (In case you missed them earlier, you can see more examples way back in Figure 2-32.)

Original PhotoSpin image   Displaced horizontally   Displaced vertically

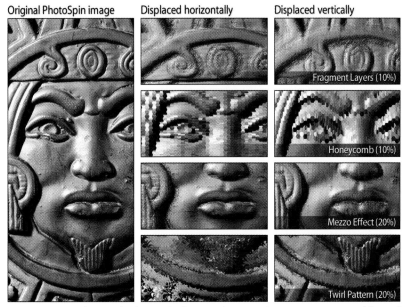

Fragment Layers (10%)

Honeycomb (10%)

Mezzo Effect (20%)

Twirl Pattern (20%)

Figure 10-31: The stock photo of what I presume to be an Aztec sun god from the PhotoSpin image library (left) displaced horizontally (middle) or vertically (right) using the dmaps featured in the previous figure.

You may notice that some of the dmap file names recommend a percentage amount for you to use, as in the case of Pentagons (10%). This happens to be the Scale value, Horizontal and Vertical, that will precisely divide the image into solid blocks of color, as in the first example in Figure 10-33. In this regard, the Displace filter map may produce an effect similar to Filter ➪ Pixelate ➪ Crystallize; but armed with a custom dmap, you have the opportunity to design an infinite array of regularly repeating shapes. Of course, you shouldn't hesitate to experiment with values other than 10 percent. Figure 10-33 offers a few suggestions.

As illustrated in Figure 10-33, many of Photoshop's predefined dmaps produce the effect of viewing the image through textured glass — an effect known in the 3D realm as *glass refraction*. Those few patterns that contain too much contrast to pass off as textured glass — including Fragment Layers, Mezzo Effect, and Schnable Effect — can be employed to create images that appear as if they were printed on coarse paper or even textured metal. Note that the Fragment Layers dmap has nothing to do with Photoshop's layers; in fact, it was so named before Photoshop even had layers. Rather, it is intended to separate an image into multiple veins of fragmented color.

When using a repeating pattern — including any of the images inside the Displacement Maps folder — as a dmap, be sure to select the Tile radio button inside the Displace dialog box. This repeats the dmap rather than stretching it out of proportion.

Fragment Layers, HScale: 5%, VScale: 5%   Honeycomb, HScale: 10%, VScale: 10%

Mezzo Effect, HScale: 8%, VScale: 12%   Twirl Pattern, HScale: 15%, VScale: 8%

Figure 10-32: More applications of Photoshop's predefined dmaps, this time using independent Horizontal and Vertical Scale values.

Creating your own textural dmaps

In Chapter 2, I also discussed a few ways to create your own textures from scratch using filters such as Add Noise, Clouds, Crystallize, and Emboss. (See Figure 2-33 and its accompanying text for more information.) These very same patterns can be put to effective use as displacement maps.

Consider Figure 10-34. The first example shows a new image I created to exactly match the dimensions of the Aztec sun god. I first applied Filter ⇨ Noise ⇨ Add Noise at 100 percent, Uniform, and Monochrome. Then I pressed Ctrl+F (⌘-F on the Mac) twice to repeat the filter. I next applied Filter ⇨ Pixelate ⇨ Crystallize with a Cell Size value of 20. And I followed that up with Gaussian Blur and a Radius value of 3 pixels. The difference between this and a similar effect illustrated back in Figure 2-33 is that I applied all three filters in the red and green channels independently. I filled the blue channel with gray.

After saving that image in the native PSD format, I returned to the sun god and chose Filter ⇨ Distort ⇨ Displace and experimented with a couple of different sets of Scale values, as labeled in Figure 10-34. The result is a custom ripple effect, unlike anything you can produce with the Ripple filter, and that I believe appears more watery than imagery created with the Ocean Ripple filter.

Pentagons, HScale: 10%, VScale: 10%   same, HScale: 25%, VScale: 25%

a third time, HScale: 48%, VScale: 62%   and a fourth, HScale: 120%, VScale: 80%

Figure 10-33: Examples of an image displaced with the Pentagons dmap. By setting the Scale values to 10 percent apiece, you assign each pentagon its own solid color (top left). Other values result in glass refraction effects.

Needless to say (but I'll say it anyway), this gooey ripple dmap is only one of an infinite number of textures that you can create with the help of Photoshop's corrective and destructive filters. Figure 10-35 starts off with a very basic dmap created by applying Filter ➪ Render ➪ Clouds to the red and green channels independently. (Again, the blue channel is gray.) The foreground and background colors were set to their defaults, black and white. That's all there was to it. And yet armed with that simple dmap, I was able to greatly distort the sun god, ultimately transforming it into a marble-like pattern, shown on the right side of Figure 10-35.

If the effect pictured in Figure 10-35 is too rough for you, you know what to do: Blur the dmap and try again. In Figure 10-36, I applied the Gaussian Blur filter with a Radius value of 40 pixels. Then I exaggerated the Scale values to generate smoother image patterns. Despite very high Scale values, the face remains discernable in the final example.

Customizing a dmap to an image

Want to get carried away? Then by all means, get carried away. Just as masking is the art of selecting an image using any tool inside Photoshop, displacing is the admittedly more arcane art of distorting an image using any tool inside Photoshop. And my experience is that the more fun you permit yourself to have with displacement maps, the more you'll come to understand how they work and the more likely you'll be to divine practical applications for them.

Add Noise x 3, Crystallize, GBlur   HScale: 5%, VScale: 5%   HScale: 18%, VScale: 32%

Figure 10-34: I created the gooey texture dmap (left) by applying the Add Noise, Crystallize, and Gaussian Blur filters to a new image, independently in the red and green color channels. I then used the Displace filter to apply the texture as a displacement map at 5 percent (middle) and 18 and 32 percent (right).

Clouds (separately in R & G)   HScale: 100%, VScale: 0%   HScale: 400%, VScale: 200%

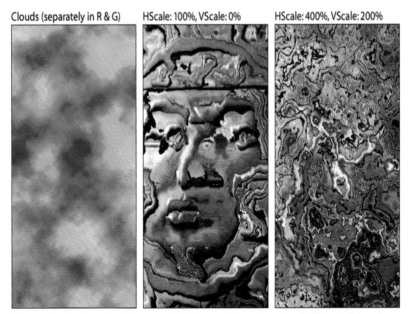

Figure 10-35: I made this dmap (left) by applying the Clouds filter in the red channel and then the green. Then I applied the dmap to the sun god exclusively horizontally (middle) and finally using very high Scale values (right).

Gaussian Blur, Radius: 40 pixels   HScale: 200%, VScale: 0%   HScale: 400%, VScale: 300%

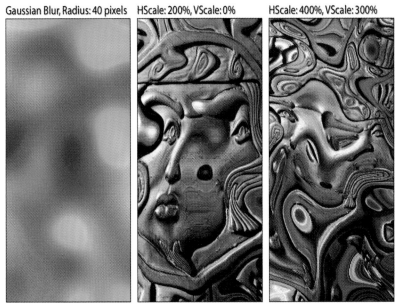

Figure 10-36: After blurring the dmap from the previous figure (left), I used it to displace the sculpted face. Even after applying a Horizontal Scale value of 400 percent (right), you can identify at least two faces in the distorted mix.

Case in point: In Figure 10-37, I once again began with a new image the same size as our Aztec friend. Working in the standard composite RGB view, I applied the Add Noise filter thrice in a row using the same 100 percent setting as before. Then I chose Filter ➪ Pixelate ➪ Color Halftone, entered a Max. Radius value of 12 pixels, and left the other values set to their defaults. (Color Halftone automatically applies different settings to different channels, so there was no need to switch channels this time around.) Last, I chose Filter ➪ Distort ➪ ZigZag and entered an Amount value of 30 percent and a Ridges value of 5. The Style was Pond Ripples. The first image in Figure 10-37 shows the finished dmap.

The second and third images in Figure 10-37 show displacements achieved using the Color Halftone dmap. Because the dmap texture is so busy, I'm able to produce dramatic effects using small Scale values. As with Figure 10-34, the results are ripple patterns that I can't achieve using any filter but Displace. That's wonderful and all, but you might reasonably wonder how many ripple patterns a person really needs, especially given the fact that the dmap has such a destructive effect on the central feature of the sun god, his face. Is there a way to design a dmap that affects one part of an image and protects another?

The answer is an unqualified yes. In fact, most artists who use displacement maps on a regular basis design a dmap with a specific image in mind. This means either creating the dmap from the image itself, or tracing the dmap over the image. For my part, I elected the latter. First, I made sure I had both the Color Halftone dmap and sun god files open. Then I copied the sun god image and pasted it into the dmap image. Photoshop registered the pasted image in place and relegated it to its own layer, thus ensuring the original pattern was unharmed.

Add Noise, Color H'tone, ZigZag   HScale: 4%, VScale: 4%   HScale: 16%, VScale: 16%

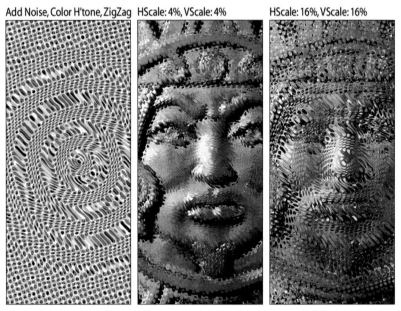

Figure 10-37: A displacement map can be as wild as you want it to be. Here I crafted a colorful dmap using the Color Halftone and ZigZag filters (left) in which red and green channels are unique. Then I applied the dmap to the sun god using small Scale values (middle and right).

I next created a new layer and used the elliptical marquee tool to approximately select the circular area around the sun god's face. I chose Select ⇨ Feather and entered a Radius of 64 pixels. Then I filled the selected area with 50 percent gray using Edit ⇨ Fill. Gray is the neutral color in a dmap — it shifts colors in the image neither horizontally nor vertically — so the face is now protected. Having finished tracing the sun god face, I deleted the pasted layer. The resulting custom dmap appears at the top of Figure 10-38.

I saved the dmap to the PSD format. (Note that when saving layered dmaps, it's necessary to include a flattened version of the image inside the PSD file. So either choose Edit ⇨ Preferences ⇨ File Handling and make sure that the Maximize PSD File Compatibility pop-up menu isn't set to Never or flatten the image before saving it.) Next, I returned to the sun god image, chose Filter ⇨ Distort ⇨ Displace, and applied the new dmap using Scale values of 30 percent each. To enhance the effect, I chose Filter ⇨ Other ⇨ Custom and banged out a few numbers to create a color emboss effect, as in the bottom example in Figure 10-38.

Now, if you're keeping up with me, you might wonder why you would go to all the effort of adding a gray area to the dmap file. Wouldn't it be easier to just select the area around the sun god's face and apply the previous dmap to the selection? After all, a selection protects an image just as well as gray pixels in a custom displacement map. But by learning how to customize a dmap to fit the needs of a specific image, you prepare yourself to take dmaps to the next level, as described in the very next section.

Fill center with gray

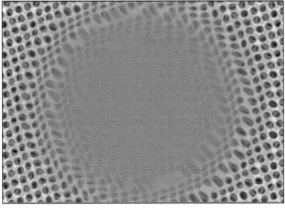

Figure 10-38: I filled the central portion of the dmap with gray to protect the face (top). This way, when I applied the Displace filter, I rippled the area around the face without harming the sun god's precious features (bottom). Finally, I used the Custom filter to emboss the image using the settings shown (inset).

Displace, HScale: 30%, VScale: 30%; Custom (settings below)

Designing custom transformations

If you ask me, Photoshop is very nearly flawless. By that, I mean, it's not actually flawless — I still have a list of a dozen or so features I'd like to see Adobe add — but gosh, it's a great application and it's been very, very good to me. Nevertheless, among the features that Photoshop is lacking is an *envelope distortion* function. Envelope distortions permit you to move areas of an image by dragging points inside a grid. Armed with an enveloping function, you could, say, precisely taper the jaw line along a face, adjust the position of a person in a photograph, or scale one part of an image independently of another.

I ask you to direct your attention to the photo in Figure 10-39. Even though it was shot by my wife's ex-husband—a good guy, I've no doubt—this image really speaks to me. Most likely, it's the frame. But it might just be the way the wind is blowing my wife's hair. Something about it makes her look like an androgynous pixie. (And, ooh baby, nobody loves an androgynous pixie more than me.) But despite the photo's elfin virtues, the balance is all wrong. The domed basilica in the background is way too far to the right. I want to tuck the basilica to the left without dramatically altering its proportions and without scaling my wife in the slightest.

Figure 10-39: My wife looks great, the basilica in the background looks great. But they've got to get closer together. This is a job for a dmap.

An envelope distortion would take care of this problem lickety-split. But as I say, Photoshop doesn't give us one. So it's fortunate that we have a workaround—the virtuous and flexible dmap. Not any dmap, mind you, but a dmap that's been specially customized for this image.

To make the dmap, I create a new image that matches the width of the pixie photo. Because I want to perform a horizontal displacement only—the vertical alignment of the elements is fine—the height of the dmap is not important. So to save memory, I create a short strip of an image, as shown at the top of Figure 10-40. I fill the dmap with 50 percent gray and white.

Gray indicates no movement; white moves pixels to the left. No black is needed. I make the white cover the distance that I want to move the basilica. Then I save the image as a PSD file, and apply it to my wife's photo using the Displace filter. Because no vertical displacement is needed, I set the Vertical Scale value to 0 percent. For this photo, a Horizontal Scale value of 100 percent happens to work well; you'll want to experiment when and if you try this technique.

The upshot is that Photoshop shifts the basilica, part and parcel, 128 pixels to the left. As shown in the second image in Figure 10-40, this corrects the composition problem, but it results in an abrupt transition between the basilica and the world around it. I could have managed something this crude by selecting the building with the rectangular marquee tool and moving it.

Gray & white dmap

Displaced image, HScale: 100%, VScale: 0%

Figure 10-40: A neutral gray dmap with a swatch of white toward the right (top) serves to shift the basilica to the left without disturbing my wife or any other elements in the photo (right). Unfortunately, the transition between displaced pixels and those around them is brusque, to say the least.

The rules we learned earlier still apply. If you want to smooth out transitions in a displacement, blur the dmap. After undoing the displacement, I return to the dmap file. Then I choose Filter ⇨ Blur ⇨ Gaussian Blur and enter a Radius value of 30 pixels. As shown in the first example in Figure 10-41, this is enough to smooth out the transitions between gray and white without eliminating the gray along the right-hand edge of the dmap.

Now when I apply the Displace filter, I get a continuous transformation effect. Granted, we end up with stretch marks along the right edge of the image, as witnessed in Figure 10-41. But that's okay. All I have to do is crop them away, and we get the work of utter perfection shown in Figure 10-42. If you inspect the final image closely, you may notice a couple of bends in the fence that weren't there before. But those bends are entirely consistent with the angle and lighting of the shot. The actual fence *could* bend in this way, so no one will be the wiser. The one drawback is that I had to buy a narrower frame. But all in all, it was worth it.

Gaussian Blur, Radius: 30 pixels

Displaced image, HScale: 100%, VScale: 0%

Figure 10-41: To soften the transitions, I apply the Gaussian Blur command to the gray-and-white dmap file (top). When I reapply the Displace filter using the same setting as before, I get a much more believable effect (bottom).

Figure 10-42: To complete my custom transformation, I crop away the stretched pixels that appeared along the right-hand side of the image. My wife looks the same, the basilica looks the same, but the space between them is quite different.

✦   ✦   ✦

Correcting Hue and Saturation

Adjusting Colors

So this is the next-to-the-next-to-the-next-to-the last chapter of this book, in case you're counting, and only now am I getting around to dealing with Photoshop's grass roots, its core functionality, the reason it was created in the first place. (I like my books to be read cover-to-cover, but maybe this one works in either direction.) Every bit as important as Unsharp Mask and other corrective filters, Photoshop's so-called *color adjustment* commands enable you to rescue overly dark shadows, tone down overly bright highlights, boost drab colors, modulate unrealistically vivid hues, and generally make a photograph look the way you want it to look.

As with filters, there are two basic varieties of color adjustments. The first are hue and saturation adjustments, which change the actual colors in an image independently of their brightness values. These commands let you remove a color cast, raise or lower the saturation of colors, colorize grayscale images, convert a photo to a duotone, and correct isolated problems such as red-eye. The second are luminosity adjustments, which give you incredibly precise control over the brightness values in an image. Because these commands work on a channel-by-channel basis, they permit you to balance colors as well.

But whereas Photoshop devotes an entire menu to its 100 or so filters, it devotes only a submenu, Image ⇨ Adjustments, to its relatively small collection of color commands. Stranger yet, although these commands are few in number, I will make no attempt to discuss or even mention all of them. Some of these commands are designed for ease of use, and others are designed to meet the needs of color and prepress technicians. But the best of the commands, the ones that serve truly unique functions, are designed to get work done efficiently and accurately.

It is this last group of efficient, accurate commands that I discuss in this and the following chapter. After introducing the larger topic of color adjustment, this chapter examines the hue and saturation commands, including Variations, the new Match Color, Hue/Saturation, and Channel Mixer. We'll also look at Photoshop CS's new red-eye defeater, the color replacement tool. Chapter 12 talks about the luminosity commands, namely Levels, Curves, and the new Shadow/Highlight.

Color effects and corrections

Color corrections can be exciting or mundane. Oftentimes the most practical modifications don't look like modifications at all. Consider Figure 11-1. The top example is an old photograph from the PhotoDisc collection, now part of Getty Images. Although an evocative photograph, this early 1990's scan is soft on focus and low on contrast. (Fortunately, the image has since been rescanned and corrected for the modern PhotoDisc library.)

Figure 11-1: Nobody's perfect, and neither is the best of scanned photos (top). You can modify colors in an image to achieve special effects (middle) or simply fix the image with a couple of well-targeted corrections (bottom).

So what we have is a beautiful image with technical shortcomings. What I decide to do with it is up to me. I can, if I choose, ignore the technical problems—in fact, abandon all semblance of realism—and enhance the otherworldly nature of the photograph by applying a color effect. The second example in Figure 11-1 shows the result of mapping the image to one of Photoshop's predefined gradients using Image ➪ Adjustments ➪ Gradient Map. But more likely, I'd choose to correct the photograph, in this case using Image ➪ Adjustments ➪ Curves and a bit of Unsharp Mask, as in the last example. Although the final example took more time to achieve, at first glance it doesn't look all that much different than the original. But a close comparison reveals that the colors are better, and the focus is better. And where image correction is concerned, that's what ultimately counts.

Scans and digital photographs are rarely perfect, no matter how much money you spend on the hardware or service. They can almost always benefit from tweaking and subtle adjustments, if not outright overhauls, in the color department. Keep in mind, however, that Photoshop can't make something from nothing. In creating the illusion of more and better colors, most color-adjustment operations actually take some small amount of color *away* from the image. Somewhere in your image, two pixels that were two different colors before you started the correction are now the same color. The irony of color correction is that, even though an image may look 10 times better, it will in fact be less colorful than when you started.

Remembering this principle is important because it demonstrates that adjusting colors is a balancing act. The first nine operations you perform may make an image look progressively better, but the tenth may send it into decline. There's no magic formula; the amount of color mapping you need to apply varies from image to image. But if you follow my usual recommendations—use the commands in moderation, know when to stop, and save your image to disk before doing anything drastic—you should be fine.

Using the adjustment dialog boxes

With the exception of the Auto commands covered in the next chapter, all the color adjustments that I discuss let you correct an image by entering values or making other changes inside a dialog box, like the one in Figure 11-2. Here are a few key points to file away in the back of your mind as you work:

✦ **Turn on the Preview check box to see what you're doing.** Only the Variations dialog box lacks a Preview check box. Otherwise, when turned on, you see the results of your changes in the image window. Assuming your computer is modern enough to provide the proper processing power, there is no reason on earth to turn this option off.

✦ **To reapply the most recent adjustment settings, press Alt (Option on the Mac) when choosing the command.** Again, the exception is Variations, which always remembers your last settings. In addition to Alt-selecting the command from the Adjustments submenu, you can also press Alt along with a command's keyboard shortcut. For example, Ctrl+Alt+U (⌘-Option-U) brings up the Hue/Saturation dialog box with the last-applied settings intact, assuming those settings were applied since you started up Photoshop.

✦ **Save your settings.** Many dialog boxes offer a Save button, which when clicked, will save your settings for later use. This is especially useful when correcting multiple images shot under similar circumstances. You can use the settings during a separate Photoshop session, or even e-mail them to a colleague to use on another computer. Macintosh users, be sure to include a three-character extension (which Photoshop automatically recommends, assuming Append File Extension is set to Always in the Preferences dialog box) with the file name if you want to use the settings on a Windows machine.

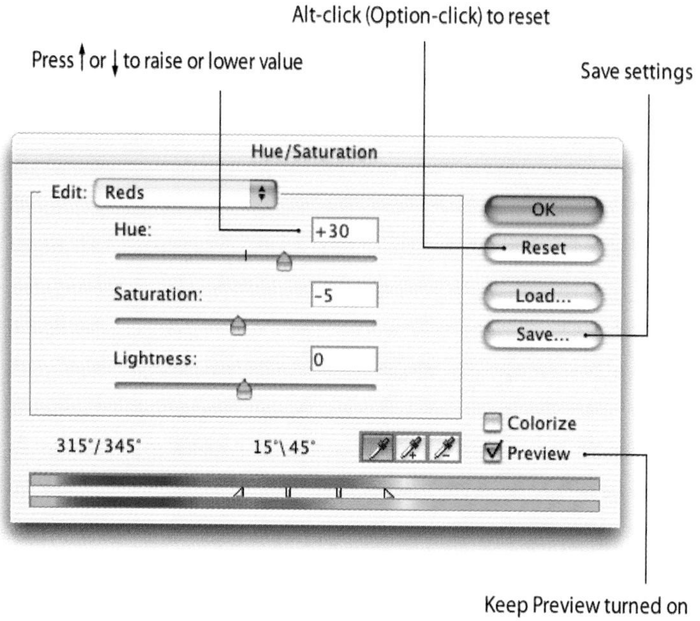

Press ↑ or ↓ to raise or lower value

Alt-click (Option-click) to reset

Save settings

Hue/Saturation

Edit: Reds

Hue: +30

Saturation: -5

Lightness: 0

OK

Reset

Load...

Save...

315°/345°   15°\45°

Colorize
☑ Preview

Keep Preview turned on

Figure 11-2: A typical color adjustment dialog box, with a few timesaving tricks labeled. For the most part, these techniques work the same as they do when applying corrective filters.

✦ **Alt-click the Cancel button to reset all options to their neutral settings.** When you press the Alt key (or Option on the Mac), the Cancel button changes to Reset. This permits you to restore an image to the way it looked when you first chose the command, so that you can begin the adjustment process over again.

✦ **Choose Edit ➪ Fade to temper an adjustment.** As always, pressing Ctrl+Shift+F (⌘-Shift-F) lets you fade the most recently applied operation, either by reducing its opacity or applying a blend mode. But the command only works immediately after applying an adjustment.

✦ **When in doubt, apply an adjustment layer.** In Chapter 8, I recommended that you float an image to an independent layer before applying a filter, thus affording you the option to mix the filtered image with the underlying original. When applying color adjustments, this technique isn't necessary. That's because most of the essential color adjustment commands can be applied as independent layers. An *adjustment layer* is editable long after it's created, it may be turned on and off, and it can affect multiple layers at a time. The main difference is that, instead of choosing a command from the Image ➪ Adjustments submenu, you choose it from the adjustment layer icon at the bottom of the Layers palette, labeled in Figure 11-3. For complete information on these wonderful tools, read "Adjustment Layers" toward the end of this chapter.

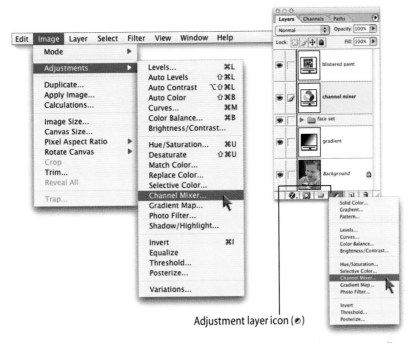

Adjustment layer icon (⊘)

Figure 11-3: In addition to applying a static adjustment from the Image ⇨ Adjustments submenu (left), Photoshop permits you to apply a dynamic adjustment layer from the Layers palette (right).

Applying Color Variations

Let's start things off with the most straightforward and unusual correction function in all of Photoshop, which also happens to be the last command in the Image ⇨ Adjustments submenu. Known simply as Variations, this ambitious command lets you correct colors and brightness values inside an image without troubling yourself with a lot of technical-sounding options and numerical values. The irony is that if you do possess a little technical knowledge, you can make better use of the command and better anticipate its outcome.

When you choose Image ⇨ Adjustments ⇨ Variations, Photoshop displays the dialog box shown in Figure 11-4, which permits you to adjust colors and brightness values in an image by clicking on one or more thumbnails that look more like the image you're hoping to achieve. To infuse color into the image, click one of the More thumbnails in the central portion of the dialog box. To lighten or darken the image, use the thumbnails on the right-hand side. Figure 11-5 shows how the buttons affect a typical high-resolution, CMYK photograph. In each case, the slider bar was set to its default position midway between Fine and Coarse and the Midtones radio button was selected.

How hues work

On first glance, the colors selected for the Variations thumbnails — red, yellow, green, cyan, blue, and magenta — may seem highly arbitrary. I mean, where's orange, indigo, and violet? If they're good enough for the rainbow, surely they should rate inclusion in the Variations dialog box. And as long as we're including magenta, we might as well throw in carmine, mauve, lilac, and fuchsia. But as it turns out, these are very specific, industry-accepted labels for six evenly spaced colors in the visible color spectrum.

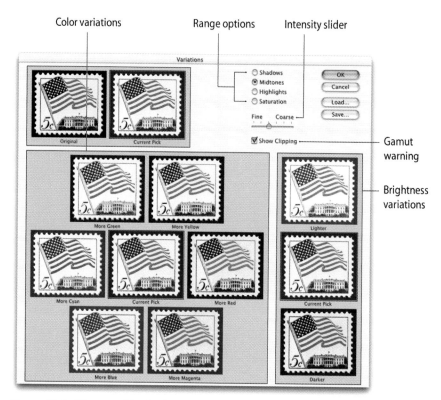

Figure 11-4: When working in the Variations dialog box, click a thumbnail to shift colors in a certain direction. Adjust the slider bar in the upper-right corner to change the sensitivity of the thumbnails. Use the radio buttons to determine which colors in the image are affected.

To fully understand how these thumbnails work, turn your attention to the diagram in Figure 11-6. Here we see all the *hues* in the visible color spectrum represented along a continuous circle. I have placed small monitors next to Red, Green, and Blue because these are the primary colors of light. Spaced evenly between them are the print pigments Cyan, Magenta, and Yellow, hence the small printer icons. (The missing CMYK ink, black, is not actually a primary, but rather a "key" color used to reinforce shadows.) In a perfect world, cyan ink exactly absorbs red light and reflects green and blue; magenta absorbs green and reflects red and blue; and yellow absorbs blue and reflects red and green. Therefore, opposite colors, such as cyan and red, are theoretical opposites (often called *complements*).

Figure 11-5: The results of applying each of the color thumbnails from the Variations dialog box to a photo of yours truly with my Little Puppet Friend, whose encyclopedic knowledge of digital imaging and dashing good looks have enlivened many a Total Training video series.

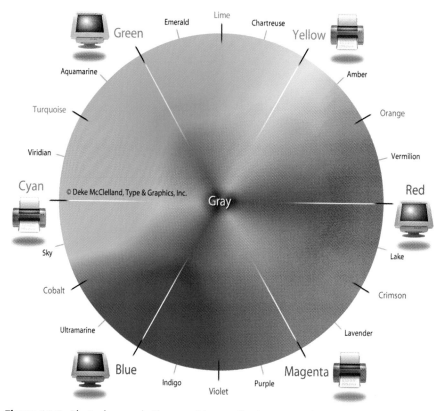

Figure 11-6: Photoshop and other graphics applications map the visible color spectrum onto a continuous circle. Red, green, and blue are the primary colors of light. Cyan, magenta, and yellow are their complementary opposites, representing the primary printed pigments.

In the real world, things aren't quite this cut and dry. But inside the Variations dialog box, theory becomes reality. Because you don't actually modify the image until you click the OK button, Variations can calculate its adjustments in a pure and perfect world. This means each thumbnail serves two purposes — to add one color and subtract its complement. If you click More Cyan, you add cyan and subtract red. If you then click More Red, you undo More Cyan and restore the original image. This means you can use More Cyan either to add cyan to an image or remove a red color cast.

In addition to the standards RGB and CMY, Figure 11-6 calls out 18 incremental colors around the perimeter of the circle, each spaced evenly, one 15 degrees from the next. Mind you, these are not industry accepted color names. In fact, I would classify them as speculative. I think we can all safely agree on Orange, but the others go by many names and many definitions. What I call Vermilion you might call Scarlet, Amber you might call Gold, and the pedestrian Sky you might call Cerulean. Most folks have never heard of the color Lake (named after a red dye made from insects), and I'm afraid carmine, mauve, lilac, and fuchsia still didn't make the cut. But while I ultimately made some subjective choices, the names are hardly random. I assembled them from a variety of sources, including several traditional art supply houses, a handful of special-interest Web sites (those serving ceramic and stamp collectors, for example), and even the occasional consumer color vendor such as Crayola. The result is a series of color signposts to help you get your bearings inside this circular rainbow.

Just as the primaries have complements, so do the composite colors. The complement of Turquoise is Crimson; the complement of Indigo is Chartreuse. This means, you can add Violet or subtract Lime by clicking More Magenta and then More Blue. To add Lavender or subtract Aquamarine, click More Red once and More Magenta twice. Alternatively, you can adjust the intensity slider to create different tints. I discuss the intensity slider in the very next section.

Intensity and range

The More thumbnails aren't the only options in the Variations dialog box; they're just the most important ones. Here are the other settings you should know about (many of which were labeled back in Figure 11-4):

✦ **Intensity slider:** To control the amount of color shifting that occurs when you click a thumbnail, move the slider triangle in the upper-right portion of the dialog box. The far left Fine setting produces very minute changes; Coarse creates massive changes, as illustrated in Figure 11-7. Each tick mark setting produces exactly twice the effect of the tick mark to the left of it, so each example in the figure is four times as blue as the example that precedes it.

Original yellow color cast

More Blue, Fine

same, medium intensity

and again, Coarse

Figure 11-7: The original scan of this 1963 postage stamp has a distinct yellow color cast (top left). I experiment with remedying this using yellow's opposite, the More Blue thumbnail, at each of three intensity settings. In this case, medium intensity (bottom left) works best.

Here's an odd and rare interface difference between the Mac and Windows versions of Photoshop: Under Windows, there are seven different intensity levels (five levels between Fine and Coarse), but on the Mac there are only six, with four intermediate levels between Fine and Coarse. As it boils down, Coarse is equally coarse on both Mac and Windows. And one tick to the left of Coarse is equal on both platforms. And so it goes, until we get to Fine on the Mac, which is actually equal to one tick up from Fine on Windows. And so, Windows' Fine level is actually finer than the Mac's. Not that I think this news should (or could) make Mac owners dump their machines and buy PCs...but it's an interesting distinction.

✦ **Range options:** The radio buttons at the top control which colors in the image are affected. Select Shadows to change the darkest colors, Highlights to change the lightest colors, and Midtones to change everything in between. Figure 11-8 shows four examples.

In fact, if you're familiar with Image ⇨ Adjustments ⇨ Levels — as you most assuredly will be after you read Chapter 12 — you might have noticed that the first three radio buttons have direct counterparts in the first set of slider triangles in the Levels dialog box. For example, when you click the Lighter thumbnail while the Highlights option is selected in the Variations dialog box, you perform roughly the same action as moving the white triangle in the Levels dialog box to the left — that is, you make the lightest colors in the image even lighter.

Figure 11-8: The effects of clicking the More Blue thumbnail when each of the first three range options is in effect, as well as all three together (bottom right). In all cases, the intensity slider triangle is two ticks over from Coarse.

✦ **Saturation:** The Saturation radio button lets you increase or decrease the saturation (vibrancy) of colors in an image. Only one thumbnail appears on each side of the Current Pick image. One decreases the saturation and the other increases it.

In Figure 11-9 notice that lowering saturation has the side effect of lightening the image while increasing saturation darkens the image. If you want to edit saturation but maintain consistent brightness levels, use Image ➪ Adjustments ➪ Hue/Saturation (discussed later in this chapter).

✦ **Show Clipping:** As you click the options — particularly when modifying saturation — you may notice that weird colors spring up inside the thumbnails. These brightly colored pixels are *gamut warnings,* Photoshop's way of highlighting colors that exceed the boundaries of the printable color space. Even if you're working in the RGB mode, the clipped pixels indicate colors that extend beyond the CMYK gamut. Although the colors won't actually appear inverted as they do in the dialog box, it's not a good idea to exceed the color space when preparing print graphics because it can result in large flat-colored regions. When creating RGB images for the Web or even for inkjet printing, turn off the Show Clipping check box to view the thumbnail representations of the image as it will really appear.

3rd-from-end ⎯⎯⎯ , Less Saturation   same, More Saturation

Figure 11-9: Clicking the Less Saturation thumbnail not only leeches away color but also increases brightness (left). More Saturation increases saturation by darkening colors (right).

When to use Variations

On balance, the Variations command is a mixed bag. On one hand, you can adjust hues and luminosity levels based on the brightness values of the pixels, something other commands cannot do. And there's no denying that the thumbnails take much of the guesswork out of the correction process.

On the other hand, the Variations dialog box takes over your screen and prevents you from previewing corrections directly inside the image window. Also frustrating, you can see at most a limited area outside a selection, which proves disconcerting when making relative color adjustments. By default, Variations lacks a keyboard shortcut (though the new Keyboard Shortcuts feature lets you assign a shortcut to it). And you cannot apply Variations as an adjustment layer.

I find myself using Variations almost exclusively to remove a color cast from a photograph or shift its hues to achieve a more naturalistic color balance. Although Variations can fix lighting problems, this is a job better suited to Levels or Curves (see the next chapter). And for more sophisticated color adjustments, choose Image ➪ Adjustments ➪ Hue/Saturation, as I explain in the next section.

But Variations is remarkably adept at one more task that you don't hear discussed very often, and that's creating quick and easy duotones, which are grayscale images colorized with two or more colors according to their brightness values. Figure 11-10 shows a grayscale scan so colorized using Variations. I started by converting the grayscale image to RGB by choosing Image ➪ Mode ➪ RGB Color. Then I chose Variations, set the intensity and range as listed in the first example, and clicked the More Yellow thumbnail. To give the image an amber tint, I reduced the intensity setting and clicked More Red. Then I selected the Shadows option, raised the intensity, and clicked More Blue to achieve the final effect.

I should mention that if you're serious about creating "real" duotones that separate out to exactly two spot-color inks, then Variations is not the ticket. Instead, Photoshop provides a command specifically designed for this purpose, Image ➪ Mode ➪ Duotone. I discuss the Duotone command at length in Chapter 18 of my softbound *Photoshop CS Bible*. But if all you're looking for is a two-color effect that's both intuitive and a breeze to apply, then Variations is the best tool on the block.

Figure 11-10: A vintage photograph first colorized with yellow (left) and amber (middle) and then imbued with deep blue shadows (right). The result is a quick and easy duotone.

Using the Match Color Command

Where Variations treats color casts like a foul scent in the air in need of immediate deodorizing, the new Match Color command takes a deep breath, fills its lungs, and says "Ah! A color cast! I can *work* with that!" Match Color excels at matching color casts between images, making the different images seem to be "cut from the same cloth," as it were. And there are a bunch of scenarios in which you might want to resolve the color cast of one image to match another. Say, for instance, that you're presenting a series of outdoor photos you took over the course of one day. Every time the clouds passed over the sun, the rich colors faded and the world of your image became a little grayish. With a little noodling around in the dialog box, Match Color does a pretty impressive job of eliminating these disparities. Or, for instance, say you want to combine two photos of people, shot in different circumstances, into one image. An inconsistency in the color cast of the skin tones can be a dead giveaway on an otherwise expert composite. While traditionally there have been ways to fix these problems manually, Photoshop CS has made it a whole lot faster and simpler with the Match Color command.

Begin by opening both the image you want to adjust and the image whose color you want to match (there are a couple of exceptions to this, which I'll discuss in a moment). If you only want to match some colors in the images, like skin tones, for example, select the colors you want to isolate in both the source and destination images. Make sure the destination image is in the active image window and choose Image ➪ Adjustments ➪ Match Color to display the dialog box shown in Figure 11-11.

The following list explains the options available to you in the Match Color dialog box.

✦ **Target:** The Target is automatically and unalterably set as whichever image and layer were active when you chose the command. If your destination image contains a selection, the Ignore Selection when Applying Adjustment check box is available. If you've made a selection, it's probably because (as I suggested above) you just want to affect certain parts of the layer, like skin tones. In that case, you'd want to leave the option off. But if instead you want to affect the entire layer, click the check box.

✦ **Image Options:** The Image Options let you make adjustments to the lightness, saturation, and strength of the destination image. Although you can use these commands on your destination image without even choosing another image to match, you'll probably instead use the Image Options as a way of tweaking Match Colors' color matching job by hand. The Luminance slider defaults to a value of 100 and lets you increase or decrease the brightness of your destination image. Color Intensity works much like clicking More Saturation in Variations. The Fade slider saves you the step of applying Match Color and then choosing Edit ➪ Fade Match Color. Increase this value to gradually bring in color elements from your unaltered destination image. A value of 100 will exactly match your pre-Match Color image.

Turn on the Neutralize check box to tell Photoshop to examine the destination image, without factoring in any values from the source image, and attempt to remove any color cast that it finds. I've found that sometimes it works really well and sometimes it just winds up dulling your image. If you don't get the results you want, try using the new Photo Filter command, which I discuss later in this chapter, to manually target a color cast.

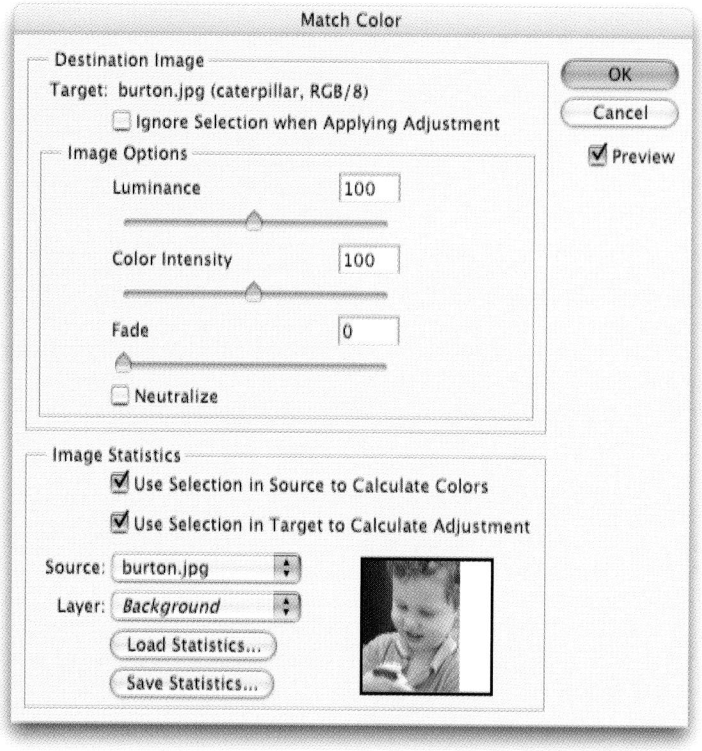

Figure 11-11: The Match Color command in Photoshop CS lets you bring the color cast of one image into another. In this case, I'm matching the color of one layer of a document to the background image of the same document.

✦ **Image Statistics:** These options let you specify a source to match your destination image to, and determine how it is interpreted. This can be any other open image, or even a layer within the destination image itself. The latter is particularly useful if you're trying to composite, say, a person from another photo on a separate layer into your destination image. If your source image contains a selection, click the Use Selection in Source to Calculate Colors check box to only analyze the statistics, or characteristics, of the selected region. When this check box is turned off, Match Color determines the statistics of the source by looking at all of the pixels in the image. Similarly, turning on the Use Selection in Target to Calculate Adjustment check box makes changes to the target image using only colors found in the selected area of that image. If you selected similarly colored areas in both your target and source images, it's a good idea to leave both of these check boxes turned on.

Use the Source pop-up menu to choose the source image from among all open images. If you select None, you still have access to the Neutralize check box and other Image Options. If you select a source with more than one layer, you can specify the layer from which you're culling statistics in the Layer pop-up menu. You also have the option of choosing a merged composite of all the layers in the source image.

Lastly, the Match Color dialog box offers you the option of both saving and then loading statistics it has calculated from a source image. This can be useful in a couple ways. First, it means you don't need to have a source image open when applying the Match Color command. It also means you can save the statistics of an image and use them to adjust an unlimited number of other images, on other machines, long after the original source image is out of the picture.

Take a look at Figure 11-12. The top and middle examples are similar in an obvious way; they both show a close-up of a ladybug on a sunflower. But the top image was taken outdoors on a day dreary enough to cause the camera's flash to fire, while the middle image was taken indoors, and in fact features a different sunflower and ladybug. I like the color in the middle image much better, so I used Match Color on the top image, and loaded the middle image as the source. The results were a bit severe, so I set the Fade to 30, giving me the bottom example in Figure 11-12. Match Color did an excellent job of giving the bright yellows a more orange tint, and of tamping down the highlights. It's not too hard to believe that you're looking at the same ladybug and sunflower in the same environment.

The Match Color command only works with images in the RGB mode.

To track the behavior of specific colors when using Match Color, display the Info palette, either by choosing Window ➪ Info or by pressing the F8 key. Then move the cursor inside the image window. The Info palette tracks the individual RGB and CMYK values of the pixel beneath your cursor. The number before the slash is the value before the color adjustment; the number after the slash is the value after the adjustment.

Hue Shifting and Colorizing

Where the Variations command enables you to shift colors in an image based on brightness values and Match Color shifts colors in an image based on the colors in a different image, another command lets you shift colors wholesale, modify some colors independently of others, raise and lower saturation values without affecting luminosity, and coat an image with a uniform tint. This wonderful command is Image ➪ Adjustments ➪ Hue/Saturation, and it's one of Photoshop's most overlooked gems.

Adjusting the Hue and Saturation values

Choose the Hue/Saturation command or press Ctrl+U (⌘-U on the Mac) to display the Hue/Saturation dialog box, shown in Figure 11-13. The figure actually shows two versions of the dialog box, first as it appears when editing all colors in a selection or layer and second as it appears when editing a specific range of colors, in this case red. I will discuss these options in more detail in a moment, but for now, be content in the knowledge that Hue/Saturation lays out a world of color challenges and opportunities before you.

Figure 11-12: Pick a destination image (top) and a source (middle), and Match Color can make everything copasetic (bottom).

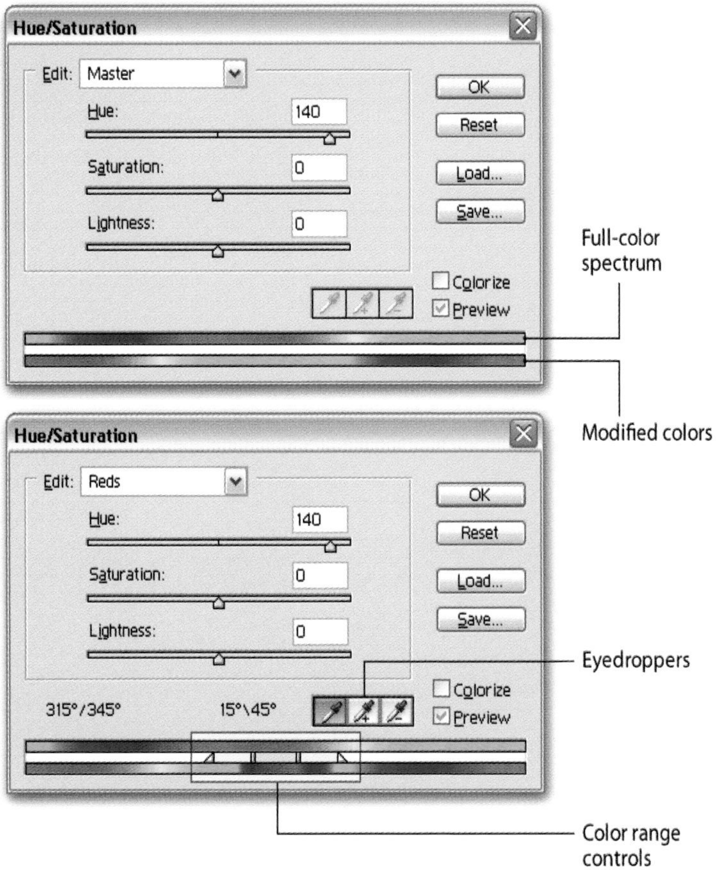

Figure 11-13: The Hue/Saturation dialog box as it appears when editing all colors in the active layer (top) and when editing a select range of colors (bottom).

Unlike Variations, Hue/Saturation relies on numerical values and more complex and equally more precise controls. But the command continues to subscribe to that most fundamental of digital color conventions, the rainbow spectrum wheel. As illustrated in Figure 11-14, Hue/Saturation sees red, yellow, green, and the others in the same positions that I diagramed for Variations in Figure 11-6. But whereas Variations presents you with strategically positioned thumbnails, Hue/Saturation measures colors in degrees. As you may recall from 8th-grade Geometry, a circle is measured in 360 degrees, starting at the 3 o'clock position (better known to us as Red), and progressing in a counterclockwise direction. The primary colors of light and pigment are spaced in 60-degree increments. As the figure shows, secondary colors occur every 30 degrees, with intermediate colors every 15 degrees.

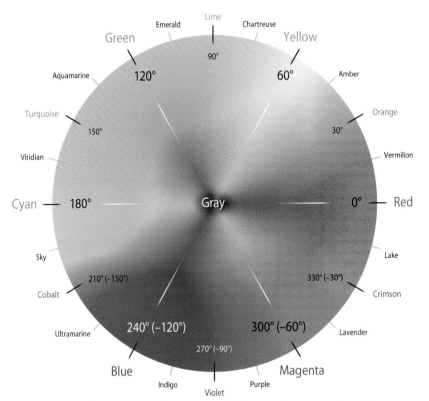

Figure 11-14: The Hue/Saturation command observes the same color circle as Variations. But instead of adding colors and subtracting complements, Hue/Saturation revolves hues around the circle by a prescribed angle, either positive or negative.

Hues can be measured absolutely—that is, yellow is at 60 degrees, green is at 120 degrees, and so on—or relatively—red shifted counterclockwise 150 degrees becomes turquoise. If all this sounds a little thick, don't worry. It'll become increasingly clear as we run through the three main options, Hue, Saturation, and Lightness:

> ✦ **Hue:** The Hue slider bar measures colors on the 360-degree rainbow wheel. Under normal circumstances (that is, when Colorize is turned off), you can adjust the Hue value from negative to positive 180 degrees. As you do, Photoshop rotates selected colors around the wheel. This means you can literally turn any color in an image into any other color just by dragging a slider triangle, a real boon when editing product and fashion photography.
>
> For example, consider the office chairs in Figure 11-15. The first image is the chair as it appeared in the original photograph, which is red. But thanks to Hue/Saturation, it doesn't have to remain that way. Change the Hue value to +60 degrees and the chair becomes yellow. Shift the Hue +120 degrees and the chair becomes green. A Hue value of either positive or negative 180 degrees produces exactly the same result, a cyan chair. A Hue value of –120 degrees is the same as a 240-degree shift (after all, 360 minus

120 equals 240), which gets me blue. To make the chair magenta, I enter –60 degrees, which is the same as a 300-degree rotation.

It stands to reason that if you can change the chair to any primary color, you can change it to a secondary or tertiary color as well. Figure 11-16 shows examples. Notice that the saturation and brightness of colors remain unchanged throughout Figures 11-15 and 11-16. This means low-saturation colors, such as the blacks and grays in the arms and legs, change very little from one Hue setting to the next. What few changes we do see look entirely consistent with the effects of colors reflected from the chair's upholstery.

Figure 11-15: Shoot one chair and make it any color you like. Here I start with a red chair and make it every other primary color by entering Hue values in multiples of 60 degrees. The Hue option accepts values only as high as +180 degrees; to achieve greater shifts, you have to enter negative values, as in the bottom row.

Bear in mind that the Hue option applies relative color transformations. So applying a Hue value of 60 degrees to an object that starts out red makes it yellow. But apply that same value of +60 degrees to an orange image, such as the pumpkin in Figure 11-17, and Photoshop converts the gourd to lime. Therefore, 60-degree Hue adjustments change the pumpkin from one secondary color to another; offset that model by 30 degrees to recolor the pumpkin in primaries.

Figure 11-16: Just because a chair starts off as a primary color doesn't mean it has to stay that way. By entering Hue values in every-other multiples of 30 degrees (according to the labels), I'm able to dye my upholstery in secondary colors.

If an image contains multiple colors, all colors rotate to new relative positions in the rainbow wheel. Figure 11-18 features multiple iterations of a decorative pin that bears the traditional red stripes of Old Glory and a slightly less traditional field of cobalt. Applying various Hue values shifts these and other colors inside the image to new relative locations.

Figure 11-17: The Hue value changes colors in an image relative to its original colors. So an orange pumpkin subject to 60-degree Hue adjustments progresses from one secondary color to another.

✦ **Saturation:** The Saturation value changes the intensity of colors. Under normal circumstances, the Saturation value varies from –100 for gray to +100 for the most vivid hues. The only exception occurs when the Colorize check box is active (as I discuss shortly), in which case saturation becomes an absolute value, measured from 0 for gray to 100 for maximum saturation.

The Saturation option is especially useful for boosting colors in images captured with consumer-grade digital cameras. Figure 11-19 shows a macro (close-up) photograph of a sandcastle wall that I built with a full-sized flag flying far in the background. No image editing here; it was all done with toy shovels and wet dirt. But alas, the colors are unacceptably drab. So I raised the Saturation value to a perilously high setting of +80 percent. (You'll rarely make changes this extreme; I do so only for the sake of demonstration.) The final image shows the result of raising the color saturation to a similar level using the Variations command. As you can see, where the Variations command deepens colors as it saturates them, Hue/Saturation protects the luminosity, making it an easier command to predict.

You'll also find the Saturation option helpful when shifting hues in an image. Thanks in part to the way Photoshop calculates CMYK conversions as well as the way our eyes perceive color, some hues naturally appear more saturated than others. The top row of Figure 11-20 shows a bright and cheerful lake-colored flower as it was originally photographed. A Hue value of +75 percent shifts the colors from lake to yellow, but what a dreary yellow it is, as the middle example shows. Fortunately, I can make the sun shine by raising the Saturation value to +40 percent.

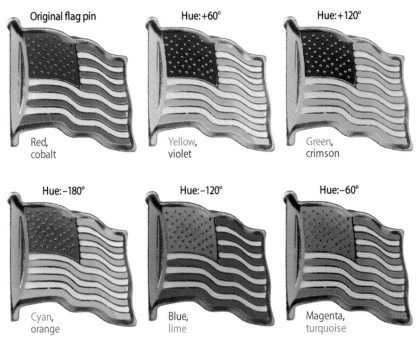

Figure 11-18: Assuming that the Edit pop-up menu is set to Master (as by default), the Hue option shifts all colors in an image to equal degrees. Saturation and luminosity levels remain constant.

The opposite turns out to be true when I shift an amber flower to sky blue (see the bottom row of Figure 11-20). Sky happens to be +150 degrees from amber, but applying such a Hue value produces absurdly vibrant colors that haven't a hope of printing properly. As the middle flower illustrates, the result is lots of flat color and little definition between one portion of the flower and the next. Fortunately, by lowering the Saturation to –50 percent, I can restore that definition without harming the hues.

It's worth noting that the Saturation value can't raise or lower the intensity of a color unless it has some intensity to work with in the first place. For example, no amount of saturation will add color to a grayscale image. To accomplish that, you have to turn on the Colorize check box, as I discuss later in "Colorizing images."

✦ **Lightness:** You can, if you wish, darken or lighten an image by varying the Lightness value from negative to positive 100. But you don't wish to. The problem with the Lightness value is that it unwisely compresses the brightness range of an image, either lightening black when you enter a positive value or darkening white when you enter a negative value. The result is a dulling of shadows or highlights and a general reduction in photographic detail. On rare occasion, you might use this option to modify the shade of a solid fill, gradient, or other very small range of colors. Otherwise, limit yourself to the Hue and Saturation values and modify the brightness of an image in a separate pass using the Levels or Curves command, as discussed in the next chapter.

Figure 11-19: Shortly after I built this sandcastle (top), my son gleefully smashed it, and then demanded I build more so he could smash them, too. But the photo lives on, with increased saturation supplied by the Hue/Saturation (middle) and Variations (bottom) commands.

Figure 11-20: Some Hue shifts result in drab colors (top middle) that necessitate an increase in the Saturation value (top right). Others produce colors so hot they violate the printable CMYK gamut (bottom middle). Often, the solution is as simple as reducing the Saturation (bottom right).

As with the Match Color command, you can track the behavior of specific colors when adjusting the Hue/Saturation options. As shown in Figure 11-21, the Info palette tracks the individual RGB and CMYK values of the pixel beneath your cursor in the image window. The number before the slash is the value before the color adjustment; the number after the slash is the value after the adjustment.

You don't have to settle for just one color readout either. Shift-click in the image window to add up to four fixed color targets, just like those created with the dedicated color sampler tool (the alternative eyedropper in the toolbox). To move a color target after you've set it in place, Shift-drag it. To delete a target, Shift+Alt-click it (Shift-Option-click it on the Mac).

Note that Shift-clicking sets targets only when the Edit pop-up menu is set to Master, because otherwise Shift-clicking adjusts the editable range (as I explain in the next section). So set your targets and then adjust the Edit option.

The Info palette and color targets are equally useful when working inside the Channel Mixer, Levels, Curves, or any other dialog box that previews its changes in the full image window. These techniques are also applicable to adjustment layers. Best of all, targets set from inside one dialog box will remain in force throughout others, so you can always rest assured of color-tracking continuity.

Original colors

Post-edit colors

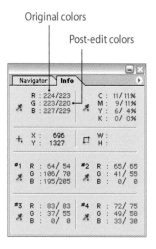

Figure 11-21: When you move the eyedropper outside a color adjustment dialog box and into the image window, the Info palette lists the color values of the pixel beneath the cursor before (red) and after (blue) the adjustment. You can also Shift-click to deposit as many as four fixed targets that the Info palette will track as you work.

Editing independent color ranges

One of the primary advantages of the Hue/Saturation dialog box is that it permits you to edit one range of colors in an image independently of another. Consider the example in Figure 11-22. The first image shows a pair of red tulips resting gracefully on a floating layer. I added a soft drop shadow (Size: 80 pixels, Distance: 160 pixels, Opacity: 50 percent) for depth. Then I set the flowers against a slate background.

Layered flowers with drop shadow   Set against slate layer

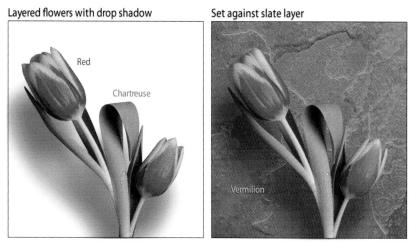

Figure 11-22: A pair of tulips relegated to an independent layer and assigned a drop shadow (left), next composited against a sturdy slate background (right).

The effect is plausible, elegant, and simple, but I don't particularly care for the colors. No problem, I can change them with Image ➪ Adjustments ➪ Hue/Saturation. In Figure 11-23, I start by shifting the colors of the slate background from predominantly vermilion to a more drab ultramarine using a Hue value of –150 degrees and a Saturation value of –50 percent.

This works beautifully, because the slate is separated off onto its own layer. But what if I want to next adjust the colors of the bright red tulip petals independently of the drab chartreuse stem and leaves? Because these elements coexist on a single layer, changing the petals to, say, bright blue likewise revolves the colors in the stem and leaves to lavender, as the second example in Figure 11-23 shows.

Background, Hue: –150°, Saturation: –50%   Flowers, Hue: –120°

Figure 11-23: By default, the Hue/Saturation command changes all colors in a selection or layer at a time, making it very easy to apply different hue and saturation settings to the slate background (left) and flowers (right). Isolating colors inside a layer, however, is another matter.

I could of course select the petals using Select ⇨ Color Range, as explained in Chapter 4. But because petal and stem are such different hues — varying by 75 degrees on the rainbow wheel — the Hue/Saturation command can isolate the colors without the help of Color Range or any other selection technique. The linchpin is the Edit pop-up menu. Labeled in Figure 11-24, the Edit option controls which colors in the active selection or layer are affected by the Hue/ Saturation command. If you select the Master option, as by default, Hue/Saturation adjusts all colors equally, as in Figure 11-23 and previous figures. If you prefer to adjust some colors in a layer independently of others, choose one of the predefined color ranges, named for the RGB and CMY primaries. You can also press a keyboard shortcut, from Ctrl+1 for Reds to Ctrl+6 for Magentas (⌘-1 to ⌘-6 on the Mac).

Figure 11-25 illustrates the extent of the six predefined Edit ranges. The Reds range from 345 to 15 degrees, lake to vermilion. Naturally, if you were to modify just the Reds while leaving all non-red pixels unchanged, you'd end up with some jagged transitions between modified and unmodified pixels. So Photoshop softens the edges with 30 degrees of extra fuzziness at either end of the red spectrum, thereby applying incremental changes to colors as far away as amber (45 degrees up north) and lavender (315 degrees down south). The tapering lines in Figure 11-25 indicate the extents of these fuzziness settings. As you can see, the fuzziness of one range of colors overlaps the fuzziness of its neighbors. Therefore, secondary colors such as orange, lime, turquoise, and others do not fall squarely inside any predefined range but rather receive partial coverage from two next-door neighbors.

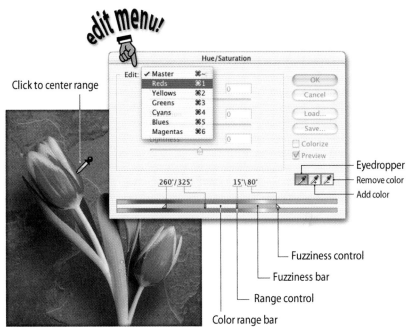

Click to center range

Eyedropper
Remove color
Add color

Fuzziness control

Fuzziness bar

Range control

Color range bar

Figure 11-24: To edit some colors in a layer independently of others, select a general range from the Edit pop-up menu. Then use the color range controls at the bottom of the dialog box to modify the range or the fuzziness.

The predefined Edit options are presets only; you can, and should, modify them to suit your needs. After you select an Edit option, you can use the color ramp controls to broaden or narrow the range of colors affected by the Hue and Saturation options.

Labeled in Figure 11-24, the color range controls work as follows:

✦ **Color range bar:** Drag the central color range bar to move the entire color range.

✦ **Fuzziness bar:** Drag one of the two horizontal fuzziness bars (located to the left and right of the color range bar) to broaden or narrow the color range without affecting the fuzziness.

✦ **Range control:** Drag the range control to change the range while leaving the fuzziness points fixed in place. This permits you to expand the range and condense the fuzziness, or vice versa.

✦ **Fuzziness control:** Drag the triangular fuzziness control to lengthen or contract the fuzziness independently of the color range.

By default, the Hue/Saturation dialog box positions red at the center of the color ramps, with cyan at either end. This is great when the range is red or some other warm color. But if you're working with a cool blue or green range, the controls get split between the two ends. To move a different color to the central position, press the Ctrl key (⌘ on the Mac) and drag inside the color ramp. The spectrum revolves around the ramp as you drag.

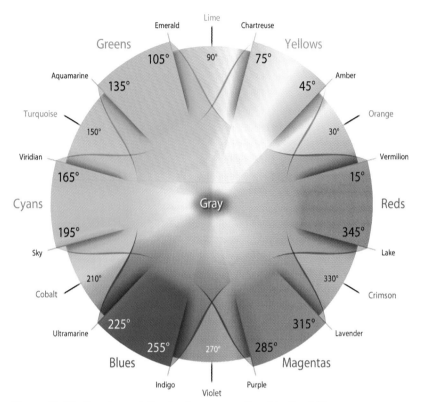

Figure 11-25: The six predefined color ranges offered by the Edit pop-up menu. Each range extends from a primary color 15 degrees in both directions. To ensure smooth transitions, the range then tapers off over the course of another 30 degrees in both directions.

Better yet, you can set a range just by clicking in the image window. Your cursor automatically changes to an eyedropper when you move it outside the Hue/Saturation dialog box. Photoshop centers the range on the exact color you clicked. For example, to change the color of the red tulip petals independently of the rest of the flowers, I first selected Reds from the Edit pop-up menu to establish the base color range. Then I clicked inside a red portion of the petals to make sure I had the right shade of red selected. The two examples in Figure 11-26 show the results of setting the Hue value to +60 degrees and –120 degrees, respectively, to achieve yellow and blue petals. Because the reds were isolated, the stem and leaves remain the same cold chartreuse.

You can also use the eyedropper to expand or condense the color range. To add colors to the editable range, Shift-click or Shift-drag inside the image window. To remove colors from the range, press the Alt key (Option on the Mac) and click or drag in the image. You can also use the alternative plus and minus eyedropper tools, but why bother? Shift and Alt do the job just fine.

It is interesting to note that you can apply multiple sets of Hue and Saturation values to different color ranges during a single visit to the Hue/Saturation dialog box. This can make an enormous difference to the way the colors behave. For example, let's say I want to take the first example in Figure 11-26 and shift the leaves to blue so that they closely match the ultramarine background. The leaves are chartreuse, so they fall into the predefined Yellows range. (This may sound strange, because to our eyes the leaves look more green than yellow. But to Photoshop, Greens trend toward emerald and aquamarine. Colors with even a hint of yellow in them are Yellows.) However, if I again choose the Hue/Saturation command, change Edit to Yellows and apply a Hue value of +165 degrees — all on top of my previous edit — I change both yellow petals and chartreuse leaves, as in the first example of Figure 11-27. This is because petals and leaves now fall inside a single range. I could of course customize the range, but I'd have a hard time distinguishing between two colors as close as yellow and chartreuse. The better approach is to restore the original red petals by undoing my previous application of Hue/Saturation, and then reapply the command to both the Reds and Yellows ranges in a single pass. This way, I can shift the red pixels to yellow and the chartreuse pixels to blue without the two operations interfering with each other.

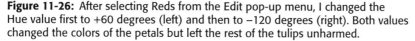

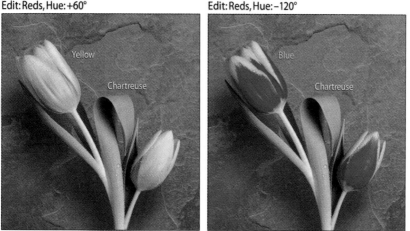

Figure 11-26: After selecting Reds from the Edit pop-up menu, I changed the Hue value first to +60 degrees (left) and then to –120 degrees (right). Both values changed the colors of the petals but left the rest of the tulips unharmed.

You can likewise combine global adjustments with range edits, but when modifying Hue values, it really doesn't matter whether you do it in the same pass or separately. Figure 11-28 shows a couple of different adjustments applied to the yellow petals and blue leaves with the Edit option set to Master. In both cases, I could have applied the Master changes at the same times I was changing the Reds and Yellows or several operations later; the outcomes would be the same.

But despite its considerable power, bear in mind that the Edit pop-up menu can't distinguish between hues that are any less than about 15 degrees apart. This means that when you edit the Reds or Yellows in an image, you run the risk of taking the flesh tones along with them. Figure 11-29 starts off with a beaming Santa. Mind you, it's not his fault — spending that much time in the wind and snow can really chap your skin — but his ruddy complexion is every bit as crimson as his outfit. So if I try to shift the Reds in his suit to green, his blushing cheeks and freckly arms go along for the ride. My only recourse is to select the areas that I want to recolor in advance, and then modify them independently of Santa's skin, as in the figure's final example.

Edit: Yellows, Hue: +165°, Saturation: –50%   one pass, Reds and Yellows together

Figure 11-27: If I first change the petals to yellow and then change the leaves to blue in two separate passes of the Hue/Saturation command, I end up modifying leaves and petals together (left). The solution is to apply the changes to the Reds and Yellows range in a single pass (right).

Edit: Master, Hue: +30°, Saturation: –70%   Edit: Master, Hue: –60°, Saturation: –50%

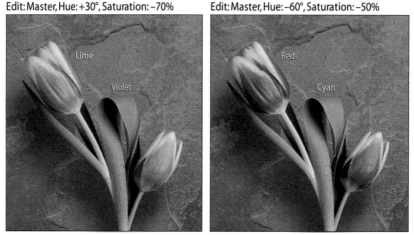

Figure 11-28: Two sets of Hue and Saturation modifications applied to the second image in Figure 11-27 with the Edit menu set to Master. Such global changes affect all colors, so it doesn't matter whether you apply them in tandem with range changes or in a separate pass.

Colorizing images

Turn on the Colorize option in the lower-right corner of the Hue/Saturation dialog box to apply a single hue and saturation level to a selection or layer, regardless of its previous coloring. All brightness levels remain intact, although you can adjust them incrementally using the Lightness slider bar (a practice that I strongly advise against, as I mentioned earlier).

Santa Claus: jolly old elf ...   or smirking green goblin?   Santa flesh protected

Figure 11-29: He's making a list...he's using Excel...Gonna find out who's naughty or swell...I've seen maraschino cherries that were less red than this Santa (left). So when I select Reds from the Edit menu and enter a Hue value of +120 degrees, the legendary man's flesh turns the same shade of green as his outfit (middle). To avoid this calamity, I carefully select around his arms and face, choose Select ⇨ Inverse to protect those areas, and then apply Hue/Saturation (right).

When the Colorize check box is active, Hue and Saturation become absolute values, measured from 0 to 360 degrees and 0 to 100 percent, respectively. A Hue value of 0 is red, 15 is vermilion, 30 is orange, and so on, as shown back in Figure 11-14, all the way around to 360 degrees, once again for red. A Saturation value of 0 percent is gray, regardless of the Hue value (although it may be black or white depending on the luminosity of the original pixels); 100 percent is color at its high-octane, ain't-gonna-print-no-matter-how-hard-you-click-Print best.

Color ranges are not permitted when colorizing. The moment you select the Colorize check box, Photoshop dims the Edit pop-up menu and sets it to Master. This means if you want to limit the extent of a colorization, you have to define a selection before choosing Hue/Saturation.

For an example, let's return to me and my Little Puppet Friend. As you can see in the first image of Figure 11-30, LPF's flesh tones (or perhaps I should say "fleece tones") appear to be blue. And not a butch navy blue, either, but a *baby* blue. For some reason, that just strikes me as wrong, particularly when he could just as easily be pink. So I take out my trusty Hue/Saturation command, set the Edit option to Blue, eyedrop and Shift-eyedrop a few colors in LPF's face, and rotate the Hue value to +120 degrees. For added emphasis, I raise the Saturation value to +40 percent. But something's not right. As the second image in Figure 11-30 so plainly shows, LPF looks less pink than unevenly sunburned. If this were intended as a cautionary illustration for puppets who spend too much time in tanning booths, I'd call this a raving success. But I'm looking for a natural pink, a pink that says, "This puppet was born pink, and pink he shall die." And this isn't it.

Original Little Puppet Friend　　　　Edit: Blues, Hue: +120°, Saturation: +40%

Figure 11-30: Once a blue puppet (left), always a blue puppet — until he's digitized and opened up in Photoshop, that is. Then, the sky's *not* the limit. (Get it? Sky? Blue? Yeah, well, it was the puppet's joke anyway.) But my attempt to change the color of LPF's fleece using the Hue/Saturation command's range controls just doesn't work (right).

The problem is that even though LPF looks blue, he isn't. Not entirely, anyway. His face is actually remarkably iridescent, reflecting light off thousands of tiny textile surfaces. (This is attributable to his stringent daily moisturizing routine.) As a result, the front of LPF's face catches an amazing array of low-saturation hues that the Edit pop-up menu can't isolate without picking up colors in my face and elsewhere.

So I turn my attention to Colorize. In the first example of Figure 11-31, I applied the Colorize check box to the entire image. This helped me get a sense of the exact shade of pink I was looking for. I finally settled on a Hue of 340 degrees and a Saturation of 25 percent, rendering LPF in a light, fetching lake.

The second image in Figure 11-31 shows my last valiant attempt to give my Little Puppet Friend a rosy glow. This time I started by making a selection using the Color Range command, which is well suited to isolating areas consistent in saturation and luminosity. Then I pressed Ctrl+Alt+U (⌘-Option-U on the Mac) to reapply my last Hue/Saturation settings, with Colorize turned on and the same lake-colored Hue and Saturation values. It's a stronger effect than I got using the Edit option, and it permitted me to avoid changing colors in my shirt, the lava lamp, and elsewhere.

If the edges of your colorized selection look a little ratty, you can touch them up in a jiffy using the brush tool. In the Color palette, switch to HSB Sliders. First, change the foreground color to match the Hue and Saturation values you used in the Hue/Saturation dialog box. You can do this by choosing the HSB Sliders command from the Color palette menu and entering the values in the H and S option boxes (in my case, 340 and 25). Set the B (Brightness) value to 100 percent. Next, select the brush tool and change the brush mode to Color by pressing Shift+Alt+C (Shift-Option-C on the Mac). Then paint as needed. The effect is identical to applying Colorize from the Hue/Saturation dialog box.

Colorize, Hue: 340°, Saturation: 25%

Select ⟷ Color Range;
Colorize, Hue: 340°, Saturation: 25%

Figure 11-31: Turning on the Colorize check box gives me a sense of the specific Hue and Saturation values I'll eventually want to use (left). Then I undo that change, select LPF's skin, and reapply Hue/Saturation with my last colorization settings (right).

When Variations and Hue/Saturation Fail

Most images with color casts and saturation problems respond well to either Hue/Saturation or Variations. But every so often, you run into an image that defies your most earnest attentions. Such is the case for the image at the top of Figure 11-32. This photograph was shot on the set of one of my *Total Training* video series. Because my natural skin coloring trends toward a deathly pale, the lighting guys generally throw a lot of red on me in an attempt to make me appear not so much rosy or even healthy as just plain human. Their efforts are futile — I am roboDeke, after all — but try they must. And while the effect appears warm and inviting to the video camera, the still camera reacts to the red like it's the only color on earth. The result is that I look like I've descended beyond the icy ninth circle of Hell in Dante's *Inferno* where I'm raising my glass in an ingratiating toast to Lucifer. (By the way, that's water in my glass. And the olives are…real olives. Some things you just can't fake.)

The first thing I try to do is selectively rotate and desaturate the red hues using the Hue/Saturation command. Problem is, just about all the colors in this image fall into the Reds range. I try making the colors a bit more orange and lowering the Saturation value, but as witnessed in the bottom-left example of Figure 11-32, the effect is awful. So I try Variations instead. But after several minutes of adjusting the range settings and intensity slider, the bottom-right image proves the best I can do.

Somehow, I can't manage to raise any volumetric details from the image — the kind of sculptural highlights and shadows that give an image depth. No matter what, my face ends up flattening out with little to define it other than my greenish eyebrows and goatee. Though I hardly thought such things were possible, I actually look more ghoulish than in real life.

A hideous example of bad color balance

Hue/Saturation is powerless   Even Variations cannot save it

Figure 11-32: Many still cameras are hypersensitive to red light (top). This particular image is so red that neither Hue/Saturation (bottom left) nor Variations (right) does a satisfactory job of fixing it.

So I restore my original image and set out on an inspection of the color channels. Sure enough, the moment I press Ctrl+1 (⌘-1 on the Mac), I am greeted by a red channel so bereft of detail that I'm tempted to throw up my hands in despair. As shown in the first example of Figure 11-33, my face is entirely ashen with sudden shading in the hair and eyes. Given that the red channel is responsible for the lion's share of the flesh tones, it's hardly surprising I'm having problems recovering the full-color face.

Red channel Green channel Blue channel

Figure 11-33: Thanks to the preponderance of red lighting, the red channel is severely blown (left), taking the flesh tones with it. Meanwhile, the green channel looks great (middle), and the blue channel is dark and noisy (right).

Somehow, I need to get better information into this red channel, but how? By borrowing brightness values from the green and blue channels, of course. So I cross my fingers and press Ctrl+2 (⌘-2) to see what the green channel has to offer. Thankfully, the news is good. As shown in the second example in Figure 11-33, the green channel is nearly perfect, with smooth gradations in luminosity from light to dark. Ctrl+3 (⌘-3) proves a bit more disappointing. The blue channel is rich with sculptural details, but it is overly dark. Worse yet, it's riddled with noise, which will only get worse when I lighten it.

If I had to grade the channels, I'd give green an A, blue a C, and red an F. So a perfect image is out of the question. Still, the three channels average to a C, and with any luck, I can tweak them into a solid B. The tweaker of choice is a command that lets you mix channels together, fittingly known as the Channel Mixer.

Mixing color channels

Choose Image ⇨ Adjustments ⇨ Channel Mixer to display the dialog box shown in Figure 11-34. Select the channel that you want to modify from the Output Channel pop-up menu. Then mix in different amounts of data from this and other channels using the Red, Green, and Blue sliders. (This assumes that you're editing in the RGB mode; the dialog box includes Cyan, Magenta, Yellow, and Black sliders in the CMYK mode.) Each slider overlays the contents of a channel using a formula very similar to the Linear Dodge blend mode set to the Opacity level indicated in the option box. You can read about Linear Dodge in Chapter 6, but the upshot is, each channel adds brightness. The slider value can be as high as +200 percent, which produces an effect very much like two layers dodging together. Negative values, as low as –200 percent, are the same as inverting the contents of a channel and applying a close cousin to Linear Burn.

Figure 11-34: The Channel Mixer dialog box, along with three variations on LPF produced entirely by mixing together his red, green, and blue channel information.

I begin Figure 11-35 by setting the Output Channel to my biggest offender, Red. Using the Source Channels values, I lower the amount of Red information to 50 percent and raise the amount of Green to slightly more, 60 percent. The blue channel is too grainy to use; if I entirely substituted the red channel with green, I'd upset the color balance. But by giving the green data a little added weight, I am able to produce a much improved image, as shown in the first example in the figure. Next, I set the Output Channel to Blue (the green channel was fine, after all). Then I raise the Green value to 30 percent, lower the Blue value to 85 percent, and click the OK button to apply my changes. Pictured in the middle of Figure 11-35, the resulting image is hardly perfect, but it's a good as I'm going to get from the Channel Mixer and good enough to serve as a starting point for Variations and other corrections.

To remove what is now a more civil red color cast, I choose Variations and click More Cyan (red's opposite) and Lighter with the intensity slider set to the middle. Then I use the Hue/Saturation command to decrease the Saturation value for the Reds by –10 percent and increase the Saturation for the Yellows by +10 percent. Shown on the right side of Figure 11-35, the corrected image looks significantly better, but it's a bit too green. So I once again choose the Channel Mixer, set the Output Channel to Blue, and insert a little more green content into the blue channel. (After years of using the Channel Mixer, I was surprised to find that you can produce effects with two or more passes of the command that are impossible to produce in a single application.) To retrieve some of the green in my shirt and eyes, I select these regions of the image and use the Hue/Saturation command to raise the Hue value to +20 degrees and the Saturation to +40 percent. Last, I apply the Unsharp Mask filter. Pictured in Figure 11-36, the end product is so far better than the original (Figure 11-32) that it looks as if I reshot the photo. It just goes to show you that as long as you have one good channel, you can work miracles in Photoshop.

Output: Red, R: 50%, G: 60%   Output: Blue, G: 30%, B: 85%   Variations & Hue/Saturation

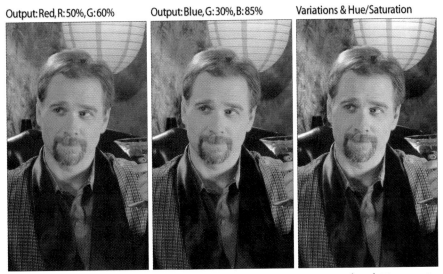

Figure 11-35: The results of changing the Red value to 50 percent Red and 60 percent Green (left) and the Blue channel to 30 percent Green, 85 percent Blue (middle). After exiting the Channel Mixer dialog box, I apply further corrections using the Variations and Hue/Saturation commands (right).

Modified eyes and shirt & Unsharp Mask

Figure 11-36: It's actually hard to believe that I was able to correct the red photograph from Figure 11-32 with this much success. But the truth is, had it not been for the Channel Mixer, it would have been next to impossible.

Reducing red-eye

Though Photoshop CS has the new color replacement tool, which is a valiant warrior in the eternal struggle against red-eye, the Channel Mixer is no slouch in this department either. We'll give the color replacement tool a spin shortly, but first let's see what the Channel Mixer can do. Illustrated in the mock book cover in Figure 11-37, red-eye affects either the pupils or, worse, both pupils and irises. It can range in brightness and saturation, but it is almost always red. That may seem like an obvious observation, but by "red," I mean neither vermilion nor lake but dead, on-the-nose, Hue-of-0 red, thus making the Channel Mixer a fine solution.

Figure 11-37: Red-eye can be handy when crafting covers for other-worldly, high-tech, sci-fi crime novels. But for just about every other purpose on earth, red-eye is a photographic crisis that must be eliminated with impunity.

Red-eye is caused by the flash entering the pupil and reflecting off the back of the retina. Why does the retina appear red? The most commonly given answer is that the flash lights up the blood vessels that line the retina. Why is blood red? Because blood contains the pigment hemoglobin. Which begs the question, why is hemoglobin red? Thankfully, this isn't the *Hemoglobin Bible*, so I'm under no obligation to tell you. But I will tell you that the retinas of animals with night vision, which include most dogs and cats, register different colors, including yellow, green, or blue. In such cases, the flash is reacting to the mirror-like *tapetum*. Located behind the retina, this highly polished membrane lights up the eye like a mirror in a small room. The tapetum therefore permits the retina to pick up very dim light that it may have missed on the first pass, and it permits the camera to register yet another wacky eye color. Humans have no tapetum — even you people who can bend spoons with your minds, pick up on other people's thoughts, and communicate with dead aliens, sorry, no tapetum — so our eyes are blood red.

Even though red-eye is a menace, it's actually a relatively rare occurrence that relies on three conditions: First, the pupil has to be dilated. Second, the flash has to be mounted close enough to the lens that it can enter the pupil and reflect back at a sufficiently acute angle that the camera will pick it up. Third, you have to be far enough away from the subject that the iris doesn't cut off the reflection. So for red-eye to occur, you generally have to be shooting at night using a consumer-grade camera positioned two or more feet from your subject. Solutions? Shoot in well-lit environments; use an external flash that's not mounted close to the lens; or get closer to your subject.

There is a fourth solution of course — the dreaded red-eye flash mode. Included with just about every consumer-grade camera on the market, the red-eye mode actually fires two strobes, one to shock the pupil into shrinking and a second to light the picture. I never use the red-eye mode for two reasons: First, a dilated eye is a more attractive eye. Babies have dilated eyes, so do young ravers in nightclubs, and those are exactly the kinds of people that get our attention. So you want to inspire dilation, not quash it. When Grandma's pupils are big, she's a fox. Second, with two strobes, you have twice the chance to miss the shot. You also have twice the opportunity to inspire your subject to blink, move the camera, and blind your children.

So take reasonable precautions to avoid red-eye. And when the precautions don't work, take advantage of the fifth solution, Photoshop. For Figure 11-37, I deliberately captured my pupils as red. Armed with a consumer-level Olympus D-40, I pointed the camera square at my face, turned off the lights, backed up, and fired. Sure enough, I got red-eye. The good news is, it's no big deal. The first example in Figure 11-38 shows my eyes as they were originally captured by the D-40. The other images show my eyes on a channel-by-channel basis. In the red channel, I look possessed. In the green and blue channels, I look normal. Surely, if I could save Figure 11-32 using one good channel, I can save my pupils using two good channels.

Naturally, you don't want to replace all the reds in your image, so you need to select the area that you want to correct, namely, the pupils. Because the pupils are round, this is easier than you might think. Using the elliptical marquee tool, drag around one pupil and then Shift-drag around the other. To soften the selection edges, choose Select ➪ Feather and enter a Radius value of 1 to 2 pixels. Then choose Image ➪ Adjustments ➪ Channel Mixer. Set the Output Channel to Reds. Then enter 0 percent for Red, +50 percent for Green, and +50 percent for Blue. As shown in Figure 11-39, these magical settings do the trick virtually every time.

Final channel-mixing tidbits

In addition to the Output Channel pop-up menu and primary color sliders, the Channel Mixer dialog box offers two options, Constant and Monochrome. The Constant value brightens or darkens the image across the board. Because it is incapable of distinguishing between highlights, midtones, and shadows, this option is sufficiently dangerous that you'll almost always want to leave it set to 0. Only when editing small selections might you want to give it a tweak.

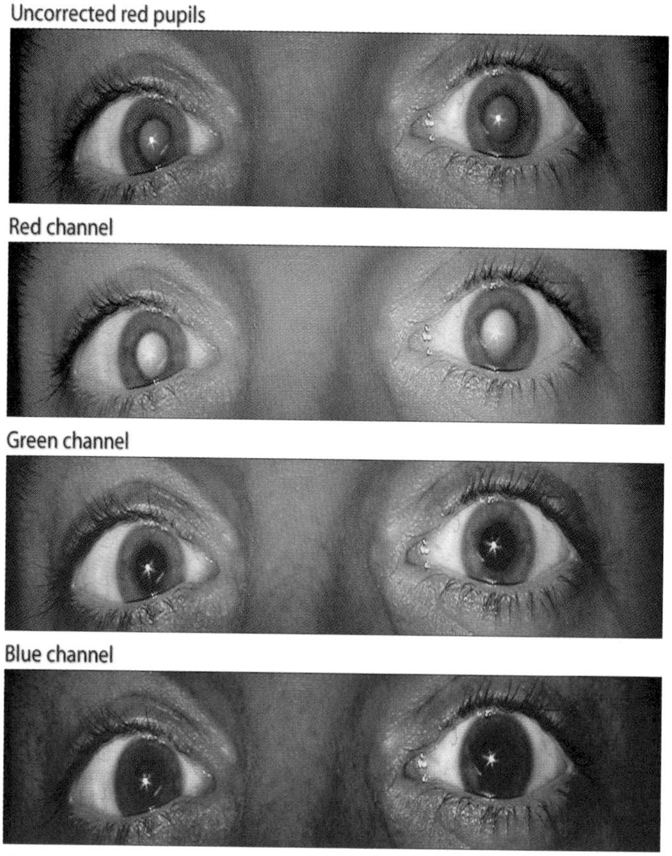

Uncorrected red pupils

Red channel

Green channel

Blue channel

Figure 11-38: My original hemoglobin-rich pupils (top), followed by their appearance in each of the color channels. Granted, we have something of a problem in the red channel, but the green and blue channels give us everything we need.

Thanks to the Monochrome check box, the Channel Mixer is a great command for creating custom grayscale images. Rather than choosing Image ➪ Mode ➪ Grayscale and taking what Photoshop gives you, you can divine your own grayscale recipe. Just select the Monochrome check box and adjust the Red, Green, and Blue values as desired.

In creating your own Monochrome recipes, you may find it helpful to know what Photoshop does as a baseline. In the world of television, the standard formula for converting RGB to grayscale is 30 percent red, 59 percent green, and 11 percent blue. The percentages used by Photoshop's Image ➪ Mode ➪ Grayscale vary depending on the active RGB color space, and the Channel Mixer dialog box employs its own special calculations, so an exact recipe is not possible. But starting with the television formula outlined above, my experiments in the Adobe RGB space suggest that placing more emphasis on red — as in Red: 40, Green: 50, Blue: 10 or Red: 45, Green: 60, Blue: 15 — should get you in the right ballpark. From there, you can experiment at will.

Figure 11-39: After selecting the pupils with the elliptical marquee tool and feathering the selection outlines, choose the Channel Mixer command and replace the red channel with an even mix of green and blue.

Using the color replacement tool

Photoshop Elements, Photoshop's adorable little goddaughter (have you noticed how that relationship keeps changing every time I mention it?), has a red eye brush tool, specifically designed to eliminate red-eye. And now, in another case of Photoshop "finding inspiration" in its second cousin once removed, Photoshop CS has a color replacement tool. Oh sure, they changed the name, and gave it some fancy new controls in the Options bar, but if they really wanted us to think they had gone to all the trouble of inventing a brand new tool for our delectation and delight, then they might have bothered to change the eye-and-brush icon in the toolbox. We're not fooled that easily, you know.

Of course, even if Photoshop CS does mooch off of Elements sometimes, it always seems to give back better than it gets. And so the color replacement tool is a lot more powerful than Elements' red eye brush tool. The color replacement tool works by taking a color sample from the area in which you first click and then applying your foreground color to any area that matches your sample. For instance, if you were trying to clean up some red-eye, you would set your foreground color to a very dark gray, select the color replacement tool, and then click and hold on the reddest section of eye you can find. What you're doing is telling the tool "You see this shade of red? A red so deep and piercing that it's as though you're staring into oblivion itself? Do your magic." As you drag with the tool, you replace any section of matching red with your more natural gray while leaving the non-red-eye components of your image untouched.

When you're dealing with a problem like red-eye, the color replacement tool can usually give you results in just one or two clicks. Figure 11-40 shows how the color replacement tool fared against my glowing red eyes from Figure 11-37.

Uncorrected red pupils

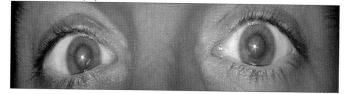

Color replacement tool with black; Mode: Color, Tolerance: 80%

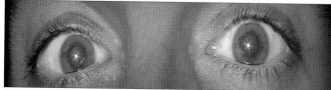

Figure 11-40: The results aren't quite as dark as in Figure 11-39, but the color replacement tool did a decent job, and it's speedy to boot.

But the tool is also capable of expertly replacing large chunks of one color with another in a variety of situations. You control the behavior and sensitivity of the color replacement tool using the settings in the Options bar. Here's how they break down:

✦ **Brush:** You don't get a whole lot of brush choices when using the color replacement tool. The minimalist controls found in the Brush option bear a closer resemblance to Photoshop 6-era brushes than the snazzy, robust Brushes palette available to a number of the other tools. But hey, "Don't look a gift horse in the mouth," as my mother always told me. And I'd smile, and nod, and pretend I knew what she meant.

✦ **Mode:** This setting tells the tool how to combine the newly painted pixels with the existing ones in your image. By default, the Mode option is set to Color, and you're generally going to want to leave it there. Because the Color mode affects hue and saturation, or the color values of an image, but doesn't affect luminance, or lightness values, it's generally the way to go. However, you can achieve some nice results by experimenting with the other choices.

✦ **Sampling:** The Sampling option lets you set how Photoshop will decide what color you're replacing. The first option, Continuous, causes the tool to keep sampling colors, nonstop, for as long as you're using the tool. Drag over your red-eye to fix it instantly, but keep dragging until you reach skin and you're left with a grayish, splotchy mess. Much more useful than Continuous is the second Sampling option, Once. This sets the color on which you click when you begin your drag as the target of your replacement. This means that for as long as you continue dragging, only the original color will be affected. The third and final Sampling setting is Background Swatch. Choosing this option tells the color replacement tool to only alter pixels in your image that share a color with the current background color. It can be a neat way of providing even more control over what the tool will affect, but I still recommend you stick with the Once setting.

✦ **Limits:** The Limits options let you set even more guidelines for which pixels the tool will affect. *Discontiguous* means that patches of color don't have to be adjacent to each other to be affected. Let's say you have a large mass of color, with little islands of the same color along the shore of the large mass. Assuming that you have a large brush with Sampling set to Once, if you click on the large mass and drag so that the color islands fall within the shape of the brush, they will also be affected by the color replacement tool. Contiguous means just the opposite; an island of color must be clicked on itself in order to be affected. Find Edges is similar to Contiguous, but as its name suggests, it finds the edges of the color mass you clicked on and is much more mindful of not changing colors beyond those edges, keeping them sharp. Experiment on your own, but I suspect you'll generally want to leave this set to Find Edges.

✦ **Tolerance:** The Tolerance value determines how exact a color match is required to be in order to deem a pixel suitable for replacement. Lower values only replace colors very similar to the sampled color, and higher values replace a broader range of colors. Most of your work with the color replacement tool will live or die based on this setting and it can be a bit tricky to get it right. Keep in mind that a value that works for one section of color in an image may not be the correct setting to affect a lighter or darker section of the same color in the image.

✦ **Anti-aliased:** This check box lets you toggle antialiasing, or softening, on or off. It's almost certainly a good idea to keep it turned on.

Figure 11-41 shows four measuring cups, before and after their makeover with the color replacement tool. I find that the tool does a decent job, and it's certainly got speed on its side. But in terms of quality, I think you're better off making a good selection and using the Hue/Saturation or Channel Mixer commands. Still, give color replacement a spin, and you might find it suits your needs.

Adjustment Layers

Variations, Hue/Saturation, and the Channel Mixer are each applicable to a single layer at a time. If you want to correct the colors in multiple layers at a time, you have to create a special kind of layer called an *adjustment layer*, which contains live, numerical correction data and applies its corrections to all layers below it without affecting any layer above.

Figure 11-41: These unsuspecting measuring cups (left) are perfect candidates for the color replacement tool. With a good bit of fiddling around with the tool's options as I worked, I was able to come up with a fairly convincing paint job (right).

Creating an adjustment layer

You can create an adjustment layer in one of two ways:

✦ Choose Layer ➪ New Adjustment Layer to display a submenu of color adjustment commands, including Hue/Saturation, Channel Mixer, and several others.

✦ Click the black-and-white circle at the bottom of the Layers palette, labeled in Figure 11-42. The first three options — Solid Color, Gradient, and Pattern — are dynamic fill layers, like shape layers discussed in Chapter 7 except that they exist independently of a vector mask. Choose any one of the remaining 12 options to make a new adjustment layer.

If you choose a command from the Layer ➪ New Adjustment Layer submenu, Photoshop displays the New Layer dialog box, which permits you to name the layer, assign a color, and set the blend mode. You can also group the adjustment layer with the currently selected layer, which means that the adjustment layer will affect that layer only. (More on this in the next section.) If you choose an option from the icon at the bottom of the Layers palette, Photoshop bypasses the New Layer dialog box and heads straight to the selected correction. Choosing Hue/Saturation, for example, displays the Hue/Saturation dialog box. (Invert is the only option that produces no dialog box whatsoever, instead simply inverting the colors.) Change the settings as desired and press Enter or Return as you normally would.

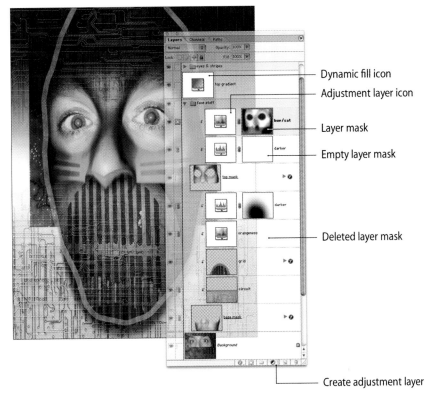

- Dynamic fill icon
- Adjustment layer icon
- Layer mask
- Empty layer mask
- Deleted layer mask
- Create adjustment layer

Figure 11-42: Virtually every figure in this chapter and elsewhere throughout this book includes at least one adjustment layer. This variation on the book cover composition features four adjustment layers and a dynamic fill.

 Hold down Alt (Option on the Mac) when choosing an adjustment layer from the Layers palette menu to force the display of the New Layer dialog box, just as if you'd chosen a command from the Layer ⇨ New Adjustment Layer submenu.

Regardless of the color adjustment you select, it appears as a new layer in the Layers palette. In the modified book cover in Figure 11-42, we can see a total of four adjustment layers as well as a dynamic gradient layer at the top. Photoshop marks adjustment layers with special icons that look like miniature versions of their respective dialog boxes. For example, the little color fountain icons indicate Hue/Saturation layers; the blue histograms indicate Levels. (In both cases, I added the colors for easier identification.) This way, you can readily tell them apart from pixel-based image layers.

The advantages of layer-based corrections

If all adjustment layers did was correct multiple layers at a time, they'd more than justify their existence. But that's just the beginning of their remarkable power. Here are a few of the wonderful things adjustment layers let you do that make them so great:

✦ **Edit an existing color adjustment:** As long as the adjustment layer remains intact — stored in one of the four formats that support layers (native Photoshop PSD, TIFF, PDF, or PSB) — you can edit the color correction over and over again without damaging the underlying pixels. Unlike standard color corrections, which alter selected pixels directly, adjustment layers have no permanent effect on the pixels. On the slightest whim, you can double-click the adjustment layer icon in the Layers palette to bring up the color correction dialog box, complete with the settings currently in force. Tweak the settings as desired and press Enter or Return to make changes on the fly. Toggle the visibility of the adjustment layer by clicking the eyeball icon in front of the layer. You can't get any more flexible than that.

When editing the settings for an adjustment layer, be sure to double-click the adjustment layer icon itself (labeled in Figure 11-42). Double-clicking in the layer mask icon displays the Layer Mask Display Options; double-clicking the layer name highlights it; and double-clicking elsewhere displays the slow-to-appear Layer Style dialog box.

✦ **Fade an adjustment:** You can fade a static color correction right after you apply it by choosing Edit ➪ Fade. But you can fade an adjustment layer any time you like by editing the blend mode and Opacity settings at the top of the Layers palette.

✦ **Correct with blend modes without ballooning file size:** You may have heard of a technique that employs blend modes to correct overly light or dark images. It works like this: Take a washed out image like the one at the top of Figure 11-43. Press Ctrl+J (or ⌘-J) to copy it to a new layer and then apply the Multiply mode. The image darkens right up, as the bottom example shows. If it becomes too dark, reduce the Opacity value. Alternatively, you can use Screen for lightening dark images, Hard Light for increasing contrast, and so on.

The problem with this trick is that it doubles the size of an otherwise flat image in memory. For example, the 5-megapixel photograph in Figure 11-43 grows from 14MB to 28MB. That's a whopping increase for such a modest and frankly narrow technique.

Adjustment layers permit you to apply this same trick without adding to file size. First, create a random adjustment layer. In Figure 11-43, I added a Channel Mixer layer, but any adjustment except Invert will do. After the dialog box appears, press Enter or Return to accept its default settings. Now select Multiply, Screen, Hard Light, or your other favorite mode from the blend mode pop-up menu in the Layers palette. The adjustment layer serves as a surrogate duplicate of the layers below it, mocking every merged pixel. And it doesn't add so much as a K to the file size. It provides all the advantages of an extra layer with none of the pain.

✦ **Paint inside the layer mask:** Adjustment layers automatically come with layer masks. If a selection is active when you create a new adjustment layer, Photoshop creates a layer mask around the selection outline. Otherwise, the layer mask is empty, ready and waiting for you to modify it as you see fit. This means you can define which areas of an image receive color adjustment and which do not just by painting inside the image window. Painting with black hides the color adjustment, painting with white applies it. Other masking techniques (see Chapters 4 and 5) work just as well.

Figure 11-44 shows an adjustment layer-heavy image that I created as a promotional piece for another of my video training series. The Clarice Starling-inspired design (crafted by artist James Dean Conklin) hinges on the idea of the butterfly as Adobe's official symbol for its high-end layout tool, InDesign. The composition started with a plain headshot of me that I colorized in ultramarine using a Hue/Saturation adjustment layer. Pictured on the right side of the figure, my stubble–ridden face is a far cry from the sleek, gleaming portrait that I'm looking for. My first step in revising this image was to bring out a little extra detail in the shadows. So I selected the darkest colors using Select ⇨ Color Range and feathered the selection with a Radius of 12 pixels. This selection appears as a mask on the left side of Figure 11-45. Then I created a Channel Mixer layer, clicked OK to accept its default settings, and set the blend mode for my new layer to Screen. (No special reason behind my continued use of Channel Mixer — just force of habit.) Photoshop automatically masked off the selected area, thus lightening just the shadows as in the second image in Figure 11-45.

Washed out digital photo

Generic adjustment layer set to Multiply blend mode

Figure 11-43: Starting with a washed out 5-megapixel digital photo (top), I created a Channel Mixer adjustment layer, clicked OK without changing any of the values, and set the blend mode to Multiply. The result is darker, richer colors (bottom) with no increase in file size.

Video promotional piece   Colorized base (Hue: 225°, Sat: 55%)

Figure 11-44: A promotional composition for a Total Training video series (left) with the base photograph colorized in ultramarine (right).

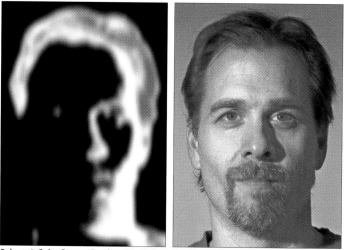

Select ➪ Color Range, Feather: 12 pixels   Random adjustment layer, Screen mode

Figure 11-45: After selecting the shadows with the Color Range command and using Select ➪ Feather to soften the selection outline (left), I create a random adjustment layer, accept the default settings, and set the blend mode for the layer to Screen (right).

Despite the fact that I applied a blend mode to an empty adjustment layer — a technique that I advertised as taking no room in memory just three paragraphs ago — my image grew by 2MB. The culprit is the layer mask, which consumes one byte for every pixel in the image. But it's the price I have to pay. After all, without a layer mask, I couldn't isolate my changes to the shadows. And a layer mask still takes up just a third as much space as a full-color image layer, even less when you save the image to disk.

Next, I use the Color Range command to select the lightest colors in the image. I blur the selection in the quick mask mode and then paint around the eyes to protect the irises and eyelids. The resulting mask appears on the left side of Figure 11-46. After exiting the quick mask mode, I create a new Channel Mixer layer, set the Output Channel to gray, and raise the Constant value to 100 percent. All other values are 0. This has the effect of filling the previously selected area with white, as in the right-hand example in Figure 11-46. Why not just fill the selection with white? That was certainly an option, and it would have looked exactly the same. But by using a masked adjustment layer, I gave myself more freedom to experiment with different colors, modify the layer's boundaries, and employ the effect in different ways later on down the line.

Select ➪ Color Range,
blur & paint in quick mask mode

Channel Mixer adjustment layer,
Output Channel: Gray, Constant: 100%

Figure 11-46: To make the highlights white, I select the light colors using the Color Range command and then edit the selection in the quick mask mode (left). Next, I make a Channel Mixer layer, set the Output Channel to Gray, and raise the Constant value to 100 percent (right).

Layer mask icons can cause layer names to get truncated. If you plan to assign an adjustment layer to an entire image or layer and you want to tidy up your palette a little, feel free to delete the mask by dragging it to the trash icon at the bottom of the Layers palette. When Photoshop asks you if you want to trash the mask, click Discard. This is precisely what I did with the Orangeness layer back in Figure 11-42.

✦ **Filter colors nondestructively:** Photographers frequently use different filters and balanced film stocks to correct the color balance in their photos. Different types of light sources produce a variety of *color temperatures*: Natural daylight generally takes on a bluish cast, or a higher color temperature, while artificial light often produces more shades of reds and yellows, or a lower color temperature. When not shooting on film that has been pre-balanced to account for these casts, photographers will often place a color filter over the lens to compensate—adding blue to an indoor scene will counteract the yellows, for instance. As demonstrated in Figure 11-47 on a photo by Laura Bigbee-Fott, Photoshop CS's new Photo Filter command can simulate the effect of photographic filters. Photo Filter can be found in the Image ⇨ Adjustments submenu, but why look for it there when you can apply Photo Filter as an adjustment layer?

Photo Filter, Filter: Warming Filter (81), Density: 40%

Figure 11-47: Photos taken outdoors often have a bluish tinge (top). Such color casts are just another burden fought and won with Photoshop CS's powerful color correction tools; a Photo Filter adjustment layer is able to nicely compensate by warming up the color temperature (bottom).

The Photo Filter dialog box gives you a few options. The first two choices in the Filter pop-up menu, Warming Filter (85) and Warming Filter (81), simulate filters that a photographer would use when the color temperature is too cool, or bluish. Warming Filter (85) produces an orange color cast while Warming Filter (81) adds more of a tan tint to your image. Conversely, Cooling Filter (80) and Cooling Filter (82) add a dark and rich or light cast of blue to your image, respectively, to account for the yellows of artificial light. The rest of the options in the pop-up menu are different color presets that let you achieve photographic effects similar to those provided by some real-life filters. You can also click the Color radio button and specify any color to use as though it were a filter. Click the color swatch to open the Color Picker and select a color. The Density slider adjusts the amount of color correction that the Photo Filter command will apply. And the Preserve Luminosity check box ensures that the brightness values will not be affected by your color adjustments.

✦ **Apply to a single layer or set:** Assuming the layer mask is empty, an adjustment layer covers the entire image like a colorful wall-to-wall carpet. However, you also have the option of limiting the adjustment to a single layer. Just select the adjustment layer in the Layers palette and press Ctrl+G (⌘-G on the Mac) to group it with the layer below it. This technique is so useful, in fact, that all the adjustment layers back in Figure 11-42 are grouped, thereby affecting only the top half of my face or the bottom.

What if you want to limit a color adjustment to a single set of layers? First, place the adjustment layer inside the set, above any layers that you want to modify. Then select the little folder icon for the set and change the blend mode in the Layers palette from Pass Through to Normal. This contains the adjustment, prohibiting it from escaping out into other layers.

✦ **Reorder your corrections:** As with any layer, you can shuffle adjustment layers up and down in the stacking order. If you decide you don't want the correction to affect a specific layer, drag the adjustment layer below the layer you want to exclude. If you're juggling multiple adjustment layers, as in Figure 11-42, you can shuffle the adjustment layers to change the order in which they're applied. Sometimes it makes a difference, sometimes it doesn't. And don't forget about the layer ordering shortcuts, Ctrl+[and Ctrl+] (⌘-[and ⌘-] on the Mac).

✦ **Change one color adjustment to another:** After applying one kind of adjustment layer, you can convert it to another kind of adjustment layer. To do so, choose the desired color adjustment from the Layer ⇨ Change Layer Content submenu. Photoshop doesn't try to preserve the prior color adjustment when making the conversion — in other words, it can't convert Hue/Saturation information into Channel Mixer data — but it does preserve the layer mask, blend mode, and other layer attributes.

One final advantage of adjustment layers is that you can move them between images. So once you find a correction that works for one image, you can apply it to others. In preparing the standard edition of the *Photoshop CS Bible* — which is mostly printed in black and white — I created virtually all the graphics in color and then applied two adjustment layers to convert the images to grayscale. The first was a Channel Mixer layer set to Monochrome that permitted me to balance brightness values in favor of one primary or other. The second was a Levels layer, which I used to boost the gamma to 1.2, which helped avoid the pitfalls of dot gain. After I had established these color adjustments inside a layer set, I was able to duplicate them over and over again to achieve consistent and flexible results.

Levels, Curves, and Shadows

Making Custom Brightness Adjustments

Photoshop's second category of color corrections enables you to adjust the luminosity levels in an image. You can make a photograph lighter or darker, enhance or reduce contrast, and even modify the balance of neutral grays and other colors. To the layman, this is known as correcting brightness and contrast. So naturally, the layman's answer to such problems is Image ⇨ Adjustments ⇨ Brightness/Contrast. As shown in Figure 12-1, the layman is a simple man and Brightness/Contrast is a simple command. They make a perfect pair.

But this is not the *Photoshop CS Bible, Layman Edition*. And although I'm sure the layman has many skills — laying presumably being one — his behavior is not to be emulated where Photoshop is concerned. Granted, Brightness/Contrast is simple, but it's also misleading, indiscriminate, and arbitrary. Because it provides no objective feedback beyond the preview in the image window, it requires you to make important decisions — decisions that could erase details in whole areas of an image — based on guesswork and speculation. In the figure, the Brightness and Contrast values read +57 and –35, respectively. But +57 and –35 *what*? You might presume percentages, or something equally relative, and you would be half right. The Contrast value scoots colors toward or away from gray as percentages of their current distance. So a value of –100 makes all colors gray, a value of +100 creates a threshold effect, turning all pixels in each channel either black or white. But Brightness is actually an absolute measurement that adds or deletes a constant amount of brightness to each and every pixel. A typical 24-bit photograph contains as many as 256 brightness levels per color channel (a topic that we'll explore at length later in this chapter), so a value of +57 shifts fully *3.5 million* of the possible 16 million colors in an image to white. By shielding you from the complexities inherent in color correction, the Brightness/Contrast command gives you no way to adjust some colors more than others and prohibits you from distributing highlights and shadows with any degree of confidence or uniformity.

This chapter is about the alternatives to Brightness/Contrast. Commands such as Levels (shown in Figure 12-1), Curves, and others demand more patience and technical knowledge, but in return they deliver reliable, exacting, unambiguous results. I'm not suggesting you use Levels and Curves to adjust your more important images; I'm suggesting you use them to adjust *all* your images. You should never — and after this chapter, I hope you will never — choose Brightness/Contrast again.

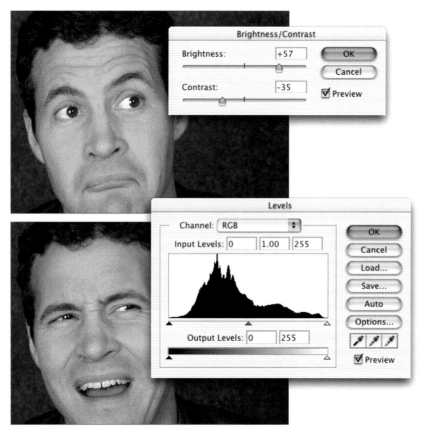

Figure 12-1: This is a layman. He is attracted to the simplicity of Brightness/Contrast. He is frightened and confused by the raw power of Levels. He should not be allowed to use Photoshop.

Automatic Levels-Based Adjustments

We'll warm up to the topics of Levels and Curves with a look at Photoshop's automatic color adjustments — Auto Levels, Auto Contrast, and Auto Color — in the order they appear in the Image⇨Adjustments submenu. Based on the Levels command, the three Auto functions analyze the colors in an image and make changes to them using a kind of crude but often serviceable artificial intelligence. They require no feedback from you — just choose the command and Photoshop does the rest. But unlike Brightness/Contrast, they work selectively, in some cases applying their changes to each color channel independently. And while Auto Levels and Auto Color may upset the color balance of an image, they are designed specifically to protect the lightest and darkest colors in an image.

Auto Levels

Assuming that you're working in the RGB mode, Image ➪ Adjustments ➪ Auto Levels visits each of the red, green, and blue channels and changes the lightest color to white and the darkest color to black. The intermediate shades of gray are stretched to fill the space in between.

In Figure 12-2, I started with the image of Giuliano de' Medici painted sometime in the late 1470s by the Florentine artist Sandro Botticelli. The unfortunate Giuliano was assassinated during mass by supporters of a gang of rival bankers. As if that weren't enough, he is now forced to endure bad scanning conditions. Thankfully, an afterlife in Photoshop has its advantages. By merely pressing Ctrl+Shift+L (⌘-Shift-L on the Mac), I instructed Photoshop to invoke Auto Levels, thereby pumping up the lights and darks and bolstering contrast. The colors ended up oversaturated, so I chose Hue/Saturation and reduced the Saturation value to –30 percent. With a small amount of work—a few seconds, max—I was able to transform a drab and murky image into a masterpiece of digital imagery.

Uncorrected RGB scan of 15th-century tempera   Auto Levels & Hue/Saturation (Saturation: –30%)

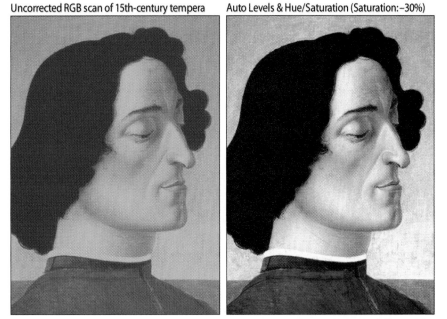

Figure 12-2: A less-than-ideal scan of Botticelli's *Giuliano de' Medici* (left) followed by that same image corrected with the Auto Levels and Hue/Saturation commands (right).

Figure 12-3 shows the effects of the Auto Levels command on the individual red, green, and blue channels, as well as its effect (sans Hue/Saturation) on the full-color painting. It's interesting to note that because Auto Levels evaluates and modifies each color channel independently, it behaves differently in the RGB mode than it does in CMYK. For the sake of comparison, Figure 12-4 shows the channel-by-channel effects of Auto Levels on a CMYK image. In the CMYK mode, Auto Levels corrects the cyan, magenta, and yellow channels, but leaves the black channel unharmed. There is good reason for this — if Auto Levels were to change to black the darkest color in the black channel, the shadows might very well grow overly dark and violate the *total ink limit*, which is the combined total of cyan, magenta, yellow, and black inks that the intended paper stock can reasonably absorb. In such a case, moderately dark colors may turn to black and, much worse, inks may smear on the printed page. But the solution — total avoidance of the black channel — goes too far in the other direction. As the final image in Figure 12-4 shows, this can result in pale or discolored shadows, which is the reason the "key" ink black exists in the first place.

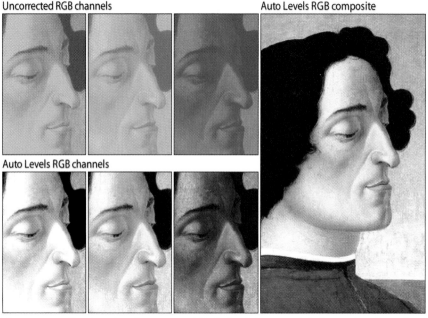

Figure 12-3: The Auto Levels command finds the lightest and darkest colors in each of the red, green, and blue channels (top row) and forces them to white and black (bottom row). The right-hand image shows the effect of Auto Levels on the RGB composite.

The moral of the story is that Auto Levels behaves most predictably in the RGB mode. I very much recommend against using it in CMYK.

Auto Contrast

The strength of Auto Levels is also its weakness. Because it modifies values on a channel-by-channel basis, it's able to correct a color cast in an image, but it's just as likely to introduce one. Look back to Figure 12-2 and you may notice that choosing the Auto Levels command not only resulted in bolder and more vibrant colors, but it also changed the background from green to blue. In this case, the color change was warranted — after all, the background is the sky, and the sky is generally blue. But what about the dollar bill detail in Figure 12-5? In its attempt to correct the washed-out scan, Auto Levels both increases the contrast and removes the green color cast (which I sort of liked, since green is the color of money). To a cold and inhuman computer, this may seem a sensible correction, and with the color schemes being introduced by the U.S. Mint right now, anything is possible. But as a taxpaying citizen of the U.S., I don't like it.

When Auto Levels takes something it's not supposed to, undo the command and try out Image ⇨ Adjustments ⇨ Auto Contrast instead. Blessed with the default keyboard shortcut Ctrl+Shift+Alt+L (⌘-Shift-Option-L on the Mac), Auto Contrast refrains from messing about with the individual color channels and satisfies itself with adjusting the composite image as a whole. The darkest pixel in any channel becomes black in that one channel only; the lightest color becomes white, again in one channel only. Auto Contrast then adjusts all the remaining channels in tandem. This fixes the contrast while preserving the color balance, as demonstrated by the final bill in Figure 12-5. It's just a dollar, but I'm all for keeping the green in the greenback.

Meanwhile, Figure 12-6 shows how Auto Contrast affects Giuliano in the RGB and CMYK modes. In the RGB image, Auto Contrast does a swell job of fixing contrast without swaying the colors. But unlike Auto Levels, which avoids changing the black channel, Auto Contrast changes all colors in kind. This means that in its attempt to increase contrast, it has cast a grim cloud over the mysterious de' Medici. Again, it's an argument for limiting your use of Auto commands to RGB only.

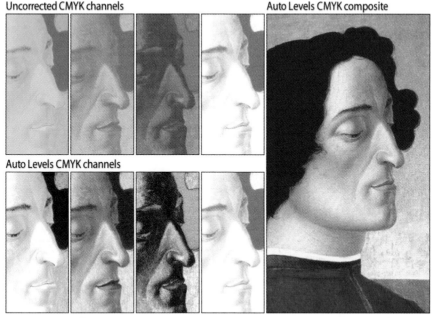

Figure 12-4: When reviewing channels in a CMYK image (top row), Auto Levels corrects the cyan, magenta, and yellow channels, but ignores black (bottom row). For Giuliano, the result is light shadows and blue hair (right). Incidentally, the CMYK channels pictured here are in no way intended to accurately stand for inked plates or pages; rather, they are color overlays used to indicate which channel is which.

Filthy lucre   Auto Levels steals the color   Auto Contrast keeps it green

Figure 12-5: Good engraving means a good economy, which is why things went in the crapper after the new bills were introduced. But just because I scanned one of the good old boys doesn't mean the image is up to snuff (left). I tried the Auto Levels command, but that took away the green (middle). Luckily, Auto Contrast fixes the bill and keeps the colors from the scan (right).

Which should you use when? If a low-contrast image suffers from a color cast that you want to correct, choose Auto Levels. If the image is washed out but the colors are okay, try Auto Contrast. (When working on a grayscale image, the two commands work the same, so choose whichever is more convenient.) Bear in mind that neither command is perfect, so you'll very likely want to make additional Levels and Variations adjustments, or try out the next command on our roster.

Auto Color

Image ➪ Adjustments ➪ Auto Color is a shining star in Photoshop's family of automatic brightness adjusters. As shown in Figure 12-7, Auto Color does far and away the better job of correcting the young, poised, and possibly snooty de' Medici. With one command, Auto Color brings to life wonderfully understated skin tones while at the same time adding a pleasing cyan-to-sky hue to the background. Compared with the overly vibrant, tangerine results of Auto Levels (Figure 12-3) and the jaundiced skin and grass green sky of Auto Contrast (Figure 12-6), Auto Color is the clear winner.

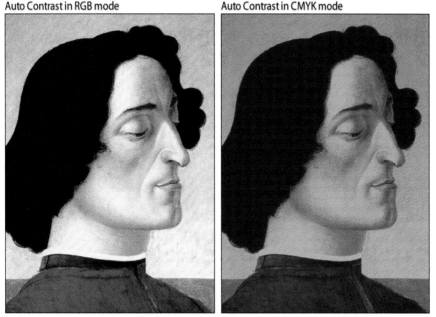

Figure 12-6: RGB (left) and CMYK (right) versions of Botticelli's painting after applications of the Auto Contrast command. Where Auto Contrast suited George admirably, it fails Giuliano.

Available exclusively in the RGB mode, choose the Auto Color command or press Ctrl+Shift+B (⌘-Shift-B on the Mac) to correct colors on a channel-by-channel basis. But where Auto Levels sets the darkest colors to black and the lightest colors to white, Auto Color seeks to neutralize the highlights, midtones, and shadows in an image, thereby restoring balance to both brightness values and colors throughout. If that sounds too good to be true, well, frankly it is. Like any automated command, Auto Color fails to achieve the desired results at least as often as it succeeds. But as it turns out, that's okay. Although Auto Color only occasionally fixes colors satisfactorily when left to its own devices, the real power comes when you customize the command using either the Levels or Curves command, a process that I discuss when we get into the Levels command.

The Histogram Palette

A *histogram* is a graph depicting the intensity of different values in your image. Histograms are certainly no stranger to Photoshop; the Levels command has boasted a histogram for years, letting you see the distribution of brightness values in your image. But just like Kelsey Grammer's Frasier Crane character on *Cheers,* the histogram has proven so popular that Adobe has spun it off into its own sitcom. Er, palette. The new Histogram palette is capable of showing the brightness values as well as the combined color and individual color values in an image. Keep it up on screen and you're never more than a glance away from knowing the distribution of levels in your image at any given time.

Auto Levels RGB channels   Auto Color RGB composite

Auto Color RGB channels

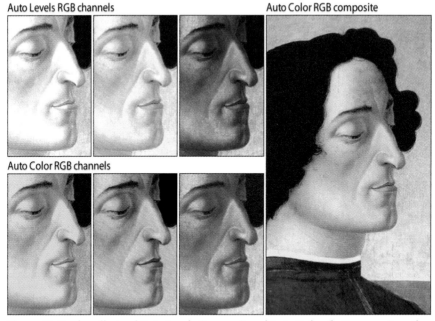

Figure 12-7: The effects of Auto Levels (top row) and Auto Color (bottom row) on the individual channels in an RGB image. Notice that Auto Color turned the red and green channels slightly darker than did Auto Levels, but the blue channel is slightly lighter, establishing a cooler color balance in the RGB composite (right).

Choose Window ⇨ Histogram to display the Histogram palette. By default, the palette will open in its Compact View, featuring only a graph that looks like a mountain range. That mountain range is in fact the histogram, which is a bar graph of all the colors in the image. The histogram comes to us from the world of statistics, where it's used to measure a fixed number of relative values. As it just so happens, the same holds true for Photoshop. Your typical scanned image or digital photograph is an 8 bits per channel, full-color RGB file that contains 256 brightness values per channel, ranging from black to white. (Photoshop CS boasts added support for 16 bits per channel images, but more on that in a bit. No pun intended.) By default, the Histogram palette shows a composite view of all color channels. So it follows that the histogram contains precisely 256 vertical bars — no fewer, no more. Each bar is one-pixel wide, so the entire histogram invariably measures 256 pixels wide, regardless of your screen resolution.

As illustrated in Figure 12-8, the histogram starts at black on the left-hand side and progresses through increasingly lighter colors, finally ending at white on the right. The numerical value for black is 0, the value for white is 255, giving you a total of 256 possible whole-number variations. The height of each bar in the graph tells you the relative number of pixels inside the selection or layer associated with that brightness value. This means you can use the histogram to gauge the distribution of darks and lights in your image. Mind you, there's no need to count pixels; the histogram is just there to give you a rough sense of what's going on. And with enough experience, it becomes an invaluable tool, serving as a kind of reality check for the colors that you see on screen.

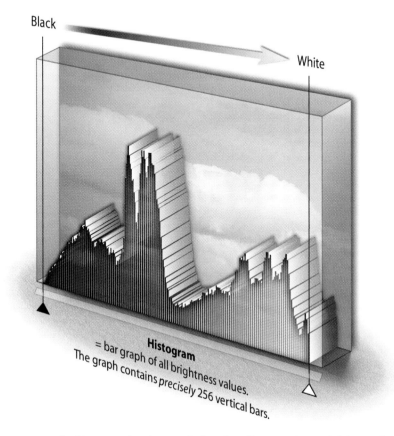

Figure 12-8: The histogram is a bar graph that describes exactly 256 brightness levels (illustrated here as alternatively light and dark vertical bars) in a single channel or throughout the composite image. The graph begins at black and ends at white. This histogram describes an image that contains predominantly dark colors.

If you aren't familiar with reading histograms, Figure 12-9 serves as a quick primer. Here we see a series of black-to-white gradients each accompanied by its histogram reading. First up is Photoshop's standard black-to-white gradient (stored as the preset Black, White). The histogram shows how the brightness values are largely evenly distributed, with Gaussian emphasis on the blacks and whites. The next example shows the effect of drawing a black-to-transparent gradient over the top of the first gradation. As the histogram shows, this (not surprisingly) shifts the balance of colors to the dark end of the spectrum. A white-to-transparent gradient results in more light colors; a gray-to-transparent gradient shifts the colors to the middle.

If Figure 12-9 seems simple, good — it's supposed to be simple. Doubtless, a histogram is a complex statistical tool that would take you hours to measure, plot, and draw by hand. Fortunately, it's Photoshop's job to do this kind of menial grunt work for us. And so far we've only seen the Histogram palette in its compact view; when you open up the palette menu and choose Expanded View or All Channels View, as shown in Figure 12-10, that's when the real grunting begins. You'll get access to the following options:

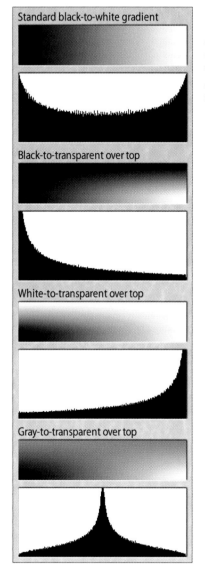

Standard black-to-white gradient

Black-to-transparent over top

White-to-transparent over top

Gray-to-transparent over top

Figure 12-9: A series of four gradients with their brightness values graphed inside histograms. A black-to-white gradient (top) includes a disproportionate number of darks and lights, which helps the colors to taper away naturally. Adding black (second), white (third), or gray (last) shifts the distribution of colors in favor of darks, lights, or medium shades.

✦ **Channel:** The Channel pop-up menu lets you determine the types of values displayed by the Histogram palette. By default it's set to the color mode in which you're working. If you're editing an image in Grayscale mode, this menu is unavailable.

From the Channel menu, you can choose to display the default combined tonal levels or any of the color channels individually. Choose Show Channels in Color from the palette menu to display the individual channels in the colors they represent. Any additional channels you have created can also be selected from the Channel pop-up menu. Choose Luminosity to display a histogram of only the brightness levels in your image. Lastly, you can call up an overlapping composite graph of all of the color channels by choosing Colors.

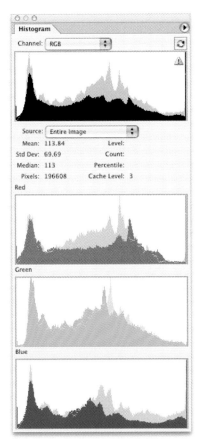

Figure 12-10: The Histogram palette in all its fully expanded, all channels, full color, statistic-showing, screen-hogging glory.

✦ **Uncached Refresh:** Whenever you make an adjustment to an image that affects its brightness or color intensity levels, the histogram redraws itself to compensate. It saves time doing this by analyzing the already-existing cache of the image and guessing how the change you've made will affect the graph. The Histogram palette will use the image cache to automatically regenerate unless you click the Uncached Refresh button in the upper-right corner, which tells the palette to redraw the graph based on the current image. Photoshop provides a number of other ways — one might even say too many ways — to refresh the histogram. You can also click the triangular cached data warning icon that appears in the top-right corner of the histogram whenever you're viewing a graph created from the cache. Additionally, you can accomplish the same thing by doubling-clicking on the histogram itself. Finally, you can choose the Uncached Refresh option from the palette menu.

✦ **Source:** In a multilayered image, you can tell the Histogram palette to display values for either the Entire Image or just the Selected Layer via the Source pop-up menu. If the image contains any adjustment layers, select one of them and choose Adjustment Composite from the Source pop-up menu to display a histogram of the layers being affected by that adjustment layer.

Beneath the Source menu in the expanded view you'll find statistical information about your image or layer, which you can toggle on or off by choosing Show Statistics from the palette menu. The details in the left column are pretty arcane. The Pixels value tells you how many pixels were used to calculate the current histogram, so if you refresh the histogram using one of the plethora of ways described above, you'll see the Pixels value update to the total number of pixels in your selection or image. The statistics on the right side update as you move your cursor within the histogram itself; you can also click and drag to create a selection within the histogram if you want to see the statistics applied to a range of values. You'll probably never need any of this statistical info, but it's here if you want it.

One of the great strengths of the Histogram palette is the fact that it updates on the fly, even while you're working within one of the color adjustment dialog boxes (but only if you have the Preview check box selected). Even better, the palette doesn't simply replace the original histogram will the new one; it keeps the original histogram visible behind the adjusted histogram in a grayed-out version. It's almost as if you're viewing the Ghost of Histograms Past, as you can see in Figure 12-10.

When you select a portion of an image, the Histogram palette only displays intensity levels and statistics for the selected area.

Although many of the other palettes become frozen when you're working inside a dialog box, you never lose access to the options inside the Histogram palette. Well, almost never. You can't access the Histogram palette options when the Filter Gallery window is open.

As I mentioned a few paragraphs ago, another new development in Photoshop CS is the greatly expanded support of 16-bit color. In case you're a little hazy on what that means, remember that everything inside your computer comes down to 1s and 0s. Think of a pixel 8 bits long as having 8 open slots, each of which could be filled with either a 0 or 1. There are 256 possible combinations — 00000000, 00000001, 00000010, 00000011, 00000100, and so on up to 11111111. So if a color channel can contain 256 luminosity values, then the three channels in an 8-bit/channel RGB image combine for a whopping 16,777,216 possible colors. But with a 16-bit/channel image, there are 65,536 possible values per channel, combining for 281,462,092,005,375 different colors. Kind of puts your box of 64 Crayolas to shame, doesn't it?

Although 281.5 trillion different colors sounds impressive in theory, theory is about as far as it goes. Your monitor can't display more than 16.8 million colors, and you'd already need a 17-megapixel digital camera to be able to theoretically capture every possible color inside one 8-bit/channel image. And the Histogram palette only shows 256 levels of brightness, no matter the mode. So what's all the big fuss about 16-bit color? Why did Adobe bother to expand its support, now letting you work in 16-bit mode with layers, text, channels, shapes, painting tools, and three times as many filters as before? Well, even though you can't actually see all those trillions of colors, they do provide a lot of wiggle room when performing drastic color adjustments to images.

In Figure 12-11, I started with the 8-bit/channel image shown back in the middle example of Figure 11-12. I chose Image ⇨ Duplicate to open a separate copy of the image, and then I chose Image ⇨ Mode ⇨ 16 Bits/Channel to set the copy to 16-bit mode. Next, I pressed Ctrl+L (⌘-L on the Mac) and dragged the black slider in the Output Levels of the Levels dialog box to 246 for both images, essentially washing them out to white. (Much more on Levels to come in just a sec.) Finally, I chose Image ⇨ Adjustments ⇨ Auto Color for each image to attempt to restore the highlights and shadows. As you can see, the 8-bit example on the left did not fare well, with heavy banding quite evident, but the 16-bit example on the right looks almost as good as new. Now, I'm certainly not recommending you start working exclusively in 16-bit mode. File sizes are twice as large as 8-bit, and you'll lose most of your file format options and filters, too. But many specialized fields like video prefer working with 16-bit/channel images, and if you're going to be performing drastic color manipulation, the option is waiting for you.

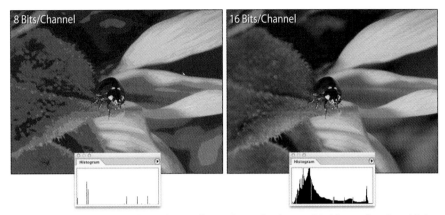

Figure 12-11: I used Levels to drastically wash out both an 8-bit/channel and 16-bit/channel copy of the central image in Figure 11-12. After choosing Auto Color to attempt to revive the images, the 8-bit/channel copy showed extreme banding (left), but the 16-bit/channel copy came out relatively undisturbed (right). The histograms beneath bear this out: The one on the left shows huge gaps between levels, while the one on the right looks much smoother.

The Levels Command

While it's misleading to call the Auto Levels, Auto Contrast and Auto Color commands just presets for Image ⇨ Adjustments ⇨ Levels — after all, each Auto command affects no two images in exactly the same way — it is accurate to say that the three Autos are based on Levels. Not only do the Auto subroutines hail from the same source as Levels, but the Levels dialog box lets you apply and modify the behavior of all three Auto commands. If the Autos are the brightness-correction drones, Levels is their queen.

The Levels command lets you adjust the specific brightness values of highlights, shadows, and midtones in each of the three (or four, in the case of a CMYK image) color channels. Like many of Photoshop's most essential commands — Unsharp Mask, Gaussian Blur, Hue/Saturation, and the upcoming Curves — Levels has been a staple of Photoshop since Version 1.0. In fact, I would go so far as to say it's one of a very few functions that put Photoshop on the map in the first place and continue to make it what it is today. If I had to choose my favorite feature in all of Photoshop, this very well might be it. Okay, I'm in love with the Levels command. There, I've said it and I'm not ashamed. We've already taken an in-depth look at the histogram, which is the most obvious aspect of Levels; let's see what else the command has that makes it so darned lovable.

Input and output levels

Although the histogram is arguably the most important occupant of the Levels dialog box, as shown in Figure 12-12, it doesn't actually *do* anything. It's just data for you to observe, ignore, embrace, or regard with absolute contempt, depending on how your day is going. As is true of most dialog boxes, you use buttons, sliders, and numerical values to put the Levels command through its paces.

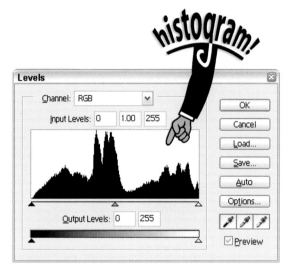

Figure 12-12: Use the Levels dialog box to map existing brightness values in the selection or layer, which Levels calls the Input Levels, to new brightness values, the Output Levels.

The numerical option boxes are arranged in two groups: Input Levels and Output Levels. You compress and expand the range of brightness values in an image by manipulating the Input Levels. Then if you like, you can convert those brightness values to new brightness values by adjusting the Output Levels options.

With that little tidbit of information in mind, let's take a look at how the individual options inside the Levels dialog box work. Throughout, I'll be demonstrating the effects of various settings on the couple pictured in Figure 12-13. It seems such a waste, but there it is, two perfectly lovely women shot under bad light. The color cast is so orange I fear they may be trapped inside a pumpkin, something like The Two Wives of Peter Peter Pumpkin Eater. And the brightness values lack such luster that the photograph could pass for the before picture in a Pledge makeover, were it only of an end table or curio cabinet. My plan, therefore, is to transform these women. As the second example in Figure 12-13 makes plain, I used the Levels command to modify the brightness and contrast levels of each color channel, one at a time. This both brightened the photograph and removed the color cast. Now the ladies are not only beautiful, they're glamorous to boot.

Now let's see how we might actually go about applying the changes. The following list explains the option boxes and slider bars in the Levels dialog box, in the order they appear on your screen.

✦ **Channel:** Select the color channel that you want to edit from this pop-up menu. Each channel presents a slightly different histogram to which you can respond with a unique set of Input Levels and Output Levels settings. You can even apply settings to the full-color composite image in addition to the individual channels. For a stroll through a typical image, see the next section, "Applying Levels one channel at a time."

Press Ctrl (or ⌘) and a number key to switch from one channel to another. For example, Ctrl+1 switches to the Red channel in an RGB image or the Cyan channel in a CMYK image. Ctrl+tilde (~) returns to the full-color composite image.

A happy couple with dysfunctional colors   Now their colors are as beautiful as they are

Figure 12-13: How happy can an alternative couple be when captured under dreary orange nostalgia lighting (left)? If their expressions are any indication, exactly as happy as they'll be after I apply a few well targeted brightness and contrast corrections from the Levels dialog box (right). The difference is that now, their happiness is mine as well.

✦ **Input Levels:** Use these options to modify the contrast of the image by darkening the darkest colors and lightening the lightest ones. The Input Levels option boxes correspond to the slider bar immediately below the histogram. You map pixels to black (or the darkest Output Levels value) by entering a number from 0 to 253 in the first option box or by dragging the black slider triangle beneath the histogram. For example, if you raise the value to 50, all colors with brightness values of 50 or less in the original image become black, darkening the image as shown in the first example of Figure 12-14.

You can map pixels at the opposite end of the brightness scale to white (or the lightest Output Levels value) by entering a number from 2 to 255 in the third Input Levels option box or by dragging the white slider triangle beneath the histogram. If you lower the value to 200, all colors with brightness values of 200 or greater become white, thus lightening the image as shown in the second example of Figure 12-14. In the last example, I raised the first value and lowered the third value, thereby increasing the amount of contrast in the image.

Although common to many of Photoshop's dialog boxes, the Tab and arrow keys are particularly useful when working with Levels. Press Tab to advance from one numeric field to the next; press Shift+Tab to back up. Then press the up and down arrow keys to modify values. Each press of an arrow key raises or lowers the value by 1 (or 0.01 in the case of the gamma value, discussed shortly). Press Shift with an arrow key to change the value in increments of 10 (or 0.1). Under Windows, you can also arrow through the Channel options.

✦ **Clipping previews:** Photoshop provides an additional hidden technique when dragging Input Levels slider triangles. If you press and hold the Alt key (Option on the Mac) while dragging the black or white triangle, Photoshop previews the *clipped colors* inside the image window. Clipped colors are those that change to black or white in at least one color channel.

Figure 12-14: The results of raising the first Input Levels value to 50 (left), separately lowering the third value to 200 (middle), and combining the two changes (right). The blue portions of the histogram show the dark colors that have turned black in the preview above; the red areas indicate the colors that have turned white.

For example, when you Alt-drag (or Option-drag) the black triangle, colors that show up as anything *but white* are turning black in one or more channels. In the first example of Figure 12-15, the yellow pixels have turned black in the blue channel, the red pixels have turned black in both the blue and green channels, and the black pixels are black in all channels. When Alt-dragging (or Option-dragging) the white triangle, colors that show up as anything *but black* are turning white. So the red pixels are white in the red channel, yellow pixels are white in the red and green channels, and white pixels are white in all channels.

By way of advice, a little clipping is inevitable, but you want to avoid as much clipping as possible. Frankly, I would judge the results in Figure 12-15 as entirely unacceptable. If I were to apply these values, fully a third of my image would turn black or white in at least one channel, as illustrated by the black and white overlays in the final image in the figure. This means partial or complete loss of detail in those areas. Higher contrast is good, but all things in moderation.

✦ **Gamma:** The middle Input Levels option box and the corresponding gray triangle in the slider bar (both labeled in Figure 12-16) control the *gamma value*, which is a handle of sorts that allows you to adjust midtones in an image without upsetting shadows or highlights. Imagine a rubber band stretched between two fixed points, black and white, as in the first example in Figure 12-17. This rubber band is the *brightness curve*. The gamma value tugs at the middle of the rubber band, arching it evenly as in the right example in the figure. (Okay, so a rubber band doesn't behave quite like this, but neither does anything else that I'm aware of, so a rubber band will have to do.) The upshot is that the gamma value transforms every color except black and white, and adjusts other colors according to their proximity to black and white. This means it affects midtones more dramatically than shadows and highlights.

Figure 12-15: The results of Alt-dragging (or Option-dragging) the black (left) and white (middle) slider triangles. The black and white overlays (right) highlight the large areas of the image that turn black or white in at least one color channel.

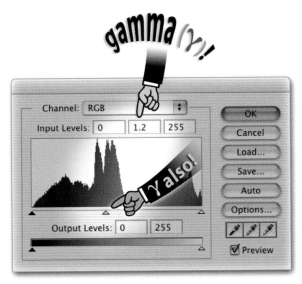

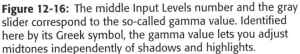

Figure 12-16: The middle Input Levels number and the gray slider correspond to the so-called gamma value. Identified here by its Greek symbol, the gamma value lets you adjust midtones independently of shadows and highlights.

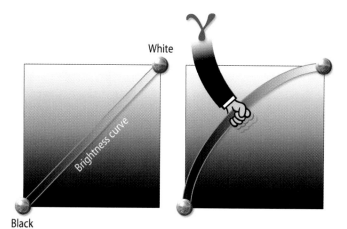

White

Black

Figure 12-17: Photoshop maps brightness values in an image along a straight line, from black to white (left). The line is called a "curve" because of its ability to bend, and the gamma value is what does the bending. Here we see the gamma value tug the curve upward (right), thereby lightening all colors except black and white.

The gamma value ranges from 0.10 to 9.99. The default value of 1.00 indicates a straight brightness curve (like the first image in Figure 12-17), which results in shadows, midtones, and highlights receiving equal amount of correction according to the first and third Input Levels values. Increase the gamma value or drag the gray slider triangle to the left to lighten the midtones independently of black and white, as in the first and second examples of Figure 12-18. Lower the gamma value or drag the gray triangle to the right to darken the midtones, as in the last example in the figure.

Photoshop typically calculates the brightness value of medium gray as 128. So you may wonder why the gamma is expressed as a decimal value instead of as a whole number, with 128 being the default. The reason is rather technical, so if math isn't your bag, consider yourself forewarned. But if you like math — or if you don't, but you like to torment yourself — here goes: Figure 12-19 diagrams the equations associated with each of the gamma corrections pictured in Figure 12-18. If y represents the old colors and x represents the new ones, the gamma value is computed as an exponent. So the new colors equal the old colors to the power of gamma. But if you were to take a brightness value such as 128 and raise it to the power of, say, 1.3, you'd blow it out of the park, sending it to 549 or more than twice the brightness of white. The trick is that the brightness levels are mapped to decimals between 0 and 1, where 0 is black, 1 is white, and 0.5 is medium gray. (The same is true of many equations inside Photoshop.) The gamma value bends the curve up or down, as shown in Figure 12-19, after which Photoshop translates the values back to the 8-bit-per-channel space.

✦ **Output Levels:** Use these options to limit the range of brightness levels in a selection by lightening the darkest pixels and darkening the lightest pixels. You adjust the brightness of the darkest pixels — those that correspond to the first Input Levels value — by entering a number from 0 to 255 in the first option box or dragging the black slider triangle. For example, if you raise the first Output Levels value to 100, no color can be darker than a brightness value of 100 (roughly 60 percent black in print lingo), which lightens the image as shown in the first example of Figure 12-20. You adjust the brightness of the lightest pixels — those that correspond to the third Input Levels value — by entering a number in the second option box or by dragging the white slider triangle. If you lower the value to 175, no color can be lighter than that brightness level (roughly 30 percent black), darkening the image as shown in the second example of Figure 12-20. For the final example in the figure, I raised the first value and lowered the second value, thus dramatically decreasing the amount of contrast in the image. Note that any change to the Output Levels values will decrease the contrast of the image.

As it turns out, you can fully or partially invert an image using the Output Levels slider triangles. Just drag the black triangle to the right and drag the white triangle to the left past the black triangle. This flips the colors, so white maps to dark and black maps to light.

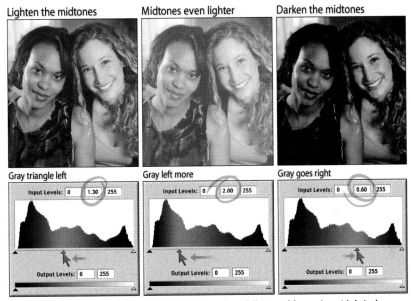

Figure 12-18: The results of raising (left and middle) and lowering (right) the gamma value to lighten and darken the midtones in an image. Notice that dark and light colors are also affected according to their proximity to black and white. Only black and white remain entirely unchanged.

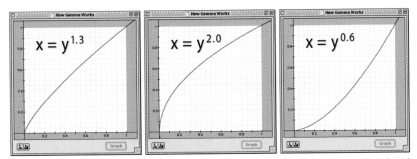

Figure 12-19: The algebraic equations and exact brightness curves associated with each of the corrections from the previous figure. Brightness values are translated to the narrow range from 0 to 1 and the gamma value is applied as an exponent.

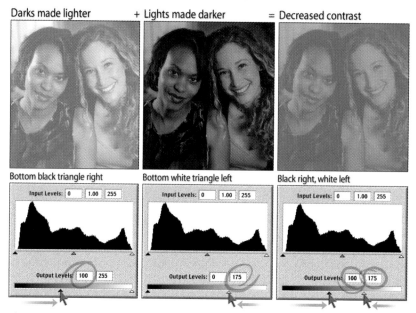

Figure 12-20: Where the Input Levels values generally increase the contrast of an image, the Output Levels values always decrease the contrast. Here I experimented with raising the first Output Levels value to 100 (left), lowering the second value to 175 (middle), and combining the two settings (right).

Applying Levels one channel at a time

Now that we've seen how the Input and Output Levels work, let's try applying them to a full-color photograph. The following steps describe how I corrected the brightness values and color cast associated with the low-contrast, shadow-heavy image that appears at the top of Figure 12-21.

STEPS: Correcting Brightness and Contrast with Levels

1. **Press Ctrl+L (⌘-L on the Mac) to display the Levels dialog box.** As illustrated in the first example in Figure 12-21, most of the colors for this image are clustered on the left side of the histogram, showing that there are far more dark colors than light.

2. **Press Ctrl+1 (or ⌘-1) to examine the red channel.** I'm editing an RGB image, so Ctrl+1 (⌘-1) displays the histogram for the red channel. The channel-specific histograms appear inset into the images in Figure 12-21.

3. **Edit the black Input Levels value as needed.** Drag the black slider triangle to below the point at which the histogram begins. In my case, there's not much going on in the histogram until the point below the "I" in the word "Input." I dragged the black triangle to the beginning of the spike, changing the first Input Levels value to 16, as you can see in the red histogram in the second example in the figure.

4. **Edit the white Input Levels value.** Drag the white slider triangle to below the point at which the histogram ends. I have a lot farther to drag on the right side of the histogram than I did on the left. As shown in the second example of the figure, I dragged the white slider triangle to the endpoint of the last peak of the histogram.

Uncorrected image

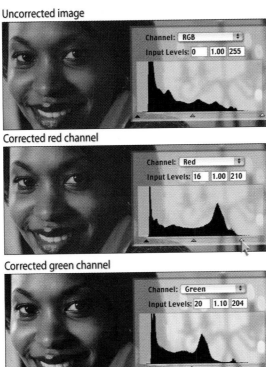

Corrected red channel

Corrected green channel

Corrected blue channel

Corrected composite

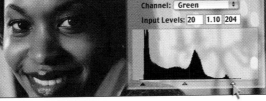

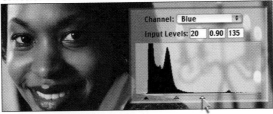

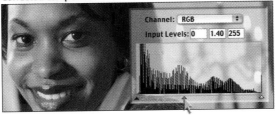

Figure 12-21: Starting with the photograph shown at top, I modified the settings for the Red (second), Green (third), and Blue (fourth) channels, according to the feedback provided to me by the histogram and the image preview. Finally, I returned to the RGB composite view and increased the gamma value to 1.40, thus lightening the midtones (bottom).

5. **Edit the gamma value.** In many cases, you'll want to drag the gray triangle to the gravitational center of the histogram. Imagine that the histogram is a big mass — a bunch of, I don't know, ants or something — and you're trying to balance the ants evenly on top of the gray triangle. If the histogram is weighted too heavily to the left, all the ants could fall off and invade your kitchen. To avoid this catastrophe, drag the gray triangle

to the left. In the case of the red channel, I thought the histogram was pretty well balanced, so I left the gamma alone. Looking ahead to the green channel, however, you can see that I dragged toward the left a little bit, changing the gamma value to 1.10.

6. **Repeat Steps 2 through 5 for the green and blue channels.** At this point, your image probably suffers from a preponderance of red. To correct this, you need to edit the green and blue channels more or less in kind. The graphs in the third and fourth examples of Figure 12-21 show how I edited my histograms. Feel free to switch back and forth between channels as much as you like to get everything just right.

7. **Press Ctrl+tilde (⌘-tilde on the Mac) to return to the full-color composite histogram.** After you get the color balance right, you can switch back to the composite mode and further edit the Input Levels. I sometimes bump up the gamma a few notches to account for dot gain.

   You may notice that your composite histogram has changed. Although the histograms in the individual color channels remain fixed, the composite histogram updates to reflect the individual channel modifications. The final RGB histogram for my image is inset into the bottom example in Figure 12-21. As you can see, the colors are well distributed across the range.

8. **Press Enter or Return to apply your changes.** Just for fun, press Ctrl+Z (or ⌘-Z) a few times to see the before and after views of your image. If your image is anything like mine, you'll be amazed by the transformation.

Customizing the Auto functions

Returning to our tour of the Levels dialog box, we transition from the painstakingly manual to the fully automatic — namely, the Auto button. The behavior of the Auto button depends upon the settings you specify in the Auto Color Correction Options dialog box (described next). The default behavior of Auto is perfectly analogous to the Auto Levels command, but you can change that by clicking the Options button.

The moment you click the Options button, Photoshop applies the default Auto function and invites you to select a different one if you prefer. But that's just the beginning of what you can do inside the Auto Color Correction Options dialog box. Pictured in Figure 12-22, this dialog box lets you modify the behavior of the Auto correction and apply your changes to any and all future adjustments. Here's how the options work:

✦ **Algorithms:** The top group of options determines the type of correction you want to apply. Despite the long, somewhat confusing names, these three choices are equivalent to Auto Contrast, Auto Levels, and Auto Color, as labeled in the figure. (If you like, you can rest your cursor over each name to see an informative tool tip telling you just this.) Turn on the Snap Neutral Midtones check box and you apply Auto Color's gamma correction, originally illustrated back in Figure 12-7. You can even combine this gamma correction with the contrast correction algorithms from Auto Levels or Auto Contrast.

✦ **Target colors:** The Target Colors & Clipping settings come into play not only when you click the Auto button but also when you choose a future Auto command. The three color swatches let you modify the target values for the shadows, midtones, and highlights in your image. Just click in a swatch and then dial in a color or click outside the Color Picker to lift a color directly from the image.

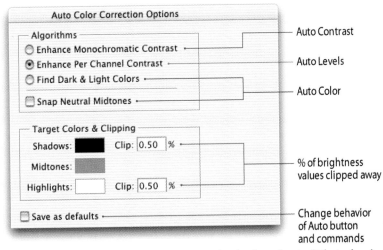

Figure 12-22: Click the Options button to take the "auto" out of Photoshop's automatic color correction functions. These options let you apply the default Auto command (usually Auto Levels), modify the behavior of the Auto button, and adjust the target colors for shadows, midtones, and highlights.

In Figure 12-23, I turned on the two Auto Color options, Find Dark & Light Colors and Snap Neutral Midtones. Then I clicked the Shadows swatch and changed the color to a dark red. (The specific red, green, and blue ingredients are called out in the figure.) Next, I clicked the Midtones swatch and changed it to a cyan, and finally I changed the Highlights to very light orange. The result is perhaps the best correction of the slain Giuliano that we have seen thus far.

✦ **Clipped values:** The two Clip values determine the percentage of total colors in the image that will be clipped away to either black and white or the alternative Shadows and Highlights colors. Enter higher values to increase the number of pixels mapped to black and white; decrease the values to lessen the effect. Figure 12-24 compares three different values applied to both Clip options. The first example illustrates 0.50-percent values, which clip away only one half of one percent of all colors in the image. Other examples show higher values of 3.50 and 9.99 percent. As you can see, raising the Clip value increases the contrast; lowering the value produces more subtle, more photographic effects.

✦ **Save as defaults:** If you select the Save as Defaults check box, your settings will be remembered the next time you use the Auto button inside the Levels or Curves dialog box. This button also saves target color and clipping changes for future applications of the Auto commands.

For an example of when this might come in handy, suppose you have a batch of photos that share similar problems or were shot under similar conditions. Make adjustments to the first photo with specific attention to the Target Colors & Clipping settings. Then turn on the Save as Defaults check box and click OK twice to exit the Levels dialog box. Now when you open another photo in that group, you can simply choose the desired Auto command to instantly apply your customized correction settings. And because it's an Auto command, Photoshop will automatically adjust the readings to reflect the needs of the specific image.

Red shadows (R: 15, G: 10, B: 10)   Cyan midtones (60, 120, 100)   Orange highlights (255, 235, 220)

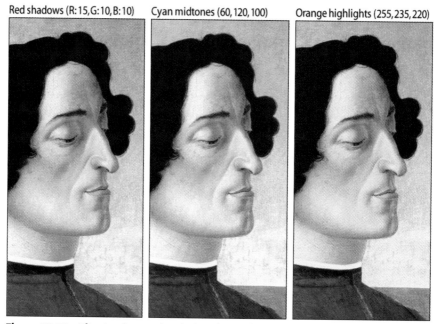

Figure 12-23: After turning on the Find Dark & Light Colors and Snap Neutral Midtones options, I changed the Shadows, Midtones, and Highlights options as shown here. Note that the effects are cumulative, so the final image shows the red shadows, cyan midtones, and orange highlights combined.

Auto Levels: Clip: 0.50%   Clip: 3.50%   Clip: 9.99%

Figure 12-24: The results of applying the Enhance Per Channel Contrast (Auto Levels) setting with the Clip values for both Shadows and Highlights set to their low (left), medium (middle), and maximum (right) values.

Eyedropping neutral colors

Like the Auto commands, the eyedropper tools in the bottom-right corner of the Levels dialog box apply automatic adjustments. But instead of permitting Photoshop to hunt down shadows and highlights automatically, you specify exactly which colors you want to change.

To use an eyedropper, click its icon and then click a pixel in the image window. If you click a pixel with the black eyedropper tool — the first of the three — Photoshop changes the color of that pixel and all darker pixels to black. If you click a pixel with the white eyedropper tool — the last of the three — Photoshop maps it and all lighter pixels to white. The remaining gray eyedropper tool works a bit differently. Rather than mapping a pixel to, say, an absolute gray, the gray eyedropper merely neutralizes a color. For example, if you click on a dark red, Photoshop shifts all colors so red becomes gray. But that pixel remains dark — its luminosity does not change.

The eyedroppers are designed to be used with photos shot using Macbeth charts, the popular professional-standard color swatch boards. Figure 12-25 starts with an image shot by Macworld Labs using a digital camera from Ricoh. The image has a severe blue cast, but thankfully, the lab tech threw in a Macbeth chart so I knew what colors the camera should have shot. After opening the scan in Photoshop, I chose the Levels command, selected the gray eyedropper tool, and clicked in one of the chart's neutral gray swatches. The result appears in the second image in the figure. Because neighboring pixels may vary widely, you may have to click more than once to hit a pixel that satisfactorily balances the colors.

Still life with Macbeth chart   Gray eyedropper on neutral gray   Black & white eyedroppers

Figure 12-25: After opening a color-flawed digital photograph (left), I clicked inside one of the gray swatches in the accompanying Macbeth chart with the gray eyedropper (middle). Then I used the black and white eyedroppers to sample blacks and whites, and adjusted the Input Levels by hand to compensate for the extreme clipping (right).

I next used the black and white eyedroppers to sample colors inside the chart's black and white squares. But because these eyedroppers map to absolute colors, they have a tendency to clip far too many colors. In the end, I was forced to visit the Input Levels values in the individual color channels to back off the black and white sliders. The final result, with adjusted blacks and whites, appears at the end of Figure 12-25.

By default, the eyedroppers map to black, white, and gray. But you can change that. Double-click any one of the three eyedroppers to display the Color Picker dialog box. For example, suppose I'm making final adjustments to a CMYK image, and I know that the lightest color my press will print is C:2, M:3, Y:5, K:0. To ensure that even my lightest highlights will print, I might double-click the white eyedropper, set the color values to the previous values, and then click a pixel in the image window. Instead of making the pixel white, Photoshop changes the clicked color — and all colors lighter than it — to C:2, M:3, Y:5, K:0, which is great for avoiding hot highlights and ragged edges.

The Curves Command

Whereas Levels permits you to modify three points on the brightness curve — black, white, and the gamma value (see Figure 12-17 if you need a refresher) — the Curves command lets you edit as many points as you like. I gather this is the reason that some folks believe Curves to be the superior command and others think that it gives you just enough latitude to hang yourself — if, indeed, it is possible to hang from latitude.

Naturally, I think both groups are right. Curves is the more powerful command, but it's likewise more cumbersome to use. Furthermore, it lacks a histogram, which is absolutely essential for gauging the proper settings for black and white points. In return, Curves lets you map out dozens of significant points on a graph. The point is, both commands have their relative advantages, and both offer practical benefits for intermediate and advanced users.

There's no substitute for a good histogram, so I prefer to use Levels for my day-to-day color correcting. But if I can't quite get the effect I want with Levels, or I know that I need to map specific brightness values in an image to other values, I'll enthusiastically take up the Curves command. And what could be better? Two very distinct commands with two very distinct purposes.

Mastering the brightness curve

When you choose Image ⇨ Adjustments ⇨ Curves or press Ctrl+M (⌘-M on the Mac), Photoshop displays the Curves dialog box, shown in Figure 12-26, which offers access to the most complex and powerful color correction options on the planet. Here's how these options work:

✦ **Channel:** As with the Levels command, Curves lets you edit the composite image and independent color channels to different degrees. Select the color channel that you want to edit from this pop-up menu or press Ctrl (⌘ on the Mac) and a number key.

✦ **Brightness graph:** The brightness graph is the core of the Curves dialog box, so it figures into many upcoming discussions. But for now, here are a few basics: You click on the brightness curve (which starts off as a straight line) to add points. Then you drag the points to map brightness values in the original image to new brightness values.

Figure 12-27 diagrams the default behaviors of the brightness graph when editing images in the RGB and CMYK spaces. In either case, the horizontal axis of the graph represents input levels, or the original colors in the image; the vertical axis represents output levels, or modified colors. To help keep them straight, I've color-coded the input levels green for RGB and magenta for CMYK; the output levels are red and cyan, respectively.

For me, it helps to think of the brightness curve as representing the original colors (hence green/magenta) that are being mapped onto a grid of new colors (red/cyan). The practical upshot of this is that, when working in the RGB color space, dragging a point up or to the left makes the image lighter; dragging a point down or to the right makes the image darker. The opposite is true when working in CMYK or grayscale.

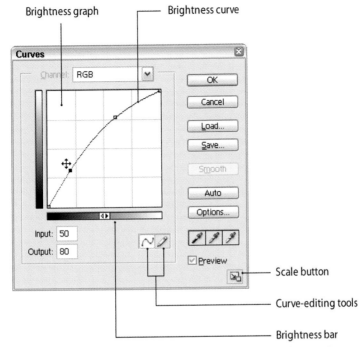

Brightness graph — Brightness curve

Scale button
Curve-editing tools
Brightness bar

Figure 12-26: The Curves dialog box lets you adjust the luminosity of one or more color channels by adding and adjusting points along the brightness curve. By default, when editing an RGB image, black is positioned in the lower-left corner of the graph and white is in the upper-right corner.

By default, a total of six grid lines — three horizontal and three vertical — crisscross the brightness graph, subdividing it into sixteenths. For added precision, you can divide the graph into horizontal and vertical tenths. Just Alt-click (or Option-click) inside the graph to toggle between the two.

✦ **Scale button:** When you first enter the Curves dialog box, the brightness graph measures a scant 171 pixels wide. (How Adobe arrived at 171 pixels, I haven't a clue — John Warnock's weight in 1990? — but there it is.) To enlarge the graph to 256 pixels, one pixel for every brightness value, click the scale button in the lower-right corner of the dialog box.

✦ **Brightness bar:** Labeled in Figure 12-26, the horizontal brightness bar shows the direction of light and dark values in the graph. When the dark end of the brightness bar appears on the left — as by default when editing an RGB image — colors are measured in terms of brightness values, as in the left example of Figure 12-28. Therefore, higher positions in the graph and larger numerical values indicate lighter colors.

If you click the brightness bar, white and black switch places, as shown in the second example in the figure. The result is that Photoshop measures the colors in terms of ink densities, from 0 to 100 percent of the primary color. Higher positions and values now indicate darker colors. As seen back in Figure 12-27, this is the default setting for CMYK and grayscale images. But if you'd rather work with brightness values, click the brightness bar to make it so.

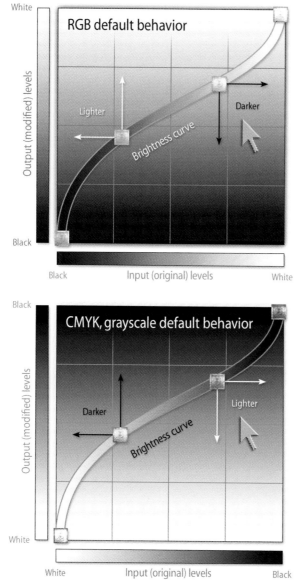

Figure 12-27: Diagrams of the Curves dialog box's brightness graph when editing an RGB image (top) versus a CMYK or grayscale image (bottom). By default, Photoshop assumes that you want to edit brightness values in RGB and ink densities in CMYK, so one graph is an inverse of the other.

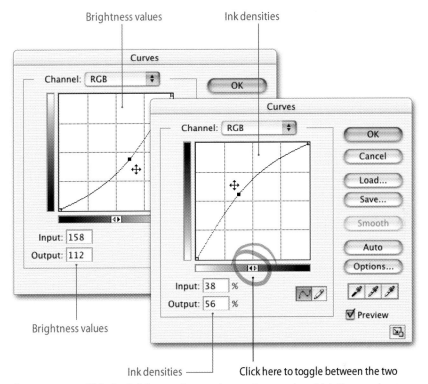

Figure 12-28: Click the brightness bar to change the way in which the graph measures color — either in terms of brightness values (left) or by ink densities (right).

✦ **Curve tools:** Use the curve tools to draw the curve inside the brightness graph. Labeled in Figure 12-29, the point tool is selected by default. When armed with this tool, you can click along the brightness curve to add a point. Drag a point to move it. Shift-click to select multiple points (or deselect selected points). To delete a point, Ctrl-click it (on the Mac, ⌘-click).

Switch to the pencil tool to draw free-form curves by dragging inside the graph, as demonstrated in Figure 12-29. This pencil works much like Photoshop's standard pencil tool. This means you can draw straight lines by clicking one location in the graph and Shift-clicking elsewhere in the graph.

✦ **Input and Output values:** Located in the bottom-left corner of the dialog box, the Input and Output values monitor the location of the selected point in the graph — or if no point is selected, the position of the cursor — according to brightness values or ink densities depending on the setting of the brightness bar. You can modify the Input and Output values when working with the point tool. Just select one or more points that you want to adjust and then enter new values. The Input number represents the brightness or ink value of the original color; the Output number records the modified brightness or ink value. When a single point is selected, the values list absolute coordinates in the graph; when multiple points are selected, they list relative positions.

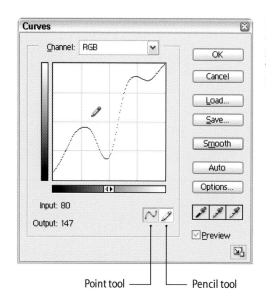

Figure 12-29: Use the pencil tool to draw free-form lines in the brightness graph. If the lines appear too rough, you can soften them by clicking the Smooth button.

Point tool — Pencil tool

 You can also nudge the Input and Output values with the arrow keys. First, select one or more points with the point tool. (You can't edit points when using the pencil tool.) Then press the right or left arrow key to raise or lower the Input value in increments of 1; press the up or down arrow key to raise or lower the Output value. To nudge a value in increments of 10, press Shift with an arrow key.

 When editing Input and Output values numerically, it's helpful to be able to select the points from the keyboard. To advance from one point to the next, press Ctrl+Tab (Control-Tab on the Mac). To select the previous point, press Ctrl+Shift+Tab (Control-Shift-Tab). To deselect all points, press Ctrl+D (⌘-D).

✦ **Smooth:** When working with the pencil tool, click the Smooth button to smooth out sharp corners and jagged lines. Doing so leads to smoother color transitions in the image window. This button is dimmed using the point tool. To see this button in use, read the section "Working with arbitrary maps" near the end of this chapter.

✦ **Auto and Options:** These buttons are identical to the Auto and Options buttons provided in the Levels dialog box. For more information, read "Customizing the Auto functions" earlier in this chapter.

Eyedropping graph points

Where I would characterize the eyedroppers in the Levels dialog box as occasionally useful, those in the Curves dialog box verge on indispensable—despite the fact that, on first blush, they seem to work the same. Located in the bottom-right corner of the dialog box, the three eyedropper tools map pixels to black, neutral gray, or white, just as in the Levels dialog box. (To map to other colors, double-click the eyedropper icons.) Figure 12-30 illustrates the result of clicking with the white eyedropper tool on a light pixel, thereby mapping that value to white.

Bear in mind that Photoshop maps the value to each color channel independently. So when editing a full-color image inside the Curves dialog box, you have to switch channels to see the results of clicking with an eyedropper. In Figure 12-30, I go so far as to recommend you switch channels before clicking with the tool just to avoid surprises. You can further adjust the brightness value of that pixel by dragging the corresponding point in the graph, as demonstrated in the last example in the figure.

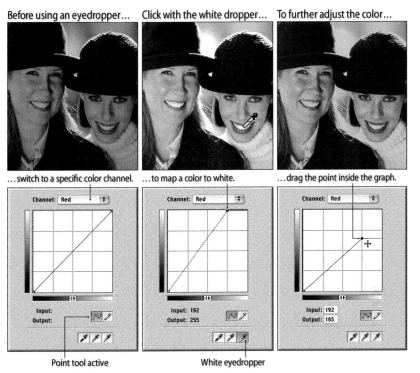

Before using an eyedropper...   Click with the white dropper...   To further adjust the color...

...switch to a specific color channel.   ...to map a color to white.   ...drag the point inside the graph.

Point tool active   White eyedropper

Figure 12-30: Because the eyedropper tools add points to the independent color channels, not to the composite view, you may want to select a channel before doing anything else (left). Then click with one of the eyedropper tools to map the color of the clicked pixel in the graph (middle) and edit the location of the point in the graph by dragging it (right).

Ironically, when no eyedropper tool is active — that is, none of the icons is highlighted in the lower-right corner of the dialog box — the eyedropper becomes even more useful. First, if a tool is active, turn it off by clicking on the active eyedropper icon. Then move your cursor into the image window to get the standard eyedropper cursor. Click and hold down the mouse button to locate the brightness of an image pixel in the graph. For as long as the mouse button is down, a circle appears in the graph and the Input and Output numbers list the values. This makes dragging in the image window a great way to locate ranges of colors.

Using the following modifier keys, you can use the eyedropper cursor to sample specific colors from the image. Bear in mind, both of these techniques work only when the point tool is active and no eyedropper is selected:

✦ **To add a color to the brightness graph, Ctrl-click (or ⌘-click) a pixel in the image window.** Photoshop adds the point to the channel displayed in the dialog box. For example, if the full-color RGB composite image is visible, the point is added to the RGB composite curve. If the Red channel is visible, Photoshop adds the point to the red graph and leaves the green and blue graphs unchanged.

✦ **To add a color to the individual channel graphs, regardless of which channel is visible, Ctrl+Shift-click (or ⌘-Shift-click) a pixel in the image window.** In the case of an RGB image, Photoshop adds points to the brightness graphs for the Red, Green, and Blue channels, but leaves the RGB composite graph unchanged. So you'll need to switch to the individual channels to see the new point.

Gradient maps

The Curves command has a partner that performs a similar function, though you wouldn't know it from its name. It all stems from the old days, when Photoshop permitted you to load a predefined gradient as a Curves map. It sounds strange, but you could actually modify brightness values to conform to the colors in a gradation. This function still exists, but nowadays you use a separate command, Image ⇨ Adjustments ⇨ Gradient Map.

Choose the Gradient Map command or adjustment layer to display the dialog box pictured in Figure 12-31. Make sure the Preview check box is turned on. Then click the down-pointing arrowhead to the right of the gradient preview to display a drop-down palette of gradient presets. Select a gradient other than Foreground To Background and watch the fireworks.

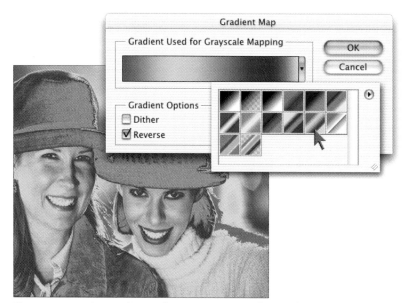

Figure 12-31: Choose the Gradient Map command to apply a preset gradient as a Curves map. Here we see the result of applying one of the most successful presets for this purpose, Copper, with the Reverse check box turned on.

What's going on? As foreign as it may sound, any gradient can be expressed as a Curves graph, progressing through a variety of brightness values in each of the three (RGB) or four (CMYK) color channels. When applied as a gradient map, the beginning of the gradient maps to black; the end of the gradient maps to white. If you apply the Violet, Orange preset, for example, the dark colors in the image map to violet and the light colors map to orange.

At this point, you might think, that's just plain weird. And I wouldn't dare disagree with you, but weirdness can be entertaining and even useful when applied properly. In the first row of Figure 12-32, I started with the classic Portrait of a Young Woman by Italian artist Pelagio Palagi. It's a wonderful composition, but that crazy Pelagio got the colors all wrong, so I decided to fix them by applying Gradient Map and experimenting with two of Photoshop's predefined gradients: Violet, Orange and Chrome. The first of the two effects looks swell because the Violet, Orange gradient transitions evenly from first color to last. But Chrome is more elaborate, and therefore results in harsh edges when expressed as a map.

So I decided to change my approach. Before applying the Gradient Map command, I copied the image to a new layer by pressing Ctrl+J (⌘-J on the Mac). Then I chose Filter ➪ Blur ➪ Gaussian Blur and entered a Radius value of 4 pixels. Next, I experimented with applying each of three gradient maps, as shown in the second row of Figure 12-32. (In the case of the Copper gradient, I turned on the Reverse check box, which reverses the order of colors in the gradient to better match the natural order of brightness values from dark to light.) The results are blurry but smooth. To complete the effect, I mixed each of the mapped images with its underlying original by choosing the Color blend mode from the Layers palette. The resulting images blend wild gradient colors with solid image details, as shown in the bottom row of the figure.

Creating and editing continuous curves

Now you know everything about how Curves and its buddy Gradient Map work, but little about how to apply the Curves dialog box's highly specialized options. That's why I spend the next two sections in this chapter exploring practical applications of this command, concentrating first on the point tool and then on the pencil tool. These discussions assume that you're working inside an RGB image and the brightness bar is set to edit brightness values, as by default.

When you first enter the Curves dialog box, the brightness curve appears as a straight line strung between two points, as shown in the first example in Figure 12-33. This maps every input level from black to white to an identical output level. If you want to perform seamless color corrections, the point tool is your best bet for editing the curve because it enables you to adjust levels while maintaining smooth transitions.

To lighten the colors, click near the middle of the curve with the point tool to create a new point and then drag the point upward, as demonstrated in the second example in Figure 12-33. To darken the image, drag the point downward, as in the third example.

Such single-point operations are analogous to modifying the gamma value in the Levels dialog box. You tap into the real power of Curves when you add two points or more. As shown in Figure 12-34, two points permit you to boost or reduce the contrast between colors in ways that Levels simply can't match. In the first example, I created one point in the darkest quarter of the curve and another in the lightest quarter. I then dragged down on the left point and up on the right point to make the dark pixels darker and the light pixels lighter, which translates to higher contrast.

In the second example in Figure 12-34, I dragged those same points in opposite directions, lifting the left point to lighten the dark pixels and lowering the right point to darken the light pixels. This decreases the contrast between colors, reducing color saturation but adding detail to the highlights and shadows.

Original painting

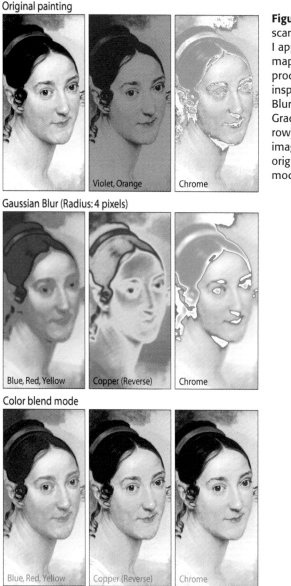

Violet, Orange   Chrome

Gaussian Blur (Radius: 4 pixels)

Blue, Red, Yellow   Copper (Reverse)   Chrome

Color blend mode

Blue, Red, Yellow   Copper (Reverse)   Chrome

Figure 12-32: After opening the scan of a 19th-century painting, I applied a couple of gradient maps (top row). The Chrome map produced jagged edges, which inspired me to apply Gaussian Blur to it and a couple other Gradient Map variations (middle row). I then mixed these fantastic images with their underlying originals using the Color blend mode (bottom row).

In the final example in Figure 12-34, I sent the contrast through the roof with special emphasis on the highlights. As shown in the brightness graph, I dragged both points down and to the left. This has the effect of springing the right half of the curve farther upward, thus dramatically increasing the brightness of the lightest pixels in the image.

Figure 12-33: Click with the point tool along the brightness curve to add a single point to the curve (left). Then drag the point upward (middle) to lighten the image evenly; drag the point downward (right) to darken the image.

Working with arbitrary maps

Back in the dim days of Photoshop — before the *Bible* even existed (if you can believe such a time is even possible) — there used to be a command called Image ⇨ Map ⇨ Arbitrary. This command made it possible to draw so-called *arbitrary maps*, which were free-form brightness graphs. The idea was you could correct an image by drawing your own graph, or altogether morph the colors in an image to produce a special effect.

The command has since disappeared, but its spirit lives on in the Curves dialog box. In fact, you can create some mind-numbing color variations by adjusting the brightness curve arbitrarily, mapping light pixels to dark, dark pixels to light, and in-between pixels all over the place. In the first example in Figure 12-35, I used the point tool to achieve an arbitrary curve. By dragging the left point severely upward and the right point severely downward, I caused shadows, highlights, and midtones to soar across the spectrum.

Although it's clearly possible to craft arbitrary effects using the point tool, the pencil tool is more versatile and less inhibiting. In fact, the pencil tool is the last vestige of what used to be the Arbitrary Map dialog box. As seen in the second example in Figure 12-35, simply switching to the pencil tool doesn't do anything — it merely converts the point-based path to a freehand line. But if I draw a quick zigzag across the graph, things change substantially, as the final example in the figure shows.

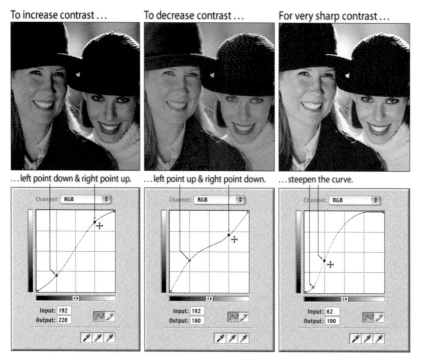

Figure 12-34: Create two points in the curve to adjust shadows and highlights independently, ideal for manipulating contrast. Here, I increased the contrast mildly (left), decreased it a bit (middle), and sent it soaring into the highlights (right).

Actually, it's a bit misleading to suggest I just dragged across the screen and got that last effect. Although it took only a few seconds, it was slightly more involved than that. To gain some control, I first drew the freehand line as a polygon by clicking and Shift-clicking my way across the graph. Then, to smooth out the corners, I clicked the Smooth button. As it turns out, the Smooth button is an integral part of using the pencil tool.

Try this little experiment: Draw a bunch of random lines and squiggles with the pencil tool in the brightness graph. As shown in the first example in Figure 12-36, your efforts will most likely yield an unspeakably hideous and utterly unrecognizable effect. Next, click the Smooth button. Photoshop automatically connects all portions of the curve, miraculously smoothing out the color-mapping and rescuing some semblance of your original image (see the second example in the figure). If the effect is still too radical, you can apply additional smoothing to the curve by once again clicking the Smooth button. I clicked the button a total of three times to create the right-hand image in Figure 12-36. Had I gone much farther, I would have eventually restored the curve to a straight line.

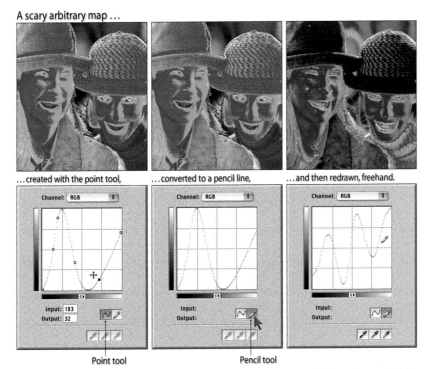

A scary arbitrary map . . .

. . . created with the point tool,   . . . converted to a pencil line,   . . . and then redrawn, freehand.

Point tool   Pencil tool

Figure 12-35: After drawing an arbitrary brightness curve with the point tool (left), I switched to the pencil tool, the modern-day successor to the ancient Arbitrary Map command (middle). Then I redrew the curve freehand to create a wildly, perhaps ridiculously surrealistic effect (right).

What might be considered ridiculous arbitrary maps when applied to continuous-tone photographs can prove extremely interesting when applied to synthetic effects, like those discussed in Chapter 9. The top row of Figure 12-37 shows three examples of synthetics created from scratch using filters and layer effects. In the first image, I applied Filter ➪ Render ➪ Clouds to each of the color channels independently, and then I blurred the composite image using Gaussian Blur set to a Radius of 4 pixels. In the second example, I filled the image with black and then applied Filter ➪ Render ➪ Lens Flare using the 35mm Prime setting. For the last image, I created a letter in Times New Roman and added a few layer effects including an Outer Glow set to the Normal blend mode and the exact same shade of emerald as the letter, which produced the effect of blurring the outline.

I next chose the Curves command and applied the arbitrary map pictured in the second example in Figure 12-36 to each of my synthetics. The results of these radical color adjustments populate the second row of Figure 12-37. Notice that even though the synthetic effects ranged from soft to downright blurry, the arbitrary map managed to draw forth colors in sharp focus. This is because, although smoothed once, the middle brightness graph in Figure 12-35 features lots of steep transitions. So the moral is, use sharp maps with soft or blurry images and smooth maps with sharp images.

To create a free-form arbitrary map . . .

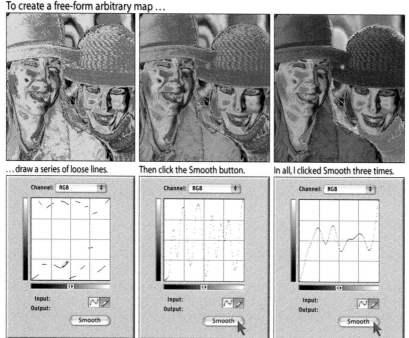

. . . draw a series of loose lines.   Then click the Smooth button.   In all, I clicked Smooth three times.

Figure 12-36: After drawing a series of random lines with the pencil tool (left), I clicked the Smooth button once to connect the lines into a frenetic curve (middle) and then twice more to even out the curve, thus preserving more of the original image (right).

In the interest of beating a dead horse, Figure 12-38 takes the three effects from the second row of Figure 12-37 and layers them on top of the original Times New Roman letter. I set each layer to the Overlay blend mode with an Opacity of 100 percent. The results make it look almost as if I had applied the effects as displacement maps (discussed in Chapter 10), but in fact, it's all a simple illusion performed with color adjustments and a blend mode. It just goes to show you that even Curves, the most button-down, industrial-grade correction function of them all, can yield an astonishing array of special effects.

Channel-by-channel brightness graphing

Now that we've seen every aspect of the Curves dialog box—from the elaborate brightness graph to the playful pencil tool and all points in between—let's turn our waning attention to how you might go about correcting a real image on a channel-by-channel basis. By way of example, Figure 12-39 shows a photograph subject to relatively basic color manipulations in the green and blue channels, followed by an arbitrary adjustment to the red channel.

Clouds in each channel; GBlur (4) Lens Flare (170%, 35mm Prime) Drop shadow, glow, emboss, & satin

Same as above, subject to free-form arbitrary map

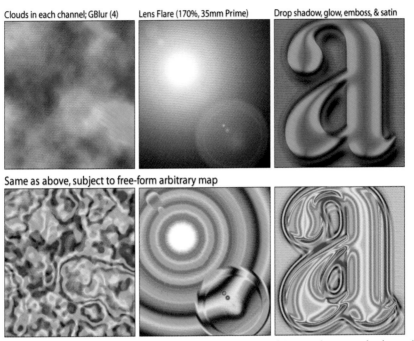

Figure 12-37: A variety of synthetic effects (top row) subject to the smoothed pencil graph featured in the second example in Figure 12-36 (bottom row). Radical arbitrary maps are especially well suited to drawing a wealth of colors from blurry or indistinct details.

Arbitrary map effects layered in front of type, Overlay blend mode

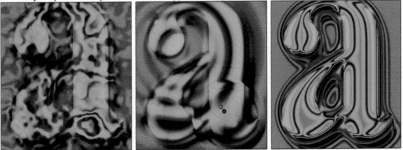

Figure 12-38: The results of layering the second row of effects in Figure 12-37 in front of the original green letter *a* and applying the Overlay blend mode. The bright, gooey colors from the effects appear to distort the colors inside the letter while leaving the character outline intact.

Corrected with Curves

Figure 12-39: The Curves command lets you correct an image with precise or even mischievous control. The first three images show the corrected image, and a couple of glimpses of how I got there, by lightening the contents of the Green channel (second) and increasing the contrast of the Blue (third). But then I thought, to heck with it and applied an arbitrary map to the Red channel. Life is just so much rosier with red accessories and eyes.

Green channel: lighten

Blue channel: increase contrast

Red channel: arbitrary map

The figure leads off with the finished image, painstakingly corrected one channel at a time using the brightness graph and the point tool. The second example shows my first tentative correction inside the Curves dialog box. Not certain where to start, I switched to the Green channel—the one that generally contains the best variations in luminosity—and lightened the channel by clicking at two points in the brightness graph and dragging up on the curve.

Then I switched to the Blue channel and clicked to set four points in the graph. I dragged the first point down to darken the darkest colors and nudged the remaining three points up to lighten the lightest colors. The result was to increase the contrast of the channel, as the third example in the figure shows.

To complete the correction, all that was required was to switch to the Red channel and lift the center of the curve slightly. This would produce the corrected image pictured at the outset. But darn it, I had a bug in my bonnet and I decided the straight and narrow was not for me. So instead, I decided to finish things off with an arbitrary map. I switched to the Red channel, added three points to the graph, and dragged the first and last points up and the middle point down. This lightened the shadows and highlights while darkening the midtones, resulting in a couple of brightly colored red hats, as we see at the figure's end. Oh, and look — after all that time spent reducing the effects of red-eye in the previous chapter, I've gone and added it to these charming young women. But it's for the best. Honestly, which image are you more likely to look at? The perfectly corrected image at the top of Figure 12-39, or the one with the shocking red hats? It's no contest — red hats win every time.

The Shadow/Highlight Command

The lens on a camera is an astonishing thing, but there are still certain areas where it just doesn't hold a candle to the good old human eye. Every waking moment of every day, for instance, the irises in our eyes are constantly adjusting our pupil size to determine the amount of light that gets in so we can perceive as much as possible. Modern cameras try their best to keep up with complicated and varied lighting situations, but you're often stuck having to choose between sacrificing the darker areas of an image or overexposing the lighter areas. For example, how many times have you photographed someone against the sky, only to find the sky perfectly exposed and your subject darker than the gothic poetry of a troubled teen?

Photoshop CS introduces a new command called Shadow/Highlight, which can help with backlighting problems like the one I just described. While the command has the power to both pull an image's shadows out from the darkness and push the highlights of an image into midtones, you'll get the most impressive immediate results by applying the command to an image with dark shadows. Choose Image ⇨ Adjustments ⇨ Shadow/Highlight to bring up the dialog box shown in Figure 12-40. (In the figure I've clicked the check box labeled Show More Options — an understatement if ever I read one.) Instantly, you should see a difference; the simple default settings go a long way toward fixing many a shadowy image.

The Shadow/Highlight command examines the image and, according to your settings, deems certain spots to be "shadows" and others "highlights." From there, you adjust the sliders to tell Photoshop just how much brightening or darkening it should perform on those areas. It's a smart feature that's deceptively easy to master. By default you're presented with just two Amount sliders, one for Shadows and one for Highlights. And in perhaps Photoshop's most counterintuitive moment — I mean, it's right up there with the naming of the Unsharp Mask filter — raising the Shadows amount *lightens* the image, and raising the Highlights amount *darkens* it. Hover your cursor over an Amount slider and a tool tip pops up to explain that you're adjusting the amount of *correction*. Ah, now I get it. To my way of thinking, that's like Gaussian Blur actually sharpening an image — unless you use negative amounts, that is. But I digress. Click on that Show More Options check box, and let's take a close look at all the controls:

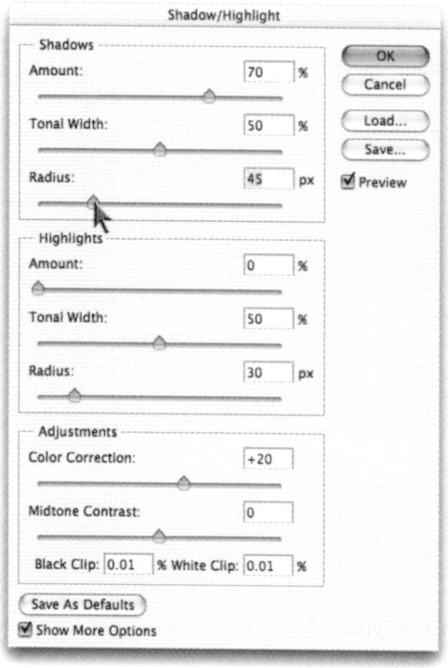

Figure 12-40: The new Shadow/Highlight dialog box lets you correct exposure problems in specific areas of an image without harming other areas.

✦ **Amount:** As I noted, in the Shadows section, the Amount slider lets you specify the degree to which the shadows in an image will be lightened. In the Highlights section, the slider controls how much the highlights will be darkened. A value of 0 percent yields no change in the image; a value of 100 percent results in maximum brightening of the shadows (in the Shadows section) or darkening of the highlights (in the Highlights section). The default Shadows Amount setting of 50 percent is a safe place to start when lightening shadows in an image.

✦ **Tonal Width:** This setting adjusts the range of the pixels that get modified by the command. In the Shadows section, higher values increase the range of shadow areas that get lightened and lower values concentrate on only the darker regions of the image. In the Highlights section, higher values increase the range of light areas that get darkened and lower values restrict the adjustment to only the lighter regions. The default Tonal Width value in both sections is 50 percent. If you find that the command is lightening too much of an image, lower the value in the Shadows section to correct it.

✦ **Radius:** The Shadow/Highlight command determines which areas are shadows and which are highlights by examining each pixel compared to the pixels that surround it. This prevents every stray dark pixel from being classified as a shadow and subsequently lightened, for example. Adjust the Radius sliders to determine the size of each pixel's "neighborhood," or, in other words, the number of surrounding pixels that are taken into account when each pixel is categorized as shadow or highlight.

Radius is the setting you'll most likely need to adjust on an image-by-image basis. The default setting of 30 pixels is a good place to start, but keep in mind that by increasing the Radius value you apply a less exacting change to the image, and by decreasing the value you lose some of the contrast.

Below the Shadows and Highlights sections is a third area labeled Adjustments. It contains the following options:

✦ **Color Correction:** Occasionally, the Shadow/Highlight command can make the colors in an image a little less vivid. The Color Correction slider lets you adjust the saturation of the color in the affected portion of the image. In grayscale images, this option is replaced with a general Brightness setting.

You can achieve an interesting effect by increasing the Amount value in the Shadows section and ramping down the Color Correction setting. The result is an image in which all pixels formerly in the shadowed areas become completely grayscale. In addition to producing an interesting effect, it also lets you glimpse exactly which pixels are being affected.

✦ **Midtone Contrast:** This setting increases or decreases the contrast of the midtone pixels in the image. Generally speaking, higher values mean a darker image and lower values produce a lighter, more even result.

✦ **Black Clip** and **White Clip:** These values let you adjust the maximum settings for how light the adjusted shadow pixels will be and how dark the adjusted highlight pixels will be. While the limit for both values is 50 percent, I advise that you never even approach that high a value. On the contrary; keep these settings as low as you can to provide for smooth transitions and healthy contrast levels in your images.

The Shadow/Highlight dialog box lets you save your settings and then load them later using the Save and Load buttons. If you want to designate your current settings as the default for the command, click the Save As Defaults button at the bottom of the dialog box.

Okay, so I've mentioned this before, but it's worth repeating: The new Histogram palette is a great way to keep track of brightness and tonal changes to an image. So it serves as a great reference while you're working in the Shadow/Highlight dialog box.

Take a gander at Figure 12-41. The first example shows what appears to be a reject from the Cirque du Soleil, rejected perhaps because he couldn't find the *soleil* to stand in. The image is a nicely composed shot that has been marred by the brightness of the sky in the background contrasting with the shadows the man is standing in, which caused the camera's iris to close and render the subject all but "noir," as they say. To create the middle image, I applied the Shadow/Highlight command with the default settings, which do a pretty great job of pulling light back into the shadows without harming the brightness or detail in the surrounding sky. In the final image on the right, I cranked up the Shadows Amount to 75 and the Tonal Width to 60. For this image, that's about as far as I can go without starting to degrade the image quality.

Figure 12-41: The Shadow/Highlight command does an expert job of recovering the detail in this man's face and costume (middle and right). On second thought, perhaps I should have left him as he was.

✦   ✦   ✦

File Management and Automation

Batching It

When I think back to my bachelor days, the concept of "baching it" conjures up images of shopping for such staples of life as coffee, ice cream, and arbitrary produce at one o'clock in the morning in an all-night grocery store. Or doing my laundry and noticing with mild dismay that I wore the same two mismatched socks all week. Or other scenarios too pitiful to mention in polite company, which when relayed to my wife make her chuckle in an "I can't decide if you're cute, stupid, or just plain disgusting" kind of way.

"Baching it" might, if pronounced a different way, suggest arranging a musical composition in the style of the late great Johann Sebastian Bach. But Photoshop has no use for any of these definitions. Taking the T from one of its several type tools, Photoshop turns "baching" into "batching" and transforms the possibly pathetic into the pregnantly powerful (helpfully illustrated in Figure 13-1). For when we are batching it, we are making full use of one of the rarely exploited advantages of computers, automation.

Photoshop's methods of automation are as vast as they are versatile, ranging from the wealth of disk-management options supplied by the File Browser, to the ability to record your own multi-step actions, to full-blown batch processing. You can rename multiple files at a time, save a folder of files in a different format, and apply a sequence of custom operations to documents that aren't even open. Some of the processes take only a few seconds to apply. Others give you a chance to go to the water cooler, catch up on your reading, or discover that cure for the common cold that you keep meaning to work on. This chapter, then, is about helping Photoshop to work smarter and more efficiently for you.

Figure 13-1: When a spouse or loved one leaves town, baching it may be a matter of survival. But inside Photoshop, batching it means kicking back, relaxing, and letting your computer do the work for you.

The File Browser

Opening an image is like putting on a pair of socks. The actual operation of applying socks to one's feet is a relatively easy one. And most of us have more socks than we know what to do with. In fact, our feet would be eternally graced by elegant, matching socks if it weren't for the fact that the darned things are so difficult to find. Washing machines, dryers, and dresser drawers harbor vast collections of socks that we'll never see again.

Images are the same way. Although easy to open, they're not so easy to find. Socked away (ow, that joke hurt even me) inside folders on external hard drives, Zips, CDs, and myriad varieties of digital camera cards, the common image is more abundant than lint and harder to locate than a clean dish towel.

Just as life would benefit from a sock browser, Photoshop benefits from the File Browser. And in Photoshop CS, the File Browser dons a whole slew of new features. This glorious window into your digital domain shows you thumbnail previews of every image contained inside a selected folder, as in Figure 13-2. You can access the File Browser by clicking the folder-and-magnifying glass icon directly to the left of the docking well in the Options bar. Clicking this icon again hides the browser. Like any window, you also can close or hide the browser using the buttons in the window's title bar. Additionally, you can display the browser by choosing File ➪ Browse, Window ➪ File Browser, or by pressing Ctrl+Shift+O (⌘-Shift-O on the Mac).

Selected image   Rotate Search   Up folder

Folder tree   Flag | Delete   Folder path menu

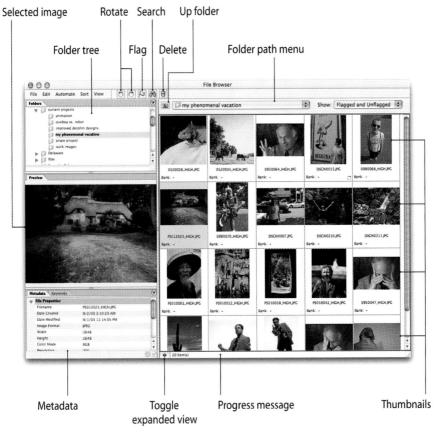

Metadata   Toggle   Progress message   Thumbnails
expanded view

Figure 13-2: The File Browser is divided into four panes, showing the folder tree, a preview of the selected image, non-pixel metadata, and thumbnail-sized previews of images inside the active folder. The browser lets you change the sorting order, rotate images, and perform a boatload of tasks way too impressive to describe in a mere caption.

Opening an image from the browser is simply a matter of navigating to its folder from the hierarchical list that's located by default in the upper-left corner of the window, and then double-clicking a thumbnail. But there's much more to the File Browser than may at first meet the eye. Photoshop CS introduces several enhancements including the expanded ability to add and edit auxiliary information about your images, improved batch processing capabilities, and new ways to organize and navigate files. The File Browser is so powerful it's like a mini-application running within Photoshop; in fact, Adobe has even given the File Browser its own menu bar. The best way to learn how it works is to run through a list of its parts. The following paragraphs explain the items shown in Figure 13-2, ranked in rough order of importance:

✦ **Folder tree:** I call the pane of the File Browser with the Folders tab at the top of it the *folder tree* because it shows folders branching off in various directions. Like the Explorer bar under Windows, the folder tree lets you dig several folders deep in search of images. Click the plus sign (or the "twirly" triangle on the Mac) next to a folder name to view all subfolders inside it. Click a folder name to make it the so-called "current" folder and view thumbnails of the images contained therein.

To update the folder tree to show changes made to a networked volume, click the right-pointing arrowhead in the top-right corner of the folder tree and choose Refresh. You can also refresh the contents of the folder tree by choosing View ⇨ Refresh from the File Browser's menu bar or simply by pressing F5. Right-click (Control-click on the Mac) in the folder tree to create new folders or rename existing ones. You can hide the folder tree and other elements along the left side of the browser by clicking the icon with the two opposite-facing arrows at the bottom of the browser window, which toggles the File Browser's expanded view mode.

If there are certain folders that you work with frequently, you might want to take advantage of the timesaving Favorite Folders feature. Favorite Folders are located near the bottom of the folder tree, marked by a cheerful little star icon. When you add a folder to your Favorite Folders, Photoshop simply creates a shortcut in the File Browser that enables you to navigate to the folder, quickly and easily. To play favorites, all you need to do is right-click (Control-click on the Mac) on the designated folder and choose Add Folder to Favorites. If the folder is selected, you can also choose File ⇨ Add Folder to Favorites from the File Browser's menu bar. To remove a folder from your list of favorites, right-click (or Control-click) the folder and choose Remove Folder from Favorites. Choosing File ⇨ Remove Folder from Favorites from the File Browser's menu bar takes you to the Remove Folder from Favorites dialog box, where you must choose the folder that has fallen out of favor from the Folder pop-up menu.

✦ **Up folder:** Click this icon to exit the current folder and view the contents of the folder one level up. Or press Ctrl+up arrow (⌘-up arrow on the Mac). This shortcut works even if a pane other than the folder tree is active.

✦ **Folder path menu:** Click here to display a menu of folders and volumes that contain the current folder. Choose any one of them to make it the current folder. This menu also gives you access to any folders you've deemed as favorites, as well as the last ten folders you've accessed with the File Browser. (You can change the number of recently accessed folders that are displayed by visiting the File Browser panel of the Preferences dialog box, which you can get by pressing Ctrl+K and then Ctrl+9 [⌘-K and ⌘-9 on the Mac] or by choosing Preferences from the File Browser's own Edit menu.)

✦ **Thumbnails:** The thumbnail view is where you do most of your work in the File Browser. Click a thumbnail to select it. Shift-click to select a range of files; Ctrl-click (on the Mac, ⌘-click) to add individual files to the selection. You can also drag and Shift-drag to select multiple files. Double-click a thumbnail or press Enter or Ctrl+O (Return or ⌘-O on the Mac) to open any and all selected files. Double-click a folder icon to view its contents. For a detailed discussion of the many other things you can do, see the next section, "Working with thumbnails."

✦ **Preview:** On the left side of the File Browser window, you'll find a scalable preview of the currently selected image. By default in Photoshop CS, the File Browser sports larger, higher-quality previews than were previously available. (You can turn this option off by unchecking the High Quality Previews check box in the File Browser panel of the Preferences dialog box.) You can make a preview bigger or smaller by dragging the horizontal and vertical lines that frame it. I'll examine this in more detail in the next section, "Customizing the workspace."

✦ **Metadata:** Of all the functions of the File Browser, this may be my favorite. Photoshop CS's new Metadata panel lets you view and edit more information about your images than you ever thought possible. The top three sections are the most important: File Properties, IPTC, and Camera Data (Exif). The Exchangeable Image File (EXIF) format is a standard for appending non-pixel information to an image file. EXIF is most widely used by digital cameras to describe a photograph's history, including the date and time it was shot, the make and model of camera, the flash setting, the focal length, and loads of other useful stuff. In the Camera Data (Exif) section of the Metadata panel, you may be able to find out all kinds of wonderful information about digital photographs that you shot and edited years ago. The remaining three sections of the Metadata panel are GPS, which shows you the Global Positioning System info that some high-end cameras can record, Camera Raw, which we'll examine at the end of this chapter, and Edit History.

This last section plays off of one of Photoshop CS's new Preferences. Located in the General panel of the Preferences dialog box (that's Ctrl+K or ⌘-K), the History Log options allow you to save information about the editing you've performed on an image. You can select a radio button to specify whether you want to save the log in a separate text file, with the image's metadata, or both. (If you choose either of the latter two options, the History Log will appear in the Edit History section of the Metadata panel.) Use the Edit Log Items pop-up menu to specify the type of information you'd like to save to the log. The Sessions Only option simply keeps track of every time you launch and quit Photoshop and open and close files. Choose the Concise option to log the session information plus the data that's recorded in the History palette. Choose Detailed to log detailed information about every edit performed on an image, giving you a permanent record of the steps you took to achieve the final results.

You may think that the Metadata panel is showing an enormous number of fields of information, but in truth, it's only showing those fields for which your image already contains information. If you click the right-pointing arrowhead in the upper-right corner of the Metadata panel and choose Metadata Display Options, Photoshop CS presents you with a list of well over 100 different fields of metadata options. Deselect the Hide Empty Fields check box and the Metadata panel will show you all available fields, whether or not your image contains information to fill those fields. You can scroll through the list and select or deselect the various check boxes to specify what's displayed in the Metadata panel. The list is truly enormous — there's a whole category devoted to Global Positioning System information; this is sure to come in handy when you need to remember exactly where in the Amazon you were when you snapped that picture of a chimp arm-wrestling a koala.

If an image was not directly captured with a digital camera, then it won't contain EXIF information. (For example, copying a digital photograph and pasting it into another image does not preserve EXIF data.) This doesn't mean, however, that you can't store non-pixel information inside of your other images. One of the areas in which the new, improved File Browser in Photoshop CS really shines is in its wide-ranging ability to view, create, and edit IPTC data. IPTC stands for International Press Telecommunications Panel, but that's not so important for our purposes. What is important is that it lets you enter a variety of non-camera-related properties for an image, including author names, descriptions and headlines, related Web addresses, and copyright information. It also helps that IPTC is a standard that can be read and edited by a number of other applications.

In previous versions, Photoshop let you access IPTC information only through the File menu. Luckily, you now have full control over it directly in the File Browser. With an image selected, click a pencil icon or in the blank space to the right of any IPTC field to reveal a stack of text boxes in which you can enter all of the IPTC information for the image (see Figure 13-3). When you have an active cursor in one of the text boxes, you can press the Tab key to jump down through the fields. When you've finished entering your IPTC information, press Enter (Return on the Mac) or click the checkmark at the bottom right of the Metadata panel. Click the cancel icon next to the checkmark to discard any changes you just made.

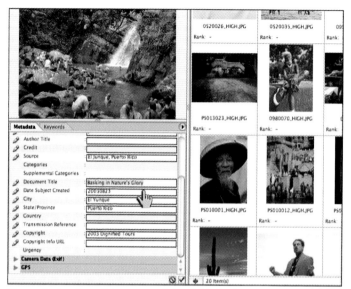

Figure 13-3: One click on any of the fields in the IPTC section of the Metadata tab lets you hop from field to field and enter a variety of different information.

Adding and editing IPTC data for multiple files at one time is also a snap in Photoshop CS. When you select more than one file in the File Browser, the Metadata panel displays information solely for characteristics shared by those files. If the files contain different values of metadata, Photoshop tells you that "Multiple values exist." When you edit any of the displayed IPTC data while multiple files are selected, your changes are applied to all of the selected files. For a closer look at changing the metadata of multiple images at once, check out the "Using the File Info command" section later in this chapter.

✦ **Keywords:** Another great new organizational tool in the File Browser is the ability to assign keywords to an image or a group of images. Click on the Keywords tab next to the Metadata tab to view a list of categories and descriptions designed to give you even more options for grouping your files. You can assign a description to any selected image or images either by clicking the check box to the left of the description or by double-clicking the description itself. The three icons that appear at the bottom of the Keywords panel let you create a new keyword set (the equivalent of a folder), create new keywords, or delete keywords, respectively. You also have the ability to drag keywords from one keyword set to another.

✦ **The menu bar:** In Photoshop CS, the File Browser is so packed with features that Adobe decided to give it its own menu bar. From this menu bar you can access some of the commands previously available in the File Browser (but with added features), plus some powerful new options. Here are a few highlights:

 • **Automate:** Now you can launch a number of automated processes directly from the File Browser using the commands in the Automate menu. For example, you can choose to create Web photo galleries, export PDF slideshows, and assemble contact sheets. The Automate menu also includes the batch processing functions, which I discuss a little later in this chapter.

- **Sort:** By default, the File Browser sorts files alphabetically by file name. However, you can rearrange them on screen by date, rank, size, and other attributes by choosing a command from the Sort menu. You can also simply click and drag around thumbnails to arrange them in any order you wish; in this case, the Sort menu setting will automatically switch to Custom.

- **View:** The options in the View menu let you customize what is displayed in the thumbnails section of the File Browser. You can set the size at which the thumbnails will appear and whether or not you'd like certain metadata displayed right next to them in the window. (The Custom Thumbnail Size option in the File Browser panel of the Preferences dialog box lets you specify the pixel width for custom thumbnails.)

✦ **Rotate:** Click one of these icons to rotate the selected thumbnail 90 degrees counterclockwise or clockwise. You can also press Ctrl+] (⌘-] on the Mac) to rotate a selected image clockwise and Ctrl+[(⌘-[on the Mac) to rotate it counterclockwise. Note that this does not change the image itself, just the thumbnail. If you double-click a rotated thumbnail, Photoshop opens the image and then rotates it in a separate operation, but you'll have to save this change to make it permanent. If you do wish to apply the thumbnail rotation to the image without opening and saving it, choose Edit ⇨ Apply Rotation from the File Browser's menu bar. This will overwrite the image with the rotated version and save you the step of opening it.

When working with a JPEG image, choosing Edit ⇨ Apply Rotation from the File Browser will cause the image to be recompressed as a JPEG, resulting in image degradation. The damage might be imperceptible to your eye, but it will occur. To prevent this, after rotating the thumbnail in the File Browser, go ahead and open the image in Photoshop, and then save it in a lossless format like PSD.

✦ **Flag:** One way to do some quick and dirty sorting of your images is by using Photoshop CS's new flag function. As opposed to the hundreds of variables you can use to classify images using metadata and keywords, the flag feature provides you with two options: Flagged and Unflagged. Select the thumbnails you wish to flag and click the flag icon in the browser's menu bar. Once images are flagged, you can choose to view all images, only flagged images, or only unflagged images from the Show pop-up menu. You can also select only flagged images by choosing Edit ⇨ Select All Flagged or by pressing Ctrl+Shift+A (⌘-Shift-A on the Mac). Flagging images is a great workflow technique for quickly separating the wheat from the chaff, without actually chucking the chaff.

✦ **Search:** Click this icon or choose File ⇨ Search to search for images by such criteria as file name, type, and metadata. Searching by metadata can be helpful, for example, if you want to track down every image on your machine that was captured with a specific digital camera. Use the Look In pop-up menu to specify the folder you want to search in; the Include All Subfolders check box, true to its name, allows the search to continue into nested folders. By clicking the plus button next to the Criteria options, you can add up to 13 criteria to really focus your search. The results of your search appear in the Search Results folder at the bottom of the folder tree.

✦ **Delete:** Click the trash icon to delete one or more selected images. You can also drag files to the trash icon to delete them. To delete the images without a warning, press the Alt (or Option) key as you click the icon or drag the files.

Be aware, however, that this does move the selected images to the Recycle Bin or Trash, just as surely as if you had done it yourself at the desktop level.

✦ **Progress message:** The File Browser often takes a while to generate thumbnails and perform other operations. As a result, it can seem like nothing's happening. If the browser keeps you waiting, take a peek at the progress message to find out what's going on.

Customizing the workspace

Don't like the layout of the File Browser? Then feel free to change it. The Folders, Preview, Metadata, and Keywords tabs can all be dragged around between the three spaces on the left side of the File Browser. Double-click a panel tab to minimize it and resize the adjacent panel to fill the empty space. You can also resize the panels by dragging the vertical and horizontal panel dividers. To hide the panels and devote the entire browser window to the thumbnails, click the double-arrow icon at the bottom of the window to switch to expanded view.

If you save your workspace by choosing Window ⇨ Workspace ⇨ Save Workspace, the current layout of the File Browser will save with it.

Working with thumbnails

The File Browser is a complex environment with more going on than you might imagine. And the thumbnail view is the hub of activity. You can select, rename, move, and even copy files from one folder to the next.

Photoshop generates thumbnail previews of all pixel-based image files that it supports. (Note that by default this rules out files that Photoshop can rasterize but which contain vector objects, such as EPS and Adobe PDF documents. However, by paying a quick visit to the File Browser panel of the Preferences dialog box, you can check the Render Vector Files check box and enable thumbnails for EPS and Adobe PDF documents too.) If you saved a preview with the image (as explained in the upcoming section "Saving previews"), the File Browser shows you that. Otherwise, it generates a new preview on the fly. This takes time, especially in the case of high-resolution or complex images. If a folder resides on a remote volume or contains lots of files — say, a few hundred — Photoshop may appear to hang for a few seconds while it gets its bearings. The progress message "Getting directory file list" tells you "Don't panic, you haven't crashed, work is being done."

When a thumbnail is active, you can advance from one thumbnail to the next using the arrow keys. To scroll to the bottom of the list, press End. To scroll to the top, press Home. Page Up, Page Down, and the scroll wheel on your mouse (if you have one) also work wonders.

Click the file name below a thumbnail to highlight the name and enter a new one. (And even though you can select the extension — *.jpg*, *.tif*, and so on — and type over it, you'll find that the changes don't stick. Photoshop protects the extension so you can't actually modify it. To override this somewhat Draconian constraint, see the upcoming section "Batch renaming.") When renaming a sequence of files, press Tab to advance from one file name to the next, press Shift+Tab to back up.

Click the Rank value to enter a grade for the image, useful for selecting a photograph from a group of proofs. Typical ranks are A through E, but you can enter other letters and numbers as you see fit.

To move an image to a different folder, drag its thumbnail and drop it into the desired folder in the folder tree. Press the Alt (or Option) key when dragging a file to copy it. Right-click (or Control-click) a thumbnail to display a shortcut menu of additional options, including ranking values, as shown in Figure 13-4.

Figure 13-4: Right-click a thumbnail to select from a shortcut menu of common operations that you can apply inside the browser. (On the Mac, press the Control key and click.)

Managing the cache

You may spend several minutes generating previews, rotating thumbnails, and ranking images inside the File Browser. And yet not a single one of these functions is necessarily saved with the image file. So how does Photoshop prevent you from losing your work? By saving a cache file that records all changes made to an entire folder full of images.

This all happens in the background without your aid or assistance, so you might assume that there's no reason to worry about it. However, although Photoshop's approach works well when viewing pictures on a local hard drive, things get a little dicey when browsing images from a network or CD. Here are two possible problem scenarios:

✦ **Sharing images over a network.** There is one cache file per folder and each resides in the system folder on your computer. This is called a *local cache* because it resides locally on your machine, and a networked version of Photoshop running on a different computer cannot share a local cache file. For example, suppose you and a coworker are browsing through images on a server. You rotate a few thumbnails, assign a few rankings, and naturally assume that the coworker can see what you've done. But she can't because her local cache is different than yours.

✦ **Browsing images on a CD.** You start with a folder of 200 images. After giving Photoshop a few minutes to generate the thumbnails, you rotate and rank the images as you see fit. Then you burn the images to a CD, having faith that the thumbnails, rotations, and ranks will be maintained. But when you put the CD in your drive and view it in the File Browser, Photoshop starts generating the thumbnails all over again. Plus the rotation and ranks have been lost. The cache remains intact, but it's linked to the local folder, not the CD folder. So Photoshop has to create a new cache for the CD. After you re-perform your work, the CD will browse as expected from that point on, *but only on this one machine.* Other computers will require their own local caches.

Are you beginning to get a sense of how messy this can get? And that's not all. Any change to a folder — renaming it, moving it to a different location — likewise breaks the link and requires you to start over again.

So what's the solution? Fortunately, a very simple one. Just choose Export Cache from the File Browser's File menu, as shown in Figure 13-5. Without any additional dialog with you, Photoshop exports three cache files to the folder itself. The files are *AdobeP8T.tb0*, which contains the thumbnails, *AdobeP8P.tb0*, which contains the previews, and *AdobeP8M.md0*, which contains the metadata, including rotation and ranking information. From that point on, the three cache files are available to other users on a network, you can burn them to a CD, or you can keep them with a folder on the off chance you move the folder or rename it.

Exporting is a manual process, so don't expect Photoshop to update your changes. If you change a rotation or ranking and you want to make it available to other users or computers, you can choose Export Cache again. When burning image CDs, get in the habit of choosing Export Cache immediately before writing the CD; this will ensure the cache is as up-to-date as possible.

If you tend to spend days and nights combing through a seemingly endless parade of images, your cache files can grow fairly quickly. Luckily, you can delete or "purge" the cache just as easily as you can export it. From the File Browser menu bar, choose File ⇨ Purge Cache to clear the cache of the particular folder you're currently viewing or File ⇨ Purge Entire Cache to clear the Photoshop cache files from your hard drive completely. The final cache-related function in the File Browser is accessed by choosing File ⇨ Build Cache for Subfolders. This command tells Photoshop to prerender the cache for all subfolders within the current folder so that you may export it all together. This also can save time for subsequent browsing.

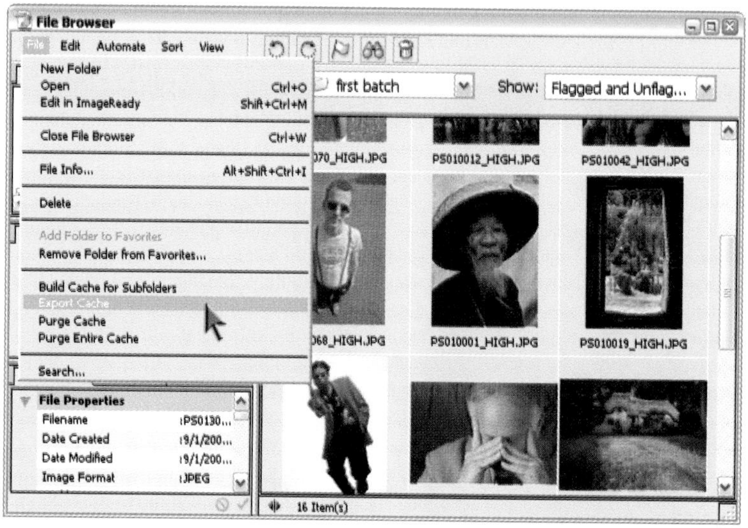

Figure 13-5: Choose File ⇨ Export Cache to save thumbnails as well as rotation and ranking data. This information is saved to the folder that contains the images, making it available to network users or to burn to a CD.

Batch renaming

I'm not thrilled by the way the browser lets you rename files. It locks you out from editing the extension and it can be slow when compared with renaming at the desktop level. However, Photoshop's File Browser gives you something the desktop doesn't—Batch Rename. This extraordinarily useful command lets you rename multiple files in one operation.

To rename a handful of specific files, click and Shift-click on their thumbnails to select them. To rename all files in a folder, choose Select All or Deselect All from the Edit menu. (If any files are selected, Batch Rename will be performed on only those selected files, but if no files are selected, Batch Rename will occur on all files within the folder.) Then right-click on an image (Control-click on the Mac) and choose Batch Rename (or choose Automate ⇨ Batch Rename from the File Browser's menu bar) to display the dialog box pictured in Figure 13-6.

Your first option in the Batch Rename dialog box (see Figure 13-6) is to rename files in the folder where they currently reside (the most common choice) or move them to a different folder. If you click Move to New Folder, the File Browser will ask you to select a destination. Note that *moving* means just that—Photoshop relocates the files as opposed to copying them to the new location.

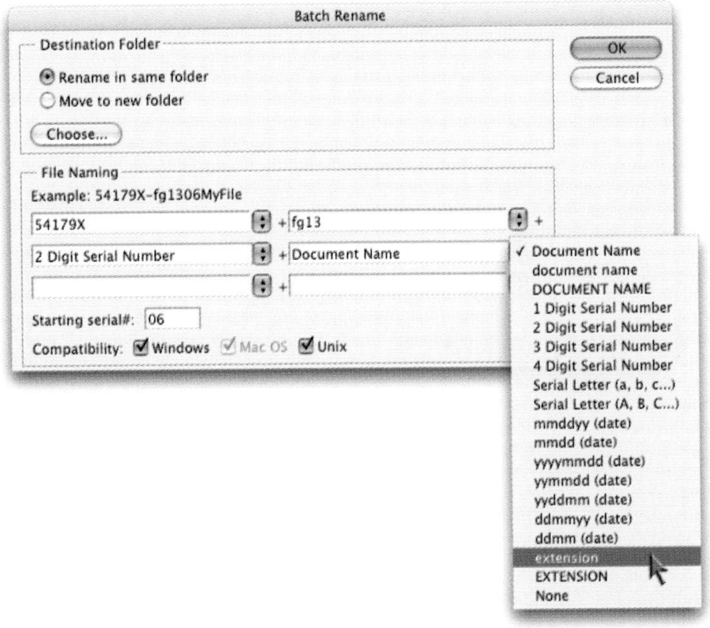

Figure 13-6: Use the Batch Rename command to rename multiple files in a single operation. You can select naming options from a pop-up menu, or enter your own name.

You can specify up to six File Naming variables, though two or three are generally sufficient. The three Document Name options retain or change the case of the name currently assigned to the file. Alternatively, you can enter your own name into an option box. For example, my publisher requires that all figures for this book begin with the last half of the ISBN number. This doesn't make much sense for my purposes, so I name the files as I see fit. Then when I have all the figures assembled in a folder, I choose Batch Rename and enter *54179X* in the first File Naming option box. The second part, *fg13*, indicates that this is a figure in Chapter 13. In the final option box, you can see me choosing *extension*, which appends a lowercase extension. This option is extremely useful for changing digital photographs with exclusively upper-case file names, so that a file ends with *jpg* instead of *JPG* (generally safer when posting graphics to the Web).

Note that Batch Rename offers several options for adding serial numbers, handy when preparing image sequences such as *Figure 13-01.tif*, *Figure 13-02.tif*, and so on. Such serial numbers normally start at 1 (or A when using letters), but if you want to start with another number, just enter it in the Starting Serial# option box. In the figure, *06* tells Photoshop to use a two-digit serial number, starting at *06*. It is Figure 13-6, after all, so I ask you — how self-referential can a figure get?

To ensure that your images are named so that they'll work on any computer, select all three Compatibility check boxes. (Either Windows or Mac OS will already be selected, depending on your platform.) Then click OK to apply your changes. Note that, as with other File Browser operations, renaming is not undoable. So be sure all settings are correct before you click OK. If you have any doubt how the command will work, experiment on a few trial images before renaming important files.

I cover actions later in this chapter, but as a little preview, I thought I'd point out that Photoshop CS gives you the ability to initiate actions to a group of selected images directly from the File Browser. If you want to perform an action on a group of images, select them in the File Browser and choose Automate ⇨ Batch from the browser's menu bar. This brings up the Batch dialog box where you can set which images will be affected, whether or not the actions will be interrupted by dialogs and warnings, and how to react if there are any errors. Additionally, you can set a naming structure in fields that are identical to those in the Batch Rename dialog box. I cover batch processing thoroughly in the upcoming section appropriately titled "Batch Processing."

Using the File Info command

As we've seen, an image file can contain a lot more information than the image data. On top of pixels, alpha channels, color profiles, and all the other image data you can cram into your image files, your images can contain a variety of reference information — where you shot the picture, who owns the image copyright, what the weather was like, relevant sonnets, and so on.

Despite the plethora of fields available to you through the File Browser's Metadata panel, sometimes you need to be able to edit and access more information than a little panel can hold. That's when you should choose File ⇨ File Info from the File Browser's menu bar or press Ctrl+Alt+I (⌘-Option-I on the Mac) to display the File Info dialog box, shown in Figure 13-7.

The File Info dialog box now contains seven panels; that's two more than there were in Photoshop 7. You switch from one panel to another by pressing Ctrl+1 through Ctrl+7 (⌘-1 through ⌘-7 on the Mac) or by selecting the panel name from the list on the left side of the window. Here's a brief overview of the options on each panel:

+ **Description:** The options in this panel are fairly straightforward. For example, if you want to create a caption, enter it into the Description option box, which can hold up to 2,000 characters. If you select Description in the Output section of the Print with Preview dialog box, the caption appears underneath the image when you print it from Photoshop. You can also add a copyright notice to your image. If you choose

Copyrighted from the Copyright Status pop-up menu, a copyright symbol (©) will appear in the window title bar and in the information box at the bottom of the screen on the PC or at the bottom of the image window on the Mac. This symbol tells people viewing the image that they can go to the Description panel to get more information about the owner of the image copyright. Choose Public Domain if you want to make it clear that the work isn't copyrighted (an Unmarked image might actually be a neglected copyrighted one).

You can also include the URL for your Web site, if you have one. Then, when folks have your image open in Photoshop, they can come to this panel and click the Go to URL button to launch their Web browsers and jump to the URL.

Click the down-pointing arrowhead to the right of an option to reveal a pop-up menu containing information that you've previously entered for the option in other images. For example, if you've entered yourself as the author of another image you recently worked on, you can click the arrowhead next to the Author option and select your name.

Because only people who open your image in Photoshop have access to the information in the File Info dialog box, you may want to embed a digital watermark into your image as well. Many watermarking programs exist, ranging from simple tools that merely imprint copyright data to those that build in protection features designed to prevent illegal downloading and reproduction of images. Photoshop provides a watermarking utility from Digimarc as a plug-in on the Filters menu; before using the plug-in, visit the Digimarc Web site (*www.digimarc.com*) to find out which, if any, of the Digimarc watermarking schemes best suits the type of work you do.

Figure 13-7: You can document your image in encyclopedic detail using the wealth of options in the File Info dialog box, which is greatly improved in Photoshop CS.

✦ **Camera Data:** Following the Description options you'll find two panels of Camera Data values. This is where the EXIF information that we discussed earlier in the chapter is displayed. As you'll remember, EXIF data is written by the digital camera, not the user, so these fields cannot be altered.

✦ **Categories:** The Categories panel may seem foreign to anyone who hasn't worked with a news service. Many large news services use a system of three-character categories to file and organize stories and photographs. If you're familiar with this system, you can enter the three-character code into the Category option box and even throw in a few supplemental categories up to 32 characters long.

✦ **History:** If you've enabled the History Log option in the General panel of the Preferences dialog box and you're saving the log in the file's metadata, this panel displays the history data for the image. Otherwise, it's blank.

✦ **Origin:** This panel provides some more option boxes into which you can enter specific information about how the image came to be, including the date, location, a headline, and a few others. Click the Today button to automatically enter the current date and time into the Date Created field. You can use the Urgency pop-up menu to indicate the editorial timeliness of the photo.

✦ **Advanced:** The Advanced panel displays all of the information you've set for the image in metadata's XMP format. On a PC, file information is only saved in image file formats that support saving extra data with the file. This includes the native Photoshop (*.psd*) format, EPS, PDF, JPEG, and TIFF. On a Mac, file information is saved with an image regardless of the format you use. Photoshop merely tacks the text onto the image's resource fork. But a resource fork won't travel with the file to a Windows machine. If you need the metadata of an image to travel with the image file, regardless of platform, application, or operating system, saving out an XMP file is the way to go. XMP stands for *eXtensible Metadata Platform,* and it's essentially a text file containing metadata that can be assigned to an image and read by many applications. The Advanced panel lets you save this type of file with the metadata you're currently viewing. From this panel you can also open an XMP file and use it in place of your current metadata, as well as append, or add the information from an XMP file on top of your image's metadata. Selecting any of the categories of metadata in the Advanced panel and clicking the Delete button will clear that specific data from your image file.

Perhaps the most exciting new metadata-related feature in Photoshop CS is the ability to create metadata templates. If you've got a collection of images with the same author or origin information, you don't want to have to go through the task of opening the File Info dialog box and manually entering metadata (or importing an XMP file) for each and every one. Naturally, Photoshop can take care of this for you. Creating a metadata template is simple: Just open the File Info dialog box for any one of the images and enter the common characteristics of the group. Next, click on the right-pointing arrowhead in the upper-right corner of the dialog box and choose Save Metadata Template. You'll be asked to enter a name but not a location (Photoshop does that for you). Click Save and you're done. Photoshop automatically adds the metadata template to the pop-up menu in the File Info dialog box, so you can easily access it time and time again.

You can assign your saved metadata templates to multiple files at once in the File Browser. Simply select the files to which you want to assign the metadata and choose Edit ⇨ Replace Metadata to display a submenu that contains all of the templates you've previously saved. If you want to add metadata from a saved template but keep the original characteristics of your image (such as name, description, or source), choose Edit ⇨ Append Metadata instead and select a template. One of the advantages of appending versus replacing metadata in an image is that it will add any keywords saved in the template to the existing keywords in the image.

Creating Custom Actions

Photoshop provides a ridiculous number of shortcuts. To be perfectly honest, it provides more shortcuts than you'll ever need. For example, I've never met anyone who regularly links layers by Ctrl+Shift+Alt-right-clicking (⌘-Shift-Option-Control-clicking) on elements in the image window. But it *is* possible. And by choosing Edit ⇨ Keyboard Shortcuts, Photoshop CS gives you the unprecedented ability to assign your own keyboard shortcuts to such important but hitherto shortcut-challenged commands as Image Size, Unsharp Mask, Variations, and Color Range.

But sometimes a simple keyboard shortcut isn't enough. If you're like me, you probably often find yourself performing certain sequences of commands in the same order each time. Maybe you've got a series of very similar images shot with a digital camera, and they all need the same saturation adjustment via Hue/Saturation, the same gamma tweak via Levels, and the same sharpening via Unsharp Mask. Even hitting three shortcuts in a row for each in a large group of images can get pretty tiresome.

Photoshop's answer is the Actions palette, which lets you record an entire sequence of commands and other operations as a single *action* and then apply those operations to an open image or an entire folder of files while you take a much-needed break. Much better than a keyboard shortcut which can only open a command, actions can actually use the command to change your image, close that command, and move on to the next one. If you spend a lot of your time performing repetitive tasks, actions can help you automate your workaday routine; then you can devote your creative energies to something more important, such as a nap.

How actions work

Choose Window ⇨ Actions or press Alt (or Option) + F9 to view the Actions palette. The icons along the bottom of the palette — labeled in Figure 13-8 — allow you to record operations and manage your recorded actions. An action may include just a single command, or you can record many operations in a row, as in the case of the *Image Size NN 200%* example (which enlarges a screen shot to twice its original size using Nearest Neighbor interpolation, a little trade secret used in just about every screen diagram in this book, including Figure 13-8 itself).

As with layers, you can organize actions into sets. But whereas sets are optional with layers, they're essential with actions. Sets are the only method for saving actions so that you can use them on another machine, transfer them to an upgraded version of Photoshop, or keep them safe in case of a crash.

With that in mind, let's see how you go about recording your own custom action:

STEPS: Recording an Action

1. **Select a set in which to store your new action**. Just click on the set that makes sense. Or create a new set by clicking the little folder icon at the bottom of the Actions palette.

   Naturally, Photoshop asks you to name the set. If you don't want Photoshop to bother you with such trivialities, Alt-click (or Option-click) the folder icon to bypass the New Set dialog box. You can likewise Alt-click other icons to skip other dialog boxes, but I don't recommend it — when recording actions, it always pays to stay as organized as possible.

2. **Create a new action.** This is very important. Much as you might like to click the record button and go, you have to first make an action to hold the recorded operations. Click the new action icon — the one that looks like a little page at the bottom of the Actions palette. Photoshop responds with the New Action dialog box, shown in Figure 13-9.

   If you accidentally start recording and immediately decide against it, press Ctrl+Z (⌘-Z on the Mac) before initiating an operation to kill the new action.

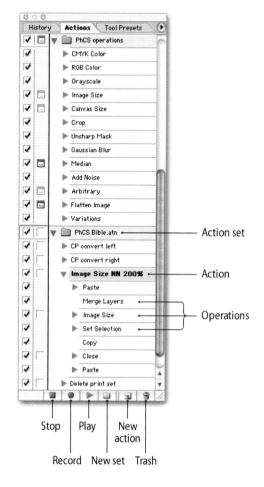

Figure 13-8: The Actions palette lets you record a sequence of operations and assign a keyboard shortcut.

3. **Enter a name for your action**. If you decide that your new action belongs in a different set than you originally imagined, choose the alternative set from the Set pop-up menu. Strange as it may sound, you can also assign a color to an action. The color affects the appearance of the action in the Actions palette's button mode, as I discuss later in "Playing actions and operations."

4. **Assign a keyboard shortcut**. For its own insidious (and, I believe, specious) reasons, Photoshop prohibits you from assigning alphanumeric shortcuts, instead limiting you to function keys in combination with Shift and/or Ctrl (⌘ on the Mac). This is particularly debilitating on the PC, where Ctrl+F4, Ctrl+F6, and all combinations of F1 are reserved by Windows. This reduces your maximum number of possible shortcuts to a scant 42, a small fraction of the quantity otherwise supplied by Photoshop. Things are slightly better on the Mac. F1 is fair game and on some keyboards function keys go as high as F15 — quite to its credit, Apple never sullied the Mac keyboard with such absurdities as Scroll Lock and Pause/Break — thus increasing your maximum number of shortcuts to 60.

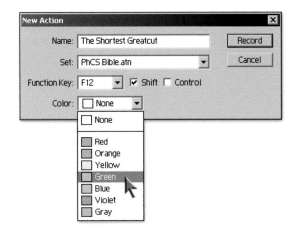

Figure 13-9: When creating a new action, you can assign a name, shortcut, and color. The shortcut must involve a function key. The color shows up in the Actions palette's button mode.

5. **Press Enter or Return to start recording.** The circular record icon at the bottom of the Actions palette turns red to show you Photoshop is now observing your every action.

6. **Perform the desired operations.** If you want to record a sequence of operations, work through the sequence as you normally would.

   But whatever you do, relax. There's no hurry and no pressure to perform. Photoshop is not recording your actions in real time. You can start to choose a command and then change your mind. You can even enter a dialog box and cancel out of it. Like a kindly grandmother, Photoshop turns a blind eye to your hesitations and false starts. Even if you mess up, just keep going. Photoshop lets you insert, delete, and reorder operations after you've finished recording an action.

   Photoshop does not necessarily record your every action. Operations that do not affect layers or selections, such as zooms, scrolls, and commands under the View or Window menu, go ignored. (To force Photoshop to record a command under the View or Window menu, see "Editing an action.") Perhaps the most important thing to remember is that Photoshop doesn't record the Undo command in actions, meaning that if you make a mistake as you're recording an action and then undo, the action will contain your goof but not your correction. If you have any concerns, keep an eye on the Actions palette. By the time you begin an operation, the previous operation will have appeared as an item inside the palette. If it fails to appear, it wasn't recorded. Switching palettes is not recorded, so you can return to the Actions palette and to your bearings any time you like.

7. **When you're finished, click the stop button.** That's the square icon at the bottom of the Actions palette. Or just press the Escape key. Congratulations, you've now successfully recorded an action.

Photoshop not only records your operations in the Actions palette, it also applies them to whatever image or images you have open. If you switch to a different image window or open an image while recording, Photoshop adds the operation to the action. For this reason, it's usually a good idea to have a dummy image open. When you're finished recording, you can choose File ➪ Revert (or press F12, if you haven't reassigned it) to restore the original, unmolested image. Also, if you want to include a Save operation, be sure to choose File ➪ Save As. This way, the original file remains intact.

Editing an action

If you take it slow and easy, you have a good chance of recording your action right the first time. But no matter if you flub it. Photoshop offers the following options to help you get it exactly right:

✦ **Adding more operations:** To add more operations at the end of an action, select the action and click the round record icon. Then start applying the operations you want to record. When you finish, click the stop icon. Photoshop automatically adds the new operations to the end of the action. To add operations at a specific point, twirl open the action, select the operation name after which you want to begin recording, and click record.

✦ **Moving an operation:** To change the order of an operation, drag the operation up or down in the list. You can even drag an operation from one action into another if you like.

✦ **Copying an operation:** To make a copy of an operation, press Alt (or Option) and drag it to a different position in the action.

✦ **Investigating an operation:** If you can't remember what settings you entered in a dialog box, or you don't recognize what an operation name such as Set Current Layer means, click the triangle in front of the operation name to expand it. Figure 13-10 shows an example of the operation Image Size expanded to show the recorded settings.

✦ **Changing a setting:** If an operation name includes an empty square to the left of it (as to the left of the hand cursor in Figure 13-10), it includes dialog box settings. When you expand the operation, Photoshop lists those settings. To modify the settings, double-click the operation name, revise the options in the dialog box, and click OK.

As when recording an action, Photoshop will go ahead and apply the settings to your current image. If this is a problem, press Ctrl+Z (or ⌘-Z) to undo the operation. This reverses the settings applied to the image, but has no effect on the changed settings in the action. The Actions palette ignores Edit ⇨ Undo, which can be a double-edged sword. When editing a setting, it's handy to be able to undo without affecting the action itself. But don't forget that Undo is also ignored while recording actions.

✦ **Leaving a setting open:** Not all images are alike, and not all images need the same settings applied to them. If you want to enter your own settings as the action plays, click inside the empty square in front of the operation name. A little dialog box icon appears to show you that you must be on hand when the action is played. In Figure 13-10, for example, a dialog box icon appears before the Close item. When I play the action, Photoshop leaves the Save Changes? alert message on screen until I confirm my decision. Then the action continues playing until it reaches the next dialog box icon or the end of the action.

Press Alt (or Option) and click the square in front of an operation name to display a dialog box icon for that one operation and hide all others. To bring up dialog boxes for everybody, Alt-click (Option-click) the same dialog box icon again or click the red dialog box icon in front of the action name.

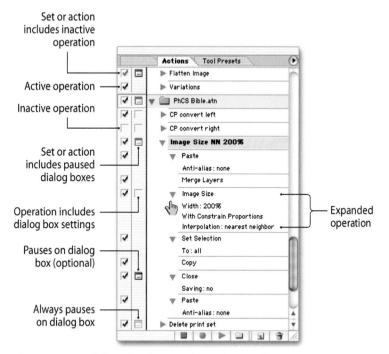

Set or action
includes inactive
operation

Active operation

Inactive operation

Set or action
includes paused
dialog boxes

Operation includes
dialog box settings

Pauses on dialog
box (optional)

Always pauses
on dialog box

Expanded
operation

Figure 13-10: Click a triangle to twirl it and expand an operation so you can view its settings. Use the checkmarks to turn whole sets, actions, or independent operations on or off. Click in the second column to force the display of a dialog box.

✦ **Forcing Photoshop to record a command:** If Photoshop seems unable or unwilling to record a command, choose Insert Menu Item from the Actions palette menu. Photoshop displays a dialog box that asks you to choose a command. Go ahead and do it — the dialog box won't interfere with your progress. Figure 13-11 shows me choosing the Button Mode command, thus setting up an action that switches between the palette's two action-display settings. (More on the button mode in the next section.)

Insert Menu Item also turns out to be the only way to record a dialog box with no settings whatsoever. This means you can capture commands such as Image Size and Canvas Size with no preconceived changes. Insert Menu Item will also recall filters such as Unsharp Mask and Gaussian Blur with the last-applied settings.

✦ **Inserting a stop:** A *stop* is a pause that permits you to convey a message to the user of an action. The user can't do anything during the stop — just read your message and then opt to continue or cancel. But it's a great way to identify a complex action so you remember its purpose and how it works later on down the line.

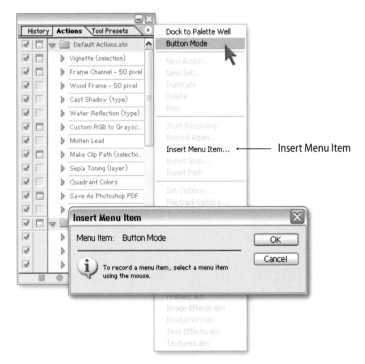

Insert Menu Item

Figure 13-11: Choose Insert Menu Item from the Actions palette menu to force Photoshop to record a command. Here I've chosen the Actions palette's own Button Mode, ironically a command that's not normally recognized.

Here's what I do: Right at the outset of a big action, I choose Insert Stop from the Actions palette menu. Then I enter a message that explains the action. (Select the Allow Continue check box to enable the user to continue the action after reading the message.) After I record the action and get all the bugs ironed out, I deactivate the stop by turning off its check in the left-hand column of the palette. This way, it's there when I need it. What do I do two years later when I forget what the action does? I turn on the stop, play the action, and read my message.

✦ **Changing the name and function key:** Renaming an action works just like it does in the Layers palette—double-click the name to highlight it and then enter a new one. To change the shortcut or color assigned to an action, press the Alt key (Option on the Mac) and double-click the action name. Note that function keys assigned to other actions will appear dimmed and unavailable.

✦ **Deleting an operation:** To delete an operation, drag it to the trash can icon at the bottom of the Actions palette. Or select the operation and Alt-click (Option-click) the trash can icon to bypass the warning.

Playing actions and operations

When it comes time to play your action, you can play all of it or just a single operation. The simplest way to play back an entire action is to press the function key you assigned to it. If you can't remember the function key or didn't assign one, you may prefer to switch to the button mode. To do so, choose the Button Mode command from the Actions palette menu, as shown in Figure 13-12. You can now see the colors you assigned to the actions, as well as the function keys. Just click the button for the action you want to play.

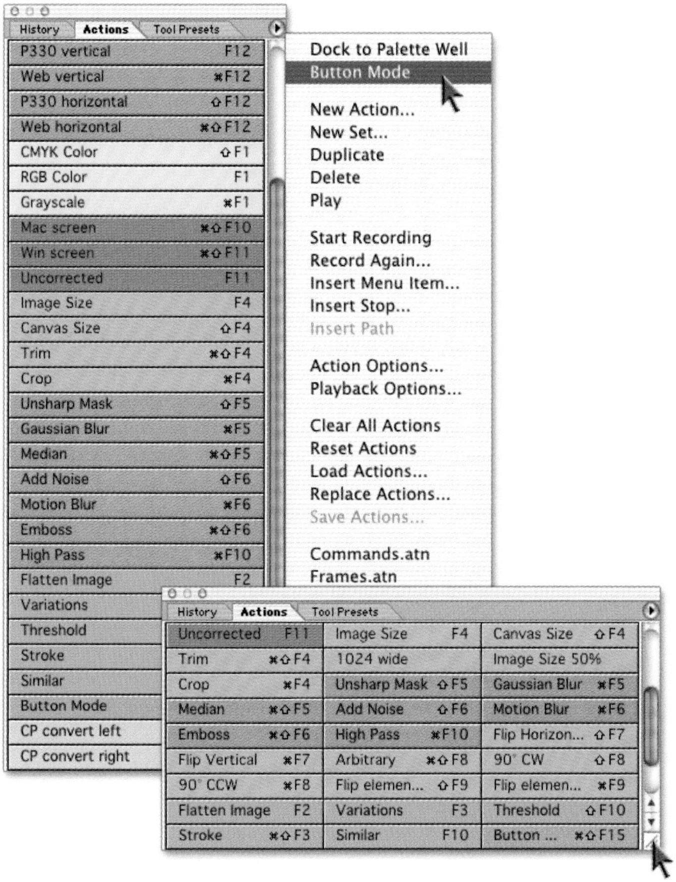

Figure 13-12: Choose the Button Mode command to view each action as an independent button, with shortcuts displayed (left). You can resize the palette to view buttons in multiple columns (bottom).

But the button mode has its drawbacks. All you can do is click buttons. You can't edit actions, you can't change the order of actions, you can't assign new function keys, and you can't play individual operations. This is a great mode if you want to protect your actions from less adept users, but it's an awful mode if you want to modify your actions and create new ones.

To return to the standard Actions palette, choose the Button Mode command again. Then try some of these less-restrictive action-playing techniques:

✦ To play a selected action, click the play icon at the bottom of the palette. You can also play an action by Ctrl-double-clicking an action name. (On the Mac, ⌘-double-click the action.)

✦ To play an action from a certain operation on, select that operation name in the palette, and then click the play icon.

✦ To play a single operation and no more, Ctrl-double-click (⌘-double-click) the operation name.

✦ You can tell Photoshop which operations to play and which to skip using the checkmarks in the on/off column (labeled back in Figure 13-10). Click a checkmark to turn off the corresponding operation. Alt-click (or Option-click) the checkmark in front of an operation to turn that one operation on and the rest off. To turn all operations on again, Alt-click (Option-click) the checkmark again or click the red checkmark by the action name.

If an action makes a mess of your image, it's generally not a problem thanks to Photoshop's multiple undos. To restore your image to its previous appearance, switch to the History palette and click the state in the list that comes directly before the first operation in your action. If you're at all concerned that an action may do irreparable damage — say, it contains more than 20 undoable steps — then record yourself saving a snapshot at the very beginning of the action. As long as the image remains open, the snapshot will remain available. For complete information on the History palette, see Chapter 3.

Saving and loading sets

Photoshop requires you to put every action inside a set. But that doesn't mean the set automatically gets saved. It's true that Photoshop saves sets and actions to a special preferences file, *but only when you quit the program.* If you crash, any actions recorded during this session are lost.

Now you might think, no biggie, Photoshop is a very stable program. But strange as it may sound, that's all the more reason to worry. My main computers — one Mac, one PC — each have 2GB of RAM apiece. Also, I leave the machines on for weeks at a time. With so much RAM, I have no reason to quit Photoshop, so Photoshop ends up running for weeks at a time. So, okay, let's say Photoshop or the computer crashes no more than once a month. That's still more often than I quit the program, because I almost never quit. And when I do, I lose those unsaved actions.

The moral — anytime you record an action, go ahead and take a moment to save or update its set. To do so, click the set name in the Actions palette. Then choose Save Actions from the palette menu. Actions are 100 percent cross-platform. But to work on any platform, the file name must include the three-character extension *.atn*.

You can also load sets of actions. By default, Photoshop displays only the Default Actions, a set of a dozen actions from Adobe. To open other predefined Adobe sets, choose one of the commands at the end of the Actions palette menu. To load some other set, choose the Load Actions command.

Turns out, you can add your own custom sets to the presets at the end of the Actions palette menu. Quit Photoshop. Then copy the action set (*.atn*) files to the Photoshop Actions folder inside the Presets folder that's inside the same folder as the Photoshop application. Then relaunch Photoshop and check out the Actions palette menu. Note that Photoshop doesn't automatically load the custom set — you have to choose the command to do that.

Batch Processing

Much of the work you do in Photoshop may be creative, involving a lengthy series of steps that are unique to a particular project. But some or even most of your work may revolve around fairly regular and repeatable activities. For example, when processing digital photos, you may want to apply a consistent set of Levels adjustments, sizing, and Unsharp Mask settings. The Actions palette is fine for adjusting such images one at a time. But if you need to attack more than one image, turn to Photoshop's Batch command.

As I mentioned earlier in this chapter, you can get to the Batch command in the File Browser's Automate menu. But this handy command also dwells in the File ➪ Automate submenu. The Batch command processes whole folders full of images in a batch, hence the term *batch processing*. And while it may sound highly technical, it's actually quite straightforward. The hardest parts, in fact, are recording the action in the first place and negotiating Photoshop's sometimes confusing (but ultimately comprehensible) options. Good luck on the first, I'm here to help you with the second.

Let's say I want to add specialty borders to a bunch of image files. Photoshop ships with a set of actions called Frames.atn that does exactly that. After choosing Frames.atn from the Actions palette menu, I test a few of the actions from that set on a photo of my wife and youngest son, as shown in Figure 13-13. Although many of the effects are interesting, I finally settle on Photo Corners, which strikes me as evocative and yet not so overstated that it'll overwhelm the photographs. Having selected my action, I am now prepared to apply Photo Corners to two, ten, or several hundred images. The question, of course, is how.

The following steps walk you through the task of batch-processing a folder of files. This isn't the only way to use the Batch command — Photoshop offers several additional variations with which you can experiment if you like. But I'm convinced these steps represent the best approach for most types of jobs.

STEPS: Applying an Action to Multiple Images

1. **Round up the image files to which you want to apply your action.** By far the easiest approach is to gather the images into a single folder. The File Browser is great for this too, incidentally. You can create a new folder by right-clicking in the thumbnail view. Then move or copy the images you want to batch.

2. **Create a folder to collect the images after Photoshop is done processing them.** If you're opening images from a folder, you can have Photoshop save to the same folder, but this saves over the original files. Better to save the files elsewhere so that you can refer to the originals if you're not pleased with the results.

3. **Inside Photoshop, select the action that you want to apply from the Actions palette.** This step isn't absolutely necessary, but it frees you from having to select an action inside the Batch dialog box, which is less convenient.

Original digital photo   Spatter Frame

Photo Corners   Brushed Aluminum Frame

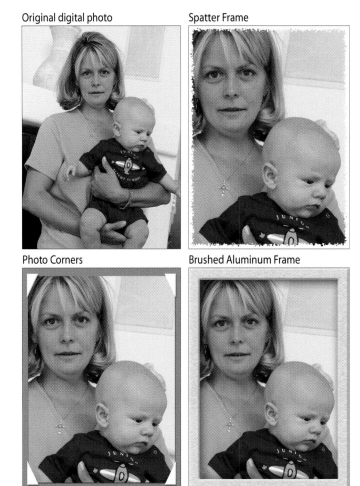

Figure 13-13: A photograph of some family members (top left) subject to three of Photoshop's predefined collection of Frames actions. Of these and others I tried out, my favorite is Photo Corners (lower left).

4. **Add a Save operation to the end of the action.** Frankly, you shouldn't have to perform this step. But the way the Batch command handles file saving leaves something to be desired (see Step 10), so it's better if you take it over yourself. All you need to do is open a sample image. You already selected the action in the last step, so just click the record button to append an operation to the end of it. Then choose File ➪ Save As and save the image in the destination folder created in Step 2. It's important to specify the file format you think you'll want to use. (Photo Corners results in layered files, so I chose the native PSD format.) However, the file name does not matter. Click the Save button to save the file and then click the stop icon at the bottom of the Actions palette to stop recording.

5. **View the images in the File Browser.** Open the File Browser and train it on the folder of images you created in Step 1. This gives you a chance to visually confirm that these are indeed the photos you want to edit.

6. **From the File Browser's menu bar, choose Automate ⇨ Batch.** Photoshop displays the dialog box shown in Figure 13-14 with the action you selected in Step 3. (See how convenient that is?) Don't be put off by the glut of options — the Batch dialog box is a peach once you get to know it.

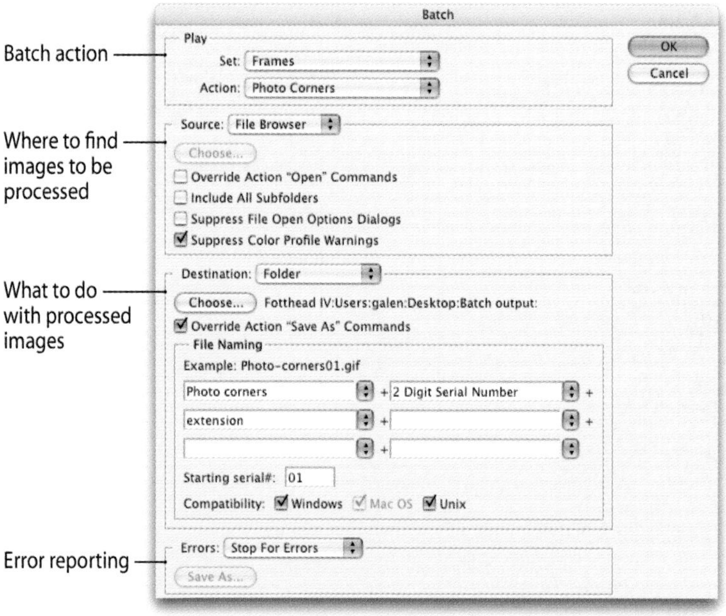

Figure 13-14: Here I have the Batch command all set up to open the images last viewed in the File Browser, run the Photo Corners action on them, and save each image to a folder on my hard drive.

7. **Turn on Suppress Color Profile Warnings.** This way, Photoshop won't bug you every time it opens an image, which defeats the purpose of batch processing. Hopefully, your current color settings won't do any damage to the files. If you have any concerns, exit out of the Batch dialog box and press Ctrl+Shift+K (⌘-Shift-K) for the Color Settings command. Then select U.S. Prepress Defaults from the Settings pop-up menu and click OK.

As for the other check boxes, leave Override Action "Open" Commands and Include All Subfolders turned off. The first one is to be used only if your action contains an Open operation, which most likely it does not; the second opens images in folders inside the current folder. If you followed my advice in Step 1, all the images are in one folder, so subfolders are irrelevant. And if you're dealing with Camera Raw images — as I'll be doing at the end of this chapter — the new Suppress File Open Options Dialogs check box keeps the Camera Raw dialog box from repeatedly opening for every file.

8. **Select the destination folder.** First, select Folder from the Destination pop-up menu. Then click the Choose button and locate the folder you created in Step 2.

9. **Turn on Override Action "Save As" Commands.** This is the most confusing step, so if you don't want to be confused, just turn on the check box and mosey along to Step 10. But if you like to learn, read on.

   When turned on, this option looks for a Save operation inside the action, which you created back in Step 4. Then it merges the naming conventions that you'll specify next (hence the term Override) with the file format you recorded into the action. It also saves the images without asking permission. Were you to turn this check box off, the Batch command would ask you to confirm the saving of each and every file, which of course would defeat the whole freaking purpose. Anyway, when you turn the option on, Photoshop displays a treatise on the subject. Feel free to tell it to bug off.

10. **Assign the File Naming conventions as desired.** I already discussed these earlier in this chapter. If you have any questions, concerns, comments, or criticism, please see the "Batch renaming" section.

11. **Ignore the Errors option.** If it fails, it fails. You'll find out soon enough.

12. **Click OK.** Photoshop begins batch processing your images, starting with the first image in alphabetical order.

It's a good idea to watch the first image from start to finish to make sure everything goes smoothly, particularly the save operation. (Photoshop should close each image after it finishes saving it.) But after the first image, you should probably leave Photoshop and your computer alone to work their wonders. A watched pot never boils, and a watched batch is a waste of your valuable time. You're supposed to be out there engaging in interesting carbon-based activities while Photoshop slaves away in your absence.

If you're looking for maximum performance, there are two ways to crank batch processing up to its top speed. First, turn down the image cache. Press Ctrl+K, Ctrl+8 (⌘-K, ⌘-8 on the Mac) to display the Memory & Image Cache panel of the Preferences dialog box and then change the Cache Levels value to 1. Second, turn off the History palette's automatic snapshot feature. Choose History Options from the History palette menu. Then deselect the Automatically Create First Snapshot check box. Both steps work wonders in improving Photoshop's response time.

Merging Images to Create a Panorama

Much like the coveted red eye brush tool, the command for quickly and easily creating a panoramic composite from a group of images was for a time the sole property of Photoshop's cuddly little lapdog, Photoshop Elements. But while Elements' red eye brush tool has been refined and revamped into Photoshop CS's new color replacement tool, the Photomerge feature first introduced in Elements has been carted over into Photoshop CS basically unchanged. That's not to say that it is a less-than-Photoshop-caliber tool, though. On the contrary, my co-author Galen Fott and I wrote in our book *Photoshop Elements 2 For Dummies* that Photomerge was "the one feature that just might make long-time Photoshop users want to spend their hard-earned money to buy Elements." And now that Adobe has rolled Photomerge into Photoshop, I'd say they pretty much killed that market. But wherever you use it, the Photomerge command is capable of doing pretty miraculous work. The only catch is that the images you plan to merge need to have been shot under some fairly specific circumstances. And sometimes, that can be a pretty big catch.

It's worth considering that you might want to reduce the size of the photos you'll be using before applying Photomerge. If you're trying to merge six photos taken in a horizontal line, and each image is 2,000 pixels wide, then your final panorama will probably be somewhere in the neighborhood of 8,000 pixels after the areas of overlap are considered. That's a pretty big image, and there's no need to make Photomerge groan under the weight of all those pixels if you're just going to reduce the whole thing after the fact anyway. Also, Photomerge only works on 8-bit/channel images. If you try to use 16-bit/channel images, Photomerge will notify you of this fact and convert them for you. If you wish to keep your original images in 16-bit mode, make sure that you undo this conversion before saving and closing the images.

Apply the Photomerge command by choosing File ➪ Automate ➪ Photomerge or by choosing Photomerge from the Automate menu in the File Browser. If you don't access the command through the File Browser with the desired photos selected, choosing Photomerge will bring up the Photomerge dialog box, as shown in Figure 13-15. At first glance, you might think Photomerge is an extremely simple command. All you need to do is choose which files you'd like to merge by clicking Browse and locating the appropriate folder or sequence of files, depending on your choice in the Use pop-up menu. If you want to merge images that are already open, you'll naturally choose Open Files. And it's pretty much a no-brainer that you want Photomerge to "Attempt to Automatically Arrange Source Images" as per the check box at the bottom of the dialog box; I mean, that's in essence what the command is supposed to do anyway. All seems pretty simple so far, huh? Alas, those sweet naïve dreams of a simple experience are soon shattered when you click OK to find yourself presented with the giant, imposing beast of a dialog box shown in Figure 13-16. How much screen real estate does this dialog box want? The answer is: How much have you got?

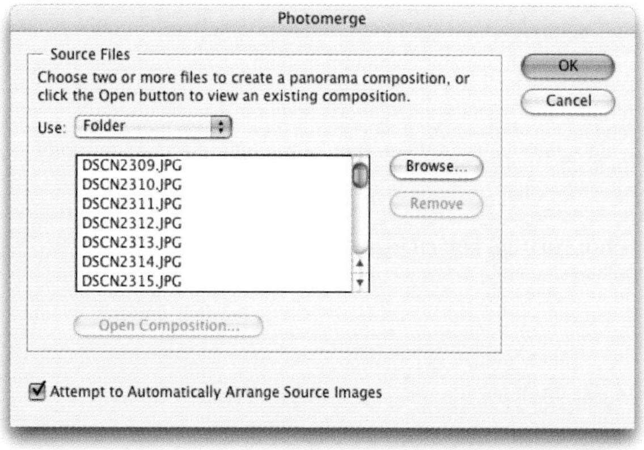

Figure 13-15: The deceptively small and simple precursor to the real Photomerge dialog box. I hesitate to even call it a hint of the behemoth that awaits you upon clicking OK.

By default, Photomerge tries its best to make sense of the pixels in your images and match certain areas of one photo with similar areas of another. But it's something of a gamble; frequently you'll see at least a few portions of the resulting image that could use some fixing. If there are images in the lightbox strip at the top of the dialog box that you want to try to place into the composition, click on them and drag them into the large window. You can adjust the individual placement and rotation of the images in a panorama using the select image and rotate image tools available in the upper-left corner of the dialog box. The bottom two tools — the zoom and hand tools — work exactly the same as they do everywhere else in the program. Between these two sets of tools is the set vanishing point tool, which we'll take a look at in a moment.

Lightbox

Select image
Rotate image
Set vanishing point

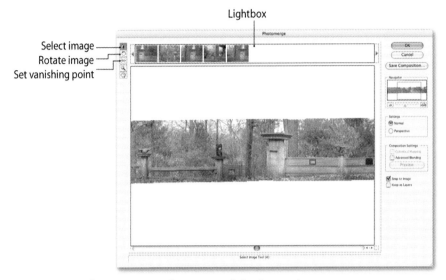

Figure 13-16: The gargantuan Photomerge dialog box makes every attempt to create a panorama from a group of photographs, but more often than not you need to manually adjust the images to get the best results.

If you can't get the results you want by fiddling with the select and rotate image tools, try removing one of the images if the area it covers is already captured by the other images on screen. To remove an image, simply select the arrow tool, click on the image, and drag it to the lightbox strip at the top of the dialog box, labeled in Figure 13-16. Believe it or not, giving the Photomerge command too much information about your scene can actually be a bad thing. The lightbox is the all-purpose depository for any image that Photoshop cannot figure out how to fit within the panorama. If you'd like to reintroduce an image, simply drag it from the lightbox and drop it back into the work area.

By default, Photomerge assembles images into a flat, jagged puzzle that rotates the images to fit each other but does not distort them in any way. If you'd like Photomerge to try bending and distorting the photos in an attempt to make them fit better, select the Perspective radio button. When the Perspective setting is selected, as it is in the middle example in Figure 13-17, the command will contort the images and present a more accurate, nearly 3-D view of your scene. Now, you can select the set vanishing point tool and alter the perspective of the composition by clicking on the different images within. You will typically want to click the centermost image, which is designated as the vanishing point by default. If you're having trouble telling where one image stops and the next one starts, hold down the Alt or Option key. A red outline will appear around the border of each image as you pass over it with the set vanishing point tool; however, the image containing the vanishing point will have a light blue border instead of a red one.

The two options available in the Composition Settings section of the Photomerge dialog box let you correct for certain problems inherent in the Photomerge process. For instance, the Perspective setting does a great job of distorting the images to ensure that they all fit together in the composition, but it also often results in a sort of "bowtie" shape for your final composition. The Cylindrical Mapping check box, available only when the Perspective setting is selected, corrects this by bending the more extreme corners of the composition back towards the center, as shown in the bottom example in Figure 13-17. Even more useful is the Advanced Blending option, which attempts to smooth over the common color and luminance shifts between images that can be dead giveaways of a computer-generated panorama. To see a preview of the eventual effects of the Composition Settings, click the Preview button.

Figure 13-17: The top example represents the original result of the Photomerge command plus a couple of minor adjustments using the select image and rotate image tools. In the middle example, I've selected the Perspective setting and enabled advanced blending, which does a great job of smoothing out exposure and color cast differences between the photos. Finally, in the bottom example I applied Cylindrical Mapping to make the distortions introduced by the Perspective setting a whole lot less dramatic.

The Keep as Layers check box is one of the very few additions that Photoshop CS has made to Elements' Photomerge command. With this check box selected, the final merge will consist of a layer for each original image plus a background layer. The final composition will maintain the positioning determined by the Photomerge command but it will lose all of the blending.

 Powerful as it may be, the Advanced Blending option can sometimes let you down when trying to stabilize the colors among the images in a panorama. A good trick for getting around this is to perform a color correction pass on your individual images before you merge them using the new Match Color command, which I discussed in Chapter 11.

If you've carefully arranged the images in your panorama and would like the ability to return sometime later and continue adjusting the settings, click the Save Composition As button to save a version of your Photomerge settings for these particular images that you can open and edit at any time. To do so, choose File ⇨ Automate ⇨ Photomerge and then click the Open Composition button in the first dialog box that appears.

As I mentioned earlier, the way in which the original images were photographed is perhaps the most important factor in determining the results of a panorama created with Photomerge. The most crucial thing to keep in mind when shooting photos that you plan to merge is that the greater the consistency in focal length, camera angle, exposure, and position, the easier it will be for Photoshop to merge the resulting images. Make sure your flash fires in either all of the photos, or none of them. While Advanced Blending can help counteract differences in exposure, it's no miracle worker. Adobe recommends an image-to-image overlap of 15 to 40 percent and to avoid using any sort of lens that will distort your images (such as a "fish-eye"). Ideally, it's best to overshoot, with large areas of overlap; then when you get inside the huge Photomerge dialog box, you can whittle down the number of photos until you have just enough for the command to do its job. And don't forget that Photomerge works vertically just as well as it does horizontally, so feel free to use it for panoramas of tall buildings. Finally, the use of a tripod or another stabilizing surface can mean the difference between an expert merge and an expressionist fiasco.

Correcting Camera Raw Images

The images produced by modern digital cameras can be nothing short of breathtaking. Yet by the time a photo leaves a digital camera and enters an image-editing program like Photoshop, even a non-compressed TIFF can be many steps removed from what the CCD or CMOS (the camera's "eye") saw. That's because the camera itself takes that input from the sensor and performs a slew of processes meant to make the image more presentable. These can include white-balance adjustments, color and brightness correction, and sharpening and compression passes over an image. It's almost as if there was a tiny little person inside your camera, using a tiny little computer running a tiny little version of Photoshop, and that little guy is trying to make your photos look better.

Although many people would welcome the help of the tiny guy—after all, the picture generally looks brighter, more balanced, and sharper by the time it's opened—the real digital photo pro knows that almost any improvement comes at a cost. In truth, a lot of the original information captured by the camera has been lost by the corrections. And who is that suspicious little guy inside the camera, anyway? Why should we trust him to correct our images willy-nilly? He may know a few things about image editing, but there's certainly no way he could have a big helpful guide like this one inside the camera for reference. For professional digital photographers and graphic designers, every last pixel counts, and there's no way those big-leaguers are going to trust the judgment of some little guy who lives in a camera over their own judgment. "Eliminate the little middle man!" is the professional's rallying cry.

Luckily, all hope is not lost. Some midrange and high-end digital cameras now offer the option of saving images as Camera Raw files, which skip all of that post-processing and save a perfect, pristine representation of the exact image as originally captured. It's very much akin to a digital negative. Between the releases of Photoshop 7 and Photoshop CS, Adobe quietly introduced a plug-in for the program that was capable of opening and making adjustments to certain Camera Raw files. With the release of Photoshop CS, a phenomenally expanded version of the Camera Raw plug-in now ships with the program. When you work directly with Camera Raw files, you have access to better image detail and a wider range of colors than would be available otherwise. In many cases, raw format images offer more than 24 bits of information in a full-color file; some cameras provide up to 30 or 36 bits, meaning you have billions and billions of potential colors to work with. For professionals who need to get the absolute most out of their digital images, getting access to this raw data is nothing short of a godsend. Camera Raw lets you *be* the little guy in the camera, taking the raw pixels captured by the camera's sensor and manipulating them *yourself* before you open the image up in Photoshop proper.

It's important to know that Camera Raw files are proprietary, meaning that each and every manufacturer adheres to a different and unique format. As I write this, Photoshop supports Camera Raw files created by 36 different cameras from Canon, Fujifilm, Leaf, Minolta, Nikon, and Olympus. Additionally, Adobe has pledged to continue expanding support to more manufacturers and models over the life of the product. Check *www.adobe.com/products/photoshop/cameraraw.html* to see if your camera has been added to the list.

Instead of the gigantic, unmanageable files you might expect them to be, Camera Raw files are very efficiently compressed, and Adobe's Camera Raw dialog box can make adjustments at an impressive speed. The only way to access the Camera Raw features in Photoshop CS is to open a file saved in a Camera Raw format. Instead of displaying the image, Photoshop first brings up the massive Camera Raw dialog box, as shown in Figure 13-18.

Figure 13-18: Think of the new Camera Raw dialog box as your first stop along the road to correcting raw images with Photoshop. Here, I'm adjusting an image captured with an Olympus E-1 digital camera.

Before we delve into the labyrinth of Camera Raw settings, here's a little-known tip: Holding down the Shift key will bypass the Camera Raw dialog box altogether and immediately open the image inside Photoshop. If you've used Camera Raw on the image before, the last settings you used will be automatically applied as the image opens. If you've never opened the image before, Camera Raw's default settings for your camera will be used instead.

Along the bottom of the Camera Raw dialog box are various settings you can adjust to determine how your image will take shape once you're through with the Camera Raw settings and you bring the image into Photoshop for regular editing. You can set the target color space of the image (probably the same as the color settings you're currently using), the number of bits per channel desired, even the size and printing resolution of the image. Camera Raw uses slightly different interpolation methods than Image Size, but the results are very good. And if you're going to downsample anyway, it will probably save you some Camera Raw processing time if you go ahead and downsample now. If your camera uses non-square pixels, the default Size amount is automatically set to try to maintain the same approximate number of pixels when the image is converted to square pixels in Photoshop. To achieve this, one dimension (width or height) will be upsampled, and the other downsampled. Setting Size to the next highest choice will cause the pixel count to be maintained along the high-resolution dimension of the image; the low-resolution dimension will be upsampled so as to achieve square pixels (almost certainly a better choice for non-square pixel images).

You can rotate the preview using the rotation buttons at the bottom right of the preview window, if you haven't already done so with the File Browser. The Camera Raw dialog box also sports a full-color histogram, mapping the red, green, and blue color channels in their respective colors. The other colored areas show where these channels overlap; white represents luminance. But the real power of the Camera Raw feature lies in the image adjustment options found in the panels on the right side of the dialog box.

Making color adjustments

As you can see in Figure 13-18, the Adjust panel in the Camera Raw dialog box is composed of two sections: settings for adjusting white balance, and settings for adjusting the tonal qualities of an image. *White balance* is a process where something white (like a sheet of paper) is typically used to calibrate the camera; with many cameras, this information is recorded at the time an image is shot and saved as metadata in the Camera Raw file. When available, the Camera Raw dialog box uses this white balance information as the default when it opens an image; hence the As Shot setting in the White Balance pop-up menu. If Camera Raw can't read white balance info from your camera, it makes a decent guess. In this case, As Shot is the equivalent of the Auto setting. The pop-up menu also contains several other options that reflect various lighting conditions that may have been present when the image was first shot. The options contain different presets for the Temperature and Tint sliders below. The White Balance pop-up menu is a good place to start when adjusting white balance. It's quite possible you'll be happy with one of the preset options. If not, you can tweak the two sliders below the pop-up menu by hand:

+ **Temperature:** This setting lets you modify the color temperature of an image. Increase the Temperature value (which is measured in Kelvins) to bring out the more yellow colors in the image, as seen in the middle example in Figure 13-19. The right example shows a decrease in Temperature to cool the image into the realm of blue.

+ **Tint:** The Tint slider adjusts and compensates for different color tints the image may contain. Drag the slider to the left to increase the amount of green in the image and drag it to the right to remove green and add in magenta values.

Temperature: 5550 (As Shot)   Temperature: 6600   Temperature: 4600

Figure 13-19: Similar to the Photo Filter command discussed in Chapter 11, Camera Raw's Temperature slider takes an image (left) and lets you warm up (middle) or cool down (right) the color temperature.

You can also set the white balance manually by selecting the white balance tool (it's the eyedropper located in the top-left corner of the dialog box) and clicking at a spot in the image that you'd like to assign as neutral, either white or gray. The White Balance settings in the Adjust panel snap into a position that adjusts the selected pixel to white and the other pixels in the image accordingly.

Below the White Balance settings are five sliders that let you make adjustments to the tonal qualities of an image. Generally, it's a good idea to adjust these controls in the order they're presented:

✦ **Exposure:** Quite simply, the Exposure setting adjusts the brightness of the image. But if you look a couple of sliders down, you'll see one labeled Brightness, so now you may quite rightly be wondering, "What gives?" The Exposure slider is based on the F-stop of a camera (a setting of +1.00 is the equivalent of opening the lens one stop wider), and adjusts in much larger increments than the Brightness setting. In fact, adjust this value more than a little and you're bound to encounter some clipping, which occurs when pixels are pushed to pure white or black and lose all detail. It's best to adjust this setting until it begins to clip, ramp it back a smidge, and then do your finer brightness adjustments with the Brightness slider.

✦ **Shadows:** Increase this value and watch as more and more pixels get sucked into darkness and, eventually, pure black. It might appear as though the Shadows slider is just upping the contrast in the image, but it's really performing a function that's more in line with the black point slider in the Input Levels section of the Levels command, discussed in the previous chapter.

Alt-drag (Option-drag on the Mac) the Exposure or Shadows slider triangles to see a dynamic depiction of any and all clipping pixels in the image. Different colors mean there is clipping only in one or two color channels. For Exposure, black means no clipping; contrariwise, white means no clipping for Shadows. Figure 13-20 shows the clipping display for the Exposure slider.

Figure 13-20: Holding down Alt or Option while using the Exposure slider on the image seen at left brings up a graphic display of which pixels are being clipped to pure white (right). In this case, the bright sunlight coming through the windows and doorway, and the reflected light on the walls and floor, are clipping.

+ **Brightness:** As I mentioned above, this setting makes gentle adjustments to the general brightness levels of the image.

+ **Contrast:** This setting increases (higher values) or decreases (lower values) the contrast in the midtone colors of the image.

+ **Saturation:** This is your basic saturation option that we've encountered a number of times before. Decrease the value to –100 to remove all colors from an image; increase the value to +100 to get colors so vibrant you may need to close your eyes.

Sharpening and smoothing

Click the Detail tab to access options you can use to adjust the sharpness and smoothness of a Camera Raw image. The Detail panel contains the following three settings:

+ **Sharpness:** The Sharpness slider works in much the same way as the Unsharp Mask filter, which I discussed in Chapter 8. The biggest difference lies in the fact that the Camera Raw dialog box does not give you controls for Radius or Threshold. This is because Camera Raw calculates these factors for you using information based on the camera model and the ISO (or light sensitivity) for the image. You'll probably want to wait to adjust sharpness as a final step with Unsharp Mask once you've opened the image inside Photoshop, but it's possible for Camera Raw to apply its Sharpness setting to only image *previews*, not the image itself. With the Camera Raw dialog box open, Macintosh users can choose Photoshop ⇨ Camera Raw Preferences, and then choose Preview Images Only from the Apply Sharpening To pop-up menu (as shown in Figure 13-21). Windows (and Macintosh) users can access the Camera Raw Preferences by selecting the Advanced radio button in the Camera Raw dialog box, clicking the right-pointing arrowhead next to the Settings pop-up menu, and choosing Camera Raw Preferences.

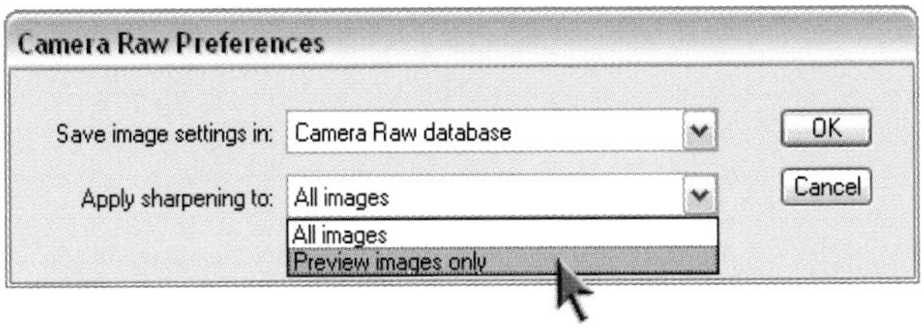

Figure 13-21: In the Advanced mode, Camera Raw has its own preferences dialog box. Here I'm telling Camera Raw to only sharpen the previews for my raw images. After I open a Camera Raw image in Photoshop, I'll use Unsharp Mask to sharpen it as a final step.

✦ **Luminance Smoothing:** This slider adjusts the amount of blurring that the Camera Raw dialog box applies in an attempt to reduce grayscale noise in an image. Depending on the ISO and general quality of the camera, a little bit of noise — those random speckles that lower the quality of an image — is a common occurrence. Increase this setting to smooth out some of the noise, but don't go overboard — too much smoothing and you'll lose valuable detail in the image.

The Camera Raw dialog box fully supports multiple undos through the usual keyboard shortcut, Ctrl+Alt+Z (⌘-Option-Z on the Mac), so don't be afraid to experiment.

✦ **Color Noise Reduction:** This slider performs the same function as Luminance Smoothing, except it works towards decreasing the amount of colored noise artifacts in the image.

Correcting for the camera lens

A camera lens is an imperfect thing. As a result of lens imperfections, which are generally more prevalent in less expensive lenses, many times an image will look terrific in the center, but subtle problems will start to creep in toward the edges and in the corners. Clicking the Advanced radio button in the Camera Raw dialog box gives you access to two additional panels full of settings. The first of these, Lens, is designed to compensate for the imperfections of a camera lens.

✦ **Chromatic Aberration R/C:** One of the problems that lenses can introduce into an image is *color fringing*, where sharp edges seem to have a fringe of pixels running along them. This happens when the color channels are slightly different sizes, creating a sort of *misregistration* like a bad printing job of the Sunday funnies. Commonly, this fringe runs red on the side of the edge toward the center of the image and cyan along the other side, as shown in Figure 13-22. The Chromatic Aberration R/C slider fixes this by slightly scaling the size of the red channel in relation to the green.

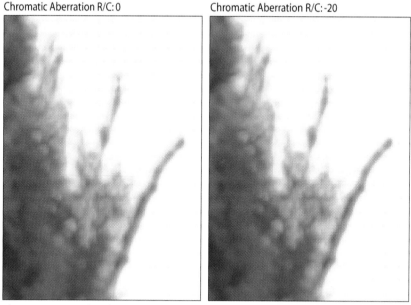

Figure 13-22: A detail from the upper-left corner of the image from Figure 13-19 shows typical color fringing (left). Adjusting the Chromatic Aberration R/C slider lets you better align the image's color channels (right).

✦ **Chromatic Aberration B/Y:** Similar to the Chromatic Aberration R/C slider, this control can eliminate a blue/yellow fringing problem on high-contrast edges found along the sides and in the corners of images by slightly scaling the blue channel in relation to the green.

If your image has both kinds of fringing, hold down the Alt (or Option) key as you adjust one slider to temporarily turn off the effects of the other slider. And remember that these sliders do nothing to the center of an image. This type of chromatic aberration only occurs along the sides and in the corners of images.

✦ **Vignetting Amount:** As shown in the top image in Figure 13-23, imperfections in lenses can also cause the edges and corners of an image to be darker than the center, creating a sort of vignette that frames the image. Drag the Vignetting Amount slider triangle to the right to lighten the edges of the image, which helps to eliminate the problem. And should you *want* this type of vignetting, drag the Vignetting Amount slider triangle to the left.

✦ **Vignetting Midpoint:** This controls the vignetting transition from dark to light. Drag to the left to increase the range of the vignetting compensation; drag to the right to decrease it.

Tweaking the profile

If you're using Camera Raw, then it's safe to assume that Photoshop has a profile based on the model of your camera. But it's possible that your particular camera might not exactly match the one Adobe used when they created the profile for your model. If you find your camera has a repeatable, predictable problem you always need to compensate for, you might want to use the controls available in the Calibrate tab of the Advanced Camera Raw settings. The first option, Shadow Tint, lets you fix a color cast lurking in the dark areas of the image. As with the Exposure and Shadows sliders in the Adjust tab, holding down the Alt or Option key gives you a look at any clipping that might occur as a result of your adjustments.

The remaining six sliders exist so you can give your Camera Raw settings a little extra tweak. Each color channel has both a hue and a saturation slider, allowing you to account for slight differences between your actual camera and the model of your camera that Adobe used to build its Camera Raw profile. There's no right or wrong way to use these sliders. The whole idea is to adjust things until they look right to you. If, after all the controls in the Adjust, Detail, and Lens tabs, those skin tones still don't look quite right, this is your chance to fix them.

Opening and saving Camera Raw images

If you feel you've thoroughly botched things with the Camera Raw dialog box, just hold down the Alt or Option key and, as with many Photoshop dialog boxes, the Cancel button changes to a Reset button. Click it, and the image will be restored to its state when you first began this session of Camera Raw adjustments. You may also notice that the OK button changes to an Update button; clicking this updates the associated Camera Raw settings to reflect your changes and closes the Camera Raw window, but it doesn't open the image in Photoshop. And holding down the Shift key makes the OK button turn into a Skip button, in case you want to open an image with its default settings (disregarding any changes you may have already made).

Once you are happy with your Camera Raw settings, click the OK button, and Photoshop will proceed to apply your adjustments and open the image. Note that you can't save the image back to the Camera Raw format. Just to thoroughly confuse things, there *is* a Photoshop Raw format available when you choose Save As, but that's a different format useful at times for saving images you plan to transfer between different computer systems. Photoshop is incapable of writing the raw format used by your digital camera. After you adjust the Camera Raw settings, Photoshop essentially opens a copy of your image, leaving the original file untouched.

Yet, here's an odd thing: The original file is untouched, but you will probably notice that the File Browser preview of your Camera Raw image has changed to reflect the adjustments you made. How can this be? Well, the changes you make with Camera Raw get saved in one of two places. By default, the changes are stored in the Camera Raw database, located on the Macintosh in the Preferences folder of the user, and under Windows in the user's Application Data folder. When the File Browser displays a raw format image, it draws the preview both from the image and from the settings for that image in the database. The problem with this is that your Camera Raw settings will fail to travel with your images to another computer. Adobe's solution can be found in the Camera Raw Preferences dialog box, which you can access by selecting the Advanced radio button, clicking the right-pointing arrowhead next to the Settings pop-up menu, and choosing Preferences. Choosing Sidecar ".xmp" Files from the Save Image Settings In pop-up menu instructs Photoshop to store the Camera Raw settings for an image not in the default database, but rather in a small file located in the same folder as the image. The data file shares the same base name as the image. For example, the image "watermelon.orf" would have its settings stored in a file called "watermelon.xmp." Keep these sidecar files along with the main image files when you move images or burn CDs, and your Camera Raw settings will travel with you.

These XMP files can be the same as those mentioned earlier in the chapter in the section "Using the File Info Command." In fact, when Camera Raw opens an image, it stores the settings in the XMP metadata. With File Info, you can export this metadata into an external XMP file and then load it back into Camera Raw.

Original

Vignetting Amount: +52, Vignetting Midpoint: 63

Figure 13-23: The top image shows typical vignetting, where the edges of the image are darker than the center. Adjusting the Vignetting Amount and Vignetting Midpoint sliders can fix the problem handily, as shown in the bottom image.

Saving your Camera Raw settings

Whether you decide to have your image's Camera Raw settings saved in the main Camera Raw database or in an individual XMP file, it's a darned good thing you *can* save them, isn't it? It would be a drag to have to try to recreate those Camera Raw settings from scratch if you should decide to open the image from the original raw file. But when you think about it, a lot of the image problems you compensated for exist not just in that image, but in every image you take with that camera. Wouldn't it be great if you could save the settings from that image and apply them to other images? Apparently, Adobe figured you'd say "Yes!" because Camera Raw lets you do just that.

When you open an image in the Camera Raw dialog box, by default the Settings pop-up menu is set to Camera Default, meaning that the default Camera Raw settings for your camera are being applied. Choosing Selected Image means that if you've ever opened that image with Camera Raw before, your last settings will be automatically applied. Previous Conversion uses the settings from the last opened raw format image that came from the same camera. To save your current settings so that they can be used by other images, click the right-pointing arrowhead next to the Settings pop-up menu and choose Save Settings. You can name the settings anything you like, but make sure you save them inside the suggested Camera Raw folder (which is inside the Presets folder in the application folder on your hard drive, in case you're curious). From then on, the settings will be available in the Settings pop-up menu. If for some reason you ignore my advice and choose to save the settings somewhere else, you'll need to use the Load Settings command (available in the same pop-up menu as the Save Settings command) to access them in the future.

When the Advanced mode is activated, it's also possible to save just a subset of settings. Maybe your camera consistently introduces chromatic aberration and vignetting to images, so you always want to apply those settings to images from that camera, but you'd rather tweak the other settings on an image-by-image basis. Click the right-pointing arrowhead next to the Settings pop-up menu and choose Save Settings Subset. You'll be presented with a column of check boxes, allowing you to specify which settings you want included in the subset. The Subset pop-up menu contains a few preset options, designed to save you from having to click a bunch of check boxes. From there, click the Save button, and save your subset in the Camera Raw folder. If you want to delete settings you previously saved, choose them from the Settings pop-up menu, click the ever-popular right-pointing arrowhead, and choose Delete Current Settings.

It's also possible to override Camera Raw's default settings for your camera model by choosing Set Camera Default from the pop-up menu that appears when you click the right-pointing arrowhead. Thereafter, the Camera Default option in the Settings pop-up menu will load your current settings. To restore Camera Raw's default settings for your camera, choose Reset Camera Default.

Applying your saved Camera Raw settings

Applying saved Camera Raw settings to a raw image before opening it in Photoshop is pretty straightforward. Start by double-clicking the raw image to open it in the Camera Raw dialog box. If you saved your settings in the Camera Raw folder as Photoshop and I suggested (see the preceding section), then the settings will appear at the bottom of the Settings pop-up menu. Just choose the settings, click OK, and go to work inside Photoshop.

But remember what happens to the OK button when you hold down the Alt or Option key inside the Camera Raw dialog box? It turns into an Update button, and clicking that button updates the Camera Raw settings for that image by changing the data saved in either the Camera Raw database or the image's XMP sidecar file. You then can see the change evident in the thumbnail and preview within the File Browser. (It's important to remember that Camera Raw never actually changes a single pixel of the raw format file. It can only change the data applied to that file which is saved in the database or the XMP file, and then open a copy of the image in Photoshop with that data applied. But you can't save back to your camera's raw format from Photoshop, so the original raw file—reflecting exactly what your camera's sensors saw—is always there on your hard drive.)

Since Photoshop is such a flexible tool, it should come as no surprise that you can actually update raw images with new Camera Raw settings without even opening the images. With one or more raw format images selected in the File Browser, either choose Automate ➪ Apply Camera Raw Settings from the File Browser's menu bar or just right-click (Control-click on the Mac) one of the images and choose Apply Camera Raw Settings. You're presented with the small Apply Camera Raw Settings dialog box, where you can select an option from the Apply Settings From pop-up menu. (If you have more than one image selected in the File Browser, the standard Selected Image option will instead appear as First Selected Image.) Click Update, and the Camera Raw data for the selected raw file or files will be updated without opening the images.

And in case that seems all too simple for a complicated feature like Camera Raw, you're exactly right. Clicking the Advanced radio button opens what is basically the Camera Raw dialog box sans preview but avec the Save Settings Subset dialog box, as shown in Figure 13-24. You can load saved settings, modify them, apply them, save them as new settings or as just a subset of settings. Seriously, go nuts. Just click Update when you're done, and the data for the selected image or images will automatically update to show the fruits of your labor.

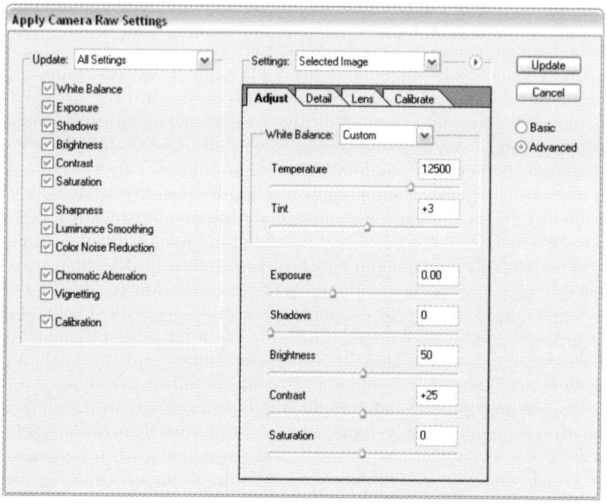

Figure 13-24: Right-clicking a camera raw image in the File Browser and choosing Apply Camera Raw Settings lets you update Camera Raw data for images without actually opening them. Pictured here is the Advanced mode of the Apply Camera Raw Settings dialog box.

And if that wasn't enough of an automated way to end this chapter on file management and automation, let me point out that Camera Raw works beautifully with actions and the Batch command. Just start recording an action, open a raw image, set the Settings pop-up menu to Selected Image so the action will draw on each image's saved Camera Raw data, perform your action, and click the stop button in the Actions palette. You can then apply that action to a whole batch of raw images with the Batch command. And really, however cool it may be, don't just sit there watching the batch processing. Go away and read a book or something. Photoshop finds you distracting.

✦   ✦   ✦

Preparing Web Graphics

The World of Web Imagery

The Internet may well be the most chaotic, anarchic force ever unleashed on an unwitting public. It has no boundaries. It has no unifying purpose. It is owned by many but controlled by no one. It's also incomprehensibly enormous, larger than any single government or business entity on the planet. In terms of pure size and volume, the Web makes the great thoroughfares of the Roman Empire look like a paperboy's route. As a result, it's difficult to get a bead on the World Wide Web. With many millions of hands in the pie and millions more groping for a slice, the Web is as subject to casual comprehension as are the depths of the oceans, the infinity of the cosmos, or the meaning of life.

Okay, that paragraph was a wild exaggeration. But in a way, exaggeration is what the Web is all about. After all, this is the force that gave us the world's biggest bookstore, the world's largest auction house, and a string of telecom companies that were poised to take over the planet. It was responsible for an economic boom and it started a subsequent economic bust. It can be fashionable to knock the Web — where once we thought it was going to revolutionize the planet, it's now clear that it's just another bourgeois medium with proletariat pretensions — and yet we're using it in bigger numbers today than we were when it was fab. Suffice it to say, the Web is a presto chango kind of place.

I include the preceding by way of a disclaimer for the general thesis of this chapter, which is simply this: Bitmapped graphics rule the Web. Sure, the audio and video content is cooler, and text-based content, databases, and hyperlinks are the main stock and trade of the Internet, but the graphics are what make the Web intelligible and invite us to come back for more. Graphics have brought the masses to the Web, images account for the vast majority of all Web graphics, and Photoshop is the world's number one image editor. As a result, Photoshop has become as inextricably linked to the Web as Internet Explorer, Macromedia Flash, QuickTime, and a hundred other programs. It's just another happy accident in Photoshop's strange and alarming success.

Photoshop and ImageReady

A few years back, Photoshop received a fair amount of flak for its relatively paltry collection of Web-savvy features. Adobe explained to Web designers they were missing the point — Photoshop was for print graphics and a separate program, ImageReady, was for the Web. But most Web designers ignored this advice and continued to grouse, so Adobe eventually caved, and started to do the right thing.

Beginning in Photoshop 5.5, Adobe's engineers expropriated a bevy of features from ImageReady 1.0 and hot-wired them directly into Photoshop. Then midway into the process they said, "Oh to heck with it!" and tossed in ImageReady for good measure. It was like a mad scientist who, after creating a half-man half-beast, decides the fellow isn't beasty enough and arms it with a pet wolverine.

Although I have nothing against wolverines, I personally wish Adobe would do away with ImageReady. Though it's faster now in CS, it's still a pain in the neck to switch back and forth between programs, and having both programs open puts a drain on system resources. But while most of its commands work the same as those in Photoshop, ImageReady is built around a central optimization window, which would change things fairly dramatically if it were integrated into Photoshop. That's Adobe's rationale, anyway. So until someone thinks of what I'm sure will turn out to be an obvious solution, ImageReady will remain in our midst and among the contents of our hard drives.

Fortunately, the most essential Web features — gamma compensation, compression optimization, color indexing, transparency management, and image slicing — are included in both Photoshop and ImageReady. As a result, this chapter focuses primarily on the one true application that we've all come to know and love: Photoshop. To be sure, ImageReady offers its share of unique capabilities. I would go so far as to suggest that it deserves its own book, albeit one much smaller than this one. But for the present, the section "Turning to ImageReady" at the end of this chapter outlines some of the interesting things ImageReady can do (as well as some that it can't) so that you can get started with the program.

So sit back, relax, and enjoy the myriad methods for preparing still images for the Web inside Adobe Photoshop CS. If you've read all the preceding chapters, you've come a long way, baby, and you deserve the premium treatment that the following sections were designed to provide. If you skipped to this chapter randomly or came to it from the index, that's okay, too. On board the cruise ship *Photoshop Bible*, every cabin is first-class, guaranteed.

By "guaranteed," I didn't mean to imply you'll get your money back. You're stuck with this book, pal. Besides, it's really taken a shine to you, I can tell.

Rules of Web Imagery

The Web provides a highly satisfying outlet for creative expression. How else can you get your work in front of gazillions of strangers without really trying? But as is the case with just about everything in life, success on the Web depends not just upon your artistic prowess, but also upon your understanding of the right and wrong ways to prepare your images. (Oh, and that losing-money-as-a-business-plan thing has lost favor. I know — it's a drag. I missed out on it, too.) To that end, the next few sections discuss a few basic rules of Web imagery.

Work large, then shrink

If you have any experience with the Web, you know that small images are speedy images. By "small," I mean both small in physical size and in the amount of disk space they consume. Physically small images are flexible, because they can coexist with text and other elements on a page displayed on a low-resolution screen. Meanwhile, disk size affects speed. A 20K image that fills your screen takes less time to download and display than a 50K file no larger than a sticky note. It's the act of getting the data through the network lines, routers, cables, and modems that takes the time.

That said, I recommend *against* making your graphics small — either physically or on disk — from the outset. The better approach is to build your images large, as if they're going to print, and then shrink them down. For example, Figure 14-1 shows an album cover I created from a digital photo of myself and Adobe's senior creative director, Russell Brown, dressed like idiots. In building this image, I experimented with a few layered permutations ranging in size from 20MB to 60MB. Having saved PSD files for what I consider to be each significant alteration in the development of the graphic, I flattened the completed image and saved it as a TIFF file. This file (Figure 14-1) weighs in at 5MB and measures a little more than 4 by 4 inches when printed at 300 pixels per inch. That's way too big to post on the Web. And it would take anywhere from about a minute to download on a 1MBps cable connection to close to 20 minutes over a 56.6Kbps modem. That's altogether unacceptable.

So naturally I have to reduce the physical size of the image and save it in a compressed, Web-friendly file format. I start by reducing the graphic to 50 percent of its previous width and height (that's 25 percent of its previous area) and saving it in the JPEG format. As shown in the first example in Figure 14-2, this makes a tremendous difference, shrinking the file size to 156K, a mere 3 percent of its previous size. That's a 2-second download over a 1MBps connection, but it still takes 30 seconds for folks with 56.6Kbps modems. And the image is too large to fit comfortably on an 800 by 600-pixel screen. It could not coexist with other elements on a page.

So I again reduced the image to 50 percent and this time tried out the GIF format. The image on the right side of Figure 14-2 shows the result of lowering the number of colors from the 8-bit RGB-standard 16 million to a mere 32. (The two images appear the same size because they're printed at different resolutions. But the GIF image actually contains just one quarter the pixels included in the JPEG image, as witnessed by the larger and tighter browser window.) Measuring 325 by 335 pixels, this image is still large by Web standards, consuming roughly a quarter of a typical Web page. And at 30K, it takes a fraction of a second to download over a 1MBps connection (good) and 6 seconds over a 56.6Kbps modem (fair). That's about right for a graphic of this size.

At this point, you may be thinking, "All very well, but why not save yourself a lot of processing power and create the graphic small in the first place?" Ah, good question, and eloquently put. The answer is *purpose*. Create a small graphic, and it has one purpose and one purpose only — early 21st-century Web. But what if you later want to print the graphic? And what about when the Web changes? It's not unrealistic to expect high-res graphics and streaming DVD-quality video to be the Internet norm in a matter of years.

So let me put a question to you: Why waste your valuable time creating an image whose death is ensured? From copious personal experience, let me assure you, there's nothing worse than spending an hour on a low-res graphic, only to watch it turn out to be one of the best images you've ever created. Only then do you realize that, had you known you were going to do such a good job, you would have done it right in the first place.

Original 300 ppi, 24-bit graphic; 1300 x 1340 pixels, 4.98MB flattened & uncompressed

Figure 14-1: In July 2002, Russell Brown (right) and I filmed a pilot for a far-fetched notion for a TV show. This album cover — and its limited-edition amber vinyl LP — was taken from a photograph shot during that pilot. (Okay, the album doesn't really exist; if it did, I would advise you not to buy it.)

World-wide color shifts

Unlike print graphics, which rely on a combination of process inks or other pigments, all Web graphics, even low-color GIF images, exist in the RGB color space. This is extremely good news because it means that what you see on screen is really, truly what you're going to get.

Well, almost. Ignoring the differences in the ways people perceive colors and the variances in ambient light from one office or dorm room to the next, there are measurable differences between monitors. Some monitors produce highly accurate colors, others — especially older screens — are entirely unreliable. But more importantly, some types of screens consistently display images more brightly than others.

For example, the typical Macintosh user is equipped with an unusually bright screen. This is because the operating system, whether Mac OS 9 or X, automatically assigns a target gamma of 1.8. Meanwhile, most PC monitors are calibrated to a gamma setting of 2.2, which results in a darker screen, roughly equivalent to television.

Reduced, 650 x 670 pixels, JPEG, Quality: 8, 156K   Reduced, 325 x 335 pixels, GIF, 32 colors, 30K

Figure 14-2: Two variations of the image from the previous figure reduced in size and saved in the JPEG (left) and GIF (right) formats. The file sizes drop to 156K and 30K, respectively.

In Chapter 12, we learned that entering higher gamma values in the Levels dialog box leads to brighter colors. And yet here we have higher gamma values leading to darker colors. What gives? Well, your monitor is incapable of interpreting the signal from its video board without distortion. This distortion manifests itself as an exponential brightening effect. As with Levels, the exponent itself is called the gamma. A gamma adjustment compensates for the overly bright screen distortion, but in the opposite direction. It's as if you inverted the image and then switched the black and white Output Levels triangles in the Levels dialog box. The result is that higher degrees of compensation — 2.2 versus 1.8, for example — lead to darker colors on screen.

Modifying the gamma

Many computers or video boards give you the option of overriding the gamma value and assigning your own. Under Mac OS X, for example, choose System Preferences from the Apple menu. Then select the Displays icon, click the Color tab, and click Calibrate. After stepping through a few panels, you'll eventually come to the Select a Target Gamma options, pictured in Figure 14-3.

Microsoft has never given color management much priority, so things are less predictable under Windows. In fact, whether or not such options exist usually depends not on your model of computer, but on the drivers supplied by the manufacturer of your video board. Right-click on the desktop and choose Properties. Then click the Settings tab and look for an Advanced button. If you find one, click it. From there, it's a matter of hunting down options like the greater trackers of yore. In other words, you're on your own.

Generally, I recommend against changing screen gammas, but there are exceptions. First, if you're a Macintosh designer who creates *nothing but* Web graphics, then you may want to switch to a gamma of 2.2 if only to see how most of your audience lives. Meanwhile, if you're working for print on the PC, you may find that you actually prefer working with a gamma of 1.8 because it tends to bring out more detail in midtones and shadows. If you do, however, bear in mind that you'll be slightly out of step with other PC users.

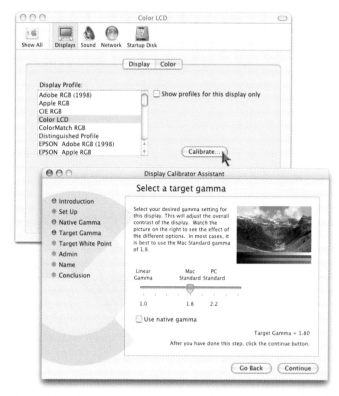

Figure 14-3: Many systems let you adjust monitor gamma, but the way you do it varies from system to system and video board to video board. Typically, you have to dig your way through an assistant (like the one shown here) or multi-part control panel to find what you're looking for. Fortunately, the instructions tend to be pretty detailed.

Anticipating PC monitors

To give you an idea of how screen gamma can affect the brightness of an image, Figure 14-4 shows a sample photograph shot with an Olympus E-20N and corrected on a calibrated display in the platform-independent color space, *sRGB*. Codeveloped by Hewlett-Packard and Microsoft, the sRGB space was reverse-engineered from the display portion of the high-definition television standard, which uses a set of phosphors known to its nearest and dearest by the unforgettable moniker ITU-R 709.BT. (You don't really need to know that last part. ITU-R 709.BT is just so plum catchy I thought you might want to bear it in mind the next time you decide to name a new pet or something.) HP, the main proponent of sRGB, is vague about what the *s* stands for, although the words *standard*, *single*, and *simple* all figure prominently into the company's press materials. (Maybe it stands for Harry Truman's middle name?) But sRGB's intention is clear—to provide a uniform standard for consumer-level digital cameras, personal printers, and screen displays from a wide variety of manufacturers.

Digital photo prepared on calibrated monitor in sRGB color space

Figure 14-4: Captured by coproducer Elisa Zazzera, this photograph tells you everything you need to know about the *Dr. Deke and Mr. Brown* show. Obviously, I'm the only one trying to provide any real content.

Although sRGB is becoming increasingly prevalent — all kinds of hardware and software, including Photoshop, assign sRGB to their images by default — support is by no means consistent or universal. Even so, it enjoys general praise and success in the preparation of Web graphics. The reason has less to do with support and more to do with design. Although originally conceived as a de facto standard for profiling vast image libraries such as those controlled by Corbis, National Geographic, and the Library of Congress, sRGB seems best suited to describing the display capabilities of a run-of-the-mill, gamma 2.2 PC monitor.

Figure 14-5 shows what I mean. Here we see the very same image introduced in Figure 14-4 as it appears when displayed first on a Mac and second on a PC. As you can see, the Mac version of the image is significantly lighter thanks to its gamma setting of 1.8. Meanwhile, the PC image is just a smidge darker and more saturated than the image from the previous figure. Although this screen is not actually calibrated to sRGB, the sRGB color space is a rough approximation. Just so you can see how wildly things can vary, however, Figure 14-5 ends with a third shot of the image as displayed on an older-model PC combined with an early flat-panel monitor whose colors were never much better than those displayed on a Palm Pilot. The image is hideously dark with exaggerated contrast.

Note that Photoshop lets you preview how your image looks on a foreign monitor. To see how an image will look on a typical Macintosh monitor, choose View ➪ Proof Setup ➪ Macintosh RGB. To see how it'll look on a typical PC, choose View ➪ Proof Setup ➪ Windows RGB. Photoshop also gives you a shortcut to toggle between the preview and the standard RGB mode — Ctrl+Y (⌘-Y on the Mac). Bear in mind that these are approximations only; Photoshop cannot anticipate aberrant screen displays like the one pictured at the end of Figure 14-5.

The lesson I draw from Figure 14-5 (not to mention my own experience) is that, while by no means perfect, sRGB represents a happy medium between the lightest and darkest screens out there. If you work inside sRGB, your graphics will appear to lighten slightly on Mac screens and darken to some extent on old PC monitors. But most folks will see something that more or less resembles the image you intended them to see, as in the middle example in the figure.

Previous image, opened in browser on modern flat-screen iMac (light)

Same, displayed on modern, professional-grade PC (best match)

And again, as seen on older consumer-model PC (very dark)

Figure 14-5: The image from the previous figure opened inside Internet Explorer on an iMac (top), a top-of-the-line PC (middle), and an old Windows 98 box that I have lying around the office just so I can kick it when I get mad at my other machines (bottom).

Working with sRGB

So the question becomes, how do you ensure that you're seeing colors in sRGB? Thankfully for Web artists, sRGB is Photoshop's default working space. To confirm that this is the case, choose Color Settings from the Edit menu (or the Photoshop menu on the Mac) or press Ctrl+Shift+K (⌘-Shift-K on the Mac). This brings up the dialog box shown in Figure 14-6. You can choose Web Graphics Defaults from the Settings pop-up menu, which changes all kinds of settings in the dialog box. Or, if you don't want to disturb your other settings, just choose sRGB IEC61966-2.1 from the first RGB menu, labeled in the figure. (IEC61966-2.1 is HP's designation for the sRGB standard. Combined with ITU-R 709.BT, you now have two cute pet names.) Hover your cursor over the sRGB option to see Adobe's official description of the sRGB space, highlighted in red at the bottom of Figure 14-6.

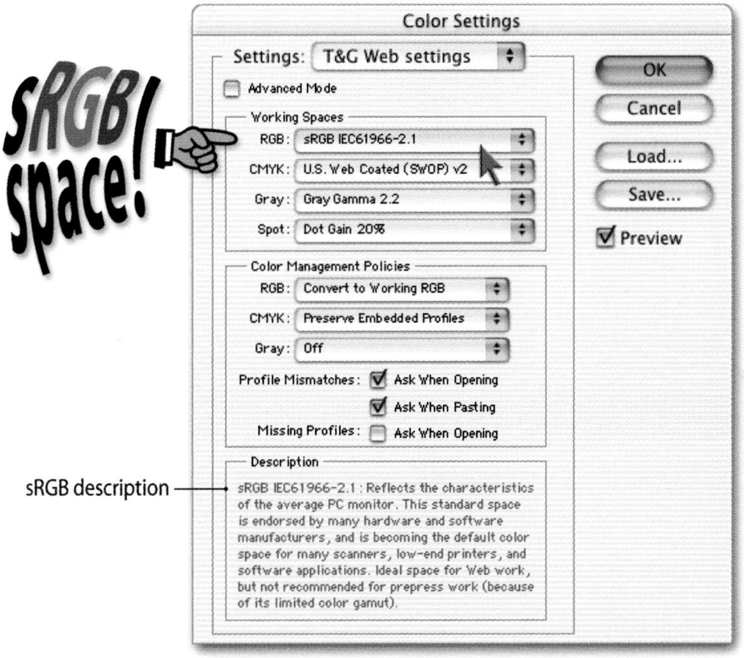

Figure 14-6: If you do most or all of your work for the Web, choose the Color Settings command and change the first RGB option to sRGB (top). You can also mouse over the word sRGB to see a description of the color space (bottom).

If you create artwork for either print or video in addition to the Web, you may prefer to work in Photoshop's recommended prepress space, *Adobe RGB*. Described at length in Chapter 16, "Essential Color Management," of the standard edition of the *Photoshop CS Bible*, Adobe RGB offers a wider gamut than sRGB, meaning that it's better suited to high-end monitors, generally anything that costs $500 or more. It also transitions better to CMYK (not to mention Adobe's video applications Premiere Pro and After Effects), making it well suited to process-color output. But it's a poor space in which to save your final Web graphics because it tends to exaggerate color saturation, leaving your images looking drab, even dingy, when displayed inside a browser that doesn't support Adobe RGB.

But just as you can work large and then shrink a graphic to make it fit the confines of a Web page, you can work in Adobe RGB and then convert to sRGB prior to saving the image in a Web file format. Choose Image ⇨ Mode ⇨ Convert to Profile. As shown in Figure 14-7, the source space, Adobe RGB, will be selected automatically; all you have to do is choose sRGB as the Destination Space. I also recommend that you set the Intent to Perceptual and turn on all check boxes except perhaps Flatten Image, which merges all layers in order to ensure the most accurate color transitions. This option you can turn on or off to suit your needs.

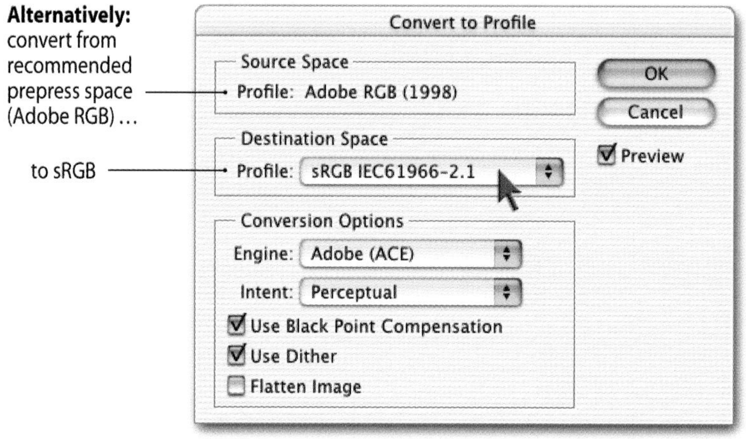

Alternatively:
convert from
recommended
prepress space
(Adobe RGB) ...

to sRGB

Convert to Profile

Source Space
Profile: Adobe RGB (1998)

OK

Cancel

☑ Preview

Destination Space
Profile: sRGB IEC61966-2.1

Conversion Options
Engine: Adobe (ACE)
Intent: Perceptual
☑ Use Black Point Compensation
☑ Use Dither
☐ Flatten Image

Figure 14-7: If you create images for both print and the Web, you'll most likely want to do most of your work in the Adobe RGB (1998) color space. Then, when optimizing the image for the Web, convert it from Adobe RGB to sRGB before scaling the image and saving it in the desired Web file format.

When saving an image using File ⇨ Save As, Photoshop asks you if you'd like to embed a source color profile, generally sRGB when saving Web graphics. If you choose to do so, this profile *may* tell the browser how to display the graphic. As I write this, only one mainstream browser in use, Internet Explorer 5 for the Mac, supports profiles. To activate profile support, choose the Preferences command, click Web Content, and turn on the Use ColorSync check box. From that point on, when IE comes across an image with an embedded sRGB profile, it will display the colors as in Figure 14-4 as opposed to the first example in Figure 14-5. (While OmniWeb 4.5 for the Mac also supports ColorSync profiles, both IE and Apple's own Safari browser are much more prevalent among Mac users.)

Meanwhile, the Windows versions of IE treat all images as if they were created in sRGB. But as we saw at the end of Figure 14-5, that by no means ensures success. So my advice is this: either create your image in, or convert your image to, sRGB. If you like, preview the image using the View ⇨ Proof Setup commands. Finally, save the image *without* a profile. The presence of a profile serves only a small group of people, but the absence of a profile saves on file size and downloading times for everyone.

More rules of Web imagery

Here are a few last-minute items to remember when creating Web graphics:

✦ **Resolution doesn't matter.** Regardless of the Resolution value you enter into the Image Size dialog box, the Web browser displays one image pixel for every screen pixel (unless you specify an alternative image size in your HTML file). Occasionally, you hear warnings that browsers may one day pay attention to resolution values, but if so, it'll be a preference setting that's off by default. Otherwise, whole Web sites would go to pieces. (Then again, little details like that rarely deter Microsoft, so you never know.) All that counts, therefore, is the pixel measurements — the number of pixels wide by the number of pixels tall.

✦ **Save in JPEG or GIF.** Discussed at length in the upcoming sections, JPEG and GIF are the most common file formats for Web graphics. GIF supports at most 256 colors, so it's better for high-contrast artwork and text. JPEG supports more than 16 million colors, but applies lossy compression, making it better suited to photographs and other continuous-tone images. There's a third format, PNG, which is essentially a 24-bit competitor to GIF that also happens to support 256 degrees of transparency, just like a Photoshop layer. But despite years of availability, PNG support among the browsers remains spotty, especially where transparency is concerned. Internet Explorer for Windows is particularly spotty in this regard. As a result, PNG images are most widely used as elements of media files that require separate plug-ins, such as Flash animations.

✦ **Save As versus Save For Web.** Photoshop lets you save images for use on the Web using either File ⇨ Save As or File ⇨ Save For Web. The latter automatically dumps all non-essential data, including paths, color profiles, and most importantly, image previews. However, the more elaborate Save For Web dialog box takes longer to display and update, and it provides no direct link to the open image. This means, to update a file on disk, you have to reoptimize and rename your image as tediously as the first time you did it. As a result, as wonderful as Save For Web is, there are lots of times when the Save As command is simply more efficient.

✦ **Save essential data only.** If you anticipate you'll be using File ⇨ Save As to save your JPEG and GIF images, the peskiest elements to eliminate are the previews. On the Mac, image previews are mostly stored in the resource fork of a file, which cannot be seen by Windows and UNIX machines and is therefore never downloaded. However, a little of the Mac preview goes in the data fork and all of the Windows preview does, so the file would be smaller without it.

To turn off previews, first press Ctrl+K, and then Ctrl+2 (that's ⌘-K, ⌘-2 on the Mac) to visit the File Handling panel of the Preferences dialog box. Next, set the Image Previews option to Ask When Saving, as in Figure 14-8. From now on, when you choose the Save As command, you'll see either a Thumbnail check box under Windows or four Image Previews check boxes on the Mac. Either way, turn all the check boxes off when saving Web graphics; leave them on for other kinds of images.

By recognizing which commands and formats to use when and how best to reduce colors inside GIF mages, you can better ensure that visitors to your Web site will spend less time sitting on their hands and more time enjoying your site. I explain the fine points of file formats, color indexing, and all the rest in the following sections.

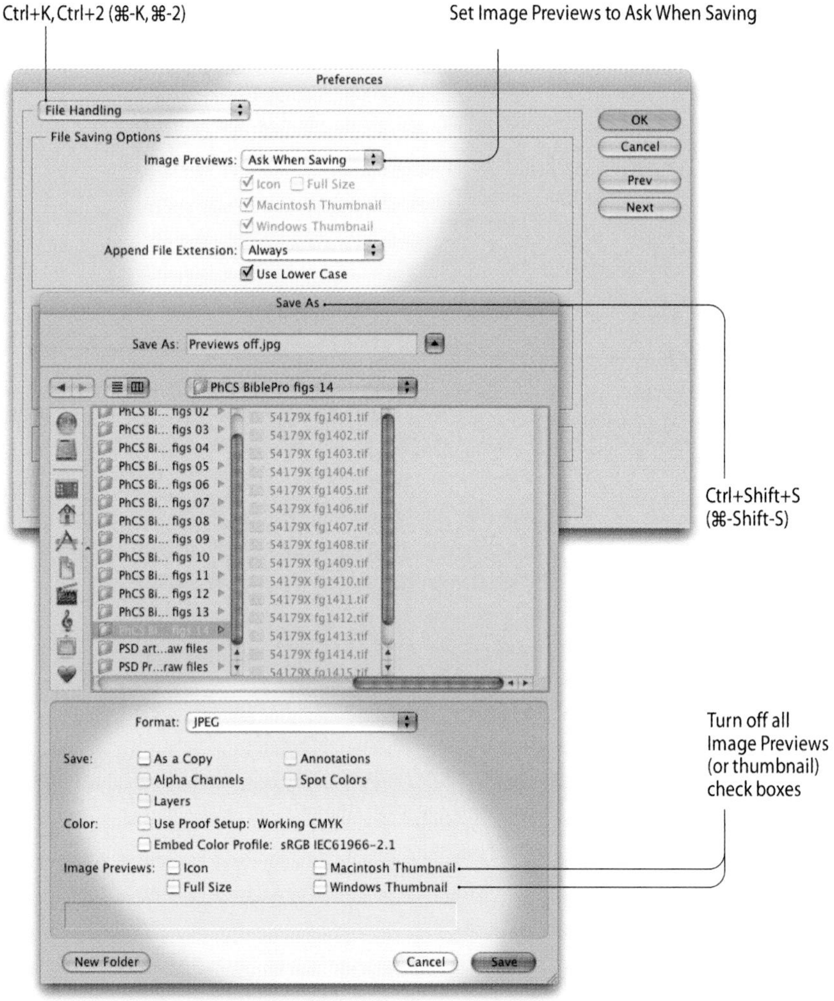

Ctrl+K, Ctrl+2 (⌘-K, ⌘-2)   Set Image Previews to Ask When Saving

Ctrl+Shift+S
(⌘-Shift-S)

Turn off all
Image Previews
(or thumbnail)
check boxes

Figure 14-8: If you intend to use the Save As command for saving Web graphics, be
sure to first set Image Previews to Ask When Saving in the Preferences dialog box (top).
Later, when confronted by the Save As dialog box, turn all check boxes off (bottom).

Saving JPEG Images

The JPEG format is named after the folks who designed it, the Joint Photographic Experts
Group. JPEG is the most efficient and essential compression format currently available and
is likely to be the compression standard for a long time to come. (New kid on the block JPEG
2000 sounds promising, but it'll be a while before the majority of in-use browsers reliably support it. If you want to check it out, you need to manually install it from your Photoshop CS
CD.) JPEG is a "lossy" compression scheme, which means it sacrifices image quality to con-
serve space on disk. You are in charge of controlling how much data is lost and how much file
size is cast to the four winds.

As with GIF and PNG, you can save an image to the JPEG format using either File ➪ Save As or the Save For Web command, which I explore later in this chapter. For the present, choose File ➪ Save As or press Ctrl+Shift+S (⌘-Shift-S), and then choose JPEG from the Format pop-up menu. (Note that none of the Web formats, JPEG included, supports layers or alpha channels.) When you click the Save button, Photoshop greets you with the JPEG Options dialog box, shown in Figure 14-9. The most vital option in this dialog box is the Quality setting, which determines how much compression Photoshop applies to your image.

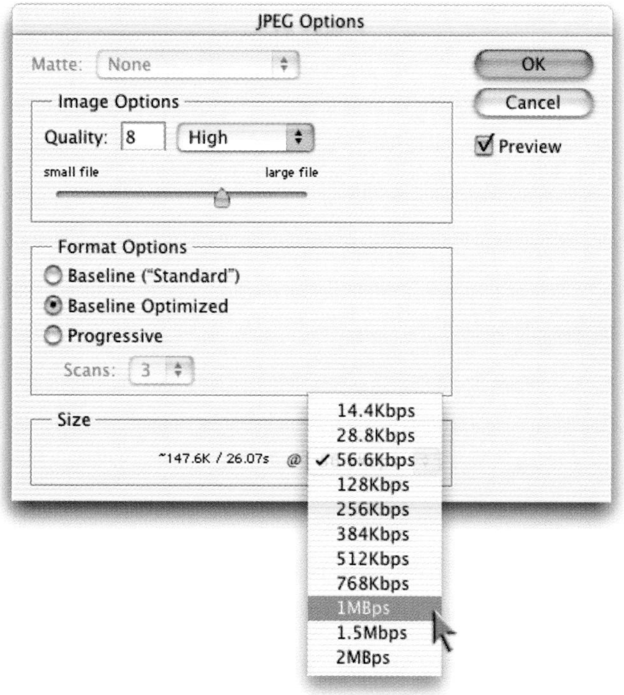

Figure 14-9: The JPEG Options dialog box provides a total of 13 compression settings, ranging from 0 (heaviest compression) to 12 (best quality). Turn on the Preview check box to not only preview the effects of your changes in the image window, but also see the approximate file size and download time of the image at various settings.

Adjusting the quality

Select an option from the Quality pop-up menu or drag the slider triangle from 0 to 12 to specify the quality setting. Of the named options, Low takes the least space on disk but distorts the image rather severely; Maximum retains the highest amount of image quality, but consumes more disk space. Of the numbered options, 0 is the most severe compressor and 12 does the least damage.

In Photoshop, JPEG evaluates an image in 8 × 8-pixel blocks, using a technique called *Adaptive Discrete Cosine Transform* (or ADCT). ADCT averages the 24-bit value of every pixel in the block, and then stores the average color in the upper-left pixel in the block and assigns the remaining 63 pixels smaller values relative to the average. Next, the lossy compression kicks in as JPEG divides the block by a formula called the *quantization matrix*, which simplifies the pixels' values by changing as many as possible to zero.

Figure 14-10 shows an image saved at each of the four named compression settings. The samples are arranged from highest image quality at top to lowest quality at bottom. The uncompressed image measures 603 by 480 pixels (admittedly large for the Web, but this being a book, the figure has to look good in print) and consumes 848K in memory. This means that the Low Quality setting, which results in a 64K file, represents a remarkable 92 percent savings. But it comes at a price. The right-hand column in Figure 14-10 shows magnified details from each of the compressed images in sharper focus, which is more analogous to the effect you see on screen. Personally, I rarely drop the Quality setting below High (8) and I never take it below Medium (5).

But you are certainly free to select any Quality value you like. To help you gauge the most desirable setting for your specific image, Photoshop displays file size information at the bottom of the dialog box (assuming that the Preview check box is turned on). The first value indicates the approximate file size you'll get if you apply the current JPEG settings. The second value estimates how long the file will take to download at a given connection speed, which you select from the neighboring pop-up menu. As shown back in Figure 14-9, your selection of connections varies from the ancient modem standard 14.4Kbps to 140 times that rate (2Mbps) with the help of a dedicated T1 connection or better. Naturally, it's always safest to assume that more visitors to your Web site suffer from the slow speeds than benefit from the fast ones — but a designer can dream, can't she?

Other JPEG options

Quality may be the most important of the JPEG settings, but it's not the only one. The remaining dialog box options work as follows (in the order they appear):

✦ **Matte:** Unlike GIF, Photoshop's implementation of JPEG does not support transparency. (The aforementioned JPEG 2000 does support alpha-channel transparency, but again, it's too early in the game to use JPEG 2000 and have any confidence that end-users will even be able to see your image.) So if your image contains transparent areas, Photoshop needs to know what color to fill them with when it saves the image as a JPEG. Select the desired color from the Matte pop-up menu. Keep an eye on the preview in the image window to make sure that you like the effect. Be aware that JPEG compression may cause the actual matte color to differ somewhat from the color you choose from the menu.

✦ **Format Options:** Most Web browsers support two variations on the JPEG format. The so-called *baseline* (or *sequentially displayed*) format draws images in line-by-line passes on screen. The second variation, *progressive*, renders an image in multiple passes, each increasing the resolution, thus permitting visitors to get an idea of how an image looks without waiting for the entire file to download.

For my part, I prefer the baseline format because it ensures compatibility with even the oldest, most ill-conceived browsers. Of the two Baseline options, I recommend you select Baseline Optimized. This setting includes better Huffman encoding (an additional component of JPEG that applies lossless compression) and may reduce the file size by an extra 5 to 10 percent.

✦ **Scans:** Okay, so I don't like Progressive. But in the name of full disclosure, if you decide to ignore my advice and select the Progressive option, Photoshop invites you to pick a number of passes from the Scans pop-up menu. A higher value results in a faster display of the initial image, but it also takes longer to render the image in its entirety because of all the incremental refreshing.

Figure 14-10: Four JPEG settings applied to a single image, with the highest Quality setting illustrated at the top and the lowest at the bottom. The first column shows each compressed photo at the standard print resolution of 300 pixels per inch; the second column shows magnified details sharpened using the Unsharp Mask command.

Preparing and Saving GIF Images

The Graphics Interchange Format, or GIF, came into being in 1987, during a time when only robber barons and captains of industry owned 1.2Kbps modems and the rest of the world's data moved at the speed of one bit per annum. Developed by CompuServe, GIF supports a maximum of 8 bits per pixel, or a maximum of 256 colors per image, and relies on LZW compression, the same "lossless" compression (meaning that it does not rewrite pixels) employed by most TIFF images.

Frankly, GIF is a tired, old format. Its reputation with the developer community took an enormous hit when CompuServe and Unisys (the holder of the patent on LZW) began demanding royalty payments eight years after the format's introduction, a fracas that ultimately inspired the development of PNG (which stands for *Portable Network Graphics* or *PNG, Not GIF*, depending whom you talk to). In the past decade, GIF has remained virtually dormant and PNG has emerged as the much better format, supporting more colors, better compression, and a wider range of transparency options. GIF's only relative advantage is that it supports animation. But what really keeps GIF alive today is inertia. It's a known quantity and even crusty old browsers running on computers that haven't been upgraded since Julius Caesar was a baby have no problems displaying GIF. So while GIF may not be the most progressive or egalitarian format on the planet, it continues to serve a very specific function.

For example, despite its obvious limitations, GIF is a better format than JPEG for saving high-contrast imagery, line art, and text. Figure 14-11 shows a public-service notice that I created for a non-profit foundation that I only wish existed. It includes high-contrast bananas (the very tastiest kind), monkey line art, scads of text, and all varieties of shape layers and sharply rendered layer effects. Given that lossy compression is best suited to soft edges and gradual color transitions, this image may very well represent JPEG's worst nightmare.

Just to prove I'm not fibbing, Figure 14-12 features magnified details from three variations on the monkey graphic. The first example shows a detail from the full-color original, which consumes 3.71MB in memory. For comparative purposes, I applied the Unsharp Mask filter using an Amount value of 100 percent and a Radius of 2.0 pixels. The second example shows the sharpened image saved to the JPEG format at an admittedly very low Quality setting, reducing the file size to a mere 132K, less than 4 percent of its uncompressed size. The resulting image suffers from an array of visible compression artifacts, especially prominent around type and other high-contrast edges. I can achieve a similar file size — 147K, still under 4 percent of the uncompressed size — by reducing the number of colors to a scant 32 and saving the image as a GIF file. And while this leads to more muted colors and noisy transitions, the GIF image is much more crisp, clear, and aesthetically pleasing, as seen in the last example in Figure 14-12.

The three routes to a GIF file

Whereas I happen to believe that File ⇨ Save As provides the most straightforward and flexible means for saving a JPEG image, I have very mixed feelings about the best way to approach GIF images. The Save As command lets you maintain a direct link between the open image window and the GIF file on disk, permitting you to make minor revisions and then update the disk file just by pressing Ctrl+S for the Save command (⌘-S on the Mac). However, for best results, you must reduce the colors and save the file in two separate steps using two separate commands. Meanwhile, the Save For Web dialog box provides all the advantages and disadvantages of shopping in a gigantic warehouse chain — it's one-stop shopping, but you have to put up with a lot of overhead and navigate through an overwhelming number of options.

Figure 14-11: This message-driven advertisement features high-contrast imagery, line art, and text, three elements that tend to work very well on the Web but react very badly to JPEG compression.

In all, there turn out to be three distinct ways to create a GIF document. Here they are, with relative advantages and disadvantages:

✦ **Index the colors and then choose Save As.** To reduce the number of colors in the image to 256 or fewer, choose Image ⇨ Mode ⇨ Indexed Color (described at length in the next section). This may seem an inconvenient first step, but it means that you have the option of modifying the pixels by hand after collapsing the color depth. (Note that Photoshop greatly limits your options when editing a low-color image. Layers and filters are entirely out of the question, for example. I generally have the most success editing individual pixels with the pencil tool, but you can also use the selection tools, paint bucket, and clone stamp, among others.)

When you're ready to save the image, choose Save As and select CompuServe GIF from the Format pop-up menu. Photoshop next displays two options, Normal and Interlaced. If you want the Web browser to display the image in incremental passes — similar to progressive JPEG — select the latter. Otherwise, select Normal, which happens to be the safer option.

Advantages: Fine-tune low-color image using limited range of tools; maintain link with file on disk. *Disadvantages*: Requires the most preparation; can't preview file size; have to use yet another dialog box (Color Table) to edit colors or make colors transparent, and even then your options are limited.

✦ **Choose Save As and *then* index the colors.** You can, if you prefer, skip the Indexed Color command and go directly to File ➪ Save As. But when you select CompuServe GIF from the Format menu, Photoshop automatically activates the As A Copy check box, breaking any link between the open image and the file you're about to save. Then Photoshop goes ahead and brings up the Indexed Color dialog box anyway. So while this approach may sound the easiest of the three, it is in fact every bit as convoluted and less flexible.

Advantages: Lets you skip Indexed Color command. *Disadvantages*: Worst of both worlds — no link to disk file; can't preview file size; no ability to edit low-color image; can't edit colors; fewer optimization options.

✦ **Choose Save For Web.** Choosing File ➪ Save For Web permits you to specify all GIF settings and color indexing preferences from one dialog box. You can also compare the effects of different settings, preview file sizes, balance GIF against JPEG, and access settings that are either unavailable otherwise or inconvenient.

Advantages: One-stop shopping; preview file sizes; compare settings; edit colors and make transparent; impose lossy compression; modify dither and color reduction using mask. *Disadvantages*: Sometimes sluggish to display dialog box and update previews; no link to disk file; can't edit low-color image by hand.

Figure 14-12: After applying the Unsharp Mask command to the full-color image (left), I saved it to the JPEG format using a very low Quality setting (middle). The saved image is a mess, riddled with compression artifacts. Fortunately, I can achieve a very similar file size by reducing the colors to 32 and saving the image as a GIF file (right).

I tend to index the colors and save the image in two separate steps, as I described in the first bullet. For this reason, I explain the more complicated of the two steps, the Indexed Color command, in the very next section. However, my preference may be one of habit. I've been creating GIF images for eons now and it's possible I got set in my ways before Save For Web existed. And I must admit, there are plenty of times when I resort to Save For Web if only to exploit its wider range of options. To learn more about the Save For Web command and decide whether you might just like it better, see the section "Making Side-by-Side Comparisons" later in this chapter.

Using the Indexed Color command

To reduce the number of colors in an RGB image so that you can save it in GIF or some other low-color format, choose Image ⇨ Mode ⇨ Indexed Color. This command strips an image of all but its most essential colors by generating a color look-up table (LUT). The LUT serves as a kind of index, describing how the few remaining colors map to the RGB space, which is why the process is called *indexing*.

When you first choose the Indexed Color command, Photoshop asks you if you want to flatten the image. Your only options are to comply or cancel — low-color images do not support layers — so be sure to save the layered image before choosing the command.

Pictured in Figure 14-13, the Indexed Color dialog box lets you specify the number of colors you want to keep, the method by which the indexed colors are recruited, and how colors are blended and made transparent. The following sections explain how these options work.

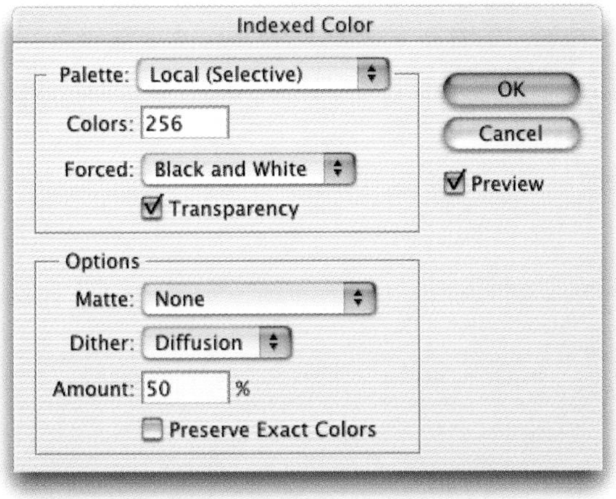

Figure 14-13: The Indexed Color options permit you to control the reduction of colors in an RGB image. The Palette settings determine which colors Photoshop keeps; the Options settings control transparency and color mixing.

Specifying the palette

Selecting colors for an image is like choosing players for a rugby team, except that you have 16 million players to choose from and you don't have to worry about being chosen last. In fact, you're kind of in charge of things. Your job is to tell the team captain, Photoshop, how to make its selections. You do this using the Palette pop-up menu.

I chose rugby for my analogy because, to the uninitiated American such as myself, the options in the Palette menu make roughly as much sense. Just as rugby looks to most Americans like a bunch of men groping each other one second, tossing and punting the ball with complete disregard for any rules the next, and finally flinging themselves in an enormous pile on top of a guy who's already been tackled, the Palette menu is all chaos and confusion. No doubt, rugby makes tons of sense and is a lot of fun if you'll just take the time to learn the rules — and wouldn't you know it, the same goes for the Palette menu. Well, except that the Palette menu isn't much fun, and it never completely makes sense. So perhaps it's more like cricket. I mean, what is up with *that* game — are those people even awake?

Now that I've offended most people outside the U.S., let's take a look at the options in the Palette menu. Thankfully, when creating Web imagery, you can safely ignore a handful of the options, including the two System settings (mostly archaic), Uniform (never was useful), and Custom (better handled by Save For Web). This leaves the following:

✦ **Exact:** Usually dimmed, Exact is only active if an image already contains fewer than 256 colors. This only occurs in extremely high-contrast situations — as when editing a screen shot or line of type. The Colors value tells you how many colors there are.

✦ **Web:** When displaying an image on an old 8-bit screen, the browser invariably changes all colors to those in the *Web (or browser-safe) palette*, which is a low-color LUT common to Internet Explorer and Netscape. The LUT comprises colors whose R, G, and B values are divisible by 51. That means each primary color can be set to 0, 51, 102, 153, 204, or 255. Calculate all possible combinations, and you get 216 colors in all, or 217 if you include Transparency.

The Web palette ensures that your GIF colors go unmodified, no matter what the capabilities of the viewer's monitor. It can also guarantee agreement between multiple images inside a table, especially when a GIF animation is involved. But generally, your images will look better and compress to smaller file sizes when you use Adaptive, Selective, or Perceptual. (To see for yourself, compare Figures 14-14 and 14-15.)

✦ **Adaptive, Selective,** and **Perceptual:** Available in both Local and Master flavors (as I describe in a moment), these three settings are variations on a common theme, intelligently culling colors based on the contents of the image window. The oldest of the three, Adaptive, is the least sophisticated, retaining the most frequently used colors in your image. Selective tries to maintain key colors that represent different parts of the spectrum, with special attention to colors in the Web palette. Meanwhile, Perceptual samples colors that produce the best transitions, great for reproducing gradients and other color blends.

My advice: Use Perceptual for photographic images, where smooth transitions are more important than specific color values. Use Selective when an image contains bright colors or sharp, graphic transitions, as with the cover of the alternate-universe *Photoshop Bible* in Figure 14-15. (Hey, I wrote *Photoshop For Dummies*; why not for *Puppets* too?) And if an image contains relatively few colors, and you want to maintain those colors as exactly as possible, go for Adaptive.

As called out in Figure 14-15, Adaptive, Selective, and Perceptual may result in smaller file sizes than the Web-safe palette, not because they compress better, but because they let you vary the number of colors. (The Web palette is locked into 216 colors, or 217 with transparency.) But colors being equal — always 32 in the case of the figure — file size remains fairly consistent. There is no inherent compression advantage of one Palette setting over another.

Original art, 27.6MB layered, 3.24MB flat   Scaled to 32%, Web-safe palette, 52K

Figure 14-14: The full-color artwork on left consumed nearly 30MB of memory with layers and just over 3MB when flattened (left). After downsampling the image and applying the 216-color Web palette, the final GIF file (magnified on right) reduced to 52K, or a scant 1.5 percent of its uncompressed size.

Adaptive, 32 colors, 34K   Selective, 32 colors, 32K   Perceptual, 32 colors, 35K

Figure 14-15: The Adaptive palette keeps the most popular colors and therefore draws lots of blues from the sky and browns from the table (left). Selective saves a wider range of color (middle) and Perceptual sacrifices variety for smooth transitions (right).

✦ **Local** versus **Master:** That's all very well and good. But once you settle on, say, Selective, how do you decide between Local (Selective) and Master (Selective)? Choose the Local option if you want Photoshop to consider the colors in the frontmost image only. However, if you have several images open and want to create a palette based on all of them, choose Master.

When you select any of the Local options, you can influence how Photoshop calculates the palette by selecting an area of your image before choosing the Indexed Color command. Photoshop favors the selected area when creating the palette. For example, Figure 14-16 shows Local (Selective) applied with just eight colors. When nothing is selected, it misses the reds of the cover art entirely. But when I draw a rough selection around the cover art using the rectangular marquee tool, Local (Selective) nabs those reds. And for only 19K — what a bargain!

✦ **Previous:** This option replays the last look-up table created by the Indexed Color command. If you're trying to create a series of high-contrast graphics that you want to look as homogeneous as possible, use this option. The Previous option is dimmed unless you've used Indexed Color at least once during the current session.

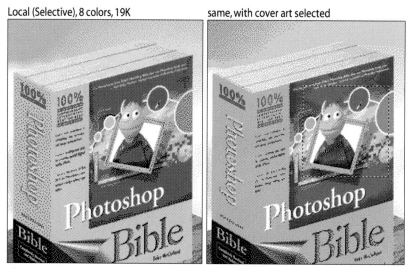

Figure 14-16: Normally, when set to a mere eight colors, the Local (Selective) option can manage mostly blues and grays, with two browns, and one gold (left). But select part of the cover art, and it replaces one of the browns with a bright red (right).

Colors, transparency, and dithering

While the Palette option may be the most complex of the Indexed Color options to understand (if not to use), it's just one of many ensemble players in the color reduction cast. Here's how the others work:

✦ **Colors:** Enter the number of colors you want to use in the Colors option box. In the old days, you controlled the number of colors by choosing a particular bit depth (the number of bits of data devoted to each pixel). But a few versions back, Adobe's engineers decided that scaling colors by whole bit values — 8-bit for 256 colors, 7-bit for 128, 6-bit for 64, and so on — wasn't absolutely necessary to achieve smaller file sizes, so you might as well free your mind and enter the exact number of colors you deem fit. Still, it was a valuable option — sacrificing an entire bit does sometimes make a difference, after all — which is why I'm glad it lives on in the Save For Web dialog box (described later).

✦ **Forced:** Useful as Adaptive, Selective, and Perceptual are, they can easily upset important colors. For example, the white background of an image might turn a pale red or blue, even if white was a predominant color. Hence the Forced option, which lets you lock down key colors so they don't change under any circumstances. Black and White locks in black and white, nearly always a good thing. Primaries protects those and RGB plus CMY. And Web protects the 216 colors in the Web-safe palette. Choose Custom to specify your own colors, such as the background color of a Web page. Click a swatch to define a color; Ctrl-click (or ⌘-click) a swatch to unlock that color.

✦ **Transparency:** If an image is set on a layer against a transparent background, selecting this check box maintains that transparency. Bear in mind, however, that transparency in a GIF file is either on or off; there are no soft transitions as in a Photoshop layer. (For an alternative to this, see "GIF optimization settings" later in this chapter.)

For example, turn your wandering gaze to Figure 14-17. After much deliberation, I decided that combining the *Bible* on a pedestal against an ethereal plane of fluffy clouds implied an endorsement that, while I was confident I had it, I had not confirmed. (My secretary has sent faxes, but so far, no response. I hear it's a really busy place.) So on my lawyer's advice, I took the clouds out, revealing the familiar checkerboard pattern of transparency. I also tossed in a drop shadow, as the first example in the figure shows. After choosing the Indexed Color command, I turned on the Transparency check box. Now here's the weird part — even though Photoshop flattened the file when I chose Indexed Color, I could still see the transparent background, as shown in the second example in Figure 14-17. Divine intervention? I can't say, but one thing's for sure: An indexed image is the only kind of Photoshop document that accommodates transparency without layers.

Full-color art sans otherworldly background   Indexed, Transparency: on, Matte: White

Figure 14-17: After deleting the cloud background from my composition (left), I applied a 32-color Local (Selective) palette and turned on the Transparency check box. Setting Matte to White adds a white backdrop to the soft and feathered edges (right).

✦ **Matte:** The Matte option works in collaboration with the Transparency check box. (If there is no transparency in an image — that is, all layers cover one another to create a seamless opacity — the Matte option is dimmed.) When you select Transparency, the specified Matte color fills the translucent pixels in the image, as demonstrated in the second example in Figure 14-17. When Transparency is turned off, the Matte color fills both translucent *and* transparent areas. To ensure smooth transitions, select the Matte color that matches the background color of your Web page, most often white.

✦ **Dither:** This option controls how Photoshop mimics the several million colors that you asked it to remove from an image. The None option makes no attempt to smooth out color transitions, but results in smaller file sizes, as in the first example in Figure 14-18. Diffusion mixes pixels to soften the transition between colors, as in the second example in the figure. Noise mixes pixels throughout the image, not merely in areas of transition. And Pattern is just plain awful. (Try it out and you'll see.) My recommendation is to stick with Diffusion and use the following option.

✦ **Amount:** This wonderful option controls the amount of dithering applied. When and only when Diffusion is active, you can modify the amount of dithering by raising or lowering this value. Lower values produce harsher color transitions, but lower the file size. Because GIF's LZW protocol is better suited to compressing uninterrupted expanses of color, quick transitions mean speedier images. As the size values in Figure 14-18 illustrate, it's a trade-off. Keep an eye on the image window to see how low you can go.

✦ **Preserve Exact Colors:** Again available only when Diffusion is active, this check box disables dithering inside areas of flat color that exactly match a color in the active palette. Say that you've created some text in a Web-safe color. The text is antialiased, but the letters themselves are flat. By selecting Preserve Exact Colors, you tell Photoshop to dither around the edges of the letters but to leave the interiors undithered. When available, I say leave it on.

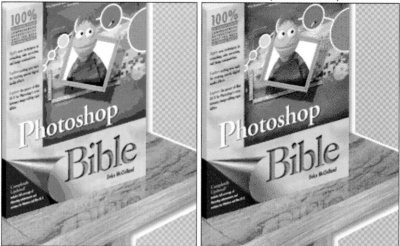

Dither: None, 24K   Dither: Diffusion, Amount: 100%, 30K

Figure 14-18: The results of combining the 32-color Local (Selective) palette with Dither turned off (left) and set to maximum Diffusion (right). A reduced amount of dithering facilitates LZW compression and therefore results in smaller file sizes.

Making Side-by-Side Comparisons

Not sure whether to use JPEG or GIF, let alone what settings to apply? Wouldn't it be nice to preview groups of settings side-by-side so you could make an educated decision as to which group provides the best trade-off between quality and file size? If your answer to that last question was Yes, you're in luck. (If your answer was No, you're nuts, but then you already knew that.) Taking a cue from ImageReady, Photoshop lets you compare palettes and dither settings for a GIF image as well as contrast different qualities of JPEG compression. You can even measure an image compressed with JPEG against that same image rendered as a low-color GIF. You know that expression "You can't compare apples and oranges"? Well obviously, it's wrong. In fact, you can compare all the fruit you want, and in just a few moments, you will. Meanwhile, throughout your many and varied comparisons, the original image remains on screen so you always know where home is.

The command at work here is Save For Web. This one command lets you apply compression, index colors, add transparency, and even resize an image to make it small enough to fit on a page, all in one operation. So there's no need to use Save As, Indexed Color, or any of the others. In fact, Save For Web works best if you start at the point you normally do when saving a file, with a full-color image open on screen, in its final state, ready and waiting to be unleashed on an eager public.

Technically, you can choose Save For Web when working with a large, layered image and then scale and flatten the image inside the ensuing dialog box. But I recommend against it. Big images can result in such slow performance that you find yourself suddenly impatient with your computer. I know, that's unlike you, but if there's one part of Photoshop that can rattle your otherwise saintly reserve, this is it. And cursing at one's computer sets such a poor example for today's suggestible youth. So increase your happiness and contentment by flattening your image and resizing it to at least approximately the right dimensions before choosing Save For Web. (Let your kids learn their curse words off the TV, like they're supposed to.) But be warned: It's pretty easy to forget you flattened and resized your original file, meaning that saving and closing the file will cause you to lose your layered, high-resolution original. (And then you'll be cursing again.) So be careful out there.

Choose File ➪ Save For Web or press Ctrl+Shift+Alt+S (⌘-Shift-Option-S on the Mac) to display the large window pictured in Figure 14-19. (Users of past versions will notice in the title bar that Save For Web is now "Powered By ImageReady." Great, that's just what Photoshop needed — product placement. What's next? "The Healing Brush — Sponsored by Johnson & Johnson"?) At first, you may think there's a lot going on here — and you'd be right — but don't fret. Many of the options duplicate functions we've already discussed. And those that don't are logical and intelligible, provided you approach them in the following order.

STEPS: Optimizing an Image for the Web

1. **Click the tab for the display you want to use.** When you first enter the Save For Web dialog box, you have to decide which image or images you'd like to preview. Photoshop defaults to the Optimized view, which shows the image with JPEG compression or color indexing applied, as it will appear when opened in a Web browser. To compare multiple settings at a time — the real power of the window — click on the 2-Up or 4-Up tab in the top-left corner of the window. Figure 14-19 shows the 4-Up view.

   To get a better look at the image in the previews, scroll and zoom using the hand tool and magnifying glass in the upper-left corner of the window. You can likewise use the standard navigation shortcuts, including spacebar for the hand tool and Ctrl+plus or minus to zoom (⌘-plus or minus on the Mac). To keep track of the active zoom ratio, keep an eye on the zoom level value in the lower-left corner of the window.

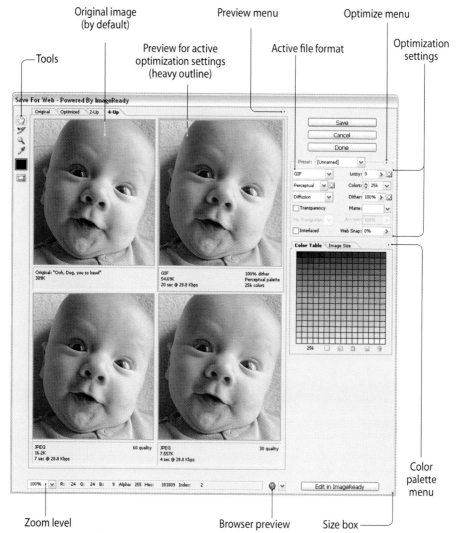

Tools

Original image
(by default)

Preview for active
optimization settings
(heavy outline)

Preview menu

Active file format

Optimize menu

Optimization
settings

Color
palette
menu

Zoom level

Browser preview

Size box

Figure 14-19: Click the 4-Up tab at the top of the window to compare the original image (upper left by default) to three sets of Web compression settings. Conveniently, zooming or scrolling inside one preview zooms or scrolls them all.

2. **Click a preview and choose the optimization settings you want to apply.** By default, the first preview shows the original image, untainted by compression settings. You probably want to leave that one alone. But the others, you can click and change to your heart's content.

The *optimization settings* — so-called because they optimize the file size for the Web — run down the right side of the dialog box and change according to the file format that you select. Each time you change a setting or advance to the next one, Photoshop rebuilds the preview to show you the result.

To preview a group of settings in your favorite Web browser, click the colorful world-and-question mark button at the bottom of the window. If the button doesn't represent your favorite browser, choose another browser from the accompanying pop-up menu.

3. **Select the preview you like best and click the Save button.** Photoshop displays a variation on the standard Save dialog box. But instead of selecting the file format — you've already done that — you specify whether you want Photoshop to create one or more image files, an HTML file describing a sample Web page, or both. Name the image and specify the location of your files on disk as usual.

Now that you understand the basic approach, the next few sections go into detail about the optimization settings for the JPEG and GIF file formats. If you would prefer to use one of the two PNG formats — which rely on subsets of the same options used by GIF — then reference the "GIF optimization settings" section.

In addition to GIF, JPEG, and PNG, Save For Web supports the Wireless Image Format (WBMP), which is a black-and-white bitmap format used by Web-surfing cell phones and other personal, wireless devices. WBMP supports dithering, but beyond that, there's not much to say about it. If you can use it, hey, way to live on the bleeding edge. However, most folks are unlikely to have any need for it.

JPEG optimization settings

When you select JPEG from the format pop-up menu, you gain access to the options shown in Figure 14-20. Most duplicate options are found in the JPEG Options dialog box (Figure 14-9), so I won't bore you and waste paper by explaining them all over again. Instead, let's take a look at the unique stuff:

✦ **Quality:** The Quality pop-up menu (labeled in Figure 14-20) and the value to its right mirror the Quality controls in the JPEG Options dialog box. But while the latter permits values from 0 to 12, this value tops out at 100. Rather than adding better quality, it provides more variety — in other words, 100 in Save For Web is roughly equivalent to 12 in JPEG Options.

If your image contains a mask channel, you can apply compression selectively by clicking the mask icon to the right of the Quality value. The resulting dialog box lets you select text, shapes, or an alpha channel to use as your mask. In Figure 14-21, I chose an edge mask I created in advance (see the steps "Creating and Using an Edge Mask" in Chapter 8). Then adjust the Minimum and Maximum settings, either using the values or sliders. Where the mask is white, Photoshop applies the Maximum quality setting (minimum compression); where the mask is black, you get Minimum quality (maximum compression). The resulting effect reduces file size without harming the edges.

✦ **Optimized:** Selecting this check box applies more efficient lossless compression to a JPEG file. It's the same as choosing Baseline Optimized in the JPEG Options dialog box (see "Other JPEG options"), and usually shaves off a K or two.

✦ **Blur:** JPEG's lossy compression scheme is better at compressing soft transitions than hard edges, meaning that it can compress blurry images better than sharp ones. So by blurring an image, you reduce its file size without applying more compression. *But you also destroy the detail!* Gee whiz, why not just fill your image with solid black — that would compress *really* small! Believe me, you're better off applying more compression than blurring the image. Leave this value set to 0.

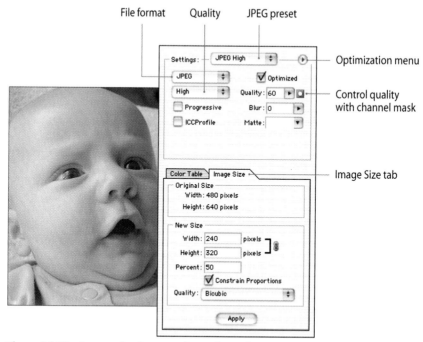

File format   Quality   JPEG preset

Optimization menu

Control quality
with channel mask

Image Size tab

Figure 14-20: Sammy the Compression Baby reclines in wonder at the site of the JPEG optimization settings. But there is also fear in his eyes. "Whatever you do," he cautions, "steer clear of the Blur value!"

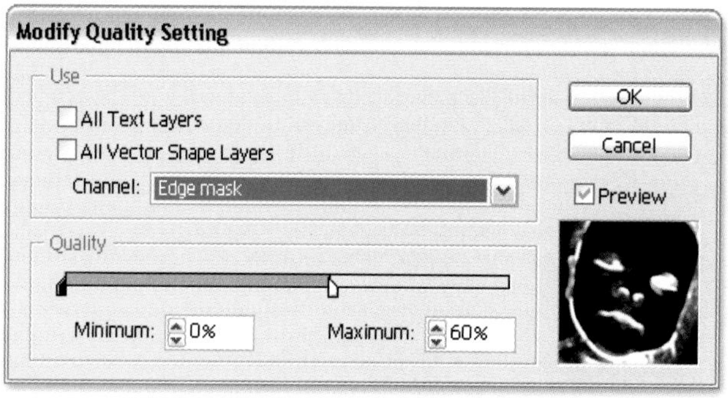

Figure 14-21: To apply variable compression settings, click the mask icon next to the Quality value. Then select the desired mask channel and adjust the Minimum and Maximum settings.

✦ **ICC Profile:** This check box embeds a color profile with the JPEG image. The color profile adds about 3K to the file size, which means an extra second of download time at 28.8Kbps. As I mentioned in "Working with sRGB" earlier in this chapter, browser support for profiles is pretty scarce. I say, leave it off.

✦ **Image Size:** Because JPEG images are full-color, the Color Table options are unavailable. However, the bottom-right side of the dialog box does not go entirely wasted. If an image is physically too large to fit snugly on your Web page, you can make it smaller it by clicking the Image Size tab and fiddling with the Width, Height, and Percent values. These options work just like those offered by Image ⇨ Image Size.

GIF optimization settings

Selecting GIF from the format pop-up menu displays the slew of options shown in Figure 14-22. Many are familiar from the Indexed Color dialog box, so I'll skip them. But the new ones I'll cover, and here they are:

✦ **Lossy:** Technically, GIF relies on lossless LZW compression, so no data is sacrificed when saving a file. But by cranking up the Lossy value, you can rearrange the pixels in an image so that they compress better. In my experience, values as high as 30 whittle away the file size while causing little damage to the appearance of an image. Higher values are rarely acceptable. Use this option prudently and keep an eye on the preview.

✦ **The mask icons:** When you index an image using Indexed Color, you can make Photoshop favor a certain area of the image by selecting that area first. In the Save For Web dialog box, you also can likewise stress one area over another using a mask that you've created in advance. Just click the mask icon next to the palette pop-up menu (labeled in Figure 14-22) and select the desired mask. Photoshop emphasizes colors inside the white portion of the mask just as it emphasizes colors in a selection.

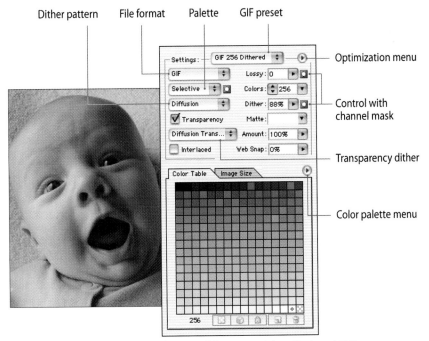

Figure 14-22: Is Sammy excited to see this mesmerizing display of GIF options, or just plain overwhelmed? It's hard to know for certain, but I suspect that glimmer in his eye means, "Diffusion Transparency rocks!"

The mask icons next to Lossy and Dither use masks to selectively rearrange and inter-mix pixels. White areas in the mask receive preferential treatment over black areas, as described in the tip in the previous section. Here again, an edge mask serves very nicely.

✦ **Colors:** As inside the Indexed Color dialog box, you can enter the specific number of colors you want to retain. But you can likewise choose presets from a pop-up menu that correlate to incremental bit-depth settings. If you can reduce down to one of these settings, you will in many cases see a significant reduction in file size. For example, if 36 colors looks good, try to get the value down to 32 colors, or 5 bits of data per pixel.

✦ **Transparency:** If an image contains transparent areas marked by the checkerboard pattern, select the Transparency check box to keep those areas transparent. Inside the Save For Web window, you also have the option of simulating translucency using a dither pattern. Choose one of the options in the pop-up menu below the Transparency check box to dither a tapering shadow or gradual fade. Figure 14-23 shows examples of this option set to No Transparency Dither with the Matte set to White alongside the same image set to Diffusion Transparency Dither.

No Transparency Dither, Matte: White   Diffusion Transparency Dither

Figure 14-23: The GIF format can express transparency but not incremental levels of translucency. So you can either matte translucent pixels (left) or dither them (right).

✦ **Web Snap:** This ingenious option replaces a specified percentage of colors in an image with members of the 216-color Web-safe palette. It's a way to hedge your bets — you can lock down some colors so they're compatible with older 8-bit monitors and permit other colors to roam free so that the image still looks great on 24-bit screens.

✦ **Color Table:** Clicking on this tab shows all the colors in an indexed image. Below the colors, you'll notice five tiny icons, which permit you to edit one or more selected swatches in the palette. (Just click a swatch to select it.) In order from left to right, these icons let you convert a swatch to transparent, change a color to its nearest Web-safe equivalent, lock the color so it can't be modified, add a color selected inside the original image with the eyedropper to the palette, or delete a color. You can also double-click a color to dial in new settings.

✦ **Color palette menu:** When the Color Table tab is active, you can modify selected colors, sort colors, and load and save palettes by choosing commands from this menu. Just click the arrowhead to the right of the tab.

The Optimize menu

Labeled back in Figure 14-19, the optimize menu supplies a few extra goodies that are equally applicable to JPEG and GIF images:

✦ **Save Settings:** Choose this command to save the current optimization settings as a preset. You can then apply the same settings by simply choosing the preset from the Settings pop-up menu.

✦ **Delete Settings:** Choose a preset and then select this command to delete it.

✦ **Optimize to File Size:** One of the best reasons to open the optimize menu, this command lets you forgo messing with a bunch of settings and instead enter a target file size. After you click OK, Photoshop automatically changes the settings to meet the target size. If you don't know whether you want to use GIF or JPEG, select Auto Select GIF/JPEG.

If the image contains slices, select Current Slice to optimize the selected slice only. Select All Slices Separately to optimize each slice to the same file size or All Slices Together to make all slices add up to the target size. For more information on slicing, see "Slicing Images" later in this chapter.

✦ **Repopulate Views:** When you're working in 4-Up view, the first preview shows your uncompressed image while the selected preview (by default, the second one) illustrates your custom optimization settings. Photoshop fills in the two remaining previews with automatic variations, each of which results in a smaller file size than your settings. If you make changes to your custom settings, you can update the two alternative previews by choosing Repopulate Views.

✦ **Link Slices:** By default, Photoshop optimizes each slice independently, applying different JPEG compression settings or calculating separate color palettes. In many cases, that's fine. But what if you have two or more neighboring slices that you want to save as GIF images using Selective palettes? Photoshop may stick completely different colors in the slices, resulting in an obvious edge between them, as demonstrated in Figure 14-24. To avoid this, Shift-click with the slice select tool (the one that looks like an X-Acto knife) to select the slices you want to link and then choose the Link Slices command. From now on, the linked slices share a common set of optimization settings, as in the final example in the figure. If you later decide you want to optimize slices independently, choose one of the two Unlink commands.

✦ **Edit Output Settings:** When you slice a document, Photoshop saves the slices as individual image files and then automatically generates the HTML code necessary to assemble the files into a cohesive Web table. This means Photoshop has to automatically name the various image files, write the code, and generate links to the images based on certain, mostly sensible assumptions. If you don't like Photoshop's assumptions, you can modify them by choosing the Edit Output Settings command. Note that this command is highly technical and requires a working knowledge of HTML scripting (which is a whole different topic worthy of — and receiving — its own *Bible*). If that's you, edit away. If not, leave well enough alone.

Figure 14-24: Optimizing slices (shown on left) independently can be dangerous, because it can result in harsh edges between one slice and its neighbor when slices are assembled inside a browser (middle). This is most evident in the banana peel, which goes from yellow to green to sudden black outlines. Link the slices to use one palette throughout (right).

The Preview menu

One last menu, loitering unpretentiously near the top of the Save For Web dialog box, controls the appearance and feedback provided by the previews. Its commands are divided into four sections:

✦ **Browser Dither:** Select this option to see how a selected preview would look if displayed on an old 8-bit monitor. When editing a GIF image, this is an exceedingly useful method for gauging the performance of the Web Snap value.

✦ **Hide Auto Slices:** In order to fill in the gaps between your slices, Photoshop has to draw in its own. This is of course a good thing, but it can lead to screen clutter. To remove this clutter from all previews, choose Hide Auto Slices. Only your custom slices remain visible. (As always, for complete information on slicing, see the section "Slicing Images," up next.)

To hide all slices — custom or automatic — click the icon at the end of the tools along the left side of the Save For Web window. (It reads Toggle Slices Visibility when you hover the cursor over it.) When no option is highlighted, use the keyboard shortcut Q.

✦ **Color Compensation:** As discussed back in "World-wide color shifts," there's no way to predict exactly how an image will look on another screen. But you can use the four color commands to get a sense. By default, Uncompensated Color is active, so Photoshop makes no attempt at a prediction. Select Standard Windows Color or Standard Macintosh Color to see how the colors might look on another platform. The final color command, Use Document Color Profile, shows the colors as they normally appear in the active color space, most likely sRGB.

✦ **Size/Download Time:** The last dozen commands change the connection speed according to which Photoshop calculates the estimated download times listed below each preview. Note that these commands affect all previews, not just the selected one.

Slicing Images

If you're like most Web designers I talk to, you rough out your pages in Photoshop. If you don't, you should — it's a great way to work. Photoshop lets you assemble all the buttons, special text, and other elements the way that you want them to appear on the final Web page. Then you can cut the elements apart and save them out to later assemble in HTML.

Consider the image in Figure 14-25. This is a first draft of the home page for my Web site, *www.dekemc.com*. Here we have a beefy cartoon of me, equipped with Sgt. Fury arms and a thick manly neck. Alas, that's what I look like. Folks keep telling me I should take some estrogen so I'll quit being so overtly virile, but I'm too much of a clean-living health nut for that. Or perhaps I should take some sodium pentothal so I can stop lying to you people. But that's so hard to self-administer.

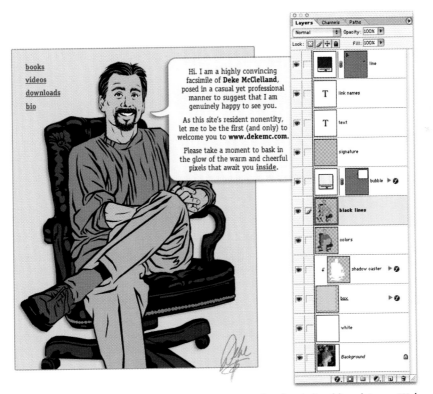

Figure 14-25: After getting email for years suggesting that I should update my Web site (my favorite leading with "Are you dead?"), I've actually gone and done it. Here's an early draft of the home page for my brand new site. Check it out for yourself online if you don't believe me. (See? I told you so.)

The image contains close to a dozen layers, including a couple of text layers. But while the text looks swell, it's just a placeholder for the text and hyperlinks I'll be including in the HTML document. The simplest way to combine text blocks and graphics on a Web page is to create an HTML table. And the simplest way to make an HTML table is to cut the graphic apart using Photoshop's slicing feature.

Illustrated in Figure 14-26, *slices* are rectangular containers that permit you to add structure to a Web page design. The eight slices in the figure act like children's blocks, each of which contains just enough of the graphic to fit together into a seamless whole. The two blocks marked in blue are my *user slices*, the ones that I drew. They indicate the boundaries of the text. The remaining blocks are *auto slices*, which Photoshop creates automatically to fill in the gaps. In the figure, a total of six auto slices are needed to keep all slices exactly rectangular.

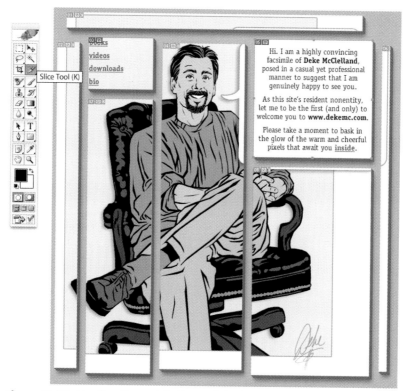

Figure 14-26: Use the slice tool (left) to subdivide a Web page design into rectangular blocks. Photoshop later assembles the blocks into an HTML table, which adds structure to the otherwise free-flowing arrangement of elements on a Web page.

Creating slices

Photoshop provides two slice tools, one for drawing slices and one for editing them. Press the K key to select the slice tool (highlighted in Figure 14-26), which lets you draw slices. That tool shares a flyout with the slice select tool, which you use to move and scale slices.

Draw a rectangle around the portion of the image that you want to slice into an independent image; Shift-drag to constrain the shape of the slice to a square. For each slice that you create, a number appears in the upper-left corner of the slice, as shown in Figure 14-26. Here are a few other things you should know:

✦ As you draw your user slices, Photoshop automatically fills in the auto slices, which it differentiates using dotted outlines. The program also numbers the slices from left to right and then top to bottom. User slice numbers appear in blue, auto slice numbers appear in gray.

✦ Simple tables are reliable tables. This means you want to draw as few slices as absolutely possible. In Figure 14-26, I drew just two slices, one for each text block, and that's it. Avoid overlapping slices and avoid having two slices that almost, but don't quite, touch, because both result in Photoshop having to draw extra auto slices.

If you need help aligning your slices, choose View ➪ Snap To ➪ Slices to snap one user slice into agreement with another. Although this option is off by default, I can't think of any reason not to always have it on.

✦ You can also align slices on the fly. While drawing a slice, press and hold the spacebar to move the slice as you drag. Release the spacebar to put the slice down and return to sizing it.

✦ To create a slice that surrounds everything on a particular layer, select the layer in the layers palette and then choose Layer ➪ New Layer Based Slice. If you later change the layer's contents, Photoshop redraws the slice boundary as necessary to include the new pixels.

Use this technique when saving slices that contain layer effects, such as drop shadows. This way, you can edit the effect without having to worry about redrawing the slice manually if the new effect takes up more space.

✦ Photoshop can also make slices from guides. First drag one or more guidelines from the horizontal and vertical rulers (View ➪ Rulers) to establish divisions inside your image. Then select the slice tool and click the Slices From Guides button in the Options bar.

✦ To hide and show the slice boundaries, press Ctrl+H (⌘-H on the Mac). By default, this hides all on-screen aids, including selection outlines and guides. (If it doesn't, choose View ➪ Show ➪ Show Extras Options and then turn on the Slices check box and try again.) To toggle the slice boundaries on and off independently, choose View ➪ Show ➪ Slices.

✦ After you get your slices just so, choose View ➪ Lock Slices to fix them in place. That way, you won't accidentally alter a slice boundary. To delete all slices, choose View ➪ Clear Slices.

Editing slices

Need to change a slice boundary? Grab the slice select tool (Shift+K) and click a slice to select it. You can also Shift-click and drag in the image window to select multiple slices. Then edit the slice or slices as described in the following list.

To temporarily access the slice select tool while the slice tool is active, press and hold Ctrl (⌘ on the Mac). This means you can Ctrl-click (⌘-click) on a slice with the slice tool to select it. Conversely, if the slice select tool is active, holding Ctrl (⌘) gets you the slice tool.

✦ A selected user slice displays corner handles. Drag a handle to change the size and shape of the slice. You can also drag inside a selected slice to change its location. Press Backspace (or Delete) to delete it.

✦ To duplicate a slice, press the Alt (or Option) key and drag the slice.

✦ When the slice select tool is active, you can promote an auto slice to a user slice. Click on the auto slice and then click the Promote to User Slice button in the Options bar. Then adjust the boundaries of the slice as desired. If the slice tool is active, right-click on an auto slice (on the Mac, Control-click) and choose Promote to User Slice.

This may make you wonder, "Hey, how do I change a user slice to an auto slice?" That's easy — just delete it.

Setting slice options

Double-click a selected slice with either of the slice tools to display the Slice Options dialog box (see Figure 14-27), which lets you assign a name to the slice image file, add a link, and set other slice attributes described in the following list. You can also access a version of this dialog box with slightly different options (as we'll see) by double-clicking a slice inside the Save For Web window.

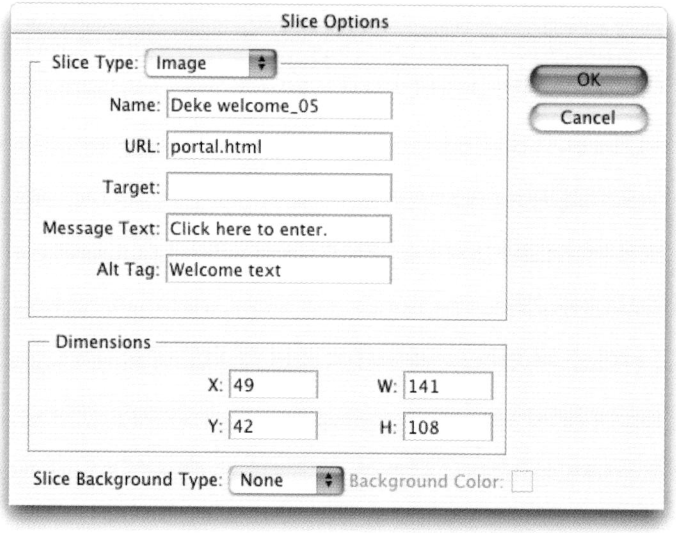

Figure 14-27: Double-click a slice with the slice tool to name the slice file that Photoshop eventually saves to disk, assign a hyperlink, and insert a status bar message.

✦ **Slice Type:** You can fill a slice with either an image or text. To keep the slice an image, leave this option unchanged. If you would prefer to fill the slice with text, select No Image.

For example, the fifth slice in Figure 14-26 features a placeholder for a text introduction to my Web site. To convey this text to the HTML document, I select the text using the type tool and copy it to the Clipboard by pressing Ctrl+C (⌘-C on the Mac). Then I switch to the slice tool, double-click on the slice, and switch the Slice Type to No Image. Photoshop gives me a text-entry box into which I can enter text. I click inside it and press Ctrl+V (⌘-V) to paste in my text, as shown in Figure 14-28. Although Photoshop cannot preview this text correctly inside the standard image window, it will save the text when you choose File ➪ Save As. Then open the resulting HTML page in your favorite browser.

You can likewise insert HTML tags into the text-entry area, but if you do, things get a bit trickier. In Figure 14-28, I added an *<a href>* tag (colorized for emphasis) around the word *inside*. This should turn the word into a hyperlink, but instead, the Web page merely ends up displaying the tags as text. The solution is to visit the Save For Web dialog box, double-click on the slice, and select an option not otherwise found in Photoshop, Text Is HTML. Highlighted in Figure 14-29, this option correctly interprets HTML tags and once selected, remains selected as long as you work on the image.

✦ **Name:** Photoshop automatically names the slices after the saved image name (in my case, *Deke welcome.psd*) followed by an underscore and number (hence Deke welcome_05 back in Figure 14-27). If you want to override the automatic naming convention, enter your preferred slice name here. (Note that this option and the four that follow apply only when you select Image as the Slice Type.)

✦ **URL:** To turn the slice into a button, enter the URL for the page you want the slice to link to. If you want to link to a page stored in the same folder as the slice, a simple file name will suffice, such as *portal.html* in Figure 14-27. For files inside other folders, enter the path name. To link to an outside Web page, enter the full URL, such as *http://www.totaltraining.com*. In fact, by all means, enter exactly that link. We love it when people do that.

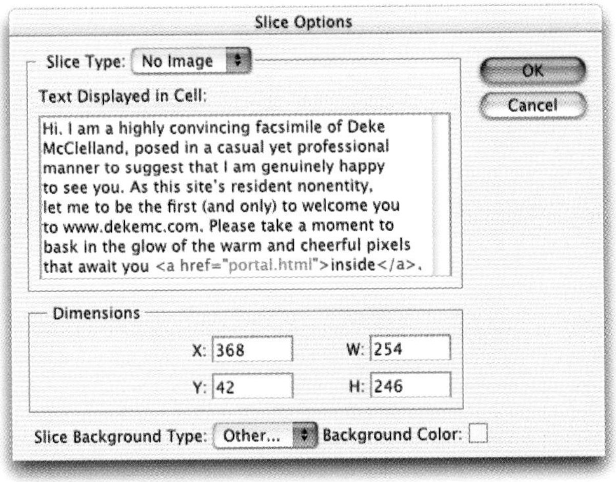

Figure 14-28: Select the No Image option to fill a slice with text and HTML tags. Here I copied the introductory type from Figure 14-26 and pasted it into the text-entry box.

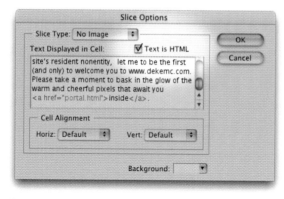

Figure 14-29: Available only inside the Save For Web dialog box (and ImageReady), select the Text Is HTML check box to properly interpret HTML tags in the text-entry area.

✦ **Target:** If your page includes frames, enter the appropriate frame tag in this option box.

✦ **Message Text:** Enter a message to appear in the status bar at the bottom of the browser window when a visitor hovers the cursor over the slice. For those familiar with JavaScript, Photoshop handles this using an *onMouseOver="window.status"* tag.

✦ **Alt Tag:** To provide a text alternate for a button, enter the text into this option box. This is generally used only if a visitor has his or her browser set to display only text.

✦ **Dimensions:** To specify the exact placement and size of a slice boundary, enter the pixel coordinates into the X and Y options and the dimensions into the W and H options. This can be useful when trying to delete auto slices by getting the user slices into exact alignment.

✦ **Slice Background Type:** If your image contains transparent areas, you can fill them with a color selected from this pop-up menu. The Matte option uses the matte color specified in the Save For Web optimization settings. Choose Other to select a color from the Color Picker. Note that you can't preview this background color in Photoshop; you must use a browser.

When working with text, the background color fills the entire slice. Back in Figure 14-28, for example, I set the background color to yellow to match the talk balloon that surrounds the text. To make sure I had the right shade of yellow, I selected the Other option; then after the Color Picker dialog box had displayed, I clicked inside the talk balloon with the eyedropper cursor.

Saving slices

I imagine that by now, your eyes are glazed over and you're thinking about how you'd rather be watching *The Sopranos* (every time I start getting a paunch, I think, "That's okay, Tony's got a gut and he kills people"), so I'll keep this final bit of slice-related data simple. After you create and edit your slices to absolute perfection, you'll want to perform *both* of the following kinds of saves:

✦ **Save the image itself.** To save your original image with all slice information, layers, and other doodads intact, choose File ➪ Save As and select either the Photoshop (PSD) or TIFF format. (Depending on your platform, other formats may also store slices, but PSD and TIFF are the safest.) When you reopen the image, choose the slice tool to redisplay the slice boundaries and make any further changes.

✦ **Save the HTML table and slice files.** To output the image in Web-ready form, choose File ➪ Save For Web. This command enables you to save all the slices as individual image files and create the HTML page that will reassemble the slices in the Web browser.

Turning to ImageReady

If you like things plain and simple, you can close this book right now and save yourself the burden of reading the few remaining pages of my tiresome prose. (Did you just call my prose *tiresome*? Hey, now that I'm chubbin' up, I don't think you want to get on my bad side.) You already know everything you need to know to create your basic Web images and sliced graphics. But if you want to add some spice to your Web site — and really, what's a *capodecina* without some garlic? — I end this chapter, not to mention this book, with a quick and dirty skim on Photoshop's tough little associate, ImageReady:

✦ **Switching to ImageReady:** As if to say, "Yes, we know we should have rolled these two programs into one, we're sorry," Photoshop and ImageReady are hot-linked to each other. (You may have already noticed the Edit in ImageReady button at the bottom right of Photoshop's Save For Web command.) To take the image that you're editing in Photoshop and open it up in ImageReady, click the icon at the bottom of the toolbox. (Note that the advent of CS means that you can no longer have a file open simultaneously in both applications.) To switch back to Photoshop — and take your ImageReady edits with you — click the icon at the bottom of the ImageReady toolbox. Figure 14-30 shows the icons and offers some advice on how to keep straight which program you're in.

You can also right-click on a thumbnail within Photoshop's File Browser and choose Edit in ImageReady to open that image directly in ImageReady. And whether you're in Photoshop or ImageReady, you'll find a list of both applications' open documents at the bottom of the Window menu. Choose one, and the document will open up in the current application.

You can also press the keyboard shortcut, Ctrl+Shift+M (⌘-Shift-M). I mention this as a cautionary note because I hate this shortcut. More often than not, I press it accidentally when trying to create a new layer (Ctrl+Shift+N) or send a selection to its own layer (Ctrl+Shift+J). Then you have to wait quite literally seconds for ImageReady to launch, during which you're quite sure you could've finished the job and shipped it off to the client — not to mention walked the dog, eaten lunch, and taken a nap. So be careful when your fingers venture near the M key. Or better yet, just reassign the shortcut (in Photoshop, at least) by visiting Edit ➪ Keyboard Shortcuts.

To switch applications without transferring images and modifications, just switch applications normally using Alt+Tab (⌘-Tab on the Mac).

✦ **Color management:** The first thing you'll notice upon transferring a Photoshop image into ImageReady is that the colors shift. This is because, by default, ImageReady unwisely ignores Photoshop's active RGB space. Fortunately, you can set things straight with a command. Assuming your image is profiled (see "Working with sRGB"), choose View ➪ Preview ➪ Use Embedded Color Profile. Like magic, ImageReady now displays the same colors you saw in Photoshop.

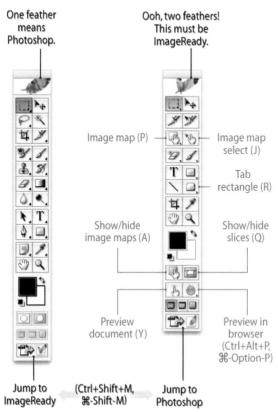

One feather
means
Photoshop.

Ooh, two feathers!
This must be
ImageReady.

Image map (P)

Image map
select (J)

Tab
rectangle (R)

Show/hide
image maps (A)

Show/hide
slices (Q)

Preview
document (Y)

Preview in
browser
(Ctrl+Alt+P,
⌘-Option-P)

Jump to
ImageReady

(Ctrl+Shift+M,
⌘-Shift-M)

Jump to
Photoshop

Figure 14-30: Photoshop (left) and ImageReady (right) are so similar that it's easy to lose track of which program you're using. The trick is to keep an eye on the top of the toolbox, which features one feather in Photoshop and two feathers in ImageReady. (ImageReady must be twice as good then, huh?) The red labels indicate tools and icons that are unique to ImageReady.

✦ **Image optimization:** Unlike Photoshop, ImageReady lacks the Save For Web command and its accompanying dialog box. That's because ImageReady was the original model for the Save For Web command. As shown in Figure 14-31, the image window itself sports the exact same four tabs found inside Save For Web — Original, Optimized, 2-Up, and 4-Up — and they serve the very same purposes. The optimization settings are contained in the floating Optimize palette (Window ➪ Optimize). To edit colors in a GIF image or make them transparent, use the Color Table palette.

✦ **Saving your work:** To save your original image — with layers, slices, and other extras — choose File ➪ Save or Save As, both of which invariably save to the PSD format. To save to a different image format, such as TIFF, choose File ➪ Export ➪ Original Document. (ImageReady cannot save a layered TIFF file.) To save Web images and HTML data, choose File ➪ Save Optimized As or press Ctrl+Alt+Shift+S (⌘-Option-Shift-S on the Mac). You can also use File ➪ Save Optimized or Ctrl+Alt+S (⌘-Option-S on the Mac) to update changes to your Web files, a real advantage over Photoshop's Save For Web.

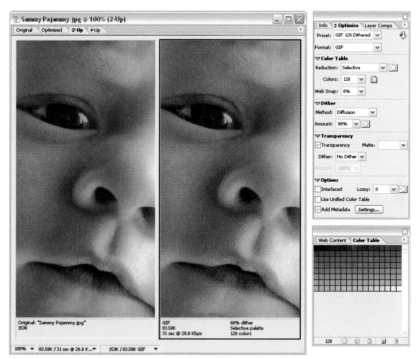

Figure 14-31: ImageReady's central image window (left), Optimize palette (upper right), and Color Table palette (lower right) were the inspiration for Photoshop's Save For Web command.

✦ **What you'll see, what you won't:** In most ways, ImageReady is a slimmed down version of Photoshop, but there are plenty of differences. For example, ImageReady has layers and even its very own Layer Comps palette, but not channels or paths. Happily, in ImageReady CS you will find some core filters that were missing before, including Median, Add Noise, Find Edges, Maximum, Minimum, and High Pass. And you can now preview most effects in the full image window. You still have Levels but not Curves, and there are still no adjustment layers. There's also one feature I'm sad to see change: Layer effects are now handled in a huge Photoshop-style dialog box, rather than inside a handy palette as before.

But the new object-based interface makes up for some of the letdowns. In ImageReady CS, it's possible to select multiple objects at once. You can Shift-click layers in the Layers palette, or even marquee-drag around elements inside the image window. And once you've got multiple items selected, you can apply layer commands to them, such as duplicate, delete, link, and merge, or group them together by pressing Ctrl+G (⌘-G on the Mac). Add the Shift key to that shortcut to ungroup layers. You can Alt-drag (or Option-drag) multiple elements to clone them. And another nifty new feature: If you're dragging an object to align it with other elements, the new smart guides (pictured in Figure 14-32) pop up to keep you from getting out of line.

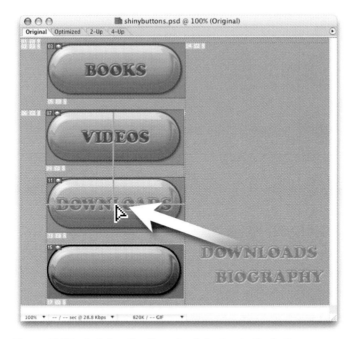

Figure 14-32: As I drag the Downloads text onto the button, ImageReady CS's new *smart guides* instantly appear to give me horizontal and vertical references for perfectly centering the text. When I don't need them anymore, the guides disappear. Pretty smart.

✦ **Creating image maps:** There's no denying that ImageReady is a derivative program, but it has a few tricks up its sleeve. These include the ability to create *image maps*. Like slicing, an image map divides a Web design or graphic into multiple pieces. But where slices are always rectangular, an image map may include ovals and polygons. A typical example of an image map is a map of the world in which each country is a separate button. Here, slicing on its own would be impractical, because a rectangular slice would overlap many countries at once. What to do about Luxembourg, for example? The better solution would be to create one big graphic with irregularly shaped buttons drawn over each country — in other words, an image map.

There are two ways to create an image map button. One is to assign an object, such as a country, to its own layer and then choose Layer ➪ New Layer Based Image Map Area. This creates a button that automatically updates with the layer contents, but by default, the button is rectangular. To rectify this, bring up the Image Map palette (Window ➪ Image Map) and in the Layer Based Settings section, select Polygon from the Shape pop-up menu, as in Figure 14-33.

The other method is to draw your buttons manually using the image map tools, which you can select from the keyboard by pressing the P key. Naturally, you can mix and match these techniques. And however you make your button, you need to tell the browser where to go when a visitor clicks inside it. To do this, select the button and enter a URL into the Image Map palette.

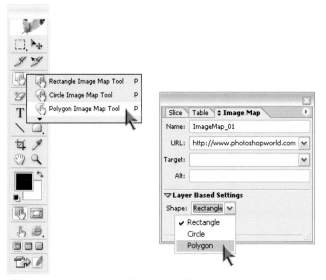

Figure 14-33: ImageReady lets you draw image map buttons using the tools shown on left. If you make a button using Layer ➪ New Layer Based Image Map Area, set the Shape option to Polygon to trace the layer's outline (bottom).

✦ **Adding JavaScript rollovers:** If there's one thing ImageReady excels at, it's rollovers. For those who aren't familiar with them, a *rollover* is a collection of JavaScript functions that makes a button change according to the actions of the mouse cursor. The most common example is a button that highlights or animates when you roll the cursor over it — hence the term "rollover."

Rollovers are composed of states — much like history states — one state for the normal appearance of a button, one for the "over" appearance, and so on. Your job is to define the contents of each state (usually by turning on and off layers or layer effects) and its boundaries. Because rollovers are more often than not buttons, the new Web Content palette (Window ➪ Web Content) tracks every slice and image map button you make. This makes it a snap to define the rollover boundaries — just click a slice or button name in the palette to tell ImageReady this is the spot you want to animate.

Next, click the tiny page icon at the bottom of the Web Content palette to add a new rollover state. By default, ImageReady makes this an Over State, meaning that this is the image you see when the cursor hovers over the button. Use the Layers palette to set up one or more layers strictly for this state, as in the right example in Figure 14-34. Then click the preview icon (or press Y) and move your mouse over the button to see the rollover in action.

✦ **Making GIF animations:** The only thing that the GIF format offers over PNG is support for animation. Although a primitive animation standard compared with, say, Flash, it can be very effective when used properly. In fact, nearly all Web advertising relies on animated GIF files. (Oops, there's another point in favor of PNG.)

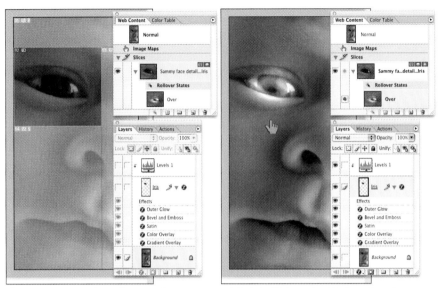

Figure 14-34: I selected my son's eye, pressed Ctrl+J (⌘-J on the Mac) to float it to a new layer, and chose Layer ➪ New Layer Based Slice. Next, I jumped over to Photoshop to add adjustment layers and effects to represent the rollover state. Then back in ImageReady I created a new state in the Web Content palette (left). I disabled the layers and effects with the normal state selected (left) and turned them on with the Over State selected (right). The result is a slice that highlights when I hover my cursor over it.

If you try to open an animated GIF file in Photoshop, the program opens the first frame and throws the rest away. Not so in ImageReady. It can read all frames in an animated GIF file and automatically separate each one to an independent layer. Figure 14-35 shows an animated GIF file that I opened in ImageReady. You can see the layers of frames in the Layers palette on the right and the Animation palette (Window ➪ Animation), with each layer assigned to a frame, along the bottom.

To make your own animation, add frames to the Animation palette, and then move and adjust the visibility of layers and effects. Notice that the Layers and Animation palettes work so closely together that they share two buttons, highlighted yellow in the figure. These take you backward or forward one frame. Other buttons appear exclusively in the Animation palette: The orange button takes you to the first frame, the green button plays, and the purple button *tweens* — that is, it automatically creates a series of inter-mediate frames between two extremes.

✦ **Export layers to Flash:** ImageReady CS provides a crucial bridge between Photoshop and Macromedia's Flash, the Web-standard software for creating vector animations. While Photoshop is an excellent place for blocking out a Web design, complete with vector shape and text layers, Flash can't import a layered Photoshop file. No problem. Just jump over to ImageReady and choose File ➪ Export ➪ Layers as Files, which brings up the Export Layers as Files dialog box shown in Figure 14-36.

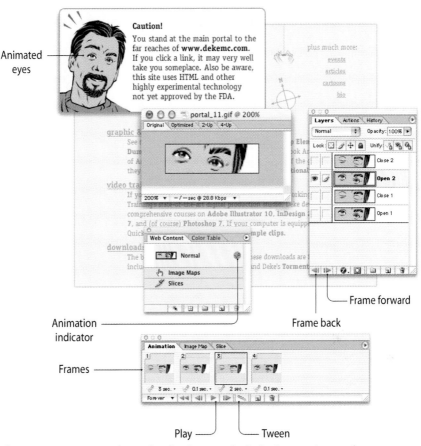

Animated eyes

Animation indicator

Frames

Frame forward

Frame back

Play

Tween

Figure 14-35: Here I animated a slice in an early draft of my main portal page to create the effect of my eyes periodically blinking. Nothing else moves, just like in a vintage Saturday morning superhero cartoon.

In the File Options section, specify a base name for your separate images, as well as file naming conventions and a destination folder for your images. In the Save Options section, you'll probably want to leave the Export pop-up menu set to All Layers, with Include Background checked. You can set the Apply pop-up menu to Separate Format for Each Layer and then use the arrows to the right of the Layer pop-up menu to move between your layers, assigning different Format Options to each layer if you wish. Then in the Format Options section, choose SWF (the native Flash format) from the Format pop-up menu.

Clicking the Set button opens the Macromedia Flash (SWF) Export dialog box, also pictured in Figure 14-36. If a text or shape layer can't be exported as vectors into Flash, the Preserve Appearance check box rasterizes the layer. You can set a background color for your Flash animation with the SWF bgcolor pop-up menu. Clicking the Generate HTML check box creates an HTML file in addition to the SWF file, containing info about the background color, image size, and formatting options. Since we're aiming for direct Flash import, clicking Enable Dynamic Text is pointless because SWF dynamic text doesn't import into Flash. Finally, the Bitmap Options allow you to set the format for exported bitmap images. Leaving the Format option set to Auto Select is usually a safe bet. Once you've exported your Photoshop layers as SWF files, you can then import them into Flash as layers by choosing File ⇨ Import ⇨ Import to Stage.

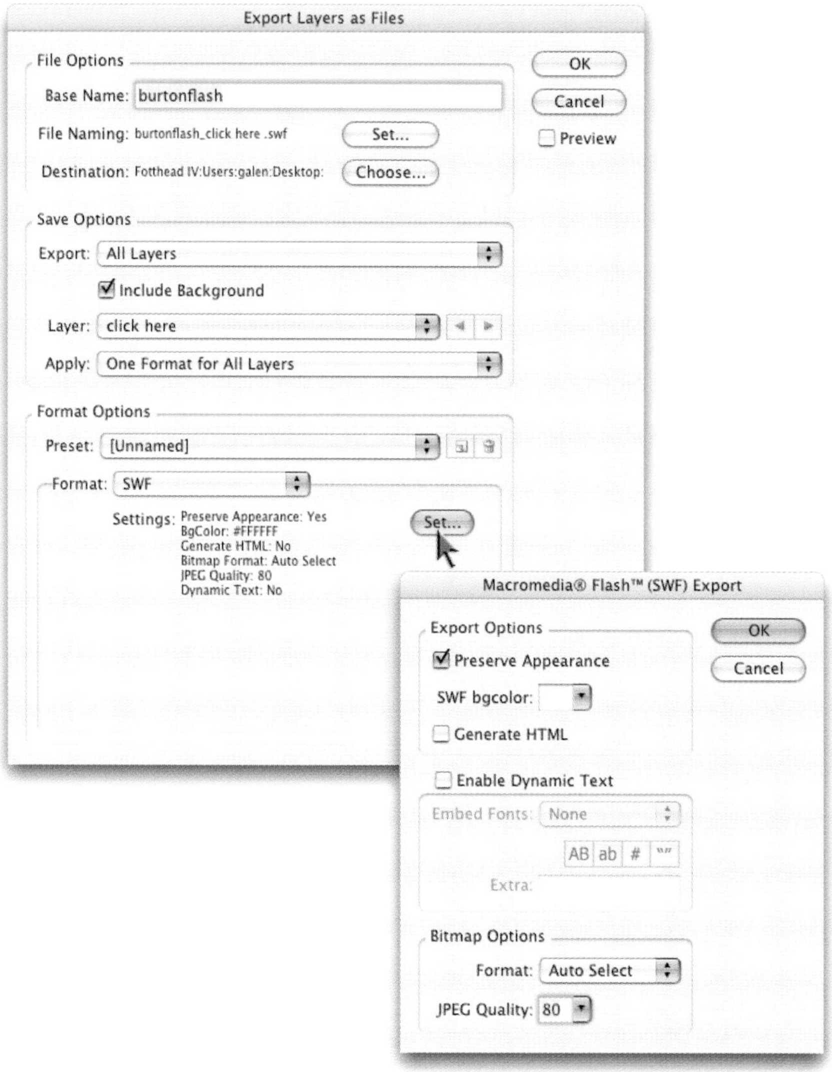

Figure 14-36: ImageReady CS's Export Layers as Files and Macromedia Flash (SWF) Export dialog boxes are just the ticket when you want to import a layered Photoshop file into Flash.

So there you have it, a quick introduction to ImageReady, a program that first spun off from Photoshop as an independent commercial application in 1998 only to be bundled with Photoshop a year later. My question: If it could spin off so easily, why can't it spin back? I hate to beat a dead horse, but if I were going to beat a dead horse, that horse's name would be One Program, One Photoshop. Seeing as it's dead, however, I don't expect this particular pony to place.

I'm really ripping on ImageReady, aren't I? I apologize. In fact, just so we end things on an up note, here's something you'll really enjoy. As you work along inside ImageReady, you may notice a puzzling difference in History. Rather than invoking the single-level undo, Ctrl+Z (⌘-Z) steps backward. Thankfully, you can bring ImageReady into agreement with Photoshop by pressing Ctrl+K (⌘-K) to bring up the Preferences dialog box and choosing Ctrl+Z from the Redo Key menu. From now on, Ctrl+Alt+Z (⌘-Option-Z) backsteps, just as it does in Photoshop.

Okay, yeah, I realize that was sort of a backhanded compliment to ImageReady: It gives you the option to make it perform as it should be doing in the first place. But here's an actual ImageReady-only plus: In ImageReady, History and Actions are linked. If you separate the History and Actions palettes, you can drag a history state and drop it into an existing action. (Only italicized states are off limits.) This means you can perform a series of steps, decide if you like them, and *then* store them as an action. And furthermore, ImageReady CS's Actions palette gives you the option to insert a *conditional step* into an action, meaning that depending on whether certain parameters (such as document size or name) are met by an image, a subsequent step in the action might or might not be performed. The flexibility boggles the mind. Heck, ImageReady can even open up frames from movie files! Why oh why doesn't Photoshop have these features? You know, perhaps Adobe shouldn't roll ImageReady into Photoshop after all; perhaps it's the other way around.

Just kidding, Photoshop. You know I love you.

Index

Continued

Continued

Continued

Continued